MACH # 491838

Market Models

Market Models

A Guide to
Financial Data Analysis

Carol Alexander

JOHN WILEY & SONS, LTD

Chichester • New York • Weinheim • Brisbane • Singapore • Toronto

Published 2001 by John Wiley & Sons Ltd, The Atrium, Southern Gate, Chichester,
West Sussex PO19 8SQ, England

Telephone   (+44) 1243 779777

Email (for orders and customer service enquiries): cs-books@wiley.co.uk
Visit our Home Page on www.wileyeurope.com or www.wiley.co.uk

Reprinted April 2002, February and November 2003

Other Wiley Editorial Offices

John Wiley & Sons Inc., 111 River Street, Hoboken, NJ 07030, USA

Jossey-Bass, 989 Market Street, San Francisco, CA 94103-1741, USA

Wiley-VCH Verlag GmbH, Boschstr. 12, D-69469 Weinheim, Germany

John Wiley & Sons Australia Ltd, 33 Park Road, Milton, Queensland 4064, Australia

John Wiley & Sons (Asia) Pte Ltd, 2 Clementi Loop #02-01, Jin Xing Distripark, Singapore 129809

John Wiley & Sons Canada Ltd, 22 Worcester Road, Etobicoke, Ontario, Canada M9W 1L1

British Library Cataloguing in Publication Data

A catalogue record for this book is available from the British Library

ISBN 0471 89975 5

Typeset in 10/12pt Times from author's disks by Dobbie Typesetting Limited, Tavistock, Devon
Printed and bound in Great Britain by Antony Rowe Ltd, Chippenham, Wiltshire
This book is printed on acid-free paper responsibly manufactured from sustainable forestry
in which at least two trees are planted for each one used for paper production.

Dedication

To Elsa, Reginald and Walter

Contents

An asterisk '*' denotes that illustrative software is on the CD. The **password** for the CD is available from http://www.wiley.co.uk/marketmodels.

Part III: Statistical Models for Financial Markets

Preface

This book is about the financial market models that are used by risk managers and investment analysts. It aims to provide a rigorous explanation of the theoretical ideas, but in practical and very clear terms. As concepts are introduced, real-world examples are provided in the text and, interactively, on the accompanying CD.

I have heard it said that too much academic research is focused on finding very precise answers to irrelevant questions. This book aims to provide academically acceptable answers to the questions that are really important for practitioners. It is written for a wide audience of practitioners, academics and students interested in the data analysis of financial asset prices.

It aims to help practitioners cut through the vast literature on financial market models, to focus on the most important and useful theoretical concepts. For academics the book highlights interesting research problems that are relevant to the day-to-day work of risk managers and investment analysts. For students, the comprehensive and self-contained nature of the text should appeal.

The book is divided into three parts:

Part I: Volatility and Correlation Analysis covers the estimation and forecasting of volatility and correlation for the pricing and hedging of options portfolios.

Part II: Modelling the Market Risk of Portfolios concerns factor modelling and the measurement of portfolio risk: the main focus is on modelling relationships between assets and/or risk factors using linear models.

Part III: Statistical Models for Financial Markets focuses on the time series analysis of financial markets.

A detailed summary of the content is provided in the introduction to each part. At the end of the book a low-level technical appendix is included; this covers the basic statistical theory that is necessary for the book to be self-contained.

Practitioners and academics share many important problems, and the communication between theory and practice is an essential part of model development. However, it is not always easy to straddle the divide between academic research and the practice of risk management and investment analysis. A common language, a common terminology and, above all, a common approach are necessary. It is hoped that this book will help to enhance the communication between these two schools.

Carol Alexander

July 2001

Acknowledgements

I liken the process of building a financial market model to that of building a musical instrument. In more than ten years of software design and development for financial institutions I have been the architect but not usually the implementer of the model. It would not have been possible to build many of the models presented in this book without the expertise provided by many mathematicians and financial engineers and the guidance of senior colleagues.

These include: Dr. Ian Giblin, Head of Research for Pennoyer Capital Management, New York; Professor Brian Scott-Quinn, Director of the ISMA Centre at Reading University; Dr. Ron Dembo, CE and President of Algorithmics, Toronto; Wayne Weddington III, CE and President of Pennoyer Capital Management, New York; Dr. Peter Williams, Reader in Cognitive Science at Sussex University; Christopher Leigh, Consultant at Abbey National Treasury Services, London; and Rajiv Thillainathan of Credit Suisse First Boston Bank, London. Their contributions are acknowledged in various parts of this text, but here I would like to say a special thanks, to all of them, for their support.

For the preparation of the CD I am greatly indebted to two outstanding students from the Financial Engineering and Quantitative Analysis (FEQA) MSc course at the ISMA Centre, University of Reading: Steffen Hennig and Sujit Narayanan. Steffen and Sujit have written excellent VBA code with graphical user interfaces for the spreadsheets that accompany each chapter. More details about Steffen and Sujit may be found on the CD.

The optimization based principal component analysis spreadsheets were kindly provided by my esteemed colleague at the ISMA Centre, Ubbo Wiersema. Many thanks also to Dr. Jurgen Doornik of Nuffield College, Oxford who has made a fully functional version of the OxMetrics software (PcGive, PcGets and STAMP) available on the CD with some of the data from the book; likewise to Dr. Mamdouh Barakat of MB Risk Management, for tailoring Universal Excel Add-ins to some of the data used in the book and for allowing readers a limited free license for this software.

Only two people apart from myself have read the entire manuscript: Richard Leigh and Jacques Pézier. Richard is a fantastic copy editor: his knowledge encompasses a surprising combination of languages and mathematics and his capacity to organize and communicate has made the copy editing process both efficient and enjoyable.

My husband, Jacques Pézier, has been a sounding board for my ideas and this has influenced my writing considerably. He made numerous contributions through constructive criticism and insightful feedback on most parts of the book. Any remaining oversights are my responsibility, but I shall probably blame him nevertheless, for not catching them(!). Finally I would like to say an enormous thank you to my young children, Boris and Helen, for sharing their mother with 'the book'.

Carol Alexander

July 2001

About the Website and the CD

The purpose of this book is to teach the reader to design and implement their own models of the relationships between important variables in financial markets. With this aim in mind, a CD has been provided that contains examples of many of the models that are described in the text. Most of the chapters have an associated spreadsheet that illustrates how important parameters, such as volatility, and important quantities, such as option prices or value-at-risk, may be obtained using the models described. These spreadsheets contain individual help files that explain their use, with references to the text that covers the technical background of the model. The **password** for these files is available from http://www.wiley.co.uk/marketmodels.

The reader may wish to use the programs as a basis for their own working models, but it should be stressed that the CD is provided free and for educational purposes only. It is not guaranteed to work and no additional software or hardware support will be given to the user. Neither are the spreadsheets guaranteed to be free of errors. Any errors should be reported to the market models user discussion forum that will be provided on the website for the book: http://www.wiley.co.uk/marketmodels. It is hoped that this forum will provide a means for users to exchange ideas on the aspects of model development that are covered in the text.

There are approximately 230 figures in this book, and more than a few have had their glorious Technicolor suppressed by the confines of monochrome print. An appealing feature of the CD is that it contains the original colour versions of these figures and, in most cases, the supporting data. The **password** for these files is available from http://www.wiley.co.uk/marketmodels. The CD includes free demonstration versions of commercial software that are particularly relevant to the subjects covered in the book, in addition to the **Market Models** spreadsheets mentioned above. An asterisk '*' is placed in the list of contents to indicate the sections that have associated software on the CD.

Carol Alexander

July 2001

WILEY COPYRIGHT INFORMATION AND TERMS OF USE

CD supplement to Market Models: A Guide to Financial Analysis

Copyright © 2001 Carol Alexander

Part I
Volatility and Correlation Analysis

Part I provides insights into the pricing and hedging of options through the understanding of volatility and correlation, and the uncertainty which surrounds these key determinants of portfolio risk. The first chapter introduces volatility and correlation as parameters of the stochastic processes that are used to model variations in financial asset prices. They are not observable in the market and can only be measured in the context of a model.

Option pricing, which models asset prices in continuous time, is covered in Chapter 2. This chapter focuses on the consequences of using the Black–Scholes model to price options. Although there can only be one true volatility for the underlying price process, different volatilities are implied by the market prices of options on the same underlying asset. If one is willing to accept these volatilities, rather than invent better option pricing models, then their behaviour can be described by modelling the 'smile' or 'skew' patterns that emerge. The relationship between underlying price changes and changes in the implied volatility of an option is analysed to support the use of different volatility assumptions for pricing and hedging.

Statistical forecasts of volatility and correlation employ discrete time series models on historical return data. Chapter 3 explains how to obtain moving average estimates of volatility and correlation and outlines their advantages and limitations. A weighted average is a method for estimation. The current estimate of volatility or correlation is sometimes used as a forecast, but this requires returns to be independent and identically distributed, an assumption which is not always supported by empirical evidence. Chapter 4 introduces generalized autoregressive conditional heteroscedasticity (GARCH) models, which are based on more realistic assumptions about asset price dynamics. This chapter aims to cut through a vast academic literature on the subject to present the concepts and models that are most relevant to practitioners. A step-by-step guide to the implementation of the GARCH models that are commonly used by risk managers and investment analysts is followed by a description of the application of GARCH models to option pricing and hedging.

Most statistical models for forecasting volatility are actually models for forecasting variance: the volatility forecast is taken as the square root of the variance forecast. However, a forecast is an expectation, taken under some probability measure, and the expectation of a square root is not equal to the square root of an expectation. The last chapter in this part of the book examines this and other key issues surrounding the use of volatility and correlation forecasts. Quite different results can be obtained, depending on the model used and on the market conditions so, since volatility can only be measured in the context of a model, how does one assess the accuracy of a volatility forecast? Rather than employ point forecasts of volatility, this part of the book ends by advocating the use of standard errors, or other measures of uncertainty in volatility forecasts, to improve the valuation of options.

Part I introduces some challenging concepts that will be returned to later as further models are introduced. For example, the principal component models of implied volatility in §6.3, the orthogonal method for generating covariance matrices in §7.4 and the normal mixture density models of §10.3 will all continue the exposition of ideas that are introduced in Part I.

1

Understanding Volatility and Correlation

This chapter introduces some of the concepts that are fundamental to the analysis of volatility and correlation of financial assets. This is a vast subject that has been approached from two different technical perspectives. On the one hand, the option pricing school models the variation in asset prices in continuous time; this perspective will be taken in Chapter 2. On the other hand, the statistical forecasting school models volatility and correlation from the perspective of a discrete time series analyst; this is the approach used in Chapters 3 and 4.

The basic concepts are introduced within a unified framework that, I hope, will be accessible to both schools. Some of these concepts are quite complex and their exposition has necessitated many footnotes and numerous pointers to other parts of the book. First, volatility and correlation are described as parameters of stochastic processes that are used to model variations in financial asset prices. Then the differing needs of various market participants to assess volatility and correlation are examined. The needs of the analyst will

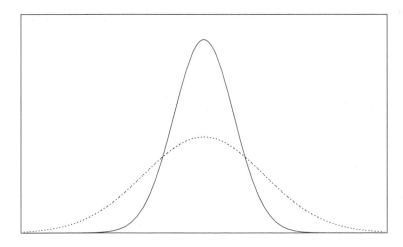

Figure 1.1 Volatility and scale.

determine whether an option pricing (implied volatility) approach or a statistical modelling (covariance matrix) approach is required (or both). Implied volatility and statistical volatility normally refer to the same process volatility, but volatility estimates often turn out to be quite different and because volatility can only be measured in the context of a model it is very difficult to assess the accuracy of estimates and forecasts. The chapter concludes with remarks on the decisions about the data and the models that will need to be made when volatility and correlation forecasts are implemented.

1.1   The Statistical Nature of Volatility and Correlation

Financial asset prices are observed in the present, and will have been observed in the past, but it is not possible to determine exactly what they will be in the future. Financial asset prices are random variables, not deterministic variables.[1] Variations of financial asset prices over a short holding period are often assumed to be lognormal random variables. Therefore returns to financial assets, the relative price changes, are usually measured by the difference in log prices, which will be normally distributed.[2]

Volatility is a measure of the dispersion in a probability density. The two density functions shown in Figure 1.1 have the same mean but the density function indicated by the dotted line has greater dispersion than the density indicated by the continuous line.[3] The most common measure of dispersion is the *standard deviation* σ of a random variable, that is, the square root of its variance.

---

[1] A *random variable*, also called a 'stochastic variable' or 'variate', is a real-valued function that is defined over a sample space with probability measure. A value x of a random variable X may be thought of as a number that is associated with a chance outcome. Each outcome is determined by a chance event, and so has a probability measure. This probability measure is represented by the *probability density function* of the random variable. For any probability density function $g(x)$, the corresponding *distribution function* is defined as $G(x) = \text{Prob}(X < x)$ $= \int_{-\infty}^{x} g(x)\,dx$. It is not necessary to specify both density and distribution: given the density one can calculate the distribution, and conversely since $g(x) = G'(x)$.

[2] The *normal density function* $\phi(x)$ is defined by two parameters, the mean μ and the variance σ^2: $\phi(x) = ((2\pi\sigma^2)^{-1/2})\exp(\frac{1}{2}(x-\mu)^2/\sigma^2)$ for $-\infty < x < \infty$. This gives the familiar symmetric bell-shaped curve, which is centred on the mean μ and has a dispersion that is determined by the variance σ^2.

A random variable is said to be *lognormally distributed* when its logarithm is normally distributed. A lognormal density function is not symmetrical; it is bounded by zero on the low side but can, in theory, reach infinitely high values. For this reason it is commonly assumed that financial assets (bonds and shares) and possibly commodity prices are better represented by lognormal than by normal variates. Conversely, investors compare financial assets on the basis of their returns; it is therefore returns that are comparable whatever the price of the underlying asset, and it is simplest to assume that returns are normally distributed. It follows that the price is lognormally distributed; indeed if $r_t = (P_t - P_{t-1})/P_{t-1}$ is normally distributed then $P_t/P_{t-1} = 1 + r_t$ and $\ln(P_t/P_{t-1}) \approx r_t$ (note that when x is small, $\ln(1 + x) \approx x$). Therefore $\ln(P_t/P_0)$ is normally distributed and P_t/P_0 is lognormally distributed. Note that this argument is based on investment assets and would not apply to interest rates. The argument has also shown that the return over small time intervals is approximated by the first difference in the log prices.

[3] If a random variable X has density function $f(x)$ then its *mean* is $\mu = E(X) = \int xf(x)dx$. The mean is like the centre of gravity of a density. It is a fundamental parameter of any density, the parameter that describes the *location* of the density. It is also called the *first moment* of the density function. The *variance* is $\sigma^2 = V(X) = \int (x - \mu)^2 f(x)dx = E(X^2) - [E(X)]^2$. This parameter measures the *dispersion* of the density function about the mean. It is also called the *second moment* about the mean of the density function.

It is hard to predict price variations of financial assets so it is usual to assume that successive returns are relatively independent of each other. This means that uncertainty will increase as the holding period increases, the distribution will become more dispersed and its variance will increase. Put another way, the variance of *n*-day returns will increase with *n*. Therefore it is not possible to compare *n*-day variance with *m*-day variance on the same scale. It is standard to assume statistically independent returns[4] and to express a standard deviation in annual terms. Thus in financial markets we define

Uncertainty will increase as the holding period increases, the distribution will become more dispersed and its variance will increase

$$\text{Annual volatility} = (100\sigma\sqrt{A})\%, \qquad (1.2)$$

where A is an annualizing factor, the number of returns per year.[5] In this way volatilities of returns of different frequencies may be compared on the same scale in a volatility term structure (§2.2.2, §3.3 and §4.4.1).

To understand what correlation is, consider a *joint density* of two random variables.[6] A joint density may be visualized as a mountain: the more symmetric this mountain is about both the axes representing the two variables, the less information can be gained about the value of one variable by knowing the value of the other; that is, the lower the *correlation* between the two variables. For highly correlated variables the joint density will have more of a ridge in a direction between the axes of the two variables.

Figure 1.2 shows three 'scatter plots', where synchronous observations on each of the returns are plotted as horizontal and vertical coordinates. A scatter plot is a sample from the joint density of the two returns series, and so if the returns have no correlation their scatter plot will be symmetrically dispersed, like the one in Figure 1.2a; a high value on one axis will be no indication that the corresponding value on the other axis will be high or low. But if they have a high positive correlation the joint density will have a ridge sloping upwards, as in Figure 1.2b; when one variable has a high value the other will also tend to have a high value. If they have negative correlation the joint density will have a downwards sloping ridge as in Figure 1.2c; when one variable has a high value the other will tend to have a low value, and vice versa.

Correlation is a measure of co-movements between two returns series. Strong positive correlation indicates that upward movements in one returns series tend to be accompanied by upward movements in the other, and similarly

---

[4] Two random variables X and Y are *independent* if and only if their joint density function $h(x, y)$ is simply the product of the two marginal densities. That is, if X has density $f(x)$ and Y has density $g(y)$ then X and Y are independent if and only if $h(x, y) = f(x)g(y)$.

[5] The annualizing factor is a normalizing constant: the variance increases with the holding period but the annualizing factor decreases. The number of *trading days* (or 'risk days') per year is usually taken for the conversion of a daily standard deviation into an annualized percentage; that is, often $A=250$ or 252 in (1.2). Note the continuation of this footnote in §2.1.1 (footnote 5).

[6] The joint density $f(x, y)$ of two random variables X and Y is a real-valued function of the two variables where the total area underneath the surface is one: $\int \int f(x, y)dxdy=1$. The joint probability that X takes values in one range and Y takes values in another range is the area under the function defined by these two ranges.

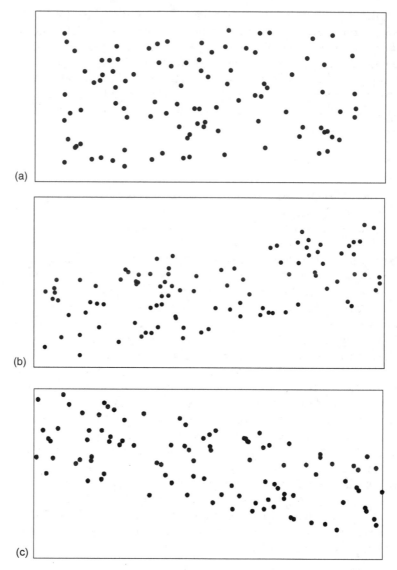

Figure 1.2 (a) Zero correlation; (b) positive correlation; (c) negative correlation.

downward movements of the two series tend to go together. If there is a strong negative correlation then upward movements in one series are associated with downward movements in the other.

A simple statistical measure of co-movements between two random variables is *covariance*, the first product moment about the mean of the joint density function. That is, $\text{cov}(X, Y) = E[(X - \mu_X)(Y - \mu_Y)]$, where $\mu_X = E(X)$ and $\mu_Y = E(Y)$. Covariance is determined not only by the degree of co-movement but also by the size of the returns. For example, monthly returns are of a much greater order of magnitude than daily returns, so the covariance of monthly returns will normally be greater than the covariance of any daily returns in the same market.

Since covariance is not independent of the units of measurement, it is a difficult measure to use for comparisons. It is better to use the correlation, which is a standardized form of covariance that is independent of the units of measurement. For two random variables X and Y the correlation is just the covariance divided by the product of the standard deviations, that is:

$$\text{corr}(X, Y) = \text{cov}(X, Y)/\sqrt{[V(X)V(Y)]}. \qquad (1.3)$$

Equivalently, using parameter notation rather than operator notation:[7]

$$\rho_{XY} = \sigma_{XY}/\sigma_X\sigma_Y. \qquad (1.4)$$

Correlation does not need to be annualized like volatility because it is already in a standardized form. Normalizing the covariance as we have in (1.3) and (1.4) will always give a number that lies between -1 and $+1$. High positive correlation indicates that the returns are strongly associated, or 'co-dependent', because they tend to move together in the same direction. High negative correlation indicates that the returns are still highly co-dependent, but they tend to move in opposite directions.

The greater the absolute value of correlation, the greater the association or 'co-dependency' between the series. If two random variables are statistically independent then a good estimate of their correlation should be insignificantly different from zero. We use the term *orthogonal* to describe such variables. However, the converse is not true. That is, orthogonality (zero correlation) does not imply independence, because two variables could have zero covariance and still be related (the higher moments of their joint density function could be different from zero).

Orthogonality does not imply independence; two variables could have zero covariance and still be related

In financial markets, where there is often a non-linear dependence between returns, correlation may not be an appropriate measure of co-dependency. Correlation is related to the slope parameter of a linear regression model (§A.1.1). Comparison of the ordinary least squares (OLS) formula with (1.3) shows that the correlation ρ and the slope coefficient β are related as

$$\beta = \rho v, \qquad (1.5)$$

where v denotes the relative volatility of Y (the dependent variable) with respect to X (the independent variable). That is, $v = \sigma_Y/\sigma_X$. Thus correlation is only a linear measure of association. If a regression line were fitted to the data in Figure 1.3a as illustrated, the estimate of the slope coefficient β will be highly

Correlation is only a linear measure of association

---

[7] Equations (1.3) and (1.4) say exactly the same thing. We tend to use parameter notation because it is concise, but often prefer operator notation for algebraic manipulation. For example $V(X + Y)=V(X)+V(Y)+2\text{cov}(X,Y)$ is perhaps easier to write than $\sigma_{X+Y}^2 = \sigma_X^2 + \sigma_Y^2 + 2\sigma_{XY}$.

significant, as reflected by its t-statistic.[8] On the other hand, if the scatter plot is curved as in Figure 1.3b the correlation will be low, even though there is obviously a strong relationship between the variables. Fitting a line to the data in Figure 1.3b would give a beta estimate that has a large standard error and correlation will not necessarily be very significant.

Correlation is a limited measure of dependency. Very often correlation estimates in financial markets lack robustness[9] so it is not surprising that alternative methods for capturing co-dependency have been considered.[10] The concept of a *copula* goes back to Schweizer and Sklar (1958). A copula is a function of several variables: in fact it is a multivariate uniform distribution function. If $u_1, \ldots, u_n$ are values of n univariate distribution functions, so each $u_i \in [0, 1]$, then a copula is a function $C(u_1, \ldots, u_n) \rightarrow [0, 1]$.

Copulas are used to combine marginal distributions into multivariate distributions. They are unique: for any given multivariate distribution (with continuous marginal distributions) there is a unique copula that represents it. They are also invariant under strictly increasing transformations of the marginal distributions. Copulas have long been recognized as a powerful tool for modelling dependence between random variables. A useful general reference text on copulas is Nelsen (1999).

Here are some simple examples of copulas:

(i) $C(u_1, \ldots, u_n) = u_1 u_2 \ldots u_n$

(ii) $C(u_1, \ldots, u_n) = \min(u_1, \ldots, u_n)$

(iii) $C(u_1, \ldots, u_n) = \max(\sum_{i=1}^{n} u_i - (n - 1), 0)$

Copula (i) corresponds to the case that the random variables are independent: the joint density will be the product of the marginal densities. Copula (ii) corresponds to *counter-monotonic dependency*, which is similar to negative correlation. Copula (iii) corresponds to *co-monotonic dependency*, which is similar to positive correlation.[11]

---

[8]Note that ρ is significant when β is significant; in fact a simple t-test (§A.2.2) for the significance of correlation is $[r\sqrt{(T-2)}/\sqrt{(1-r^2)}] \sim t_{T-2}$.

[9]In Chapter 11 we shall see that correlation estimates will not be very robust if the two series are not jointly covariance-stationary.

[10]In Chapter 12 we ask whether one should be using return data at all to measure the co-dependency of financial returns. There it is argued that return data have all the memory taken out of them before the analysis even begins. So return data can only be used to pick up short-term associations between returns series. To investigate the possibility of any long-run associations it is necessary to use a long-memory model, such as a cointegration analysis on the price series.

[11]Two random variables X_1 and X_2 are 'counter-monotonic' if there is another random variable X such that X_1 is a decreasing transformation of X and X_2 is an increasing transformation of X. If they are both increasing (or decreasing) transformations of X then X_1 and X_2 are called 'co-monotonic'. (Note that the transformations do not have to be *strictly* increasing or decreasing.)

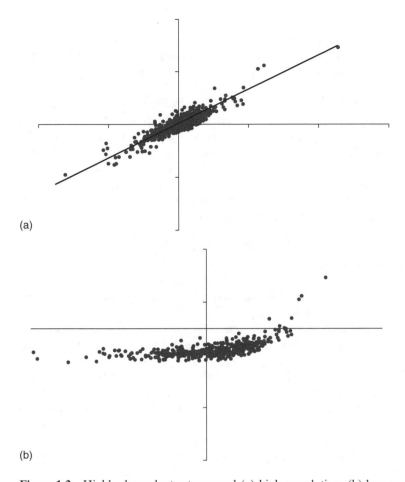

(a)

(b)

Figure 1.3 Highly dependent returns and (a) high correlation; (b) low correlation.

In the last few years copulas have been used as a powerful tool in financial risk management (Embrechts *et al.*, 1999a). They have important applications to the aggregation of individual loss distributions into an overall loss distribution, particularly when correlation is difficult to assess, as it is, for example, in operational risk measurement.

1.2 Volatility and Correlation in Financial Markets

The only significant risks are the 'irreducible' risks: those that cannot be reduced by hedging or diversification. Thus the concerns of a portfolio manager focus not on the total volatility of a portfolio, but on the volatility that is collinear with the market. This volatility is represented by the portfolio 'beta'; it represents the irreducible part of the total volatility of the portfolio. In a capital asset pricing model framework (§8.1.1) a high beta can be attributed to a high positive correlation with the index and a high relative volatility for the portfolio — this was shown in (1.5) above. Of course, if the relative volatility of the portfolio is very high it can have a large irreducible risk even when the correlation with the market is low (as long as it is positive).

Similarly, what matters for pricing an option is only the volatility of underlying price movements and not the trend in prices. Whatever the trend in an asset price, an option position can be hedged by the proper position on the underlying asset. All market participants would agree about the same 'fair' price of an option if the volatility of underlying price movements could be forecast accurately, but usually it cannot. Then, if sensitivity to volatility changes cannot be hedged away, different traders will have different market views that give rise to a large bid/offer spread.

Thus the estimation and forecasting of volatility and correlation is at the heart of financial risk modelling:

➤ Traders writing options need to forecast the volatility of the price process over the lifetime of the option.
➤ The risk management of their positions, which is based on optimal hedging, also requires volatility and correlation forecasts, but mainly over the short term.
➤ Implied volatility and correlation are necessary to compute the appropriate hedge ratios for their positions.
➤ Statistical volatility and correlation forecasts for all possible risk factors in the markets are necessary to net positions and to calculate a total market risk capital requirement for the entire firm.
➤ To validate the pricing and hedging models that are used in the front office, the middle office risk management and control functions will require independent assessments of all the implied and statistical volatilities and correlations.

An option price depends on a whole volatility surface so it is a little simplistic to talk about 'the' implied volatility for a time horizon

Implied volatility is the volatility forecast over the life of an option that equates an observed market price with the model price of an option. An option price depends on the choice of model and, after, on a whole volatility surface (§2.2.3) so it is a little simplistic to talk about 'the' implied volatility for a time horizon. However, the Black–Scholes model price of a simple call (or put) option will depend on 'the' implied volatility. This implied volatility is the volatility of the geometric Brownian motion process that is assumed to govern price variations from now until the option matures, that will equate the model price with the market price (Chapter 2). In that sense it is more accurate to refer to the Black–Scholes implied volatility, or for short, the Black–Scholes volatility.

Statistical volatility depends on the choice of statistical model that is applied to historical asset returns data. The statistical model is usually a time series model, such as a moving average or generalized autoregressive conditional heteroscedasticity (GARCH) process (these will be discussed extensively in

Chapters 3 and 4). Applying the model to historical data will generate statistical estimates of volatility for the past, where historical data are available. It will also generate forecasts of volatility from now until some future point in time, called the *risk horizon*. It is convenient to present the statistical estimates (or forecasts) of volatility and correlation between all asset (or risk factor) returns in a portfolio in the form of a covariance matrix (Chapter 7).

Unlike prices, volatility and correlation are not directly observable in the market. They can only be estimated in the context of a model. It is important to understand that implied and statistical volatility models normally provide estimates or forecasts of the same thing — that is, the volatility parameter in some assumed underlying price process.[12] The volatility of the stochastic process that governs price movements (or equivalently returns) is called the *process volatility*.

Unlike prices, volatility and correlation are not directly observable in the market. They can only be estimated in the context of a model

In practice there can be substantial differences between implied and statistical forecasts of the process volatility; there are many reasons for this, some of which are discussed in §2.1.3.

Our knowledge of the process volatility will depend on the model of the price process. The Black–Scholes model (§2.1.1) assumes that the underlying price process is a geometric Brownian motion, which has a *constant volatility*. More advanced price process models may assume other diffusion or jump models where the process volatility is stochastic. When volatility is stochastic it may have its own diffusion or jump model; so the price process model may have two random factors, one to represent the price process for a given volatility and another to represent the volatility process. Often we seek to represent the volatility process and, in particular, its dependence on the underlying price through time, by a volatility surface (§2.2.3). In multi-factor models, this dependence — and, in particular, the correlation between price changes and volatility changes — will be a key determinant of option prices; empirical modelling of the relationship between prices and volatility will be discussed in §2.3 and §6.3.

Realized volatility is a realization of the process volatility. It can be measured using historical price data. For example, if the price process is one of constant volatility then the realized volatility is the sample standard deviation of the observed returns.[13] If the price process has a time-varying volatility that is governed by a GARCH model, then the realized volatility is the GARCH volatility that is estimated over the historical data period. Realized volatility, the ex-post estimate of the process volatility, is a very difficult thing to forecast

---

[12] It is normally assumed that underlying asset returns are generated by a *stationary stochastic process*. In a stochastic process the return that is observed at time t is an observation on a density $f(r_t; \theta_t)$ where θ_t are the parameters of the density function at time t and the functional form $f(\cdot)$ is the same throughout the process. The term 'stationary' is defined in §11.1.2.

[13] That is, $s = \sqrt{[(r_1 - \bar{r})^2/(n-1)]}$, where $\bar{r}$ is the average return over the sample of size n. Often we assume $\mu = 0$ so the standard deviation has the unbiased estimate $\sqrt{[r_t^2/n]}$ (see §3.1.1).

ex ante; it will be greatly affected by an extreme market movement occurring at any time up to the risk horizon of the model.

Remember, volatility can only be observed in the context of a model. Most implied volatilities are based on the Black–Scholes model, and equally weighted moving average models are still the most common method of estimating statistical volatilities and correlations. These models are based on similar assumptions, but they are not very good models. The assumptions upon which these models are based just do not hold in practice. Therefore, much of the discussion in Part I of the book will focus on the implications of using the wrong model for volatility.

1.3   Constant and Time-Varying Volatility Models

Constant volatility models only refer to the unconditional volatility of a returns process. This is a finite constant σ, the same throughout the whole data generation process. It can be defined in terms of the variance parameter of the unconditional distribution of a stationary returns process. In fact, unconditional volatility is only defined if one assumes that the asset return series is generated by a stationary stochastic process (§11.1.2), but this assumption seems far more reasonable than many other assumptions that are commonly made in financial models.

Suppose one were to take together all the returns that were observed over some historic period. Consider a single density function that could have generated them. The variance of this distribution is the unconditional variance

One of the properties of a stationary series is that it has a finite 'unconditional' variance σ^2. To understand what this means, suppose one were to take together all the returns that were observed over some historic period, forgetting about any dynamic ordering. Consider a single density function that could have generated them (some idea of this density function may be obtained by plotting the histogram of the observed returns). This density is called the unconditional density, and its associated distribution is the unconditional distribution of the return process. The variance of this distribution is the unconditional variance and its square root is the *unconditional volatility*.[14]

Time-varying volatility models describe a process for the *conditional volatility*. A conditional distribution, in this context, is a distribution that governs a return at a particular instant in time[15] and the conditional volatility at time t is the square root of the variance of the conditional distribution at time t. The conditional mean at time t is denoted $E_t(r_t)$ or μ_t and the conditional variance at time t is denoted $V_t(r_t)$ or σ_t^2. An estimation procedure for the time-varying parameters of the conditional distributions is based on a model where anything that has happened in the past is not considered to be an observation on the

---

[14] The unconditional mean and variance operators are written $E(\cdot)$ and $V(\cdot)$. The unconditional mean is denoted $E(r_t)$ or μ and the unconditional variance is denoted $V(r_t)$ or σ^2.

[15] In more general terms, a conditional distribution is any distribution that is conditioned on a set of known values for some of the variables, that is, on an *information set*. In time series models the information set at time t, I_t, is often taken as all the past values that were realized in the process.

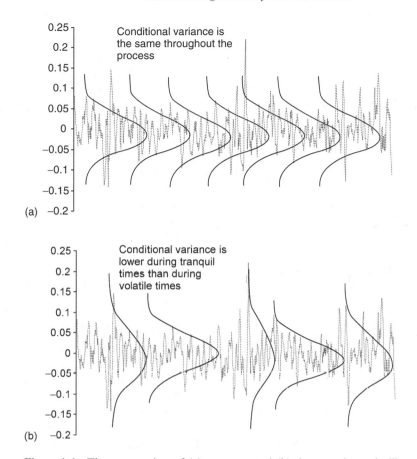

Figure 1.4 The assumption of (a) constant and (b) time-varying volatility.

current random variable. Its value is known, and so past observations become part of the information set. That is, the actual rather than the expected values of anything that happened in the past will be used to estimate the current value of a time-varying volatility parameter. Put another way, the current (and future) conditional distributions of the random variable will be 'conditioned' on the current information set.[16]

The actual rather than the expected values of anything that happened in the past will be used to estimate the current value of a time-varying volatility parameter

Figure 1.4 illustrates the distinction between constant and time-varying volatility models. The majority of time-varying volatility models assume that returns are normally distributed, in which case each conditional distribution is completely determined by its conditional mean and its conditional variance. Both the conditional mean and the conditional variance could change at every

---

[16] A simple example to illustrate the difference between the conditional and the unconditional mean and variance is given by the AR(1) model $y_t = \alpha y_{t-1} + \varepsilon_t$, where the ε_t are independent and identically distributed with mean 0 and variance σ^2, denoted $\varepsilon_t \sim$ i.i.d $(0, \sigma^2)$. The conditional mean at time t is $E_t(\alpha y_{t-1}) + E_t(\varepsilon_t) = \alpha y_{t-1}$ and the conditional variance is $V_t(\alpha y_{t-1}) + V_t(\varepsilon_t) = \sigma^2$ because y_{t-1} is known at time t. In §11.1.2 it is shown that $E(y_t) = 0$ and $V(y_t) = \sigma^2/(1 - \alpha^2)$.

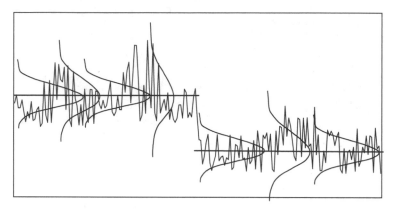

Figure 1.5   The importance of the conditional mean.

time period throughout the process, but for the purposes of estimating and forecasting conditional volatility it is often assumed that the conditional mean is a constant.

A linear regression model such as the capital asset pricing model introduced in §8.1.1 could be used to estimate and forecast the conditional mean. Not necessarily very well though, since returns are extremely difficult to predict. However, there are some notable exceptions where the exclusion of a proper time-varying conditional mean could produce misleading results. The returns series depicted in Figure 1.5 shows the same sort of characteristics as, for example, internet stocks during 1999 and 2000. In the 1999 technology boom, returns on many internet-related companies were high, but in 2000 the boom turned into a slump and below normal returns were experienced in many such companies.

Figure 1.5 shows that the conditional volatility would be very high if a constant conditional mean were assumed throughout the entire period. However, if the model had a conditional mean that varied over time (being high during the first part of the data period and low during the second part of the data period) then the conditional volatility would be much lower at every point in time.

The conditional volatility has no place in the standard framework for linear regression, because standard linear regression assumes that returns are *homoscedastic* — that is, their conditional variance is the same throughout the process (this assmption is depicted in Figure 1.4a). The term *conditional heteroscedasticity* means that the conditional variance changes over time (this is depicted in Figure 1.4b). The most popular models for time-varying volatility are the GARCH models described in Chapter 4.

1.4   Constant and Time-Varying Correlation Models

Suppose that two stationary return processes r_1 and r_2 are jointly covariance-stationary (§11.4). That is, their joint distribution has certain stability properties over time. One of these properties is that the contemporaneous covariance $\text{cov}(r_{1t}, r_{2t})$ is a constant, irrespective of the time at which it is measured; at every point in time t, $\text{cov}(r_{1t}, r_{2t}) = \sigma_{12}$.

It is only under this assumption of joint stationarity that one can define the *unconditional correlation*. It is the constant correlation given by

$$\text{corr}(r_{1t}, r_{2t}) = \text{cov}(r_{1t}, r_{2t})/\sqrt{(V(r_{1t})V(r_{2t}))} \qquad (1.6)$$

Thus the correlation is independent of the time at which it is measured; in alternative notation it is denoted $\rho_{12} = \sigma_{12}/\sigma_1\sigma_2$.

A scatter plot of two return series, such as those in Figures 1.2 and 1.3, gives a graphical representation of unconditional correlation. Scatter plots may be regarded as observations on the joint density function: the denser the points, the higher the frequency of joint values in that range. Where there is insignificant correlation scatter plots correspond to flat joint densities, like the Table Top mountain. Concentrated scatter plots come from joint densities with peaks or 'ridges', and here the unconditional correlation may be significantly different from zero.

It is important to note that there is nothing in an unconditional model to explain the variation in volatility or correlation estimates over time, except for sampling error

If it exists, the unconditional correlation is one parameter, ρ, that has the same value throughout the process, just like unconditional volatility. But the estimates of unconditional volatility and correlation will be different at different times because of differences in the sample data. The smaller the sample the bigger the differences, because sampling errors are inversely proportional to the square root of sample size. It is important to note that there is nothing in an unconditional model to explain the variation in volatility or correlation estimates over time, except for sampling error.

Unfortunately, the 'correlation' one speaks of in financial markets does not always exist. Although it is generally satisfactory to assume that individual return processes are stationary it is by no means always the case that two return processes will be jointly stationary. For example, two arbitrary returns series such as a Latin American Brady bond and a stock in the Nikkei 225 could be totally unrelated. In that case they are not likely to be jointly stationary, so unconditional correlations between these returns do not exist. Of course, it is always possible to calculate a number, according to some statistical formula, and to suppose that this number represents correlation. But often these numbers change considerably from day to day, and this is a sure sign that the two returns processes are not jointly stationary — that unconditional correlation does not exist.

Of course, it is always possible to calculate a number, according to some statistical formula, and to suppose that this number represents correlation

It is not only in obviously unrelated markets that joint stationarity might fail to hold. In currency markets, commodity markets and equity markets it is not uncommon for time-varying correlation estimates to jump around considerably from day to day. Commonly, cross-market correlation estimates are even

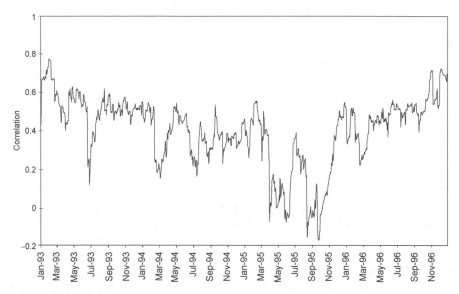

Figure 1.6 Bivariate vech GARCH correlation estimates of US dollar–sterling and Japanese yen–sterling exchange rates.

Some standard correlation estimation methods induce an apparent stability that is purely an artefact of the method

more unstable. Unfortunately, some standard correlation estimation methods induce an apparent stability that is purely an artefact of the method, and the unstable nature of underlying conditional correlations may be obscured (§3.1).

If correlation estimates are very unstable, what can be done to hedge correlation risk? In the absence of any specialized derivatives contract to hedge correlation it will be necessary to adjust mark-to-model values for uncertainty in correlation estimates (§5.3.1). Alternatively, one might consider using other measures of co-movement between assets, as described in Chapter 12.

The joint distribution between two returns series can also be viewed in a conditional framework, where the parameters that govern the joint distribution of returns are assumed to vary over time. *Conditional correlation* models allow the correlation in the conditional joint distribution to be different at different points in time. The notation is a natural extension of the notation for conditional volatility introduced above: the conditional covariance $\text{cov}_t(r_{1t}, r_{2t})$, also denoted $\sigma_{12,\,t}$, is divided by the product of the conditional standard deviations of each return. Thus (1.6) is extended to the parameters of the conditional joint distribution, to give the conditional correlation, denoted $\text{corr}_t(r_{1t}, r_{2t})$, or $\rho_{12,\,t}$.

A time-varying correlation model, such as the bivariate GARCH model described in §4.5.2, can be used to obtain time series estimates (and forecasts) of the conditional correlations between two returns series. However, these estimates are often quite unstable over time. Figure 1.6 illustrates a daily series of GARCH conditional correlation estimates for the US dollar–sterling and the Japanese yen–sterling exchange rates between 1993 and 1996. These correlation estimates show large jumps during the data period. Several times they either double or halve in value, more or less overnight.

This type of instability is quite common in conditional correlation estimates, but is much less apparent in unconditional correlation estimates. The past does not have the same role in conditional models as it does in unconditional correlation models. In unconditional correlation models the variation in correlation estimates is only due to sampling error, and events that happened far in the past can still affect the sampling error as much as if they happened only yesterday, so sampling errors can be perpetuated over a long period of time. However, in conditional correlation models the variation in successive estimates is also due to variation in the process parameters. The parameters vary because conditional correlation measures the co-dependency of two returns at a particular instant in time, assuming that everything that has happened in the past is *predetermined*. Current estimates are still influenced by past data, because it is in the information set, but the long-term past is less relevant than it may be in an unconditional model.

1.5   Remarks on Implementing Volatility and Correlation Models

It is important to have some consistency between the data frequency and the time-varying characteristics of the model that is used. For example, a time-varying volatility model would normally be based on high-frequency returns — in fact it is standard to use at least daily if not intra-day data. Any lower frequency of data will not capture the volatility clustering that is a characteristic of most financial markets (§4.1.1). Any attempt to estimate a time-varying volatility model for daily variations using low-frequency data would not give very meaningful results. Even daily data cannot capture the huge market swings that are sometimes experienced during the course of the day. However, the management of intra-day databases poses enormous practical problems and many institutions would not have such data readily available.

Any attempt to estimate a time-varying volatility model for daily variations using low-frequency data would not give very meaningful results

On the other hand, if a volatility or correlation model has no need to account for short-term variations in volatility or correlation, and is only required to generate forecasts of the unconditional volatility or correlation over a long-term risk horizon, there is no need to use high-frequency data. In fact the excess variation in high-frequency data will only be attributed to 'noise' or sampling errors, because there is nothing else in the model to explain it. Therefore, very high-frequency data can give misleading results when simple unconditional volatility or correlation estimates are all that is called for.

It is also important to employ a statistical volatility or correlation model that is consistent with the horizon of the forecast. To forecast a long-term average volatility it makes little sense to use a high-frequency time-varying volatility model. On the other hand, little information about short-term variations in daily volatility would be forthcoming from a long-term moving average volatility model.

A common option maturity is 3 months, so should one use a time-varying volatility model or a constant volatility model to price such an option? The answer depends on the volatility characteristics of the underlying asset returns — in particular, on their volatility term structure (§2.2.2). If 3-month volatility is close to the long-term average volatility then it is satisfactory to use a constant volatility model with a long averaging period (Chapter 3). However, if 3-month volatility often differs considerably from the long-term average it is better to use the 3-month forecast from a time-varying volatility model (§4.4.1).

Forecasts of volatility and correlation may just not be available for distant time horizons. Often implied volatilities cannot be obtained because there is no real market for options of the appropriate maturity. Sometimes statistical forecasts cannot be made because the underlying market is only very recent. In this case, if pricing a long-term option is a necessity, it is important to decide how uncertainties in volatility will be taken into account (§5.3).

If the underlying asset with missing or inaccurate data lies in a highly correlated system then much can be done to get around the problem by using principal component analysis

Missing data is a common problem that can affect both long-term and short-term volatility and correlation forecasting. Trading may be very thin, not just in long-term options, and if quotes are left stale for a long period of time then implied volatilities are never going to be very accurate. Lack of liquidity can also present problems when trying to obtain meaningful parameter estimates in statistical models. Short-term uncertainties will be impossible to quantify if there is currently no market in the underlying. However, if the underlying asset with missing or inaccurate data lies in a highly correlated system then much can be done to get around the problem by using principal component analysis (§6.4.2).

To obtain a statistical estimate or forecast of correlation, the historic data on the two asset returns need to be of the same frequency and measured at synchronous points in time. There may be a problem with obtaining data at exactly the same time for cross-market correlation estimates. If data on one series is measured before the data on the other, correlation estimates may be seriously biased. When it is impossible to obtain synchronous daily data, for example when two markets are never open at the same time, it may be better to move to a different frequency.

1.6 Summary

The aim of this chapter has been to introduce the reader to some of the important but complex concepts that will be discussed in Part I of the book. Volatility and correlation have been described as parameters of stochastic processes that are used to model variations in financial asset prices. Unlike market prices, they are unobservable and can only be estimated within the context of a model. Therefore the analysis of volatility and correlation is a very complex subject. In this introductory chapter some basic distinctions have been drawn, in particular between:

➤ implied and statistical volatility estimates and forecasts;
➤ constant parameter and time-varying parameter models for volatility and correlation.

It is necessary to understand these distinctions in order to motivate the exposition in the next four chapters.

2

Implied Volatility and Correlation

What is the 'correct' price of an option? If a model price is not the same as the market price, which is the 'right' price?

In game theory, the concept of a solution is determined by the 'rationality' of the players; in finance theory the concept of the correct price is determined by the nature of the modeller. The British, being practical and empirical, might say that the market is right and their model is wrong. The French — rationalists and theoreticians — might say that their model is right and the market is wrong. However, the Americans, pragmatic and diplomatic as they are, would most likely say that both the market and their model are wrong. But, to be serious, investors will attempt to trade on market prices that are close to their model price; on the other hand, quantitative analysts will calibrate an option pricing model by training it on market price. These two types of market participants are always trying to catch up with each other, and this is one of the ways in which we achieve market efficiency, if not necessarily rationality.

The observed market prices of options may have resulted from the use of several different models. However, most simple options are priced using models of the Black–Scholes type, which are based on two basic assumptions: first, that markets are complete and efficient (arbitrage-free), so there is a perfect hedge for any financial asset; and second, that underlying prices $S(t)$ are governed by a *geometric Brownian motion* (*GBM*) diffusion process with constant volatility σ:

$$dS(t)/S(t) = r\,dt + \sigma\,dZ(t),$$

where r is the risk-free rate of return and Z is a Wiener process.[1] These two assumptions are simple and powerful, but most people would agree that the Black–Scholes model is only a crude approximation of reality. In fact, the assumptions underlying the Black–Scholes model are incorrect.

This chapter will focus on some of the consequences of using the wrong model to price options. Section 2.1 shows that although there can only be one true

---

[1]That is, increments dZ are independent and normally distributed with mean zero and variance dt. The assumption that prices are governed by a GBM diffusion process implies that log returns are independently and normally distributed with constant volatility (§4.4.2).

volatility for the underlying price process, many different Black–Scholes volatilities are found to be implicit in the market prices of options on the same underlying price. If one is willing to accept these volatilities (rather than invent better models that are based on the observed empirical qualities of the underlying price), then their behaviour can be described by certain patterns. First, the volatility smile pattern found in options of different strikes on the same underlying is described and explained in §2.2. The volatility smile is a result of using an over-simplistic model and would not be found if options were priced using an appropriate model. This section also looks at the term structure of implied volatilities and the shape of the whole volatility smile surface in different types of markets.

The volatility smile is a result of using an over-simplistic model and would not be found if options were priced using an appropriate model

Section 2.3 looks at the relationship between underlying price changes and changes in the implied volatility of an at-the-money option. For equity indices, empirical observation on the correlation in this relationship supports the use of different volatility assumptions for pricing and hedging, depending on the current market conditions. At the end of §2.3 some joint distributions for price and volatility changes are derived and their applications to probabilistic scenario analysis are discussed. The chapter concludes with a brief account of implied correlation and its use in pricing and hedging options.

2.1   Understanding Implied Volatility

A simple option pricing model will give a theoretical price for an option as a function of a constant volatility for the underlying price process (§1.3) and other known values such as interest rates, time to maturity, exercise prices and so on. Option writers might use a statistical model to forecast some value for the volatility of the underlying process, and then substitute this volatility into the pricing model to obtain the theoretical or 'model price' of the option. Of course, if the option is traded, the market price may not be the same as the model price. In that case one might ask, which volatility forecast does one have to use in the model so that the model price and the market price are the same? This is the implied volatility. In a constant volatility framework implied volatility is the volatility of the underlying asset price process that is implicit in the market price of an option according to a particular model. It is a volatility forecast, not an estimate of volatility, with horizon given by the maturity of the option.[2]

Implied volatility is the volatility of the underlying asset price process that is implicit in the market price of an option

Implied volatility is a forecast of the process volatility. If process volatility is stochastic, implied volatility may be thought of as the *average* volatility of the underlying asset price process that is implicit in the market price of an option. Now, whatever the assumption made about the process volatility, it is very

---

[2]Note that in an option pricing model there may be other factors with no known value, such as dividends or average tax effects. Unfortunately, volatility is often the only parameter that is adjusted to match model prices to market prices.

likely that different options on the same underlying asset will give different implied volatilities. When real-world data are used to infer parameter values, different data will give different inferences. In a way, one might view the differences between different implied volatilities for the same underlying asset as a form of sampling error.

However, there is a problem which time and time again will lead to unresolved questions and irreconcilable differences. And that is, that the generic geometric Brownian motion model for the price process is wrong.

2.1.1 Volatility in a Black–Scholes World

It is not always possible to compute 'the' volatility that is implicit in the market price of an option according to a certain model.[3] However, most implied volatilities are based on the *Black–Scholes formula* for European options (Black and Scholes, 1973).[4] In this formula the price of a call option with strike price K and time to maturity τ, on an underlying asset with no dividend and current price S and volatility σ, is given by

$$C = S\Phi(x) - Ke^{-r\tau}\Phi(x - \sigma\sqrt{\tau}). \qquad (2.1a)$$

Here r denotes the risk-free rate of interest, used to discount the strike into present value terms, and $\Phi(\cdot)$ is the normal distribution function.

The terms $\Phi(x)$ and $\Phi(x - \sigma\sqrt{\tau})$ allow uncertainty in the price process to be accounted for in the option price. The quantity x provides a measure of the *moneyness* of the option (as described in more detail below); it is given by

$$x = \ln(S/Ke^{-r\tau})/\sigma\sqrt{\tau} + \sigma\sqrt{\tau}/2.$$

The process volatility is σ and τ is the maturity of the option in years, so the term $\sigma\sqrt{\tau}$ is the τ-maturity standard deviation of returns under the assumption of constant volatility (§3.3).[5] The first term in x measures the divergence between the current price and the discounted value of the strike, relative to the standard deviation. The second term is there because of the volatility dependence of C.

The price of a put option on the same underlying with the same strike, maturity and volatility is

---

[3]It is also possible that a given market price could be justified with several different volatilities if the option in question is not European, or is in some other way 'exotic'. Or there may be no volatility that equates the model price with the market price.

[4]A *European option* is one that can only be exercised on the maturity date; *American options* may be exercised before their maturity date and are much more difficult to price than European options.

[5]If volatility is quoted in annualized percentage form it should be divided by $100\sqrt{A}$ when calculating x. Note that the number of *trading days* (or *risk days*) per year is usually taken for the conversion of a daily standard deviation into an annualized percentage; that is, often $A = 250$ or 252 in (1.2). But note, on the other hand, that the maturity of the option is used to discount values to today and therefore an option having h days to expiry will have $\tau = h/365$ (or 366 in a leap year).

$$P = -S\Phi(-x) + Ke^{-r\tau}\Phi(-(x - \sigma\sqrt{\tau})). \tag{2.1b}$$

Therefore, we have the following relationship, referred to as *put–call parity*:

$$C - P = S - Ke^{-r\tau}. \tag{2.2}$$

Intuitively, the left-hand side is the value of a bought call and a sold put with the same strike, maturity and volatility. Now either $S > Ke^{-r\tau}$, in which case the put would be worth nothing if exercised now but the call would be worth $S - Ke^{-r\tau}$ in present value terms. Or $S < Ke^{-r\tau}$, in which case the call would be worth nothing if exercised now but the put has worth $-(S - Ke^{-r\tau})$.

Some people speak of call options being *in the money* (ITM) if the current price is above the discounted value of the strike; *out of the money* (OTM) if the current price is below the discounted value of the strike; and *at the money* (ATM) if the current price is equal to the discounted value of the strike. However, it is more natural to define the 'moneyness' of an option so that options are ITM, OTM or ATM according as moneyness is positive, negative or zero. A number of slightly different measures of moneyness are used (and so there are corresponding differences in the definition of the ATM strike). Many people use x itself for the moneyness; this is done in Figure 2.1. Thus an option is ITM, ATM or OTM according as $x > 0$, $x = 0$, or $x < 0$. Under constant volatility this definition of the moneyness is approximately the same as $\Delta - \frac{1}{2}$, where Δ is the option *delta* (§2.3.3). However, there are other less formal definitions of moneyness that have slipped into common use.[6]

Black–Scholes call option prices increase monotonically with volatility

As is obvious from formulae (2.1), the Black–Scholes price of an option has a non-linear relationship with volatility. Some graphs of a call price (left-hand scale) and the moneyness measure x (right-hand scale) against volatility are shown in Figure 2.1. The reader may generate their own figures using the **implied volatility** spreadsheet on the CD. These figures show that Black–Scholes call option prices increase monotonically with volatility. Intuitively, the greater the volatility, the more uncertainty and the greater the value of the option.[7] Note that ATM call option prices are approximately linear with respect to volatility, but this is not the case for ITM and OTM call option prices. The sensitivity of an option price to changes in volatility is commonly called the option *vega*.[8] ATM options have the greatest sensitivity to volatility because they can so easily move ITM or OTM even with low levels of volatility (§2.3.3 and §5.4).

---

[6]Other definitions include: $S - Ke^{-r\tau}$; the same without discounting the strike; the ratio S/K (with or without discounting K); and $\ln(S/K)$ with or without discounting the strike. With these definitions the moneyness is not comparable between different options because it will vary with the price of the underlying. The reason why x is often the preferred definition for moneyness is that in the first term of x the numerator, $\ln(S/Ke^{-r\tau})$, measures the deviation between the underlying and the discounted strike and the denominator, $\sigma\sqrt{\tau}$, is the τ-period volatility. Therefore, in x the deviation is normalized by the volatility, which makes x comparable between different options.

[7]Without uncertainty, options would have no intrinsic value.

[8]This is a term that was invented by Americans, and intended to sound like a Greek letter. Some people call it the option *zeta*, and at least in this case there is no confusion about the letter of the alphabet that should be used in the notation.

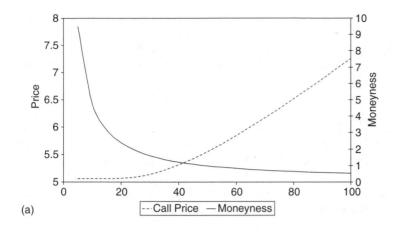

(a)

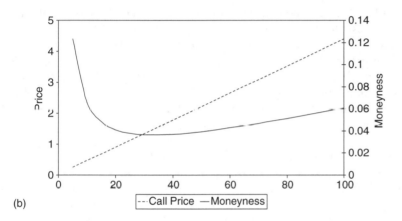

(b)

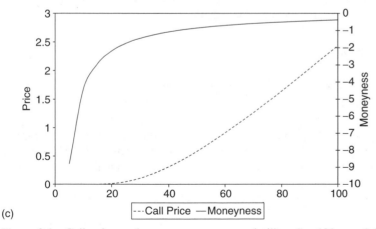

(c)

Figure 2.1 Call price and moneyness versus volatility: $S = 100$, $t = 0.012$, $r = 0.055$ and (a) $K = 95$; (b) $K = 100$; (c) $K = 105$.

Exactly the same implied volatility should be implicit in the prices of all options of the same type on the same underlying asset. However, this assumes that the pricing model is correct, and generally it is not

If the market price of an option can be observed, along with the current price of the underlying S, then every variable in the Black–Scholes option pricing model has a known value — except the volatility. Therefore, the pricing model may be used with the known quantities K, r and τ, and the observed quantities C and S, to 'back out' the volatility. In fact implied volatility is really just an inverse option price in the sense of the inverse function theorem.

There is no closed-form solution for implied volatility, even when the option pricing model has an analytic form. We know that implied volatility is usually increasing with option prices, but there is no simple formula that relates implied volatility to the market price of the option, the underlying price and the other variables. Instead one has to use numerical methods to solve for volatility as an implicit function of the known quantities:[9]

$$\text{Implied Volatility} = f(C, K, S, \tau, r).$$

Within the Black–Scholes assumptions there is a constant volatility for the underlying process, so all options on the same underlying should give the same implied volatility. Put another way, exactly the same implied volatility should be implicit in the prices of all options of the same type on the same underlying asset. However, this assumes that the pricing model is correct, and generally it is not. When the Black–Scholes model is used, one obtains different implied volatilities for different strikes and maturities on the same underlying asset.

Rather than changing the model, a 'quick fix' is to change the only unknown factor — the volatility

Therefore either the market information is not accurate or the market does not believe in the assumptions of the Black–Scholes model: in particular, the constant volatility and the normality of returns may be questioned by the market. Market prices often reflect properties of the price process that are not assumed in the Black–Scholes model. Rather than changing the model, a 'quick fix' is to change the only unknown factor — the volatility. There is nothing else that appears to be unknown so the Black–Scholes model uses different implied volatilities for different strikes and maturities.

2.1.2 Call and Put Implied Volatilities

In a simple European option, if the pricing model is applied correctly then it should not matter whether one uses a call price or a put price to back out implied volatility. If a put and a call of the same maturity are both available for a given strike, the implied volatility in the call should be the same as the implied volatility in the put. Even though one is ITM and the other is OTM, the same constant volatility is implicit in both option prices.[10] However, some sources

---

[9]Often Newton–Raphson iteration is the preferred method, much faster than the simple 'method of bisections' (Chriss, 1997). See the **implied volatility** spreadsheet on the CD.

[10]Also, in the put–call parity relationship (2.2) the right-hand side is independent of volatility. Therefore, if the price of a call of a fixed strike K goes up due to an increase in volatility, the price of the put of the same strike must go up by an equal amount.

Table 2.1: Prices, implied volatilities and volume of trade on call and put options

Strike	Calls			Puts		
	Price	*Implied volatility*	*Volume*	*Price*	*Implied volatility*	*Volume*
6250	223	—	10	4	23.65	120
6300	176	—	1	6.5	21.55	37
6350	132	29.21	2	12.5	20.4	2
6400	92	26.32	18	23	19.28	22
6450	58.5	24.26	30	40	17.9	64
6500	33	22.51	178	66.5	16.57	12
6550	16	21.42	400	102.5	14.48	0
6600	5.5	19.53	1966	149	14.05	3
6650	2	19.23	0	199	—	0
6700	0.5	18.59	1	249	—	0

of implied volatility data show discrepancies between call and put implied volatility. Why should this be so?

Consider the data on option prices and associated implied volatilities for FTSE 100 index options shown in Table 2.1. A plot of these implied volatilities against strike is shown in Figure 2.1.

Notice that the call implied volatility is considerably greater than the put implied volatility for all strikes, as shown in Figure 2.2.[11] Generally speaking, if call implied volatilities are significantly different from put implied volatilities it is because the evaluation model is not applied correctly. Probably it is a model based on spot price when the appropriate hedging instrument is a future, and the future is not quite in line with the spot price. In a rising market, or whenever the future trades above its 'fair' or theoretical value, calls will appear more expensive than they should because market prices are based on a higher underlying price than the underlying price taken in the model. The way that the model is adjusted to account for the high market price is to jack up the volatility. Similarly, puts will appear less expensive than they should, so the implied volatility that is backed out of the model will be lower. The opposite is true in a falling market, or whenever the future trades below its fair value.

If call implied volatilities are significantly different from put implied volatilities it is because the evaluation model is not applied correctly

In the example above the closing value of the FTSE 100 index was 6451.2, so the theoretical fair value of the future was 6453.92. However, the FTSE 100 future closed at 6486.[12] The call implied volatilities are too high because the

---

[11]These are American options and they only have 3 days to expiry. Compared to the time value, the early exercise premium may have a large effect. However, the early exercise premium only increases the value of put options and so makes the point even more strongly in this example.

[12]The index closes 30 minutes later than the future, so the index had fallen back.

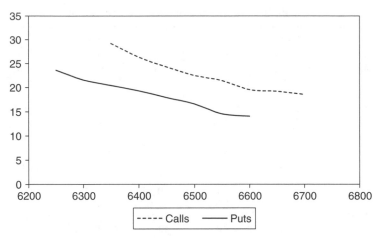

Figure 2.2   Implied volatilities on the FTSE 100 index option, 15 June 1999.

market price is based on a higher price than is assumed in the model, and put implied volatilities are too low.

This sort of anomaly would disappear with a model that takes into account the actual futures price. Whenever possible, implied volatilities should be taken from futures options rather than options on the underlying cash instrument, unless the cash market can be used for hedging. Then, when the model is applied correctly, the implied volatility in an ITM call should be about the same as the implied volatility in an OTM put of the same strike.

2.1.3   Differences between Implied and Statistical Volatilities

Implied volatilities should be viewed differently from statistical volatilities, even though they both forecast the volatility of the underlying asset over the life of the option. The two forecasts differ because they use different data and different models.[13] Implied methods use current data on market prices of options, so implied volatility contains all the forward expectations of investors about the likely evolution of the underlying. The model for implied volatility assumes complete markets, no arbitrage and a GBM constant volatility continuous time diffusion process for the underlying asset price. Contrast this with statistical methods for generating volatility forecasts, which use historic data on the underlying asset returns in a discrete time model for the variance of a time series.

If the option pricing model were an accurate representation of reality, and if investors' expectations were taken as correct, then any observed differences

---

[13]The model for the underlying price process in a statistical analysis should not differ from the model used for option pricing.

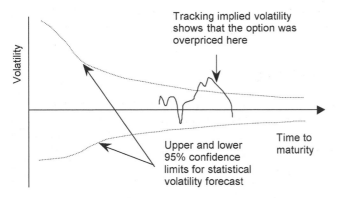

Figure 2.3 Volatility cones.

between implied and statistical volatility would reflect inaccuracies in the statistical forecast. Alternatively, if statistical volatilities were accurate, then differences between the implied and statistical forecasts of volatility would reflect a mispricing of the option by the market.

Implied volatilities can be compared with the statistical forecasts of volatility over a horizon equal to the term of the option. This type of comparison has been used as a means of evaluating whether an option is cheap or expensive. Upper and lower confidence limits can be taken from statistical volatility forecasts (§5.2) and any substantial mispricing of the option in the market will show up when the implied volatility exceeds one of these limits. If the implied volatility exceeds the upper limit the market may be overpricing the option, and if it falls below the lower limit the market may be underpricing the option.

This type of comparison has been used as a means of evaluating whether an option is cheap or expensive

To trade on this type of observation, of course, one needs to gain some sense of the volatility history of the option. This is what is gained by looking at *volatility cones*. To construct a cone, estimate confidence limits for volatility forecasts of several different horizons, as described in §5.2. If implied volatilities are available then these should be used to construct the cones. Otherwise one might construct an empirical distribution of historical volatility from all h-period volatilities during the last few years and record the upper and lower 95% confidence limits. Repeat this for a number of different holding periods, from 1 day to 1 year say, and this will give the upper and lower limits of the cones, as in Figure 2.3.

Cones are used to track implied volatility over the life of a particular option, and under- or overshooting the cone can signal an opportunity to trade, as shown in the figure. However, if the cone is constructed from the confidence limits for statistical forecasts they should be used with caution, particularly if overshooting is apparent at the long end. This is because differences between long-term statistical and implied volatility are to be expected. In particular, transaction costs can be substantial for long-term positions when there is a real imbalance between supply and demand, and these are implicit in implied volatilities but not in the statistical volatilities (Swidler and Diltz, 1992).

2.2 Features of Implied Volatility

We have just seen that the constant volatility assumption does not fit the market prices of options very well. One consequence of this is that, if model prices are to be close to market prices, then different volatilities for options of different strikes and maturity on the same underlying asset must be used. This section describes, and attempts to explain, some well-known patterns in the behaviour of Black–Scholes implied volatility as the strike and the maturity of the option change.

2.2.1 Smiles and Skews

The *smile effect* refers to the empirical fact that for most underlying assets a plot of implied volatility against strike has a smile shape.[14] Implied volatility is usually higher for OTM puts and calls than for ATM options. Why should this be so?

If returns are fat-tailed then large price changes will be more likely, and consequently an OTM option will have a higher chance of becoming ITM, than is assumed in the Black–Scholes model. The only way that the Black–Scholes price can match the market price is to increase the volatility

Most options are priced using the Black–Scholes formula, but it is well known that the assumptions upon which this formula is based are not justified empirically. In particular, return distributions may be 'fat-tailed' (§10.2) and their volatility is certainly not constant (§4.1). Therefore, it is not really appropriate to model the underlying price as a geometric Brownian motion. If prices are not governed by a geometric Brownian motion then large price changes may be observed empirically with a frequency that is greater than that assumed in the Black–Scholes model. If returns distributions are normal but volatility is stochastic, or if volatility is constant but returns are fat-tailed — or, indeed, both — then large price changes will be more likely, and consequently an OTM option will have a higher chance of becoming ITM, than is assumed in the Black–Scholes model. Therefore, the Black–Scholes model price will be less than the market price for an OTM option. Now the only way that the Black–Scholes price can match the market price is to increase the volatility — this is the only parameter that the model is free to change. Thus the implied volatility for OTM options will be greater than the ATM implied volatility.

Symmetric smiles where both OTM call and put options have higher implied volatilities than ATM options are commonly observed in foreign exchange markets. However, in equity markets the smile has a negative skew appearance, with higher implied volatilities for the low strike options and lower implied volatilities for the high strike options. This can only be due to the fact that the market price of low strike options (ITM calls and OTM puts) is much higher than the Black–Scholes model predicts. The main reason for this is that equity

---

[14]It is also common to plot a volatility smile as implied volatility against moneyness instead of strike. In §2.3.3 we see that the moneyness, as measured by x, and the Black–Scholes delta of an option have a simple relationship: $\Delta_{\text{BS}}(S, \sigma) = \Phi(x)$. Therefore it is also common to plot volatility smiles with respect to delta.

markets are not symmetric. A price fall is bad news for the shareholders, whereas a price rise is good.[15] The negative skew is often very noticeable in the index market, where a very large price fall could precipitate 'doom and gloom' for the economy as a whole. Traders will therefore use a high volatility to price an OTM put, and they are able to do this because there is a high demand for the insurance offered by these puts from risk-averse investors. This highly priced supply of OTM puts will normally be met by an equal demand as long as investors hold pessimistic views about the possibility of a market crash. It is notable that the skew in equity markets has only been pronounced since the 1987 global crash in equity markets.

A secondary reason for the negative skew in equity markets is that equity markets become much more turbulent after a large price fall than they do after a price rise of the same magnitude. This so-called 'leverage effect' is discussed in §4.1.2. The market price of an ITM call (or equivalently an OTM put) reflects the fact that if there is a large fall in price (so the ITM call option becomes OTM) the underlying asset volatility will remain high for some time. Then the prices of all options will increase and, in particular, the call option will have a high probability of becoming ITM again because of the increased volatility. The higher than expected market price of ITM calls and OTM puts can therefore be attributed to more than just the 'doom and gloom' in the economy — the leverage effect also plays a secondary role.

2.2.2 Volatility Term Structures

Now consider the relationship between maturity and implied volatility for a fixed strike option. For example, reading across a single row in Table 2.2 gives the market prices of different maturity options of the same strike, and backing out the volatilities implied in these prices will give a term structure of volatility. Figure 2.4 shows the implied volatility, plotted as a function of the option maturity, which corresponds to the call prices given in the second row of Table 2.2 ($K = 6325$).

The volatility term structure converges to the long-term average volatility level. This is a consequence of the mean-reverting behaviour of volatility; the fact that volatility comes in bursts or 'clusters'

The volatility term structure converges to the long-term average volatility level, which is about 21% in the figure, and this is a typical feature of implied volatility. It is a consequence of the mean-reverting behaviour of volatility; the fact that volatility comes in bursts or 'clusters' (§4.1.1). If the current period is very volatile, short-term volatilities will be well above the long-term average. Expectations may be that volatility will be high over the next few days, but over a longer period it is usually expected that volatility will fall back to its average level. On the other hand, if markets are relatively tranquil then short-term volatility will be below the long-term average and volatility term structures will converge from below.

---

[15]The opposite is usually the case in commodity markets: price falls are good news and price rises are bad news. The volatility skew in commodity markets is normally the other way around, that is, OTM calls (high strike options) have higher volatilities than OTM puts (low strike options).

Table 2.2: Market prices of FTSE 100 call and put options with different strikes and maturities

Expiry end: Strike	Jun Call	Jun Put	Jul Call	Jul Put	Aug Call	Aug Put	Sep Call	Sep Put	Dec Call	Dec Put
6275	169	11	281	101	366.5	182				
6325	126.5	19	245	115	332.5	197.5	397	244	582.5	373
6375	89	31	214	133.5	300	215			517.5	405.5
6425	57	49	184	154	269.5	233.5	333	279	517.5	405.5
6475	33	75	154.5	174	240	254				
6525	16	108	128.5	197.5	213	276	272	316.5	272	448
6575	6.5	148.5	104	223	187	300				
6625	2	194	83	252	163.5	326	219	362	219	495.5

Source: *Financial Times.*

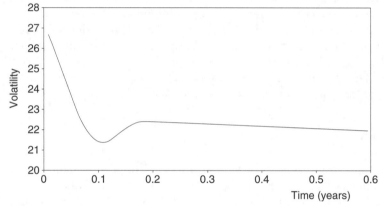

Figure 2.4 Term structure of implied volatilities on 15 June 1999; $S = 6451.2$, $K = 6325$, $r = 0.055$.

GARCH models are statistically tractable models of volatility that give convergent volatility term structure forecasts. However, if GARCH models are used there are many implications that will warrant careful consideration, and these will be discussed in Chapter 4. For example, the Black–Scholes delta (or gamma or vega) will no longer be appropriate, and pricing and hedging become uncertain because one can no longer assume the risk-neutrality hypothesis.[16]

2.2.3   Volatility Surfaces

Combining the smile (or skew), which is a cross section of implied volatilities from different strike options of the same maturity, with a volatility term structure for each of these strikes, one obtains a three-dimensional plot of

---

[16]The risk neutrality hypothesis rests on the completeness of markets and the arbitrage that results when it is possible to perfectly hedge any asset. However, when volatility is stochastic it will not be possible to hedge every type of asset perfectly (§4.4.2).

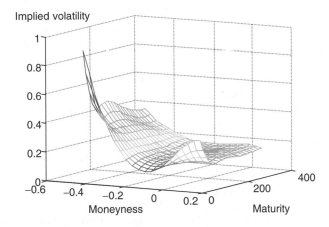

Implied volatility

Figure 2.5 Black–Scholes smile surface for FTSE 100 index options, December 1997.

implied volatility against strike price[17] and maturity, which is called a *volatility smile surface*. In most markets there is little trading in long-term or far-OTM options, therefore considerable skill is required to fit a smile surface to the available market data.

For example, the prices of the FTSE 100 Index European options on 15 June 1999 are shown in Table 2.2. Although some prices are quoted for the longer-term expiry dates, these options are very sparsely traded and the quoted prices will be rather unreliable. In general, only a few data points will be available at the long end of the smile surface, and it is necessary to interpolate and extrapolate between these points to get a smooth surface such as that shown in Figure 2.5.[18]

In this figure the smile and skew effects are much more noticeable in short-term options, and this is often found to be the case. If an OTM option has a long time to expiry, there will still be a good chance that it will end up ITM even with a relatively low level of volatility. However, short-term OTM option prices must reflect higher volatility expectations than short-term ATM option prices. With only a few days left to expiry an OTM option will require a big change in the underlying price — that is, a high volatility — if it is to be worth something at maturity.

The volatility smile surface over the (K, τ) or the (x, τ) domain should not be confused with the *volatility surface* — they are quite different. The volatility smile surface $\sigma(K, \tau)$ is a surface of the implied volatility (and usually the Black–Scholes implied volatility) viewed as a function of (K, τ). On the other hand, the volatility surface $\sigma(S, t)$ is a specification of the *process* volatility as a function of the underlying asset price S and time t. Of course, if the process

---

[17]It is also common to use a moneyness metric instead of a strike metric for the smile surface, as in Figure 2.5.

[18]This smile surface was fitted using the cubic spline method from Press *et al.* (1992). Many thanks to Chris Leigh for providing this.

volatility is constant this surface is flat; it is only when the process volatility is assumed to be non-constant that the question of the specification of the volatility surface arises.

To calibrate an option pricing model, which may include a volatility surface, the analyst will need to use market data on option prices. But is it really possible to specify a volatility surface by assuming a functional form and then to use market data on option prices to estimate the parameters of this function? The implied volatilities that are backed out from option prices are forecasts of the process volatility, so these could be used to estimate the parameters of a volatility surface. However, it is not consistent to use Black–Scholes implied volatilities in this way, because the Black–Scholes model assumes constant volatility.[19] Therefore, what is often done is that the Black–Scholes implied volatility for a particular option (usually ATM) is regarded as a forecast of the *average* volatility of the process over the lifetime of the option. If options are available for many different maturities then the time dimension of the volatility surface can be calibrated in this way.[20] The space dimension, S (i.e. the underlying price dimension), is more difficult, as we shall see in the next section.

2.3 The Relationship between Prices and Implied Volatility

Implied volatilities are derived from market prices. Therefore, you may ask, if the underlying price changes to some level, how will the implied volatilities change? An answer to this question will indicate how to calibrate the volatility surface in the space dimension[21] (§2.3.1). It will also tell us how to construct scenarios for prices and implied volatilities for use in risk management (§2.3.2). This is also a very interesting question for option traders, because the answer will give us the *volatility sensitivity to price* term, $\partial\sigma/\partial S$, which is an important determinant of the option delta (§2.3.3).

2.3.1 Equity Prices and Volatility Regimes

This subsection follows the work of Derman (1999) that is based on binomial trees with local volatilities rather than volatility surfaces.[22] Derman (1999) shows how local volatilities may be fixed by the strike of the option in some

---

[19]To be consistent, one should really use the implied volatilities that are backed out from market prices using a model with a time- and space-varying volatility process. However, this leads to a circular argument: the volatility process cannot be specified before one knows the parameters of the volatility surface, so one cannot back out the implied volatilities corresponding to that process from market prices.

[20]For example, if 1-week ATM volatility is $\sigma_1(t)$ at time t, and 2-week ATM volatility is $\sigma_2(t) = \sqrt{[(\sigma_1(t)^2 + \sigma_1(t+1)^2)/2]}$, then $\sigma_1(t+1) = \sqrt{[(2\sigma_2(t)^2 - \sigma_1(t)^2]}$. In a Brownian process, the variances are additive, not the volatilities.

[21]Assuming that Black–Scholes implied volatilities are forecasts of the average of a time-varying process volatility.

[22]A binomial tree is a discretization of a price process in space and time that is calibrated so that it will fit a deterministic volatility surface. The trend in nodes over time is equal to the risk-free rate and the 'local volatility' of a node is a measure of the dispersion at that node.

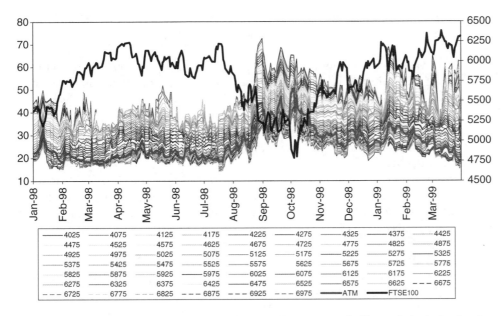

Figure 2.6 One-month fixed strike volatilities, at-the-money volatility and the index level.

circumstances (the 'sticky strike' model). That is, there will be a different tree relevant for pricing each option with a different strike, and all the local volatilities in this tree will be the same. In other circumstances (in fact when markets are trending but stable) the tree should have local volatility that is determined by the delta of the option, rather than the strike (the 'sticky delta' model). When markets are jumpy there is a single tree that can be used for all options, with local volatilities that really do vary from node to node (the 'sticky implied tree' model).

Figure 2.6 shows the 1-month implied volatilities for European options of all strikes on the FTSE 100 index for the period from 4 January 1998 to 31 March 1999.[23] The bold grey line indicates the ATM volatility and the bold black line the FTSE 100 index price (on the right-hand scale).

Look at the movements in the index and the way that ATM volatility is behaving in relation to the index. In the spring of 1998 the index was trending upwards while ATM volatility remained relatively constant. From mid-July until the end of August 1998 the index fell by over 1000 points in the wake of the Russian crisis. ATM volatility rose from 18% to 44% around this time, and

---

[23]The fixed maturity implied volatility data used in this section have been obtained by linear interpolation between the two adjacent maturity option implied volatilities. However, this presents a problem for the 1-month volatility series because data on the near maturity option volatilities are often totally unreliable during the last few working days before expiry. Therefore, the 1-month series rolls over to the next maturity, until the expiry date of the near-term option, and thereafter continues to be interpolated linearly between the two option volatilities of less than and greater than 1 month.

in the early part of 1999 it fell back from 35% to 18% as the FTSE index was jumpy but appeared to be bounded between 6300 and 5800.[24]

Observation of data similar to Figure 2.6, but on the S&P500 index option 3-month volatilities, has motivated Derman (1999) to formulate three different types of market regime:

(a) *range-bounded*, where future price moves are likely to be constrained within a certain range and there is no significant change in realized volatility;
(b) *trending*, where the level of the market is changing but in a stable manner so there is again little change in realized volatility in the long run; and
(c) *jumpy*, where the probability of jumps in the price level is particularly high so realized volatility increases.

Taking a cross-section from Figure 2.6 will normally give a line similar to that shown in Figure 2.7. In Derman's models the skew is approximated by a linear function of the strike. Derman hypothesizes that the form of this linear function should depend on the market regime. Denote by $\sigma_K(\tau)$ the implied volatility of an option with maturity τ and strike K, $\sigma_{ATM}(\tau)$ the volatility of the τ-maturity ATM option, S the current value of the index and σ_0 and S_0 the initial implied volatility and price used to calibrate the tree. Then:

(a) In a range-bounded market skews should be parameterized as

$$\sigma_K(\tau) = \sigma_0 - b(\tau)(K - S_0). \tag{2.3a}$$

Thus fixed strike volatility $\sigma_K(\tau)$ is independent of the index level in the sense that if the index changes, fixed strike volatilities will not change. This implies that σ_{ATM} will decrease as the index increases, as can be seen by substituting $S = K$ above, giving:

$$\sigma_{ATM}(\tau) = \sigma_0 - b(\tau)(S - S_0). \tag{2.4a}$$

The range-bounded model (2.3a) is called the 'sticky strike' model because local volatilities will be constant with respect to strike. That is, each option has its own binomial tree, with a constant volatility that is determined by the strike of the option. As the index moves all that happens is that the root of the tree is

---

[24]To understand why this should be so, suppose a firm's asset value X and equity price Y vary over time, but in the short run debt k is constant. Equity volatility will be greater than asset volatility ($Y = X - k$ so $\Delta Y/Y = \Delta X/(X - k)$, which is greater than $\Delta X/X$ if $k > 0$). In fact equity volatility divided by asset volatility is $X/(X - k)$. Now suppose the equity price jumps down. Then the asset value will go down in the short run, because debt is constant. Then equity volatility will become very much greater than the underlying (but unmeasurable) asset volatility. Therefore a downward jump in equity price should lead to a significant increase in equity volatility in the short run. In an upward-trending market asset values will go up and the equity volatility will go down, becoming closer to the underlying asset volatility. If asset values continue to stay high the asset volatility declines and the firm may wish to take advantage of this. Most likely it will increase its debt level, and if it does, the equity volatility will move up again. The net effect is that equity volatilities can appear to be negatively correlated with price movements, although they remain relatively constant over the longer term.

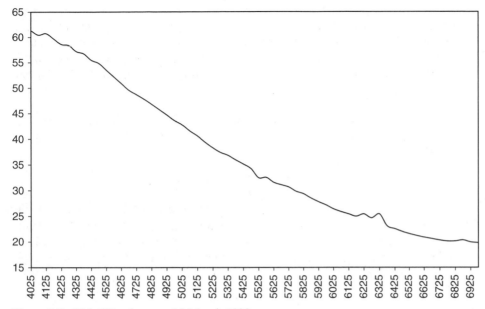

Figure 2.7 Volatility skew on 15 March 1999.

moved to the current level of the index. The same tree is still used to price the option.

(b) In a stable trending market skews should be parameterized as

$$\sigma_K(\tau) = \sigma_0 - b(\tau)(K - S). \tag{2.3b}$$

Fixed strike volatility $\sigma_K(\tau)$ will increase with the index level but $\sigma_{\text{ATM}}(\tau)$ will be independent of the index, since

$$\sigma_{\text{ATM}}(\tau) = \sigma_0. \tag{2.4b}$$

When the index moves, ATM volatility will remain constant. The trending markets model (2.3b) is called the 'sticky delta' model because local volatilities are constant with respect to the moneyness (or equivalently the delta) of the option. That is to say, it is the moneyness of the option that determines the (still constant) local volatility in the tree. As the index moves, the delta of the option changes and we consequently move to a different tree, the one corresponding to the current option delta.

(c) In jumpy markets skews should be parameterized as

$$\sigma_K(\tau) = \sigma_0 - b(\tau)(K + S) + 2b(\tau)S_0 \tag{2.3c}$$

Fixed strike volatility $\sigma_K(\tau)$ will decrease when the index goes up, and increase when the index falls. Since

$$\sigma_{\text{ATM}}(\tau) = \sigma_0 - 2b(\tau)(S - S_0), \tag{2.4c}$$

the ATM volatility will also decrease as the index goes up and increase as the index falls, and twice as fast as the fixed strike volatilities do. In the 'sticky tree' model (2.3c) the local volatilities in the binomial tree are no longer constant. There is, however, one unique tree that can be used to price all options, that is determined by the current skew. This is the implied tree described in Derman and Kani (1994).

All three 'sticky' models take the same form when they are expressed in terms of deviations of fixed strike volatility from the ATM volatility

Alexander (2001a) points out that all three 'sticky' models take the same form when they are expressed in terms of deviations of fixed strike volatility from the ATM volatility. That is,

$$\sigma_K(\tau) = \sigma_{\text{ATM}}(\tau) = -b(\tau)(K - S). \qquad (2.5)$$

In fact, one can view each of the sticky models as (2.5) together with the alternative parameterization given in equations (2.4a), (2.4b) and (2.4c). Note that each of these equations corresponds to a linear parameterization for the volatility surface $\sigma(S, t)$ in the space dimension. In fact we could specify the deterministic surface

$$\sigma(S, t) = b(t)S + c(t),$$

where the coefficient $b(t)$ jumps between three different levels (0, b and $-b$) as the market moves between different regimes and the coefficient $c(t)$ represents additional variation in the time dimension.

Not until Chapter 6 shall we develop the tools that allow us to use a more general model, where volatility surfaces are parameterized as a quadratic in S. Therefore, any further discussion of this topic will have to be postponed until §6.3, where Derman's 'sticky' models will be extended to a more flexible framework. For the present let us continue with the linear model framework, and ask how one should determine which value of $b(t)$ should be used. To distinguish which of the 'sticky' models is currently appropriate, a simple approach that is explained in the next subsection is to examine the recent behaviour of ATM volatility and its relationship with the index movements.

2.3.2 Scenario Analysis of Prices and Implied Volatility

A scenario-based risk management of options portfolios requires the definition of scenarios for implied volatilities and underlying asset prices. Given the current smile or skew, what is the appropriate way to change it as the price level moves? In the absence of an effective model of how implied volatilities change with market price, these scenarios may be rather simplistic. Constant volatility scenarios are often augmented with just a few simple scenarios. For example, the 1996 Basle Accord Amendment (§9.1.1) recommends using parallel shifts in all volatilities that are independent of movements in underlying prices.

This section describes a simple method for generating correlated movements between the underlying price and ATM volatility. The discussion above has shown how these correlations may depend on the current market regime. A joint distribution over all possible price and ATM volatility changes is generated, so that probabilistic scenario analysis methods can be employed (§9.6.2). The principal component model that is described in §6.3 will allow these scenarios to be extended to scenarios for the whole smile or skew.

In equity index options there is sometimes a clear negative correlation between ATM volatility and the underlying price, but at other times this correlation can seem very weak. Figure 2.8 shows, for three different 2-month periods during 1998, a scatter plot of the daily changes in 1-month ATM volatility against daily changes in index price for the FTSE 100 European option. The periods chosen were: (a) February and March 1998; (b) May and June 1998; and (c) August and September 1998.

Casual observation of these scatter plots indicates a significant negative correlation between the 1-month implied volatility and the index price, but the strength of this correlation depends on the data period. Period (a), when the UK equity market was very stable and trending, shows less correlation than period (b), when daily movements in the FTSE 100 index were limited to a 'normal' range; but the negative correlation is most obvious during the mini-crash period (c) that followed the Russian crisis in July 1998. These observations are not peculiar to the 1-month ATM FTSE 100 volatilities, and not just during the periods shown: negative correlations, of more or less strength depending on the data period, are also evident in other fixed term ATM volatilities and in other equity markets.

Realistic scenarios for ATM volatility and index prices would, therefore, be for movements in ATM volatility to occur in the opposite direction to the index price movements. The volatility regime models of §2.3.1 imply that the size of the relative movements will depend on current market regime. In stable trending markets ATM volatility changes should be independent of changes in the index; in range-bounded markets there should be a negative correlation between ATM volatility changes and index price changes; and the magnitude of this correlation will double when the market enters a jumpy regime.

The following simple model for the joint density of daily price changes and daily ATM implied volatility changes, denoted $\text{Prob}(\Delta S \text{ and } \Delta\sigma)$, can be used to assess the current market conditions and quantify the correlation effect. By the theorem of conditional probability,

$$\text{Prob}(\Delta S \text{ and } \Delta\sigma) = \text{Prob}(\Delta\sigma \mid \Delta S)\,\text{Prob}(\Delta S).$$

Now suppose that price changes are normally distributed,

$$\Delta S \sim N(\mu, \sigma^2), \tag{2.6}$$

and that the conditional distribution $\text{Prob}(\Delta\sigma \mid \Delta S)$ is given by the linear model

$$\Delta\sigma = \alpha + \beta\Delta S + \varepsilon, \tag{2.7}$$

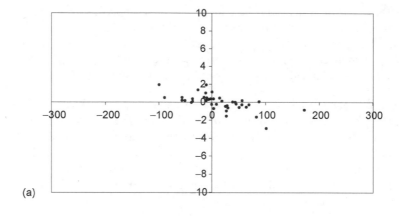

(a)

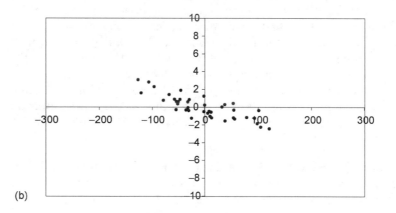

(b)

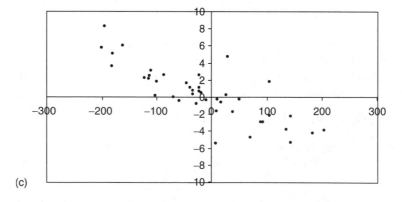

(c)

Figure 2.8 At-the-money volatility versus FTSE 100 (daily changes): (a) February and March 1998; (b) May and June 1998; (c) August and September 1998.

where $\varepsilon \sim N(0, \sigma_\varepsilon^2)$. Then $\Delta\sigma \,|\, \Delta S \sim N(\alpha + \beta\Delta S, \sigma_\varepsilon^2)$ and the joint density will be bivariate normal, that is, the product of two normal densities $N(\alpha + \beta\Delta S, \sigma_\varepsilon^2)$ and $N(\mu, \sigma^2)$.

Estimation of the parameters α, β, σ_ε^2, μ and σ^2 could be done using any type of distribution fitting method. A simple and transparent method is to estimate all parameters using equally weighted historic data over a prespecified time period. Thus the parameters in (2.6) are estimated by taking the sample mean and variance of all the daily price changes during the recent past. The parameter estimates in (2.7) can be obtained by ordinary least squares regression of $\Delta\sigma$ on ΔS over same data window. It is important not to use too much historic data for the parameter estimation, so that the parameter estimates will capture only the most recent market behaviour. However, obviously there is a trade-off between accuracy in the estimates and their ability to isolate the current market regime.

Figure 2.9 shows a joint density for 31 July 1998 that has been constructed using this method. The parameter estimates in Table 2.3 were obtained using two months of daily data.

The data period in Table 2.3 corresponds to a relatively stable market, and this is evident from the joint density shown in Figure 2.9. There is a significantly negative but relatively small correlation between the changes of

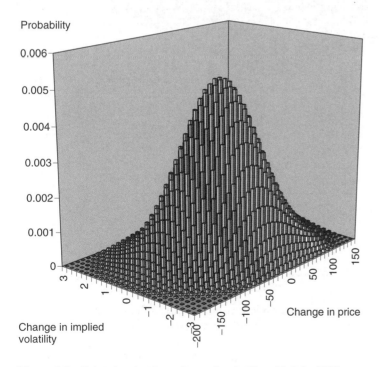

Figure 2.9 Joint density for price and volatility, 31 July 1998.

Table 2.3: Parameter estimates for joint density of $\Delta\sigma$ and ΔS on 31 July 1998

α	0.044386985
β	-0.018945946
σ_ε	1.234698494
μ	-4.637254902
σ	65.81748084

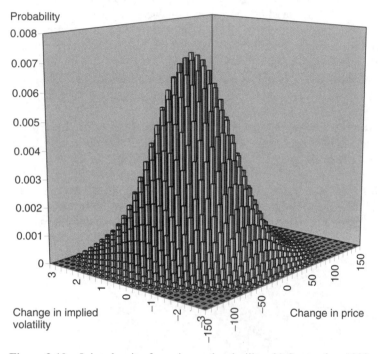

Figure 2.10 Joint density for price and volatility, 30 September 1998.

Table 2.4: Parameter estimates for joint density of $\Delta\sigma$ and ΔS on 30 September 1998

α	0.044386985
β	-0.035899089
σ_ε	1.23452389
μ	-10.6478327
σ	45.2964378

the index and the changes in implied volatility, as reflected in the estimate of β, and the mean daily change in the index is only -4.6.

Contrast this with the density shown in Figure 2.10, which is given by the parameter estimates of Table 2.4. On 30 September 1998 the market had been through an extremely jumpy period and the probability of large downward moves in the index, accompanied by large upward moves in the ATM volatility, was much higher than it was on 31 July. This is evident from the estimate of beta having risen (in absolute terms) to -0.0359. The mean daily change in index price was -10.6.

This section has illustrated a simple method for examining the correlations of price changes and ATM volatility changes. Knowledge of this correlation provides information about the current market regime, and therefore the appropriate sticky model to use for calibrating binomial trees for option pricing and hedging. It shows how to construct a joint density for prices and ATM volatilities that can be used to compute the expected loss in probabilistic scenario analysis (§9.6).

However, it has told us nothing about the relationship between fixed strike volatilities and changes in the underlying price. Since positions are likely to move ITM and/or OTM during the risk horizon, we need to know what scenarios are most probable for the whole volatility skew. More than this, in the next section we show how it is extremely important to have an accurate estimate of the volatility sensitivity to price, $\partial\sigma/\partial S$, for options of all strikes. The simple model that has been presented in this section will not provide these estimates and we shall have to return to this problem later in the book, in §6.3, after some more sophisticated tools have been developed.

It is extremely important to have an accurate estimate of the volatility sensitivity to price, $\partial\sigma/\partial S$, for options of all strikes

2.3.3   Implications for Delta Hedging

In this section we write an option price as $f = f(S, \sigma)$, ignoring the dependence on strike, maturity, discount rates and so on for ease of notation. The *delta* of an option is its price sensitivity to changes in the underlying price S:

$$\Delta(S, \sigma) = \partial f(S, \sigma)/\partial S. \qquad (2.8)$$

Standard delta hedging strategies are to match each unit of the option with Δ units of the underlying. Therefore if one is short x units in the option one goes long Δx units of the underlying, and this hedged portfolio has value $V = \Delta x S - x f(S, \sigma)$. The delta hedged portfolio is called *delta neutral* because the portfolio value will remain unchanged for small changes in the underlying: $\partial V/\partial S = 0$.

The amount of the underlying required to maintain delta neutrality will usually change every time the underlying price changes. That is, the option delta will depend on the underlying price level unless the option gamma is zero. The *gamma* of an option measures the sensitivity of delta to changes in the underlying price:

$$\Gamma(S, \sigma) = \partial^2 f(S, \sigma)/\partial S^2 = \partial\Delta(S, \sigma)/\partial S. \qquad (2.9)$$

Gamma is usually greatest for ATM options, and typically it will increase as the option approaches expiry. Therefore to maintain delta neutrality the portfolio will have to be delta hedged on a dynamic basis, and very frequently as the option approaches expiry. This rebalancing can be very costly so it is obviously important to get the delta right. What is the right delta to use?

If one assumes volatility is constant as in the Black–Scholes model, the *Black–Scholes delta* is simply

$$\Delta_{BS}(S, \sigma) = \partial f / \partial S.$$

From the Black–Scholes formula (2.1), $\Delta_{BS}(S, \sigma) = \Phi(x)$ and the delta is easily calculated as the value of the normal distribution $\Phi(\cdot)$ at x, the moneyness of the option.[25]

However, the discussion in this section has focused on the fact that the smile surface changes each time the underlying moves. We should *not* be assuming that volatility is constant, and instead we shall suppose that that the volatility surface $\sigma(S, t)$ is deterministic. In this case applying the chain rule to compute the option delta gives:

$$\Delta(S, \sigma) = \partial f / \partial S + [\partial f / \partial \sigma][\partial \sigma / \partial S] = \Delta_{BS} + \text{vega}[\partial \sigma / \partial S], \qquad (2.10)$$

where

$$\text{vega} = \partial f(S, \sigma) / \partial \sigma. \qquad (2.11)$$

The option *vega* is the sensitivity of the option price to changes in implied volatility. ATM options can have very large vegas; in fact the option gamma and the option vega are often proportional.[26] When volatility is not constant and an option has a non-zero vega, the Black–Scholes delta will not be very accurate. From (2.10) an extra term which contains the vega and the volatility price sensitivity $\partial \sigma / \partial S$ will have to be included.

When volatility is not constant and an option has a non-zero vega, the Black–Scholes delta will not be very accurate

Option traders often approximate the term $\partial \sigma / \partial S$ by $\partial \sigma / \partial K$. That is, they evaluate the slope of the current skew or smile and use that in place of the volatility price sensitivity to calculate the option delta by (2.10). Note that the sticky models given in equations (2.3) will determine different values for $\partial \sigma / \partial S$ according to the market regimes. In range-bounded markets one should take $\partial \sigma / \partial S = 0$, but in trending markets $\partial \sigma / \partial S = b$ and in jumpy markets $\partial \sigma / \partial S = -b$. These models do not, however, provide a measure for this coefficient b. In any case, how does one know which model to apply?

---

[25] $\partial C / \partial S = \Phi(x) + S\phi(x)\partial x / \partial S - Ke^{-rt}\phi(y)\partial y / \partial S$, where $y = x - \sigma\sqrt{\tau}$. Since $\partial y / \partial S = \partial x / \partial S$, this may be written $\partial C / \partial S = \Phi(x) + (\partial x / \partial S)[S\phi(x) - Ke^{-rt}\phi(y)]$, where $\phi(x) = \Phi'(x)$. A little algebra shows that the term in the square brackets is zero.

[26] For a simple example to illustrate this, suppose the pay-off function is $(S_t - S_0)^2$, where the variance $V(S_t)$ is $\sigma^2 S_0^2 t$, such as would be the case under geometric Brownian motion starting from an initial price $S = S_0$. Then the value $f(S, \sigma) = E((S_t - S_0)^2) = V(S_t) = \sigma^2 S_0^2 t$. Therefore, gamma $= 2\sigma^2 t$ and vega $= 2\sigma S_0^2 t$. That is, vega $= (S_0^2 / \sigma)$gamma.

An alternative method for estimating $\partial\sigma/\partial S$ is presented in §6.3. There we show how Derman's sticky models are limited to only parallel shifts in the equity skew, corresponding to a volatility surface that is linear in the space dimension. Section 6.3 presents a different model that has a quadratic parameterization of the volatility surface and includes non-parallel as well as parallel shifts in the skew. Using principal component analysis, the model will be used to provide an estimate of the $\partial\sigma/\partial S$ term that is so important for dynamic delta hedging.

2.4   Implied Correlation

In some circumstances an implied correlation may be derived from associated implied volatilities—for example, in currency markets, when there are options available on two foreign exchange rates and the cross rate, or whenever there are traded spread options. Rearranging the formula for the variance of a difference,

$$\sigma_{x-y}^2 = \sigma_x^2 + \sigma_y^2 - 2\sigma_x\sigma_y\rho,$$

to solve for the correlation ρ gives

$$\rho = \frac{\sigma_x^2 + \sigma_y^2 - \sigma_{x-y}^2}{2\sigma_x\sigma_y}.$$

If there are traded options on X, Y and $X - Y$, putting these implied volatilities in the above formula gives the associated implied correlation. For example, X and Y could be two US dollar foreign exchange rates (in logarithms) so $X - Y$ is the cross rate, and the implied correlation between the two foreign exchange rates is calculated from the implied volatilities of the two US dollar rates σ_x and σ_y and the implied volatility of the cross rate σ_{x-y}.

There is a convenient graphic representation of this implied correlation in the unique triangle with the length of each side equal to the implied volatility. The implied correlation is the cosine of the opposite angle, as shown in Figure 2.11. This idea can be extended to higher-dimensional simplices.

Similar calculations can be used for equity implied correlations, but they are based on some rather severe assumptions. If the correlation between all pairs of equities in an index is constant then the implied value of this constant correlation is approximated from implied volatilities of stocks in the index, σ_i and the implied volatility of the index, σ_I as

$$\rho = (\sigma_I^2 - \Sigma\omega_i^2\sigma_i^2)/(2\,\Sigma\Sigma\omega_i\omega_j\sigma_i\sigma_j), \tag{2.12}$$

where ω_i denotes the weight of stock i in the index. Of course, the constant correlation assumption is very restrictive, and not all equities will be optionable, so they have to be omitted from the formula. The approximation (2.12) is therefore very crude and can lead to implied correlation estimates that are

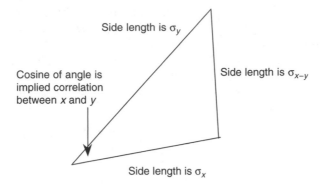

Figure 2.11   Graphical representation of implied correlation.

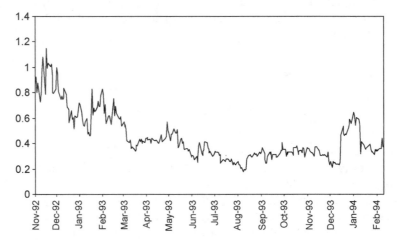

Figure 2.12   Implied correlation in FTSE 100 equities.

greater than 1. Figure 2.12 shows that this was in fact the case at the end of 1992, for a constant implied correlation of the form (2.12) calculated using all the optionable stocks in the FTSE 100.

A *quanto correlation* is the correlation between an equity and an exchange rate. The issuer of a quanto option offers purchasers a protection against currency risk by determining the pay-off at a fixed exchange rate. The Black–Scholes type formula for pricing a quanto option on an underlying foreign equity with foreign currency price S and strike K is:

$$C = \bar{X}(Se^{(R-r)\tau}\Phi(x) - Ke^{-r\tau}\Phi(x - \sigma\sqrt{\tau})), \qquad (2.13)$$

where r is the domestic discount rate, $\bar{X}$ is the predetermined domestic/foreign exchange rate, $x = \ln(S/Ke^{-R\tau})/\sigma\sqrt{\tau} + \sigma\sqrt{\tau}/2$, and R is determined by the foreign discount rate r_f and the covariance between the equity and the exchange rate, as $R = r_f - \rho\sigma_E\sigma_X$, where ρ is the quanto correlation and σ_E and σ_X are the equity and the exchange rate implied volatilities.

Quanto implied correlations can be obtained by inverting this formula to back out the correlation between the equity and the exchange rate: The market price of a quanto option, the domestic and foreign interest rates, the equity and exchange rate implied volatilities (backed out from vanilla options) and values for all the quantities that appear in (2.13) except ρ must be obtained. Then they can be substituted in (2.13) to back out an implied correlation between the equity and the exchange rate.

In summary, there are some ways in which implied correlations can be backed out from option prices, but they can be very unstable. Instability arises because the true underlying asset returns have a non-linear relationship, and/or they are not jointly stationary, and/or because there are a number of rather questionable assumptions that are used for calculating implied correlations. In short, implied correlations should be used with more caution than implied volatilities.

3

Moving Average Models

Moving averages have many uses in financial data modelling. For example, in technical analysis, where they are called 'stochastics', the relationship between moving averages of different lengths can be used as a signal to trade. Simple moving averages have also been used to estimate and forecast unconditional volatility and correlation. The terms *historic volatility* and *historic correlation* are applied to the statistical forecasts that are based on equally weighted moving averages. This rather confusing terminology remains standard, even though several other types of statistical forecast based on historic data are now in common use.

In this chapter, §3.1 describes how historic volatility and correlation measures are obtained, and outlines their advantages and limitations. The equally weighted average is calculated on a fixed size data window that is rolled through time, each day adding the new return and taking off the oldest return. Another common form of weighted average measure for volatility and correlation is an exponentially weighted moving average; this is described in §3.2. If exponentially weighted moving averages are used correctly they can produce much more reasonable estimates of short-term volatility or correlation than equally weighted moving averages. In fact in some cases an exponentially weighted moving average correlation model may be preferred to a more sophisticated correlation model, including some of the GARCH correlation models that are described in §4.5. The reader should use the **moving averages** spreadsheet to see how these models work in practice.

In some cases an exponentially weighted moving average correlation model may be preferred to a GARCH correlation model

Perceived changes in volatility and correlation can have important consequences, so it is essential to understand what is the source of variability in any particular model. Any weighted average model is only appropriate for estimating *unconditional* volatility or correlation (§1.3 and §1.4). As such it provides no reason for estimates to differ as the data window moves through time, except for sampling error, or 'noise'. It is important to realize that the unconditional volatility or correlation of the time series is one number, a constant for the whole series, and so the variation observed as weighted average volatility or correlation estimates are moved through time can only be attributed to sampling errors.

An important but subtle point, that will be returned to with a more detailed discussion in §10.3.3, is that in this chapter, and in Chapter 4, the fundamental

*We can, of course, say
that our current estimate
of volatility or
correlation is the
forecast, and this is what
is generally done*

parameters that are being forecast are the variance and the covariance. These are the parameters that determine the returns distributions, and it is standard to base statistical forecasts on a model for these parameters. However, a forecast is an expectation, taken under some probability measure, and the expectation of a square root is not equal to the square root of an expectation, that is, $E(\sigma) \neq \sqrt{E(\sigma^2)}$. Despite this observation, most statistical models for 'forecasting volatility' are actually models for forecasting variance: they first forecast a variance, and then the volatility forecast is taken as the square root of the variance forecast (and if necessary annualized in the usual way, as in (1.2)).

It should also be understood that a weighted average is really just an estimation method. We can, of course, say that our current estimate of volatility or correlation is the forecast, and this is what is generally done, but there are more sophisticated models available. For example, GARCH models can provide forecasts of the whole term structure of volatility for any point in the future (§4.4.1).

3.1   Historical Volatility and Correlation

3.1.1   Definition and Application

Historical estimates of volatility and correlation are obtained in two stages. First one obtains unbiased estimates of the unconditional variance and covariance that are based on equally weighted averages of squared returns and cross products of returns. Then these are converted into volatility and correlation estimates by applying formulae (1.2) and (1.3), respectively.

An n-day 'historic' volatility estimate is often based on an equally weighted average of n squared daily returns. An unbiased estimate of unconditional variance at time t, using the n most recent daily returns and assuming the mean is zero,[1] is

$$\hat{\sigma}_t^2 = \sum_{i=1}^{n} r_{t-i}^2 / n \qquad (3.1)$$

Using (1.2), the estimate at time t of an n-day historic volatility is the square root of this estimate multiplied by the number of daily returns per year. Note that (3.1) gives an estimate of the variance, σ^2, that is to say, the hat ˆ should be written over σ^2 and not just σ. It is *not* the square of the unbiased

---

[1]It is usual to apply moving averages to squared returns $r_t^2(t = 1, 2, 3, \ldots, n)$ rather than squared mean deviations of returns $(r_t - \bar{r})^2$, where $\bar{r}$ is the average return over the data window. Standard statistical estimates of variance are based on mean deviations, but empirical research on the accuracy of variance forecasts in financial markets has demonstrated little advantage in using mean deviations, except if the returns are very low-frequency. The volatility of monthly returns may be better estimated using a non-zero value for $\bar{r}$, in which case the unbiased estimate of variance will have $n - 1$ rather than n in the denominator. For analysing daily financial series it has become standard to base variances on squared returns and covariances on cross products of returns (Figlewski, 1997; Alexander and Leigh, 1997).

estimate of the standard deviation. For typesetting reasons, however, the notation $\hat{\sigma}^2$ is used throughout this book to denote the variance estimate or forecast.

The current n-day historic volatility estimate is sometimes taken as the forecast of future volatility to plug into the pricing model for an option that matures in n days. Historic volatility estimates are also commonly used in the n-day covariance matrix for measuring portfolio risk. Sometimes one looks back exactly n days in order to forecast forward n days: only recent market conditions are thought to be more appropriate for short-term forecasts, but for long-term forecasts one should take a longer averaging period. It is, however, more common to use a historic period of more than n days for an n-day forecast, especially if n is small. For example, for a 10-day forecast most practitioners would look back 30 days or more.

Long-term historic forecasts need not be based on daily returns, provided the number of observations remains sufficiently large. Weekly or monthly returns may be used in a similar way. For example, a historic forecast of volatility over the next six months that is based on weekly returns data could use the last 26 weekly returns in (3.1) and an annualizing constant of 52.

Similarly, n-day 'historic' correlations are calculated by dividing the equally weighted covariance estimate over the last n days by the square root of the product of the two n-day variance estimates:[2]

$$\hat{\rho}_t = \frac{\sum_{i=1}^{n} r_{1,t-i} r_{2,t-i}}{\sqrt{\sum_{i=1}^{n} r_{1,t-i}^2 \sum_{i=1}^{n} r_{2,t-i}^2}}. \tag{3.2}$$

If these estimates are based on a small sample size they will not be very precise. The larger the sample size the more accurate the estimate, because sampling errors are proportional to $1/\sqrt{n}$. Therefore a short moving average will be more variable than a long moving average. Put another way, short-term volatility or correlation estimates have much more variability over time than long-term estimates. For example a 30-day historic volatility (or correlation) will always be more variable than a 60-day historic volatility (or correlation) that is based on the same daily return data. It is important to realize that, whatever the length of the averaging period, and whenever the estimate is made, the 'historic' estimates are always estimating the same parameter: the unconditional volatility (or correlation) that is a constant for the whole process. The variation in n-day historic estimates can only be attributed to sampling error; there is nothing else in the model to explain it.

The variation in n-day historic estimates can only be attributed to sampling error; there is nothing else in the model to explain it

---

[2]Again, assuming zero means is simpler, and there is no convincing empirical evidence that this degrades the quality of correlation estimates and forecasts in financial time series.

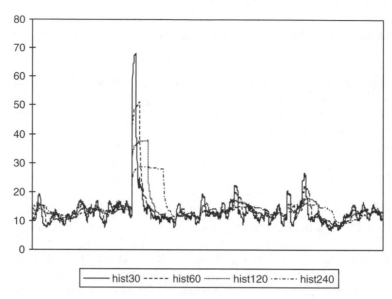

Figure 3.1 Historic volatilities of the FTSE 100 index, 1984–1995.

Of course, if one really believes in the assumption of constant volatility that underlies this estimation method one should always use as long a history as possible, so that sampling errors are reduced. Long-term predictions should be unaffected by short-term phenomena such as 'volatility clustering' (§4.1), so it is appropriate to take the average over a long historic period. Short-term predictions should reflect current market conditions, which means that only the immediate past returns should be used.

Extreme events are just as important to current estimates, whether they occurred yesterday or at any other time in the averaging period

This apparently sensible approach hides a major problem: extreme events are just as important to current estimates, whether they occurred yesterday or at any other time in the averaging period. Even just *one* unusual return will affect the *n*-day historic volatility or correlation to the same extent for exactly *n* days following that day, although a conditional volatility or correlation may have long ago returned to normal levels.

3.1.2 Historic Volatility in Financial Markets

Figure 3.1 illustrates equally weighted volatility estimates of different periods for the FTSE 100 index. Daily squared returns are averaged over the last *n* observations for *n* = 30, 60, 120 and 240 days, and this variance is transformed to an annualized volatility using (1.1). The 240-day volatility of the FTSE jumped up to 26% the day after Black Monday and it stayed at that level for almost a whole year because that one, huge squared return had exactly the same weight in the average for 240 days. Exactly 240 days after the event the large return fell out of the moving average, and so the volatility forecast returned to its normal level of around 13%. But nothing of note happened in

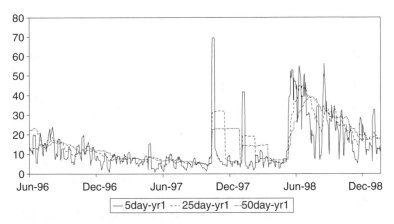

Figure 3.2 Historic volatilities of South African rand 1-year swap rates.

the markets on the 240th day after 17 October 1987, or 30 or 60 or 120 days after Black Monday. The drastic fall in volatility on those dates is just a *ghost* of Black Monday, an artefact of the method. Certainly it is no reflection of the real market conditions.

Short term equally weighted averages have more pronounced *ghost features* because an extreme event is being averaged over just a few observations, but at least these ghost features last for a relatively short period of time: they last for as long as the averaging period.

Following an extreme event there will be very noticeable differences between volatility estimates obtained from equally weighted averages of different lengths. On the other hand, if the market has been quite stable for some time, there will be little difference between historic volatility estimates of different lengths.

Figure 3.2 illustrates this. Historic 5-day, 25-day and 50-day volatilities of the South African rand 1-year swap rate show a number of 'ghost' effects of the swap rate jumps in October 1997 and January 1998. Following both of these there are enormous differences between the 5-day, 25-day and 50-day estimates. For example, during the month of December 1997, the 25-day volatility had returned to more normal levels around 6%, but the 50-day volatility recorded 23% because it was still affected by the one event in October 1997.

If the market has been quite stable for some time, there will be little difference between historic volatility estimates of different lengths

From June 1998 to the end of the data period the South African fixed income market could be characterized by high volatility without any really extreme market moves. The marked discrepancies between the 25-day and the 50-day estimates were not so noticeable at this time. Of course, the 5-day historic volatility is still jumping around all over the place at the end of the data period, because there is such a large sampling error when the sample size is only 5.

3.1.3   Historic Correlation in Energy Markets

Following just one event that affects both markets in a similar way, the n-day historic correlation will remain high for exactly n days. This makes n-day historic correlation estimates appear more stable as n increases. Figures 3.3 and 3.4 illustrate this point with historic correlation estimates in energy markets.[3]

In the earlier days of the KCBOT contract, the use of 30-day historic correlations would have substantially overestimated, and then underestimated, the correlation that should be used to calculate the proxy hedge ratio

In the natural gas market some futures contracts have a relatively low volume of trade and some traders may be inclined to use a more liquid proxy, if it is highly correlated. Consider the Kansas City 'Western' KCBOT, and the NYMEX natural gas prompt future contracts. The NYMEX has always traded at a higher price. When the KCBOT was first introduced both volume and volatility were very low relative to the NYMEX, but as the KCBOT contract trading volume increased the spread decreased substantially. In the last few years of the sample shown in Figure 3.3, their correlation was very high and stable: although the KCBOT closes later, trading on this contract after the NYMEX has closed is still very thin. Spread volatility is now relatively low and consequently correlations are much larger.

However close in price two futures contracts appear to be, caution should always be exercised when historic correlation estimates are used for the proxy hedge. During the second half of the data period the 30-day correlations shown in Figure 3.3 were indeed very similar to the exponentially weighted average correlations, with $\lambda = 0.94$ (§3.2.1). However, in the earlier days of the KCBOT contract, the use of 30-day historic correlations would have substantially overestimated, and then underestimated, the correlation that should be used to calculate the proxy hedge ratio.

On 26 March 1996 the price of the KBOT future increased quite sharply and then remained more or less around this new level. The spread between the two contracts narrowed significantly; the 30-day historic correlation between the two futures prices rose from about 0.85 to about 0.93 and stayed around this level for exactly 30 days afterwards. Then 30 days later, on 9 May 1996, the 30-day correlation fell from 0.94 to 0.74, although nothing of note happened in the market on that day. The apparent drop in correlation was just an artefact of the equal weighting of historical data.

Figure 3.3 compares the 30-day historic correlation, which remains a standard measure of correlation in energy markets, with an exponentially weighted moving average correlation measure. The exponentially weighted moving average more accurately reflects what is happening between the two markets. After the spread decreased sharply on 26 March 1996 it gradually rose again, peaking in the summer of 1996 before falling back to very low levels. While the correlation rose sharply on 26 March 1996, it should have declined gradually

[3]A fuller discussion of correlation in energy markets is given in Alexander (1999a). Many thanks to Enron for providing the data used in these examples.

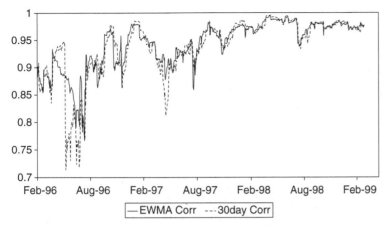

Figure 3.3 EWMA and 30-day correlation of NYMEX and KCBOT prompt futures.

again until the summer of 1996 before rising again to more comfortable levels.

Spot–future correlations are meaningful only for assets with uncertain carry costs or assets that cannot be stored or shorted. Otherwise the spot–future relationship is deterministic: Future Price = Spot Price + Carry Cost. Spot–future correlation can be far lower in commodity markets than in financial markets, because of transportation costs, storage constraints, and other logistic problems. Figure 3.4 shows correlations between West Texas Intermediate (WTI) spot and futures crude oil prices calculated using equal weighting over 3 months, 6 months, 1 year and 2 years. These correlations are generally quite stable over the latter part of the period and substantially less than 1. However, increased volatility during the Gulf war induced a marked change in spot–future correlations.

Spot–future correlation can be far lower in commodity markets than in financial markets, because of transportation costs, storage constraints, and other logistic problems

The ghost effects of the Gulf war on correlation measures is less intense, but longer-lasting, as the averaging period increases. On 17 January 1991 when spot and future prices dropped from about $32 to about $22 overnight with the outbreak of war, equally weighted correlations increased substantially by an amount in inverse proportion to the length of average. On 18 January 1991 the 3-month correlation rose from 0.8 to 0.91, staying above 0.9 until 17 April 1991 when it jumped down from 0.94 to 0.83. The 2-year correlation jumped from 0.81 to 0.86, staying at around this level for exactly 2 years, long after the other averages had returned to more realistic levels. But nothing special happened on 17 April 1991, or on 18 July 1991, long after the outbreak of the Gulf war. The sharp declines in correlation measures on these dates are just an artefact of the estimation method.

The sharp declines in correlation measures on these dates are just an artefact of the estimation method

Energy producers that are exposed to many commodities may wish to hedge revenues with *basket options*. There is no need to pay for greater protection than the risk one is exposed to. If the exposure is to the sum of several commodities,

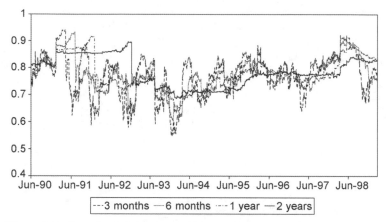

Figure 3.4   Equally weighted correlations of WTI crude oil spot and futures.

The lower the correlation, the smaller the basket volatility and the cheaper the option

buying individual put options can be more of a gamble than a hedge. Not only this, basket options are generally far cheaper than buying options on individual markets. This is because basket volatility is related to the volatility of individual options as $\sigma^2_{x+y} = (\sigma_x + \sigma_y)^2 - 2(1 - \rho)\sigma_x\sigma_y$, so the basket volatility is less than the sum of individual volatilities unless $\rho = 1$. The lower the correlation, the smaller the basket volatility and the cheaper the option.

Figure 3.5 shows some historic correlation measures between NYMEX prompt futures on crude oil and natural gas. The long-term correlations are in the region of 0.1–0.2, so long-term basket options on natural gas and crude oil should be relatively cheap. However, among other factors, differences in settlement dates and procedures across different markets produce highly unstable short-term correlations. For example, the 30-day correlation in Figure 3.5 can fluctuate between 0.3 and −0.3 in the course of a few days. Even though they may be cheaper, there will be far more uncertainty when hedging with short-term basket options because their prices will be much more variable.

3.1.4   When and How Should Historic Estimates Be Used?

In what circumstances, if at all, should one consider applying equally weighted volatility or correlation measures? Long-term volatility could be forecast with this method, but only when one assumes that the past is an accurate reflection of the future. How long a look-back period should be used? A long-term volatility based on all the FTSE 100 index data in Figure 3.1 is around 15%, but if Black Monday were excluded and the data period started in 1988 then long-term volatility forecasts would be lower, at about 13%.

One should ask whether it is appropriate to measure long-term volatility and correlation with extreme events in the data set

Since market events on a single day have such a prolonged effect on long-term volatility and correlations that are calculated using equally weighted moving averages, one should ask whether it is appropriate to measure long-term

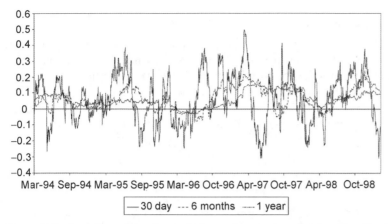

Figure 3.5 Equally weighted correlations of natural gas and crude oil.

volatility and correlation with extreme events in the data set. Should these be filtered out first?

One cannot give an objective answer to this question. Equally weighted averages can give some idea of the possible range for long-term volatility or correlation, with and without extreme market moves. The decision about which of these forecasts to use depends on one's subjective beliefs about the possible occurrence of extreme events during the risk horizon. Users may define their beliefs about long-term volatility by a probability distribution over the range that seems plausible from historic calculations, and this distribution should really be carried through the rest of the analysis. For example, instead of a single mark-to-market (MtM) value of a long-term option, use the mean MtM, with an MtM standard error based on the distribution of long-term volatility (§5.3.1).

Are equally weighted averages at all successful for short-term volatility forecasting? Most of the empirical evidence indicates that the historical method is not very effective for short-term horizons (§5.1). Although shorter averages are supposed to capture more of the 'clustering' in volatility, the equal weighting does not properly account for the dynamic properties of returns. The 'historic' model is essentially a static model which should not be forced into a time-varying framework with little regard for the consequences.

The 'historic' model is essentially a static model which should not be forced into a time-varying framework with little regard for the consequences

3.2 Exponentially Weighted Moving Averages

An exponentially weighted moving average (EWMA) puts more weight on the more recent observations, and thus takes some account of the dynamic ordering in returns. When an EWMA is applied to squared returns the resulting volatility estimate will react immediately following an unusually large return. Then the effect of this return in the EWMA gradually diminishes over time. The reaction of EWMA volatility estimates to market events therefore persists over time, and with a strength that is determined by the *smoothing constant* λ. This is a number between 0 and 1. The larger the value of λ the more weight is placed on past observations and so the smoother the series becomes.

An *n*-period exponentially weighted moving average of a time series x is defined as

$$\frac{x_{t-1} + \lambda x_{t-2} + \lambda^2 x_{t-3} + \ldots + \lambda^{n-1} x_{t-n}}{1 + \lambda + \lambda^2 + \ldots + \lambda^{n-1}}.$$

One does not need to define a look-back period $\{x_{t-1}, \ldots, x_{t-n}\}$ with an exponentially weighted moving average. Since $0 < \lambda < 1$, $\lambda^n \to 0$ as $n \to \infty$ and the exponentially weighted moving average will eventually place no weight at all on observations far in the past. Also the denominator converges to $1/(1 - \lambda)$ as $n \to \infty$, so an infinite exponentially weighted moving average may be written

$$(1 - \lambda) \sum_{i=1}^{\infty} \lambda^{i-1} x_{t-i}.$$

This is the formula that is used to calculate EWMA estimates of volatility and correlation. For volatility one first calculates an exponentially weighted variance estimate of squared returns:

$$\hat{\sigma}_t^2 = (1 - \lambda) \sum_{i=1}^{\infty} \lambda^{i-1} r_{t-i}^2.$$

Then one converts this to annualized volatility in the usual way. For correlation, the covariance estimate

$$\hat{\sigma}_{12,t} = (1 - \lambda) \sum_{i=1}^{\infty} \lambda^{i-1} r_{1,t-i} r_{2,t-i}$$

is divided by the square root of the product of the two variance estimates with the same value of λ. As with equally weighted moving averages, it is standard to square daily returns and cross products of daily returns, not in mean deviation form. These formulae may be rewritten in the form of recursions that are normally used for calculation:

$$\hat{\sigma}_t^2 = (1 - \lambda) r_{t-1}^2 + \lambda \hat{\sigma}_{t-1}^2 \qquad (3.3)$$

and

$$\hat{\sigma}_{12,t} = (1 - \lambda) r_{1,t-1} r_{2,t-1} + \lambda \hat{\sigma}_{12,t-1}. \qquad (3.4)$$

How should the smoothing constant λ be interpreted? There are two terms on the right-hand side of (3.3). The first term, $(1 - \lambda) r_{t-1}^2$, determines the intensity

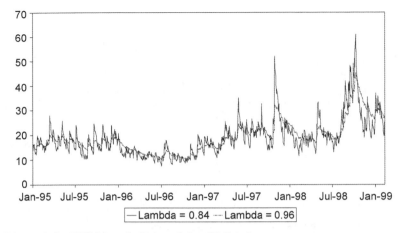

Figure 3.6 EWMA volatilities of the CAC index.

of *reaction* of volatility to market events: the smaller is λ the more the volatility reacts to the market information in yesterday's return. The second term, $\lambda\hat{\sigma}^2_{t-1}$, determines the *persistence* in volatility: irrespective of what happens in the market, if volatility was high yesterday it will be still be high today.

The effect of a single event diminishes because $0 < \lambda < 1$. The closer λ is to 1, the more persistent is volatility following a market shock. Thus a high λ gives little reaction to actual market events, but great persistence in volatility, and a low λ gives highly reactive volatilities that quickly die away. An unfortunate restriction of EWMA models is that the reaction and persistence parameters are not independent, because they sum to one. If this holds in any market, it is perhaps most likely to be the case in some foreign exchange markets, such as the major US dollar rates.

An unfortunate restriction of EWMA models is that the reaction and persistence parameters are not independent, because they sum to one

The effect of different λ on EWMA volatility forecasts can be quite substantial, as shown in Figure 3.6. Which is the best value to use for the smoothing constant?[4]

As a rule of thumb EWMA volatility in most markets should take values of λ between about 0.75 (volatility is highly reactive but has little persistence) and 0.98 (volatility is very persistent but not highly reactive). If you want to use the EWMA model for forecasting, very commonly lower values for λ are used for short-term forecasts and higher values of λ are used for long-term forecasts.

As with the equally weighted moving average, an EWMA is just an estimation method. Additional assumptions need to be made to turn it into a forecasting model. The recursion (3.3) is similar to a simple GARCH model. In fact an

---

[4]In GARCH models there is no question of 'how' we should estimate parameters, because maximum likelihood estimation is an optimal method that always gives consistent estimators (§4.3.2). Statistical methods may also be used for EWMA—for example, λ could be chosen to minimize the root mean square forecasting error (§A.5.3). But given the problems with assessing the accuracy of volatility forecasts described in Chapter 5, statistical methods are not necessarily the best means of estimating λ.

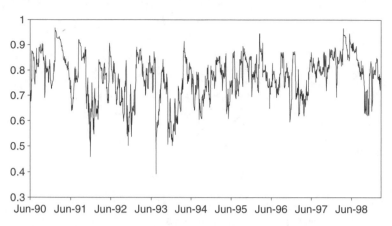

Figure 3.7   EWMA correlations of WTI spot and futures.

An EWMA is equivalent to an I-GARCH model, without a constant term

EWMA is equivalent to an I-GARCH model, without a constant term. In §4.2.3 it will be shown that term structure forecasts from I-GARCH models are constant. Similarly, term structure forecasts of volatility under any given EWMA model — that is, for a given choice of λ — will not converge. The current EWMA estimate of volatility is the volatility forecast for all risk horizons (§3.3).

An EWMA with a smoothing constant of 0.94 such as is used in the RiskMetrics data (§7.3) has a half-life of around 25 days. Thus it is similar to an equally weighted average of 20–30 days, and this is illustrated in Figure 3.7. This shows estimates of the same unconditional correlation parameter as that estimated in Figure 3.4 between WTI crude oil spot and futures. Figure 3.4 was based on an equally weighted moving average model, whereas Figure 3.7 is based on an EWMA model. The main difference between the estimates from these two models is evidenced following major movements in both markets at the same time: the equally weighted model will produce 'ghost' effects of this event, as seen in Figure 3.4, whereas in the exponential model correlations will overshoot and then gradually decay.

When all is said and done, the smoothing constant is just a parameter in the estimation model. In §5.3 we shall see that single-point estimates of volatility and correlation can be very misleading if there is uncertainty surrounding the best choice for the model parameter. When an MtM value is based on volatility estimates one must be aware of the uncertainty that is introduced in the MtM value by the errors in volatility estimates. One should consider using not just one single value of λ but instead some distribution over λ. Then instead of a single MtM value, a whole distribution of MtM values will be obtained.[5]

---

[5]The same remark applies to all parameters in the valuation model, not just volatility but drifts, discount rates, betas, yields and so on.

3.3   Constant Volatility and the Square Root of Time Rule

Term structure volatility forecasts are forecasts of the volatility of h-day returns for every maturity h. Denote by r_{th} the return over the next h days at time t, so that approximately

$$r_{th} = \ln P_{t+h} - \ln P_t,$$

where P_t denotes the price at time t (see footnote 2 in §1.1). Converting the forecasted variance $V(r_{th})$ for every h to a volatility gives the volatility term structure.

The underlying model for both equally weighted moving averages and EWMAs is a constant volatility model, so term structure volatility forecasts that are consistent with moving average models will be constant. Note that

$$r_{th} = r_{t1} + r_{t+1,1} + \ldots + r_{t+h-1,1},$$

Term structure volatility forecasts that are consistent with moving average models will be constant

so if the return process is independent and identically distributed (i.i.d.) with constant variance σ^2, taking variances of the above gives $V(r_{th}) = h\sigma^2$. If there are A returns a year, then the number of h-day returns per year is A/h, and so annualizing $V(r_{th})$ into a volatility gives

$$
\begin{aligned}
h\text{-day volatility} &= 100\sqrt{(A/h)}\sqrt{(h\sigma^2)} \\
&= 100\sqrt{(A\sigma^2)} \\
&= 1\text{-day volatility.}
\end{aligned}
$$

In general, if 1-period returns are i.i.d. then h-period standard deviations are just $\sqrt{h}$ times the 1-period standard deviation: this is the 'square root of time' rule. It is widely used, although it may not be supported by empirical observations.

The constant volatility assumption underlies both moving average statistical models and Black–Scholes type pricing models. In that sense the pricing model and the estimation model are coherent. However, constant volatility term structures are not generally observed in market implied volatilities (§2.2.2). Volatility term structures normally mean-revert, with short-term volatility lying either above or below the long-term mean, depending on whether current conditions are high or low volatility. It is unrealistic to assume that current levels of volatility will remain unchanged for ever. One of the main advantages of GARCH models is that their term structures reflect the mean-reversion of volatility that is expected in financial markets (§4.4.1).

If 1-period returns are i.i.d. then h-period standard deviations are just $\sqrt{h}$ times the 1-period standard deviation: this is the 'square root of time' rule

4

GARCH Models

The moving average models of volatility and correlation that were discussed in Chapter 3 assume that asset returns are independent and identically distributed. There is no time-varying volatility assumption in any weighted moving average method. They only provide an estimate of the unconditional volatility, assumed to be a constant, and the current estimate is taken as the forecast. The volatility estimates do change over time, but this can only be ascribed to 'noise' or sampling errors in a moving average model. There is nothing else in the model that allows for variation in volatility.

However, the returns in many financial markets are not well modelled by an independent and identically distributed process. At very high frequencies returns may show signs of autocorrelation, so they are not independent. Lower-frequency returns may not be autocorrelated, but there is often a strong autocorrelation in squared returns, and so again returns are not independent (§13.1.3).

Positive autocorrelation in squared returns indicates that financial market volatility comes in 'clusters' where tranquil periods of small returns are interspersed with volatile periods of large returns. The technical term given to this is *autoregressive conditional heteroscedasticity*. This phenomenon has been documented for a very long time. As long ago as 1963, Benoit Mandlebrot observed that financial returns time series exhibit periods of volatility interspersed with tranquillity, where 'Large returns follow large returns, of either sign'. However, it is only relatively recently that useful models of volatility clustering have been developed.

Financial market volatility comes in 'clusters' where tranquil periods of small returns are interspersed with volatile periods of large returns. The technical term given to this is autoregressive conditional heteroscedasticity

This chapter describes a framework for modelling time-varying volatility that has engendered a truly remarkable number of academic papers. Autoregressive conditional heteroscedasticity (ARCH) models of volatility and correlation were first introduced by Rob Engle (1982). Consequently a bibliography of research papers on GARCH during the last twenty years would run to hundreds of pages, so it is not an easy task to cut through all this literature to find the work that is most relevant to practitioners. Sometimes academic research seems to exist only to perpetuate more research in the area, but, of course, one never knows whether research that presently seems to lack real-world application will have practical relevance in the future. There is currently so much academic interest in GARCH models that it is quite possible that most financial institutions will be using sophisticated GARCH models some time in the future. Nevertheless, at the present time the majority of practitioners do not use GARCH models at all, and if they do it is in a relatively basic form. Part of the problem is the divide between academic research and practical applications. This chapter aims to present some of the most relevant academic research on GARCH models in a form that is accessible to practitioners. Many empirical examples are provided in the text and the reader should use the **MBRM-GARCH** spreadsheet and the **PcGive demo** on the CD, to generate their own models for the data used in this chapter. The aim is to highlight some of the problems that are most important for practical applications and to help direct academic research towards the areas that have most practical relevance.

At the present time the majority of practitioners do not use GARCH models at all, and if they do it is in a relatively basic form

Section 4.1 describes the nature of GARCH models from both financial and statistical perspectives. Volatility clustering and the 'leverage effect' are both accommodated in a GARCH framework by simply extending the linear regression model with another equation called the conditional variance equation. The section ends by emphasizing the tremendous scope of this framework for financial modelling. Section 4.2 outlines the mathematical specification of several univariate GARCH models—not all of them by any means, as this would take up a whole book on its own. There is a vast literature on different specifications of the conditional variance equation, so this section just gives a brief overview of some of the most common GARCH models. Their estimation by maximum likelihood methods is detailed in §4.3, which emphasizes the choice of data period, and the way it affects long-term volatility and the stability of GARCH parameters.

Section 4.4 looks at some of the most important practical applications of GARCH models. Although it has received relatively little attention in the academic literature, one of the most useful applications of GARCH models is the generation of volatility term structure forecasts that converge to a long-term average level of volatility as the maturity increases. In §4.4.1 we describe how to construct these forecasts, and how to relate their properties to the GARCH parameters. Univariate GARCH models are also used to price and hedge options. Some of the fundamental concepts for GARCH option pricing are discussed in §4.4.2. The section ends with an explanation of how to use GARCH models for smile fitting and forecasting.

The last part of this chapter examines some of the extensive research on multivariate GARCH models. The bivariate GARCH models described in §4.5.1 have found some very useful applications to the computation of time-varying hedge ratios and the pricing of options that are based on two correlated assets. Bivarate GARCH models are relatively easy to estimate, but GARCH models on more than two variables have been less successful. Section 4.5.2 reviews some different ways of parameterizing multivariate GARCH models: the computational aspects of multivariate GARCH become more and more problematic as the dimension increases. At the moment there is no chance that multivariate GARCH models can be used to estimate *directly* the very large covariance matrices that are required to net all the risks in a large trading book. However, it is possible to generate GARCH covariance matrices using only univariate GARCH volatilities, and the chapter ends with an overview of these methods.

The financial community has benefited enormously from the work of many academics. One professor whose pioneering work on GARCH stands out above the rest is Rob Engle (http://weber.ucsd.edu/~mbacci/engle/index.html). Much of the important development and validation work on different GARCH models is attributable to Rob Engle and his co-authors and numerous research students, particularly Torben Andersen, Tim Bollerslev, Ken Kroner, Joshua Rosenberg and Victor Ng. Since his first seminal article in 1982, Rob Engle has continued to produce path-breaking work in this area. More recently, a number of intriguing new developments and applications of GARCH models have come from Jin-Chuan Duan. His lecture notes, research papers and computer programs, available on his website (www.rotman.utoronto.ca/~jcduan), are well worth a visit!

4.1 Introduction to Generalized Autoregressive Conditional Heteroscedasticity

In a generalized autoregressive conditional heteroscedasticity (GARCH) model, returns are assumed to be generated by a stochastic process with time-varying volatility. Instead of modelling the data after they have been collapsed into a single unconditional distribution, a GARCH model introduces more detailed assumptions about the conditional distributions of returns. These conditional distributions change over time in an autocorrelated way — in fact the conditional variance is an autoregressive process (§11.2.1).

4.1.1 Volatility Clustering

Many financial time series display volatility clustering, that is, autoregressive conditional heteroscedasticity. Equity, commodity and foreign exchange markets often exhibit volatility clustering at the daily, even the weekly, frequency, and volatility clustering becomes very pronounced in intra-day data. A typical example of a conditionally heteroscedastic return series is shown in Figure 4.1. Note that two types of news events are apparent. The second volatility cluster shows an anticipated announcement, which turned out to be good news: the market was increasingly turbulent before the announcement, but the large positive return at that time shows that punters were pleased, and the volatility soon decreased. The first cluster of volatility indicates that there is turbulence in the market following an unanticipated piece of bad news.

Volatility clustering implies a strong autocorrelation in squared returns, so a simple method for detecting volatility clustering is to calculate the first-order autocorrelation coefficient in squared returns

Volatility clustering implies a strong autocorrelation in squared returns, so a simple method for detecting volatility clustering is to calculate the first-order autocorrelation coefficient in squared returns:

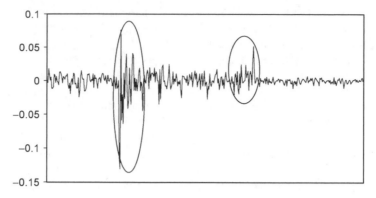

Figure 4.1 Volatility clustering.

$$\frac{\sum_{t=2}^{T} r_t^2 r_{t-1}^2}{\sum_{t=2}^{T} r_t^4}.$$

A basic test for the significance of autocorrelation is the Box–Pierce LM test (§11.3.2). To test for conditional heteroscedasticity in the data, this test may be applied to the squared return.[1] However, simply calculating the Box–Pierce statistic is not enough. In fact one might perform a Box–Pierce test that shows insignificant autocorrelation in squared returns even though volatility clustering is present in the data.

To illustrate why this happens, daily data on 20 US stocks from 2 January 1996 to 2 October 2000 has been analysed in Table 4.1. The table gives a number of summary statistics for the daily returns, including the first-order autocorrelation coefficient of squared returns (column 6) and the Box–Pierce statistic for first-order correlation (column 7). Bold type is used to pick out the statistics that indicate a potential problem.

Looking first at columns 6 and 7, there are seven stocks that have low autocorrelation in squared returns (Ford, Hewlett Packard, Microsoft, BankOne, Procter and Gamble, Rockwell and AT&T). But does this really mean that there is no volatility clustering? Actually not. Even though the data are adjusted for dividends and splits, these stocks have at least one very extreme negative return during the data period. How do we know this (other than of course by looking at the data)? The first four sample moments, up to skewness and excess kurtosis, are given in columns 2–5. From the negative

---

[1]The Box–Pierce test for first-order autocorrelation is asymptotically a chi-squared variable with 1 degree of freedom, so the 1% critical value for this test is 6.635. This test is simple but not very robust. Robust but complex test procedures for GARCH models are given in Wooldridge (1991).

Table 4.1: Statistics for 20 US stocks (daily data from 2 January 1996 to 2 October 2000)

Stock	Mean	s.d.	Skewness	Excess kurtosis*	GARCH Auto-correlation	GARCH LM	A-GARCH Auto-correlation	A-GARCH LM
(1)	(2)	(3)	(4)	(5)	(6)	(7)	(8)	(9)
America Int'l Group	0.0012	0.0196	0.2813	1.8360	0.1466	25.7847	−0.0037	0.0162
America Online	0.0026	0.0411	0.1906	1.5125	0.1136	15.4735	−0.0693	5.7641
American Express	0.0013	0.0231	0.0679	1.9543	0.2342	65.8048	−0.0696	5.8184
AT&T	−0.0004	0.0246	−1.4018	20.4217	0.0343	1.4109	0.0270	0.8720
Bank of America	0.0005	0.0228	−0.0441	1.6671	0.1748	36.6869	0.0014	0.0022
BankOne Corp.	0.0002	0.0237	−1.0432	13.8524	0.0278	0.9269	−0.0424	2.1577
Boeing Corp.	0.0004	0.0223	−0.3948	7.3615	0.1459	25.5560	−0.0180	0.3901
Cisco Systems	0.0021	0.0294	−0.1270	1.6547	0.1778	37.9210	−0.1253	18.8389
Citigroup	0.0014	0.0250	0.2046	2.8857	0.1365	22.3706	0.0184	0.4068
Coca Cola Co.	0.0004	0.0197	0.0158	2.5512	0.1833	40.3056	−0.0452	2.4496
Walt Disney	0.0006	0.0213	0.2910	4.0542	0.1594	30.4738	−0.0493	2.9179
Exxon Mobil	0.0007	0.0166	0.1900	1.2463	0.1276	19.5358	−0.0846	8.5854
Ford Motor Co.	0.0003	0.0236	−3.5109	60.3539	0.0159	0.3018	−0.0072	0.0621
General Electric Co.	0.0013	0.0178	0.0352	1.1232	0.1145	15.7423	−0.1093	14.3312
Hewlett Packard	0.0007	0.0287	−0.2401	3.2223	0.0664	5.2907	0.0374	1.6769
Merrill Lynch	0.0014	0.0286	0.1233	1.8895	0.2108	53.3221	−0.0396	1.8812
Microsoft Co.	0.0014	0.0238	−0.4704	4.1963	0.0345	1.4311	0.0100	0.1190
Procter and Gamble	0.0004	0.0221	−3.7453	60.0698	0.0263	0.8322	−0.0382	1.7465
Rockwell Int.	−0.0001	0.0219	−0.9535	11.4014	0.0627	4.7140	−0.0365	1.6010
Unicom Corp.	0.0006	0.0158	0.0429	3.4449	0.1499	26.9722	0.0158	0.2985

*Excess kurtosis is obtained by subtracting 3 from the value of kurtosis, so that the normal distribution has excess kurtosis equal to zero.

skewness and extreme excess kurtosis on these particular stocks it is clear that the apparently low autocorrelation in squared returns is due to one, or even a few, extreme negative returns.

If these outliers were removed from the data, then volatility clustering would be evident from the first-order autocorrelation statistics. For example, the price of Ford stock fell 30% on 8 April 1998, and the effect of removing that one single return on that day is to change the excess kurtosis from 60.35 to 1.79 and the GARCH Lagrange multiplier (LM) statistic from 0.3 to 17.33. Obviously one should either remove or 'dummy out' that return from the historic data set used to estimate the GARCH model parameters. The message to take home for GARCH modelling is: always examine your data carefully before you begin the analysis. The potential saving of time and trouble with non-convergent GARCH models can be considerable.

Always examine your data carefully before you begin the analysis. The potential saving of time and trouble with non-convergent GARCH models can be considerable

Excess kurtosis is discussed in detail in §10.1. It is not always due to single outliers, and it may not affect our tests for volatility clustering. For example, Boeing, Disney and Unicom all show signs of significant excess kurtosis, but the GARCH autocorrelation diagnostics are still highly significant.

4.1.2   The Leverage Effect

If volatility is higher following a negative return than it is following a positive return then the autocorrelation between yesterday's return and today's squared return will be large and negative

In equity markets it is commonly observed that volatility is higher in a falling market than it is in a rising market. The volatility response to a large negative return is often far greater than it is to a large positive return of the same magnitude. The reason for this may be that when the equity price falls the debt remains constant in the short term, so the debt/equity ratio increases. The firm becomes more highly leveraged and so the future of the firm becomes more uncertain. The equity price therefore becomes more volatile. This 'leverage effect' has already been mentioned in §2.2.1 as a secondary cause of the implied volatility skew in equity markets. It also implies an asymmetry in volatility clustering in equity markets: if volatility is higher following a negative return than it is following a positive return then the autocorrelation between yesterday's return and today's squared return will be large and negative.

The asymmetric GARCH tests in the last two columns of Table 4.1 investigate the leverage effect in 20 US stocks. A very simple test of this effect is to compute the first-order autocorrelation coefficient between lagged returns and current squared returns:

$$\frac{\sum_{t=2}^{T} r_t^2 r_{t-1}}{\sqrt{\sum_{t=2}^{T} r_t^4 \sum_{t=2}^{T} r_{t-1}^2}} \ .$$

If this is negative and the corresponding Box–Pierce test (the LM test in the last column) is significantly different from zero, then there is an asymmetry in volatility clustering which will not be captured by a symmetric GARCH model. Instead one of the asymmetric GARCH models should be employed (§4.2.4).

Where implied volatility smiles have noticeable skew effects, these may or may not be indicative of a leverage effect

It is interesting that the asymmetric GARCH tests in Table 4.1 fail to reject the null hypothesis of no asymmetry in many cases. Only three out of the 20 stocks in Table 4.1 show significant leverage effects in the data period: Cisco Systems, General Electric and Exxon Mobil. Using robust test statistics that are much more sophisticated than the simple LM procedure used for Table 4.1, Hagerud (1997) has also found that relatively few Nordic stocks show signs of asymmetric volatility clustering. Only 12 out of his sample of 45 stocks exhibited a noticeable leverage effect. The volatility skew may still be very pronounced in these stocks, so where implied volatility smiles have noticeable skew effects, these may or may not be indicative of a leverage effect.

Table 4.2 examines the results of applying the simple Box–Pierce tests for symmetric and asymmetric GARCH to 12 international equity indices. While all except Taiwan have very significant GARCH effects, only seven out of the 12 indices have asymmetric GARCH effects that are significant at the 1% level.

Table 4.2 LM tests for symmetric and asymmetric GARCH effects in equity indices (daily data from 2 January 1996 to 6 October 2000)

Index	GARCH	A-GARCH
AEX	52.9	24.1
AORD	205.4	52.2
CAC	44.5	9.6
DAX	27.7	19.6
FTSE 100	18	6.2
Hang Sang	176.2	43.6
Ibovespa	46.8	30.8
JSA	31.8	0.23
Nikkei 225	164.7	77.2
S&P 500	51.8	24.7
Straights Times	67.9	7.6
Taiwan	7.6	5.5

Neither the UK, France, South Africa, Singapore nor Taiwan have had pronounced leverage effects in their equity indices since 1996. However, index options in all these markets have pronounced skews in their volatility smiles.

Literally dozens of different variants of asymmetric GARCH models have been proposed and tested in a vast research literature. Some of these models are outlined in §4.2.4. However, we have just seen that asymmetric GARCH models have a fairly limited practical use. It is a good thing to be able to include the possibility of asymmetry in the GARCH model so that any leverage effect will be captured, but one should do so with caution because the estimation of asymmetric GARCH can be much more difficult than the estimation of symmetric GARCH.

Literally dozens of different variants of asymmetric GARCH models have been proposed and tested in a vast research literature

4.1.3 The Conditional Mean and Conditional Variance Equations

A simple linear regression can provide a model for the conditional mean of a return process. For example, in a factor model regression the expected value of a stock return will change over time, as specified by its relationship with the market return and any other explanatory variables. This expectation is the conditional mean. The classical linear regression model assumes that the unexpected return ε_t, that is, the error process in the model, is *homoscedastic*. In other words, the error process has a constant variance $V(\varepsilon_t) = \sigma^2$ whatever the value of the dependent variable (§A.1.1). The fundamental idea in GARCH is to add a second equation to the standard regression model: the conditional variance equation. This equation will describe the evolution of the conditional variance of the unexpected return process, $V_t(\varepsilon_t) = \sigma_t^2$.

The fundamental idea in GARCH is to add a second equation to the standard regression model: the conditional variance equation

The dependent variable, the input to the GARCH volatility model, is always a return series. Then a GARCH model consists of two equations. The first is the conditional mean equation. This can be anything, but since the focus of

GARCH is on the conditional variance equation it is usual to have a very simple conditional mean equation. Many of the GARCH models used in practice take the simplest possible conditional mean equation $r_t = c + \varepsilon_t$. In this case the unexpected return ε_t is just the mean deviation return, because the constant will be the average of returns over the data period. In some circumstances it is better to use a time-varying conditional mean (recall Figure 1.5), but the modeller must be very careful not to use many parameters in the conditional mean equation otherwise convergence problems are likely (§4.3.3). If there is a significant autocorrelation in returns, you should use an autoregressive conditional mean, and in almost all cases an AR(1) model will suffice (§11.2.1). If there is a structural break, where the mean return jumps to a new level although the volatility characteristics[2] of the market are unchanged, then a dummy variable can be included in the conditional mean (§A.4.4).

The second equation in a GARCH model is the conditional variance equation. Different GARCH models arise because the conditional variance equations are specified in different forms; some of the more common GARCH models are overviewed in the next section. There is a fundamental distinction between the symmetric GARCH models that are used to model ordinary volatility clustering and the asymmetric GARCH models that are required to capture leverage effects. In symmetric GARCH the conditional mean and conditional variance equations can be estimated separately, as described in §4.3.2. However, this is not possible for asymmetric GARCH models. Their estimation is much more complex, and for more details the reader is referred to the specific papers cited in §4.2.4.

A GARCH model focuses on the time-varying variance of the conditional distributions of returns. Underlying every GARCH model there is also an unconditional returns distribution. The unconditional distribution of a GARCH process will be stationary under certain conditions on the GARCH parameters, as shown in the next section, and if necessary these conditions can be imposed on the estimation. However, if these constraints are indeed binding, one should really ask whether the GARCH model is appropriate to the data.[3]

4.2   A Survey of Univariate GARCH Models

Very many different types of GARCH models have been proposed in the academic literature, but not all have found good practical applications. This section gives an overview of some of the better-known GARCH models that are currently used by academics and financial practitioners. The first autoregressive conditional heteroscedasticity (ARCH) model, introduced by

---

[2] E.g., the degree of persistence in volatility, and the extent of reaction in volatility to market news (§4.2.2).

[3] I prefer to estimate GARCH without imposing constraints on the parameters, and if the freely estimated parameters do not satisfy these constraints I would use a different data period or a different GARCH model.

Engle (1982), was applied to economic data. For financial data it is more appropriate to use a generalization of this model, the symmetric GARCH introduced by Bollerslev (1986). Following this very many different GARCH models have been developed, notably the exponential GARCH model of Nelson (1991), one of the first asymmetric GARCH models to be introduced. For excellent reviews of the enormous literature on GARCH models in finance, see Bollerslev *et al.* (1992, 1994) and Palm (1996).

4.2.1 ARCH

The ARCH(p) process captures the conditional heteroscedasticity of financial returns by assuming that today's conditional variance is a weighted average of past squared unexpected returns:

$$\sigma_t^2 = \alpha_0 + \alpha_1 \varepsilon_{t-1}^2 + \ldots + \alpha_p \varepsilon_{t-p}^2$$
$$\alpha_0 > 0, \ \alpha_1, \ldots, \alpha_p \geqslant 0 \quad \varepsilon_t | I_t \sim N(0, \sigma_t^2).$$

$$(4.1)$$

If a major market movement occurred yesterday, the day before or up to p days ago, the effect will be to increase today's conditional variance because all parameters are constrained to be non-negative (and α_0 is constrained to be strictly positive). It makes no difference whether the market movement is positive or negative, since all unexpected returns are squared on the right-hand side of (4.1).

ARCH models are not often used in financial markets because the simple GARCH models perform so much better. In fact the ARCH model with exponentially declining lag coefficients is equivalent to a GARCH(1,1) model, as is shown in (4.3) below, so the GARCH process actually models an infinite ARCH process, with sensible constraints on coefficients *and* using only very few parameters. The convergence of ARCH(p) models to GARCH(1,1) as p increases is illustrated in Figure 4.2. Here ARCH(5), ARCH(20) and GARCH(1,1) volatilities have been estimated on the CAC. The volatility from an ARCH(5) model is too variable because the lag is too short. The ARCH(20) volatility is similar to the GARCH(1,1) volatility, except there is a certain amount of noise around the estimate that we could very well do without.

As the lag increases in an ARCH model it becomes more difficult to estimate parameters because the likelihood function becomes very flat (§4.3.3). Add to this the inadequate dynamics in an ARCH model with only a few lags, and the differences between volatility estimates in Figure 4.2 are easily accounted for. Since we need very many lags to get close to a GARCH(1,1) model, which has only three parameters, the use of standard ARCH models for financial volatility estimation is not recommended.

The use of standard ARCH models for financial volatility estimation is not recommended

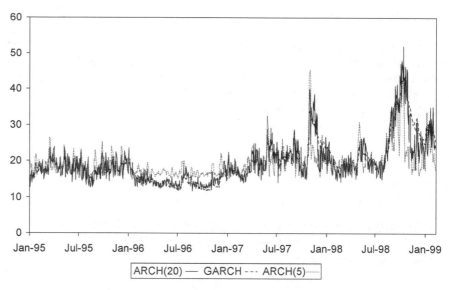

Figure 4.2   ARCH and GARCH volatilities of the CAC index.

4.2.2   Symmetric GARCH

The full GARCH(p, q) model adds q autoregressive terms to the ARCH(p) specification, and the conditional variance equation takes the form

$$\sigma_t^2 = \alpha_0 + \alpha_1 \varepsilon_{t-1}^2 + \ldots + \alpha_p \varepsilon_{t-p}^2 + \beta_1 \sigma_{t-1}^2 + \ldots + \beta_q \sigma_{t-q}^2$$
$$\alpha_0 > 0, \; \alpha_1, \ldots, \; \alpha_p, \; \beta_1, \ldots, \; \beta_q \geqslant 0.$$

However, it is rarely necessary to use more than a GARCH(1,1) model, which has just one lagged error square and one autoregressive term. Using the standard notation for the GARCH constant ω, the GARCH error coefficient α and the GARCH lag coefficient β, the symmetric GARCH(1,1) model is:

$$\sigma_t^2 = \omega + \alpha \varepsilon_{t-1}^2 + \beta \sigma_{t-1}^2$$
$$\omega > 0, \; \alpha, \; \beta \geqslant 0 \tag{4.2}$$

Equation (4.2) is the generic or 'vanilla' GARCH model that many financial institutions use today. Note that this model may also be written

$$\begin{aligned}
\sigma_t^2 &= \omega + \alpha \varepsilon_{t-1}^2 + \beta \sigma_{t-1}^2 \\
&= \omega + \alpha \varepsilon_{t-1}^2 + \beta(\omega + \alpha \varepsilon_{t-2}^2 + \beta(\omega + \alpha \varepsilon_{t-3}^2 + \beta(\ldots))) \\
&= \omega/(1 - \beta) + \alpha(\varepsilon_{t-1}^2 + \beta \varepsilon_{t-2}^2 + \beta^2 \varepsilon_{t-3}^2 + \ldots)
\end{aligned} \tag{4.3}$$

so the GARCH(1,1) model is equivalent to an infinite ARCH model with exponentially declining weights, as mentioned in §4.2.1 above.

The sizes of the parameters α and β determine the short-run dynamics of the resulting volatility time series. Large GARCH lag coefficients β indicate that shocks to conditional variance take a long time to die out, so volatility is 'persistent'. Large GARCH error coefficients α mean that volatility reacts quite intensely to market movements, and so if alpha is relatively high and beta is relatively low then volatilities tend to be more 'spiky'. In financial markets it is common to estimate lag (or 'persistence') coefficients based on daily observations in excess of 0.8 and error (or 'reaction') coefficients no more than 0.2. Much of the discussion in this section and §4.3 concerns the values that one should expect for these 'reaction' and 'persistence' coefficients in different markets, and their stability over time.

Large GARCH lag coefficients β indicate that shocks to conditional variance take a long time to die out, so volatility is 'persistent'. Large GARCH error coefficients α mean that volatility reacts quite intensely to market movements, and so if alpha is relatively high and beta is relatively low then volatilities tend to be more 'spiky'

Estimating vanilla GARCH models using a statistical package such as PcGive or TSP (http://www.tspintl.com) is very simple. Most market data are sufficiently well behaved for the GARCH(1,1) model to be estimated on just a few years of daily data. For example, daily returns on 20 US stocks between 1 January 1996 and 1 October 2000 were used to estimate GARCH(1,1) models in TSP, and the parameter estimates are given in Table 4.2.

The GARCH models for Ford, BankOne, Rockwell and Unicom did not converge, which, following the discussion after Table 4.1, should come as no surprise.[4] We already know the reasons for this: for example, in the case of Ford it is a single observation on 8 April 1998 that upsets the GARCH model, and removing it will resolve the problem. A discussion of more general convergence problems is given in §4.3.3.

Some dubious results are highlighted in italics in Table 4.3. Boeing, Hewlett Packard and AT&T all have excessive excess kurtosis (see Table 4.1) so for these stocks a non-normal symmetric GARCH model will be better than a normal one. Cisco Systems also shows a marked leverage effect, and really needs an asymmetric GARCH model to capture its volatility clustering. The result of applying symmetric normal GARCH to these four stocks is that, although the models do converge, the conditional volatilities on these stocks are very spiky (large reaction, low persistence) and not at all similar to the volatilities on the other stocks.[5]

The result of applying symmetric GARCH to these four stocks is that, although the models do converge, the conditional volatilities on these stocks are very spiky (large reaction, low persistence) and not at all similar to the volatilities on the other stocks

Figure 4.3 shows some of the GARCH volatility estimates that are obtained from the GARCH models for America Online, Citigroup, General Electric, Microsoft and Exxon Mobil. America Online was very volatile for most of the period, and only in the last few months did its volatility come down to more normal levels. Microsoft was also very volatile around the time of the court case between it and the Department of Justice. The other stocks, notably

---

[4]The PcGive demo version on the CD has a tutorial that will discuss this problem.

[5]Of course, it may be the case that some of these stocks, like Cisco, do in fact have very spiky volatilities that are not at all like the other stocks. However, it is likely that the normal GARCH model where $\varepsilon_t | I_t \sim N(0, \sigma_t^2)$ should be replaced by one with a fat-tailed conditional distribution for ε_t; see also the remarks at the beginning of §4.2.5.

Table 4.3: GARCH(1,1) parameter estimates for US stocks

Stock	Omega	Omega (*t*-stat)	Alpha	Alpha (*t*-stat)	Beta	Beta (*t*-stat)
America Int'l Group	2.59E-06	2.12187	0.045359	5.29153	0.948155	93.7937
America Online	2.66E-05	3.12595	0.04889	5.02992	0.935099	73.1338
American Express	7.72E-06	2.83625	0.062286	5.67418	0.923646	66.4884
AT&T	*3.58E-05*	*5.5276*	*0.178474*	*7.61225*	*0.787171*	*28.8813*
Bank of America	5.43E-06	3.276	0.038714	5.17009	0.950696	95.5138
Boeing Corp.	*1.28E-04*	*4.90809*	*0.139733*	*4.86066*	*0.611529*	*8.89522*
Cisco Systems	*7.01E-05*	*3.74729*	*0.134544*	*6.94339*	*0.785827*	*23.128*
Citigroup	2.55E-05	3.30053	0.043641	3.53104	0.915207	39.3103
Coca-Cola Co.	7.53E-06	3.22137	0.063769	7.61847	0.919065	85.7738
Walt Disney	2.64E-06	2.0579	0.040962	6.16269	0.954436	119.476
Exxon Mobil	4.42E-06	1.94717	0.047186	4.34822	0.937404	60.9217
General Electric Co.	6.48E-06	2.32103	0.062028	4.56579	0.918307	48.5241
Hewlett Packard	*8.56E-05*	*3.80309*	*0.099437*	*5.57272*	*0.801407*	*20.9742*
Merrill Lynch	1.19E-05	2.78178	0.055077	5.20405	0.931259	64.3563
Microsoft Co.	1.82E-05	3.43548	0.065529	5.17813	0.901895	47.2069
Procter and Gamble	1.63E-08	0.02115	0.056208	8.0493	0.953651	178.097

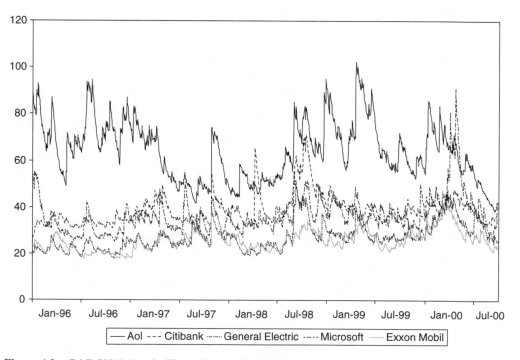

Figure 4.3 GARCH(1,1) volatility estimates for US stocks.

Citibank, have volatilities that are more affected by global events, such as the crises in equity markets in the autumns of 1997 and 1998.

Putting $\sigma_t^2 = \sigma^2$ for all t in (4.2) gives an expression for the long-term steady-state variance in a GARCH(1,1) model:

$$\sigma^2 = \omega/(1 - \alpha - \beta). \tag{4.4}$$

The sum $\alpha + \beta$ must be less than 1 if the returns process is to be stationary. Only in this case will GARCH volatility term structures described in §4.4.1 converge to a long-term average level of volatility that is determined by (4.4). The sum of the α estimate and the β estimate in Table 4.2 is generally less than 1, except for Proctor and Gamble. American International Group and Walt Disney have an estimate of $\alpha + \beta$ equal to 0.993514 and 0.9954, respectively. These stocks may be better modelled by a different GARCH model, such as the integrated GARCH model described in §4.2.3, or a simple exponentially weighted moving average (EWMA) model with the smoothing constant λ set equal to the estimated GARCH beta (§3.2).

The sum $\alpha + \beta$ must be less than 1 if the returns process is to be stationary. Only in this case will GARCH volatility term structures converge to a long-term average level of volatility that is determined by (4.4)

The GARCH(1,1) process is the most common specification for GARCH volatility models, being relatively easy to estimate and generally having robust coefficients that are interpreted naturally in terms of long-term volatilities and short-run dynamics. However, it should be stressed that all three parameter estimates, and particularly that of ω, will be sensitive to the data used. Thus the choice of historic data will affect the current volatility forecasts. In particular, long-term volatility forecasts will be influenced by the inclusion of stress events in the historic data. The problems of which data to use for GARCH volatility estimation, the stability of GARCH coefficients, and the possible advantages of imposing a value for long-term volatility on the GARCH model, are all discussed in §4.3.

4.2.3 Integrated GARCH and the Components Model

Most financial markets have GARCH volatility forecasts that 'mean-revert'. That is, there is a convergence in term structure forecasts to the long-term average volatility level, and by the same token the time series of any GARCH volatility forecast will be stationary. However, currencies and commodities tend to have volatilities that are not as mean-reverting as the volatility of other types of financial assets. In fact, they may not mean-revert at all. In some currency markets not only are exchange rates themselves a random walk, but the volatilities of exchange rates may also be random walks. In this case the usual stationary GARCH models will not apply.

Currencies and commodities tend to have volatilities that are not as mean-reverting as the volatility of other types of financial assets. In fact, they may not mean-revert at all

When $\alpha + \beta = 1$ we can put $\beta = \lambda$ and rewrite the vanilla GARCH (4.2) as

$$\sigma_t^2 = \omega + (1 - \lambda)\varepsilon_{t-1}^2 + \lambda\sigma_{t-1}^2 \quad (0 \leqslant \lambda \leqslant 1). \tag{4.5}$$

Table 4.4: GARCH(1, 1) parameters of the cable rate

Omega	Omega (*t*-stat)	Alpha	Alpha (*t*-stat)	Beta	Beta (*t*-stat)
0.33E-06	5.31182	0.043201	10.5196	0.947753	196.236

Note that the unconditional variance (4.4) is no longer defined and term structure forecasts (§4.4.1) do not converge. Since in this case the variance process is non-stationary, (4.5) is called the *integrated GARCH* (I-GARCH) model.[6] When $\omega = 0$ the I-GARCH model (4.5) becomes an EWMA, hence EWMAs may be viewed as simple GARCH models without an ω and with constant term structures.

I-GARCH is often encountered in foreign exchange markets (Gallant *et al.*, 1991). For example, using daily data on cable (sterling–US dollar) rates from 5 January 1988 to 6 October 2000, the estimated GARCH(1,1) model parameters produce an estimate of $\alpha + \beta = 0.991$, as shown in Table 4.4. Thus the volatilities of the cable rate that are estimated by an I-GARCH model will be very similar to those estimated by an EWMA with $\lambda = 0.94$, as shown in Figure 4.4a.

It is not just in foreign exchange markets that GARCH(1,1) models can become close to being integrated. For example, in Table 4.7 below (§4.3.1) the GARCH(1,1) model for the CAC equity index has an estimate of $\alpha + \beta = 0.993$. Again, the persistence parameter is around 0.94 so the similarity of the GARCH volatility with the EWMA ($\lambda = 0.94$) volatility of the CAC will be obvious, as shown in Figure 4.4b.

The currency and the equity index I-GARCH models that were mentioned above both have persistence parameters that are near 0.94, the same as the RiskMetrics daily data persistence parameter (§7.3). However, I-GARCH models can arise with other values for the persistence parameter. For example, estimating GARCH(1,1) models on the WTI spot and futures data used in Chapter 3 gives the I-GARCH(1,1) parameter estimates shown in Table 4.5. The resultant GARCH volatility estimates are shown in Figure 4.5.

The exponentially weighted moving average correlation that was shown in Figure 3.7 has a smoothing constant of 0.94, but the parameter estimates in Table 4.5 show that this value of lambda is likely to be too high if the whole data period were used. However, it is evident from Figure 4.5 that the excessively high volatility around the time of the Gulf war may be exerting a significant influence on the model parameter estimates, and if the Gulf war period were excluded from the data the beta parameter estimates are closer to

---

[6]Integrated time series processes are discussed in §11.1.3.

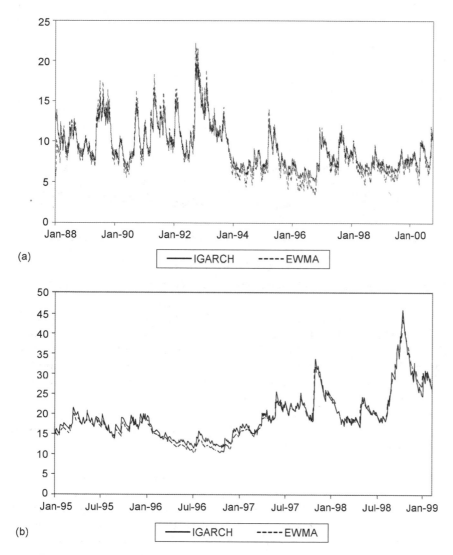

Figure 4.4 I-GARCH and EWMA volatitlies: (a) US dollar–sterling exchange rate; (b) CAC equity index.

Table 4.5: GARCH(1,1) parameters for crude oil

3 July 1988 to *26 Feb 1999*	**Omega**	**Omega** (***t*-stat**)	**Alpha**	**Alpha** (***t*-stat**)	**Beta**	**Beta** (***t*-stat**)
Spot	0.57E-05	5.0276	0.1193	16.7606	0.8807	110.332
Future	0.72E-05	7.2581	0.1403	17.5326	0.8538	95.856
1 July 1992 to *26 Feb 1999*	**Omega**	**Omega** (***t*-stat**)	**Alpha**	**Alpha** (***t*-stat**)	**Beta**	**Beta** (***t*-stat**)
Spot	0.18E-05	2.5032	0.0435	8.8674	0.9545	171.087
Future	0.23E-05	2.9712	0.0717	12.0442	0.9257	125.935

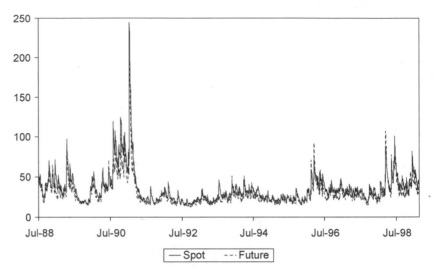

Figure 4.5   GARCH(1, 1) volatility estimates of WTI spot and prompt futures.

Notably, whatever the data period, the estimated model is an I-GARCH model

0.94. When the data period starts in July 1992 instead of July 1988, the alpha and beta estimates are quite different. If the whole data period were used the GARCH volatility would be 'spiky': highly reactive but not very persistent. However, when the Gulf war period is excluded from the data the resultant GARCH volatility is less reactive and more persistent. Notably, whatever the data period, the estimated model is an I-GARCH model.[7] Thus, term structure forecasts will not converge and the estimated GARCH volatility will be approximately the same as an EWMA volatility series with a smoothing constant equal to the estimate of the GARCH beta coefficient.

When a GARCH model is estimated over a rolling data window, different long-term volatility levels will be estimated, corresponding to different estimates of the GARCH parameters (this will be discussed further, in §4.3.1). The *components GARCH* model extends this idea to allow variation of long-term volatility within the estimation period (Engle and Lee, 1993a, 1993b; Engle and Mezrich, 1995). It is most useful in currency and commodity markets, where GARCH models are often close to being integrated and so convergent term structures that fit the market implied volatility term structure cannot be generated. The components model is an attempt to regain the convergence in GARCH term structures in currency markets, by allowing for a time-varying long-term volatility.

The GARCH(1,1) conditional variance may be written in the form

$$\sigma_t^2 = (1 - \alpha - \beta)\sigma^2 + \alpha\varepsilon_{t-1}^2 + \beta\sigma_{t-1}^2$$
$$= \sigma^2 + \alpha(\varepsilon_{t-1}^2 - \sigma^2) + \beta(\sigma_{t-1}^2 - \sigma^2)$$

---

[7]Another example that demonstrates the I-GARCH nature of volatility in energy markets is given in §4.5.1.

where σ^2 is defined by (4.4). In components GARCH σ^2 is replaced by a time-varying 'permanent' component given by

$$q_t = \omega + \rho(q_{t-1} - \omega) + \zeta(\varepsilon_{t-1}^2 - \sigma_{t-1}^2) \qquad (4.6)$$

Therefore the conditional variance equation in the components GARCH model is

$$\sigma_t^2 = q_t + \alpha(\varepsilon_{t-1}^2 - q_{t-1}) + \beta(\sigma_{t-1}^2 - q_{t-1}). \qquad (4.7)$$

Equations (4.6) and (4.7) together define the components model. If $\rho = 1$, the permanent component to which long-term volatility forecasts mean-revert is just a random walk. While the components model has an attractive specification for currency markets, parameter estimation is not straightforward. Estimates may lack robustness and it seems difficult to recommend the use of the components model — except in the event that its specification has passed rigorous diagnostic tests.

4.2.4 Asymmetric GARCH

During the last few years the leverage effect (§4.1.2) has become quite noticeable, particularly in equity markets. For example, three out of the 20 stocks in Table 4.1 had pronounced asymmetry in their volatility clustering, so that volatility increased more when the stock price was falling than when it was rising by the same amount. It therefore came as no surprise that the application of symmetric GARCH to these three particular stocks produced some dubious parameter estimates in Table 4.2.

The vanilla GARCH model of §4.2.2 specifies a symmetric volatility response to market news. That is, the unexpected return ε_t always enters the conditional variance equation as a square, so it makes no difference whether it is positive or negative. However, there is an enormous literature on different specifications of the GARCH conditional variance equation to accommodate an asymmetric response.

The first asymmetric GARCH model that precipitated considerable academic interest was the *exponential GARCH* or E-GARCH model introduced by Nelson (1991).[8] The conditional variance equation in the E-GARCH model is defined in terms of a standard normal variate z_t:

$$\ln \sigma_t^2 = \omega + g(z_{t-1}) + \beta \ln \sigma_{t-1}^2. \qquad (4.8)$$

---

[8]The continuous time limit of the AR(1)–exponential ARCH model gives a conditional variance process whose stationary distribution is lognormal. See Nelson (1990), where he also develops a class of diffusion approximations based on the exponential ARCH.

Table 4.6: Asymmetric GARCH(1, 1) models for major equity indices

Parameter	France	Germany	Japan	UK	US
ω	1.2E-05	1.01E-05	0.85E-05	0.84E-05	0.114E-05
	(9.7)	(8.29)	(8.41)	(6.58)	(3.38)
α	0.111	0.112	0.151	0.084	0.07
	(11.48)	(13.68)	(19.67)	(12.17)	(23.68)
λ	0.0024	0.003	0.004	0.003	0.00038
	(3.14)	(4.26)	(8.2)	(4.09)	(6.39)
β	0.805	0.823	0.8	0.851	0.905
	(60.47)	(75.45)	(68.09)	(65.8)	(182.15)

where $g(\cdot)$ is an asymmetric response function defined by[9]

$$g(z_t) = \lambda z_t + \varphi(|z_t| - \sqrt{2/\pi}).$$

The standard normal variable z_t is the standardized unexpected return ε_t/σ_t. When $\varphi > 0$, and $\lambda < 0$ negative shocks to returns ($z_{t-1} < 0$) induce larger conditional variance responses than positive shocks.

Exponential GARCH is difficult to use for volatility forecasting because there is no analytic form for the volatility term structure

Many GARCH models have to place non-negativity constraints on the parameters to avoid generating negative variances, even though this may unduly restrain the model dynamics. The E-GARCH model eliminates the need for such constraints by formulating the conditional variance in logarithmic terms. Several studies have found that the exponential GARCH model fits financial data very well, often better than other GARCH models. Even without significant leverage effects, the logarithmic specification appears to have considerable advantages (Taylor, 1994; Heynen *et al.*, 1994; Lumsdaine, 1995). But unfortunately, exponential GARCH is difficult to use for volatility forecasting because there is no analytic form for the volatility term structure.

The *asymmetric GARCH* or A-GARCH model of Engle and Ng (1993) is easier to estimate than exponential GARCH and its volatility term structure forecasts may be generated in a simple analytic way (§4.4.1). The A-GARCH model has the conditional variance equation

$$\sigma_t^2 = \omega + \alpha(\varepsilon_{t-1} - \lambda)^2 + \beta\sigma_{t-1}^2 \quad \text{(for } \omega > 0, \, \alpha, \beta, \lambda \geq 0). \tag{4.9}$$

Asymmetric GARCH(1,1) models for the five major equity indices using a very long period of daily data (from 17 February 1981 to 28 April 1995) have been estimated, and the results are shown in Table 4.6 and Figure 4.6. Parameter estimates and *t*-ratios in parentheses may be obtained using the **PcGive demo** on the CD, or by using the BHHH algorithm in RATS (Regression Analysis of Time Series, an econometrics package produced by Estima and available from http://www.estima.com).

---

[9]The last term $(|z_t| - \sqrt{(2/\pi)})$ is the mean deviation of z_t since $\sqrt{(2/\pi)} = E(|z_t|)$.

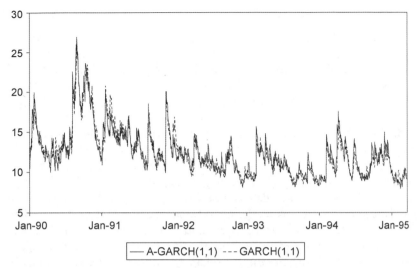

Figure 4.6 Asymmetric and symmetric GARCH volatility estimates for the S&P 500 index.

The estimates of the leverage coefficient λ are of a similar order of magnitude as daily returns, but they are much less significant than the other GARCH coefficient estimates. This implies that the volatility estimates from these asymmetric GARCH(1,1) models will be fairly close to the volatility estimates from a symmetric GARCH model, as shown in the figure. The volatility forecasts made from an A-GARCH model differ from the forecasts made with a symmetric GARCH(1,1) model, and this is discussed in more detail in §4.4.1.

For option pricing and hedging (§4.4.2), Duan (1995) advocates the *non-linear asymmetric GARCH* or N-GARCH model:

$$r_t = r - 0.5\sigma_t^2 + \sigma_t \xi_t$$
$$\sigma_t^2 = \omega + \alpha\sigma_{t-1}^2(\xi_{t-1} - \theta - \lambda)^2 + \beta\sigma_{t-1}^2 \qquad (4.10)$$
$$\xi_t = \varepsilon_t + \lambda.$$

When volatility is stochastic the perfect markets assumption that is necessary for a risk-neutral probability measure no longer holds, but Duan shows that a form of local risk neutrality does hold if prices follow this model. Thus option prices can be calculated as discounted expected values under a unique risk neutral probability measure, in the usual way. An empirical example of the model is given in §4.4.3, where we discuss the work of Duan (1996) on using this model to fit a volatility smile surface.

Many other asymmetric GARCH models have been developed, notably the asymmetric power GARCH of Ding *et al.* (1993), the GJR model of Glosten *et al.* (1993), the threshold GARCH of Zakoian (1994), and the quadratic GARCH model of Sentana (1995). The ability of these models to capture the dynamics of conditional volatility is compared in Hagerud (1997).

4.2.5 GARCH Models for High-Frequency Data

Most of the GARCH models that are used in practice assume that the errors in the conditional mean equation, that is, the unexpected part of returns, are conditionally normally distributed. Nevertheless, the unconditional returns distributions generated by a normal GARCH model will have fat tails, because the conditional volatility is time-varying.

GARCH models for high-frequency data that have error distributions defined by mixtures of normal distributions are required

The normal GARCH models that have been described in this section are commonly used for modelling the volatility of daily returns. However, there is some evidence to suggest that normal GARCH models cannot capture the full extent of excess kurtosis in high-frequency data (Terasvirta, 1996).[10] In this case a leptokurtic distribution, such as a Student t error distribution, could be assumed for the error process in the conditional mean equation (Bollerslev, 1987; Baillie and Bollerslev, 1989b; Engle and González-Riviera, 1991). The absence of analytic derivatives makes optimization rather slow and unreliable, nevertheless t-GARCH (where the 't' refers to Student's t-distribution) is available in many statistical packages such as MFIT (Oxford University Press) and from Ken Kroner's GAUSS programs at Rob Engle's home page: http://weber.ucsd.edu/~mbacci/engle/index_data.html.

Other non-normal GARCH models can be programmed just by changing the likelihood function that is given in §4.3.2. In tandem with other recent developments on modelling fat tails in financial data (§10.3), GARCH models for high-frequency data that have error distributions defined by mixtures of normal distributions are required. However, these have yet to be incorporated in standard statistical packages.

Is it better to predict high-frequency volatility with a low-frequency model, or a low-frequency volatility with a high-frequency model?

Intra-day data are useful for modelling very short-term volatility but there are some additional problems here, to do with time aggregation. In §13.1.3 it is shown that ARCH effects in very high-frequency data are far stronger than one might suppose from the analysis of daily data. The question arises whether a GARCH model estimated on intra-day returns will predict the same daily volatility as a GARCH model estimated on daily returns; and whether a GARCH model estimated on daily returns will predict the same intra-day volatility as a GARCH model estimated on intra-day returns. If not, is it better to predict high-frequency volatility with a low-frequency model, or a low-frequency volatility with a high-frequency model?

Drost and Nijman (1993) use symmetric GARCH models to imply conditional heteroscedasticity at both a lower frequency than the data used to estimate the model, and a higher frequency than the model data. Müller *et al.* (1997) also compare GARCH volatilities that are estimated at different frequencies. They

---

[10]High-frequency foreign exchange data are highly leptokurtic. For example, in §10.1.1 the excess kurtosis of 1-hourly returns on the DEM–USD exchange rate is calculated as 8.34. Equity returns can be very leptokurtic even at the daily frequency (see §4.4.2).

support the findings of Drost and Nijman: that a GARCH model that is estimated on high-frequency data does not predict lower-frequency volatility well, and that it is better to predict a high-frequency volatility with a low-frequency model.

A number of studies have shown that the aggregation properties of GARCH models are not straightforward (Guillaime *et al.*, 1994; Ghose and Kroner, 1995; Andersen *et al.*, 1999a; Galbraith and Zinde-Walsh, 2000). The persistence in volatility seems to be lower when measured on intra-day data than when it is measured on daily or weekly data. One would expect, for example, that fitting a GARCH(1, 1) to daily data would yield a sum of alpha and beta parameter estimates that is greater than the sum of alpha and beta parameter estimates that is obtained when fitting the same GARCH(1, 1) to 2-day returns. The 'square root of time' rule does not hold, of course, but one should expect some similarity between the long-term volatilities that are inherent in GARCH(1, 1) implementations on different data frequencies. In fact, from the long-term variance equation (4.17), it is clear that we should observe

The 'square root of time' rule does not hold, of course, but one should expect some similarity between the long-term volatilities that are inherent in GARCH(1, 1) implementations on different data frequencies

$$[1/(1 - \alpha_1 - \beta_1)] \approx [2/(1 - \alpha_2 - \beta_2)] \approx \ldots \approx [n/(1 - \alpha_n - \beta_n)]$$

where α_i and β_i are the GARCH parameters based on i-day returns. This does not always turn out to be the case. Andersen and Bollerslev (1996) attribute this to a variety of volatility components in the data, possibly due to the different investment strategies of heterogeneous agents.

These observations have prompted Müller *et al.* (1997) and Dacorogna *et al.* (1996) to develop a GARCH model that is based on a number of independent volatility components in high-frequency data. In the simple ARCH model (4.1) the conditional variance is a weighted sum of squared returns. The *heterogeneous interval autoregressive conditional heteroscedasticity* (HARCH) model modifies this so that the squared returns are taken at different frequencies. It is extremely burdensome computationally to use all possible data frequencies, so the most recent formulation of the HARCH model in Dacorogna *et al.* (1998) uses exponentially smoothed squared sums of returns measured at only a few different frequencies. The 'partial volatilities' that are used in the HARCH model are designed to capture volatility clustering at different frequencies. They are defined as

$$\sigma_{j,t}^2 = (1 - \lambda_j) \left(\sum_{i=1}^{K_j} \varepsilon_{t-i\Delta t} \right)^2 + \lambda_j \sigma_{j,t-\Delta t}^2. \tag{4.11}$$

The number of returns taken in the sum, K_j, is increasing with j, so as j increases, the time span in the memory of the partial volatility also increases.[11]

---

[11]Dacorogna *et al.* (1998) use K_j=1, 2, 5, 17, 65, . . . for j=1, 2, 3, 4, ... This is similar to the data preprocessing stage of a neural network, where partial sums of different frequencies are used to capture certain patterns in the data (§13.2).

The HARCH conditional variance equation is then similar to the ARCH(p) equation (4.1) but with the partial sums $\sigma_1^2, \ldots, \sigma_p^2$ in place of $\varepsilon_{t-1}^2, \ldots, \varepsilon_{t-p}^2$. For example, one might take 1 hour as the basic interval of time, and form the partial sums of 1-hour returns by taking the sum of K_j consecutive returns for each $j=1, \ldots, p$. Then the exponentially smoothed partial sums (4.11) are taken in the conditional variance equation

$$\sigma_t^2 = \alpha_0 + \alpha_1 \sigma_1^2 + \ldots + \alpha_p \sigma_p^2. \tag{4.12}$$

4.3 Specification and Estimation of GARCH Models

In a GARCH model there is a trade-off between having enough data for parameter estimates to be stable as the data window is rolled, and so much data that the forecasts do not properly reflect the current market conditions

How should one choose the data period for a GARCH model on daily data? Obviously the data should run up to the present date, but how far should one look back? An example of how GARCH parameter estimates depend on the choice of data period has already been given (Table 4.5). In §4.3.1 we show that in a GARCH model there is a trade-off between having enough data for parameter estimates to be stable as the data window is rolled, and so much data that the forecasts do not properly reflect the current market conditions.[12] Then, in §4.3.2, a brief mathematical description of the algorithms that are used to estimate GARCH parameters is provided. However, it is unlikely that a market model developer will need to code up any programs. The most common GARCH models are already available as preprogrammed procedures in econometric packages such as the OxMetrics suite given with the CD, S-PLUS, TSP, EVIEWS, SAS, RATS and MICROFIT. A critical review of the available GARCH software is given in Brooks *et al.* (2001).

Even vanilla GARCH models can encounter convergence problems, although this is relatively rare; most often the cause of non-convergence is simply trying to apply the wrong model or using some rather difficult data. Section 4.3.3 gives some hints for helping GARCH models to converge; the section finishes by outlining, in §4.3.4, some simple diagnostics that will help you choose the correct specification for the GARCH model.

4.3.1 Choice of Data, Stability of GARCH Parameters and Long-Term Volatility

It is usual to take daily or intra-day returns, because GARCH effects at lower frequencies are not so apparent. In choosing the time span of historical data used for estimating a GARCH model, the first consideration is whether major market events from several years ago should be influencing forecasts today. For example, including Black Monday (October 1987) in equity GARCH models will have the effect of raising current long-term volatility forecasts by several per cent. For another example, including the Gulf war period in a crude

---

[12]In §4.2.3 it was shown that EWMA models can be considered as simple GARCH models. However, the estimation of EWMA volatility normally takes the smoothing constant parameter as given, so the data period has little influence on results. It makes no difference to the current estimate whether a time series of EWMA volatility has been taken over the past 50 days or the past 100 days. This is not the case with GARCH models.

Table 4.7: GARCH(1,1) parameter estimates and long-run volatility (daily data from 2 January 1996 to 6 October 2000)

Index	Omega $(\times 10^{-5})$	Alpha	Beta	1-day Forecasts (% Vol)	LR Forecasts (% Vol)
AEX	0.2	0.093	0.898	11.8	24.03701
AORD	0.98	0.153	0.714	11.28	13.8412
CAC	0.14	0.052	0.941	19.11	22.80351
DAX	0.26	0.087	0.9025	16.62	25.3734
FTSE 100	0.05	0.047	0.949	14.21	18.02776
Hang Seng	0.53	0.115	0.88	34.06	52.49762
Ibovespa	2.31	0.186	0.786	32.56	46.31414
JSA	0.31	0.180	0.820	13.71	N/A*
Nikkei 225	0.67	0.083	0.886	20.24	23.70518
S&P 500	0.37	0.089	0.886	15.6	19.61632
Straights Times	0.34	0.152	0.848	19.2	N/A*
Taiwan	3.28	0.157	0.74	38.8	28.77431
From November 1997					
AORD	0.446	0.091	0.852	12.31	14.26319
JSA	1.81	0.183	0.735	16.78	23.95626
Straights Times	0.69	0.144	0.822	21.47	22.97057

*These models are integrated so no long run volatility forecast exists.

oil GARCH model will give large reaction and low persistence coefficient estimates and consequently make current volatility estimates very 'spiky' (Figure 4.5 and Table 4.5).

The long-term level of volatility to which a current volatility term structure will converge depends on the estimates of the GARCH parameters. For example, in the GARCH(1, 1) model the long-term volatility is related to the GARCH constant ω as in (4.4). All parameter estimates, and in particular the estimate of the GARCH constant, are sensitive to the historic data used for the model. Thus even if the market has been stable for some time, the estimate of long-term volatility can be high if the data period covers several years with many extreme market movements. Therefore, in choosing how far to go back with the data, one has to take a view on whether or not current forecasts should be influenced by events that occurred many years ago.

In choosing how far to go back with the data, one has to take a view on whether or not current forecasts should be influenced by events that occurred many years ago

Table 4.7 reports the GARCH(1, 1) parameter estimates and corresponding long-run volatility forecasts for international equity indices, that were applicable on 6 October 2000, using GARCH models based on daily data since 2 January 1996.[13] The corresponding GARCH volatility estimates are shown in Figure 4.7.

In the European markets, the Netherlands (AEX) and Germany (DAX) are less persistent and more reactive in volatility than France (CAC) and the UK (FTSE 100), and so their GARCH volatilities are more 'spiky' (see Figure 4.7)

---

[13]For Taiwan the data start on 2 January 1997.

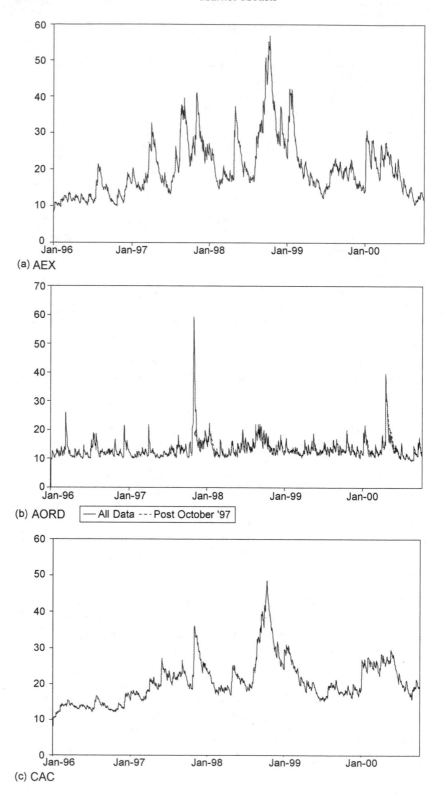

(a) AEX

(b) AORD [— All Data --- Post October '97]

(c) CAC

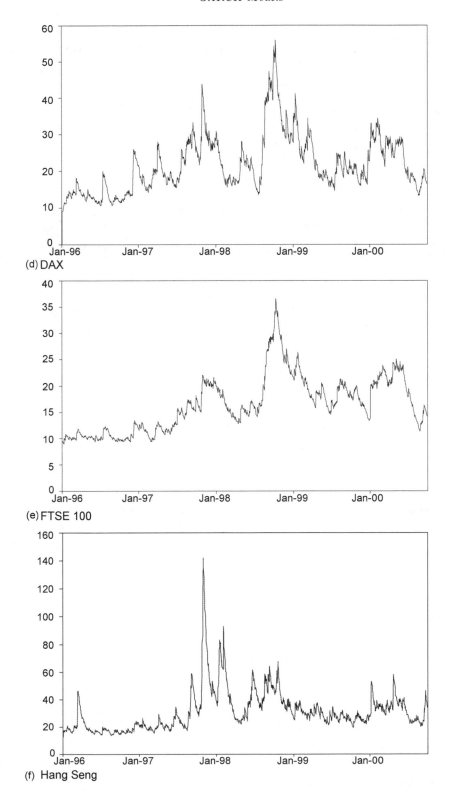

(d) DAX

(e) FTSE 100

(f) Hang Seng

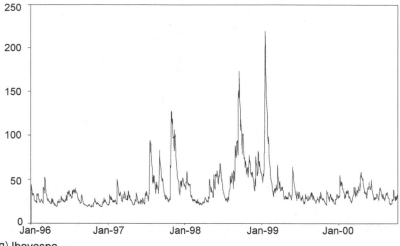

(g) Ibovespa

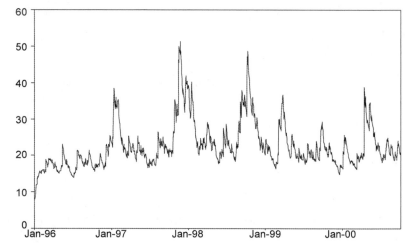

(h) Nikkei 225

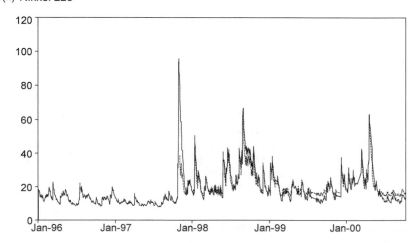

(i) Johannesburg   —— All Data ---- Post October '97

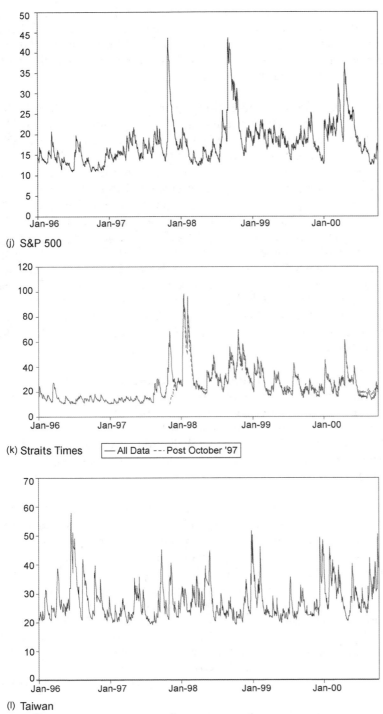

(j) S&P 500

(k) Straits Times — All Data --- Post October '97

(l) Taiwan

Figure 4.7 GARCH(1, 1) volatility: (a) AEX; (b) AORD; (c) CAC; (d) DAX; (e) FTSE 100; (f) Hang Seng; (g) Ibovespa; (h) Nikkei 225; (i) Johannesburg; (j) S&P 500; (k) Straits Times; (l) Taiwan.

and their long-run volatility forecasts are correspondingly a little higher (but more uncertain). Currently the reaction and persistence parameters in the USA (S&P 500) and Japan (Nikkei 225) are very similar, but the higher estimate of omega in Japan yields a long run volatility of 23.7% for Japan, compared with 19.6% for the USA based on the same sample period.

On the basis of these results, and looking at the graphs in Figure 4.7, the indices that are most reactive in volatility seem to be in Australia (AORD), Hong Kong (Hang Seng), Brazil (Ibovespa), South Africa (Johannesberg) and Taiwan. The equity markets in Hong Kong, Singapore and Brazil have been generally rather volatile since 1998. For example, having fallen 17.2% on 10 September 1998, the Brazilian Ibovespa then proceeded to recover, and in the early part of 1999 some quite spectacular gains were made: on 15 January 1999 it rose 28.8%. Singapore has been less fortunate, although a gain of 12.87% was made on a single day on 2 February 1998. It is not surprising, therefore, that the long-run volatility forecasts for 6 October 2000 that are based on these data come in at around 50% for Brazil and Hong Kong.[14] The long-run volatility forecast for Taiwan is much lower because, although it often experiences volatilities in the 60% range, it has the least persistent volatility. This type of over-reactive and low persistent volatility is a well-documented feature of Asian-Pacific equity and currency markets (Alexander and Thillainathan, 1995).

The Australian equity market volatility seems to have more in common with that of the South African equity market than the other Asian-Pacific markets, except that both were badly affected by the Asian crisis in 1997. Australia and South Africa were uncharacteristically volatile during that time: on 28 October 1997 the Australian index fell by 7.5% and the South African index fell by 11.85%. And volatility in both markets, particularly South Africa, has increased since that time.

In this case there is a good reason to choose the starting date for the data to be after the mini-crash in equities of the summer of 1997

Now suppose it is 6 October 2000 and you want to make a volatility forecast a year ahead. You consider that it is very unlikely that the spectacular losses associated with the Asian crisis will be repeated during your forecast horizon, and you also believe that the relatively tranquil equity markets experienced in Australia and South Africa before the 1997 mini-crash will not be seen again for at least another year. Then there is a good reason to choose the starting date for the data to be after the mini-crash in equities of the summer of 1997. In fact the South African equity index GARCH model is not well specified when data before the mini-crash are included in the sample: the results for South Africa (and in fact for Singapore) in the upper part of the table correspond to an I-GARCH model, which has no long-run volatility because volatility is a random walk (§4.1.2). However, when the data period starts on 1 November

---

[14]Long-run forecasts are not available for Singapore because the estimate of $\alpha + \beta$ is 0.999, close enough to 1 for the GARCH model to be integrated. This indicates that the model is not well specified for the data and should be re-run using a different historic period, as has been done for South Africa and Australia, or a different (asymmetric) GARCH model.

1997, the GARCH model for South Africa is well specified, and it gives a long-run volatility forecast of about 24% on 6 October 2000. The last two rows of Table 4.7 show that if the Australian and South African GARCH models were estimated on data from 1 November 1997, instead of from 2 January 1996, they would tell quite a different story for 6 October 2000.

The results for Australia and South Africa in Table 4.7 are improved when one only uses about 3 years of data, rather than the original sample of almost 5 years. Thus you may well ask whether it would be even better to use only 2 years of data instead of 3. However, it is important to understand that a certain minimum amount of data will be necessary for the likelihood function to be well defined. Usually a few years of daily data are necessary to ensure proper convergence of the model and, even if there are sufficient data to avoid convergence problems, parameter estimates may lack robustness if too few observations are used. That is, as the data window is rolled forward day by day, the estimates of the GARCH parameters might lack stability. Therefore it is always a good idea to check the robustness of GARCH parameter estimates by doing some rolling GARCH regressions.

A certain minimum amount of data will be necessary for the likelihood function to be well defined

Figure 4.8 shows the GARCH(1, 1) parameter estimates and corresponding long-run GARCH volatility forecasts for five of the US stocks from Table 4.2. Instead of using the entire data period from 1 January 1996 to 2 October 2000 to estimate the GARCH model as in Table 4.3, only 4 years of data were used. The GARCH model was rolled weekly from December 1999 until the end of the data set, each time recording the parameter estimates, and these are shown in Figure 4.8.

From Figure 4.8a it is evident that the GARCH omega constants for Microsoft and America Online declined significantly during the estimations, but for other stocks the GARCH constants were relatively stable. Looking at Figures 4.8b and 4.8c, America Online started off with a higher alpha and lower beta, that is, a high reaction but low persistence, giving a 'spiky' volatility. However, by the end of the period its volatility characteristics had changed to become more similar to those of the other stocks.

The reaction coefficients (alpha) and the persistence coefficients (beta) shown in Figures 4.8b and 4.8c are more variable in all stocks. After the technology bubble burst most American stocks seem to have settled down again sometime during the second quarter of 2000, Microsoft being an exception. At the beginning of the data period the Microsoft GARCH models gave incredibly high reaction and low persistence volatilities, but this may have had something to do with the legal battle between Microsoft and the US Monopolies Commission. Indeed, all the GARCH parameters for Microsoft underwent considerable change leading up to the court ruling to split in April 2000. Around that time the reaction coefficient for Microsoft was extremely variable, and this has fed through to the long-term volatility forecasts shown in Figure 4.8d.

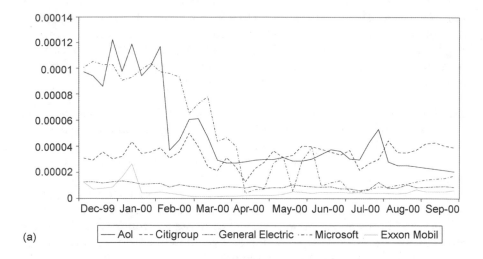

(a)

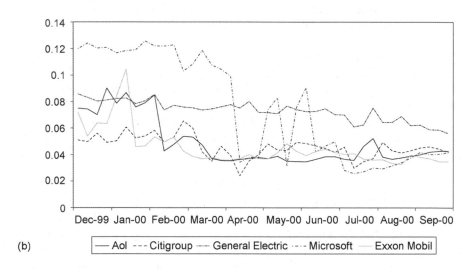

(b)

Figure 4.8 (a) and (b).

One does not need to estimate the GARCH constant freely. Instead one can fix the long-term volatility level by imposing the constant before model estimation

Despite the changes in GARCH parameter estimates during the period, Figure 4.8d shows that the long-term volatility forecasts from these GARCH models do not change much. The long-term volatility of Microsoft did increase somewhat in April 2000, reflecting developments in the court case brought by the Monopolies Commission. If the GARCH parameter estimates do vary considerably when the model is rolled over time it may be that the model is not well specified. In fact there is some evidence to suggest that specification of the GARCH model will depend on the current market regime (Hamilton and Susmel, 1994).

In summary, one should use several years of daily data, enough to ensure that parameter estimates are relatively stable as the data window is rolled, but not

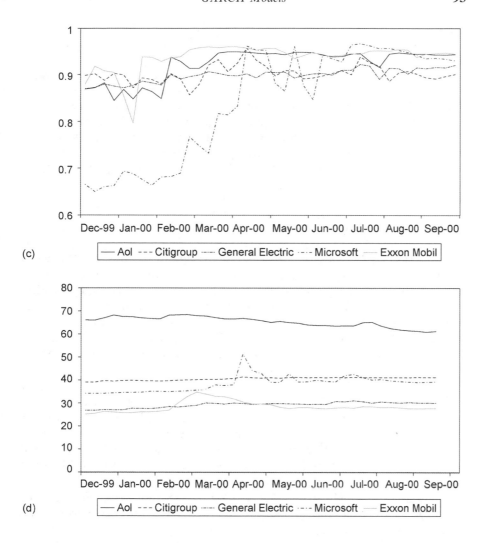

Figure 4.8 Parameter estimates for US stocks in 2000: (a) rolling GARCH omega; (b) rolling GARCH alpha; (c) rolling GARCH beta; (d) long-run GARCH volatilities.

so much that these estimates do not reflect changes in current market conditions. When there are outliers in the data, however far in the past, this can upset convergence of the GARCH model and give misleading results for parameter estimates. A very long data period with several outliers is unlikely to be suitable because extreme moves from very long ago can have a great influence on the long-term volatility forecasts made today.

One does not need to estimate the GARCH constant freely. Instead one can fix the long-term volatility level by imposing the constant before model estimation. To illustrate the idea, consider the GARCH(1,1) model (4.2).

Substituting for ω using (4.4) gives an alternative formulation of the GARCH(1, 1) model in terms of deviations from long-term variance σ^2:

$$\sigma_t^2 - \sigma^2 = \alpha(\varepsilon_{t-1}^2 - \sigma^2) + \beta(\sigma_{t-1}^2 - \sigma^2). \tag{4.13}$$

Scenario analysis on long-term volatility may be quite simply extended to the whole volatility term structure using the GARCH model

Thus a GARCH(1,1) model on the deviations of squared unexpected returns from some assumed level for the long-term variance gives estimates of the GARCH reaction and persistence parameters while fixing the long-term volatility. In this way a scenario analysis on long-term volatility may be quite simply extended to the whole volatility term structure using the GARCH model.

4.3.2 Parameter Estimation Algorithms

The mathematical foundations of computer programs that estimate GARCH model parameters are now described. It is worthwhile to have some understanding of the mathematical principles used because if a statistical package does not offer in-built commands for GARCH model estimation then procedures must be written. For example, in GAUSS the GARCH procedures are explained in the manual. Several GARCH programs in GAUSS written by Ken Kroner are available free from http://weber.ucsd.edu/~mbacci/engle/index_data.html.

Following Bollerslev (1986), GARCH model parameters are normally estimated by maximum likelihood, a powerful and general parameter estimation procedure that is widely used because it almost always produces consistent, asymptotically normal and efficient estimates (§A.6). The general idea is to choose estimates of the parameters θ to maximize the likelihood of the data under an assumption about the shape of the distribution of the data generation process. The parameter estimation method is therefore one of optimizing a function of several variables, for which there is often no analytic solution but there are many standard routines.

Most algorithms are iterative, that is, the parameter estimates are updated using a scheme:

$$\theta_{i+1} = \theta_i + \lambda_i \delta_i,$$

where λ_i is a step length and δ_i is a direction vector, chosen so that the likelihood of the data under θ_{i+1} is greater than the likelihood under θ_i. The gradient descent methods that are used for GARCH model estimation in most packages define the direction vector in terms of the gradient of the likelihood function and the Hessian matrix of second derivatives of the likelihood function, both evaluated at θ_i.

For an i.i.d. normal data generation process with mean μ and variance σ^2, the likelihood of a sample of returns $r_1, r_2, \ldots, r_T$ is

$$L(\mu,\sigma^2|r_1,r_2,\ldots,r_T) = \prod_{t=1}^{T} f(r_t)$$

where $f(\cdot)$ is the normal density function. Choosing μ and σ^2 to maximize L, or equivalently and more simply to minimize $-2\ln L$, yields the maximum likelihood estimates of these parameters, as described in Appendix 6.

In GARCH models the likelihood functions are more complex because the variance is time-varying (Engle, 1982; Bollerslev, 1986). For a normal symmetric GARCH model the log-likelihood of a single observation r_t is, ignoring the term in $\ln(2\pi)$ because it does not affect the estimates:

Most univariate GARCH models should encounter few convergence problems if the model is well specified and the data are well behaved

$$l_t = -\tfrac{1}{2}\left[\ln\sigma_t^2 + (\varepsilon_t^2/\sigma_t^2)\right]$$

and Σl_t should be maximized with respect to the variance parameters. Denote the variance parameters by θ, so in the case of GARCH(1,1) the variance parameters are $\theta = (\omega, \alpha, \beta)'$. Then the first derivatives may be written

$$\partial l_t/\partial\theta = (1/(2\sigma_t^2))[(\varepsilon_t^2/\sigma_t^2) - 1]\mathbf{g}_t \qquad (4.14)$$

where the gradient vector is[15]

$$\mathbf{g}_t = \partial\sigma_t^2/\partial\theta.$$

These derivatives may be calculated recursively, taking the ordinary least squares estimate of unconditional variance as pre-sample estimates of ε_t^2 and σ_t^2 in (4.14) and calculating the gradient vectors by the recursion

$$\mathbf{g}_t = \mathbf{z}_t + \beta\mathbf{g}_{t-1},$$

where $\mathbf{z}_t = (1, \varepsilon_{t-1}^2, \sigma_{t-1}^2)$. Solving the first-order conditions $\partial_t/\partial\theta = \mathbf{0}$ yields a set of non-linear equations in the parameters that may be solved using some quasi-Newton variable metric algorithm such as the Davidon–Fletcher–Powell (DFP) or the *Berndt–Hall–Hall–Hausmann (BHHH) algorithm* that is recommended by Bollerslev (1986). The BHHH iteration is

$$\boldsymbol{\theta}_{i+1} = \boldsymbol{\theta}_i + \lambda_i\mathbf{H}_i^{-1}\mathbf{g}_i, \qquad (4.15)$$

where λ_i is a variable step length chosen to maximize the likelihood in the appropriate direction, $\mathbf{H}_i$ is the Hessian matrix $\Sigma(\mathbf{g}_t\mathbf{g}_t')$ and $\mathbf{g}_i = \Sigma\mathbf{g}_t$, both evaluated at $\boldsymbol{\theta}_i$. The iteration is deemed to have converged when the gradient vector $\mathbf{g}$ is zero.

---

[15] The algorithm may take a long time unless analytic derivatives are used to calculate the gradient. This problem has limited the usefulness of t-distributed GARCH models for very leptokurtic data, since they require numerical derivatives to be calculated at each iteration.

4.3.3   Estimation Problems

Sometimes convergence problems arise because the more parameters in the GARCH model the 'flatter' the likelihood function becomes, therefore the more difficult it is to maximize. The likelihood function becomes like the surface of the moon (in many dimensions) so it may be that only a local optimum is achieved. In that case a different set of estimates may be obtained when the starting values for the iteration are changed (§4.3.2). In order to ensure that the estimates correspond to a global optimum of the likelihood function one would have to run the model with many starting values and each time record the likelihood of the optima. If this type of convergence problem is encountered one should use a more parsimonious parameterization of the GARCH model, if possible.

Convergence problems with GARCH models can also arise because the gradient algorithm used to maximize the likelihood function has hit a boundary. If there are obvious outliers in the data then it is very likely that the iteration will return the value 0 or 1 for either the alpha or the beta parameter (or both). It may be safe to remove a single outlier (as in the Ford example given above) if the circumstances that produced the outlier are thought to be unlikely to happen in future. Alternatively, the boundary problem might be mitigated by changing the starting values of the parameters, or changing the data set so that the likelihood function has a different gradient at the beginning of the search. Otherwise the model specification will have to be changed. A sure sign of using the wrong GARCH model is when the iteration refuses to converge at all, even after you have checked the data for outliers, changed the starting values or chosen a different data period.

Most univariate GARCH models should encounter few convergence problems if the model is well specified and the data are well behaved. Changes in the data will induce some changes in the coefficient estimates, as was evident in the rolling estimates of GARCH parameters that were shown in Figure 4.8. However, if the model is 'well tuned' the parameter estimates should not change greatly as new data arrive, except when there are structural breaks in the data generation process.

4.3.4   Choosing the Best GARCH Model

Which is the best GARCH model to use and when? The vanilla GARCH model already offers many advantages, even without asymmetric effects, and is widely used. But does it capture the right type of volatility clustering in the market? When should an asymmetric or non-linear or other more complex GARCH model be used?

The first question to answer for a chosen GARCH model is how well it models the conditional volatility of the process. If a GARCH model is capturing volatility clustering adequately, the returns should have no significant autoregressive conditional heteroscedasticity once they have been standardized by their conditional volatility. An indication of the success of GARCH models to really capture the volatility clustering is that, even in very high-frequency exchange rate data where GARCH effects are strong and complex (§4.2.5), returns are nearly normally distributed when divided by their conditional volatility (Andersen *et al.*, 1999a, 1999b).

If a GARCH model is capturing volatility clustering adequately, the returns should have no significant autoregressive conditional heteroscedasticity once they have been standardized by their conditional volatility

In §4.1.1 we saw that standard tests for autoregressive conditional heteroscedasticity are based on autocorrelation in squared returns. Returns themselves may not be autocorrelated, but if volatility clustering is present in the data they will not be independent because squared returns will be autocorrelated. Therefore a simple test for a GARCH model is that the standardized returns squared, $r_t^{*2} = r_t^2 / \hat{\sigma}_t^2$, where $\hat{\sigma}_t^2$ is the estimate of the GARCH conditional variance, should have no autocorrelation.

Such tests may be based on an autocorrelation test statistic such as the Box–Pierce statistic described in §11.3.2. For large sample sizes T, the Box–Pierce test statistic $Q \sim \chi_p^2$ is:

$$Q = T \sum_{n=1}^{p} \varphi(n)^2,$$

where $\varphi(n)$ is the nth-order autocorrelation coefficient in squared standardized returns,

$$\varphi(n) = \frac{\sum_{t=n+1}^{T} r_t^{*2} r_{t-n}^{*2}}{\sum_{t=1}^{T} r_t^{*4}}.$$

If there is no autocorrelation in the squared standardized returns the GARCH model is well specified. But what if several GARCH models account equally well for GARCH effects? In that case choose the GARCH model which gives the highest likelihood in post-sample predictive tests, as explained in §5.5.1 (see also Appendix 5).

4.4 Applications of GARCH Models

Whilst the 'square root of time' rule might be a useful approximation to reality over very short-term horizons, the clustering of volatility means that there will be a large approximation error if this rule were to be applied over the longer term (§3.3). One needs a model that generates volatility term structures that converge to the long-term average volatility level as maturity increases, rather than the constant term structures that result from moving average volatility models. This is one of the main advantages of GARCH models.

Whilst the 'square root of time' rule might be a useful approximation to reality over very short-term horizons, the clustering of volatility means that there will be a large approximation error if this rule were to be applied over the longer term

Having obtained a GARCH conditional variance for the next observation period, its square root may be taken and it may be annualized in the usual way to obtain a GARCH volatility estimate. However, this current estimate is not taken to be the forecast of volatility over all future time horizons, as it is in the moving average methods described in Chapter 3. Instead, mean-reverting volatility term structures that converge to the long-term average volatility are derived analytically from the estimated GARCH model parameters, as explained in §4.4.1.

GARCH volatility forecasts are very flexible and can be adapted to any time period. The forward volatilities that are generated by GARCH models have many applications. Valuing path-dependent options or volatility options, measuring risk capital requirements, calibration of binomial trees — all of these require forecasts of forward volatilities that have a proper mean-reverting property.

There is no need to hold a GARCH model together with bits of string and sticky plaster, to force it into a framework that is inconsistent with its basic assumptions

Perhaps the most important of all the advantages of GARCH models is that they are based on a statistical theory that is justified by empirical evidence. Unlike constant volatility models, there is no need to hold a GARCH model together with bits of string and sticky plaster, to force it into a framework that is inconsistent with its basic assumptions. This coherency has led to many applications of GARCH models to the pricing and hedging of options.

Some GARCH models have diffusion limits that will provide a model for stochastic volatility.[16] In §4.4.2 the motivation behind their use to price and hedge any type of option, path-dependent or otherwise, is explained. GARCH models have also been used to fit and forecast implied volatility smiles, as described in §4.4.3.

4.4.1   GARCH Volatility Term Structures

Long-term (steady-state) forecasts of volatility from a GARCH(1,1) model have already been referred to in §4.3.1. There it was also noted that one can fix this long-term volatility at a level that reflects any reasonable scenario, and use the formulation (4.13) to estimate the GARCH reaction and persistence parameters using historic data.

Volatility forecasts for any maturity may be obtained from the one estimated model

Whether the long-term volatility is fixed or estimated freely, the real strength of the GARCH model is that volatility forecasts for any maturity may be obtained from the one estimated model. Forecasts are very simple to construct in many GARCH models because they take a simple analytic form. No approximations or lengthy simulations are necessary. Term structure forecasts that are constructed from GARCH models mean-revert to the long-term level

---

[16]In his PhD dissertation, Nelson (1988) made the bold conjecture that it was not possible to find a conditionally heteroscedastic diffusion limit for a GARCH process. He later corrected this mistake (Nelson, 1990).

of volatility at a speed that is determined by the estimated GARCH parameters. This is the great advantage of GARCH over moving average methods, which are based on the less realistic assumption of constant volatility term structures (§3.3).

The first step is to construct forecasts of instantaneous forward volatilities — that is, the volatility of r_{t+j}, made at time t for every step ahead j. For example, in the GARCH(1, 1) model the 1-day forward variance forecast is

$$\hat{\sigma}_{t+1}^2 = \hat{\omega} + \hat{\alpha}\varepsilon_t^2 + \hat{\beta}\hat{\sigma}_t^2 \tag{4.16}$$

and the j-step ahead forecasts are computed iteratively as[17]

$$\hat{\sigma}_{t+j}^2 = \hat{\omega} + (\hat{\alpha} + \hat{\beta})\hat{\sigma}_{t+j-1}^2.$$

Putting $\hat{\sigma}_{t+j}^2 = \hat{\sigma}^2$ for all j gives the steady-state variance estimate

$$\hat{\sigma}^2 = \hat{\omega}/(1 - \hat{\alpha} - \hat{\beta}) \tag{4.17}$$

and this determines the long-term volatility level to which GARCH(1,1) term structure forecasts converge if $\hat{\alpha} + \hat{\beta} < 1$.

The forecasts from an A-GARCH model (4.9) also have a simple analytic form. The one-step-ahead forecast is

$$\hat{\sigma}_{t+1}^2 = \hat{\omega} + \hat{\alpha}(\varepsilon_t - \hat{\lambda})^2 + \hat{\beta}\hat{\sigma}_t^2 \tag{4.18}$$

and the steady-state variance estimate is

$$\hat{\sigma}^2 = (\hat{\omega} + \hat{\alpha}\hat{\lambda}^2)/(1 - \hat{\alpha} - \hat{\beta}). \tag{4.19}$$

Comparison of (4.17) and (4.19) shows that the leverage coefficient λ would have the effect of increasing long-term volatility forecasts, *ceteris paribus*. That is, if the ω, α and β estimates were not changed very much by moving from a symmetric GARCH(1,1) to an A-GARCH(1,1) model, the long-term volatility forecasts from the A-GARCH model would be higher than those from a symmetric GARCH model. However, there will be a change in the ω, α and β estimates and the steady-state variance estimate in (4.19) should not differ from the GARCH(1,1) steady state (4.17).

The most noticeable differences between the forecasts made by symmetric and asymmetric GARCH models are in the short-term volatility forecasts following a large fall in market price

The most noticeable differences between the forecasts made by symmetric and asymmetric GARCH models are in the short-term volatility forecasts following a large fall in market price. Comparison of (4.16) with (4.18) shows that the difference between one-step ahead variance forecasts will be dominated by the term $\hat{\alpha}\hat{\lambda}(\hat{\lambda} - 2\varepsilon_t)$. Differences in volatility forecasts may be considerable if a very large unexpected negative return is experienced at time t, as shown in Table 4.8.

---

[17]The unexpected return at time $t+j$ is unknown for $j > 0$. But $E(\varepsilon_{t+j}^2) = \sigma_{t+j}^2$.

Table 4.8: Approximate increase in 1-day volatility forecast due to λ

Lambda		Alpha				
		0.15	**0.125**	**0.1**	**0.075**	**0.05**
$\varepsilon_t = -0.01$	**0.0001**	0.868	0.793	0.709	0.614	0.501
	0.0005	1.961	1.790	1.601	1.386	1.132
	0.001	2.806	2.562	2.291	1.984	1.620
$\varepsilon_t = -0.05$	**0.0001**	1.937	1.769	1.582	1.370	1.119
	0.0005	4.341	3.963	3.544	3.070	2.506
	0.001	6.154	5.618	5.025	4.352	3.553
$\varepsilon_t = -0.1$	**0.0001**	2.739	2.501	2.237	1.937	1.582
	0.0005	6.131	5.597	5.006	4.336	3.540
	0.001	8.682	7.925	7.089	6.139	5.012

We construct h-*day forecasts by adding the* j-*step-ahead GARCH variance forecasts for* j = 1, . . ., h

To construct a term structure of volatility forecasts from any GARCH model, first note that the log return at time t over the next h days is

$$r_{t,h} = \sum_{j=1}^{h} r_{t+j}.$$

Since

$$V_t(r_{t,h}) = \sum_{i=1}^{h} V_t(r_{t+i}) + \sum_i \sum_j \mathrm{cov}_t(r_{t+i}, r_{i+j}) \qquad (4.20)$$

the GARCH forecast of h-period variance is the sum of the instantaneous GARCH forecast variances, plus the double sum of the forecast autocovariances between returns. This double sum will be very small compared to the first sum on the right-hand side of (4.20) — indeed, in the majority of cases the conditional mean equation in a GARCH model is simply a constant, so the double sum is zero.[18] Hence we ignore the second term and construct h-day forecasts simply by adding the j-step-ahead GARCH variance forecasts. These are square-rooted and annualized with the appropriate factor as in (1.2) to give GARCH h-day volatility forecasts.[19]

Since all 1-day forward variance forecasts are computed it is also a simple matter to generate h-day forward volatility forecasts at any future date. For example, the average volatility over the next h days in n months' time may be used to price path-dependent options. This is a feature of MBRM's Universal Add-in for GARCH that is on the CD.

---

[18]Even in an AR(1)–GARCH(1,1) model with autocorrelation coefficient ρ in the conditional mean equation, (2.31) becomes $\hat{\sigma}^2_{j,n} = \sum_{i=1}^{n} \hat{\sigma}^2_{i+i} + \hat{\sigma}^2_i[\rho(1 - \rho^n)/(1 - \rho)]^2$, and the first term clearly dominates the second.

[19]For a GARCH model that is based on daily returns with A daily returns per year, the annualizing factor for the h-day forecast is A/h.

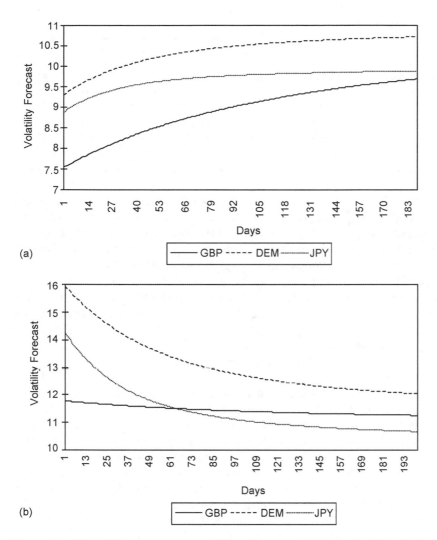

Figure 4.9 GARCH term structures of US dollar rates: (a) 2 March 1995; (b) 13 April 1995.

The speed of convergence of the GARCH(1,1) volatility term structure depends on the estimate of $\alpha + \beta$. The smaller this quantity the more rapid the convergence to the long-term volatility estimate that is determined by (4.16).[20] Figure 4.9 illustrates some GARCH(1,1) term structure volatility forecasts. Using seven years of daily data on US dollar rates the model is estimated up to 2 March 1995, a period of low volatility (Figure 4.9a) and up to 13 April 1995, a period of high volatility (Figure 4.9b). In both cases a term structure of volatility is generated up to 200 days. The estimated parameters are given in Table 4.9.

The speed of convergence of the GARCH(1,1) volatility term structure depends on the estimate of $\alpha + \beta$

---

[20]The half-life of the return to the long-term average is $1/(1 - \alpha - \beta)$. So if $\alpha + \beta$ is estimated as 0.95 it is 20 days, and if $\alpha + \beta$ is estimated as 0.99 it is 100 days.

Table 4.9: GARCH(1, 1) parameter estimates for US dollar rates

Date		$\hat{\omega}$ $(\times 10^{-6})$	$\hat{\alpha}$	$\hat{\beta}$	$\hat{\alpha} + \hat{\beta}$	Half-life
2 March 1995	GBP	0.69	0.0467	0.9384	0.9851	67.1
	DEM	0.19	0.0609	0.9010	0.9619	26.2
	JPY	0.24	0.0603	0.8811	0.9414	17.1
13 April 1995	GBP	0.76	0.0490	0.9353	0.9843	63.7
	DEM	0.18	0.0635	0.9005	0.9640	27.8
	JPY	0.23	0.0636	0.8819	0.9455	18.3

As expected (see §4.2.3) the estimates of $\alpha + \beta$ are high and the parameter estimates do not change very much between 2 March and 13 April. The GBP rate is least reactive and most persistent of the three, having the lowest estimate of α and the highest estimate of β; the estimate $\hat{\alpha} + \hat{\beta}$ is about 0.985, so the half-life of the return to the long-term average is over 60 days. This is much shorter for the JPY and even shorter for the DEM. These rates have similar intensities of reaction to market events in both periods (the estimates of α increasing slightly in the second period) but the DEM volatility is more persistent than the JPY. The estimated long-term volatility level (approximately $100\hat{\sigma}\sqrt{250}$, where $\hat{\sigma}$ is given by (4.16)) changes hardly at all between the two dates, being approximately 10% for JPY, 10.7% for GBP and 11% for DEM.

The term structures in Figure 4.9 are quite different on 2 March and 13 April. On 2 March the GBP 1-day volatility forecast was very low, around 7.5%. Because of the slow convergence in GBP volatility, even the 200-day volatility was only 9.7%, well below its long-term average. The other two rates have higher short-term volatility, around 9%, and are much quicker to reach their average levels. GBP short-term volatility was much less than the other two on 13 April, in fact it was near its long-term average, whereas DEM volatility was rather high, at 16% in the short term. The 200-day forecast of DEM volatility on that day was 12%, a little more realistic than assuming it would be 16% for ever, as would be the case with a moving average model.

Convergence of GARCH volatility term structures is typically rather slow in foreign exchange markets

Convergence of GARCH volatility term structures is typically rather slow in foreign exchange markets; often the GARCH models are close to being integrated. Equity markets often have more rapidly convergent volatility term structures, as is evident from the estimated GARCH parameters in Table 4.6. For General Electric, for example, five time series of GARCH volatility forecasts, over the next 1, 10, 30, 60 and 120 days, are shown in Figure 4.10a.[21]

GARCH volatility term structures on every day from 16 October 1997 to 11 September on the FTSE 100 indices are shown in Figure 4.10b. A rolling

---

[21]In order to generate a time series of GARCH term structure volatility forecasts as in this figure one should really re-estimate the GARCH model every day, and each time record the GARCH term structure. But General Electric has such stable parameter estimates (Figure 4.6) that simply generating all the GARCH forecasts from one model gives a good indication of the history of the General Electric term structure.

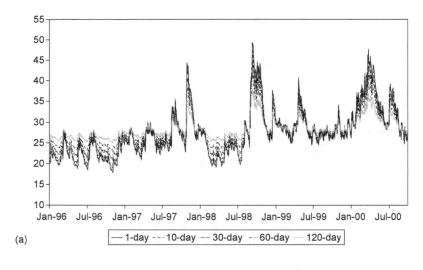

(a)

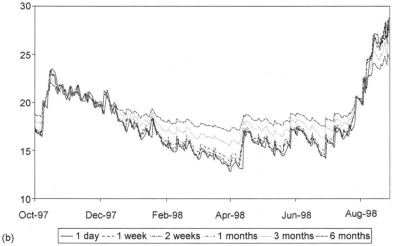

(b)

Figure 4.10 GARCH volatility term structure forecasts for: (a) General Electric; (b) FTSE 100.

window of 1 year of data has been used to estimate the models, much less than in other examples of this chapter, and 1 year is really the minimum historic period that one should use in a GARCH model. The volatility forecasts in Figure 4.10b reflect the average volatilities during the last year and they are a little higher than they would be if several years of data were used, since equity markets have been much more volatile since 1997 (see Figure 4.7e).

4.4.2 Option Pricing and Hedging

The classic paper of Hull and White (1987) examined the pricing of options when volatility is stochastic. The assumptions of the Black–Scholes model no longer hold, risk-neutral valuation breaks down and returns to risky assets should have a risk premium. This is, therefore, one reason why Black–Scholes prices can differ from market prices of options. Engle and Mustafa (1992) examine the stochastic volatility that could be implied from observed market prices of options. Subsequently, Noh *et al.* (1994) and Engle and Rosenberg (1994, 1995) consider how the GARCH stochastic volatility can be incorporated into model prices of options. This is particularly important for short-maturity out-of-the-money equity options where practitioners may require more than a simple Black–Scholes valuation model. Amin and Ng (1993) and Hafner and Härdle (2000) have all found that the GARCH prices of such options are closer to the observed market price than the Black–Scholes prices.

Standard pricing methods for an option on a single asset assume that the underlying price $S(t)$ follows the geometric Brownian motion diffusion process

$$dS(t)/S(t) = r \, dt + \sigma \, dZ(t),$$

where r is the risk-free rate of return and Z is a Wiener process. Since volatility σ is assumed to be known, there is only one source of uncertainty, Z. If simulation methods are used at all it is only necessary to use Monte Carlo on the independent increments dZ to generate price paths $S(t)$ over the life of the option. The simulation is based on the discrete form of GBM, adjusted for risk neutrality,[22]

$$S_t = S_{t-1} \exp(r - 0.5\sigma^2 + \sigma z_t),$$

where the z_t are i.i.d. $N(0, 1)$. Starting from the current price S_0, Monte Carlo simulation of an independent series on z_t for $t = 1, 2, \ldots, T$ will generate a terminal price S_T. Thousands of these terminal prices should be generated starting from the current price S_0, and the discounted expectation of the option pay-off function at the risk-free interest rate gives the price of the option.

For example, a call option on an average price (known as an *Asian call*) has price

$$C(S_0) = e^{-rT} E(\max\{A_m - K, 0\}),$$

where T is the option maturity, K is the strike and A_m is the arithmetic average of m prices at times $t_1, t_2, \ldots, t_m$ (and normally $t_m = T$):

$$A_m = \sum_{j=1}^{m} S_{t_j}/m$$

The price of the Asian call may be estimated from the simulated distribution of average prices A_{mi}, for $i = 1, \ldots, N$ and N very large, by

---

[22]To derive this from the continuous form, use Itô's lemma on $\ln S$ and then make time discrete.

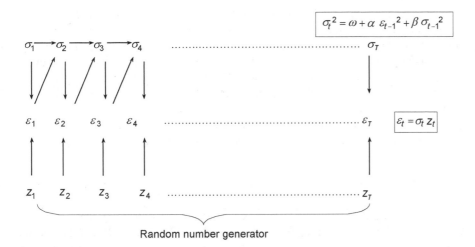

Figure 4.11 Simulation with a GARCH process.

$$\hat{C}(S_0) = e^{-rT}(\Sigma_i \max\{A_{mi} - K, 0\}/N).$$

Engle and Rosenberg (1995) describe how to extend simulation methods for option pricing when the underlying returns have time-varying volatility generated by a GARCH process. A *single* random variable z_t drives the two diffusion processes in discrete time:

$$S_t = S_{t-1}\exp(r - 0.5\sigma_t^2 + \varepsilon_t),$$
$$\sigma_t^2 = \omega + \alpha\varepsilon_{t-1}^2 + \beta\sigma_{t-1}^2,$$

where $\varepsilon_t = \sigma_t z_t$ and the z_t are independent standard normal variates. Monte Carlo simulation on z can be used to price the option exactly as described above and following the scheme shown in Figure 4.11.[23]

Corresponding GARCH option deltas and gammas may be calculated using finite-difference approximations, such as the central differences:

$$\delta = [\hat{C}(S_0 + \eta) - \hat{C}(S_0 - \eta)]/2\eta,$$
$$\gamma = [\hat{C}(S_0 + \eta) - 2\hat{C}(S_0) + \hat{C}(S_0 - \eta)]/\eta^2.$$

Corresponding GARCH option deltas and gammas may be calculated using finite-differences

When calculating deltas and gammas by simulation, errors can be very large unless large numbers of simulations are used. Simulation errors will be reduced by using correlated random numbers because the variance of delta and gamma estimates will be reduced when $\hat{C}(S_0 + \eta)$ and $\hat{C}(S_0 - \eta)$ are positively correlated.

---

[23]Note that there is still only one source of uncertainty in this discrete time formulation. However, in continuous time the diffusion processes corresponding to GARCH models do have an additional error process. See Nelson (1990).

As noted by Engle and Rosenberg (1995), when volatility is stochastic a perfect hedge would not normally exist, so the risk-neutral pricing assumption will not hold. However, Duan (1995) explains that there is a *local* risk-neutral valuation relationship with the N-GARCH volatility model defined in §4.2.4. However, Duan's option pricing model still depends on a risk premium parameter λ. If this is non-zero there will be a risk premium in the asset return, indicating that a perfect hedge will not exist, and if the estimates of the risk premium parameter are not very robust the model will have to be used very carefully in practical applications. One of these is described in the next subsection.[24]

When volatility is stochastic a perfect hedge would not normally exist, so the risk-neutral pricing assumption will not hold

4.4.3   Smile Fitting

Instead of using time series data, a cross-section of market prices on options at different strikes and maturities is used to estimate the GARCH model parameters. Parameters are fitted by iterating on the root mean square error between the GARCH and the market implied volatility smile surfaces. How is a GARCH smile surface obtained?

GARCH option prices are put into the Black–Scholes formula, and the GARCH 'implied' volatility is then backed out of the formula just as one would do with ordinary market implied volatilities

Initial values for the GARCH model parameters are fixed, and then GARCH option prices obtained, as explained above, for options of different strikes and maturity that also have reliable market prices. These GARCH option prices are put into the Black–Scholes formula, and the GARCH 'implied' volatility is then backed out of the formula just as one would do with ordinary market implied volatilities, only this time the GARCH price is used instead of the price observed in the market. Comparison of the GARCH smile surface with the observed market smile surface leads to a refinement of the GARCH model parameters by iteration on the root mean square error between the two smiles, and so the GARCH smile is fitted, as in Figure 4.12.[25]

Duan (1996) reports that estimating the parameters of an N-GARCH model using current market data gives very similar results to those obtained using time series data. However, one must be very careful to check the stability of parameter estimates; parameter estimates that are based on a snapshot of option prices on one day, rather than a long historical series on the underlying price, may vary considerably from day to day. For example, Table 4.10 shows that comparing Duan's estimates for the FTSE on 31 March 1995 with the estimates we obtained on 2 March 1998 gives quite different values for $\theta + \lambda$ and β.

Looking at Figure 4.12, on 2 March 1998 the volatility term structure was sloping upwards, because the market had been relatively quiet for some time, and convergence to the 1-year volatility level was also relatively rapid.

---

[24]In later work Duan *et al.* (1998) and Duan (1999) have derived an analytic approximation to the univariate N-GARCH option pricing model, and Duan and Wei (1999) have extended the framework to a bivariate N-GARCH model for pricing foreign exchange options and currency-protected options.

[25]Many thanks to Chris Leigh for providing this figure.

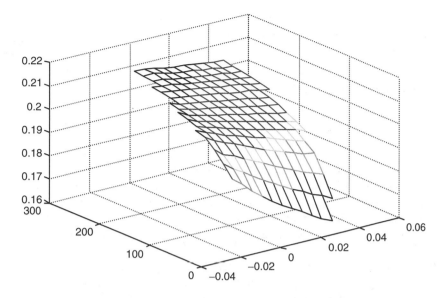

Figure 4.12 GARCH smile of the FTSE 100 index on 2 March 1998.

Volatility smile surfaces can change so quickly from day to day that it may be misguided to expect stability in parameter estimates of a GARCH model that is based on snapshots of option prices from the market

Table 4.10: N-GARCH parameter estimates from two different days

	2 March 1998	31 March 1995
ω	8.26×10^{-6}	1.95×10^{-6}
β	0.6802	0.8355
α	0.1377	0.1062
$\theta + \lambda$	0.9218	0.5507

Interestingly, both these observations could have been made from the time series models of the FTSE 100 GARCH volatilities in Figures 4.7e and 4.10b. At this rather general level the GARCH models estimated on snapshots of option market data are corroborated by the GARCH estimates based on time series of the underlying. However, volatility smile surfaces can change so quickly from day to day that it may be misguided to expect stability in parameter estimates of a GARCH model that is based on snapshots of option prices from the market.

4.5 Multivariate GARCH

This section begins by discussing the main use of time-varying correlations, which is to construct short-term hedge ratios that accurately reflect current market conditions. Then it reviews some of the most common multivariate GARCH models, and discusses the computational problems that are inevitable if one attempts direct estimation of full multivariate GARCH models for large-dimensional systems. The last part of this section describes how to deal with the complications that arise when using GARCH to build the large covariance matrices that are necessary for netting the risks from all positions in a large trading book.

4.5.1 Time-Varying Correlation

Computational problems are inevitable if one attempts direct estimation of full multivariate GARCH models for large-dimensional systems

In §1.4 the distinction was drawn between unconditional and conditional correlation. Conditional correlation is a time-varying parameter: there is not one true value for the parameter, as so many economic models would assume. Of course, all correlation estimates will change over time, whether the model is based on constant correlation or time-varying correlation. In a constant correlation model this variation in the estimates with time is only due to sampling error, but in a time-varying parameter model this variation in the estimates is also ascribed to changes in the true value of the parameter.

Conditional correlations can be estimated by any n-dimensional GARCH model ($n > 1$), but estimates of the same conditional correlation parameter can be quite different, depending on the model chosen. In this section only bivariate GARCH models are discussed. Like univariate GARCH models, bivariate GARCH models normally converge rapidly, in fact the only problems that might arise are lack of proper specification by the user, or the use of inappropriate data (e.g. there may be problems if the data generation processes are not jointly stationary).

The simplest parameterization of a bivariate GARCH(1,1) model is the *diagonal vech* parameterization.[26] In addition to the two conditional mean equations, one for each return, it has the conditional variance equations:

$$\sigma_{1,t}^2 = \omega_1 + \alpha_1 \varepsilon_{1,t-1}^2 + \beta_1 \sigma_{1,t-1}^2$$
$$\sigma_{2,t}^2 = \omega_2 + \alpha_2 \varepsilon_{2,t-1}^2 + \beta_2 \sigma_{2,t-1}^2 \qquad (4.21)$$
$$\sigma_{12,t} = \omega_3 + \alpha_3 \varepsilon_{1,t-1} \varepsilon_{2,t-1} + \beta_3 \sigma_{12,t-1}.$$

where ε_1 and ε_2 are the unexpected returns from the two conditional mean equations. This model is fairly restrictive on the dynamics of conditional correlation. For example, yesterday's variances $\sigma_{1,t-1}^2$ and $\sigma_{2,t-1}^2$ do not enter the equation for today's covariance, so the model does not capture the increase in correlation that often accompanies increased volatilities. This is a severe limitation, and additional constraints on the coefficients in (4.21) are necessary to ensure positive definiteness of the covariance matrices.

The bivariate diagonal vech model (4.21) is just one of a large number of different parameterizations of the same bivariate normal GARCH(1,1) model. These parameterizations will be discussed in §4.5.2 and §4.5.3. For the moment

---

[26]The 'vech' operator stacks all columns of a matrix into a column vector. Thus if the columns of $\mathbf{X}$ are $\mathbf{x}_1, \ldots, \mathbf{x}_n$ then vech($\mathbf{X}$) is the column vector that stacks $\mathbf{x}_1$ above $\mathbf{x}_2$ above...above $\mathbf{x}_n$.

the only point to make is that when a different parameterization is used for the three GARCH(1,1) equations, the estimates of the same time-varying correlation will be different. Figure 4.13 compares diagonal vech correlation estimates with orthogonal GARCH and BEKK correlation estimates (these are described in §4.5.2 and §7.4). Figure 4.13a does not include the BEKK correlation because there were difficulties in convergence. In fact the convergence problems for univariate GARCH models that were outlined in §4.3.3 are even more substantial in multivariate GARCH.

If the model does converge then the mean-reverting term structure forecasts that have been described for univariate GARCH models in §4.4 can be extended to correlation. Simply iterate the GARCH conditional variance and covariance forecasts[27] and then take the sum over the next h days. These h-day variance and covariance forecasts are then converted to correlation term structures using

$$\hat{\rho}_{t,h} = \hat{\sigma}_{12,t,h}/\hat{\sigma}_{1,t,h}\hat{\sigma}_{2,t,h}.$$

Correlation-dependent market parameters, such as market betas or statistical hedge ratios, may also be regarded as time-varying. In §8.1 the market sensitivity β in a CAPM model is defined as the ratio of the covariance between the market return X and the asset return y to the variance of the market. It can also be written $\beta = \rho v$, where v denotes the relative volatility and ρ is the correlation (cf. (1.5)). The definition of a conditional market beta may be derived from the definitions of conditional covariances and variances in the natural way. A time-varying beta is defined as

$$\beta_t = \sigma_{Xy,t}/\sigma_{X,t}^2 = \rho_t v_t$$

where, at time t, $\sigma_{Xy,t}$ is the conditional covariance, $\sigma_{X,t}^2$ is the conditional variance of the market, ρ_t is the conditional correlation and v_t is the ratio of conditional volatilities.

Correlation-dependent market parameters, such as market betas or statistical hedge ratios, may also be regarded as time-varying

In §8.2.1 we note that, for risk management purposes, it is better to use estimates of market betas that are based on recent daily data, so that they respond to current market conditions, rather than the equally weighted estimates that are calculated when a CAPM is estimated by ordinary least squares using monthly data over several years (§A.1.4). In the covariance VaR models described in §9.3 the net betas for each risk factor should be estimated from models that assume that the true beta is *not* constant over time. As a rule the time-varying beta estimates of any stock will change rapidly and frequently. It is normal for a time-varying beta to oscillate between values much less than 1 and much more than 1 in the space of a few days. This casts some doubt on the wisdom of categorizing stocks into high and low risk according to their ordinary least squares market betas.

This casts some doubt on the wisdom of categorizing stocks into high and low risk according to their ordinary least squares market betas

---

[27]Note that $\mathrm{cov}_t(R_{1,t,h}, R_{2,t,h}) = \sum_{i,j=1}^{h} \mathrm{cov}_t(r_{1,t+i}, r_{2,t+j})$. Ignoring non-contemporaneous covariances gives $\hat{\sigma}_{12,t,h} = \sum_{i=1}^{h} \hat{\sigma}_{12,t+i}$.

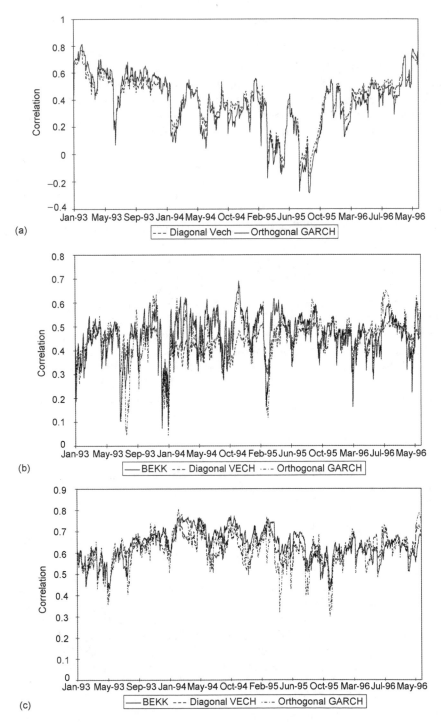

Figure 4.13 GARCH models correlation comparison: (a) US dollar–sterling and Japanese yen–sterling exchange rates; (b) FTSE 100 and DAX equity indices; (c) FTSE 100 and CAC equity indices.

Currently many practitioners prefer to use EWMA rather than GARCH correlations. They do have limitations, including the fact that their term structure forecasts do not mean-revert (§3.3), and GARCH is certainly the superior method for modelling volatility: one of the great advantages of univariate GARCH models is that they generate mean-reverting term structure forecasts for volatility in a very simple analytic form. But is there really a robust term structure of correlation that mean-reverts? Correlation is such a limited concept anyway, because it assumes that co-dependencies are linear and it ignores the co-dependency through common trends in prices.

Given the uncertainties surrounding correlation in financial markets, it may indeed be sufficient, from a modelling perspective, to use EWMA correlations. They can be particularly useful for constructing a time-varying commodity futures hedge because univariate GARCH models of commodity volatilities are often close to being integrated. An EWMA is an approximation to an I-GARCH model (§4.3.3) and they are very easy to compute. In short, the end results from a skilful parameterization and calibration of a bivariate GARCH model may just not be worth the effort.

In short, the end results from a skilful parameterization and calibration of a bivariate GARCH model may just not be worth the effort

Figure 4.14 compares two different estimates of beta for Danone stock in the CAC from July 1994 to February 1999. At certain times these estimates differ substantially, for example during most of 1996 and in the first few months of 1998. The 120-day equally weighted estimate is the beta that would be obtained when applying ordinary least squares to a CAPM with about 6 months of daily data. It ranges between about 0.6 and 1, but typically an even longer period would have been used for the betas supplied by data analytics firms, and these betas would have stayed roughly within the 0.7–0.8 range for the whole time. However, the exponentially weighted beta (with $\lambda = 0.94$) ranges from less than 0.3 to over 1.7, and changes rapidly over the course of a few days. This EWMA beta estimate uses about 100 days of data ($0.94^{100} \approx 0.002$) so the statistical error of these estimates is certainly higher than the error on the 120-day equally weighted average (§5.2.1). However, it is not so much greater that all the differences between the two estimates in Figure 4.14 could be attributed to sampling error.

There has been some interesting research on the use of bivariate GARCH to calculate the optimal futures hedge (Cecchetti *et al.*, 1988; Baillie and Myers, 1991; Kroner and Claessens, 1991; Lien and Luo, 1994; Park and Switzer, 1995). Recall from §4.2.3 that the daily WTI spot and prompt futures prices have integrated GARCH models for their volatilities. This is often the case for commodities. Table 4.11 shows the GARCH(1, 1) parameter estimates for the natural gas futures prices that were discussed in Chapter 3. Figure 4.15a shows the GARCH volatilities that are estimated from these models.

Since the GARCH models are near to being integrated, an EWMA model will be adequate for the calculation of an optimal time-varying proxy hedge ratio and there is no real need to use a bivariate GARCH. Figure 4.15b shows the

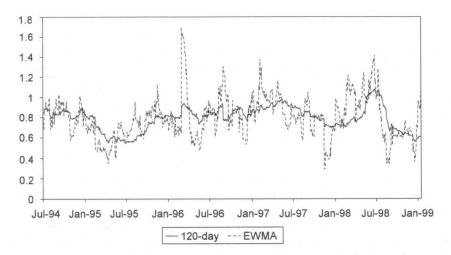

Figure 4.14   Equally and exponentially weighted betas for Danone in CAC.

Table 4.11: GARCH(1, 1) models for natural gas futures

	Omega	Omega (*t*-stat)	Alpha	Alpha (*t*-stat)	Beta	Beta (*t*-stat)
NYMEX	0.284E-04	2.5010	0.1161	5.3033	0.8781	40.6964
KCBOT	0.203E-04	2.4885	0.1237	7.03357	0.8704	48.5538

EWMA hedge ratio corresponding to $\lambda = 0.87$. It is more variable than the hedge ratios that were based on the equally weighted average methods that were discussed in §3.1.3. Therefore, there may be a greater need for rebalancing during the course of the hedge than is normally assumed in practice.

Another important application of time-varying correlation is the derivation of optimal weights in a minimum-risk portfolio (§7.2). However, since the correlations used to derive these weights must be consistent with a positive definite covariance matrix, it is not possible to estimate them in a bivariate setting. Instead we must use a full multivariate GARCH model on all the assets in the portfolio. These models are described in the next subsection, and if there are very many assets in the portfolio the methods that are outlined in §4.5.3 will be necessary to overcome the difficulties of computing a large-dimensional GARCH covariance matrix.

4.5.2   Multivariate GARCH Parameterizations

In an *n*-dimensional multivariate GARCH model there are *n* conditional mean equations, which can be anything, but for the sake of parsimony it is normal to assume the form

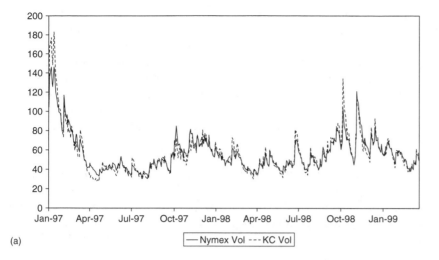

(a)

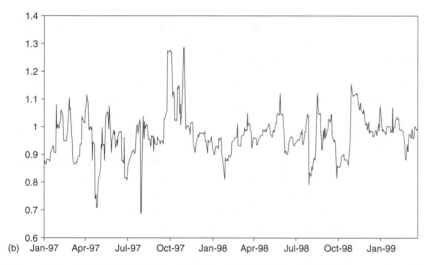

(b)

Figure 4.15 (a) GARCH(1, 1) volatilities of NYMEX and KCBOT natural gas futures; (b) optimal time-varying hedge ratio.

$$r_{it} = c_i + \varepsilon_{it} \quad \text{for } i = 1, \ldots, n.$$

The multivariate GARCH models that are described below all assume that the conditional distributions of returns are normal and differ only in the form assumed for the conditional variance and covariance equations.

The diagonal vech model described in §4.5.1 imposes severe cross equation restrictions because each equation is a separate GARCH(1,1). The *n*-dimensional *vech model* is written as

$$\text{vech}(\mathbf{H}_t) = \mathbf{A} + \mathbf{B}\text{vech}(\xi_{t-1}\xi'_{t-1}) + \mathbf{C}\text{vech}(\mathbf{H}_{t-1}), \qquad (4.22)$$

where $\mathbf{H}_t$ is the conditional covariance matrix at time t and vech($\mathbf{H}_t$) is the vector that stacks all the elements of the covariance matrix. In the bivariate diagonal vech $\xi_t = (\varepsilon_{1t}, \varepsilon_{2t})'$, $\mathbf{A} = (\omega_1, \omega_2, \omega_3)'$, $\mathbf{B} = \mathrm{diag}\,(\alpha_1, \alpha_2, \alpha_3)$ and $\mathbf{C} = \mathrm{diag}(\beta_1, \beta_2, \beta_3)$, but more general forms of the coefficient matrices are possible, provided that restrictions are imposed on their parameters to ensure positive definiteness. In some markets these restrictions can lead to substantial differences between the vech estimates and those from other multivariate GARCH parameterizations, so the vech model should be employed with caution.

A general parameterization that involves the minimum number of parameters while imposing no cross equation restrictions and ensuring positive definiteness for any parameter values is the *BEKK model*, after Baba, Engle, Kraft and Kroner who wrote the preliminary version of Engle and Kroner (1993). The conditional covariance matrix has the following multivariate GARCH(1,1) parameterisation:

$$\mathbf{H}_t = \mathbf{A}'\mathbf{A} + \mathbf{B}'\,\xi_{t-1}\xi'_{t-1}\mathbf{B} + \mathbf{C}'\mathbf{H}_{t-1}\mathbf{C}, \qquad (4.23)$$

where $\mathbf{A}$, $\mathbf{B}$ and $\mathbf{C}$ are $n \times n$ matrices and $\mathbf{A}$ is triangular.

The BEKK parameterization for a bivariate model involves 11 parameters, only two more than the vech parameterization, but for higher-dimensional systems the extra number of parameters in the BEKK increases, and completely free estimation becomes very difficult indeed. Often it is necessary to impose restrictions and so reduce the number of parameters to estimate (Bollerslev *et al.*, 1994). It may be assumed that all elements of $\mathbf{B}$ are the same if the market reaction coefficients of all variables in the system are assumed to be identical. If persistence in volatility and correlation are the same throughout, all elements of $\mathbf{C}$ could be imposed to be identical. This is the *scalar BEKK* model. The forecasting performance of a scalar BEKK is often inferior to that of the *diagonal BEKK* model, where $\mathbf{B}$ and $\mathbf{C}$ are assumed to be diagonal (Engle, 2000b). Engle and Mezrich (1995) is a very accessible reference on multivariate GARCH model parameterization, and a general framework for asymmetric multivariate GARCH models is described in Kroner and Ng (1998).

4.5.3 Time-Varying Covariance Matrices Based on Univariate GARCH Models

The conditional variance of an n-dimensional multivariate process is a time-series of $n \times n$ covariance matrices, one matrix for each point in time, denoted $\mathbf{H}_t$. Each of the $n(n+1)/2$ distinct elements of these covariance matrices has its own GARCH model. If there are just three parameters in each conditional variance or conditional covariance equation, as in the diagonal vech and BEKK models described above, there will be $3n(n+1)/2$ parameters in total, plus the n parameters, one in each conditional mean equation. Thus the three-variate GARCH model has a minimum of 21 parameters. This is already a large number, but just think of a 10-dimensional system, with at least 175 parameters to estimate!

It is therefore not surprising that estimation of multivariate GARCH models can pose problems. Since all parameters are estimated simultaneously the convergence problems outlined in §4.3 can become insurmountable. Even in relatively low-dimensional systems parameterizations of multivariate GARCH models should be as parsimonious as possible. The lack of robustness to alternative parameterizations in conjunction with the inevitable computational difficulties in systems with more than five or so variables, even with the most parsimonious of parameterizations, casts considerable doubt on the practicalities of full multivariate GARCH for modelling large covariance matrices. However, there are some approximations that allow multivariate GARCH covariance matrices $\mathbf{H}_t$ to be generated by univariate GARCH models alone. Three of these models are described here.

The lack of robustness to alternative parameterizations in conjunction with the inevitable computational difficulties casts considerable doubt on the practicalities of full multivariate GARCH for modelling large covariance matrices

The first model, introduced by Bollerslev (1990), approximates the time-varying covariance matrix as a product of time-varying volatilities and a correlation matrix that does not vary over time. The *constant GARCH correlation* may be written:

$$\mathbf{H}_t = \mathbf{D}_t \mathbf{C} \mathbf{D}_t,$$

where $\mathbf{D}_t$ is a diagonal matrix of time-varying GARCH volatilities, and $\mathbf{C}$ is the constant correlation matrix. Individual return data are used to estimate GARCH volatilities, using one of the models described in §4.2, and the correlation matrix is estimated by taking equally weighted moving averages over the whole data period.

Recently this model has been generalized by Engle (2000b) to the case where the correlation matrix is time-varying. Obviously it would defeat the point if now a multivariate GARCH model were used to estimate this time-varying correlation matrix, so to keep the model as simple as possible, Engle advocates using a GARCH(1,1) model with the same parameters for all the elements of the correlation matrix—or, as in the RiskMetrics matrices (§7.4) using an EWMA with the same smoothing constant throughout.

Another method for generating *n*-dimensional GARCH covariance matrices using only univariate GARCH is to use a capital asset pricing model framework (§8.1). These *factor GARCH* models allow all the individual asset volatilities and correlations to be generated from univariate GARCH models of the market volatility and the specific risk (Engle *et al.*, 1990). In the CAPM individual asset returns are related to market returns X_t by the regression equation

Factor GARCH models allow all the individual asset volatilities and correlations to be generated from uni-variate GARCH models of the market volatility and the specific risk

$$r_{it} = \alpha_i + \beta_i X_t + \varepsilon_{it} \text{ for } i = 1, 2, \ldots, n. \tag{4.24}$$

Simultaneous estimation of the n linear regression equations in (4.24) as described in Appendix 2 will give factor sensitivities β_i and specific components ε_{it}.

Now denote by $\sigma_{i,t}$ the conditional standard deviation of asset i and by $\sigma_{ij,t}$ the conditional covariance between assets i and j. Assuming no conditional correlation between the market and specific components, taking variances and covariances of equation (4.24) yields

$$
\begin{aligned}
\sigma_{i,t}^2 &= \beta_i^2 \sigma_{X,t}^2 + \sigma_{\varepsilon_i,t}^2, \\
\sigma_{ij,t} &= \beta_i \beta_j \sigma_{X,t}^2 + \sigma_{\varepsilon_i \varepsilon_j,t}.
\end{aligned}
\tag{4.25}
$$

Thus all the GARCH variances and covariances of the assets in a portfolio are obtained from the GARCH variance of the market risk factor, and the GARCH variances and covariances of the stock-specific components. From a computational point of view there is much to be said for ignoring the covariance between specific components, the second term of the covariance equation. Then (4.25) gives the individual asset conditional variances and covariances in terms of univariate GARCH models only. It is not straightforward to generalize this framework to the case where the underlying factor models have more than one risk factor: firstly, generalized least squares should be used for the factor sensitivity and residual estimation (§A.3.3); and secondly, multivariate models for the covariances between risk factors will need to be employed.

In the orthogonal GARCH model, the GARCH covariance matrices are obtained from univariate GARCH estimates of the variances of the principal components of the system

The last model that allows GARCH covariance matrices to be generated using only univariate GARCH models is only mentioned here very briefly. In the *orthogonal GARCH* model, full details of which will be given in §7.4.3, the GARCH covariance matrices are obtained from univariate GARCH estimates of the variances of the principal components of the system. This method has many practical advantages, particularly for the generation of very large positive semi-definite covariance matrices (Alexander, 2001b).

5
Forecasting Volatility and Correlation

Previous chapters have described how volatility and correlation forecasts may be generated using different models. In some cases there are very noticeable differences between the various forecasts of the same underlying volatility or correlation, and in some cases there are great similarities. It is a generic problem with volatility forecasting that rather different results may be obtained, depending on the model used and on the market conditions. Correlation forecasting is even more problematic because the inherent instability of some correlations compounds the difficulties.

Which volatility is being forecast?

Even if only one particular type of model were always used, the forecasts will depend on the parameters chosen. For example, in Figure 3.6 the exponentially weighted moving average volatility of the CAC at the end of 1997 could be 30% or 45% depending on whether the smoothing constant is chosen to be 0.96 or 0.84. Many other such examples have been encountered in previous chapters, such as the different 'historic' forecasts of the rand 1-year swap rate volatilities in Figure 3.2. There are also differences between various types of GARCH correlation estimates, as shown in Figure 4.13.

The underlying market conditions will also affect results. When markets are stable, in that they appear to be bounded above and below or that they are trending with a relatively stable realized volatility, differences between the various forecasts are relatively small. It is following extreme market events that differences between forecasts tend to be greatest.

When markets are stable, in that they appear to be bounded above and below or that they are trending with a relatively stable realized volatility, differences between the various forecasts are relatively small

If one decides to approach the difficult problem of forecast evaluation, the first consideration is: which volatility is being forecast? For option pricing, portfolio optimization and risk management one needs a forecast of the volatility that governs the underlying price process until some future risk horizon. A geometric Brownian motion has constant volatility, so a forecast of the process volatility will be a constant whatever the risk horizon. Future volatility is an extremely difficult thing to forecast because the actual realization of the future process volatility will be influenced by events that happen in the future. If there is a large market movement at any time before the risk horizon but after $t = 0$, the forecast that is made at $t = 0$ will need to take this into account. Process volatility is not the only interesting volatility to forecast. In some cases one might wish to forecast implied volatilities, for example in short-term volatility trades with positions such as straddles and butterflies (Fitzgerald, 1996).

The second consideration is the choice of a benchmark forecast. The benchmark volatility forecast could be anything, implied volatility or a long-term equally weighted average statistical volatility being the most common. If a sophisticated and technical model, such as GARCH, cannot forecast better than the implied or 'historical' forecasts that are readily available from data suppliers (and very easily computed from the raw market data) then it may not be worth the time and expense for development and implementation.

Which type of volatility should be used for the forecast?

A third consideration is, which type of volatility should be used for the forecast? Since both implied and statistical volatilities are forecasts of the same thing, either could be used. Thus a model could forecast implied volatility with either implied volatility or statistical volatility. Price process volatilities could be forecast by statistical or implied volatilities, or indeed both (some GARCH models use implied volatility in the conditional variance equation).

There is much to be said for developing models that use a combination of several volatility forecasts. When a number of independent forecasts of the same time series are available it is possible to pool them into a combined forecast that always predicts at least as well as any single component of that forecast (Granger and Ramanathan, 1984; Diebold and Lopez, 1996). The Granger–Ramanathan procedure will be described in §5.2.3; the focus of that discussion will be the generation of confidence intervals for volatility forecasts.

When a number of independent forecasts of the same time series are available it is possible to pool them into a combined forecast that always predicts at least as well as any single component of that forecast

This chapter begins by outlining some standard measures of the accuracy of volatility and correlation forecasts. Statistical criteria, which are based on diagnostics such as root mean square forecasting error, out-of-sample likelihoods, or the correlation between forecasts and squared returns, are discussed in §5.1.1. Operational evaluation methods are more subjective because they depend on a trading or a risk management performance measure that is derived from the particular use of the forecast; these are reviewed in §5.1.2.

Any estimator of a parameter of the current or future return distribution has a distribution itself. A point forecast of volatility is (usually) just the expectation of the distribution of the volatility estimator,[1] but in addition to this expectation one might also estimate the standard deviation of the distribution of the estimator, that is, the standard error of the volatility forecast. The standard error determines the width of a confidence interval for the forecast and indicates how reliable a forecast is considered to be. The

---

[1]Similarly, a point forecast of correlation is just the expectation of the distribution of the correlation estimator.

wider the confidence interval, the more uncertainty there is in the forecast.[2] Standard errors and confidence intervals for some standard forecasting models are described in §5.2.

Having quantified the degree of uncertainty in a forecast, one should make an adjustment to the mark-to-market value of an option portfolio when some options have to be marked to model. The scale of this adjustment will of course depend on the size of the standard error of the volatility forecast, and in §5.3.1 it is shown that the model price of out-of-the-money options should normally be increased to account for uncertainty in volatility. Section 5.3.2 shows how uncertainty in volatility is carried through to uncertainty in the value of a dynamically delta hedged portfolio. It answers the question: how much does it matter if the implied volatility that is used for hedging is not an accurate representation of the volatility of the underlying process?

5.1 Evaluating the Accuracy of Point Forecasts

How can it be that so many different results are obtained when attempting to forecast volatility and correlation using the same basic data? Unlike prices, volatility and correlation are unobservable. They are parameters of the data generation processes that govern returns. Volatility is a measure of the dispersion of a return distribution. It does not affect the shape of the distribution but it still governs how much of the weight in the distribution is around the centre, and at the same time how much weight is around the extreme values of returns. Small volatilities give more weight around the centre than large volatilities, so it may be that some volatility models give better forecasts of the central values, while other volatility models give better forecasts of the extreme values of returns.

In financial markets the volatility of return distributions can change considerably over time, but there is only one point against which to measure the success of a fixed horizon forecast: the observed return over that horizon. The results of a forecast evaluation will therefore depend on the data period chosen for the assessment. Furthermore, the assessment of forecasting accuracy will depend very much on the method of evaluation employed (Diebold and Mariano, 1995). Although we may come across statements such as 'We employ fractionally integrated EWMA volatilities because they are more accurate', it is unlikely that a given forecasting model would be 'more accurate' according to all possible statistical and operational evaluation criteria. A forecasting model may perform well according to some evaluation criterion but not so well according to others. In short, no definitive answer can ever be given to the question 'which method is more accurate?'.

The assessment of forecasting accuracy will depend very much on the method of evaluation employed

---

[2]Classical statistics gives the expected value of the estimator (point estimate) and the width of the distribution of the estimator (confidence interval) *given* some true value of the underlying parameter. It is a good approximation for the distribution of the true underlying parameter only when the statistical information (the sample likelihood) is overwhelming compared to one's prior beliefs. This is not necessarily so for volatility forecasts, especially for the long term (§8.3.3).

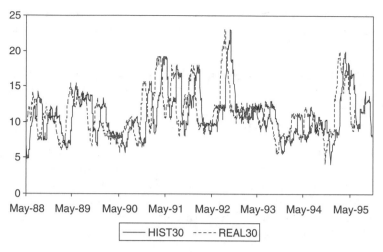

Figure 5.1   Historic and realized volatility of the German mark–US dollar exchange rate.

A realization of a constant volatility process is just a lag of historical volatility, and trying to predict the lag of a time series by its current value will not usually give good results!

Much research has been published on the accuracy of different volatility forecasts for financial markets: see, for example, Andersen and Bollerslev (1998), Alexander and Leigh (1997), Brailsford and Faff (1996), Cumby *et al.* (1993), Dimson and Marsh (1990), Figlewski (1997), Frennberg and Hansson (1996) and West and Cho (1995). Given the remarks just made about the difficulties of this task it should come as no surprise that the results are inconclusive. However, there is one finding that seems to be common to much of this research, and that is that 'historic' volatility is just about the worst predictor of a constant volatility process. Considering Figure 5.1, this is really not surprising.[3] A realization of a constant volatility process is just a lag of historic volatility,[4] and trying to predict the lag of a time series by its current value will not usually give good results!

Some operational and statistical criteria for evaluating the success of a volatility and/or correlation forecast are described below. Whatever criterion is used to validate the model it should be emphasized that, however well a model fits in-sample (i.e. within the data period used to estimate the model parameters), the real test of its forecasting power is in out-of-sample, and usually post-sample, predictive tests. As explained in §A.5.2, a certain amount

---

[3]Let $t = T$ be the forecast horizon and $t = 0$ the point at which the forecast is made. Suppose an exceptional return occurs at time $T - 1$. The realized volatility of the constant volatility process will already reflect this exceptional return at time $t = 0$; it jumps up T periods before the event. However, the historical volatility only reflects this exceptional return at time T; it jumps up at the same time as the realized volatility jumps down.

[4]This is the case if the historical method uses an equally weighted average of past squared returns over a look-back period that is the *same* length as the forecast horizon. More commonly, historical volatilities over a very long-term average are used to forecast for a shorter horizon—for example, 5-year averages are used to forecast 1-year average volatilities.

of the historic data should be withheld from the period used to estimate the model, so that the forecasts may be evaluated by comparing them to the out-of-sample data.

5.1.1 Statistical Criteria

Suppose a volatility forecasting model produces a set of post-sample forward volatility predictions, denoted $\hat{\sigma}_{t+1}, \ldots, \hat{\sigma}_{t+T}$. Assume, just to make the exposition easier, that these forecasts are of 1-day volatilities, so the forecasts are of the 1-day volatility tomorrow, and the 1-day forward volatility on the next day, and so on until T days ahead. We might equally well have assumed the forecasts were of 1-month volatility over the next month, 1 month ahead, 2 months ahead, and so on until the 1-month forward volatility in T months' time. Or we might be concerned with intra-day frequencies, such as volatility over the next hour. The unit of time does not matter for the description of the tests. All that matters is that these forecasts be compared with observations on market returns of the same frequency.[5]

A process volatility is never observed; even ex post we can only ever know an estimate, the realization of the process volatility that actually occurred. The only observation is on the market return. A 1-day volatility forecast is the standard deviation of the 1-day return, so a 1-day forecast should be compared with the relevant 1-day return. One common statistical measure of accuracy for a volatility forecast is the likelihood of the return, given the volatility forecast. That is, the value of the probability density at that point, as explained in §A.6.1. Figure 5.2 shows that the observed return r has a higher likelihood under $f(x)$ than under $g(x)$. That is, r is more likely under the density that is generated by the volatility forecast that is the higher of the two. One can conclude that the higher volatility forecast was more accurate on the day that the return r was observed.

A process volatility is never observed; even ex post we can only ever know an estimate, the realization of the process volatility that actually occurred

Suppose that we want to compare the accuracy of two different volatility forecasting models, A and B.[6] Suppose model A generates a sequence of volatility forecasts, $\{\hat{\sigma}_{t+1}, \ldots, \hat{\sigma}_{t+T}\}_A$ and model B generates a sequence of volatility forecasts, $\{\hat{\sigma}_{t+1}, \ldots, \hat{\sigma}_{t+T}\}_B$. For model A, compare each forecast $\hat{\sigma}_{t+j}$ with the observed return on that day, r_{t+j}, by recording the likelihood of the return as depicted in Figure 5.2. The *out-of-sample likelihood* of the whole sequence of forecasts is the product of all the individual likelihoods, and we can denote this L_A. Similarly, we can calculate the likelihood of the sample given the forecasts made with model B, L_B. If over several such post-sample predictive tests, model A consistently gives higher likelihoods than model B, we can say that model A performs better than model B.

---

[5] If implied volatility is being forecast, then the market implied volatility is the observed quantity that can be used to assess the accuracy of forecasts.

[6] These could be two EWMA models, but with different smoothing constants; or a 30-day and a 60-day historic model; or an EWMA and a GARCH; or two different types of GARCH; or a historic and an EWMA, etc.

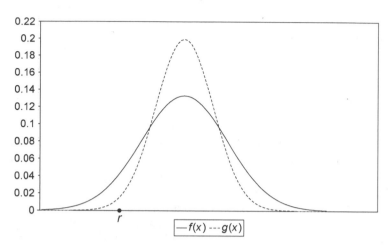

Figure 5.2   Volatility and the likelihood.

Different volatility forecasting models may be ranked by the value of the out-of-sample likelihood, but the effectiveness of this method does rely on the correct specification of the return distributions. Generally speaking, we assume that these return distributions are normal, but if they are not normal then the results of out-of-sample normal likelihood tests will not be reliable. If likelihood criteria are to be used it is advisable to accompany results with a test for the assumed distribution of returns (§10.1).

Much of the literature on volatility forecasting uses a root mean square error (RMSE) criterion instead of a likelihood (§A.5.3). But while a RMSE may be fine for assessing price forecasts, or any forecasts that are of the mean parameter, there are problems with using the RMSE criterion for volatility forecasting (Makridakis, 1993). In fact, the 'minimize the RMSE' criterion is equivalent to the 'maximize the likelihood' criterion when the likelihood function is normal with a *constant* volatility.[7] Hence RMSEs are applicable to *mean* predictions, such as those from a regression model, rather than variance or covariance predictions.[8]

Not only is the RMSE criterion applicable to means rather than variances, one statistical performance measure that has, unfortunately, slipped into common

---

[7]To see this, suppose returns are normal so (from §A.6.3) the likelihood L is most easily expressed as:

$$-2\ln L = T\ln(2\pi) + T\ln\sigma^2 + \Sigma(x_i - \mu)^2/\sigma^2.$$

Now maximizing L is equivalent to minimizing $-2\ln L$, and when volatility is constant this is equivalent to minimizing $\Sigma(x_i - \mu)^2$. This is the same as minimizing $\sqrt{(\Sigma(x_i - \mu)^2)}$, that is, the root of the sum of the squared errors between forecasts x_i and the *mean*.

[8]Of course, a variance is a mean, but the mean of the *squared* random variable, which is chi-squared distributed, not normally distributed, so the likelihood function is totally different and does not involve any sum of squared errors. Many thanks to Peter Williams for explaining these issues during enlightening discussions when we were colleagues at Sussex University.

use is an RMSE between a volatility forecast and the realized volatility, which is just one observation on the process volatility. As a statistical criterion this makes no sense at all, because the correct test is an F-test, not an RMSE.[9] In fact the only justification for using the RMSE between a forecast and the ex-post realized volatility is that it is a simple distance metric.

Notwithstanding these comments, a popular approach to assessing volatility forecasting accuracy is to use the RMSE to compare the forecast of variance with the appropriate squared return. The difference between the variance forecast and the squared return is taken as the forecast error. These errors are squared and summed over a long post-sample period, and then square-rooted to give the post-sample RMSE between the variance forecast and the squared returns. However, these RMSE tests will normally give poor results, because although the expectation of the squared return is the variance, there is a very large standard error around this expectation. That is, the squared returns will jump about excessively while the variance forecasts remain more stable. The reason for this is that the return r_t is equal to $\sigma_t z_t$, where z_t is a standard normal variate, so the squared return yields very noisy measurements due to excessive variation in z_t^2.

The only justification for using the RMSE between a forecast and the ex-post realized volatility is that it is a simple distance metric

Another popular statistical procedure is to perform a regression of the squared returns on the variance forecast. If the variance is correctly specified the constant from this regression should be zero and the slope coefficient should be one. But since the values for the explanatory variable are only estimates, the standard errors-in-variables problem of regression described in §A.4.2 produces a downward bias on the estimate of the slope coefficient.

The R^2 from this regression will assess the amount of variation in squared returns that is explained by the successive forecasts of σ^2. However, the excessive variation in squared returns that was mentioned above also presents problems for the R^2 metric. In fact this R^2 will be bounded above, and the bound will depend on the data generation process for returns. For example, Andersen and Bollerslev (1998) show that if returns are generated by the symmetric GARCH(1, 1) model (4.2), then the true R^2 from a regression of the squared returns on the variance forecast will be

$$R^2 = \alpha^2/(1 - \beta^2 - 2\alpha\beta). \tag{5.1}$$

Relation (5.1) provides an upper bound for the R^2 for GARCH(1, 1) forecasts, and similar upper bounds apply to other standard forecasting models. Table 5.1 shows how the true R^2 varies with some common values for the estimates of α and β. Most of the R^2 are extremely small, and the largest value in the table is around 1/3, nothing like the maximum value of 1 that one normally expects with R^2. Therefore it is not surprising that most of the R^2 that are reported in

---

[9]Hypothesis tests of the form H_0: $\sigma_A = \sigma_B$ would be relevant; that is, to test whether the process volatility underlying the forecast is the same as the process volatility that generated the realization we have observed, ex post. Therefore an F-test based on the test statistic $\hat{\sigma}_A^2/\hat{\sigma}_B^2$ for the equality of two variances would apply.

Table 5.1: R^2 from regression of squared returns on GARCH(1, 1) variance forecast

The fact that the R^2 from a regression of squared returns on the forecasts of the variance is low does not mean that the model is misspecified

Alpha	Beta	R^2	Alpha	Beta	R^2	Alpha	Beta	R^2
0.05	0.85	0.0130	0.075	0.83	0.0301	0.1	0.8	0.0500
0.05	0.86	0.0143	0.075	0.84	0.0334	0.1	0.81	0.0550
0.05	0.87	0.0160	0.075	0.85	0.0375	0.1	0.82	0.0611
0.05	0.88	0.0182	0.075	0.86	0.0428	0.1	0.83	0.0689
0.05	0.89	0.0210	0.075	0.87	0.0500	0.1	0.84	0.0791
0.05	0.9	0.0250	0.075	0.88	0.0601	0.1	0.85	0.0930
0.05	0.91	0.0309	0.075	0.89	0.0756	0.1	0.86	0.1131
0.05	0.92	0.0406	0.075	0.9	0.1023	0.1	0.87	0.1447
0.05	0.93	0.0594	0.075	0.91	0.1589	0.1	0.88	0.2016
0.05	0.94	0.1116	0.075	0.92	0.3606	0.1	0.89	0.3344

the literature are less than 0.05. Earlier conclusions from this literature, that standard volatility models have very poor forecasting properties, should be reviewed in the light of this finding. The fact that the R^2 from a regression of squared returns on the forecasts of the variance is low does not mean that the model is misspecified.

5.1.2   Operational Criteria

An operational evaluation of volatility and correlation forecasts will focus on the particular application of the forecast. Thus any conclusions that may be drawn from an operational evaluation will be much more subjective than those drawn from the statistical methods just described. The advantage of using an operational criterion is that the volatility forecast is being assessed in the actual context in which it will be used. The disadvantage of operational evaluation is that the results might imply the use of a different type of forecast for every different purpose.

Some operational evaluation methods are based on the P&L generated by a trading strategy. A measurement of trading performance is described in §A.5.3 that is relevant for price forecasting, where an underlying asset is bought or sold depending on the level of the price forecast. A performance criterion for volatility or correlation forecasts should be based on hedging performance (Engle and Rosenberg, 1995) or on trading a volatility- or correlation-dependent product.

The metric for assessing a forecast of implied volatility could involve buying or selling straddles

For example, the metric for assessing a forecast of implied volatility could involve buying or selling straddles (a put and a call of the same strike) depending on the level of the volatility that is forecast. Straddles have a V-shaped pay-off and so will be in-the-money if the market is volatile, that is, for a large upward or downward movement in the underlying. The forecast of volatility $\hat{\sigma}$ can be compared with the current implied volatility level σ, and then a trading strategy can be defined that depends on their difference.

The choice of strategy is an entirely subjective decision. It depends on how one proposes to implement the trades. For example, a simple trading strategy for an implied volatility forecast $\hat{\sigma}$ that relates to a single threshold τ, might be: 'buy one at-the-money straddle if $\hat{\sigma} - \sigma > \tau$; otherwise do nothing'. An alternative volatility strategy could be: 'buy one ATM straddle if $\hat{\sigma} - \sigma > \tau_1$; sell one ATM straddle if $\hat{\sigma} - \sigma < \tau_2$; otherwise do nothing'. Or the strategy may go long or short several straddles, depending on various thresholds: 'buy n_1 straddles if $\hat{\sigma} - \sigma > \tau_1$; sell n_2 straddles if $\hat{\sigma} - \sigma < \tau_2$; otherwise do nothing'.

The P&L results from this strategy will depend on many choices: the number of trades n_1 and n_2, the thresholds τ_1 and τ_2, the frequency of trades, the strike of the straddles and, of course, the underlying market conditions during the test, including the current level of implied volatility σ. Clearly an evaluation strategy that is closest to the proposed trading strategy needs to be designed and the trader should be aware that the optimal forecasting model may very much depend on the design of the evaluation strategy.

When volatility and correlation forecasts are used for risk management the operational evaluation of volatility and correlation forecasts can be based on a standard risk measure such as value-at-risk. The general framework for backtesting of VaR models will be discussed in §9.5. But if the model performs poorly it may be for several reasons, such as non-normality in return distributions, and not just the inaccuracy of the volatility and correlation forecasts.

Alexander and Leigh (1997) perform a statistical evaluation of the three types of statistical volatility forecasts that are in standard use: 'historical' (equally weighted moving averages), EWMAs and GARCH. Given the remarks just made, it is impossible to draw any firm conclusions about the relative effectiveness of any volatility forecasting method for an arbitrary portfolio. However, using data from the major equity indices and foreign exchange rates, some broad conclusions do appear. While EWMA methods perform well for predicting the centre of a normal distribution, the VaR model backtests indicate that GARCH and equally weighted moving average methods are more accurate for the tails prediction required by VaR models. These results seem relatively independent of the data period used.

GARCH forecasts are designed to capture the fat tails in return distributions, so VaR measures from GARCH models tend to be larger than those that assume normality. The 'ghost features' of equally weighted averages that follow exceptional market moves have a similar effect on the 'historical' VaR measures. Therefore it is to be expected that these two types of forecasts generate larger VaR measures for most data periods, and consequently better VaR backtesting results (§9.5.1).

5.2   Confidence Intervals for Volatility Forecasts

The standard error of the volatility forecast is not the square root of the standard error of the variance forecast

We have examined the ability of point forecasts of volatility to capture the constant volatility of a price process. These point forecasts are the expectation of the future volatility estimator distribution. Another important quality for volatility forecasts is that they have low standard errors. That is, there is relatively little uncertainty surrounding the forecast or, to put it another way, one has a high degree of confidence that the forecast is close to the true process volatility. In §A.5.1 it is shown how standard errors of statistical regression forecasts are used to generate confidence intervals for the true value of the underlying parameter. These principles may also be applied to create confidence intervals for the true volatility, or for the true variance if that is the underlying parameter of interest.

The statistical models described in chapters 3 and 4 are variance forecasting models.[10] When the variance is forecast, the standard error of the forecast refers to the variance rather than to the volatility. Of course, the standard error of the volatility forecast is not the square root of the standard error of the variance forecast, but there is a simple transformation between the two. Since volatility is the square root of the variance, the density function of volatility is

$$g(\sigma) = 2\sigma h(\sigma^2) \qquad \text{for } \sigma > 0, \qquad (5.2)$$

where $h(\sigma^2)$ is the density function of variance.[11] Relationship (5.2) may be used to transform results about predictions of variances to predictions of volatility.

5.2.1   Moving Average Models

A confidence interval for the variance $\hat{\sigma}^2$ estimated by an equally weighted average may be obtained by a straightforward application of sampling theory. If a variance estimate is based on n normally distributed returns with an assumed mean of zero, then $n\hat{\sigma}^2/\sigma^2$ has a chi-squared distribution with n degrees of freedom.[12] From §A.2, a $100(1 - \alpha)\%$ two-sided confidence interval for $n\hat{\sigma}^2/\sigma^2$ would therefore take the form $(\chi^2_{n,1-\alpha/2}, \chi^2_{n,\alpha/2})$ and a straightforward calculation gives the associated confidence interval for the variance σ^2 as:

$$(n\hat{\sigma}^2/\chi^2_{n,\alpha/2}, \ n\hat{\sigma}^2/\chi^2_{n,1-\alpha/2}). \qquad (5.3)$$

For example a 95% confidence interval for an equally weighted variance forecast based on 30 observations is obtained using the upper and lower chi-squared critical values:

---

[10]The volatility forecast is taken to be the square root of the variance forecast, even though $E(\sigma) \neq \sqrt{E(\sigma^2)}$.

[11]If y is a (monotonic and differentiable) function of x then their probability densities $g(\cdot)$ and $h(\cdot)$ are related by $g(y) = |dx/dy|h(x)$. So if $y = \sqrt{x}$, $|dx/dy| = 2y$.

[12]The usual degrees-of-freedom correction does not apply since we have assumed throughout that returns have zero mean.

$$\chi^2_{30,0.025} = 46.979 \text{ and } \chi^2_{30,0.975} = 16.791.$$

So the confidence interval is $(0.6386\hat{\sigma}^2, 1.7867\hat{\sigma}^2)$ and exact values are obtained by substituting in the value of the variance estimate.

Assuming normality,[13] the standard error of an equally weighted average variance estimator based on n (zero mean) squared returns is $[\sqrt{(2/n)}]\sigma^2$. Therefore, as a percentage of the variance, the standard error of the variance estimator is 20% when 50 observations are used in the estimate, and 10% when 200 observations are used in the estimate.

The (infinite) EWMA variance estimator given by (3.3) has variance[14]

$$2\frac{1-\lambda}{1+\lambda}\sigma^4.$$

Therefore, as a percentage of the variance, the standard error of the EWMA variance estimator is about 5% when $\lambda = 0.95$, 10.5% when $\lambda = 0.9$, and 16.2% when $\lambda = 0.85$.

To obtain error bounds for the corresponding volatility estimates, it is of course not appropriate to take the square root of the error bounds for the variance estimate. However, it can be shown that[15]

$$V(\hat{\sigma}^2) \approx (2\sigma)^2 V(\hat{\sigma}).$$

The standard error of the volatility estimator (as a percentage of volatility) is therefore approximately one-half the size of the standard error of the variance estimator (as a percentage of the variance)

The standard error of the volatility estimator (as a percentage of volatility) is therefore approximately one-half the size of the variance standard error (as a percentage of the variance).[16] As a percentage of the volatility, the standard error of the equally weighted volatility estimator is approximately 10% when 50 observations are used in the estimate, and 5% when 200 observations are used in the estimate; the standard error of the EWMA volatility estimator is about 2.5% when $\lambda = 0.95$, 5.3% when $\lambda = 0.9$, and 8.1% when $\lambda = 0.85$.

The standard errors on equally weighted moving average volatility estimates become very large when only a few observations are used. This is one reason

---

[13]It follows from footnote 11 that if X_i are independent random variables ($i = 1, \ldots, n$) then $f(X_i)$ are also independent for any monotonic differentiable function $f(\cdot)$. Moving average models already assume that returns are i.i.d. Now assuming normality too, so that the returns are NID(0, σ^2), we apply the variance operator to $\hat{\sigma}_t^2 = \Sigma_{i=1}^n r_{t-i}^2/n$. Since the squared returns are independent $V(\hat{\sigma}_t^2) = \Sigma_{i=1}^n V(r_{t-i}^2)/n^2$. Now $V(r_t^2) = E(r_t^4) - [E(r_t^2)]^2 = 3\sigma^4 - \sigma^4 = 2\sigma^4$ by normality, and it follows that the variance of the equally weighted moving average variance estimator is $2\sigma^4/n$.

[14]Applying the variance operator to (3.3): $V(\hat{\sigma}^2) = [(1-\lambda)^2/(1-\lambda^2)]V(r_{t-1}^2) = [(1-\lambda)/(1+\lambda)]2\sigma^4$.

[15]Taking a second-order Taylor expansion of $f(x)$ about μ, the mean of X, and taking expectations gives $E(f(X)) \approx f(\mu) + \frac{1}{2}V(X)f''(\mu)$. Similarly, $E(f(X)^2) \approx f(\mu)^2 + V(X)[f'(\mu)^2 - f(\mu)f''(\mu)]$, again ignoring higher-order terms. Thus $V(f(X)) \approx f'(\mu)^2 V(X)$.

[16]For the equally weighted average of length n, the variance of the volatility estimator is $(2\sigma^4/n)(1/2\sigma)^2 = \sigma^2/(2n)$, so the standard error of the volatility estimator as a percentage of volatility is $1/\sqrt{(2n)}$; For the EWMA, the variance of the volatility estimator is $(2[(1-\lambda)/(1+\lambda)]\sigma^4)(1/2\sigma)^2 = [(1-\lambda)/(1+\lambda)]\sigma^2/2$, so the standard error of the volatility estimator as a percentage of volatility is $\sqrt{[(1-\lambda)/2(1+\lambda)]}$.

why it is advisable to use a long averaging period in 'historical' volatility estimates. On the other hand, the longer the averaging period, the longer-lasting the 'ghost effects' from exceptional returns (see Figure 3.1).

5.2.2   GARCH Models

The covariance matrix of the parameter estimates in a GARCH model can be used to generate GARCH confidence intervals for conditional variance. For example, the variance of the one-step-ahead variance forecast in a GARCH(1, 1) model is

$$
\begin{aligned}
V_t(\hat{\sigma}_{t+1}^2) = {} & V_t(\hat{\omega}) + V_t(\hat{\alpha})\varepsilon_t^4 + V_t(\hat{\beta})\hat{\sigma}_t^4 + 2\,\mathrm{cov}_t(\hat{\omega},\,\hat{\alpha})\varepsilon_t^2 \\
& + 2\,\mathrm{cov}_t(\hat{\omega},\,\hat{\beta})\hat{\sigma}_t^2 + 2\,\mathrm{cov}_t(\hat{\alpha},\,\hat{\beta})\varepsilon_t^2\hat{\sigma}_t^2
\end{aligned}
\tag{5.4}
$$

The estimated covariance matrix of parameter estimates is part of the standard output in GARCH procedures. It will depend on the sample size used to estimate the model: as with the error bounds for moving average estimates given above, the smaller the sample size the bigger these quantities. However, in the GARCH forecast by far the largest source of uncertainty is the unexpected return at time t. If there is a large and unexpected movement in the market, in either direction, then ε_t^2 will be large and the effect in (5.4) will be to widen the confidence interval for the GARCH variance considerably.

The GARCH confidence intervals are much wider following a large unexpected return — rather than uncertainty in parameter estimates, it is market behaviour that is the main source of uncertainty in GARCH forecasts

Consider the GARCH(1, 1) models discussed in §4.3.2. Table 5.2 reports upper and lower bounds for 95% confidence intervals for the 1-day-ahead GARCH variance forecasts that are generated using (4.16) with a number of different values for unexpected daily return. Note that these returns will be squared in the symmetric GARCH(1, 1), so it does not matter whether they are positive or negative. The confidence interval for the variance is quoted in annualized terms assuming 250 days a year.

Note that the GARCH confidence intervals are much wider following a large unexpected return — rather than uncertainty in parameter estimates, it is market behaviour that is the main source of uncertainty in GARCH forecasts. These confidence intervals are for the variance, not the volatility, but may be translated into confidence intervals for volatility.[17] For example, the confidence intervals for an unexpected return of 0.005 translate into a confidence interval in volatility terms of (30.8%, 33.1%) for the S&P 500, (44.6%, 46%) for the CAC and (36.5%, 37.9%) for the Nikkei 225.

5.2.3   Confidence Intervals for Combined Forecasts

Suppose a process volatility σ is being forecast and that there are m different

---

[17]Percentiles are invariant under monotonic differentiable transformations, so the confidence limits for volatility are the square root of the limits for variance.

Table 5.2: GARCH variance 95% confidence interval bounds on 11 September 1998

Unexpected return	S&P 500		CAC		Nikkei 225	
	Lower	Upper	Lower	Upper	Lower	Upper
0.001	0.10080	0.10345	0.20367	0.20649	0.13829	0.14022
0.002	0.099647	0.10460	0.20273	0.20742	0.13722	0.14130
0.003	0.098144	0.10610	0.20144	0.20871	0.13606	0.14245
0.004	0.096568	0.10768	0.20006	0.21009	0.13489	0.14362
0.005	0.094967	0.10928	0.19865	0.21151	0.13371	0.14480

forecasting models available.[18] Denote the forecasts from these models by $\hat{\sigma}_1$, $\hat{\sigma}_2, \ldots, \hat{\sigma}_m$ and suppose that each of these forecasts has been made over a data period from $t = 0$ to $t = T$. Now suppose we have observed, ex post, a realization of the process volatility over the same period. The combined forecasting produce of Granger and Ramanathan (1984) applied in this context requires a least squares regression of the realized volatility σ on a constant and $\hat{\sigma}_1, \hat{\sigma}_2, \ldots, \hat{\sigma}_m$. The fitted value from this regression is a *combined volatility forecast* that will fit at least as well as any of the component forecasts: the R^2 between realized volatility and the combined volatility forecast will be at least as big as the R^2 between realized volatility and any of the individual forecasts. The estimated coefficients in this regression, after normalization so that they sum to one, will be the optimal weights to use in the combined forecast.

Figure 5.3 shows several different forecasts of US dollar exchange rate volatilities for sterling, the Deutschmark and the Japanese yen. Some general observations on these figures are as follows:

➤ The GARCH forecasts seem closer to the implied volatilities.
➤ The historic 30-day and the EWMA forecasts with $\lambda = 0.94$ are similar (because the half-life of an EWMA with $\lambda = 0.94$ is about 30 days).
➤ The EWMA forecasts are out of line with the other 90-day forecasts (because the EWMA model assumes a constant volatility, the 90-day forecasts are the same as the 30-day forecasts).
➤ There is more agreement between the different 30-day forecasts than there is between the different 90-day forecasts (because uncertainties increase with the risk horizon).
➤ The volatility forecasts differ most at times of great uncertainty in the markets, for example during 1994 in sterling and during 1990 in the Deutschmark. On the other hand, they can be very similar when nothing unusual is expected to happen in the market, for example during 1990 in the yen.

Now suppose that a combination of these forecasts is to be used as a single forecast for realized volatility. Table 5.3 summarizes the results of the ordinary

---

[18]For the Granger–Ramanathan procedure these forecasts should also be independent.

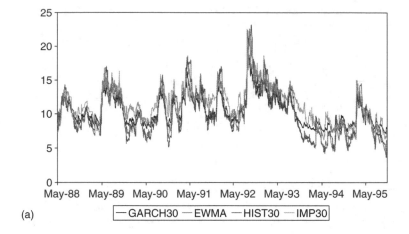

(a)

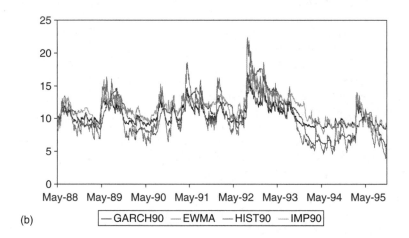

(b)

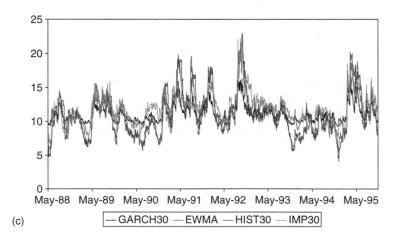

(c)

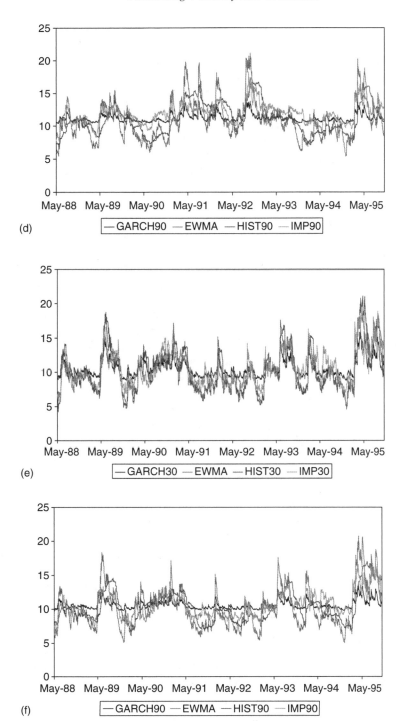

(d)

(e)

(f)

Figure 5.3 Volatility forecasts: (a) 30-day US dollar–sterling; (b) 90-day US dollar–sterling; (c) 30-day German mark–US dollar; (d) 90-day German mark–US dollar; (e) 30-day Japanese yen–US dollar; (f) 90-day Japanese yen–US dollar.

Table 5.3: Combined forecasts of realized volatility

| | GBP | | DEM | | JPY | |
	30-day	*90-day*	*30-day*	*90-day*	*30-day*	*90-day*
Intercept	−2.02	0.44	−3.73	−3.06	−6.08	−4.67
	(−2.78)	*(0.35)*	*(−3.83)*	*(−1.41)*	*(−6.23)*	*(−2.09)*
GARCH	**1.13**	**1.02**	**1.16**	**1.48**	**1.56**	**1.49**
	(6.58)	*(5.12)*	*(8.33)*	*(6.52)*	*(10.36)*	*(5.94)*
Historic	−0.26	**0.19**	−0.10	**0.11**	0.24	−0.24
	(−3.56)	*(4.48)*	*(−1.36)*	*(2.97)*	*(3.36)*	*(−5.90)*
EWMA	−0.24	−0.14	−0.27	−0.03	−0.81	−0.10
	(−1.77)	*(−1.45)*	*(−2.35)*	*(−0.59)*	*(−7.19)*	*(−1.57)*
Implied	**0.50**	−0.12	**0.51**	−0.27	**0.54**	**0.26**
	(8.32)	*(−1.6)*	*(9.21)*	*(−4.3)*	*(11.2)*	*(5.00)*
Est s.e.	2.87	2.47	2.83	2.22	2.65	2.20
R^2	0.56	0.46	0.47	0.3	0.51	0.34

least squares regressions of realized volatility on the GARCH, historic, EWMA and implied volatility forecasts shown in Figure 5.3. Some general conclusions may be drawn from the estimated coefficients and the *t*-statistics (shown in parentheses). Firstly, the GARCH forecasts take the largest weight in the combined forecast, although they are not always the most significant. In fact implied volatilities are often very significant, particularly for the 30-day realized volatilities. Historic and EWMA forecasts have low weights, in fact they are often less than zero, so they appear to be *negatively* correlated with realized volatility.[19] In each case the fitted series gives the optimal combined forecast for realized volatility. Note that the intercept is quite large and negative in most cases, which indicates that the forecasts have a tendency to overestimate realized volatility.

Figure 5.4a shows two combined forecasts of 30-day realized volatility of the GBP–USD rate. Forecast 1 uses all four forecasts as in Table 5.3, and forecast 2 excludes the EWMA forecast because of the high multicollinearity with the historic 30-day forecast (§A.4.1). In each case the model was fitted up to April 1995 and the last 6 months of data are used to compare the model predictions with the realized volatility out-of-sample in Figure 5.4b. Since the 30-day realized volatility jumps up 30 days before a large market movement, it is a very difficult thing to predict, particularly when markets are jumpy. There is, however, a reasonable agreement between the forecast and the realized volatility during less volatile times, and the out-of-sample period marked with a dotted line on the figures happened to be relatively uneventful.

---

[19] The low and insignificant coefficients on the historic 30-day forecast and the EWMA are a result of a high degree of multicollinearity of these variables (§A.4.1). In fact their unconditional correlation estimate during the sample is over 0.95 in all three models. When there is a high level of correlation between some explanatory variables the standard errors on coefficient estimators will be depressed, and the danger is that the model will be incorrectly specified.

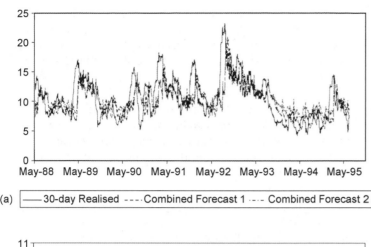

(a)

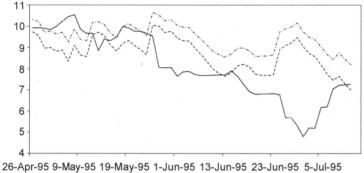

(b)

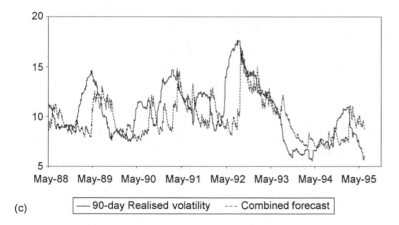

(c)

Figure 5.4 (a) Thirty-day realized volatility and combined forecasts of the US dollar–sterling rate; (b) out-of-sample performance of the US dollar–sterling combined forecast; (c) 90-day realized volatility and combined forecasts of the US dollar–sterling rate.

The 90-day realized volatility jumps up 90 days before a large market movement, so it is even more difficult to predict. Not surprisingly the models in Table 5.3 have much lower R^2 for 90-day realized volatility in all three rates. Figure 5.4c shows the combined forecast from the GBP–USD model in the second column of Table 5.3.

The linear regression approach to the construction of combined volatility forecasts allows one to use standard results on confidence intervals for regression predictions (§A.5.1) to construct confidence intervals for volatility forecasts

The linear regression approach to the construction of combined volatility forecasts allows one to use standard results on confidence intervals for regression predictions (§A.5.1) to construct confidence intervals for volatility forecasts. For example, a two-sided confidence interval for the realized volatility will be

$$(\hat{\sigma}_t - \xi_t, \ \hat{\sigma}_t + \xi_t), \tag{5.5}$$

where $\hat{\sigma}_t$ is the combined volatility forecast value at time t, and

$$\xi_t = Z_\alpha s \sqrt{(1 + \mathbf{R}_t (\mathbf{X'X})^{-1} \mathbf{R}_t)},$$

where Z_α is an appropriate critical value (in this case normal since very many points were used for the regression), s is the estimated standard error of the regression, $\mathbf{X}$ is the matrix of in-sample data on the different volatility forecasts and $\mathbf{R}_t = (1, \ \hat{\sigma}_{1t}, \ \hat{\sigma}_{2t}, \ \ldots, \ \hat{\sigma}_{mt})'$ the vector of the individual volatility forecasts at the time when the combined forecast is made.

As an example, return to the realized volatility forecasts shown Figure 5.3. The $\mathbf{X}$ matrix for the GBP 30-day realized 'combined forecast 2' in Figure 5.4a contains data on 1s (for the constant), 30-day GARCH volatility, 30-day historic and 30-day implied, and

$$(\mathbf{X'X})^{-1} = \begin{pmatrix} 0.04200 & -0.00543 & 0.00274 & -0.00110 \\ -0.00543 & 0.00115 & -0.0066 & 0.00001 \\ 0.00274 & -0.0066 & 0.00042 & -0.00021 \\ -0.00110 & 0.00001 & -0.00021 & 0.00011 \end{pmatrix}.$$

The vector $\mathbf{R}_t$ depends on the time period. For example, on 7 July 1995 it took the value $(1, \ 9.36, \ 9.55, \ 8.7)'$ and so $\mathbf{R}_t (\mathbf{X'X})^{-1} \mathbf{R}_t = 0.0023$. Since the estimated in-sample standard error of regression was $s = 2.936$, and the 5% critical value of $N(0, 1)$ is 1.645, the value ξ_t for a 90% confidence interval based on (5.5) for the realized volatility on 7 July 1995 was 4.83. The point prediction of realized volatility on that day was 8.44, so the interval prediction is 8.44 ± 4.83. Therefore from this model one can be 90% sure that realized volatility would be between 3.61% and 13.27%. Similarly, a 95% confidence interval is (2.68%, 14.2%). These interval predictions are very imprecise. Similar calculations for the other rates and for 90-day volatilities show that all interval predictions are rather wide. This is because the standard errors of regression are relatively large and the 'goodness' of fit in the models is not particularly good.

5.3 Consequences of Uncertainty in Volatility and Correlation

Volatility is very difficult to predict — and correlation perhaps even more so. This section considers how one should account for the uncertainty in volatility and correlation when valuing portfolios. When portfolios of financial assets are valued, they are generally *marked-to-market* (MtM). That is, a current market price for each option in the portfolio is used to value the portfolio. However, there may not be any liquid market for some assets in the portfolio, such as OTC options. These must be valued according to a model, that is, they must be *marked-to-model*. Thus the MtM value of a portfolio often contains marked-to-model values as well as marked-to-market values.

Uncertainty in volatility is captured by a distribution of the volatility estimator; this will result in a distribution of mark-to-model values

There are uncertainties in many model parameters; volatility and correlation are particularly uncertain. When uncertainty in volatility (or correlation) is captured by a distribution of the volatility (or correlation) estimator; this distribution will result in a distribution of mark-to-model values. In this section the MtM value of an options portfolio is regarded as a random variable. The expectation of its distribution will give a point estimate of MtM value. However, instead of the usual MtM value, this expectation will be influenced by the uncertainty in volatilities. The adjustment to the usual value will be greatest for portfolios with many OTM options; on the other hand, the variance of the adjusted MtM value will be greatest for portfolios with many ATM options.

We shall show that volatility and correlation uncertainty give rise to a distribution in MtM values. Distributions of MtM values are nothing new. This is exactly what is calculated in VaR models. However, in VaR models the value distribution arises from variations in the risk factors of a portfolio, such as the yield curves, exchange rates or equity market indices. This section discusses how to approach the problem of generating a value distribution where the only uncertainty is in the covariance matrix forecast.

5.3.1 Adjustment in Mark-to-Model Value of an Option

In the first instance let us consider how the uncertainty in a volatility forecast can affect the value of an option. Suppose that the volatility forecast is expressed in terms of a point prediction and an estimated standard error of this prediction. The point prediction is an estimate of the mean $E(\sigma)$ of the volatility forecast, and the square of the estimated standard error gives an estimate of the variance $V(\sigma)$ of the volatility forecast. Denote by $f(\sigma)$ the value of the option as a function of volatility, and take a second-order Taylor expansion of $f(\sigma)$ about $E(\sigma)$:

$$f(\sigma) \approx f(E(\sigma)) + (\partial f/\partial \sigma)(\sigma - E(\sigma)) + \tfrac{1}{2}(\partial^2 f/\partial \sigma^2)(\sigma - E(\sigma))^2. \qquad (5.6)$$

Thus the expectation of the option value is

$$E(f(\sigma)) \approx f(E(\sigma)) + \tfrac{1}{2}(\partial^2 f/\partial \sigma^2)V(\sigma), \qquad (5.7)$$

and this can be approximated by putting in the point volatility prediction for $E(\sigma)$ and the square of the estimated standard error of that prediction for $V(\sigma)$.

When the uncertainty in the volatility forecast is taken into account, the expected value of the option requires more than just plugging the point volatility forecast into the option valuation function

It is common practice for traders to plug a volatility forecast value into $f(\sigma)$ and simply read off the value of the option. But (5.7) shows that when the uncertainty in the volatility forecast is taken into account, the expected value of the option requires more than just plugging the point volatility forecast into the option valuation function. The extra term on the right-hand side of (5.7) depends on $\partial^2 f/\partial\sigma^2$.[20] For the basic options that are usually priced using the Black–Scholes formula, $\partial^2 f/\partial\sigma^2$ is generally positive when the option is OTM or ITM, but when the option is nearly ATM then $\partial^2 f/\partial\sigma^2$ will be very small (and it may be *very* slightly negative).

We have already seen that Black–Scholes 'plug-in' option prices for OTM and ITM options are too low and that this is one reason for the smile effect (§2.2.1). The adjustment term in (5.7) means that when some account is taken of the uncertainty in forecasts of volatility, the Black–Scholes 'plug-in' price will be revised upwards. On the other hand, the Black–Scholes price of an ATM option will need negligible revision. It may be revised downwards, but only by a very small amount. We shall return to this problem in §10.3.3, when the volatility uncertainty will be modelled by a mixture of normal densities. The empirical examples given there will quantify the adjustment for option prices of different strikes and it will be seen that simple ATM options will require only very small adjustments, if any, because they are approximately linear in volatility.

However, the variance of the model value due to uncertain volatility will be greatest for ATM options. To see this, take variances of (5.7):

$$V(f(\sigma)) \approx (\partial f/\partial\sigma)^2 V(\sigma). \tag{5.8}$$

This shows that the variance of the value is proportional to the variance of the volatility forecast, and it also increases with the square of the option volatility sensitivity, that is, the option vega (§2.3.3). Options that are near to ATM will have the largest contribution to the variance of the option portfolio value due to uncertain volatility, since they have the greatest volatility sensitivity.

The adjustments that need to be made to the value of a portfolio of options to account for uncertainty in the correlation forecasts are not easy to express analytically. A simple graphical method is to plot the value as a function of correlation and examine its convexity in the local area of the point correlation forecast. Figure 5.5a illustrates a hypothetical option value as a function of correlation. If the correlation forecast is $\hat{\rho}_1$ then the value should be adjusted downwards for uncertainty in correlation because the function is concave at this point, but if the correlation forecast is $\hat{\rho}_2$ then the value should be adjusted

---

[20] $\partial^2 f/\partial\sigma^2$ is similar to the new Greek 'psi' that was introduced by Hull and White (1997) to capture kurtosis sensitivity in options (§10.3.3).

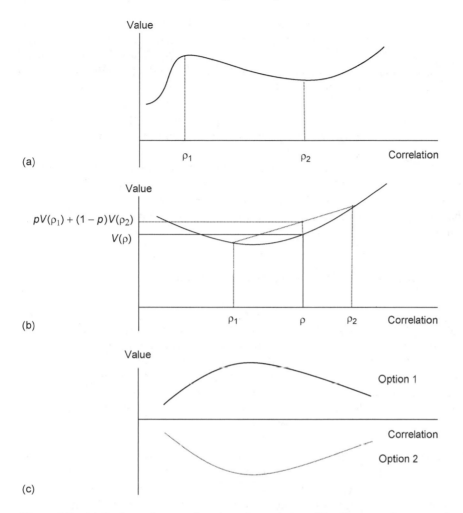

Figure 5.5 (a) Option value as a function of correlation; (b) adjustment for uncertainty in correlation; (c) options with opposite correlation characteristics.

upwards for uncertainty in correlation because the function is convex at this point. Figure 5.5b shows that the amount of this adjustment depends on the degree of uncertainty in correlation and the shape of the value as a function of correlation. If correlation is known to be ρ then the option value is $V(\rho)$. However, if correlation is unknown, suppose it takes the value ρ_1 with probability p and the value ρ_2 with probability $1 - p$: in this case, because the option value is convex in correlation, the option value $pV(\rho_1) + (1 - p)V(\rho_2)$ is greater than $V(\rho)$. Thus the uncertainty in correlation, in this case, would lead to an upward adjustment in the option value.

Rather than making an *ad-hoc* adjustment in portfolio values, it may be preferable to hedge this correlation risk by taking a position with the opposite characteristics. For example, if value is a concave function of correlation this

Rather than making an ad-hoc adjustment in portfolio values, it may be preferable to hedge this correlation risk by taking a position with the opposite characteristics

portfolio could be hedged with a portfolio that has a value which is a convex function of correlation, as depicted in Figure 5.5c. Unfortunately, it is not always possible to find such products in the market, although recently there has been some growth in the markets for OTC products such as currency correlation swaps to hedge correlations between two currency pairs.

Before ending this section, it is worthwhile to comment that the method for adjusting portfolio values due to uncertain correlation that is depicted in Figure 5.5 should be applied to *all* parameters in the portfolio pricing model. Volatility is easier, because the adjustments have a simple analytic form described by (5.7) and (5.8). But for correlation, and all other parameters, it is worthwhile to investigate the degree to which they affect the value and, if necessary, make adjustments for uncertainties in parameter estimates.

5.3.2   Uncertainty in Dynamically Hedged Portfolios

How much does it matter if there are errors in the implied volatilities that are used to calculate deltas for dynamic hedging of an option portfolio? It is possible to answer this question with an empirical analysis, as the following example shows. Consider a short position on a 90-day call option that is delta hedged daily using an implied volatility of 15%. The process volatility is unknown, of course, but suppose you believe that it could take any value between 8% and 18% and that each value is equally likely. What is the error in the value of the delta hedged portfolio?

For a given process volatility we can estimate the value of the option in h days' time, and so also the value of the delta hedged portfolio. Using 1000 Monte Carlo simulations on the underlying price process, with a fixed process volatility, we obtain an expected value for the option (taking the discounted expected value of the pay-off distribution as described in §4.4.2) and a measure of uncertainty in this option value (either the standard error of the option value distribution over 1000 simulations, or the 1% lower percentile of this distribution). In each simulation, the evolution of the underlying price and the fixed delta (corresponding to an implied volatility of 15%) allow us to compute the expected value of the delta hedged portfolio in h days time, along with a measure of uncertainty (standard error or percentile). We can do this for each process volatility $x\%$ ($x = 8, 9, \ldots, 18$) and thus generate a curve that represents the expected value of the hedged portfolio as a function of the process volatility. Then, taking the time horizons $h = 1, 2, \ldots, 90$ gives a surface that represents the expected value of the hedged portfolio as a function of the process volatility x and time horizon h.

For the uncertainty around this surface, the 1% lower percentile of the value change distribution is a good measure since it corresponds to the 1% h-day VaR measure. Figure 5.6 shows the 1% VaR for each possible process

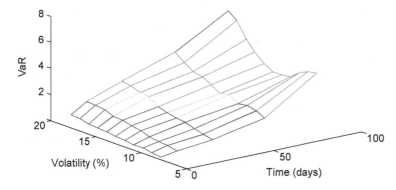

Figure 5.6 One per cent VaR of a dynamically delta hedged call.

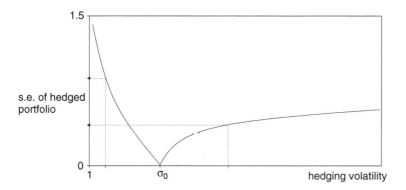

Figure 5.7 The effect of using an incorrect hedging volatility.

volatility between 8% and 18% and for each holding period from 1 to 90 days. The figure shows that VaR measures can be high even when process volatility is low, if the option is hedged for a long period using the wrong hedging volatility.[21] So much is obvious, but what is more interesting is that the VaR measures are much greater when the process volatility is above 15%. That is, when the (wrong) hedging volatility of 15% is underestimating the process volatility, some VaR measures can be very considerable indeed.

There is a simple explanation for the shape of this surface. With continuous rebalancing, the variance of a delta hedged portfolio due to using the wrong hedging volatility is approximately $(\sigma_h - \sigma_0)^2 (\text{vega})^2$, where σ_h denotes the implied volatility used for hedging and σ_0 denotes the process volatility.[22] This is only a local approximation. In fact the standard error of the hedged portfolio value has the asymmetric shape shown in Figure 5.7.

---

[21]Many thanks to Chris Leigh for providing this figure.

[22]Discrete rebalancing increases the standard error of the hedged portfolio by a factor that depends on $1/\sqrt{(2n)}$, where n is the number of rebalancings, and on the process volatility; the standard error curve still has an asymmetric smile shape.

The standard error of the value of the portfolio (option plus hedge) is zero if $\sigma_h = \sigma_0$. If the hedging volatility is correct the option can be perfectly hedged. But σ_0 is unknown, and if the implied (hedging) volatility is not equal to the process volatility, the standard error of the portfolio value increases with the volatility error, as shown in Figure 5.7. It is not symmetric: if the process volatility is less than the hedging volatility then there is less uncertainty in the value of the hedged portfolio; if the process volatility is greater than the hedging volatility then there is more uncertainty in the value of the hedged portfolio. This means that if one does not know whether the hedging volatility is accurate, it is better to use a higher value than a lower value. That is, there will be less uncertainty in the value of the hedged portfolio if one over-hedges the position.

If one does not know whether the hedging volatility is accurate, it is better to use a higher value than a lower value

Part II

Modelling the Market Risk of Portfolios

The first two chapters in this part of the book introduce principal component analysis (PCA) and covariance matrices as key tools for the statistical analysis of market risk. Investment appraisal and the risk management of financial assets will, typically, be modelled by systems that have hundreds of different risk factors. The purpose of PCA is to reduce dimensions, so that only the most important sources of information are used, and to orthogonalize the variables, so that covariance matrices are diagonal. Chapter 6 begins with the traditional application of PCA to modelling term structures of interest rates and futures. Then some of the latest PCA applications, to models for implied volatilities and for overcoming data problems, are described.

Chapter 7 covers the use of covariance matrices in risk and investment analysis. An algebraic approach is taken to introduce the variance of a linear portfolio as a quadratic form of a positive semi-definite covariance matrix. Section 7.2 shows how covariance matrices are used to diversify investments and obtain minimum risk portfolios, and to generate the efficient frontier for optimal asset allocation. Optimal portfolios are determined by the risk attitude of investors, and so this section also contains a brief introduction to utility theory. The chapter concludes by describing methods for generating large covariance matrices, including a new orthogonal method that employs PCA. The linear theme is continued in Chapter 8, which examines fundamental factor models and their implications for diversifiable and non-diversifiable risk.

The first three chapters of this part provide the background for the comprehensive and detailed description of value-at-risk (VaR) models in Chapter 9. Following a summary of the Basel regulations for market risk capital, the chapter gives an overview of various alternative measures of risk. The core of this chapter is in the description of different VaR models and in the supporting examples from the text and on the CD. The chapter concludes with a brief account of VaR model validation and the application of stress testing and scenario analysis to daily risk management.

The final chapter in this part concerns the testing, modelling and application of non-normal distributions in financial markets. It begins with a description of standard statistical tests for skewness and kurtosis and a brief description of the extreme value and hyperbolic distributions. The main focus of this chapter is on normal mixture densities, their estimation and their application to risk measurement, option pricing and hedging. It makes concrete the ideas on modelling uncertainty in volatility that were introduced at the end of Part I.

6

Principal Component Analysis

Many financial markets are characterized by a high degree of collinearity between returns. Term structures such as yields of different maturities on similar bonds exhibit a very high level of correlation, that is, they are highly collinear. Variables are highly collinear when there are only a few important sources of information in the data that are common to many variables. This chapter is about a standard method for extracting the most important uncorrelated sources of variation in a multivariate system, which is called principal component analysis (PCA). Not only term structures but also implied volatilities of different options on the same underlying asset, and futures of different maturities on the same underlying, lend themselves to PCA. It also has very useful applications to modelling equity markets, or currency markets, or indeed any market where there is a reasonably high level of correlation between the returns.

Variables are highly collinear when there are only a few important sources of information in the data that are common to many variables

It is a common problem in risk management that risk measures and pricing models are applied to a very large set of scenarios based on movements in all possible risk factors. The dimensions are so large that the computations become extremely slow and cumbersome, so it is quite common that over-simplistic assumptions are made. For example, smile surfaces may be assumed constant, or at least only parallel shifts in the smile will be considered. Yield curves might be interpolated between just a few points along the curve, rather than taking scenarios for all maturities in the term structure.

This chapter describes a modelling tool for correlated financial systems that is based on only a few key market risk factors. Large systems for the pricing and risk management of financial assets use hundreds of different risk factors. One of the aims of principal component analysis is to reduce dimensions so that only the most important sources of information are used. The two main advantages of this approach are:

➢ The computational efficiency that results from the lack of correlation between the principal components and the dimension reduction from taking just a few of them.
➢ That it provides a tractable and intuitive framework that will often aid understanding of the dynamics of market behaviour.

In many cases the objective of PCA is to reduce dimensionality by taking only the first m principal components in the representation (6.2) below. This is certainly useful in highly correlated systems because there will only be a few independent sources of variation and most of it can be explained by just a few principal components. The reduction in dimensionality achieved by a principal component representation can greatly facilitate calculations. Transformations to the principal components may be applied, and then the factor weights are used to relate these transformations to the original system. This has enormous advantages in scenario analysis (§9.6). The significant reduction in computation time makes principal components a very useful tool for risk measurement in large portfolios.

Another very useful application of principal component analysis is the construction of large positive definite covariance matrices

Another very useful application of principal component analysis is the construction of large positive definite covariance matrices. In this case the advantage of PCA is not so much in the reduction of dimensionality; rather it is due to the orthogonalization of variables.[1] Since principal components are orthogonal their unconditional covariance matrix is diagonal. The variances of the principal components can be quickly transformed into a covariance matrix of the original system using the factor weights. Only the m principal component variances need to be calculated, instead of the $k(k + 1)/2$ different elements of the $k \times k$ covariance matrix of the original system. Full details of the method are given in §7.4.

A linear algebraic approach to PCA is taken in §6.1.[2] Section 6.2 will help the reader to gain an intuitive grasp of principal components, and their factor weights, through empirical examples of the application of PCA to term structures (term structures lend themselves to PCA and many financial analysts are familiar with PCA in this context). Section 6.3 describes some of the latest research on the application of PCA to modelling volatility smiles and skews (Alexander, 2000b, 2001a). This section shows how non-linear movements of smiles and skews, corresponding to a quadratic parameterization of the volatility surface, may be modelled using PCA.

PCA can be used to fill in missing data points for new issues or illiquid assets

The final section of this chapter explains how PCA may be used to overcome various problems with data. A common problem that arises with many models, such as multi-factor models and benchmark tracking models that are based on regression analysis, is that explanatory variables are often highly collinear. This 'multicollinearity' can cause difficulties with model estimation (§A.4.1). Section 6.4.1 shows how PCA provides a robust and efficient method for estimating parameters in these models. The second data problem concerns missing data on relatively new assets that do, however, have a reasonably high correlation with other assets in the system. Section 6.4.2 explains how PCA can be used to fill in missing data points for such assets: an empirical example that simulates an artificial price history over more than 2 years from just a few months of real

---

[1] If two random variables have zero unconditional correlation they are called *orthogonal*.

[2] Such an approach presents a useful background for the applications of PCA that will be explored in this and subsequent chapters. The CD contains spreadsheets that illustrate the optimization approach. Jolliffe (1986) gives more details on the theoretical background.

data is given. It has obvious applications to new issues, and to financial assets that are not heavily traded.

6.1 Mathematical background

The data input to PCA must be stationary (§11.2). Prices, rates or yields are generally non-stationary and so they will have to be transformed, commonly into returns, before PCA is applied. These returns will also need to be normalized before the analysis, otherwise the first principal component will be dominated by the input variable with the greatest volatility. We therefore assume that each column in the $T \times k$ stationary data matrix $\mathbf{X}$ has mean 0 and variance 1, having previously subtracted the sample mean and divided by the sample standard deviation.[3]

PCA is based on an eigenvalue and eigenvector analysis of $\mathbf{V} = \mathbf{X'X}/T$, the $k \times k$ symmetric matrix of correlations between the variables in $\mathbf{X}$. Each principal component is a linear combination of these columns, where the weights are chosen in such a way that:

➢ the first principal component explains the greatest amount of the total variation in $\mathbf{X}$, the second component explains the greatest amount of the remaining variation, and so on;
➢ the principal components are uncorrelated with each other.

It is now shown that this can be achieved by choosing the weights from the set of eigenvectors of the correlation matrix. Denote by $\mathbf{W}$ the $k \times k$ matrix of eigenvectors of $\mathbf{V}$. Thus

$$\mathbf{VW} = \mathbf{W\Lambda},$$

where $\mathbf{\Lambda}$ is the $k \times k$ diagonal matrix of eigenvalues of $\mathbf{V}$. Order the columns of $\mathbf{W}$ according to size of corresponding eigenvalue. Thus if $\mathbf{W} = (w_{ij})$ for i, $j = 1, \ldots, k$, then the mth column of $\mathbf{W}$, denoted $\mathbf{w}_m = (w_{1m}, \ldots, w_{km})'$, is the $k \times 1$ eigenvector corresponding to the eigenvalue λ_m and the column labelling has been chosen so that $\lambda_1 > \lambda_2 > \ldots > \lambda_k$.

Define the mth principal component of the system by

$$P_m = w_{1m}X_1 + w_{2m}X_2 + \ldots + w_{km}X_k,$$

where X_i denotes the ith column of $\mathbf{X}$, that is, the standardized historical input data on the ith variable in the system. In matrix notation the above definition becomes

---

[3] Other forms of standardization are occasionally applied, which explains why different statistical packages may give different results. Note that if, after normalizing the data in $\mathbf{X}$, the observation at time t is weighted by an exponential smoothing constant λ^{T-t}, then $\mathbf{V} = (1 - \lambda)\mathbf{X'X}$ will be the exponentially weighted correlation matrix of the input data. An example of this is given on the CD. Normalization of the eigenvectors also plays a role, as the reader will discover when using the different spreadsheets for PCA on the CD. A full explanation of differences due to normalization is given in their help and tutorial files.

$$P_m = \mathbf{X}\mathbf{w}_m.$$

Each principal component is a time series of the transformed $\mathbf{X}$ variables, and the full $T \times m$ matrix of principal components, which has P_m as its mth column, may be written

$$\mathbf{P} = \mathbf{X}\mathbf{W}. \tag{6.1}$$

To see that this procedure leads to uncorrelated components, note that

$$\mathbf{P'P} = \mathbf{W'X'XW} = T\mathbf{W'W\Lambda}.$$

However, $\mathbf{W}$ is an orthogonal matrix, that is $\mathbf{W'} = \mathbf{W}^{-1}$ and so $\mathbf{P'P} = T\Lambda$. Since this is a diagonal matrix the columns of $\mathbf{P}$ are uncorrelated, and the variance of the mth principal component is λ_m.

Since the variance of each principal component is determined by its corresponding eigenvalue, the proportion of the total variation in $\mathbf{X}$ that is explained by the mth principal component is $\lambda_m/$(sum of eigenvalues). However, the sum of the eigenvalues is k, the number of variables in the system.[4] Therefore the proportion of variation explained by the first n principal components together is

$$\sum_{i=1}^{n} \lambda_i/k.$$

Because of the choice of column labelling in $\mathbf{W}$ the principal components have been ordered so that P_1 belongs to the first and largest eigenvalue λ_1, P_2 belongs to the second largest eigenvalue λ_2, and so on. In a highly correlated system the first eigenvalue will be much larger than the others, so the first principal component alone will explain a large part of the variation.

Since $\mathbf{W'} = \mathbf{W}^{-1}$, equation (6.1) is equivalent to $\mathbf{X} = \mathbf{P}\mathbf{W'}$, that is,

$$X_i = w_{i1}P_1 + w_{i2}P_2 + \ldots + w_{ik}P_k \tag{6.2}$$

Thus each vector of input data may be written as a linear combination of the principal components. This is the *principal components representation* of the original variables that lies at the core of PCA models. Often only the first few principal components are used to represent each of the input variables, because they are sufficient to explain most of the variation in the system. However, even without this dimension reduction, calculations of covariance for the original variables are greatly facilitated by the representation of these variables by (6.2); the principal components are orthogonal so their unconditional covariance matrix is diagonal.

---

[4] To see why, note that the sum of the eigenvalues is the trace of Λ, the diagonal matrix of eigenvalues of $\mathbf{V}$. However, the trace of Λ equals the trace of $\mathbf{V}$ (because trace is invariant under similarity transforms), and because $\mathbf{V}$ has 1s all along its diagonal, the trace of $\mathbf{V}$ is the number of variables in the system.

6.2 Application to Term Structures

This section shows how, in any highly correlated system, the first principal component captures an approximately parallel shift in all variables. Term structures are special because they impose an ordering on the system that provides an intuitive interpretation of *all* the principal components, not just the first. After interpreting the principal components of a single yield curve, we shall consider how PCA should be applied to modelling multiple yield curves. Finally, an empirical example of PCA is given for modelling futures prices on the same underlying asset.

Term structures are special because they impose an ordering on the system that provides an intuitive interpretation of all the principal components, not just the first

6.2.1 The Trend, Tilt and Convexity Components of a Single Yield Curve

Figure 6.1 shows monthly data on US semi-annualized zero-coupon rates using monthly data from 1944 to 1992.[5] There are three different programs on the CD that analyze these data; each one illustrates a slightly different approach to programming PCA.

The data for PCA must be stationary, so that the unconditional correlation matrix $\mathbf{X'X}$ can be calculated (§3.1) but the yields in Figure 6.1 are not stationary. Therefore, the input to PCA should be the first differences of the yields. For ease of exposition we shall refer to these first differences as the bond 'returns'.[6] Other transformations, such as taking deviations from a trend, do not generally make financial data stationary (§11.1.5).

The return correlation matrix $\mathbf{X'X}$ for the US data is shown in Table 6.1. It exhibits the typical behaviour of the yield curve: correlations tend to decrease with the spread, and the 1-month rate and long rate have lower correlations with other rates. The trace of this matrix (the sum of the diagonal elements) is the number of variables in the system, that is, 14.

The results of a PCA are shown in Tables 6.2a and 6.2b. From Table 6.2a, the largest eigenvalue is 11.01, so the proportion of total variation that it explains is 11.01/14, or 78.6%. The second largest eigenvalue, 1.632, explains a further $1.632/14 = 11.7\%$ and the third largest eigenvalue (0.4963) explains another 3.5% of the total variation. Thus 93.8% of the total variation in the zero-coupon bond returns is explained by the linear model with just three principal components, that is,

$$X_i = w_{i1}P_1 + w_{i2}P_2 + w_{i3}P_3$$

for the *i*th maturity bond, where X_i is the standardized return (with zero mean and unit variance).

---

[5] Copyright Thomas S. Coleman, Lawrence Fisher, Roger G. Ibbotson, 'U.S Treasury Yield Curves 1926–1992', Ibbotson Associates, Chicago. See Coleman *et al.* (1992).

[6] The returns on zero-coupon bonds are often represented by the process $\partial B/B = r\,dt + t\,dr$, where dr is the difference in rates.

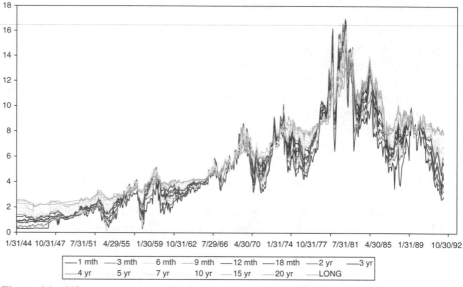

Figure 6.1   US zero-coupon yields from January 1944 to December 1992.

Table 6.1 Correlation matrix for US zero-coupon bonds

	1 mth	3 mth	6 mth	9 mth	12 mth	18 mth	2 yr	3 yr	4 yr	5 yr	7 yr	10 yr	15 yr	long
1 mth	1.00													
3 mth	0.79	1.00												
6 mth	0.73	0.93	1.00											
9 mth	0.69	0.89	0.97	1.00										
12 mth	0.66	0.84	0.93	0.99	1.00									
18 mth	0.63	0.81	0.91	0.97	0.98	1.00								
2 yr	0.60	0.77	0.88	0.94	0.94	0.99	1.00							
3 yr	0.54	0.71	0.82	0.89	0.91	0.96	0.97	1.00						
4 yr	0.49	0.66	0.77	0.85	0.86	0.92	0.93	0.99	1.00					
5 yr	0.48	0.63	0.75	0.82	0.84	0.90	0.92	0.98	0.99	1.00				
7 yr	0.44	0.58	0.69	0.77	0.78	0.85	0.87	0.93	0.94	0.98	1.00			
10 yr	0.39	0.53	0.65	0.72	0.74	0.81	0.83	0.88	0.90	0.94	0.97	1.00		
15 yr	0.31	0.45	0.56	0.62	0.64	0.70	0.72	0.77	0.77	0.81	0.84	0.94	1.00	
long	0.22	0.36	0.43	0.49	0.51	0.55	0.56	0.61	0.63	0.68	0.72	0.75	0.70	1.00

An upward shift in the first principal component therefore induces a roughly parallel shift in the yield curve

The factor weights w_{i1}, w_{i2} and w_{i3} are given in Table 6.2b. Note that the correlations are quite high, and this is reflected in the similarity of the weights on the first principal component w_{i1}, except perhaps for the very short and very long maturities that have lower correlation with the rest of the system. An upward shift in the first principal component therefore induces a roughly parallel shift in the yield curve, as shown in Figure 6.2a. For this reason the first principal component is called the trend component of the yield curve, and in this example 78.6% of the total variation in the yield curve over the sample period can be attributed to (roughly) parallel shifts.

Table 6.2a: Eigenvalues of correlation matrix

Component	Eigenvalue	Cumulative R^2
P_1	11.01	0.786
P_2	1.632	0.903
P_3	0.4963	0.938

Table 6.2b: Eigenvectors of correlation matrix

	P_1	P_2	P_3
1 mth	0.63451	0.57207	0.34291
3 mth	0.80172	0.50173	0.16278
6 mth	0.89228	0.37901	0.033712
9 mth	0.94293	0.27852	−0.04566
12 mth	0.9451	0.21936	−0.08602
18 mth	0.97481	0.11973	−0.12606
2 yr	0.97181	0.061225	−0.14593
3 yr	0.97585	−0.07672	−0.1628
4 yr	0.95465	−0.15533	−0.1684
5 yr	0.95542	−0.22317	−0.10985
7 yr	0.9234	−0.31032	−0.02539
10 yr	0.89628	−0.39553	0.056755
15 yr	0.79469	−0.4439	0.12832
long	0.65674	−0.48628	0.46605

The factor weights on the second principal component, w_{i2}, are monotonically decreasing from 0.57207 on the 1-month rate to −0.48628 on the long rate. Thus an upward movement in the second principal component induces a change in slope of the yield curve, where short maturities move up but long maturities move down, as shown in Figure 6.2b. Therefore, the second principal component is called the 'tilt' component, and in this example 11.7% of the total variation is attributed to changes in slope.

An upward movement in the second principal component induces a change in slope of the yield curve, where short maturities move up but long maturities move down

The factor weights on the third principal component, w_{i3}, are positive for the short rates, but decreasing and becoming negative for the medium-term rates, and then increasing and becoming positive again for the longer maturities. Therefore, the third principal component influences the convexity of the yield curve, and in this example 3.5% of the variation during the data period is due to changes in convexity (Figure 6.2c).

6.2.2 Modelling Multiple Yield Curves with PCA

It is often necessary to model more than one yield curve, for example when risk factors for fixed income portfolios include both government and corporate

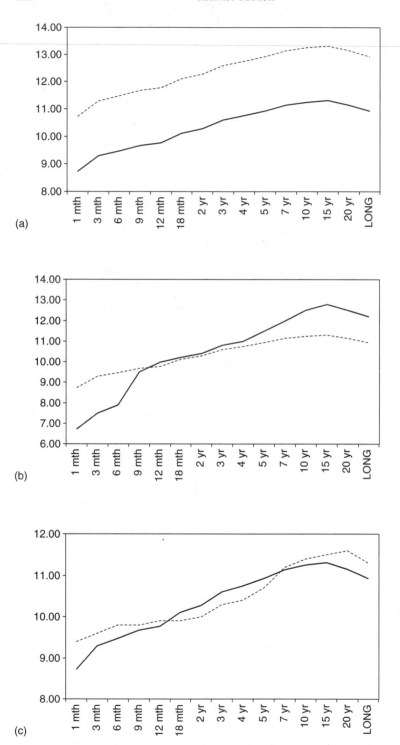

Figure 6.2   Effect of (a) first, (b) second and (c) third principal component.

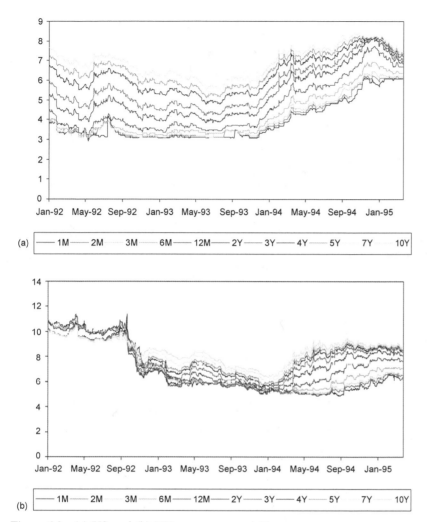

Figure 6.3 (a) US and (b) UK zero-coupon yields.

bond yields. In this case PCA can be a very useful computational tool because it allows a great reduction in dimensions. Moreover, when PCA is applied to more than one yield curve, the natural ordering in the system still gives a meaningful interpretation to the principal components.

To see this, consider an example where four principal components are used to represent a system of 20 yields. Contemporaneous data on both US and UK yields are illustrated in Figure 6.3. The data are daily from 1 January 1992 to 24 March 1995. There are 21 variables in the system: 10 maturities in the US yield curve and 11 maturities in the UK yield curve.

The results of PCA with four principal components are shown in Table 6.3. The largest eigenvalue of the correlation matrix is 14.97, so the first principal

Table 6.3a: Eigenvalues of correlation matrix

Component	Eigenvalue	Cumulative R^2
P_1	14.97137	0.713
P_2	5.168187	0.959
P_3	0.362979	0.976
P_4	0.262027	0.989

Table 6.3b: Eigenvectors of correlation matrix

	P_1	P_2	P_3	P_4
UKM1	0.64582	0.71303	0.14858	0.18207
UKM2	0.6813	0.70169	0.1331	0.14556
UKM3	0.71295	0.67832	0.10494	0.093967
UKM6	0.76527	0.62764	0.089948	0.049379
UKM12	0.83606	0.53436	0.063978	−0.00348
UKY2	0.91328	0.38855	−0.00028	−0.07951
UKY3	0.93443	0.32647	−0.05142	−0.11222
UKY4	0.93975	0.29785	−0.08806	−0.13611
UKY5	0.93674	0.28619	−0.11627	−0.14116
UKY7	0.93368	0.25919	−0.1471	−0.14114
UKY10	0.918	0.18919	−0.08847	−0.15481
USM1	0.84639	−0.47163	0.21786	−0.06231
USM2	0.82833	−0.51836	0.19453	−0.03943
USM3	0.81062	−0.554	0.17545	−0.04109
USM6	0.77976	−0.60844	0.13337	−0.04118
USM12	0.75182	−0.65003	0.071129	−0.01245
USY2	0.79801	−0.59524	−0.01148	0.050071
USY3	0.84423	−0.52032	−0.06705	0.090413
USY5	0.89964	−0.38509	−0.14294	0.14517
USY7	0.92243	−0.29515	−0.18522	0.16065
USY10	0.93392	−0.21314	−0.21979	0.16915

component explains 71.29% of the total variation. The weights on the first principal component in Table 6.3b show that it captures a shift in the same direction, of approximately the same magnitude, for both curves.

The second eigenvalue explains a further 24.7% of the variation in the system. The factor weights in Table 6.3b show that it represents an upwards shift and tilt up at the short end in the UK curve contemporaneous with a downwards shift and tilt down at the short end in the US curve.

The last two principal components capture relatively minor movements due to simultaneous tilts in both curves. Together they explain only an additional 3% of the variation. The third principal component represents a similar tilt in both curves, up at the short maturities and down at the long maturities. The fourth and least significant component represents a tilt up in the short and down in the long of the UK, but down at the short and up in the long in the US.

In the US–UK example the first two principal components already explain nearly 96% of the variation in the system between January 1992 and March 1995. Thus a very useful reduction in dimensionality, from 21 to 2, has been achieved with a high degree of accuracy.

The results shown here are not specific to these countries, or to a system with just two yield curves. In fact it is often necessary to analyse portfolios based on a number of different yield curves, within and/or across countries. In such cases PCA enables dimensions to be very substantially reduced, but to what extent depends very much on the empirical nature of the system. As a very rough guide, note that 2^{n-1} principal components will capture all possible combinations of up/down shifts of n yield curves.[7] Thus if variation is limited to this type of movement, one needs only 4 components for three yield curves, 8 components for four yield curves, and so on. Empirically, of course, some of the more important components are likely to include tilts as well as shifts and the shifts will be of differing magnitudes.

It is often necessary to analyse portfolios based on a number of different yield curves, within and/or across countries. In such cases PCA enables dimensions to be very substantially reduced

6.2.3   Term Structures of Futures Prices

The NYMEX sweet crude oil futures prices from 1 to 12 months for the period from 4 February 1993 to 24 March 1999 are shown in Figure 6.4.[8] This was a relatively quiet period in oil prices. Basis risk for these very liquid contracts is minimal, as all the futures prices are tightly pegged to the spot price. Therefore, it should be expected that a PCA applied to this system would reveal only one major source of information.

As usual, the PCA routine first calculates the return correlation matrix and determines its eigenvalues and eigenvectors. The eigenvalue and eigenvalue analysis shown in Tables 6.4a and 6.4b indicate that indeed there is only one major source of variation: 96% of the variation in these prices over the period could be attributed to roughly parallel shifts in all prices. The tilt component adds only another 3% to the explanation of variation, and there is little need to use more than these two components. Of all the systems examined in this section, the term structure of crude oil futures prices has the strongest correlation. This high correlation is reflected in the factor weights on the first principal component, which are not only very similar but also close to 1.

This high correlation is reflected in the factor weights on the first principal component, which are not only very similar but also close to 1

---

[7] There are 2^n possible combinations of up–down shift in n yield curves, but the principal component that captures a shift up in all curves is the same as the one that captures a shift down in all curves, and so on. Assuming that the up–down shifts are of similar magnitude, only half of these movements ($2^n/2 = 2^{n-1}$) are needed.

[8] Many thanks to Enron for providing these data.

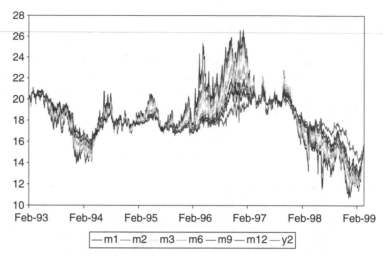

Figure 6.4 NYMEX sweet crude prices.

Table 6.4a: Eigenvalues of correlation matrix

Component	Eigenvalue	Cumulative R^2
P_1	11.5107	0.959
P_2	0.396962	0.992
P_3	0.06899	0.998

Table 6.4b: Eigenvectors of correlation matrix

	P_1	P_2	P_3
M1	0.89609	0.40495	0.18027
M2	0.96522	0.24255	−0.06305
M3	0.98275	0.15984	−0.085
M4	0.99252	0.087091	−0.08012
M5	0.99676	0.026339	−0.06514
M6	0.99783	−0.0209	−0.04637
M7	0.99702	−0.06221	−0.02359
M8	0.99451	−0.09858	0.000183
M9	0.99061	−0.13183	0.020876
M10	0.98567	−0.16123	0.04027
M11	0.97699	−0.19269	0.06493
M12	0.97241	−0.21399	0.075176

6.3 Modelling Volatility Smiles and Skews

Principal component analysis greatly facilitates the construction of appropriate scenarios for movements in the implied volatility smile surface corresponding to movements in the underlying price. Various attempts to model volatility smiles and skew with PCA have almost invariably used daily changes in implied volatilities, by strike or by moneyness, as input. Derman and Kamal (1997) analyse S&P 500 and Nikkei 225 index options where the volatility surface is specified by delta and maturity. Skiadopoulos *et al.* (1998) apply PCA to log differences of implied volatilities for fixed maturity buckets. Fengler *et al.* (2000) employ a common PCA that allows options on equities in the DAX of different maturities to be analysed simultaneously.

There is an important difference between the research just cited and the approach taken in this section. Instead of applying PCA to daily changes in implied volatilities themselves, a PCA is applied to daily changes in the *deviations from at-the-money volatility*. The advantages of this approach are both empirical and theoretical. On the empirical front, time series data on fixed strike or fixed delta volatilities often display very much negative autocorrelation, possibly because markets overreact, so the 'noise' in daily changes of fixed strike volatilities is a problem for PCA. However, the daily variations in fixed strike deviations from ATM volatility, $\Delta(\sigma_K - \sigma_{\text{ATM}})$, are much less noisy than the daily changes in fixed strike (or moneyness) volatilities. Consequently, the application of PCA to fixed strike deviations gives results that are very much more robust than the results cited above.

Instead of applying PCA to daily changes in implied volatilities themselves, a PCA is applied to daily changes in the deviations from at-the-money volatility

On the theoretical level, it was shown in §2.3 that Derman's models of the skew in equity markets can be expressed in the form (2.5), where the particular market regime will be determined by the different behaviour of the ATM volatility specified by equations (2.4). There it was shown that in every market regime, whether it is trending, range-bounded or jumpy, the relationship between fixed strike deviations and the underlying price is always the same. In fact for any maturity *t* there is a *linear* relationship between the deviation of a fixed strike (K) volatility from ATM volatility and the underlying price, given by

$$\sigma_K - \sigma_{\text{ATM}} = -b(K - S). \tag{6.3}$$

For any given maturity τ, the deviations of all fixed strike volatilities from ATM volatility will change by the same amount $b(\tau)$ as the index level changes, as shown in Figure 6.5a. Four strikes are marked on this figure: a low strike K_L, the initial ATM strike K_1, the new ATM strike after the index level moves up K_2, and a high strike K_H. The volatilities at each of these strikes are shown in Figure 6.5b, before and after an assumed unit rise in index level ($\Delta S = 1$). In each of the three market regimes the range of the skew between K_L and K_H, $\sigma_L - \sigma_H$, will be the same after the rise in index level. Thus as the underlying price moves, the fixed strike volatilities will undergo a parallel shift, and the range of the skew will remain constant. The direction of the movement in fixed strike volatilities depends on the relationship between the original ATM volatility σ_1 and the new ATM volatility σ_2.

Recall from §2.3 that the movement in ATM volatility as the underlying price moves depends on the current market regime:

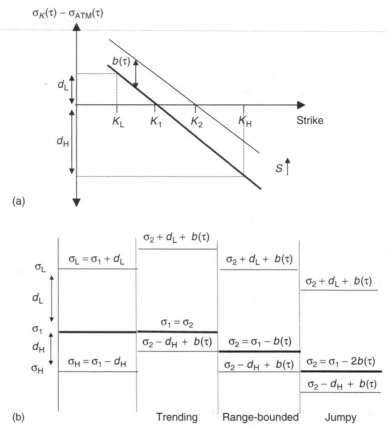

Figure 6.5 Parallel shifts in (a) skew deviations and (b) fixed strike volatilities, as price moves up.

➢ In a range-bounded market $\sigma_2 = \sigma_1 - b$, but fixed strike volatilities have all increased by the same amount b, so a static scenario for the skew by strike should be applied.

➢ When the market is stable and trending, $\sigma_2 = \sigma_1$ and there is an *upward* shift of b in all fixed strike volatilities.

➢ In a jumpy market $\sigma_2 = \sigma_1 - 2b$, so a parallel *downward* shift of b in the skew by strike should be applied.

These observations suggest a method for the empirical validation of the 'sticky' models for volatility regimes in §2.3. The method consists of performing a PCA of $\Delta(\sigma_K - \sigma_{ATM})$ and examining the significance of the second and higher principal components. The sticky models imply that only the first principal component should be significant, but if it is found that the second or higher principal components are significant factors for determining movements in $\Delta(\sigma_K - \sigma_{ATM})$, then the parallel shifts in the skew that are implied by the sticky models will not be justified in practice. Instead, movements in the skew will be

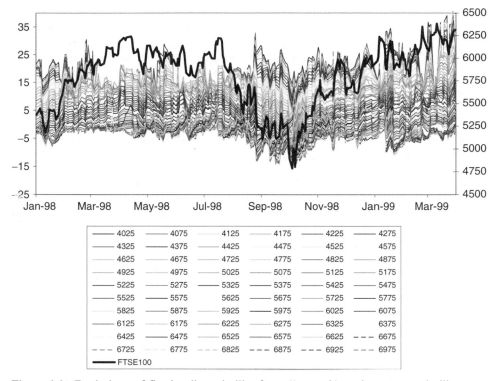

Figure 6.6 Deviations of fixed strike volatility from (1-month) at-the-money volatility.

characterized by a widening or narrowing of the range, depending on the current market conditions.

The principal component model described in this section extends Derman's linear models to allow non-linear movements in fixed strike implied volatilities as the underlying price changes. The data used to describe the model are FTSE 100 index options, but it should be noted that this framework is quite general and has applications to other types of financial assets.

6.3.1 PCA of Deviations from ATM Volatility

Time series data on implied volatilities, such as the 1-month volatilities for the FTSE 100 shown in Figure 2.6, should contain all the information necessary to parameterize the skew. However, there are around 60 different strikes represented there, and their implied volatilities form a correlated, ordered system that is similar to a term structure. It is therefore natural to consider using PCA to identify the uncorrelated sources of information. Both analytic simplicity and computational efficiency will result from a model that is based on only a few key risk factors.

Both analytic simplicity and computational efficiency will result from a model that is based on only a few key risk factors

A PCA of daily changes in the fixed strike volatilities shown in Figure 2.6 may not give very good results, because the data will be rather noisy as mentioned above. However, look at the deviations of the same fixed strike volatilities from the ATM volatility, shown in Figure 6.6. The fixed strike deviations display much less negative autocorrelation and they are even more highly correlated and ordered than the fixed strike volatilities themselves. A strong *positive* correlation with the index is very evident during the whole period. These stylized facts are also revealed in the 3-month FTSE 100 implied volatility data: compare the fixed strike volatilities shown in Figure 6.11a with the fixed strike deviations from ATM volatility shown in Figure 6.11b.

The PCA of fixed strike deviations is based on the model

$$\Delta(\sigma_K - \sigma_{\text{ATM}}) = w_{K1}P_1 + w_{K2}P_2 + w_{K3}P_3, \tag{6.4}$$

where the volatility maturity and the strike of the volatility are both fixed. Time series data on $\Delta(\sigma_K - \sigma_{\text{ATM}})$ are used to estimate the time series of principal components P_1, P_2 and P_3, and the constant factor weights w_{K1}, w_{K2} and w_{K3}.

A PCA for 3-month implied volatility skew deviations based on the data shown in Figure 6.11b gives the output in Table 6.5. From Table 6.5a it is clear that the first principal component only explains 74% of the movement in the volatility surface and that the second principal component is rather important, as it explains an additional 12% of the variation over the period. It is interesting that the factor weights shown in Table 6.5b indicate the standard interpretation of the first three principal components in a term structure, as parallel shift, tilt and convexity components. Note that sparse trading in very out-of-the money options implies that the extreme low strike volatilities show less correlation with the rest of the system, and this is reflected by their lower factor weights on the first component.

Principal component analysis of $\Delta(\sigma_K - \sigma_{\text{ATM}})$ for a fixed maturity has given some excellent results. Alexander (2000b) shows that for fixed maturity volatility skews in the FTSE 100 index option market during most of 1998, 80–90% of the total variation in skew deviations can be explained by just three key risk factors: parallel shifts, tilts and curvature changes. The parallel shift component accounted for around 65–80% of the variation, the tilt component explained a further 5–15%, and the curvature component another 5% or so. The precise figures depend on the maturity of the volatility (1, 2 or 3 months) and the exact period in time that the principal components were measured.

The immediate conclusion must be that linear parameterizations such as (6.3) and the consequent limitation of movements in volatility surfaces to parallel shifts alone is an over-simplification of what is actually happening in the data. The next subsection explains how the principal component representation (6.4) provides a more general framework in which to analyse the dynamics of the skew.

Table 6.5a: Eigenvalues of correlation matrix

Component	Eigenvalue	Cumulative R^2
P_1	13.3574	0.742078
P_2	2.257596	0.8675
P_3	0.691317	0.905906

Table 6.5b: Eigenvectors of correlation matrix

	P_1	P_2	P_3
4225	0.53906	0.74624	0.26712
4325	0.6436	0.7037	0.1862
4425	0.67858	0.58105	0.035155
4525	0.8194	0.48822	−0.03331
4625	0.84751	0.34675	−0.19671
4725	0.86724	0.1287	−0.41161
4825	0.86634	0.017412	−0.43254
4925	0.80957	−0.01649	−0.28777
5025	0.9408	−0.18548	0.068028
5125	0.92639	−0.22766	0.13049
5225	0.92764	−0.21065	0.12154
5325	0.93927	−0.22396	0.14343
5425	0.93046	−0.25167	0.16246
5525	0.90232	−0.20613	0.017523
5625	0.94478	−0.2214	0.073863
5725	0.94202	−0.22928	0.073997
5825	0.93583	−0.22818	0.074602
5925	0.90699	−0.22788	0.068758

6.3.2 The Dynamics of Fixed Strike Volatilities in Different Market Regimes

Which type of skew scenarios should accompany different scenarios on movements in the underlying? In Derman's models the skew always shifts parallel, whatever the underlying market regime, and it is only the reaction of ATM volatility to underlying price movements that depends on the regime, as specified in equations (2.4a)–(2.4c). However, the PCA in §6.3.1 indicates that the simple static or parallel shift scenarios for the volatility skew that are a consequence of these models may not be appropriate.[9]

Which type of skew scenarios should accompany different scenarios on movements in the underlying?

In the model described below the movement in fixed strike volatilities as the underlying moves is determined by the way the principal components move as the underlying moves. It encompasses changes in the tilt and curvature of the volatility skew as well as a parallel shift. Therefore, the range of the skew can

[9] However, if they are appropriate, is the volatility by strike static, so the volatility by moneyness has a parallel shift, or is volatility by moneyness static, which is equivalent to a parallel shift in volatility by strike?

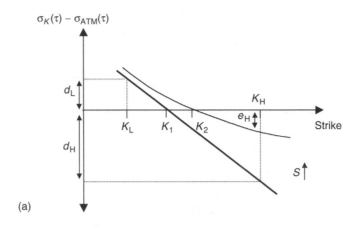

(a)

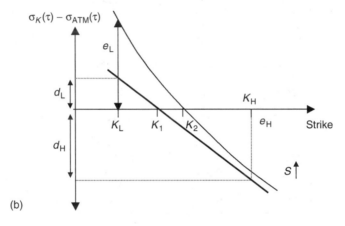

(b)

widen or narrow as the underlying price moves up or down, and change convexity in the process. However, does the movement occur at in-the-money volatilities as much as out-of-the-money volatilities? And how do the magnitudes of these movements depend on the current market regime?

Each component P_i ($i = 1$, 2, or 3) is assumed to have a linear relationship with daily changes ΔS in the underlying. A linear model with a time-varying parameter $\gamma_{i,t}$ is defined for each component:

$$P_{i,t} = \gamma_{i,t}\Delta S + \varepsilon_{i,t}, \tag{6.5}$$

where the ε_i are independent i.i.d. processes. Thus the movement in fixed strike volatilities in response to movements in the underlying will be determined by (a) the factor weights in the principal components representation (6.4) and (b) the gamma coefficients in (6.5).

Figure 6.7 depicts the movement in skew deviations as the index price moves up, according to the signs of γ_2 and γ_3. Note that γ_1 is always assumed to be positive, an assumption that is justified by the empirical analysis below. The

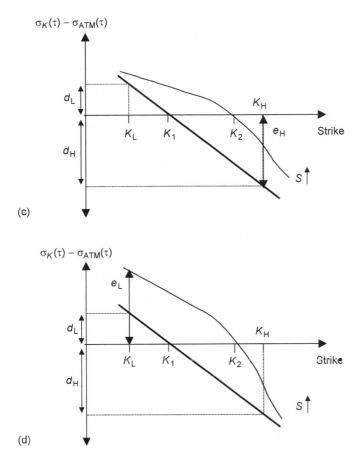

Figure 6.7 Non-parallel shift in skew deviations as price moves up: (a) $\gamma_1 > 0$, $\gamma_2 < 0$, $\gamma_3 > 0$; (b) $\gamma_1 > 0$, $\gamma_2 > 0$, $\gamma_3 > 0$; (c) $\gamma_1 > 0$, $\gamma_2 < 0$, $\gamma_3 < 0$; (d) $\gamma_1 > 0$, $\gamma_2 > 0$, $\gamma_3 < 0$.

coefficient γ_2 determines the tilt of the fixed strike deviations and γ_3 determines the convexity, so the four combinations shown represent stylized movements in the skew deviations.

Later on, estimates of the gamma coefficients will be used to generate empirical sensitivities for fixed strike deviations with respect to the index. However, for the present qualitative analysis, the important observation is that the sign of γ_2 will determine whether the range of the skew narrows or widens when the index moves up. When the range narrows, most of the movement will come from low strike volatilities. However, when the range widens, much of the movement also comes from the high strike volatilities.

To see this, consider the effect on fixed strike deviations from ATM volatility as the index moves up, depicted in Figure 6.7. A result of the upward movement in the underlying is that one of the high strike deviations, at strike

The sign of γ_2 will determine whether the range of the skew narrows or widens when the index moves up. When the range narrows, most of the movement will come from low strike volatilities. However, when the range widens, much of the movement also comes from the high strike volatilities

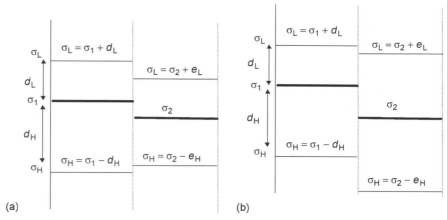

Figure 6.8   Effect on fixed strike volatilities as price moves up: (a) $\gamma_2 < 0$; (b) $\gamma_2 > 0$.

K_2 say, will change from a negative value to a value of zero because the ATM strike has moved from K_1 to K_2. Strikes above K_2 will still have volatilities that are lower than the ATM volatility, strikes between K_1 and K_2 now have volatilities that are above ATM volatility, and strikes below K_1 will still have volatilities above the ATM volatility. For the lowest strikes there will be little change: their volatility deviation from the new ATM volatility is about the same as it was before the movement in the underlying.

When γ_2 is negative, as in Figures 6.7a and 6.7c, the range of the skew will narrow as the index moves up, and the deviation from ATM volatility of high strike options will decrease. On the figures the deviation at the high strike K_H is denoted d_H before the move and e_H after the move, and when γ_2 is negative it is clear that $e_H < d_H$. This translates in Figure 6.8a to a narrowing of the range of the skew as the index moves up (and a widening as the index moves down), with most of the movement coming from low strike volatilities.

When γ_2 is positive, as in Figures 6.7b and 6.7d, the range of the skew will widen as the index moves up, and the deviation from ATM volatility of low strike options will increase. On the figures the deviation at the high strike K_L is denoted d_L before the move and e_L after the move, and when γ_2 is positive it is clear that $e_L > d_L$. This translates in Figure 6.8b to a widening of the range of the skew as the index moves up (and a narrowing as the index moves down), with much the movement coming from high strike volatilities.

Let us now make some estimates of the gamma response coefficients for the principal components of the FTSE 100 skew deviations. The principal components have zero unconditional covariance; however, by (6.5) their conditional covariance is

$$\mathrm{cov}_t(P_{i,t},\ P_{jt}) = \gamma_{i,t}\gamma_{j,t}\sigma_t^2,$$

where σ_t^2 is the conditional variance of the index, $V_t(\Delta S_t)$. The time-varying gamma parameters are estimated using an exponentially weighted moving average model as an approximation to a bivariate GARCH(1, 1).[10] Thus

$$\gamma_{i,t} = \mathrm{cov}_t(P_{i,t}, \Delta S_t)/V_t(\Delta S_t),$$

where the covariance and variance are estimated using an EWMA, as described in §3.2. For the sake of conformity with standard covariance calculations such as those in JP Morgan/Reuter's RiskMetrics (§7.3) the smoothing constant $\lambda = 0.94$ has been used.

EWMA estimates (with $\lambda = 0.94$) of γ_1, γ_2 and γ_3 for each of the 1-, 2- and 3-month maturities have been calculated, and these are shown in Figure 6.9. The first point to note about all the graphs is that the estimate of γ_1 is positive throughout. It is higher and more stable than the estimates of γ_2 and γ_3, and for the 1- and 2-month maturities it is generally declining over the sample period.

For the 2-month maturity the gamma estimates are shown in Figure 6.9b. The index seems to have little effect on the second and third principal components, in fact the estimates of γ_2 and γ_3 are close to zero for almost all the sample period. Therefore, it would be reasonable to apply parallel shift scenarios for fixed strike volatilities of 2-month maturities. In fact it is quite clear in Figure 6.10 that the skew deviations were moving parallel throughout the period, and so the fixed strike volatilities themselves were also moving parallel.

However, the 1- and 3-month volatilities shown in Figures 6.9a and 6.9c show that the estimate of γ_2 is often negative, particularly during the spring of 1998 and the spring of 1999. This is the range-narrowing regime defined above where most of the movement will be coming from the low strike volatilities. However, in the 1-month volatilities there are two notable periods, just before the beginning of the crash and during the market recovery, when the estimate of γ_2 was positive. On 14 July 1998, several days before the FTSE 100 price started to plummet, there was a dramatic increase in γ_2 and decrease in γ_3 so that $\gamma_2 > 0$ and $\gamma_3 < 0$. During this period the range of the 1-month skew will have narrowed, as the index fell. Then between 8 and 12 October 1998, the FTSE 100 jumped up 8% in 2 days' trading, from 4803 to 5190. At the same time γ_2 jumped up and γ_3 jumped down, so that again $\gamma_2 > 0$ and $\gamma_3 < 0$, and the range of the 1-month skew will have widened as the index moved up.

It would be reasonable to apply parallel shift scenarios for fixed strike volatilities of 2-month maturities

The analysis of Figure 6.8b reveals that the narrowing of the range of the skew as the index fell, and the consequent widening again as the market recovered, would have been driven by movements in high strike volatilities. During this unusual period the high strike volatilities did indeed move much more than usual, as was evident in Figure 2.6.

---

[10] This choice allows one to bypass the issue of parameterization of the bivariate GARCH which is a difficult issue in its own right (§4.5.2). It does of course introduce another issue, and that is which smoothing constant should be chosen for the exponentially weighted moving averages.

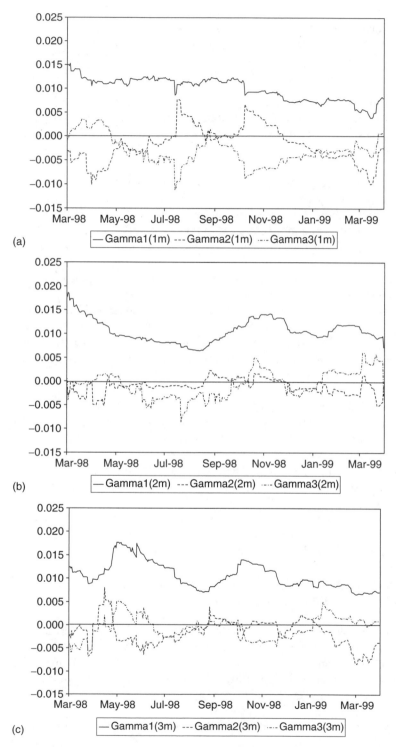

Figure 6.9 Gamma estimates for (a) 1-month, (b) 2-month and (c) 3-month volatilities.

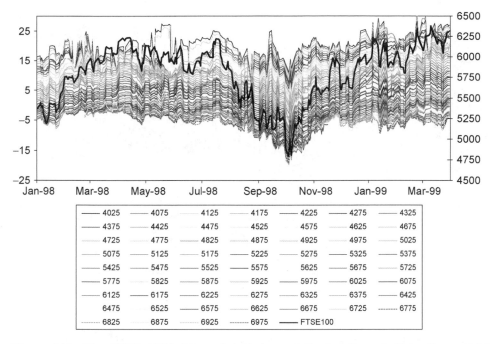

Figure 6.10 The FTSE 100 index and deviations of fixed strike volatilities from ATM volatility (2 months).

The second principal component also plays a role in movements of the 3-month skew, but it is not as important as it is for the 1-month skew. In Figure 6.9c the estimate of γ_2 is negative during the springs of 1998 and 1999. Therefore, we may draw the same conclusions as for the 1-month volatilities, that the range in the skew of 3-month volatilities will generally narrow as the index increases and widen as the index falls, with most of the movement coming from the low volatilities. However, during the jumpy period in the summer of 1998 the estimates of γ_2 and γ_3 were very close to zero. Therefore, during the crash period the movements in 3-month volatilities will have been approximately parallel.

To see whether these observations are valid, look at the 3-month fixed strike volatilities shown in Figure 6.11. Some of the very low strikes have unrealistically high volatilities. In fact the 4025 and 4125 strikes have already been removed from the data set because their movements were quite out of line with the rest. The range narrowing and widening in the skew as the index moves up and down is very noticeable in the spring of 1999. And as predicted, most of the movement is coming from the low strikes. The 3-month fixed strike deviations graph in Figure 6.11b gives a somewhat clearer picture of what is happening during the crash period. The parallel shifts that the principal component model predicts are very evident in this picture.

The range narrowing and widening in the skew as the index moves up and down is very noticeable in the spring of 1999

The principal component model of fixed strike deviations has identified two different market regimes. When index moves are negatively correlated with the

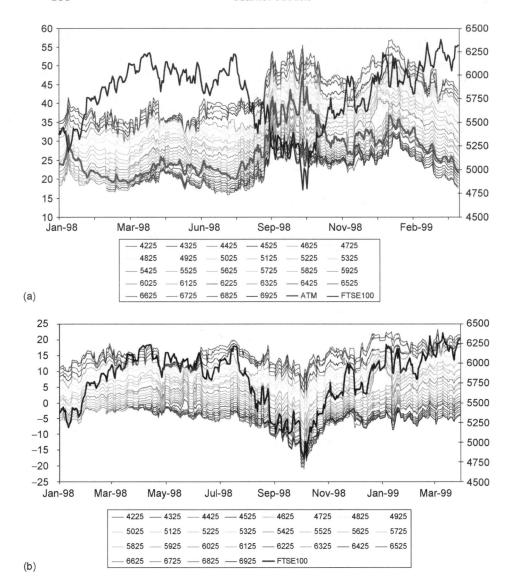

Figure 6.11 Three-month ATM volatility and the FTSE 100 index. (a) Fixed strike volatilities; (b) deviations of fixed strike volatilities from ATM volatility.

second principal component ($\gamma_2 < 0$) the range of the skew will narrow as the index moves up and widen as the index moves down, with most of the movement coming from low strike volatilities and little movement in the high strike volatilities. This regime has been apparent in the FTSE 100 index options during the springs of 1998 and 1999. However, during the 1998 crash the index moves appear to have zero, or even a positive, correlation with the second principal component. In this regime the skew will shift parallel as the index moves ($\gamma_2 = 0$). However, in the short-term volatilities where it seems that γ_2

was positive during the pre- and post-crash periods, the range of the skew actually narrows as the index moves down and widens as the index moves up. Both cases are characterized by movements the volatilities of all strikes, including the high strikes, which in normal circumstances do not move as much as the low strike volatilities.

6.3.3 Parameterization of the Volatility Surface and Quantification of $\partial\sigma/\partial S$

The principal component model of fixed strike implied volatilities has, so far, been based on their deviations from ATM volatility. Thus it is not complete without a model for the behaviour of ATM volatility as the index moves. Following (2.6), we assume for a fixed maturity τ of 1, 2 or 3 months that

$$\Delta\sigma_{ATM} = \alpha + \beta\Delta S + \varepsilon. \qquad (6.6)$$

To give some idea of the orders of magnitudes of α and β, a simple ordinary least squares (OLS) regression over the whole period gives the following estimates (with t-statistics in parentheses):

Maturity (months)	α	β
1	0.044 (0.64)	-0.019 (-22.14)
2	0.036 (0.68)	-0.015 (-23.47)
3	0.032 (0.65)	-0.013 (-21.74)

Though larger than the estimates of β, the estimates of α are very insignificant, so it seems reasonable to assume that α is zero. However, the estimates of β are all highly significant. If we are to capture the dependence of ATM volatility sensitivity on the current market conditions it is, of course, best to estimate a time-varying parameter β_t instead of a constant parameter. A sensible approach, which complements the estimation of the gamma response coefficients for the principal components in (6.5), is to estimate β_t with an EWMA (again with $\lambda = 0.94$). Hence

It is very clear indeed that the sensitivity of ATM volatility moves with the level of the index. It does not jump unless the index jumps

$$\beta_t = \text{cov}_t(\Delta\sigma_{ATM,t}, \Delta S_t)/V_t(\Delta S_t).$$

These estimates are shown in Figure 6.12. As expected, the sensitivity of ATM volatility to changes in the FTSE is greater in 1-month than in 2-month options, which in turn have greater sensitivity than 3-month options. There is a striking pattern in Figure 6.12a, that is verified in Figure 6.12b when the level of the FTSE is superimposed on these sensitivities. It is very clear indeed that the sensitivity of ATM volatility moves with the level of the index. It does not jump unless the index jumps.

In the Derman models presented in §2.3.1, ATM volatility sensitivity jumped between three levels, according to the current market regime. This assumption led to a linear parameterization of the volatility surface:

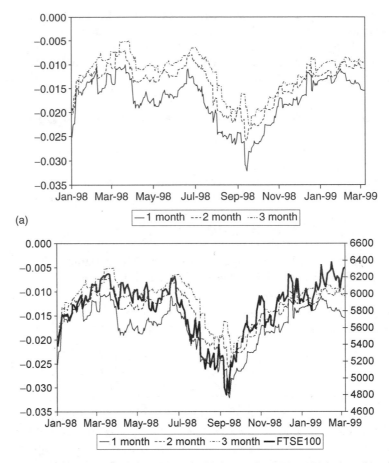

Figure 6.12 (a) ATM volatility sensitivity to the FTSE 100 index; (b) with the level of the index superimposed.

$$\sigma(S, t) = b(t)S + c(t),$$

where the coefficient $b(t)$ jumps between three different levels (0, b and $-b$) as the market moves between different regimes. However Figure 6.12 suggests that the ATM volatility sensitivity changes over time because the level of the index changes over time. It seems more reasonable to suppose, therefore, that

$$\partial\sigma/\partial S = 2a(t)S + b(t),$$

where $a(t) < 0$, and $a(t)$ and $b(t)$ may be calibrated from the estimates of β_t for different maturity options. Now this gives a quadratic parameterization of the volatility surface:

$$\sigma(S, t) = a(t)S^2 + b(t)S + c(t).$$

The finding of time-varying ATM volatility sensitivity that depends on the index level is therefore equivalent to a second-order Taylor approximation to the volatility surface.

The discrete-time framework of PCA also allows one to measure the $\partial \sigma / \partial S$ term in (2.10) for the delta hedging of options with different strikes at any point in time, when the volatility surface is not constant. In fact, combining (6.4), (6.5) and (6.6) yields a model that shows how to change all fixed strike volatilities as the index moves:

$$\Delta \sigma_{K,t} \approx \beta_{K,t} \Delta S_t,$$

where

$$\beta_{K,t} = \beta_t + \Sigma w_{Ki} \gamma_{i,t}. \tag{6.7}$$

The fixed strike volatility sensitivities to the underlying moves can therefore be obtained as a simple sum of the coefficient estimates in the models (6.4), (6.5) and (6.6). Figure 6.13 illustrates the estimates of $\beta_{K,t}$ for 1-month maturity options for strikes K between 4675 and 5875. These lowest and highest strikes are picked out in black and grey. The index sensitivities of all fixed strike volatilities are negative, so they move up as the index falls but by different amounts. During the crash period the sensitivities of all volatilities are greater and the change in the 5875 strike volatility sensitivity is very pronounced at this time. Before the crash it ranged between -0.005 and -0.01, indicating an increase of between 0.5 and 1 basis points for every FTSE point decrease. At

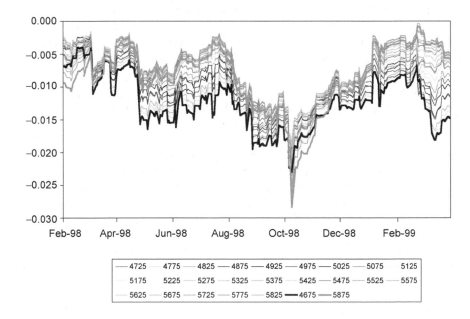

Figure 6.13 Change in 1-month fixed strike volatility per unit increase in index.

the beginning of the crash the 5875 sensitivity increased to about 1.5 basis points, and since the FTSE fell by 1500 points during the crash, that corresponds to a 22.5% increase in 5875 volatility. Then, at the height of the crash between 1 and 9 October, the 5875 sensitivity became increasingly large and negative as the FTSE index reached a low of 4786 on 5 October. On 9 October the 5875 sensitivity was an impressive -0.028, indicating a 2.8 basis point increase in volatility for every point off the FTSE at that time.

The method outlined here explains how to use PCA to calculate the volatility sensitivity to underlying price changes directly, and for options with different strikes

An increase in low strike sensitivities is much less pronounced around the time of the crash. What is interesting about the 4675 volatility sensitivity is that it is often far greater (in absolute terms) than the high strike volatility sensitivities. Therefore, most of the movement will be coming from the low strikes as the range of the skew narrows when the index rises and widens when the index falls. Very approximately the 4675 volatility gains about 1 or 2 basis points for every point fall in the FTSE index during the period, although the sensitivity varies considerably over the period. At the end of the data period it is extraordinarily large, and it can be seen in Figure 6.6 that range narrowing of the skew was very considerable at this time.

6.3.4   Summary

This section has presented a new principal component model of fixed strike volatility deviation from ATM volatility. It has been used to estimate the change that should be made to any given fixed strike volatility per unit change in the underlying, that is $\partial\sigma/\partial S$. This quantity is an important determinant of an option delta when volatility is not constant. Market traders often approximate this sensitivity by $\partial\sigma/\partial K$ but the method outlined here explains how to use PCA to calculate the volatility sensitivity to underlying price changes directly, and for options with different strikes.

Non-parallel movements in the volatility surface are particularly important for short-maturity volatilities

The model also shows how to construct scenarios for the volatility surface that should accompany given moves in the underlying price. A quadratic parameterization of the volatility surface is consistent with the model, and this allows non-parallel movements in the surface as the underlying price moves. Derman's 'sticky' models that were discussed in §2.3 correspond to a local linear approximation for the volatility surface and only allow for parallel shifts. However, the principal component approach that has been developed here shows that non-parallel movements in the volatility surface are particularly important for short-maturity volatilities.

Empirical application of the model to the FTSE 100 index options has revealed two distinct regimes of volatility in equity markets. In the first regime the range of the skew narrows as the index moves up and widens as the index moves down. Most of the movement is in low strike volatilities; high strike volatilities remain relatively static as the underlying moves. The second regime corresponds to a market crash and recovery period, where the range of the skew is quite static and the volatilities of all strikes will shift parallel and in line with the (considerable) changes in the ATM volatility.

During the very jumpy markets before and after the 1998 crash the very short-term volatilities behaved a little differently from the volatilities of 2- and 3-month maturities. The 1-month volatilities actually exhibited a narrowing in the range of the skew as the index fell during the initial period of the crash (mid-July to mid-August). In the recovery period (mid-October to mid-November) the skew range widened as the index moved up. At both times the high strike volatilities were moving more than usual, just like the 2- and 3-month high strike volatilities, but there was less movement in very short-term very low strike volatilities. It was not until the height of the crash that the low strike 1-month volatilities became more responsive to the index, so that the skew shifted parallel, in line with the ATM volatility changes.

Because the model admits non-linear movements in the volatility smile as the underlying moves, it has very general applications. It should be particularly useful in currency option markets, where smiles are non-linear, and a parameterization of the swaption skew would be useful for several interest rate option models.

6.4 Overcoming Data Problems Using PCA

Principal component analysis provides a means of coping with several common data problems. Data may be unavailable, or just difficult and time-consuming to gather on a regular basis. Even when data are available, they could be full of measurement errors, and this will bias parameter estimates (§A.4.2). This section shows how PCA can be used to fill in missing or erroneous data. It also shows how PCA can be used to overcome the difficulty with model specification that is often encountered when data on explanatory variables are highly collinear (§A.4.1).[11]

Section 6.4.1 shows how PCA provides a means of performing regressions on totally uncorrelated variables, so that collinearity problems in regression are minimized. Sometimes, however, collinearity of variables in a system can be an advantage. In §6.4.2 it is shown how PCA can be used to fill in observations on missing data; the method works very well when the missing data are from a reasonably highly correlated system. Otherwise the modeller will have to take some views on the likely correlation of the missing variable within a system.

Some of the models presented in this section will use principal components in time series regression analysis, and the reader should be aware of a tricky statistical issue surrounding this. In order to compute the principal components of a system, one

---

[11] If explanatory variables are highly collinear their *t*-statistics will be depressed, and this can augment the attenuation bias caused by data errors. More details are given in Appendix 4.

The value of a principal component at time $t = 1$ will actually depend on the future values of the input variables. Depending on how the model is used, this may or may not be acceptable

has to use a quantity of data to calculate the correlation matrix of the input variables. Therefore the value of a principal component at time $t = 1$ will actually depend on the future values of the input variables. Depending on how the model is used, this may or may not be acceptable. For example, it would not be acceptable if the model is used to predict the values of another variable at time $t = 1$, because it will be using data from the future.

The bottom line is really whether the model that is built on an historical data set will be able to perform in the same way in real time. If not, the principal components will have to be computed in a time series framework as follows: begin with a data set from the start of the data history that is long enough for the principal component specification to be reasonably robust.[12] Say it runs from $t = 1$ to $t = T$. Perform a PCA on this data set, save the factor weights w_{ij} and then calculate the value of each component at time $T + 1$ as

$$P_m = w_{1m}X_1 + w_{2m}X_2 + \ldots + w_{km}X_k,$$

where the data on the input variables $X_1, X_2, \ldots, X_k$ are taken at time $T + 1$. Then roll the data period one time interval and again do a 'post-sample' computation for the values of the principal components. Repeating in this way, a set of data on all principal components starting at time $T + 1$ may be obtained, where each value of each component depends only on the past and not on the future.

6.4.1   Multicollinearity

When explanatory variables are highly collinear then model parameter estimates and their standard errors will be affected

In Appendix 4 some of the problems with linear regression that are common to factor models, index tracking models and other linear portfolio models are outlined. The choice of explanatory variables in a linear model may pose a difficult problem. What stocks should be selected for a benchmark tracker, or what factors should be chosen in a multi-factor model? Theoretical consider-ations are important in determining this choice, but there is another practical aspect to the problem. When explanatory variables are highly collinear then model parameter estimates and their standard errors will be affected.

PCA is one of the most efficient means of dealing with multicollinearity. Other methods, such as changing the data, excluding one or more collinear variables, or employing a ridge estimator all have their drawbacks (§A.4.1). However, an orthogonalization of the variables using PCA is a simple way to obtain efficient parameter estimates for the original model with nothing more than OLS estimation.

The idea is straightforward. Let $X_1, \ldots, X_k$ be the explanatory variables for the linear model with dependent variable Y. Both Y and the explanatory variables are assumed to be stationary.

---

[12] This will depend, of course, on how highly correlated the system is.

Step 1: Normalize the explanatory variables so that $X_1^*, \ldots, X_k^*$ have mean 0 and variance 1 over the estimation period. Thus $X_i^* = (X_i - \mu_i)/\sigma_i$ where μ_i and σ_i are the mean and standard deviation of X_i for $i = 1, \ldots, k$.

Step 2: Pass $X_1^*, \ldots, X_k^*$ through PCA to obtain all k principal components $P_1, \ldots, P_k$, along with their factor weights matrix.

Step 3: Perform an OLS regression of Y on $P_1, \ldots, P_k$ to obtain the intercept estimate a and slope coefficient estimates $\mathbf{b} = (b_1, \ldots, b_k)'$.

Step 4: Use the factor weights from the PCA to convert these estimates into coefficients for the original model and their covariance matrix estimate.

To see this in mathematical terms, consider the PCA written in matrix form as in (6.1), that is,

$$\mathbf{X}^* = \mathbf{PW}',$$

where $\mathbf{W}$ is the factor weights matrix. Following §A.1.2, the OLS estimated model in step 3 is

$$\mathbf{y} = \mathbf{a} + \mathbf{Pb} + \mathbf{e}, \tag{6.8}$$

where $\mathbf{a} = (a, a, \ldots, a)'$, and by (A.1.10) the vector $\mathbf{b}$ of OLS estimates is

$$\mathbf{b} = (\mathbf{P}'\mathbf{P})^{-1}\mathbf{P}'\mathbf{y} = \mathbf{\Lambda}^{-1}\mathbf{P}'\mathbf{y}$$

because $\mathbf{P}'\mathbf{P} = \mathbf{\Lambda}$, the $k \times k$ diagonal eigenvalue matrix of $\mathbf{X}^{*'}\mathbf{X}^*$. By (A.1.13) their covariance matrix is $\sigma^2\mathbf{\Lambda}^{-1}$. Now the 'orthogonal regression' model is obtained by substituting in $\mathbf{P} = \mathbf{X}^*\mathbf{W}$ to (6.8). That is,

$$\mathbf{y} = \mathbf{a} + \mathbf{X}^*\mathbf{b}^* + \mathbf{e}, \tag{6.9}$$

where the coefficients $\mathbf{b}^* = \mathbf{Wb}$. In terms of the non-standardized original variables, (6.9) becomes

$$\mathbf{y} = \mathbf{c} + \mathbf{Xd} + \mathbf{e}, \tag{6.10}$$

where $\mathbf{d} = (b_1^*/\sigma_1, \ldots, b_k^*/\sigma_k)' = \mathbf{\Sigma}\mathbf{b}^*$, in which $\mathbf{\Sigma}$ is a diagonal matrix with $1/\sigma_i$ on the ith diagonal. Therefore the orthogonal regression slope coefficients can be obtained as a simple transformation of the direct regression slope coefficients $\mathbf{b}$ using the PCA factor weights $\mathbf{W}$ and the diagonal matrix $\mathbf{\Sigma}$:

$$\mathbf{d} = \mathbf{\Sigma}\mathbf{Wb}.$$

The constant in (6.10) is $\mathbf{c} = \mathbf{a} + \mathbf{\mu}$ where $\mathbf{\mu} = (\mu_1, \ldots, \mu_k)'$, the vector of means of the explanatory variables. The t-statistics and other model diagnostics for (6.10) are obtained from the (diagonal) covariance matrix of $\mathbf{d}$. This is simply computed as[13]

---

[13] $V(\mathbf{d}) = \mathbf{\Sigma}\mathbf{W}V(\mathbf{b})\mathbf{W}'\mathbf{\Sigma} = \mathbf{\Sigma}\mathbf{W}\sigma^2\mathbf{\Lambda}^{-1}\mathbf{W}'\mathbf{\Sigma} = \sigma^2\mathbf{\Sigma}\mathbf{\Lambda}^{-1}\mathbf{\Sigma}.$

Table 6.6: Calculation of orthogonal regression coefficients

	Σ		b	W			ΣW			ΣWb
Paribas	0.019969	P_1	0.01043	0.85004	0.84801	0.70791	42.56798	39.96654	45.6539	**0.3984**
SocGen	0.021218	P_2	−0.00008	0.28896	0.29994	−0.70628	14.47043	14.13611	−45.5488	**0.1531**
Danone	0.015506	P_3	−0.00003	0.44038	−0.43694	−0.00538	22.05318	−20.5929	−0.34727	**0.2465**

$$V(\mathbf{d}) = \sigma^2 \Sigma \Lambda^{-1} \Sigma,$$

where σ^2 is the variance of $\mathbf{y}$, and Λ is the diagonal matrix of eigenvalues of $\mathbf{X}^{*\prime}\mathbf{X}^*$.

To summarize the procedure, instead of regressing Y on a set of correlated variables in $\mathbf{X}$, the regression (6.8) is performed on the uncorrelated principal components. The OLS coefficients $\mathbf{b}$ that are estimated on the principal components are simply transformed into coefficient estimates for the original model. In fact $\mathbf{d} = \Sigma\mathbf{W}\mathbf{b}$, where Σ is a diagonal matrix with $1/\sigma_i$ on the diagonal (σ_i is the standard deviation of the ith explanatory variable) and $\mathbf{W}$ is the PCA factor weights matrix.

As an example, consider a regression of the CAC index daily returns on the daily returns to three stocks, Paribas, Société Générale and Danone. An OLS procedure using daily returns gives the following estimates, with t-statistics in parentheses:

$$rcac = 0.0003 + 0.1943 \text{ rparibas} + 0.2135 \text{ rsocgen} + 0.2995 \text{ rdan.} \quad (6.11)$$
$$\;\;\;(1.45)\qquad\;\;(14.71)\qquad\qquad\;(17.21)\qquad\qquad\;(20.55)$$

If this model were to be used for portfolio optimization the capital allocation to each stock as determined by the estimated coefficients would be approximately 27.5% to Paribas, 30% to Société Générale and 42.5% to Danone. However, the stocks were highly correlated during the data period: Paribas and Société Générale had a correlation of 0.615 and Danone had a correlation of almost 0.4 with each of the other two stocks. This high level of collinearity will have affected the coefficient estimates in the OLS regression above.

The same model is estimated by an orthogonal regression, and the results are shown in Table 6.6. This is a much better model because the portfolio weights will not be distorted by multicollinearity. The coefficient estimates $\mathbf{d} = \Sigma\mathbf{W}\mathbf{b}$ in the last column of the table indicate that approximately 50% of the capital should actually be allocated to Paribas, only 19% to Société Générale and 31% to Danone.

6.4.2   Missing Data

This section will show that when data are missing from a variable that lies in a correlated system, it is possible to use PCA to fill in appropriate values for the missing variable from data that are available on the correlated variables. Values for the missing data should be created in a way that reflects the correlation in the system, and PCA is the natural way to do this.

Suppose the new stock has a daily return X_1, and suppose $X_2, \ldots, X_k$ are the daily returns on the correlated stocks.

Step 1: Perform a PCA on X_1 and $X_2, \ldots, X_k$ using only the most recent data (as far back as you can go to include data on X_1) to obtain principal components and factor weights as in (6.2). Choose only the first m principal components for the representation, where $m < k$. The choice of m will depend on how highly correlated the system is.[14] Save the factor weights of the representation of X_1, and denote these factor weights as $w_{11}, \ldots, w_{1m}$.

Values for the missing data should be created in a way that reflects the correlation in the system, and PCA is the natural way to do this

Step 2: Perform another PCA, this time using a long history of data on just $X_2, \ldots, X_k$, and take the same number m of principal components. Call these components $P_1, \ldots, P_m$. They will be time series going from the start of the data set on $X_2, \ldots, X_k$ up to the present.

Step 3: Recreate an artificial data history on X_1 for the same long period, using the factor weights from step 1 and the principal components from step 2, as:

$$X_1^* = w_{11}P_1 + w_{12}P_2 + \ldots + w_{1m}P_m.$$

Step 4. To calibrate the model, decisions about the other variables to include and the size of m are necessary. The real data on X_1 that are available should be compared with the simulated data on X_1^* over the recent period from step 3. The variables $X_2, \ldots, X_k$ and the number of components m will need to be chosen so that there is a reasonably small root mean square error between X_1 and X_1^*.

To illustrate the procedure, suppose that a new stock has been issued in the US banking sector and that daily prices are available from 2 March to 6 October 2000. First choose some related stocks that have a long price history and that are reasonably highly correlated with the new stock. For this illustration I have chosen just seven such stocks, because a PCA of these seven stock returns and the new stock return between 2 March and 6 October 2000 already gives quite good results. In fact four principal components explain about 72% of the variation in the system and the new stock return has the principal component representation:

$$0.85867P_1 + 0.047495P_2 + 0.091244P_3 + 0.35181P_4. \qquad (6.12)$$

A price series for the new stock from the beginning of 1998 was simulated by taking the returns from the seven banking stocks (all have price histories going

---

[14] As a rule of thumb, we need to take enough principal components to explain at least 60–70% of the variation.

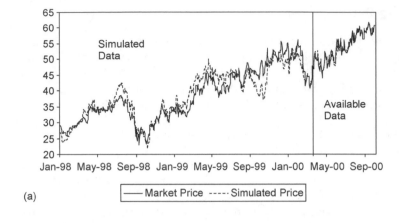

(a)

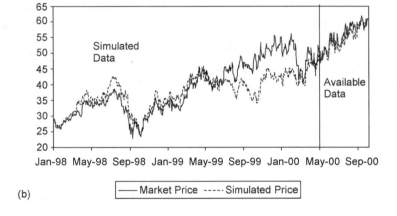

(b)

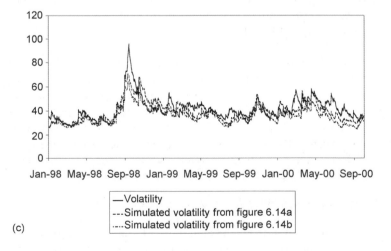

(c)

Figure 6.14 Using PCA to simulate a price history from (a) 150 and (b) 100 recent prices; (c) GARCH(1, 1) volatilities from market prices and simulated prices.

back that far) and performing a PCA of the period from 2 January 1998 to 2 March 2000. The first four principal components are taken and substituted in (6.12) to simulate a return series for the new stock over the same period. The results are illustrated in Figure 6.14a. For the purposes of this illustration I have only pretended that the stock is a new stock, but market prices were actually available.[15] The actual market prices are shown on the figure so that the reader can compare them with the simulated prices.

Note that the returns that are simulated by (6.12) will be standardized, and will need to be multiplied by their standard deviation and added to their mean before transforming into a price series. Which mean and standard deviation should be used? I have found that good results are obtained by taking the standard deviation equal to the in-sample standard deviation of the new stock, but that for the mean it is better to use an average of the in-sample mean of the new stock and the mean of the seven other stock returns during the pre-sample period.

The returns that are simulated by (6.12) will be standardized, and will need to be multiplied by their standard deviation and added to their mean before transforming into a price series. Which mean and standard deviation should be used?

If an astute choice of the related stocks and the number of principal components has been made there should be a good fit between the actual market price of the new stock and the price that is simulated by the representation (6.12). The success of the next stage will depend on a successful calibration here, so it may be necessary to choose different stocks, possibly more stocks, and/or more principal components in the representation (6.12). The RMSE between the actual and simulated returns in this example was 0.0098, which is very low, so the model appears to fit very well.

Figure 6.14b shows that the results of a similar analysis, which only assumes that data on the new stock are available for 100 days, are not quite as good.[16] Finally, Figure 6.14c compares the GARCH(1, 1) volatility estimates that are generated by the actual market prices and both series of simulated market prices. Although the simulated volatilities both underestimate the effect of the September 1998 crash in equity markets, they are otherwise similar to the actual GARCH(1, 1) volatility characteristics of the stock, even as far back as January 1998.

The methodology just described has applications beyond the simulation of missing data. In fact it may be applied to great effect in the construction of a hedging basket for a stock. If a basket of seven related stocks can be used to simulate a historical price series for a stock, then it could also be used to simulate a future price series. This means that a hedging basket can be based on a principal component representation such as (6.12). To illustrate this, return to the example of the banking stocks and consider the example of hedging a banking stock X_1 with seven other banking stocks $X_2, \ldots, X_8$. Suppose that the hedging basket on 6 October 2000 will be based on data since 6 March

A hedging basket can be based on a principal component representation

---

[15] The stock was in fact American Express.

[16] The model was not recalibrated to use different stocks so it is possible that better results would be obtained by choosing different stocks in the first stage.

2000, and so it is defined by (6.12), the principal component representation of X_1 using four components in the eight-variable system. The weight for each stock $X_2, \ldots, X_8$ in the hedging basket is obtained by substituting into (6.12) the representations of P_1, P_2, P_3 and P_4 in terms of these seven stock returns — that is, using (6.1) based on data only for $X_2, \ldots, X_8$. Normally this second PCA will be based on a longer data period. Then rebalancing the hedge is straightforward: all that is necessary is for the weights in the hedging basket to be reset by recalculating the weights in (6.12). For example, if the hedge is to be rebalanced on 31 October, (6.12) should be revised using a PCA of all eight stocks from 31 March 2000 to 31 October 2000.

Another example of the use of PCA to fill in missing data is when a mark-to-market price is required for a portfolio that contains securities from different markets but some of these are closed, either because of a bank holiday or because of time differentials. Or perhaps trading is very thin in some markets, with stale quotes imparting a lack of variability in some returns. Of course, if derivative securities are being traded on an exchange that is currently open, the securities prices may be inferred from the current derivatives price. If this is not possible, however, one can use a principal components representation to infer prices, if their movements are correlated with the movements of the other security prices in the system.

The accuracy of these prices will depend on the strength of the correlation within a system and the number of securities that do have a current price. If the correlation is reasonably high then of course the system can be represented by just a few principal components. And if there are still many securities that do have a current price, these principal components can be updated to their current value using just those securities. Then the current value for the missing prices can be deduced by applying their factor weights to the current principal components. This type of marking-to-market is possible when there is a strong correlation between different market returns and it copes with the problem of market closures.

7

Covariance Matrices

The covariance matrix of a set of k time series $X_1, \ldots, X_k$ is a square, symmetric matrix of the form[1]

$$\mathbf{V} = \begin{pmatrix} V(X_1) & \text{cov}(X_1, X_2) & \ldots & \ldots & \text{cov}(X_1, X_k) \\ \text{cov}(X_1, X_2) & V(X_2) & \ldots & \ldots & \text{cov}(X_2, X_k) \\ \text{cov}(X_1, X_3) & \text{cov}(X_2, X_3) & V(X_3) & \ldots & \text{cov}(X_3, X_k) \\ \ldots & \ldots & \ldots & \ldots & \ldots \\ \text{cov}(X_1, X_k) & \ldots & \ldots & \ldots & V(X_k) \end{pmatrix}$$

In financial analysis the series $X_1, \ldots, X_k$ will be returns (for short holding periods these are often taken to be the first difference in log prices) on the different assets in a portfolio, or on the risk factors of a portfolio. Note that the covariance matrix is a concise and convenient form for the information on all the volatilities and correlation in a system: volatilities and correlations can be obtained through simple operations on the elements of the covariance matrix, as described in Chapter 1.

This chapter begins with the applications of covariance matrices in financial analysis. A covariance matrix lies at the heart of risk management: statistical forecasts of the variances and covariances of asset or risk factor returns are summarized in such a matrix to obtain a forecast of portfolio risk (§7.1). Covariance matrices are also a cornerstone of investment analysis, and §7.2 shows how they are used to diversify investments and obtain minimum risk portfolios, and to generate the efficient frontier for optimizing linear portfolios.

Typically hundreds of risk factors, such as all yield curves, interest rates, equity indices, foreign exchange rates and commodity prices, need to be encompassed by a very large-dimensional covariance matrix. Covariance matrices must always be positive semi-definite, for reasons that are explained in §7.1.3 and it has become quite a challenge to generate large, meaningful, positive semi-definite covariance matrices that are necessary to net the risks across all positions in a firm. Simplifying assumptions may be necessary. For example the RiskMetrics methodology designed by J.P. Morgan uses either simple equally weighted

---

[1] The series should be not only stationary but also jointly stationary, otherwise the covariances will not be stable over time, as explained in §11.4.2.

moving averages, or exponentially weighted moving averages with the same smoothing constant for all volatilities and correlations of returns. There are some limitations with the RiskMetrics methodology; these are discussed in §7.3.

It is easy to implement and will produce matrices that have very desirable characteristics, so I believe that many large banks will eventually adopt this approach

Section 7.4 describes a new method for generating large covariance matrices. It is easy to implement and will produce matrices that have very desirable characteristics (§7.4.5), so I believe that many large banks will eventually adopt this approach. The basic principles of the method are explained in §7.4.1. Then the orthogonal EWMA method is described in §7.4.2; it provides a simple but computationally efficient way to apply EWMA to generate a covariance matrix that will always be positive semi-definite. Moreover, the degree of smoothing on each variable will be determined by its correlation in the system.

The orthogonal approach can also be applied with GARCH models. The flexibility and accuracy of GARCH forecasting techniques place them in a unique position to fulfil many of the needs of back office risk management and front office trading systems, but without a feasible method for computing large covariance matrices using GARCH techniques, this potential will not be realized. Given the insurmountable problems in direct estimation of large GARCH covariance matrices (§4.5.3), but given also the need for mean-reverting covariance forecasts for measuring portfolio risk, the orthogonal GARCH model presented in §7.4.3 is of great significance.

7.1 Applications of Covariance Matrices in Risk Management

The first section of this chapter sets out some fundamental concepts for the measurement of portfolio risk. The exposition centres on the risk models that are used to measure the variance of portfolio returns for a volatility analysis, or the variance of portfolio P&L for value-at-risk analysis. It provides a background for Chapters 8 and 9.

7.1.1 The Variance of a Linear Portfolio

Suppose the return on a linear portfolio[2] can be described as a sum of individual asset returns, say

$$R_P = w_1 R_1 + \ldots + w_k R_n, \tag{7.1}$$

where $\Sigma w_i = 1$. So there are n risky assets in the portfolio, asset i has return R_i and the proportion of capital that is invested in it is w_i. Using the rule for variance of a sum of random variables,[3] the variance of the portfolio, V_P, is

---

[2] A linear portfolio is one whose pay-off function is a linear function of underlying risk factors. Option and bond portfolios are therefore non-linear but cash or simple future positions are linear.

[3] $V(w_1 R_1 + w_2 R_2) = w_1^2 V(R_1) + w_2^2 V(R_2) + 2w_1 w_2 \text{cov}(R_1, R_2)$.

$$V_P = w_1^2 V(R_1) + \ldots + w_k^2 V(R_n) + 2w_1 w_2 \text{cov}(w_1, w_2) + 2w_1 w_3 \text{cov}(w_1, w_3) \quad (7.2)$$
$$+ 2w_1 w_n \text{cov}(w_1, w_n) + \ldots + 2w_{n-1} w_n \text{cov}(w_{n-1}, w_n).$$

It is more convenient to use matrix notation. Denote the portfolio weights by $\mathbf{w} = (w_1, \ldots, w_n)'$ and the asset returns $\mathbf{r} = (R_1, \ldots, R_n)'$, so that (7.1) may be written

$$R_P = \mathbf{w}'\mathbf{r}. \quad (7.1a)$$

Denote the covariance matrix of asset returns by $\mathbf{V_R}$. Then the portfolio variance (7.2) is more succinctly expressed as

$$V_P = \mathbf{w}'\mathbf{V_R}\mathbf{w}. \quad (7.2a)$$

Thus the variance of a linear portfolio is a quadratic form.[4]

If a portfolio has very many assets it may be appropriate to use a factor model to describe its returns by those of a smaller set of risk factors (Chapter 8). For example, a large international equity portfolio may be represented as a weighted sum of equity index returns where the weights correspond to the net portfolio betas with respect to that index (§8.1.1). Alternatively, a multi-factor model may be used that is based on the arbitrage pricing theory (§8.1.2) or on statistical factors using principal component analysis.

The variance of a linear portfolio is a quadratic form

When a factor model is used, let $X_1, \ldots, X_k$ denote returns to the k different risk factors and $\mathbf{B}$ be the $n \times k$ sensitivity matrix, whose (i, j)th element is the sensitivity of the ith asset to the jth risk factor.[5] In this case the portfolio variance due to market risk factors is the quadratic form

$$V_P = \mathbf{w}'\mathbf{B}\mathbf{V_X}\mathbf{B}'\mathbf{w}, \quad (7.3)$$

where $\mathbf{w}$ is the $n \times 1$ vector of portfolio weights and $\mathbf{V_X}$ is the $k \times k$ risk factor covariance matrix (see equation (8.6) in §8.1.2).

So far we have shown how the covariance matrix is used to compute the variance of a portfolio return as a quadratic form; but the variance of the portfolio P&L is also a quadratic form.[6] We can obtain the variance of the portfolio P&L simply by multiplying the portfolio weights vector by the nominal amount invested in the portfolio. This gives the vector $\mathbf{p}$ of nominal amounts invested in each of the assets, and then the variance of portfolio

---

[4] A quadratic form is a scalar quantity (that is, a single number, not a matrix or vector) that can be written as the product of a row vector, a square matrix and the column vector (transpose of the row vector), for example $\mathbf{x}'\mathbf{A}\mathbf{x}$. It is called a quadratic form because every term in the expansion has a square or cross product of elements of $\mathbf{x}$.

[5] For example, the risk factors for international equity portfolios are normally taken to be the relevant equity indices in different countries and the exchange rates.

[6] For example, suppose a portfolio of bonds or loans is represented by a cash flow map $\mathbf{p} = (PV_1, PV_2, \ldots, PV_k)$, where PV_t denotes the present value of the income flow at time t for fixed maturity dates $t = 1, \ldots, k$. Then the variance of the portfolio P&L is $\mathbf{p}'\mathbf{V}\mathbf{p}$, where $\mathbf{V}$ is the $k \times k$ covariance matrix of interest rates at maturity dates $t = 1, \ldots, k$. For more details, see §9.3.2.

P&L is $\mathbf{p}'\mathbf{V_R}\mathbf{p}$ at the individual asset level, or $\mathbf{p}'\mathbf{BV_X}\mathbf{B}'\mathbf{p}$ at the risk factor level.[7] The variance of P&L is the crucial determinant of the portfolio VaR when it is measured using the covariance method (§9.3).

7.1.2 Simulating Correlated Risk Factor Movements in Derivatives Portfolios

Independent Monte Carlo simulation on each of these returns will produce very odd yield curves

Another application of covariance matrices is to generate correlated paths for the underlying risk factors in an options portfolio. As a simple example, consider a portfolio of domestic swaps where the risk factor is an AA zero-coupon yield curve. Suppose that the cash flow map is to k different maturities along this curve, so the risk factor returns are summarized by a vector of returns to zero-coupon AA bonds of k different maturities denoted $\mathbf{r} = (R_1, \ldots, R_k)'$. Independent Monte Carlo simulation on each of these returns will produce very odd yield curves and we need to use the covariance matrix of $\mathbf{r}$, denoted $\mathbf{V}$, to produce simulations that accurately reflect the correlation in the system.

To see how this is done, let $\mathbf{z} = (z_1, \ldots, z_k)'$ be the vector of observations on independent standard normal variates that is simulated by Monte Carlo. Then the covariance matrix $V(\mathbf{z}) = \mathbf{I}$, the identity matrix. Denote by $\mathbf{C}$ the Cholesky decomposition of $\mathbf{V}$. The Cholesky decomposition of $\mathbf{V}$ is a triangular matrix $\mathbf{C}$ such that $\mathbf{V} = \mathbf{CC}'$. Transform $\mathbf{z}$ into $\mathbf{r} = \mathbf{Cz}$. Since $V(\mathbf{r}) = \mathbf{C}V(\mathbf{z})\mathbf{C}' = \mathbf{CIC}' = \mathbf{V}$, the random sample $\mathbf{z}$ has been converted to a set of normal returns $\mathbf{r}$ that reflects the appropriate covariance structure.

Figure 7.1 illustrates a set of 10 simulations on a yield curve. In Figure 7.1a each of the simulations is uncorrelated and in Figure 7.1b each of the simulations is correlated. That is, on each curve in Figure 7.1b the six maturities have been moved in a correlated fashion, rather than independently as in Figure 7.1a. The correlated simulations were achieved by pre-multiplying the simulation vector by the Cholesky decomposition of the covariance matrix of the yield curve, as described above.

Vanilla options will have the underlying price, the implied volatility and the interest rate as risk factors

Most derivative portfolios have many risk factors other than a yield curve. Even vanilla options will have the underlying price, the implied volatility and the interest rate as risk factors, so the simulation of a correlated price path requires specification of a 3×3 covariance matrix for the underlying asset return, the implied volatility and the interest rate. This type of correlated simulation for option risk factors is illustrated in the **Monte Carlo VaR** spreadsheet on the CD.[8] A certain amount of historic data will be required to obtain statistical estimates of the variances of these risk factors, and of the covariance between the underlying asset and the implied volatility (unless the

---

[7] At the risk factor level this is only the P&L variance due to market risk factors. There will be another term for P&L variance due to specific risk factors (§8.1.2 and §9.3.3).

[8] However, it should be noted that the dependency between price changes and volatility changes is highly non-linear, as we have seen in §2.3. Therefore it is not well captured by the linear covariance matrix.

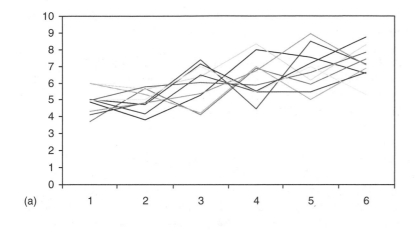

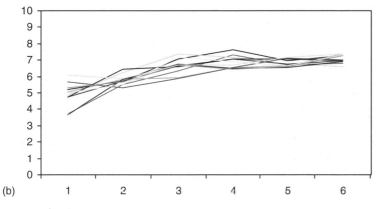

Figure 7.1 Yield curves generated by: (a) independent Monte Carlo; (b) correlated Monte Carlo.

underlying is a bond, it is often assumed that the correlation between the interest rate and the other two risk factors is small, if not zero).

7.1.3 The Need for Positive Semi-definite Covariance Matrices

In §7.1.1 it was shown that the variance of a linear portfolio is a quadratic form $\mathbf{w}'\mathbf{V}\mathbf{w}$, where $\mathbf{w}$ contains the portfolio weights or, in a factor model representation, their net sensitivities. A symmetric matrix $\mathbf{A}$ is *positive semi-definite* if and only if $\mathbf{x}'\mathbf{A}\mathbf{x} \geq 0$ for all non-zero $\mathbf{x}$. Thus if the covariance matrix $\mathbf{V}$ were not positive semi-definite there would be some non-trivial portfolios that have a negative variance. This is not possible, since variance must always be non-negative. Another reason why covariance matrices should be positive definite is that in order to generate correlated scenarios as described above, either the Cholesky or the singular value decomposition of the covariance matrix is usually employed (§7.1.2). The Cholesky decomposition is like the square root of a matrix: it only exists if the matrix is positive definite.[9]

A symmetric matrix $\mathbf{A}$ is positive semi-definite if and only if none of its eigenvalues are negative.[10] Thus tests for positive semi-definiteness are based on calculating the eigenvalues and ensuring that they are all non-negative. It is always prudent to pass a covariance matrix through a simple eigenvalue check for positive semi-definiteness.

The covariance matrix is commonly estimated by $(\mathbf{X'X})/T$, where T is the number of data points and $\mathbf{X}$ is the $T \times k$ matrix of data on the asset (or risk factor) returns. This matrix, which corresponds to using equally weighted averages of squared risk factor returns, will always be positive definite when $T > k$.[11] But if other covariances and variances are used in a covariance matrix, such as EWMA or GARCH estimates, positive semi-definiteness is not always guaranteed (§7.4 and §4.5).

In some cases a covariance matrix that is not positive definite is a blatant case of misspecification.[12] In some cases non-positive semi-definiteness is simply a result of rounding error (this will happen if, for example, linear interpolation is used between risk factors); in that case it may happen that some eigenvalues are negative, but then they will be extremely small. Then it may not alter the original covariance greatly if one simply gives these negative eigenvalues a value of zero. Whenever negative eigenvalues are made zero, it is of course necessary to check the new variance and covariances to ensure that they accurately reflect the volatilities and correlations in the system.

7.1.4 Stress Testing Portfolios Using the Covariance Matrix

Sections 7.1.1 and 7.1.2 explained the role of a covariance matrix for the calculation of portfolio risk. To obtain an 'everyday' or 'normal markets' risk measure for a portfolio it is appropriate to use a covariance matrix that is currently relevant for the risk horizon of the measure. This covariance matrix will often be a forecast of variances and covariances that are obtained using the statistical methods described in Chapter 3 or 4. But in addition to an 'everyday' risk measure, risk management will require estimates of the portfolio risk under extreme market conditions. A 'stress' covariance matrix is applied in the

---

[9] In fact if $\mathbf{V}$ has eigenvalues $\lambda_1, \ldots, \lambda_k$ and $\mathbf{V} = \mathbf{M\Lambda M'}$, where $\mathbf{M}$ is the matrix of eigenvectors and $\mathbf{\Lambda}$ is the diagonal matrix of eigenvalues, then $\mathbf{C} = \mathbf{M\Lambda}^{1/2}$, where $\mathbf{\Lambda}^{1/2}$ is the diagonal matrix with the square roots of the eigenvalues along the diagonal. If $\mathbf{V}$ is not positive semi-definite some of these eigenvalues will be negative, so $\mathbf{C}$ does not exist. If $\mathbf{V}$ is not positive definite because some eigenvalues are zero, then $\mathbf{C}$ is not defined uniquely.

[10] This can be seen by writing $\mathbf{x'Ax} = \mathbf{u'\Lambda u}$, where $\mathbf{\Lambda}$ is the diagonal matrix of eigenvalues of $\mathbf{A}$.

[11] A matrix of the form $\mathbf{A'A}$ is always positive definite, since $\mathbf{x'A'Ax}$ is the sum of the squares of the elements of $\mathbf{Ax}$, so it will always be non-negative for non-zero $\mathbf{x}$.

[12] Even if the result is positive semi-definite, some methods of estimating the covariance matrix may still be quite ridiculous.

risk model, keeping the other parameters such as the portfolio weights and the estimates of pricing model parameters constant. These are the 'stress tests' that are explained in more detail in §9.6.3.

In linear portfolios a stress test only requires the substitution of a stress covariance matrix in place of the current covariance matrix in the quadratic form for portfolio risk (§7.1.1). This will give an estimate of portfolio volatility, or portfolio VaR, in the extreme market circumstances that are captured by the covariance matrix. However, this analysis rests on some strong distributional assumptions and the standard normality assumption for VaR models becomes even more difficult to justify when the focus is on the very extreme returns.

Standard normality assumption for VaR models becomes even more difficult to justify when the focus is on the very extreme returns

In options portfolios a stress covariance matrix may be used to generate correlated movements in the underlying risk factors in Monte Carlo simulations. But the stress test will also require scenarios for exceptional movements in the underlying asset price movements and the implied volatility movements; these scenarios must be consistent with the covariance matrix used in the Monte Carlo simulations. For example, if the covariance matrix has a negative correlation between price and volatility, then only consider scenarios where the smile shifts in the opposite direction to the price (§2.3.4, §6.3 and §9.6.2).

Risk management should have a 'library' of stress covariance matrices containing covariance matrices that have actually been experienced historically as well as a set of covariance matrices that reflect extreme scenarios for volatility and correlation. The historical library might contain the covariance matrix for equity portfolios that pertained on Black Monday, or during the Asian crisis in 1998, and so forth. The library for extreme scenarios for volatility requires covariance matrices that are perturbations of the current covariance matrix, artificially making certain volatilities very large. Whatever the values used for volatilities, the stress covariance matrix will always remain positive semi-definite.[13]

Correlation stress testing is not as straightforward as volatility stress testing. It is not always clear which values for correlation will produce extreme scenarios. The reader can verify this using the **stress testing** functions in the VaR spreadsheets on the CD. Correlations could be set to zero, to unity, to minus unity or to some other values; it depends on the construction of the portfolio (§7.2.2). Also note that the perturbed covariance matrices for correlation stress testing may not be positive semi-definite; they will need to be checked for this, as explained in §7.1.3.

Perturbed covariance matrices for correlation stress testing may not be positive semi-definite

---

[13] To see this, write $V = DCD$, where C is the correlation matrix and D is the diagonal matrix with standard deviations along the diagonal. It follows that V is positive semi-definite if and only if C is positive semi-definite, whatever volatilities are used in D (as long as they are positive).

7.2 Applications of Covariance Matrices in Investment Analysis

The efficient allocation of sparse resources is the fundamental problem of microeconomics. Therefore, it is not surprising that this section draws on many concepts, such as utility functions and optimization, that will be familiar to readers with an economics background. The exposition will focus on the mean–variance analysis that was introduced by Markovitz (1959) and has since formed the basis of the portfolio theory and investment analysis developed by Sharpe (1970) and others.

The long-term capital allocation problem should be viewed in terms of risk-adjusted returns

Senior managers make capital allocation decisions that require comparison of the performance of different desks throughout the organization. Simple VaR figures are based on risk alone and are only appropriate for short risk horizons. But the long-term capital allocation problem should be viewed in terms of risk-adjusted returns. The choice becomes one of selecting allocations to different parts of the organization to minimize risk while maximizing returns, and while also accounting for the preferences of senior managers.

Global asset management can be regarded as a two-stage process: first select the optimal weights to be assigned to country indices; and then allocate funds optimally to each country. Probably the first stage will be the most important, but there will also be constraints. For example, allocations may need to be restricted within a certain range, so inequality constraints such as 'no more than 10% of the fund invested in Japan', have to be imposed.

The mathematical concepts that are introduced in the context of asset allocation may also be applied to other financial agents that face allocation decisions

The reader should bear in mind that the mathematical concepts that are introduced in the context of asset allocation may also be applied to other problems in the efficient allocation of sparse resources. Throughout the text the opportunity set is referred to in terms of portfolios of assets, and the decision-makers are called 'investors' or 'asset managers'. But exactly the same analysis can apply to other financial agents that face allocation decisions. For example, a senior manager in an investment bank faces the two-stage decision problem: first select the optimal allocations to global product lines; and then assign weights optimally at the desk level. The performance of a trader, just like the performance of a portfolio or of a product line, might be compared in terms of risk-adjusted returns (§7.2.3). If risk managers base trading limits on the risk *and* returns from different traders, they face an allocation problem that can be viewed from the same perspective. Trading limits cannot be negative, which is the same in mathematical terms as the constraint that no short sales are allowed.

In §7.2.4 it is shown how a portfolio manager's attitude to risk will influence his choice of optimal portfolio. Similarly, the risk aversion of a manager will determine the trading limits that are optimal for his particular utility, and his choice of allocation to global product lines. Mathematically speaking, these problems are all equivalent.

This section examines the role of covariance matrices in the construction of optimal portfolios. Section 7.2.1 solves the problem of how to construct minimum risk portfolios and gives empirical examples of the application of the solution. Then in §7.2.2 the trade-off between risk and return is discussed in the context of efficient frontier analysis, both with and without short sales. The relationship between correlation and portfolio diversification is analyzed in some detail. In §7.2.3 capital allocation decisions are framed in terms of risk-adjusted performance measures. Utility theory is introduced in §7.2.4, and it is shown that the problem of maximizing expected utility of an investment cannot usually be reduced to the problem of maximizing a function of the mean and the variance of returns. One of the reasons why exponential utility functions are commonly used, despite the fact that they are limited by their constant absolute risk-aversion characteristics, is that they allow utility maximization to be viewed in a mean–variance perspective.

One of the reasons why exponential utility functions are used is that they allow utility maximization to be viewed in a mean–variance perspective

The final part of this section examines efficient portfolios in practice. There is a fundamental problem with the use of return data in mean–variance analysis. The long-run trends and any common trends in the prices will have been taken out of the data already before they are used for analysis. Return data have very short memory and it is very difficult to use them for anything other than short-term analysis. If the short-term volatilities and correlations that are generated by an EWMA model or a GARCH model are used to construct the efficient frontier, it will change considerably from day to day. In §7.2.5 the problems presented by the use of different types of covariance matrices are discussed, and practical examples are given.

7.2.1 Minimum Variance Portfolios

Assume that portfolio allocation decisions are made only on the basis of risk characteristics and that the standard deviation of portfolio returns is taken to be the appropriate measure of risk. If there are n risky assets in the portfolio having weights $\mathbf{w} = (w_1, \ldots, w_n)'$ and if the covariance matrix of asset returns is $\mathbf{V}_R$ then the portfolio variance is $\mathbf{w}'\mathbf{V}_R\mathbf{w}$, as in (7.2a). In larger linear portfolios which are best described by factor models, the portfolio variance is derived in §8.1.2. It is measured using the $k \times k$ covariance matrix of risk factor returns $\mathbf{V}_X$, the $n \times k$ matrix of the asset sensitivities to the different risk factors $\mathbf{B}$ and the $n \times n$ specific risk covariance matrix $\mathbf{V}_\varepsilon$. Whether portfolios are represented at the asset or the risk factor level, the minimum variance portfolio is the solution to a simple optimization problem, viz.

$$\min_{\mathbf{w}} \mathbf{w}'\mathbf{V}\mathbf{w} \quad \text{such that} \quad \Sigma w_i = 1, \tag{7.4}$$

where

$$\mathbf{V} = \begin{cases} \mathbf{V}_R & \text{at the asset level,} \\ \mathbf{B}\mathbf{V}_X\mathbf{B}' + \mathbf{V}_\varepsilon & \text{at the risk factor level.} \end{cases}$$

If we assume that weights can be negative or zero then (7.4) has a straight-forward solution for the optimal weights $\mathbf{w}^* = (w_1^*, \ldots, w_n^*)'$ of the minimum variance portfolio. The solution is given by

$$w_i^* = \psi_i / \Sigma \psi_i, \tag{7.5}$$

where ψ_i is the sum of the elements in the ith column of $\mathbf{V}^{-1}$, and $\Sigma \psi_i$ is the sum of all the elements of $\mathbf{V}^{-1}$. The variance of the global minimum variance portfolio, V^*, is then $1/\Sigma \psi_i$.

To illustrate the method, consider a portfolio of the following US stocks: American International, American Express, Boeing, Citigroup, General Electric, Coca-Cola and Merrill Lynch. Suppose that the minimum variance portfolio of these stocks is computed using long-term equally weighted average estimates of each element in $\mathbf{V_R}$, the covariance matrix of the returns to these stocks (§3.1). These estimates, and so also the minimum variance portfolio weights, will depend on the sample period chosen, and in Table 7.1 the results of applying (7.5) are given for three different samples. All three samples are daily data up to 6 October 2000, but they start at the beginning of January 1997, 1998 and 1999, respectively.

Table 7.1a: Minimum variance portfolio weights (%)

	Since		
Stock	Jan 1997	Jan 1998	Jan 1999
American Int'l	1.55	−3.90	−2.70
American Express	21.14	16.63	15.00
Boeing	22.13	22.70	25.85
Citigroup	0.68	5.69	7.50
General Electric	31.61	34.31	28.75
Coca-Cola	25.61	26.30	22.87
Merrill Lynch	−2.72	−1.72	2.74

Table 7.1b: Volatility estimates of stocks and the minimum variance portfolio (%)

	Since		
Stock	Jan. 1997	Jan. 1998	Jan. 1999
American Int'l	33.43	35.86	35.56
American Express	39.00	41.71	41.00
Boeing	37.85	39.38	37.19
Citigroup	42.20	43.46	39.13
General Electric	29.93	30.79	31.91
Coca-Cola	33.32	34.87	36.95
Merrill Lynch	48.79	52.02	49.61
Minimum Variance Portfolio	**23.53**	**23.54**	**22.25**

The weights in the minimum variance portfolios in Table 7.1a change relatively little because long-term equally weighted averages are used to compute the covariance matrix. Table 7.1b shows that a considerable risk reduction is obtained with this method. But suppose one requires the minimum variance portfolio to respond more rapidly to changes in market conditions, aiming at a greater reduction in risk through more frequent rebalancing. In this case it is possible to use GARCH or EWMA estimates of the variances and covariances in $\mathbf{V}_R$ (§7.3 and §7.4).

Figure 7.2a shows the weights that should be allocated to a portfolio of just three US stocks, to minimize the variance when daily estimates of $\mathbf{V}_R$ are obtained using EWMAs with $\lambda = 0.94$. They change considerably during the data period, particularly in July 1999 when most US stocks were very volatile. This type of reaction to market conditions is impossible to capture with long-term equally weighted averages. Figure 7.2b shows that American Express was particularly volatile and so it is not surprising that the minimum variance portfolio weight allocated to American Express is much smaller at this time. Around July 1999 the minimum variance portfolio had a volatility of between 30% and 40%, much higher than during other periods; the rest of the time it was possible to find a portfolio of just these three stocks that had a volatility of between 10% and 20%.[14]

This type of reaction to market conditions is impossible to capture with long-term equally weighted averages

7.2.2 The Relationship between Risk and Return

The unconstrained problem (7.4) ignores the portfolio return characteristics. Rather than always seeking to minimize risk, the view may be taken that more risk is perfectly acceptable if it is accompanied by higher returns. In fact managers are in danger of under-utilizing resources if insufficient capital is allocated to high-risk, high-return activities.

The portfolio return is $\mathbf{w}'\mathbf{r}$, where $\mathbf{r} = (R_1, \ldots, R_n)'$ is the vector of asset returns, or, for large portfolios that are represented by a risk factor model, $\mathbf{r} = \mathbf{Bx} + \boldsymbol{\varepsilon}$ where $\mathbf{x}$ is the $k \times 1$ vector of risk factor returns, $\mathbf{B} = (\beta_{ij})$ is the $n \times k$ matrix of factor sensitivities and $\boldsymbol{\varepsilon}$ is the $n \times 1$ vector of specific returns (an alternative matrix form will be given in §8.1.2). The capital allocation problem of finding minimum variance portfolios having a given minimum level of return μ becomes:

Managers are in danger of under-utilizing resources if insufficient capital is allocated to high-risk, high-return activities.

$$\min_{\mathbf{w}} \mathbf{w}'\mathbf{V}\mathbf{w} \quad \text{such that} \quad \Sigma w_i = 1 \text{ and } \mathbf{w}'\mathbf{r} \geqslant \mu, \qquad (7.6)$$

where $\mathbf{V}$ is defined in (7.4). In this case the optimal weights $\mathbf{w}^\dagger = (w_1^\dagger, \ldots, w_n^\dagger)'$ are given by

---

[14] One would not normally wish to rebalance daily to maintain the absolute minimum variance portfolio at all times. Usually one sets rebalancing bounds and uses the daily chart analysis such as Figure 7.2 to monitor when the bounds have been exceeded.

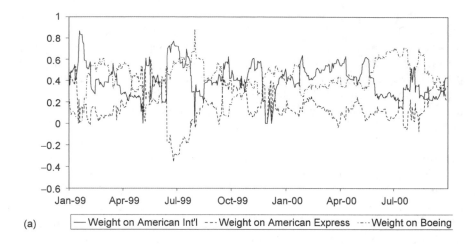

(a)

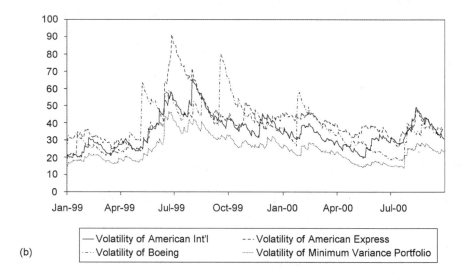

(b)

Figure 7.2 (a) Minimum variance portfolio weights; (b) volatility of minimum variance portfolio compared to individual stocks.

$$w_i^\dagger = ((a\psi_i - b\xi_i) + \mu(V^*\xi_i - b\psi_i))/(V^*b - a^2), \qquad (7.7)$$

where V^* is the variance of the global minimum variance portfolio, ψ_i is the sum of the elements in the ith column of $\mathbf{V}^{-1}$, ξ_i is the returns-weighted sum of the ith column of $\mathbf{V}^{-1}$, $a = \psi'\mathbf{r}$ and $b = \mathbf{r}'\mathbf{V}^{-1}\mathbf{r}$.

Figure 7.3a shows a stylized plot of portfolio returns $\mathbf{w}'\mathbf{r}$ against portfolio risk $(\mathbf{w}'\mathbf{V}\mathbf{w})^{1/2}$ for all possible portfolio allocations $\mathbf{w}$ among n risky assets with returns vector $\mathbf{r}$ and covariance matrix $\mathbf{V}$. This is called the *opportunity set*. It is the convex hull of the points in risk–return space defined by the n risky assets.

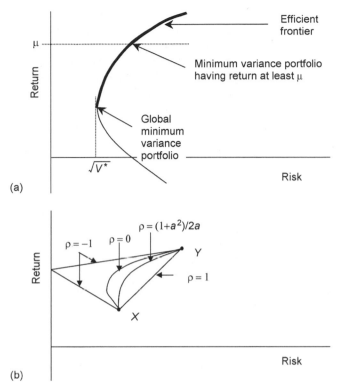

Figure 7.3. (a) Efficient frontier and minimum variance portfolios; (b) efficient frontier with no short sales.

In general, optimal capital allocations will be to portfolios that lie on the *efficient frontier* (illustrated by the thick line in Figure 7.3a) where it is not possible to adjust allocations to gain higher return for the same level of risk, or less risk for the same level of return. The efficient frontier will be a concave curve, the upper boundary of the opportunity set from the minimum variance portfolio. Also marked on the figure are the global minimum variance portfolio, and the minimum variance portfolio having a given minimum level of return μ.

If no short sales are allowed the analytic solutions given above to the global minimum variance problem (7.4) and to the constrained minimum variance problem (7.6) are no longer valid, since the additional constraints $w_i \geqslant 0$ must be imposed. Without short sales the opportunity set cannot extend infinitely along the risk axis. In fact the efficient frontier is the envelope of all portfolios lying between the global minimum variance portfolio and the maximum return portfolio.

The efficient frontier is the envelope of all portfolios lying between the global minimum variance portfolio and the maximum return portfolio

The concavity of the boundary of the opportunity set between two assets (or portfolios) X and Y depends on their correlation, becoming more concave as correlation decreases, as illustrated in Figure 7.3b. Note that when X and Y are perfectly correlated the efficient frontier between them is a straight line. Since their returns are essentially the same, the majority of investors would not diversify. As their correlation decreases there is more incentive to reduce risk by diversification. To see this, consider (7.4) as the problem of choosing a proportion p for a portfolio of just two assets, with p invested in X and $1 - p$ invested in Y, add the constraint $0 \leqslant p \leqslant 1$ and assume without loss of generality that Y is more variable than X. The portfolio variance is

$$V = p^2\sigma_x^2 + (1 - p)^2\sigma_y^2 + 2p(1 - p)\rho\sigma_x\sigma_y. \tag{7.8}$$

Differentiating with respect to p and setting to zero gives the unconstrained optimal value for p as

$$p^* = (\sigma_y^2 - \rho\sigma_x\sigma_y)/(\sigma_x^2 + \sigma_y^2 - 2\rho\sigma_x\sigma_y).$$

The denominator is always positive, being the variance of the portfolio $X - Y$, and the assumption that $\sigma_y/\sigma_x > 1$ means that the numerator must also be positive. In fact one can put $\sigma_y = \sigma$ and $\sigma_x = a\,\sigma$ into (7.8), where $0 < a < 1$ is the relative volatility of X with respect to Y. Then

$$p^* = (1 - a\rho)/(1 + a^2 - 2a\rho),$$

and substituting this into (7.7) gives the variance V^* of the minimum variance portfolio as

$$V^* = (1 - \rho^2)a^2\sigma^2/(1 + a^2 - 2a\rho).$$

As correlation decreases there is more incentive to diversify

Note that this is less than $a^2\sigma^2$, the variance of X, if and only if $1 + a^2 - 2a\rho > 0$, that is, when the correlation is less than $(1 + a^2)/2a$. So when $\rho < (1 + a^2)/2a$ the optimal portfolio has a variance reduction as shown in Figure 7.3b. For example, if $\rho = 0$ then $p^* = 1/(1 + a^2)$ and the minimum variance portfolio has variance $V^* = a^2\sigma^2/(1 + a^2)$ which is less than the variance of X. If $\rho = -1$ then $p^* = 1/(1 + a)$ and $V^* = 0$. But if $\rho \geqslant (1 + a^2)/2a$ then $p^* = 1$ and X is the minimum variance portfolio.

The analysis so far has been simplified by the assumption that no risk-free asset exists. Many other possibilities are introduced if there is a risk-free asset with return R_f and unlimited lending and borrowing at this rate. In Figure 7.4, suppose an investor forms a new portfolio Y by placing a fraction w of funds in an arbitrarily chosen portfolio Q and a fraction $1 - w$ in the riskless asset, where w can be greater than 1. The expected return on Y is given by the line between Q and R_f at a point that is determined by w:

$$R_y = wR_q + (1 - w)R_f. \tag{7.9}$$

The variance of the new portfolio Y is

$$\sigma_y^2 = w^2\sigma_q^2 + (1 - w)^2\sigma_f^2 + 2w(1 - w)\sigma_{qf} = w^2\sigma_q^2,$$

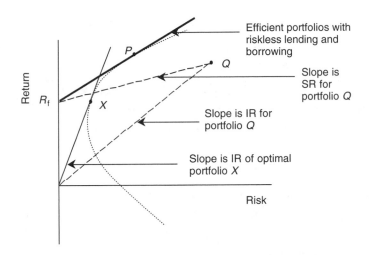

Figure 7.4 Risk-adjusted performance measures.

assuming the risk-free rate has zero variance. So $w = \sigma_y/\sigma_q$ and the line (7.9) becomes

$$R_y = R_f + ((R_q - R_f)/\sigma_q)\sigma_y. \qquad (7.10)$$

This is the equation of a line through Q with slope $((R_q - R_f)/\sigma_q)$ that cuts the returns axis at R_f, shown in Figure 7.4.[15] Efficient portfolios will lie along the thick line in Figure 7.4. They are all combinations of riskless lending or borrowing with the efficient portfolio P. Portfolios to the left of P are combinations of lending at rate R_f and portfolio P. Portfolios to the right are combinations of borrowing at rate R_f and portfolio P. The actual portfolio that is chosen along this line depends on the risk attitude of the investor: the less risk-averse, the more he will borrow at the riskless rate to achieve both higher return and higher risk.

7.2.3 Capital Allocation and Risk-Adjusted Performance Measures

Efficient capital allocation needs to consider both risk and return characteristics of portfolios. If one only considers return then too much capital would be allocated to a high-return but high-risk activity, and if one only considers the risk then too little capital would be allocated to the same activity. By taking the ratio of return to risk in a risk-adjusted performance measure (RAPM) it is possible to compare activities with different risk–return characteristics.

Figure 7.4 also illustrates two of the standard RAPMs for investment analysis. If there is unlimited riskless lending and borrowing at a risk-free rate R_f, the

---

[15] It is worthwhile noting that (7.9) forms the basis of the Sharpe–Lintner capital asset pricing model described in §8.1.1. Without an error process the portfolio will be perfectly correlated with the market, so the CAPM (8.1) becomes $y = \alpha + \beta X$, where α is the risk-free rate of return R_f, X is the excess return of the market over the risk-free rate and the portfolio beta is just the relative volatility σ_y/σ_X.

appropriate RAPM to use is the *Sharpe ratio* (SR) given by the slope of the line (7.9):

$$SR = (R_q - R_f)/\sigma_q.$$

If risk-free returns are assumed to be zero the *information ratio* (IR) is the appropriate RAPM, given by the slope of the line from the origin to the point (μ_x, σ_x) in risk–return space that represents the optimal portfolio X, that is,

$$IR = \mu_x/\sigma_x.$$

In either case the efficient utilization of capital should allocate funds to activities or investments with the highest RAPM.

7.2.4 Modelling Attitudes to Risk

Which is regarded as 'best' of all efficient portfolios will depend on the risk attitude of the investor. If an investor is very averse to taking risks, he is more likely to choose a low-return, low-risk portfolio over a high-risk, high-return portfolio. To formulate the problem in a mathematical framework, and hopefully find an analytic solution, it is convenient if the preferences of an investor are represented by a utility function.[16] In an uncertain environment risk preferences can still be expressed rationally if decision-makers accept a few elementary rules of behaviour which, to most, will appear natural. The three elementary rules are as follows:

➤ *Transitive preferences*: If an investor says he prefers outcome A to outcome B and he also prefers B to C, then he should prefer A to C.
➤ *Independence*: If the investor is indifferent between outcomes A and B, then he is also indifferent between the two gambles $\{A$ with probability p and C with probability $1 - p\}$ and $\{B$ with probability p and C with probability $1 - p\}$ for any outcome C.
➤ *Certainty equivalence*: For any gamble there is a *certainty-equivalent* value such that the investor is indifferent between the gamble and the certainty equivalent.

These three rules are sufficient to prove the existence of a *utility function* $U(W)$ that assigns a real number to any monetary amount W and such that if an investor has a choice between two risk investments he should always prefer the investment that has maximum expected utility. The *expected utility* is defined by

$$EU(P) = \Sigma p_i U(W_i),$$

---

[16] A utility function is a function $U: \Omega \to \Re$ from the space of all possible outcomes Ω to the real numbers $\Re$. Thus a utility function assigns a real number to every possible outcome, and outcomes may be ranked in order of preference by the size of their utility.

where $W_1, \ldots, W_n$ are the possible outcomes in terms of end of period wealth resulting from an investment P, and these occur with probabilities $p_1, \ldots, p_n$.

Note that the expectation operator is a linear operator, so a utility function is only unique up to an increasing affine transformation. That is, if we define $V(x) = a + bU(x)$, $b > 0$, then the choices resulting from the use of U and V will be the same.

Usually we assume that more is better—that is, $U' > 0$. The risk preference of an investor is expressed by the curvature of the utility function—in particular, the convexity U''. To see this, return first to the concept of certainty equivalence, that is, the monetary value Q_P that has the same utility as the expected utility of an investment P:

$$U(Q_P) = EU(P).$$

The risk preference of an investor is expressed by the curvature of the utility function

Call μ_P and σ_P^2 the mean and the variance of the investment P; then, using a second-order Taylor series expansion of U around μ_P and taking expectations, we obtain

$$EU(P) \approx \mu_P + \tfrac{1}{2}\sigma_P^2 U''.$$

Thus when:

➤ $U'' = 0$ locally, $Q_P = \mu_P$ and the investor is *risk-neutral* (that is, he is willing to play the average because his certainty equivalent is the mean return);
➤ $U'' < 0$ locally, $Q_P < \mu_P$ and the investor is *risk-averse* (the certainty equivalent of an investment is less than its expected value);
➤ $U'' > 0$ locally, $Q_P > \mu_P$ and the investor is *risk-loving* (because of the pleasure in gambling the investor puts a greater certainty equivalent on an investment than its expected value).

Diminishing marginal utility of wealth implies the investor is risk-averse. The degree of risk aversion—that is, the concavity of the utility function—is commonly measured by the *coefficient of absolute risk aversion* $A(W) = -U''/U'$, or the *coefficient of relative risk aversion* $R(W) = -WU''/U'$. These coefficients are not independent of the level of wealth. The investor may have increasing absolute risk aversion, $A' > 0$, so that as his wealth increases he holds less in risky assets in absolute terms, or increasing relative risk aversion, $R' > 0$, so that as his wealth increases he holds proportionately less in risky assets. Or he may have constant or decreasing absolute or relative risk aversion, depending on the functional form assumed for the utility function.

The utility function can be encoded by recording the choices that the investor or the decision-maker for the firm would make when presented with simple investment alternatives

The quantification of risk attitude through the construction of a utility function is a useful discipline that allows decision-makers to choose more consistently between risky opportunities. The utility function of an investor, or of a firm, can be encoded by recording the choices that the investor or the decision-maker for the firm would make when presented with simple investment alternatives. For example, the first encoding of a utility function may show domains where the investor is risk-averse and some domains where he is risk-loving. It is not uncommon to find investors showing risk aversion for a range of positive returns but a risk-loving attitude for extremely positive or negative returns. This may be the result of cognitive biases or the consequence of conflict between the incentive of an individual and those of the firm for which he is acting. For example, it may not matter to an individual what losses he makes beyond a certain threshold because his career would already have been ruined; or an individual may take a very small chance of winning a return that will change his life.

If a decision-maker is risk-averse for some levels of returns and risk-loving for others, then a more consistent decision-maker can take advantage of this pattern

When examining a utility function and realizing the different degrees of risk attitude expressed for different levels of returns, a decision-maker has the opportunity to revise his preferences and perhaps choose to follow a more consistent pattern of behaviour. To illustrate, if a decision-maker is risk-averse for some levels of returns and risk-loving for others, then a more consistent decision-maker can take advantage of this pattern; he could make systematic gains at the expense of the first by offering a series of transactions that the first will find attractive, even though they will result in a net loss for him. Most organizations would want to avoid falling into this trap and should therefore adopt a utility function that is always convex ($U'' < 0$); it is normally expected that organizations are risk-averse.

Other, stronger conditions on a utility function may lead to specific functional forms. For example, the Swiss mathematician Daniel Bernoulli (who was the first to promote the concept of utility functions) argued strongly for the *logarithmic utility function* $U(W) = \ln W$ defined on positive wealth W. He argued that a man, no matter how poor, still has some positive net worth as long as he is alive. The main property of a logarithmic utility is that of *constant relative risk aversion* (CRRA): if Q is the certainty equivalent of an uncertain state of wealth W then λQ is the certainty equivalent of the uncertain wealth λW for any $\lambda > 0$. The other utility function commonly used to reflect CRRA is the *power utility function* $U(W) = W^{1-\gamma}/(1 - \gamma)$, $W > 0$.

CRRA may well reflect the risk attitude of decision-makers faced with extreme circumstances that may have a considerable effect on their state of wealth. However, it is more common that investment decisions will affect the wealth of the decision-maker only marginally. If that is the case many decision-makers like to adopt a *constant absolute risk aversion* (CARA) that is independent of their state of wealth. CARA corresponds to the following *delta property*: if Q is the certainty equivalent of an uncertain state of wealth W then $Q + \delta$ is the certainty equivalent of an uncertain state of wealth $W + \delta$, where δ is any known change to the state of wealth. The only utility functions showing the delta property of CARA are the linear utility function and the *exponential utility function*

$$U(W) = -e^{-\lambda W}. \qquad (7.11)$$

The exponential utility function has two convenient properties. Because of the delta property it is not necessary to make explicit the initial state of wealth. It is sufficient to maximize the expected utility of any new investment. Furthermore, if the returns of the new investment are normally distributed with mean μ_P and variance σ_P^2 then it is easy to show that

$$Q_P = \mu_P - (\lambda/2)\sigma_P^2.$$

In other words, maximizing the expected utility (or equivalently, maximizing the certainty equivalent) of an investment is the same as satisfying a mean–variance criterion with a constant trade-off ratio between mean and variance equal to $\lambda/2$. That is, with an exponential utility the capital allocation problem becomes the simple optimization:

$$\max_{\mathbf{w}} \mathbf{w}'\mathbf{r} - (\lambda/2)\mathbf{w}'\mathbf{V}\mathbf{w} \quad \text{such that } \Sigma w_i = 1. \tag{7.12}$$

If an exponential utility function is not appropriate, perhaps because an investor has constant relative risk aversion,[17] there is no such simple link between the expected utility of a portfolio and its mean-variance characteristics.

Mean–variance analysis requires that an investor's preferences are defined purely in terms of the risk and return of the portfolio. It is unfortunate that so few utility functions allow the link to be made from preferences in a risky environment to mean–variance analysis. Some portfolio models will just assume from the outset that preferences are represented by *indifference curves* in risk-return space and, unfortunately, throw away the idea of expected utility of a portfolio defined in terms of end-of-period wealth. Indifference curves are isoquants of a utility function $U(\mu, \sigma)$ that is defined over risk σ and return μ. That is, they are curves in risk–return space that join all points having the same utility, like contour lines on a map. A risk-averse investor has diminishing utility with respect to risk, and diminishing marginal utility of extra returns:

$$\partial U/\partial\mu > 0, \ \partial U/\partial\sigma < 0; \ \partial^2 U/\partial\mu^2 < 0, \ \partial^2 U/\partial\sigma^2 < 0.$$

In this case the indifference curve will be convex downwards, as illustrated in Figure 7.5a. The investor is indifferent between certain high-risk, high-return and certain low-risk, low-return portfolios, that is, he is willing to accept more risk only if it is accompanied by more return, because he is risk-averse. Since the efficient frontier is a concave curve, and the indifference curves of a risk-averse investor are convex downwards, there should be a unique optimal portfolio. Three curves are drawn on the figure representing increasing levels of

It is unfortunate that so few utility functions allow the link to be made from preferences in a risky environment to mean–variance analysis

---

[17] The exponential utility function has constant absolute risk aversion (the coefficient of absolute risk aversion is λ) so the exponential utility is an appropriate choice for an investor who holds the same dollar amounts in risky assets as wealth increases. An investor who does not change the percentage invested in risky assets as his wealth increases might be assumed to have the logarithmic utility function, because this has decreasing absolute risk aversion and constant relative risk aversion. Alternatively, if investment in risky assets decreases with wealth the *quadratic utility function* $U(W) = W - aW^2$ would be appropriate, since this has increasing absolute and relative risk aversion.

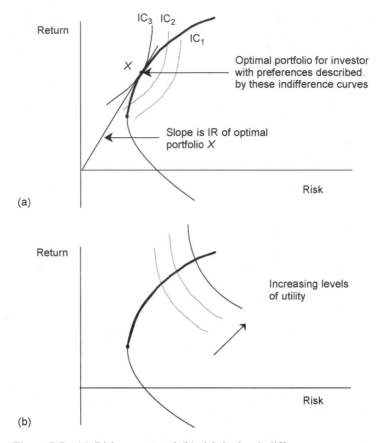

Figure 7.5 (a) Risk-averse and (b) risk-loving indifference curves.

utility. The maximum achievable utility is on the indifference curve IC_3 that is tangential to the efficient frontier, and the optimum portfolio X is at the point of tangency. Any other portfolio in the opportunity set will have a lower utility level.

Without the assumption of risk aversion, indifference curves will be straight lines (risk neutrality) or concave downwards (risk-loving). Neither of these assumptions can necessarily guarantee a unique optimal portfolio. In fact risk-loving indifference curves do not determine finite solutions, at least when short sales are allowed. The risk-loving investor would seek to go infinitely short the risk-free asset and long the risky asset to achieve the highest possible risk and return (Figure 7.5b).

7.2.5 Efficient Portfolios in Practice

It is not advisable to use mean–variance analysis as a 'black box' technique. In particular, the recommended weights in optimal portfolios will require careful

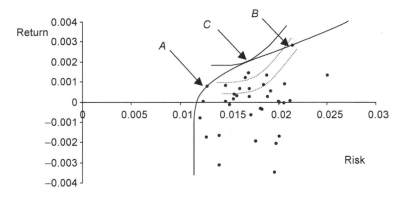

Figure 7.6 Efficient frontiers and optimal portfolios in practice.

scrutiny of high-risk, high-return investments. High-risk, high-return assets can have a huge effect on the shape of the efficient frontier and therefore the construction of optimal portfolios, particularly for an investor who is not very risk-averse and can go short on other assets. To see why, consider Figure 7.6 which shows an opportunity set for portfolios of up to 35 assets, whose risk and return are marked as points within the set. The efficient frontier, assuming short sales are allowed, is marked in bold and an optimal portfolio *C* is indicated for a risk-averse investor with the indifference curves shown. Because of the high risk and return of asset *B*, and the high correlation between assets *A* and *B*, the efficient frontier is virtually a straight line through these two points and the optimal portfolio will just be a combination of these two assets. The less risk-averse the investor, the greater proportion will be invested in the high-risk, high-return asset *B*.

High-risk, high-return assets can have a huge effect on the shape of the efficient frontier and therefore the construction of optimal portfolios, particularly for an investor who is not very risk-averse and can go short on other assets

In the practical application of mean–variance analysis to stock selection and asset allocations it is quite common that optimal portfolio will be dominated by just a few assets that appear to have high-return, high-risk characteristics.[18] For example, a risk-neutral investor in Nikkei 225 stocks would have chosen the portfolio shown in Table 7.2 that is dominated by the high-risk, high-return power stocks.

If measured over the short term the estimates of parameters that determine the shape of the efficient frontier (the mean, variance and correlation between the asset returns) can be extremely unstable and the efficient frontier will be changing all the time. For example, a risk-neutral investor who employs an efficient frontier based on 30-day averages of FTSE 100 stocks would have made the allocations shown in Tables 7.3a and 7.3b. The optimal portfolio on 6 April is quite well diversified, with no more than about 10% or 11% in any one

---

[18] When the covariance matrix and mean returns are calculated using equally weighted averages, an asset can appear to go through a prolonged period of high risk and high return following single jump in the share price. That single extreme return will affect the efficient frontier, and the optimal portfolio selection, for as many days as it remains in the equally weighted average (§3.1).

Table 7.2: Mean–variance analysis of Nikkei 225
on 4 June 1998

Tokyo Electric Power	0.444
Chubu Electric Power	0.180
Tokyo Gas Supply	0.192
Osaka Gas Supply	0.027

Table 7.3a: FTSE 100 allocations on 6 April 1998

Allied Domecq	0.054	Lucas Variety	0.017
Boots	0.028	Misys	0.049
British Energy	0.092	P&O	0.112
Unilever	0.106	Vodafone	0.117
Cadburys	0.057	Reckitt	0.090
National Grid	0.048	Rentokil	0.093
GKN	0.021	Schroders	0.027
Compass Group	0.004	Shell	0.086

Table 7.3b: FTSE 100 allocations on
19 June 1998

ASDA	0.168
SmithKline Beecham	0.069
British Telecom	0.433
Misys	0.001
Railtrack	0.234
Rank	0.004
Rentokil	0.019
Sainsbury	0.073

stock. However, 6 weeks later the same model recommends a completely different optimal portfolio that is very concentrated, with 43.3% in BT, 23.4% in Railtrack, 18.8% in ASDA, 7.3% in Sainsbury, 8.9% in SmithKline Beecham (and a little in Misys and Rank).

Optimal portfolios will not stay optimal for very long and will require constant rebalancing

Although efficient frontiers that are based only on recent data will reflect current market conditions more accurately, optimal portfolios will not stay optimal for very long and will require constant rebalancing. Common methods for cutting rebalancing costs include:

➢ using very long-term averages to construct the covariance matrix and mean returns, so that the efficient frontier becomes more stable over time. But then, from §3.1 we know that a single extreme return far in the past will have a prolonged effect on the shape of the efficient frontier and the choice of optimal portfolio — until it drops out of the averaging period, when the efficient frontier will suddenly jump for no apparent reason.

➢ assigning current portfolio weights as a weighted average of current and past optimal allocations. This has the effect of smoothing allocations over time, but the resulting portfolio may be far from optimal because it may not respond enough to current market conditions.

➤ setting rebalancing limits so that allocations are changed only if the weights recommended by the optimal portfolio exceed them. Depending on the range of these limits, which is an arbitrary choice, rebalancing cost can be substantially reduced, but then portfolios may be far from optimal.

➤ using strong priors for the values in the covariance matrix and the mean return (§8.3.3).

➤ doing a limited amount of rebalancing in the direction indicated by the latest mean–variance analysis.

The problems with efficient frontier analysis that have been outlined in this section have a common root. In fact there is a fundamental and insurmountable difficulty with mean–variance analysis, and this is that the basic data for mean–variance analysis consist of asset returns. Price data are detrended before the analysis even begins, but the return data are 'short memory processes' (Granger and Teräsvirta, 1993). The result is that one has to use one of the *ad hoc* procedures outlined above when mean–variance analysis is used for investment analysis. The question arises whether mean–variance analysis, or indeed any other analysis that is based on return data, should be used for anything other than short-term models. We shall return to this question in Chapter 12.

7.3   The RiskMetrics™ Data

J.P. Morgan launched the first version of RiskMetrics in October 1994, and over the course of the next two years made several updates to the methodology and the scope of the data. The data are downloadable from the internet at www.riskmetrics.com. They consist of large covariance matrices of the returns to many risk factors: major foreign exchange rates, money market rates, equity indices, interest rates and some key commodities. For the statistical methodology for calculating these covariance matrices, and a description of how the data should be implemented in VaR models, see the *RiskMetrics Technical Document* (J.P. Morgan and Reuters, 1996).

The availability of data sets that can be used to produce VaR measures is the great advantage of RiskMetrics. The disadvantage is that there are some limitations with the methodology that underpins the calculation of some of the data. The RiskMetrics data are based on weighted average models for volatility and correlation. There are three types of covariance matrix: a 1-day matrix, a 1-month (25-day) matrix and a 'regulatory' matrix, so called because it complies with the quantitative standards for internal models for market risk requirements that were set out in the 1996 Amendment to the 1988 Basle Accord (§9.1).

The availability of data sets that can be used to produce VaR measures is the great advantage of RiskMetrics. The disadvantage is that there are some limitations with the methodology that underpins the calculation of some of the data

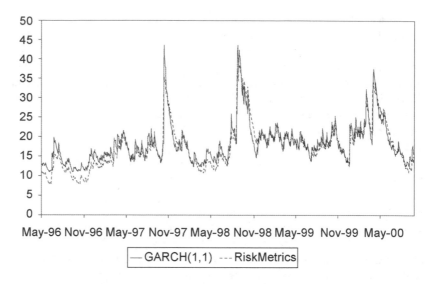

Figure 7.7   RiskMetrics and GARCH(1, 1) volatility estimates of the S&P 500 index.

An EWMA model on squared returns is used for the 1-day matrix, with smoothing constant $\lambda = 0.94$ (§3.2). Many of its elements are very similar to GARCH(1, 1) 1-day estimates (§4.2). For example, the GARCH(1, 1) models for the CAC and the FTSE 100 equity indices that were reported in Table 4.7 indicate that the RiskMetrics volatility data for these indices will be very close indeed to the GARCH(1, 1) 1-day volatility forecasts illustrated in Figure 4.7. On 6 October 2000, using data since January 1996, the GARCH(1, 1) estimates of the volatility persistence and market reaction parameters on the FTSE 100 and CAC were very similar to the RiskMetrics values of 0.94 and 0.06.

In general, the GARCH(1, 1) parameter estimates will not be as close to 0.94 and 0.06 as they were in the CAC and FTSE 100. For example, the GARCH(1, 1) model estimates of the market reaction and volatility persistence parameters for the S&P 500 index were 0.089 and 0.886 (see Table 4.7). Thus there will be a difference between the volatility forecasts over the 1-day horizon, as shown in Figure 7.7.

There are a few limitations of the RiskMetrics 1-day data that should be noted:

➢ The same value of the exponential smoothing constant $\lambda = 0.94$ must be used for all markets. This is necessary, otherwise the covariance matrix would not be positive semi-definite (see J.P. Morgan and Reuters, 1996). There is much discussion in J.P. Morgan and Reuters (1996) about the optimal value for λ. However, on the basis of estimating GARCH(1, 1) models it appears that for many risk factors the value $\lambda = 0.94$ is a little too high, so the RiskMetrics 1-day volatility data tend to overestimate volatility for some time after a market shock. If an average value of λ has to be taken for all markets it may be better if it were slightly lower.[19]

➤ To provide VaR measures of holding periods greater than 1 day it is possible to follow the BIS recommendations and use the 'square root of time' rule (§3.3) and assume that current levels of volatility and correlation persist forever. But the EWMA method is not really suitable for forecasts of more than a few days, so 10-day VaR measures that are obtained using the RiskMetrics daily data can be substantially overestimated (or indeed underestimated, depending on the construction of the portfolio).

➤ The 1-day matrix does not conform to the current international regulators' quantitative standards for internal VaR models, so it may not be admissible to base market risk capital reserves on VaR measures produced with this matrix. Regulators are requiring that at least one year (about 250 trading days) of historical data be used to construct the covariance matrices. Unfortunately, a value of $\lambda = 0.94$ in an EWMA means that only a few days of data are used. For example 0.94^{50} is less than 0.05 and 0.94^{224} is approximately zero.[20]

The 1-day matrix does not conform to the current international regulators' quantitative standards for internal VaR models

Portfolio market risk estimates relevant for a 1-month (25-day) horizon could be based purely on the 1-day covariance matrix. Assuming returns are independent and identically distributed and using the square-root-of-time rule, a covariance matrix for measuring portfolio risk over the next 25 days is obtained by multiplying every element in the 1-day covariance matrix by 25. But the EWMA methodology is only really applicable to very short-term forecasting, assuming as it does that volatility and correlation are constant.

Thus RiskMetrics have produced different data for the 1-month covariance matrix. If the EWMA methodology is to be applied, one approach would be to apply exponential smoothing to 25-day (monthly) returns. However, there is not enough historical data to base covariance matrix on non-overlapping monthly returns, so instead RiskMetrics apply exponential smoothing to the daily squared and cross-products of returns with a smoothing constant $\lambda = 0.97$ and multiply the resulting variance and covariance estimates by 25.

The same smoothing constant has to be used to calculate all volatilities and correlations in the RiskMetrics 1-day and 1-month covariance matrices, otherwise they would not necessarily be positive semi-definite. However, the RiskMetrics 'regulatory' matrix is based on equally weighted moving averages over the past year of data and so needs no constraints to be positive definite (§7.1.3). Following the discussion in §3.1, it is clear that one large return will continue to keep the 'regulatory' volatility estimates high for exactly one

---

[19] The persistence parameters from GARCH(1, 1) models that are tailored to daily data on each individual risk factor are rarely as high as 0.94.

[20] What is zero depends on the tolerance level used for calculations. In RiskMetrics the tolerance level is 10^{-6}, but if a higher tolerance were set then more historic data would be used.

year, and exactly one year after a major market event the equally weighted volatility estimate will jump down again as abruptly as it jumped up. By the same token, the 'regulatory' correlation estimates will appear too stable for the whole year following a single event that affects both markets. These 'ghost features' in the regulatory covariance matrix that will certainly follow large market movements are going to bias VaR measures for a whole year, but the direction of the bias is not always easy to determine as it depends on the portfolio construction.

7.4 Orthogonal Methods for Generating Covariance Matrices

Many covariance matrices, including the RiskMetrics matrices, are obtained by applying computations to the full set of assets (or risk factors). But the dimensions of the problem are normally so large that the problem is intractable. That is why restrictive assumptions often need to be made. However, there is an alternative: to apply computations to only a few key market risk factors that capture the most important uncorrelated sources of information in the data, that is, to the principal components. This section describes how to use the principal component analysis that was explained in Chapter 6 to construct large covariance matrices that have many desirable characteristics:

➢ They are always positive semi-definite.
➢ They have relatively few constraints imposed on the movements in volatility and correlation.
➢ Exponentially weighted moving averages can be used to produce EWMA covariance matrices where the persistence in volatilities and correlation is not the same for all factors. Instead it will be determined by the correlation in the system.
➢ Univariate GARCH can be used to produce covariance matrix term structures that are mean reverting. The usual GARCH analytic formulae for computing the term structure of volatility and correlation are applied so that the n-day covariance matrix converges to the long-term average as n increases.

The method is computationally very simple: it takes the univariate volatilities of the first few principal components of a system of risk factors, together with the factor weights matrix of the principal components representation, to produce a full covariance matrix for the original system. The method can be used with either GARCH or EWMA volatilities of the principal components. In orthogonal EWMA there is no need to impose the same value of the smoothing constant on all variables, as there is in the RiskMetrics data sets.

There are many advantages with the orthogonal method for generating covariance matrices. First, the computational burden is much lighter when all of the $k(k + 1)/2$ volatilities and correlations are simple matrix transformations of just a few variances. Second, some data may be difficult to obtain directly, particularly on some financial assets that are not actively traded. When data are sparse or unreliable for some of the variables in the system, a direct estimation of volatilities and correlation may be very difficult. However, if there is sufficient information to infer their factor weights in the principal components representation, their volatilities and correlations may be obtained using the orthogonal method. For example, some bonds or futures may be relatively illiquid for certain maturities, and statistical forecasts of their volatilities may be difficult to generate directly on a daily basis. But if the principal components and factor weights of the term structure are known, the orthogonal method will give a full covariance matrix that generates forecasts of all maturities, including the illiquid ones. Other advantages of the orthogonal method include the ability to reduce the amount of noise in the system so that correlation estimates are more stable. The method may also be used to obtain volatility and correlation forecasts of securities for which only a short price series is available (e.g. new issues — see §6.4.2).

The orthogonal method will give a full covariance matrix that generates forecasts of all maturities, including the illiquid ones. Other advantages of the orthogonal method include the ability to reduce the amount of noise in the system so that correlation estimates are more stable

Given these considerable advantages for generating high-dimensional covariance matrices, one would not necessarily expect orthogonal GARCH to perform as well as other multivariate GARCH models when the system has only a few dimensions. Indeed, some multivariate GARCH models are designed for the specific purposes of estimating single correlations, so they are only based on a bivariate GARCH specification. Nevertheless, Engle (2000b) shows that the orthogonal GARCH model performs very well according to three out of the four diagnostics that he has chosen for assessing the accuracy of correlation forecasts.

7.4.1 Using PCA to Construct Covariance Matrices

This section shows how to obtain the full covariance matrix of a large system from the covariance matrix of the principal components. This method is computationally efficient because the covariance matrix of asset or risk factor returns, which may have hundreds of elements, can be obtained as a simple transformation of the variances of the first few principal components.

Recall the principal components representation (6.2), which may also be written in vector form as

$$\mathbf{x}_i = w_{i1}\mathbf{p}_1 + \ldots + w_{ik}\mathbf{p}_k, \tag{7.13}$$

where $\mathbf{x}_i$ is the $T \times 1$ vector of normalized data on the ith variable in the system, $\mathbf{p}_j$ is the $T \times 1$ vector of data on the jth principal component and $\mathbf{W} = (w_{ij})$ is the matrix of factor weights. In terms of the original variables the representation (7.13) is equivalent to

$$\mathbf{y}_i = \mu_i + w_{i1}^* \mathbf{p}_1 + \ldots + w_{im}^* \mathbf{p}_m + \varepsilon_i, \tag{7.14}$$

where $w_{ij}^* = w_{ij}\sigma_i$ and the error term in (7.14) picks up the approximation from using only the first m of the k principal components.

Since principal components are orthogonal, their unconditional covariance matrix is just the diagonal matrix of their variances

One of the attractions of using principal component factor models is that they have a particularly simple risk structure. Since principal components are orthogonal, their unconditional covariance matrix is just the diagonal matrix of their variances. Since the principal components are also orthogonal to the error, taking variances of (7.14) gives the covariance matrix of $\mathbf{Y} = (\mathbf{y}_1, \ldots, \mathbf{y}_n)$ as:

$$\mathbf{V} = \mathbf{ADA}' + \mathbf{V}_\varepsilon, \tag{7.15}$$

where $\mathbf{A} = (w_{ij}^*)$ is the matrix of denormalized factor weights, $\mathbf{D} = \mathrm{diag}(V(\mathbf{p}_1), \ldots, V(\mathbf{p}_m))$ is the diagonal matrix of variances of principal components and $\mathbf{V}_\varepsilon$ is the covariance matrix of the errors. Ignoring $\mathbf{V}_\varepsilon$ in (7.15) gives the approximation

$$\mathbf{V} = \mathbf{ADA}' \tag{7.16}$$

with an accuracy that is controlled by choosing more or less components to represent the system.

Note that $\mathbf{V}$ will always be positive semi-definite, and one might indeed be content with this. However, $\mathbf{V}$ may not be strictly positive definite unless $m = k$.[21] The approximation (7.16) will normally produce a strict positive definite covariance matrix when the representation (7.13) is made with enough principal components to give a reasonable degree of accuracy. Nevertheless when covariance matrices are based on (7.16) with $m < k$, they should be run through an eigenvalue check to ensure strict positive definiteness.

There is a very high degree of computational efficiency in calculating only m variances instead of the $k(k+1)/2$ variances and covariances of the original system

The first advantage of using this type of orthogonal transformation to generate risk factor covariance matrices is now clear. There is a very high degree of computational efficiency in calculating only m variances instead of the $k(k+1)/2$ variances and covariances of the original system, and typically m will be much less than k. For example, in a single yield curve with, say, 15 maturities, only the variances of the first two or three principal components need to be computed, instead of the 120 variances and covariances of the yields for 15 different maturities.

7.4.2 Orthogonal EWMA

Exponentially weighted moving averages of the squares and cross products of returns are a standard method for generating covariance matrices. But a

[21] Although $\mathbf{D}$ is positive definite because it is a diagonal matrix with positive elements, there is nothing to guarantee that $\mathbf{ADA}'$ will be positive definite when $m < k$. To see this write $\mathbf{x}'\mathbf{ADA}'\mathbf{x} = \mathbf{y}'\mathbf{Dy}$, where $\mathbf{A}'\mathbf{x} = \mathbf{y}$. Since $\mathbf{y}$ can be zero for some non-zero $\mathbf{x}$, $\mathbf{x}'\mathbf{ADA}'\mathbf{x}$ will not be strictly positive for all non-zero $\mathbf{x}$. It may be zero, and in that case $\mathbf{ADA}'$ will only be positive semi-definite.

limitation of this type of direct application of EWMAs is that the covariance matrix is only guaranteed to be positive semi-definite if the same smoothing constant is used for all the data. That is, the reaction of volatility to market events and the persistence in volatility must be assumed to be the same in all the assets or risk factors that are represented in the covariance matrix.

A major advantage of the orthogonal factor method described here is that it allows EWMA methods to be used without this unrealistic constraint. Each principal component EWMA variance in **D** can be calculated with a different smoothing constant and the matrix **V** given by **ADA**′ will still be positive semi-definite.

The net effect will be that the degree of smoothing in the variance of any particular asset or risk factor will depend on the factor weights in the principal components representation. These factor weights are determined by the correlation with other variables in the system, so the degree of smoothing on any variable is determined by its correlation with other variables in the system. Put another way, in orthogonal EWMA the market reaction and volatility persistence of a given asset will not be the same as the other assets in the system, instead it will be related to its correlation with the other assets. Even if the EWMA variances of the principal components all have the same smoothing constant the transformation of these variances using the factor weights will induce different decay rates for the variances and covariances of the variables in the original system.[22]

In orthogonal EWMA the market reaction and volatility persistence of a given asset will not be the same as the other assets in the system, instead it will be related to its correlation with the other assets

Figure 7.8 uses the daily data on the same three French stocks that were used in the example of §6.4.2. Figure 7.8 compares the volatilities and correlations that are obtained using the orthogonal EWMA method with the volatilities and correlations that are obtained using EWMAs directly on the squared returns.[23]

Comparative plots such as these are a crucial part of the orthogonal model calibration. If these volatilities and correlations are not similar it will be because (a) the data period used for the PCA is too long, or (b) there are variables included in the system that are distorting the volatilities and correlations of other variables computed using the orthogonal method. Both these problems may be encountered if there is insufficient correlation in the system for the method to be properly applied. If one or more of the variables has a low degree of correlation with the other variables over the data period, the factor weights in the PCA will lack robustness over time. The model could

Comparative plots such as these are a crucial part of the orthogonal model calibration

---

[22] Choosing identical smoothing constants for all principal components is in fact neither necessary for positive definiteness nor desirable for optimal forecasting. The optimal smoothing constants may be lower for the higher, less important principal components, whereas the volatility of the first component may be the most persistent of the principal component volatilities in a highly correlated system because the first component picks up the common trend.

[23] The smoothing constant λ has been set arbitrarily as 0.95 for all EWMAs in this section.

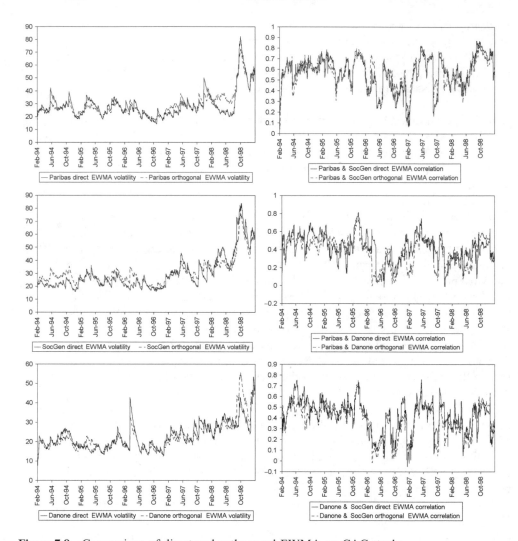

Figure 7.8 Comparison of direct and orthogonal EWMA on CAC stocks.

be improved by using a shorter data period, and/or omitting the less correlated variables from the system.

Figure 7.8 shows that the orthogonal EWMA method replicates the direct EWMA method well, even though the PCA on these three stocks is not very informative because their correlation is not that high. One might expect that the orthogonal EWMA method would be even closer to direct EWMA in systems that are highly correlated, such as yield curves and other term structures.

Having explained the method with a simple 3 stock example, let us now see its real strength by applying it to a larger and highly correlated system. Figure 7.9

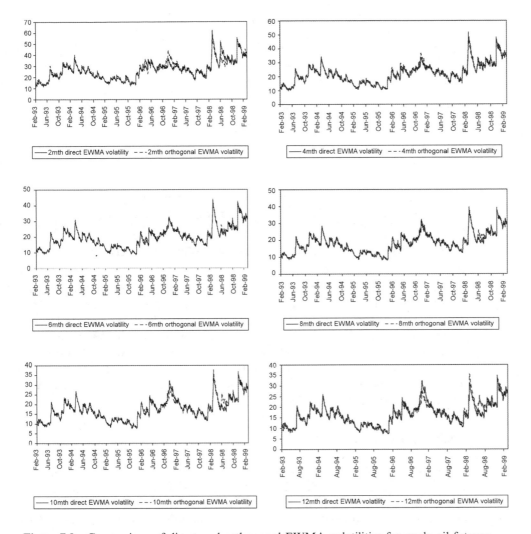

Figure 7.9 Comparison of direct and orthogonal EWMA volatilities for crude oil futures.

illustrates some of the output of using the orthogonal EWMA method with three principal components of the crude oil futures data shown in Figure 6.4. The PCA of these data has already been discussed in §6.2.3. The great advantage in using the orthogonal EWMA method on term structure data is that all the volatilities and correlations in the system can be derived from just two or three EWMA variances. That is, instead of estimating 78 EWMA volatilities and correlations directly, using the same value of the smoothing constant throughout, only two or three EWMA variances of the trend, tilt and perhaps also the curvature principal components need to be generated. In some term structures, including the crude oil futures term structure used for Figure 7.9, a mere two components already explain over 99% of the variation, so adding a third component makes no discernible difference to the covariance results.

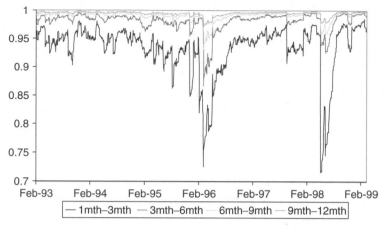

Figure 7.10 Some correlations from the orthogonal EWMA model.

From just two EWMAs, the entire 12×12 covariance matrix of the original system is recovered with negligible loss of precision. The orthogonal EWMA correlations shown in Figure 7.10 are very similar indeed to the correlations generated by direct EWMA. But there is a problem with using EWMAs at all in the crude oil futures market because there are some price decouplings between some of the near-maturity futures. This problem will be a point of discussion based on Figure 7.12 below, where the same correlations are measured by the orthogonal GARCH model.

7.4.3 Orthogonal GARCH

It is extremely difficult to use multivariate GARCH to generate covariance matrices of more than a few dimensions

It has been shown in §4.5 that large covariance matrices that are based on GARCH models would have many advantages. But it was also shown that it is extremely difficult to use multivariate GARCH to generate covariance matrices of more than a few dimensions. Some models that use only univariate GARCH to generate covariance matrices were discussed in §4.5.3, and there we referred to the orthogonal GARCH model that is now described.

A principal components representation is a multi-factor model, and the idea of using factor models with GARCH is not new. Engle *et al.* (1990) use the capital asset pricing model to show how the volatilities and correlations between individual equities can be generated from the univariate GARCH variance of the market risk factor. Their results have a straightforward extension to multi-factor models, but unless the factors are orthogonal a multivariate GARCH model on the risk factors will still be required.

The orthogonal GARCH model is a generalization of the factor GARCH model introduced by Engle *et al.* (1990) to a multi-factor model with orthogonal factors. The idea of using PCA for multivariate GARCH modelling goes back to Ding (1994). However, there Ding used the full number of principal components in the representation and the strength of the orthogonal GARCH model rests, crucially, on using a reduced space of principal components, as explained by Alexander and Chibumba (1996) and more recently developed in Alexander (2000a, 2001b) and Klaassen (2000).[24]

The orthogonal GARCH model allows $k \times k$ GARCH covariance matrices to be generated from just m univariate GARCH models. Normally m, the number of principal components, will be much less than k, the number of variables in the system. This is so that extraneous 'noise' is excluded from the data and the volatilities and correlations produced become more stable. In the orthogonal GARCH model the $m \times m$ diagonal matrix of variances of the principal components is a time-varying matrix denoted $\mathbf{D}_t$, and the time-varying covariance matrix $\mathbf{V}_t$ of the original system is approximated by

$$\mathbf{V}_t = \mathbf{A}\mathbf{D}_t\mathbf{A}', \qquad (7.17)$$

where $\mathbf{A}$ is the $k \times m$ matrix of rescaled factor weights. The model (7.17) is called orthogonal GARCH when the diagonal matrix $\mathbf{D}_t$ of variances of principal components is estimated using a GARCH model. In the examples given here the standard 'vanilla' GARCH(1, 1) model (4.2) is used.

The representation (7.17) will give a positive semi-definite matrix at every point in time, even when the number m of principal components is much less than the number k of variables in the system. Of course, the principal components are only unconditionally uncorrelated, but the assumption of zero conditional correlations has to be made, otherwise it misses the whole point of the model, which is to generate large GARCH covariance matrices from GARCH volatilities alone. The degree of accuracy that is lost by making this assumption is investigated by a thorough calibration of the model, comparing the variances and covariances produced with those from other models such as EWMAs or, for small systems, with full multivariate GARCH. Care needs to be taken with the model calibration, in terms of the number of components used and the time period used to estimate them, but once calibrated the orthogonal GARCH model may be run very quickly and efficiently on a daily basis.

The strength of the orthogonal GARCH model rests on using a reduced space of principal components

The remainder of this section examines how to calibrate orthogonal GARCH(1, 1) models to term structures and to equity/foreign exchange systems. The first example of an orthogonal GARCH model is a straightforward extension of the crude oil term structure example presented in §7.4.2, using GARCH(1, 1) variances of the first two principal components in place of EWMAs.

Table 7.4 presents the GARCH(1, 1) parameter estimates of the first two principal components. The orthogonal GARCH volatilities that result are very close indeed to the direct GARCH volatilities. In fact, they are almost identical

---

[24] Commercial software that generates large orthogonal GARCH matrices has been available since 1996 from S-Plus GARCH and since 1998 from www.algorithmics.com. Excel add-ins for the orthogonal GARCH model may be available from cleigh@dial.pipex.com and MBRM (details on the CD).

Table 7.4: GARCH(1, 1) models of the first and second principal components

	1st Principal Component		2nd Principal Component	
	Coefficient	t-statistic	Coefficient	t-statistic
Constant	0.650847E-02	0.304468	0.122938E-02	0.066431
ω	0.644458E-02	3.16614	0.110818	7.34255
α	0.037769	8.46392	0.224810	9.64432
β	0.957769	169.198	0.665654	21.5793

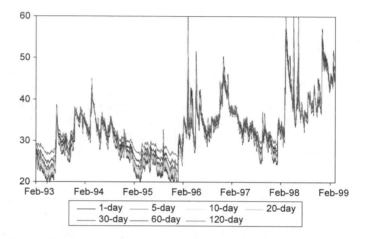

Figure 7.11 Orthogonal GARCH term structure volatility forecasts for 1-month crude oil futures.

to the EWMA volatilities illustrated in Figure 7.10. Why use GARCH, then? There are two important reasons. The first is that EWMA volatility term structure forecasts do not converge to the long-term average, but GARCH forecasts do, provided $\alpha + \beta < 1$. Although univariate GARCH analysis of the crude oil data indicated IGARCH behaviour and therefore no convergence in term structures (§4.2.3), Table 7.4 shows that the principal components do have convergent volatility term structures.[25] It is therefore a simple matter to extend the orthogonal GARCH parameter estimates to provide forecasts of the average volatility over the next n days, for any n (using the formulae given in §4.4.1). Orthogonal GARCH volatility terms structures for the 1-month future are shown in Figure 7.11, for every day during the six year period.

Another good reason to use orthogonal GARCH rather than orthogonal EWMA is that the orthogonal GARCH correlations will more realistically reflect what is happening in the market. As already mentioned, the correlations

---

[25] Recall from §4.4.1 that the size of $\alpha + \beta$ determines the speed of convergence of the volatility term structure. So the second (tilt) component in Table 7.4 has a more rapidly convergent volatility term structure than the first (trend) component. This reflects the fact that the prices of short-maturity crude oil futures are more variable than the prices of long-maturity futures.

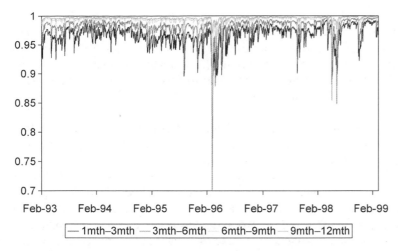

Figure 7.12 Some of the correlations from the orthogonal GARCH model.

shown in Figure 7.10 that were generated by the orthogonal EWMA are a little worrying. One would expect correlations between commodity futures to be more or less perfect most of the time, but the EWMA correlations between the 1-month futures and other futures, and between other pairs at short maturities, appear to be considerably below 1 for long periods of time. For example, during long periods of 1996 and 1998 the EWMA correlations are nearer to 0.8 than 1.

The reason for this is that the smoothing constant of 0.95 — which from Table 7.4 is an appropriate choice for the EWMA volatility of the first and most important principal component — is clearly too large for the correlations. Unfortunately, if one were to reduce the values of the smoothing constants used in the orthogonal EWMA model so that the correlations were less persistent, the volatilities would also be less persistent.

In the crude oil futures market, price decoupling only occurs over very short time spans so correlations may deviate below 1, but only for a short time. Now, if the orthogonal model were to be used with just one principal component (the results from §6.2.3 indicate that this trend component explains over 95% of the variation) the correlations would of course be unity. So all the variation in the orthogonal GARCH correlations is coming from the movements in the second principal component. This second principal component is the tilt component, and it only explains about 3% of the movement (see Table 6.4a).

The GARCH(1, 1) models of the first two principal components of this term structure, given in Table 7.4, indicate that the second principal component has a lot of reaction (α is about 0.22) but little persistence (β is about 0.66). In other words these tilt movements in the term structure of futures prices are intense but short-lived. So one would expect the correlations given by the orthogonal GARCH model in Figure 7.12 to be more accurately reflecting real market conditions than the orthogonal EWMA correlations in Figure 7.10.

This example has shown how 78 different volatilities and correlations of the term structure of crude oil futures between 1 month and 12 months can be generated, very simply and very accurately, from just two univariate GARCH models of the first two principal components. It has also shown how volatility forecasts of different maturities can be generated as simple transformations of these two basic GARCH variances.

The orthogonal GARCH model is particularly useful for term structures that have some illiquid maturities

The orthogonal GARCH model is particularly useful for term structures that have some illiquid maturities. When market trading is rather thin, there may be little autoregressive conditional heteroscedasticity in the data and what is there may be rather unreliable, so the direct estimation of GARCH volatilities is very problematic. The orthogonal GARCH model has the advantage that the volatilities of such assets, and their correlations with other assets in the system, are derived from the principal component volatilities that are common to all assets and the factor weights that are specific to that particular asset.

To illustrate this point let us step up the complexity of the data a little. Still a term structure, but a rather difficult one: the daily zero-coupon yield data in the UK with 11 different maturities between 1 month and 10 years from 1 January 1992 to 24 March 1995, shown in Figure 6.3b. It is not an easy task to estimate univariate GARCH models on these data directly because yields may remain relatively fixed for a number of days. Particularly on the more illiquid maturities, there may be insufficient conditional heteroscedasticity for GARCH models to converge well and the direct estimation of GARCH models on these data is rather problematic. Since it has not always been possible to obtain convergence for even univariate GARCH models on these data, the orthogonal GARCH volatilities in Figure 7.13 have been compared instead with EWMA volatilities.[26]

The orthogonal GARCH volatilities are not as closely aligned with the EWMA volatilities as they were in the previous example, but there is sufficient agreement between them to place a fairly high degree of confidence in the orthogonal GARCH model. Again two principal components were used in the orthogonal GARCH, but the PCA of Table 7.5 shows that these two components only account for 72% of the total variation (as opposed to over 99% in the crude oil term structure).

Clearly the lower degree of accuracy from a representation with two principal components is one reason for the observed differences between the orthogonal GARCH volatilities and the EWMA volatilities. Another is that the 10-year yield has a very low correlation with the rest of the system, as reflected by its low factor weight on the first principal component, which is quite out of line with the rest of the factor weights on this component. The fit of the orthogonal

---

[26] Interest rates have less persistence in volatility than equities or commodities, so a smoothing constant of 0.9 has been used.

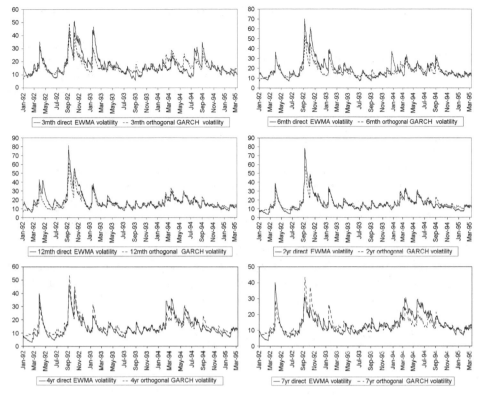

Figure 7.13 Calibration of an orthogonal GARCH model to UK zero-coupon yields.

Table 7.5a: Eigenvalue analysis

Component	Eigenvalue	Cumulative R^2
P_1	5.9284117	0.53894652
P_2	1.9899323	0.71984946
P_3	0.97903180	0.80885235

Table 7.5b: Factor weights

	P_1	P_2	P_3
1 mth	0.50916	0.60370	0.12757
2 mth	0.63635	0.62136	−0.048183
3 mth	0.68721	0.57266	−0.10112
6 mth	0.67638	0.47617	−0.10112
12 mth	0.83575	0.088099	−0.019350
2 yr	0.88733	−0.21379	0.033486
3 yr	0.87788	−0.30805	−0.033217
4 yr	0.89648	−0.36430	0.054061
5 yr	0.79420	−0.37981	0.14267
7 yr	0.78346	−0.47448	0.069182
10 yr	0.17250	−0.18508	−0.95497

model is good, but could be improved further if the 10-year yield were excluded from the system.

The GARCH(1, 1) model estimates for the first two principal components are given in Table 7.6. This time the second principal component has a better-conditioned GARCH model: the tilts in the UK yield curve are less temporary and more important than they are in the crude oil term structure discussed above. As a consequence the orthogonal GARCH correlations will be more stable than the correlations in Figure 7.12.

Figure 7.14 shows some of the orthogonal GARCH correlations for the UK zero-coupon yields. Not only does the orthogonal method provide a way of estimating GARCH volatilities and volatility term structures that may be impossible to obtain by direct univariate GARCH estimation, they also give very sensible GARCH correlations, which would be very difficult indeed to *All elements of the* estimate using direct multivariate GARCH. All elements of the covariance *covariance matrix are* matrix are obtained from the variances of just two principal components that *obtained from the* represent the most important sources of information—other variations are *variances of just two* ascribed to 'noise' and are not included in the model.

principal components
that represent the most
important sources of
information—other
variations are ascribed to
'noise' and are not
included in the model

Table 7.6: GARCH(1, 1) models of the first and second principal component

	1st Principal Component		2nd Principal Component	
	Coefficient	*t*-stat	Coefficient	*t*-stat
Constant	0.769758E-02	0.249734	0.033682	1.09064
ω	0.024124	4.50366	0.046368	6.46634
α	0.124735	6.46634	0.061022	9.64432
β	0.866025	135.440	0.895787	50.8779

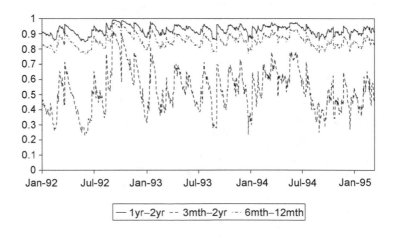

Figure 7.14 Orthogonal GARCH correlations of UK zero-coupon yields.

A useful technique for parameterizing multivariate GARCH models is to compare the GARCH volatility estimates from the multivariate GARCH with those obtained from direct univariate GARCH estimation. Similarly, when calibrating an orthogonal GARCH model one could compare the volatility and correlation estimates with those obtained from other models, such as an EWMA correlation model or other multivariate GARCH models. There are, of course, problems with this. What choice of smoothing constants should be made when the comparison is with EWMA volatilities? If the system is large, convergence problems may very well be encountered, so how sure can one be about the validity of the diagonal vech or BEKK multivariate GARCH parameter estimates?

We now show some results from calibrating orthogonal GARCH models to multivariate GARCH models. Since multivariate GARCH is not easy to use for large systems, a relatively small system of four European equity indices is used: France (CAC), Germany (DAX), the Netherlands (AEX) and the UK (FTSE 100).[27] A PCA on daily return data from Morgan Stanley Index prices, from 1 April 1993 to 31 December 1996 gives the results in Table 7.7.

Table 7.7a: Factor weights

	P_1	P_2	P_3	P_4
AEX	0.866	0.068	0.224	0.441
CAC	0.834	−0.238	−0.496	0.036
DAX	0.755	0.615	−0.027	−0.226
FTSE	0.818	−0.397	0.294	−0.296

Table 7.7b: Eigenvalue analysis

Component	Eigenvalue	Cumulative R^2
P_1	2.686141	0.671535
P_2	0.596853	0.820749
P_3	0.382549	0.916386
P_4	0.334456	1

The weights on the first principal component are comparable and quite high. Since this is the trend component the indices are, on the whole, moving together, and the eigenvalue analysis in Table 7.7b indicates that common movements in the trend explain 67% of the total variation over the 4-year period.

The third and fourth principal components are often more important in equity systems than in term structures, and this case is no exception. Thus all four principal components have been used in the orthogonal GARCH model, that

---

[27] Many thanks to Dr Aubrey Chibumba for producing these results as part of his MPhil thesis at Sussex University.

Table 7.8: GARCH(1, 1) models of the principal components

	1st PC		2nd PC		3rd PC		4th PC	
	Coefficient	*t*-stat	Coefficient	*t*-stat	Coefficient	*t*-stat	Coefficient	*t*-stat
Constant	0.00613	0.19446	0.00262	0.09008	−0.0801	−0.26523	0.00267	0.087511
ω	0.032609	1.90651	0.066555	3.10594	0.089961	2.12915	0.203359	1.80057
α	0.033085	2.69647	0.086002	4.57763	0.067098	2.92511	0.070417	2.00423
β	0.934716	35.9676	0.846648	25.9852	0.841618	14.4038	0.726134	5.22888

is, the matrix $\mathbf{D}_t$ is a 4×4 diagonal matrix. Table 7.8 reports results from estimating univariate GARCH(1, 1) models on each of the four principal components to give the elements of $\mathbf{D}_t$ at each point in time.

The results of applying the orthogonal GARCH model are the four volatilities and six correlation graphs shown in Figure 7.15. These graphs compare the orthogonal GARCH volatilities and correlations with those estimated from two other multivariate GARCH models, the diagonal vech and the BEKK (§4.5.2).

The reason that this system has been confined to only four variables is that there are no convergence problems with the multivariate GARCH models that are being used for comparison. The four-dimensional diagonal vech model has 10 equations, each with three parameters. The 30 parameter estimates and their *t*-statistics (in italics) are reported in Table 7.9. The four-dimensional BEKK model has 42 parameters and the estimates of the matrices $\mathbf{A}$, $\mathbf{B}$, and $\mathbf{C}$ are given in Table 7.10.

Some care must be taken with the initial calibration of orthogonal GARCH. Then it can be used to compute large GARCH covariance matrices that are reliable and computationally efficient on a daily basis

It is important to realize that *all* the 10 graphs in Figure 7.15 come from the models reported in Tables 7.8–7.10. That is, all the BEKK volatilities and correlations come from the same BEKK model estimated in Table 7.10. Similarly, there is only one diagonal vech model, in Table 7.9, generating all the vech series for the graphs and one orthogonal GARCH model in Table 7.8 for the orthogonal GARCH graphs. However, there are cases where the orthogonal GARCH volatilities coincide quite closely with the BEKK volatilities but not the vech volatilities (graphs f, h and j). In some cases the orthogonal GARCH are more similar to the vech volatilities than the BEKK volatilities (graphs d, e and i) and in some cases all three volatilities differ noticeably (graphs a, b, c and g). Having said this, there is not a huge difference between the three models in any of the graphs. Given how volatility and correlation estimates *can* differ when different multivariate GARCH models are used, these graphs are nothing abnormal.

To summarize the discussion, some care must be taken with the initial calibration of orthogonal GARCH. Then it can be used to compute large

Table 7.9: Diagonal vech parameter estimates

	Variance equations				Covariance equations					
	AEX	CAC	DAX	FTSE	AEX–CAC	AEX–DAX	AEX–FTSE	CAC–DAX	CAC–FTSE	DAX–FTSE
	ω_1	ω_2	ω_3	ω_4	ω_5	ω_6	ω_7	ω_8	ω_9	ω_{10}
	5.8×10^{-6}	3.4×10^{-6}	5.0×10^{-6}	1.8×10^{-6}	1.9×10^{-6}	9.3×10^{-6}	1.8×10^{-6}	8.6×10^{-6}	3.0×10^{-6}	1.6×10^{-6}
	3.11	*2.19*	*1.71*	*2.11*	*2.45*	*1.63*	*2.25*	*3.24*	*1.58*	*2.28*
	α_1	α_2	α_3	α_4	α_5	α_6	α_7	α_8	α_9	α_{10}
	0.054900	0.028889	0.028264	0.024601	0.021826	0.031806	0.028069	0.059739	0.022341	0.028377
	4.14	*3.15*	*2.28*	*2.68*	*3.75*	*2.40*	*3.68*	*3.56*	*2.18*	*2.88*
	β_1	β_2	β_3	β_4	β_5	β_6	β_7	β_8	β_9	β_{10}
	0.82976	0.89061	0.83654	0.91227	0.95802	0.74503	0.926414	0.829753	0.861387	0.934363
	18.23	*21.17*	*9.58*	*25.2*	*79.49*	*5.20*	*36.36*	*17.93*	*10.67*	*38.74*

Table 7.10: BEKK parameter estimates

	AEX	CAC	DAX	FTSE
A	0.00160	0	0	0
	0.00008	−0.00176	0	0
	0.00094	0.00197	−0.0087	0
	0.00142	−0.00003	−0.00051	2.5×10^{-6}
B	0.22394	−0.04156	0.019373	0.04785
	−0.07147	0.18757	−0.05247	0.031895
	−0.06286	−0.04764	0.29719	0.07003
	−0.016277	−0.027589	−0.017405	0.178563
C	0.951805	0.027231	−0.050236	0.026130
	0.033141	0.9615723	0.023822	0.013623
	0.067985	0.053024	0.844291	0.005211
	0.022278	0.029257	−0.014482	0.948453

GARCH covariance matrices that are reliable and computationally efficient, on a daily basis. The model calibration will depend on two important factors:

➤ *The assets that are included in the system.* PCA works best in a highly correlated system. An asset that has very idiosyncratic properties compared to other assets in the system (such as the 10-year bond in the UK yield curve above) will corrupt the volatilities and correlations of the other assets in the system, because they are all based on the principal components that are common to all assets.
➤ *The time period used for estimation.* The GARCH volatilities of the principal components change over time, but it is only their current values that matter for forecasting the covariance matrix. However, the factor weights are also used in this forecast, and these take different values depending on the estimation period. So changing the time period for estimation affects current forecasts of the covariance matrix primarily because it affects the factor weights matrix, not because it affects the parameter estimates for the principal component volatilities in $\mathbf{D}_t$.

The main focus of this long subsection on orthogonal GARCH has been to explain and empirically validate a new method of obtaining large GARCH correlation matrices using only univariate GARCH estimation techniques on principal components of the original return series. Empirical examples on commodity futures, interest rates and on international equity indices have been presented and used to explain how best to employ the method in different circumstances. It has been found that when the systems are suitably tailored, the orthogonal method compares very well with the general multivariate GARCH models. In many cases the divergence between the orthogonal GARCH estimates and the BEKK estimates is far less than between the vech and the BEKK estimates.

7.4.4 'Splicing' Methods for Obtaining Large Covariance Matrices

This subsection describes the use of PCA to generate large-dimensional covariance matrices. It has many advantages over the RiskMetrics approach, for example:

> ➤ Very large covariance matrices that are generated using this method will be very much more robust than the covariance matrices obtained by applying EWMA to each returns series separately.
> ➤ There is no need to reduce dimensions by using linear interpolation along the yield curve.
> ➤ The method will conform to regulators' requirements on historic data if at least one year of data is used to compute the principal components and their factor weights.
> ➤ Positive definiteness can be assured without having to use the same EWMA smoothing constant for all markets.

The 'splicing' method amounts to a two-stage orthogonal model (Alexander, 1997). First all risk factors, such as equity market indices, exchange rates, commodities, government bond and money market rates, must be grouped into reasonably highly correlated categories. These categories will normally reflect geographic locations and instrument types. Principal component analysis is then used to extract the key risk factors from each category and the orthogonal GARCH model or the orthogonal EWMA model is applied to generate the covariance matrix for each category. Then, in the second stage, the factor weights from the principal component analysis are used to 'splice' together a large covariance matrix for the original system.

The method is explained for just two categories; the generalization to any number of categories is straightforward. Let the first category be European equity indices, and let the second be European exchange rates. Suppose there are n variables in the first and m variables in the second. It is not the dimensions that matter. What does matter is that each category of risk factors is suitably co-dependent, so that it justifies the categorization as a separate and coherent category.

Stage 1: Find the principal components of each category, $\mathbf{P} = (P_1, \ldots, P_r)$, and separately $\mathbf{Q} = (Q_1, \ldots, Q_s)$ where r and s are number of principal components that are used in the representation of each category. Generally r will be much less than n and s will be much less than m. Denote by $\mathbf{A}$ $(n \times r)$ and $\mathbf{B}$ $(m \times s)$ the normalized factor weights matrices obtained in the PCA of the European equity and exchange rate categories, respectively. Then the 'within-factor' covariances, that is, the covariance matrix for the equity category and for the exchange rate category separately, are given by $\mathbf{A}\mathbf{D}_1\mathbf{A}'$ and $\mathbf{B}\mathbf{D}_2\mathbf{B}'$, respectively. Here $\mathbf{D}_1$ and $\mathbf{D}_2$ are the diagonal matrices of the univariate GARCH or EWMA variances of the principal components of each system.

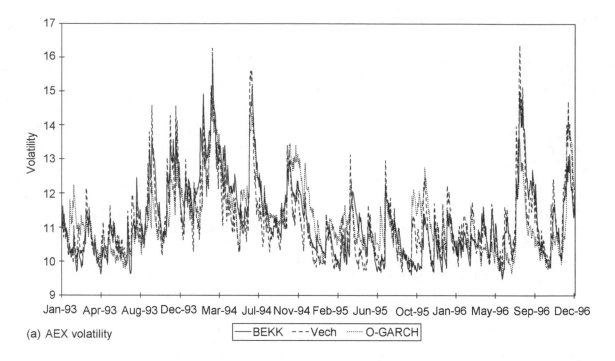

(a) AEX volatility

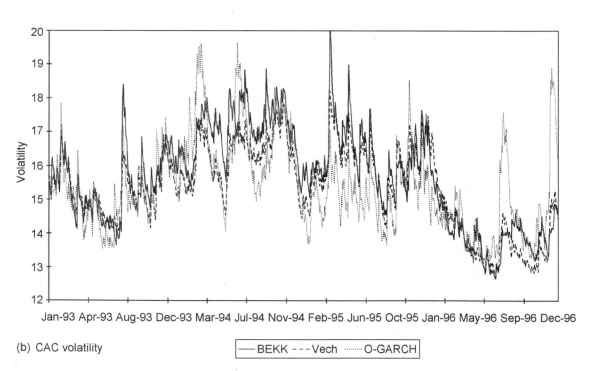

(b) CAC volatility

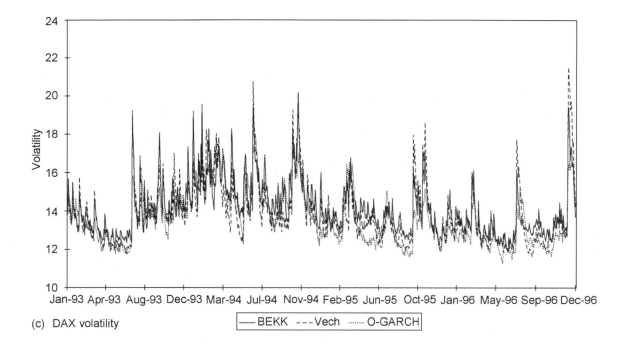

(c) DAX volatility

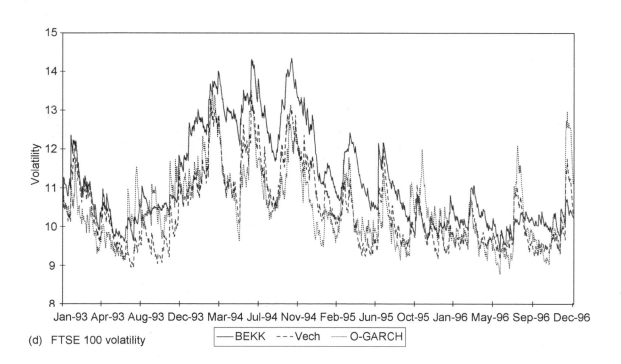

(d) FTSE 100 volatility

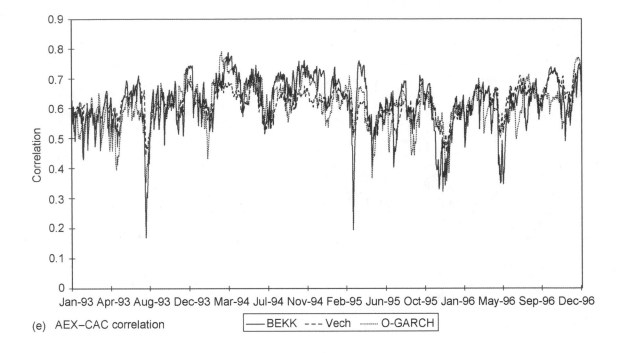

(e) AEX–CAC correlation

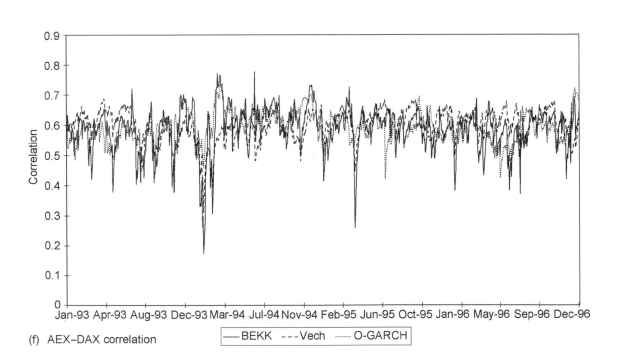

(f) AEX–DAX correlation

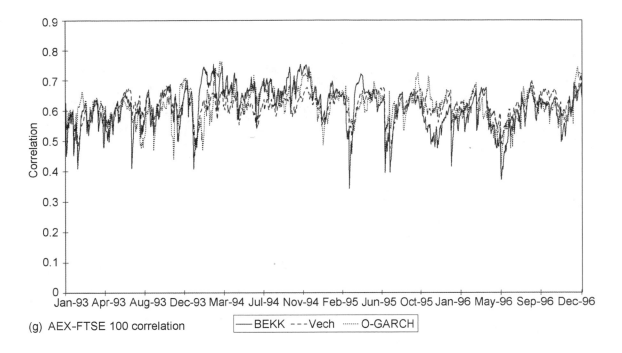

(g) AEX–FTSE 100 correlation   ——BEKK - - -Vech ·······O-GARCH

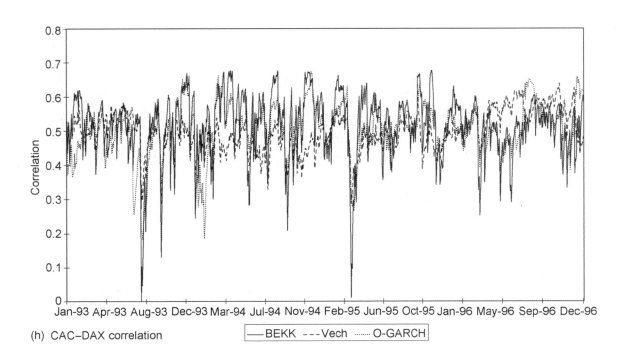

(h) CAC–DAX correlation   ——BEKK - - -Vech ·······O-GARCH

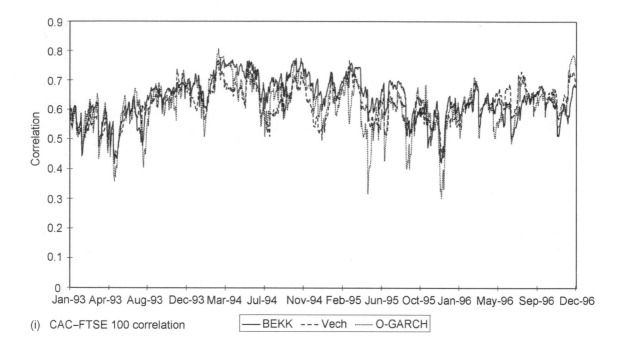

(i) CAC–FTSE 100 correlation   BEKK - - - Vech ········ O-GARCH

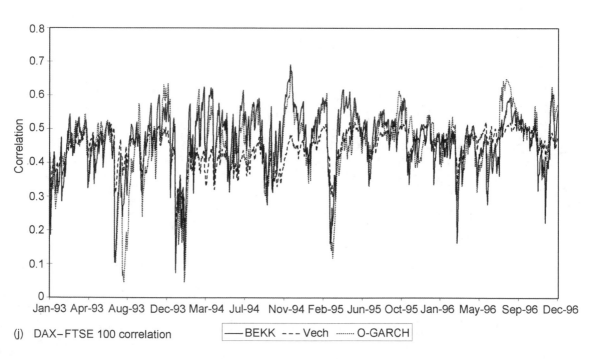

(j) DAX–FTSE 100 correlation   BEKK - - - Vech ········ O-GARCH

Figure 7.15 GARCH model volatility comparison: (a) AEX; (b) CAC; (c) DAX; (d) FTSE 100. GARCH model correlation comparison: (e) AEX–CAC; (f) AEX–DAX; (g) AEX–FTSE 100; (h) CAC–DAX; (i) CAC–FTSE 100; (j) DAX–FTSE 100.

Stage 2: Denote by $\mathbf{C}$ the $r \times s$ matrix of covariances of principal components across the two systems, that is, $\mathbf{C} = \{\text{cov}(P_i, Q_j)$. It is possible to estimate each element of the covariance $\mathbf{C}$ directly, using EWMA or bivariate GARCH. But it is better to estimate all elements of $\mathbf{C}$ simultaneously, and this can be done by using orthogonal EWMA or orthogonal GARCH a second time, now on a system of the $r + s$ principal components $P_1, \ldots, P_r, Q_1, \ldots, Q_s$. The cross-factor covariances of the original system will then be given by $\mathbf{ACB}'$ and the full covariance matrix of the original system is:

$$\begin{pmatrix} \mathbf{AD_1A'} & \mathbf{ACB'} \\ \mathbf{(ACB')'} & \mathbf{BD_2B'} \end{pmatrix}.$$

The within-factor covariance matrices $\mathbf{AD_1A'}$ and $\mathbf{BD_2B'}$ will always be positive semi-definite. But it is not always possible to guarantee positive semi-definiteness of the full covariance matrix of the original system, unless the off-diagonal blocks $\mathbf{ACB'}$ are set to zero.[28]

7.4.5 Summary

The examples presented in this section have been chosen to illustrate some of the many advantages of the orthogonal approach to generating covariance matrices:

➤ Computational difficulties are kept to a minimum:
  ○ only univariate GARCH models are necessary for orthogonal GARCH;
  ○ computation time is very significantly reduced.
➤ Market reaction and persistence parameters do not have to be the same for all assets:
  ○ these parameters will be determined by the correlation in the system;
  ○ therefore orthogonal EWMA is quite different from the RiskMetrics daily matrix.
➤ Mean-reverting covariance forecasts can be obtained:
  ○ the orthogonal GARCH model covariance matrix forecasts are based on the usual simple form for GARCH term structure forecasts (§4.4.1);
  ○ they may have convergent term structure forecasts even when univariate estimation gives IGARCH models.
➤ Block-diagonal covariance matrices will be positive semi-definite:
  ○ this is because each block is given by $\mathbf{AD_tA'}$, where $\mathbf{D_t}$ is a diagonal matrix of GARCH or EWMA volatilities and $\mathbf{A}$ is a matrix of constant factor weights;
  ○ however, when 'splicing' together the blocks into a very large covariance matrix, positive semi-definite checks will need to be employed.

---

[28] This may be a sensible thing to do, in the light of the huge instabilities often observed in cross-factor covariances.

➤ Choosing a few principal components to represent the system:
  ○ allows one to control the amount of 'noise' and therefore produce more stable correlation estimates;
  ○ it also allows one to forecast volatilities and correlations for all variables in the system, including those illiquid variables for which direct computation of forecasts is difficult.

8

Risk Measurement in Factor Models

Few equity portfolios are so small that they can be analysed using their representation as a weighted sum of the constituent assets. Instead the returns and risks of large equity portfolios are usually represented by a factor model. This is a linear model where portfolio returns are written as a sum of risk factor returns, weighted by sensitivities to these risk factors, plus a specific or idiosyncratic return that is not captured by the risk factors. The success of factor models in predicting returns in financial asset markets and analysing risk depends on both the choice of risk factors and the method for estimating factor sensitivities. Factors may be chosen according to economics (interest rates, inflation, gross domestic product, . . .), finance (market indices, yield curves, exchange rates, . . .), fundamentals (price/earning ratios, dividend yields, . . .) or statistics (principal component analysis, factor analysis, . . .). Depending on the type of factor model, sensitivities may be estimated using cross-sectional regression, time series techniques or eigenvalue methods.

The success of factor models depends on both the choice of risk factors and the method for estimating factor sensitivities

Factor models are normally used to model relationships between underlying assets, rather than between an underlying asset and its derivatives. Traditionally these models are based on an economic perspective. That is, returns are modelled by exogenous variables that are not always considered to be stochastic. And if they are, only their basic properties such as correlation really matter for the model. This is in contrast to the option pricing approach, where the probability distributions of underlying factors are fundamental to the model.

Portfolios that are constructed or analysed by factor models typically have pay-offs that are a linear function of the underlying asset, hence the term 'linear portfolios'. In options portfolios these pay-offs are non-linear. Quite different techniques are used to analyse options because there is a deterministic — not a statistical — relationship between the option price and the underlying price. Also, option pricing models are generally based on continuous time diffusion processes for the underlying risk factors, but a discrete time series approach is normally used for factor models.

The statistical modelling procedures for factor models have much in common with tracking models (§12.5). Both use linear statistical models to analyse portfolio risk and return, and the mean–variance analysis developed by Markovitz (1959) is a common tool for asset allocations (§7.2). But whereas factor models attempt to explain individual asset returns by returns to market indices or other factors, tracking models turn the problem around, seeking to explain a market index as a linear function of its constituents, or more generally to track the performance of a portfolio to another benchmark return.

This chapter examines how the volatility of a linear portfolio depends on the volatility of the underlying risk factors, the factor sensitivities and the specific risks. After describing some common specifications for linear factor models in §8.1, it looks at different modelling perspectives and how these relate to methods for estimating factor sensitivities. A number of classical statistical methods are described in §8.2, and then §8.3 discusses how Bayesian methods have been applied to the estimation of factor models. The chapter closes with general guidelines for specifying and estimating factor models and some quite cautionary conclusions.

8.1 Decomposing Risk in Factor Models

8.1.1 The Capital Asset Pricing Model

One of the most common applications of a simple linear regression model in financial markets is the capital asset pricing model (CAPM).[1] The CAPM model is written

$$y_t = \alpha + \beta X_t + \varepsilon_t \qquad (t = 1, \ldots, T), \tag{8.1}$$

where y_t denotes the return to a stock, X_t the return to a market index and ε_t the stock-specific return, all measured at time t.[2] In the original derivation of the model, based on the mean–variance analysis of Markovitz (1959), investors have access to risk-free lending and borrowing and so the returns X and y are excess over some risk-free rate (Sharpe, 1964; Lintner, 1965). Without this assumption, the Black (1972) version of the model is based on real returns. Linear regression provides a method, though not necessarily the best method, for estimating:

➢ the mispricing of the stock relative to the market, α;
➢ the stock sensitivity to the market risk factor, β;
➢ the residual return, ε.

Active portfolio managers seek to gain incremental returns with a positive alpha, but if markets are efficient and the Sharpe–Lintner version of the

---

[1] This is not a text on portfolio theory and it is not intended to describe the fundamental assumptions and developments of the CAPM here. There are already many excellent texts that cover this topic — for example, Campbell *et al.* (1997).

[2] The subscript t is used throughout, assuming time series data are used to fit the model. However cross-sectional or panel data might also be used.

CAPM is the correct model, alpha should be zero. Statistical procedures such as those described in Appendix 2 may be used to test the hypothesis that $\alpha = 0$; in fact these form the basis of many empirical tests of the validity of different versions of the CAPM.

Beta provides a measure of how the stock responds to changes in the index: If β is insignificantly different from 0 the index has no statistical effect on the stock, and if it is insignificantly different from 1 then changes in the index are matched by changes in the stock. The residual returns are assumed to be diversifiable and therefore unimportant: if the portfolio has many assets the stock-specific returns will tend to cancel each other out. The market represents the *undiversifiable risk* this is common to all stocks and therefore the stock beta reflects the 'riskiness' of the stock relative to the market: stocks that have a beta significantly less than 1 are regarded as 'low risk' investments, those with beta significantly greater than 1 are categorized as 'high risk'. Assuming the true value of beta is a constant, it is defined as

The residual returns are assumed to be diversifiable and therefore unimportant: if the portfolio has many assets the stock-specific returns will tend to cancel each other out

$$\beta_y = \sigma_{Xy}/\sigma_X^2, \tag{8.2}$$

where σ_{Xy} is the unconditional covariance of the return of stock y with the return of the market X, and σ_X^2 is the unconditional variance of the return of the market.

The estimation of beta in a CAPM can be very sensitive to the definitions of the market portfolio and the risk-free rate. The market portfolio should include all risky assets, but most indices only contain a subset. So betas with respect to the Dow Jones 30 can be very different from betas with respect to the S&P 500, for example. It is not always easy to know what is the appropriate risk-free rate either. Short-term treasury bills are often taken as 'risk-free', thus ignoring uncertainties about inflation and assuming bills are held to maturity. However, the beta may equally well be measured in terms of total returns if the risk-free rate really does have zero variance.[3]

Portfolio betas may be measured directly by using return data at the portfolio level. An artificial history of portfolios returns is constructed using the current portfolio weights and historic data on each asset. Alternatively, the individual stock betas may be weighted by the proportion of the fund that is invested in stock with return y, denoted w_y. Then summation gives the net beta of the portfolio as

$$\beta_Y = \sum w_y \beta_y.$$

When ordinary least squares is used to estimate the betas the two methods will give the same results (§8.2.2).

The portfolio beta provides a very simple framework for predicting portfolio

---

[3] Denote by r the risk-free rate, so the estimate of beta is $\text{cov}(X-r,y-r)/V(X-r) = [\text{cov}(X,y) - \text{cov}(X,r) - \text{cov}(y,r) + V(r)] / [V(X) - 2\text{cov}(X,r) + V(r)] = \text{cov}(X,y)/V(X)$ if $V(r)=0$.

returns and modelling portfolio risk. A 1% fall in the market is expected to be matched by a $\beta\%$ fall in the portfolio, so a portfolio with beta greater than 1 is considered more risky than a portfolio with beta less than 1. A portfolio manager seeking only to track an index will diversify the portfolio to achieve a beta of 1, an alpha of 0 and residual returns as small as possible to minimize the tracking error. On the other hand, active portfolio managers that seek positive alpha may have betas that are somewhat greater than 1 if they are willing to accept an increased risk for the incremental return above the index.

The CAPM attributes risk to three sources: assuming $\text{cov}(X_t, \varepsilon_t) = 0$ for all t, taking variances of (8.1) gives

$$V(y) = \beta^2 V(X) + V(\varepsilon).$$

More generally, recall that for n assets with returns r_i $(i = 1, \ldots, n)$ in a portfolio with weights $\mathbf{w} = (w_1, \ldots, w_n)'$ where $\Sigma w_j = 1$, the portfolio return is $R_P = w_1 r_1 + \ldots + w_n r_n = \mathbf{w}'\mathbf{r}$. The portfolio variance $V(P)$ is given by the quadratic form $\mathbf{w}'\mathbf{V}\mathbf{w}$, where $\mathbf{V}$ is the covariance matrix of individual asset returns (§7.1.1). For equities, which are modelled by the CAPM and it is assumed that $\text{cov}(X_t, \varepsilon_{it}) = 0$ for all i and t, the diagonal elements of $\mathbf{V}$ are $\beta_i^2 V(X) + V(\varepsilon_i)$ and the off-diagonal elements of $\mathbf{V}$ are given by $\beta_i \beta_j V(X) + \text{cov}(\varepsilon_i, \varepsilon_j)$. Thus

$$\mathbf{V} = \boldsymbol{\beta} V(X) \boldsymbol{\beta}' + \mathbf{V}_\varepsilon, \tag{8.3}$$

where $\boldsymbol{\beta} = (\beta_1, \ldots, \beta_n)'$ is the vector of equity betas and $\mathbf{V}_\varepsilon$ is the $n \times n$ specific risk covariance matrix. Portfolio risk, as measured by the portfolio variance, is given by

$$V(P) = \mathbf{w}' \boldsymbol{\beta} V(X) \boldsymbol{\beta}' \mathbf{w} + \mathbf{w}' \mathbf{V}_\varepsilon \mathbf{w}. \tag{8.4}$$

This illustrates the three sources of risk in a factor model:

➤ factor sensitivities (the beta vector, $\boldsymbol{\beta}$);
➤ market risk (the variance of the market risk factor, $V(X)$);
➤ specific risks (the residual covariances, $\mathbf{V}_\varepsilon$).

An example of the application of (8.4) will be given in §8.2.4, after the methods used to estimate factor sensitivities have been described. See also the **risk decomposition** spreadsheet on the CD.

If relevant risk factors are omitted from the model the assumption $\text{cov}(X_t, \varepsilon_t) = 0$ will not hold

This risk decomposition is totally dependent on the assumption $\text{cov}(X_t, \varepsilon_t) = 0$ and this in turn depends very much on the model specification (§8.5). If relevant risk factors are omitted from the model, the variation from these factors can only be attributed to the specific risks, and if these omitted factors are correlated with the market risk factor then the assumption $\text{cov}(X_t, \varepsilon_t) = 0$ will not hold. This is one of the reasons why it is important to include all possible risk factors in the model for a linear portfolio, and often there are too many sources of risk to capture with the simple CAPM alone.

8.1.2 Multi-factor Fundamental Models

Suppose a portfolio consists of two groups of stocks, a low-beta group in industry sector A and a high-beta group in industry sector B, and suppose that the net portfolio beta is 1, so that the CAPM predicts that the portfolio should move in line with the market. Any differences between the portfolio return and the market return are attributed to stock-specific risks, which in a sufficiently large portfolio should be diversified away. However, if the market index contains stocks from other industry sectors that have different characteristics to sector A and sector B, the portfolio will not necessarily move in line with the market.

The arbitrage pricing theory (APT), introduced by Ross (1976), resolves this problem by extending the CAPM to a more general linear model. In the APT model the returns from each asset are represented as a linear sum of several economic 'risk factors' that are common to all assets. The no-arbitrage principle implies that the expected returns to portfolios that have the same net exposure to these common risk factors will be equalized provided the number of assets in the portfolios is large in relation to the number of risk factors and that specific risks have been diversified away.

More general factor models that are based on APT represent the returns to each asset in a portfolio by many risk factors:

$$R_{jt} = \beta_{1j}X_{1t} + \beta_{2j}X_{2t} + \ldots + \beta_{kj}X_{kt} + \varepsilon_{jt}, \tag{8.5}$$

where R_j denotes the returns to the jth asset in the portfolio ($j = 1, \ldots, n$), X_i denotes the return to the ith risk factor ($i = 2, \ldots, k$, and $X_1 = 1$), β_{ij} denotes the sensitivity of the jth asset to the ith risk factor, and ε_j denotes the residual of the jth asset. The model (8.5) is a system of n general linear regression equations. A matrix form of this model is[4]

$$\mathbf{r}_j = \mathbf{X}\boldsymbol{\beta}_j + \boldsymbol{\varepsilon}_j,$$

where $\mathbf{r}_j$ is the $T \times 1$ vector of returns to asset j, $\mathbf{X}$ is the $T \times k$ matrix whose ith column is the $T \times 1$ vector $\mathbf{X}_i$ of data on the ith risk factor returns, $\boldsymbol{\beta}_j$ is the $k \times 1$ vector $(\beta_{1j}, \ldots, \beta_{kj})'$ and $\boldsymbol{\varepsilon}_j$ is the $T \times 1$ vector $(\varepsilon_{j1}, \ldots, \varepsilon_{jT})'$.

How should the risk factors in an APT model be specified? Economic theory would imply that factors are at levels of increasing granularity: international equity market indices; industrial sector indices within each market; and the input–output criteria used for national accounts within each sector (wage rates, exchange rates, interest rates, taxes, commodity prices and other variables in the Standard Industrial Classification code). However, an enormous quantity of data are required to estimate such models with a complete specification, and it is more usual to determine potential factors by a consensus view from market

---

[4] Note that an alternative matrix form, $\mathbf{r} = \mathbf{Bx} + \boldsymbol{\varepsilon}$, was used in §7.2.2.

Certain factors such as prices/earnings ratio, book-to-price ratio, debt/ equity ratio and market capitalization have emerged as standard 'fundamental' factors

analysts. Certain factors such as prices/earnings ratio, book-to-price ratio, debt/equity ratio and market capitalization have emerged as standard 'fundamental' factors:

The S&P/BARRA Growth and Value Indexes are constructed by dividing the stocks in an index according to a single attribute: book-to-price ratio. This splits the index into two mutually exclusive groups designed to track two of the predominant investment styles in the U.S. equity market. The value index contains firms with higher book-to-price ratios; conversely, the growth index has firms with lower book-to-price ratios. Each company in the index is assigned to either the value or growth index so that the two style indices 'add up' to the full index. Like the full S&P indexes, the value and growth indexes are capitalization-weighted, meaning that each stock is weighted in proportion to its market value. The design of the indexes is an outgrowth of research into investment styles in the U.S. equity market performed by 1990 Nobel Laureate William F. Sharpe. Sharpe found that the value/growth dimension (as represented by price-to-book ratios), along with the large/small dimension (as represented by market capitalization), appears to explain many of the differences in returns to U.S. equity mutual funds.

(www.barra.com, 1999)

For international equity markets, data analysis firms such as Barra use certain common fundamental factors such as: volatility, momentum, size, trading activity, growth, earnings yield, value, earnings variability, leverage, labour intensity and foreign currency exposure. But some country models may require quite idiosyncratic factors (e.g. the 'family control indicator' in Thailand, or foreign exports in South Africa). The point to note is that a vast number of decisions must be made about the nature of the variables and the data that are relevant for analysis in order to apply the APT framework to equity markets. We shall return to this problem at the end of the chapter.

The point to note is that a vast number of decisions must be made in order to apply the APT framework

The risk decomposition (8.4) for portfolios of assets modelled by the simple CAPM may be generalized to portfolios where assets are modelled by multi-factor models. Stacking the estimates of the betas in (8.5) in an $n \times k$ estimated sensitivity matrix $\mathbf{B}$ gives an estimated portfolio beta with respect to each risk factor as follows: for an $n \times 1$ vector of portfolio holdings $\mathbf{w} = (w_1, \ldots, w_n)'$, where $\Sigma w_j = 1$, the net portfolio beta vector is a $k \times 1$ vector $\mathbf{B}'\mathbf{w}$, where the ith element is the estimated net portfolio sensitivity with respect to the ith risk factor. With this notation it can be seen that multi-factor models allow the decomposition of portfolio variance into two terms corresponding to the risks due to fundamental and specific factors:

$$V_P = \mathbf{w}'\mathbf{B}\mathbf{V}_x\mathbf{B}'\mathbf{w} + \mathbf{w}'\mathbf{V}_\varepsilon\mathbf{w}, \qquad (8.6)$$

where $\mathbf{V}_x$ is the $k \times k$ covariance matrix of risk factor returns and $\mathbf{V}_\varepsilon$ is the $n \times n$ specific risk covariance matrix.

The residuals $\mathbf{e}_1, \ldots, \mathbf{e}_n$ from the estimation of (8.5) are used to estimate their covariance matrix $\mathbf{V}_\varepsilon$. This specific risk covariance matrix has a number of applications in addition to the risk decomposition (8.6), that is used by portfolio risk analysts. For example, if the choice of risk factors differs for different stocks in the portfolio, the most efficient parameter estimates will be obtained using generalized least squares (§A.3.3) which requires the matrix $\mathbf{V}_\varepsilon$. The specific risk covariance matrix is also necessary to measure the contribution of the specific risks to the total value-at-risk of a portfolio. This can reduce market risk capital charges considerably compared to the standard methods (§9.3.3).

The specific risk covariance matrix is also necessary to measure the contribution of the specific risks to the total value-at-risk of a portfolio

8.1.3 Statistical Factor Models

Statistical factor models are a common alternative to fundamental factor models. They have no need for data on possible explanatory variables and no problems with multicollinearity, but there is no economic interpretation of the variables. One of the most popular statistical techniques for developing multi-factor models for asset risk management is principal component analysis. Although the first principal component will still represent a simultaneous shift in all assets if they are highly correlated (§6.2), the interpretation of lesser principal components will depend on an ordering in the system. This is possible in term structures and in implied volatilities (according to strike or moneyness), but otherwise an ordering is not normally possible.

If the risk factors are taken as the principal components of a system we have an orthogonal factor model. To see this, suppose that the ith asset return is X_i, so that the normalized variables are $X_i^* = (X_i - \mu_i)/\sigma_i$, where μ_i and σ_i are the mean and standard deviation of X_i for $i = 1, \ldots, k$. Write the principal components representation (6.2) as

$$X_i^* = w_{i1}^* P_1 + w_{i2}^* P_2 + \ldots + w_{ik}^* P_k, \tag{8.7}$$

where w_{ij}^* is the factor weight on the jth component in the representation for the ith normalized asset return. In terms of the original asset returns this can be written

$$X_i = \mu_i + w_{i1} P_1 + w_{i2} P_2 + \ldots + w_{im} P_m + \varepsilon_i, \tag{8.8}$$

where $w_{ij} = w_{ij}^* \sigma_i$ and the error term in (8.8) picks up the approximation from using only m of the k principal components. The factors $P_1, \ldots, P_m$ are orthogonal with each other and with the error term, and the model parameters w_{ij} are easily calculated from the principal component factor weights and the asset return standard deviations.

Risk decomposition in statistical factor models is analogous to (8.6). The factor weights $w_{ij} = w_{ij}^* \sigma_i$ are equivalent to the beta estimates, and to calculate the specific risk matrix in (8.6) calculate the model errors in (8.8) and take an equally weighted average covariance matrix of these as described in §3.1.[5]

With statistical factor models the difficult model specification issues that will be discussed in §8.4 are avoided. It is only necessary to decide on the number of principal components and the length of data used to calculate them; the choice will depend on the results of backtesting the model.

8.2   Classical Risk Measurement Techniques

The diversity of multi-factor model implementations is not only due to differences in risk factors or different estimation periods. The choice of estimation methods will also influence results: in particular, it will affect the ability of the model to capture portfolio risk characteristics. Portfolio risk has been ascribed to sensitivities, risk factors and specific components. This section shows how estimates of all these quantities will depend on a number of different covariance matrices: covariances between the risk factors, covariances between the assets and the risk factors, and covariances between residuals of different assets. We discuss the different methods that are available for estimating these covariance matrices and the context where each could be applied.

8.2.1   The Different Perspectives of Risk Managers and Asset Managers

Classical economics assumes that there is one true value for each model parameter. However, from a risk management perspective it is better to assume that the 'true' betas vary over time

Many asset managers simply take an average beta over a long period of time; typically 5 years of monthly data will produce robust results when fitting a CAPM. In doing so they are taking the economist's perspective. Classical economics assumes that there is one true value for each model parameter. In this case OLS is often the most efficient estimator (§A.2.4) and better results are obtained when long periods of data are used, because any differences in estimates are only due to sampling error and the more data are used the lower the sampling variation (§5.2.1). It is fine to estimate betas using long-term equally weighted averages when considering long-term 'buy–hold' strategies. However, conditions in a firm or an industry can change quite abruptly, so covariances may be quite unstable. Risk managers are concerned by the accurate estimation of factor sensitivities from day to day, since these factor sensitivities are crucial inputs to the risk model. For modelling short-term risk exposures such as 1-day VaR, rather than assuming there is one true value for the underlying parameter it is preferable to assume that the parameters themselves change over time. So from a risk management perspective it is better to assume that the 'true' betas vary over time. In this case OLS is not the appropriate modelling methodology. For accurate daily measures of

---

[5] Since principal components are based on the equally weighted correlation matrix, it is consistent to apply equal weighting for the specific covariance matrix also.

sensitivities to be used in risk models such as the covariance VaR model of §9.3, we require a theoretical model that is based on the time-varying parameter assumption.

8.2.2 Methods Relevant for Constant Parameter Assumptions

The ordinary least squares method of estimating the covariance matrices that determine portfolio risk in factor models is described in Appendix 2. It gives equal weighting to all observations in the sample. Thus OLS betas are related to the unconditional correlation ρ between the risk factor return and the asset return. For example, in the simple CAPM defined by (8.1) and (8.2) the unconditional correlation ρ and the OLS beta are related by

$$\beta = \rho v, \qquad (8.9)$$

where v denotes the relative volatility of the asset relative to the market. Thus if the asset is perfectly correlated with the market, so that there is no specific return, the beta is just the relative volatility. Stocks that tend to move in the opposite direction to the market may have negative betas; and when stocks are relatively volatile, betas may be much greater than one.

If the asset is perfectly correlated with the market, so that there is no specific return, the beta is just the relative volatility

In multi-factor models the OLS sensitivity estimates, which are determined by the covariance and variances of stock and market excess returns, are obtained by applying the formulae in §A.1.2. The OLS estimator of $\boldsymbol{\beta}_j$ is the inverse of the covariance matrix between risk factors, times the vector of covariances between the jth asset returns and the risk factors:

$$\mathbf{b}_j = (\mathbf{X}'\mathbf{X})^{-1}\mathbf{X}'\mathbf{r}_j. \qquad (8.10)$$

These estimates are $k \times 1$ vectors in which the ith element is the estimated asset sensitivity to the ith risk factor. To obtain the OLS specific risk covariance matrix first obtain the OLS estimates from (8.10) and then calculate the OLS residuals as $\mathbf{e}_j = \mathbf{r}_j - \mathbf{X}\mathbf{b}_j$. Then $\mathbf{e}_i'\mathbf{e}_j/T$ is the estimate of the (i, j)th element of $\mathbf{V}_\varepsilon$.

Note that fitting the model (8.10) for each stock separately makes some oversimplistic assumptions about the behaviour of stock returns. In particular, it should not be assumed that the movements of some stocks in a portfolio will be unrelated to the behaviour of other stocks in a portfolio. Instead, if the return on one asset is unusually high, this should give some useful information about the returns on some of the other assets in the portfolio. However, this type of useful information will be overlooked if each parameter vector is estimated on an individual basis using OLS applied to each equation in (8.10) separately.

Generalized least squares is a more general method of estimation that takes account of the relations between different asset returns by allowing the error processes $\varepsilon_1, \ldots, \varepsilon_n$ to be correlated with each other. In §A.3.3 it is shown that if all the risk factors are identical in each equation, generalized least squares is equivalent to ordinary least squares. But if different assets in the portfolio have a different set of risk factors there will be considerable efficiency gains when generalized least squares is used to estimate factor sensitivities.

If different assets in the portfolio have a different set of risk factors there will be considerable efficiency gains when generalized least squares is used to estimate factor sensitivities

8.2.3 Methods Relevant for Time-Varying Parameter Assumptions

The OLS method gives equal weights to all observations in the sample used to estimate the beta. Therefore, it does not emphasize the importance of the most recent market conditions. If a stock and the index have even just one large synchronous movement during the sample period, this single event will have a great effect on the beta estimate; and this effect will not diminish with time — until it drops out of the average. Similarly, if the stock experiences an exceptional return at any point in the data period, this will also increase the current beta estimate for as long as that return remains in the averaging period. In fact OLS beta estimates have exactly the same problems of 'ghost features' and artificial stability as the equally weighted measures of volatility and correlation (§3.1).

For the purpose of measuring short-term risk exposures, therefore, it may be better to use a model that does not assume that the beta is constant over time. Instead one can assume that the true parameter beta takes different values at different points in time. This time-varying parameter assumption is an extension of the time-varying conditional correlation parameters introduced in §1.4. To see this, note that one can extend the definition (8.2) of a CAPM market beta to conditional covariances and variances in the natural way:

$$\beta_t = \sigma_{Xy,t}/\sigma_{X,t}^2 = \rho_t \nu_t, \tag{8.11}$$

OLS beta estimates have exactly the same problems of 'ghost features' and artificial stability as the equally weighted measures of volatility and correlation

where $\sigma_{Xy,t}$ is the conditional covariance, $\sigma_{X,t}^2$ is the conditional variance of the market, ρ_t is the conditional correlation and ν_t is the relative conditional volatility at time t. Similarly, in a multi-factor model, where in (8.10) the beta estimate is given by the inverse risk factor covariance matrix multiplied by the vector of covariances between the stock and the risk factors, the use of conditional covariance matrices in place of unconditional covariance matrices will extend the constant parameter estimate to an estimate of a time-varying beta vector. In this way the estimates of time-varying market betas can be obtained from time-varying volatility and correlation estimates. An example of the estimation of a time-varying beta was given in §4.5.1.

8.2.4 Index Stripping

Having estimated a stock beta and found the residuals, a useful technique for the risk analysis of a stock is to use (8.3) to decompose the total volatility of the stock into market and specific components. This can also be done at the

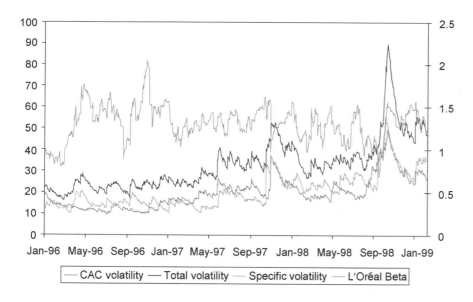

Figure 8.1 Decomposing L'Oréal total volatility into market and specific components.

portoflio level, using (8.4). At any point in time the total volatility of the stock or portfolio is attributed to two components: market volatility and specific volatility.

Figure 8.1 shows the exponentially weighted moving average estimates of total, market and specific volatilities for the stock L'Oréal in the CAC index from 2 January 1996 to 9 February 1999. The specific volatility is calculated from the stock-specific return series: $y_t - \beta_t X_t$, where y_t is the stock return, X_t is the market return and β_t is the EWMA stock beta which is also shown on the graph on the right-hand scale. All EWMAs have been calculated with a smoothing constant of 0.94. For most of the period the L'Oréal beta has been greater than 1, and the riskiness of this stock is augmented by a specific volatility of an order of magnitude similar to the market volatility. On 12 October 1998 L'Oréal volatility reached almost 90%, but only part of this was attributed to increase volatility in the CAC during the global equity market crash. A large part of this volatility was attributed to specific risk that has not been captured by the market factor. Other examples can be generated using the **risk decomposition** spreadsheet on the CD.

8.3 Bayesian Methods for Estimating Factor Sensitivities

Classical statisticians assume that at any point in time there is one true value for a model parameter. This 'frequentist' approach to statistics focuses on the question 'what is the probability of the data given the model parameters?'. That is, the functional form and the parameters of the model are as fixed, so that probabilistic statements are only made about the likelihood of the sample data given assumed parameter values.

This section examines what can be said about the uncertainty of model parameters. There may well be one true value at any point in time, but since we shall never know what it is, we could represent the possible true values of a parameter by a probability distribution. In this way probabilistic statements can also be made about model parameters, thus turning around the question above to ask 'what is the probability of the parameter given the data?'.

This approach has been named after the Rev. Thomas Bayes, whose 'Essay towards solving a problem in the doctrine of chances' was published posthumously in the *Philosophical Transactions of the Royal Society of London* in 1764. The Bayesian process of statistical estimation is one of continuously revising and refining our subjective beliefs as more data become available. It can be considered as an extension of, rather than an alternative to, classical inference: indeed, some of the best classical estimators may be regarded as basic forms of Bayesian estimator.[6]

Some securities firms (for example, Merrill Lynch) have published stock betas based on Bayesian methods. Bayesian methods extend the classical viewpoint so that prior information about model parameters becomes part of the model fitting process. In this section it will be shown that Bayesian betas can be substantially different from OLS beta estimates, depending on the strength of one's prior beliefs about the true value of a beta.

The idea is to express uncertainty about the true value of a model parameter with a 'prior' density that describes one's beliefs about this true value

Bayesian estimates are a combination of prior beliefs and sample information. The idea is to express uncertainty about the true value of a model parameter with a 'prior' density that describes one's beliefs about this true value. Note that these beliefs can be entirely 'subjective' if so wished. Then more 'objective' information is added, in the form of a historic sample. This information is summarized in a likelihood function[7] that is used to update the prior density to a 'posterior' density, using the method for multiplying conditional probabilities which is referred to as Bayes' rule.

8.3.1 Bayes' Rule

The cornerstone of Bayesian methods is the theorem of conditional probability of events X and Y:

$$\text{Prob}(X \text{ and } Y) = \text{Prob}(X|Y)\text{Prob}(Y) = \text{Prob}(Y|X)\text{Prob}(X).$$

[6] In fact the maximum likelihood estimator is a Bayesian estimator with a non-informative prior.

[7] The difference between the prior and the likelihood is that sample information is always rooted in some real observable quantities (the new data) whereas prior densities reflect one's views prior to collecting the new data. These views may or may not have an empirical basis.

This can be rewritten in a form that is known as Bayes' rule, which shows how prior information about Y may be used to revise the probability of X:

$$\text{Prob}(X|Y) = \text{Prob}(Y|X)\text{Prob}(X)/\text{Prob}(Y).$$

When Bayes' rule is applied to distributions about model parameters, it becomes

$$\text{Prob}(\text{parameters}|\text{data}) = \text{Prob}(\text{data}|\text{parameters})\text{Prob}(\text{parameters})/\text{Prob}(\text{data}).$$

The unconditional probability of the data, Prob(data), only serves as a scaling constant, and the generic form of Bayes' rule is usually written:

$$\text{Prob}(\text{parameters}|\text{data}) \propto \text{Prob}(\text{data}|\text{parameters})\text{Prob}(\text{parameters}).$$

Prior beliefs about the parameters are given by the *prior density*, Prob(parameters); and the likelihood of the sample data, Prob(data|parameters), is called the *sample likelihood*. The product of these two densities defines the *posterior density*, Prob(parameters|data), which incorporates both prior beliefs and sample information into an updated view of the model parameters, as depicted in Figure 8.2.

If prior beliefs are that all possible values of parameters are equally likely, this is the same as saying there is no prior information. The prior density is just the uniform density and the posterior density is just the same as the sample likelihood. On the other hand, if sample data are not available then the posterior density is the same as the prior density. More generally, the posterior density will have a lower variance than both the prior density and the sample likelihood. The increased accuracy reflects the value of additional information, whether subjective, as encapsulated by prior beliefs, or objective, as represented in the sample likelihood.

Subjective beliefs may have a great influence on model parameter estimates if they are expressed with a high degree of confidence

Subjective beliefs may have a great influence on model parameter estimates if they are expressed with a high degree of confidence. Figure 8.3 shows two posterior densities based on the same likelihood. In Figure 8.3a the prior beliefs are rather uncertain, which is represented by the large variance of the prior

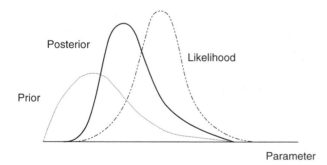

Figure 8.2 The posterior density is the product of the prior density and the sample likelihood.

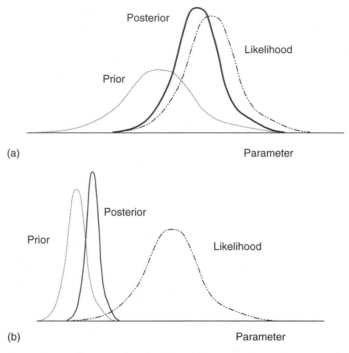

Figure 8.3 The posterior density with: (a) an uncertain prior; (b) a certain prior.

density. In this case the posterior mean will be close to the sample mean and prior beliefs will have little influence on the parameter estimates. But in Figure 8.3b, where prior beliefs are expressed with a high degree of confidence, the posterior density is much closer to the prior density and parameter estimates will be much influenced by subjective prior beliefs.

We have seen that it is not just prior expectations that influence the Bayesian estimate: the degree of confidence held in one's beliefs also has an effect. In Bayesian analysis the posterior density will take more or less account of objective sample information, depending on the confidence of beliefs as represented by the variance of prior densities. How confident should prior beliefs be? One should always use a prior that reflects all the information, views and opinions that one has *a priori*—no more, no less. This is crucial for rational descriptions and decision-making.

8.3.2 Bayesian Estimation of Factor Models

In the context of specifying a multi-factor model $\mathbf{r} = \mathbf{X}\boldsymbol{\beta} + \boldsymbol{\varepsilon}$, Bayes' rule becomes[8]

---

[8] We assume that the variance of the error term, σ^2 is known, so that it is only the factor sensitivities $\boldsymbol{\beta}$ that will be estimated by the Bayesian method. See Greene (1998) for the generalization to the case where σ^2 is also estimated by Bayesian methods.

$$f(\boldsymbol{\beta}|\mathbf{r}, \mathbf{X}, \sigma^2) = Kg(\mathbf{r}|\boldsymbol{\beta}, \mathbf{X}, \sigma^2)h(\boldsymbol{\beta}), \tag{8.11}$$

where:

➤ $h(\boldsymbol{\beta})$ is a prior density function that expresses uncertain views about the model parameters $\boldsymbol{\beta}$ before adding any sample information on $\mathbf{r}$, $\mathbf{X}$ and σ^2;

➤ $g(\mathbf{r}|\boldsymbol{\beta}, \mathbf{X}, \sigma^2)$ is the joint density function of the dependent variable when the parameters and explanatory variables are regarded as fixed. This is obtained from the likelihood of the sample (see appendix 6);

➤ $f(\boldsymbol{\beta}|\mathbf{r}, \mathbf{X}, \sigma^2)$ is the posterior density function that expresses revised views on parameter uncertainties, given the beliefs about $\boldsymbol{\beta}$ expressed in the prior density and the sample information on $\mathbf{r}$, $\mathbf{X}$ and σ^2;

➤ K is the normalization constant that makes $f(\boldsymbol{\beta}|\mathbf{r}, \mathbf{X}, \sigma^2)$ into a proper density function.

The strength of Bayesian methods is their ability to take into account, via the prior density $h(\boldsymbol{\beta})$, any sort of prior information about model parameters. It may be purely subjective views on model parameters, or prior densities can be based on information from a previous model fitting exercise. Of course, in a proper density function the area under the curve is 1, but it is usual to express total lack of prior information about the parameters by an improper density function, the 'non-informative' prior $h(\boldsymbol{\beta}) = 1$.[9] With a non-informative prior the posterior density is just the normalized likelihood of the sample, so with a non-informative prior Bayesian estimates reduce to the estimates from standard sampling theory, such as the maximum likelihood estimates; one would not expect anything else.

The strength of Bayesian methods is their ability to take into account, via the prior density $h(\boldsymbol{\beta})$, any sort of prior information about model parameters

For convenience, informative priors are commonly described using the same shape of density function as the likelihood, otherwise (8.11) would give some rather strange functional forms for the posterior density. Even with these so called *conjugate priors* the algebra of normalization can become quite burdensome. However, retaining the assumption of normal disturbances, $\boldsymbol{\varepsilon} \sim N(0, \sigma^2 \mathbf{I})$, with known variance σ^2 does simplify things considerably. Since $\boldsymbol{\varepsilon} \sim N(0, \sigma^2 \mathbf{I})$ implies $\mathbf{r} \sim N(\mathbf{X}\boldsymbol{\beta}, \sigma^2 \mathbf{I})$, an informative prior on $\boldsymbol{\beta}$ that has the same functional form as the likelihood will take the form

$$\boldsymbol{\beta} \sim N(\boldsymbol{\beta}_0, \boldsymbol{\Sigma}_0).$$

In this case, after rather a lot of algebra (see Greene, 1998; Griffiths *et al.*, 1993), it may be shown that the Bayesian estimators will also be normally distributed. The revised estimators of the model parameters will lie on the line between the prior and sample parameter estimates:

$$\mathbf{b}^* = \mathbf{F}\boldsymbol{\beta}_0 + (\mathbf{I} - \mathbf{F})\mathbf{b},$$

where

---

[9] The appropriate K for normalization is found after the functional form of the posterior has been derived. Because this normalization comes at the end it is not a problem to use improper densities in the prior.

$$\mathbf{F} = \mathbf{\Sigma}^* \mathbf{\Sigma}_0^{-1}$$

and $\mathbf{\Sigma}^*$ is the covariance matrix of the Bayesian estimators given by

$$\mathbf{\Sigma}^{*-1} = \mathbf{\Sigma}_0^{-1} + \mathbf{\Sigma}^{-1},$$

in which $\mathbf{\Sigma}$ is the covariance matrix of the OLS sample estimators, viz. $\sigma^2(\mathbf{X}'\mathbf{X})^{-1}$.

Bayesian estimates of beta will move closer to the value of beta that is assumed in the prior beliefs as more confidence is expressed in those beliefs

Thus Bayesian betas are linearly interpolated between the OLS estimate (the mean of the likelihood) and the prior belief (the mean of the prior density). The exact point for the posterior estimate on the line between these two estimates will depend on the standard errors of these densities. In fact Bayesian estimates of beta will move closer to the value of beta that is assumed in the prior beliefs as more confidence is expressed in those beliefs, as the example below demonstrates.

Since σ^2 is really unknown, it is common to replace it in the above by its posterior estimate s^2. In this case Greene (1998) shows that the posterior density will be t-distributed with expectation

$$\mathbf{b}^* = \mathbf{\Sigma}^*(\mathbf{\Sigma}_0^{-1}\boldsymbol{\beta}_0 + \mathbf{\Sigma}_1^{-1}\mathbf{b}), \qquad (8.12)$$

and the estimated variance $\mathbf{\Sigma}^*$ is given by

$$\mathbf{\Sigma}^{*-1} = c(\mathbf{\Sigma}_0^{-1} + \mathbf{\Sigma}_1^{-1}), \qquad (8.13)$$

where $\mathbf{\Sigma}_1$ is the estimated covariance matrix of the OLS sample estimators, viz. $s^2(\mathbf{X}'\mathbf{X})^{-1}$ and c is a degrees-of-freedom-adjustment, $c = m/(m-2)$, in which m represents the degrees of freedom in the model.

To illustrate how to calculate Bayesian estimates of asset betas, consider the example of estimating a CAPM for Eletrobrás in the Ibovespa index based on daily data for the period 1 August 1994 to 30 December 1997. The OLS estimate of the stock beta is 1.211, with a standard error of 0.021586 (§A.1.3 and §A.2.2). Now suppose that a prior density on this beta is normal with expected value 0.8 with a standard error of 0.1. Since the sample size is so large the t-distributed posterior converges to a normal posterior, and the degrees-of-freedom correction in (8.13) is approximately 1. Thus the estimated variance of the posterior estimator computed from (8.13) is simply

$$((0.021586)^{-2} + (0.1)^{-2})^{-1} = 0.0004452.$$

Putting this in (8.12) gives the revised estimate for the stock beta, given both sample data and prior beliefs, as

$$0.0004452(1.211/(0.021586)^2 + 0.8/(0.1)^2) = 1.193.$$

Thus the Bayesian beta estimate is 1.193 with standard error 0.0211, not very different from the OLS beta of 1.211 with standard error 0.0216.

However, if the prior were stated with far more certainty, with a standard error of 0.01 instead of 0.1 as in Figure 8.3b, then the Bayesian beta estimate would become quite different from the OLS estimate. From (8.13) the posterior variance estimate is

$$((0.021586)^{-2} + (0.01)^{-2})^{-1} = 0.0000823,$$

so the standard error of the posterior is just 0.009. With conjugate normal distributions the standard error of the posterior will always be less than the sample or prior standard errors, reflecting the value of more information (even if it is totally subjective). However, in the first case when the prior had a standard error of 0.1, the posterior standard error was not much different from the sample standard error. This rather small reduction in the precision of the estimate reflects the fact that the prior density was not very certain, compared to the weight of the empirical evidence given by the sample data.

With conjugate normal distributions the standard error of the posterior will always be less than the sample or prior standard errors, reflecting the value of more information (even if it is totally subjective)

Now (8.13) gives the posterior mean, that is the Bayesian beta estimate:

$$0.0000823(1.211/(0.021586)^2 + 0.8/(0.01)^2) = 0.872,$$

quite far from the OLS beta of 1.211 and much nearer to the prior beta of 0.8.

8.3.3 Confidence in Beliefs and the Effect on Bayesian Estimates

Bayesian estimates of factor sensitivities can be substantially different from OLS estimates, depending on the certainty with which prior beliefs about the value of betas are expressed. Prior beliefs could be formed as a result of historic information, such as would be the case if the beta of a stock was observed to have varied between a certain range over a period of time. Alternatively, the model developer could specify a prior density using arbitrary parameters. The only proviso for using the formulae (8.12) and (8.13) is that the prior density be normal.

The example in §8.3.2 demonstrated that if the degree of certainty in prior information is greater than in the sample information, the posterior estimates will be closer to the prior estimates. Also the standard error of the posterior will be much less than the sample standard error when prior beliefs are expressed with a high degree of certainty (note that the standard error of the posterior is much smaller in the second case, when the prior had a standard error of 0.01). Therefore if the prior beliefs are expressed with a great deal of certainty the Bayesian estimates will be close to the prior expectation *and* they will be viewed as having a high degree of precision. This can happen even if the information in the prior beliefs is purely subjective, so the model developer should be wary of regarding Bayesian methods as a licence to 'massage' sample

If the prior beliefs are expressed with a great deal of certainty the Bayesian estimates will be close to the prior expectation and they will be viewed as having a high degree of precision

To express one's views in the form of a probability distribution without under- or overstating one's degree of knowledge is an art

data in order to obtain whatever results are desired. The point is that it is just as dangerous not to include information that is available as it is to overstate one's views. To express one's views in the form of a probability distribution without under- or overstating one's degree of knowledge is an art.

8.4   Remarks on Factor Model Specification Procedures

A standard econometric approach to model specification is to begin by throwing in everything that could possibly influence the dependent variable. This 'testing down' procedure involves examining the t-ratios on all the explanatory variables (§A.2.2) and throwing out those that have insignificant t-ratios, one by one, until a satisfactory model has been achieved. The rationale for this approach is that the quality of parameter estimates will deteriorate substantially if important variables are omitted from the specification, but will be less affected if irrelevant variables are included. OLS will be biased if important explanatory variables are omitted from the model, unless the omitted variables are completely uncorrelated with the included variables. Whether the bias on a coefficient is upward or downward depends on whether the variable has positive or negative correlation with an important but excluded variable.

However, leaving irrelevant variables in the model does not cause a problem for the estimates of parameters on the relevant variables. They will still be unbiased, and the only effect will be that the precision of all estimates will be depressed since degrees of freedom are lost as more variables are included. This causes no problems in reasonably large data sets, of course, where very many degrees of freedom are available. But one should be very wary of extreme movements in irrelevant variables. During normal times the irrelevant variables will have little effect on predictions, since their coefficients will be small. But if a large idiosyncratic movement occurs in one of these variables, the model predictions will be knocked off course. This is one of the reasons why models have to be thoroughly backtested.

It can be that two variables both appear to have little effect in the model, until one of them is removed and then the other becomes very significant

Of course there are problems with the testing down approach, particularly if data are missing, but it is a framework for model development that is commonly considered. The main problem is caused by *multicollinearity* (§A.4.1). When there is a high degree of multicollinearity it becomes very difficult to distinguish what is and what is not a relevant variable for the model. If some of the variables that are initially 'thrown in with the kitchen sink' are highly collinear, this will depress the precision of parameter estimates. Thus some useful variables may appear to have little effect in the model. It can be that two variables both appear to have little effect in the model, until one of them is removed and then the other becomes very significant. Alternatively, a variable that seemed very useful suddenly may become insignificant when another (related) variable is taken out of the model.

Multicollinearity is a common problem with multi-factor models: a factor that seems to be an important determinant of returns may suddenly appear insignificant when another collinear factor is included, and factor sensitivity estimates may lack robustness as different model specifications are tested. For this reason many firms are now favouring a more objective framework, where stock returns are modelled by statistical factors alone. These models do not contradict the APT. Different APT models assume that different factors are the driving forces, but statistical factor models rely on the data alone to tell the story. The economic principles are not denied but, given the difficulty in defining a single 'true' factor model, let alone the difficulties in estimation, more robust results may be obtained by using a statistical analysis from beginning to end.

The testing down procedure can be a little haphazard, leaving much to the integrity of the model builder. However, that is always the case with the development of fundamental models. Financial and economic theory are a great guide to model specification, but nevertheless the developer will be faced with many decisions about the variables to use and the data on these variables. Model development is as much an art as a science: it is a rare and valuable quality to be able to use a model to its greatest potential. Just as a musician who performs well on an instrument is appreciated, perhaps above the technician who built the instrument, so a practitioner who can 'play' a model really well may be valued more than the quantitative analyst who understands how to build the model but cannot play it!

Model development is as much an art as a science: a practitioner who can 'play' a model really well may be valued more than the quantitative analyst who understands how to build the model but cannot play it

A few words of warning are appropriate before finishing this chapter. A linear model is only a very basic formulation of a functional relationship. It is possible to capture a certain amount of non-linearity in relationships by transforming variables (e.g. with exponential or logarithmic transformations), but in the end a linear model may just be an inadequate description of the multivariate data generation process. In fact there may not be *any* sort of stable relationship between variables, let alone a linear one. This will show itself in the residual analysis, where no amount of inclusion of new variables or transformation of existing variables removes econometric problems such as autocorrelation, heteroscedasticity or structural breaks.

In this scenario the typical econometrician's response is to employ a more advanced method of estimation. *Instrumental variables* are a favourite with economists because, whatever the explanatory variables in the actual model, if they are 'instrumented' in a creative manner, one might obtain estimators that do indeed take values that are in line with whatever economic theory the researcher seeks to uphold—and these estimators will normally be consistent (§A.1.3). This is just one example of a problem that is endemic in statistical analysis: advanced techniques are sometimes regarded as methods for establishing relationships that would otherwise be obscured, rather than more sophisticated tools for refining models of relationships that are already established. But if one has to take a sledgehammer to crack a nut, one wonders

Advanced techniques are sometimes regarded as methods for establishing relationships that would otherwise be obscured. But if there is a real, stable relationship between the underlying variables it should shine through, whatever the estimation methods employed

whether the nut is worth cracking in the first place! How reliable are risk estimates that are based on highly technical estimation methods? If there is a real, stable relationship between the underlying variables it should shine through, whatever the estimation methods employed. If nothing is obvious from a 'first pass' at the data using a method such as OLS, which may not be the best method but which should be good enough to gain some insight, then it is unlikely that any *informative* relationships are going to be revealed by a more sophisticated analysis.

9

Value-at-Risk

During the last few years there have been many changes in the way financial institutions evaluate risk. Improvements are continuously being sought to relate the regulatory capital that must be available to the underlying risks that a firm takes. Hence regulations have played a major role in the development of risk measurement techniques. The Basel Committee on Banking Supervision now recommend two types of models for measuring market risk on a daily basis; details of these models are given in the Basel Accord Amendment of 1996.

These internal models have become industry standards for measuring risk not only for external regulatory purposes, but also for internal risk management and control. One approach is to quantify the maximum loss over a large set of scenarios for movements in the risk factors over a certain time horizon. Another approach is to weight scenarios with probabilities and to assess the level of loss that has some low probability of being exceeded over a fixed time horizon.[1] This measure is called the portfolio value-at-risk (VaR).[2] Both approaches assume the portfolio is not managed during the fixed time horizon.

This chapter is about the VaR approach to measuring market risk, for capital requirements and for internal risk management. The first section looks at the current risky environment in financial markets and gives a brief overview of the developments in risk capital regulation during the last few years. It outlines the limitations with current regulations and discusses how they are being addressed by the new proposals from the Basel Committee that are currently under consultation (Basel 2). The theoretical and practical advantages and limitations of VaR as a measure of portfolio risk are described in §9.2. Here some of the traditional 'sensitivity-based' risk measures and some of the new alternative risk measures are also described.

The next two sections look at the VaR models that have emerged as industry standard during the last few years. The covariance VaR model is described in

---

[1] In our uncertain environment loss is a random variable, so it is only possible to make *probabilistic* statements about the loss from a portfolio.

[2] Or more precisely, the *market VaR* of the portfolio. Although VaR was introduced in the context of market risk, recently the context has been extended to credit VaR and operational VaR.

§9.3, with examples of its application to different types of linear portfolios. Option portfolios have too many non-linear characteristics to be measured by a covariance VaR model; instead one of the simulation methods described in §9.4 will normally be applied.

Section 9.5 describes the methods that are normally used to validate a VaR model and the impact of backtesting results on risk capital requirements. This section also deals with the sensitivity of VaR estimates to assumptions about model parameters, something that deserves careful investigation by both internal and external risk control functions. The chapter concludes by reviewing the methods by which market VaR estimates of current or potential positions can be complemented by stress testing and scenario analysis to control the impact of extreme market movements.

There are three workbooks on the CD to supplement this chapter: **covariance VaR**, **historical VaR** and **Monte Carlo VaR**. The reader can use these to specify portfolios, compute VaR and perform stress tests.

9.1 Controlling the Risk in Financial Markets

Are financial markets more risky than ever? They are certainly more volatile. One of the reasons for this is the increased ability of financial institutions to create leverage. Hedge funds can take extraordinarily highly leveraged positions because their models are supposedly designed to diversify most of the risks. New derivative products are continually being structured to allow companies and banks to increase leverage in more ingenious ways than ever.

Financial activity is unstable and risky by its very nature. As new markets are opened and new products are developed, market liquidity may be insufficient to accommodate our growing appetite for leverage. In young markets for new products sometimes it is just not possible to understand the risks completely. Even when proper pricing models have been developed they may be so new that they are only understood by 'quants'. In established markets that are better understood there can always be an event that has never been experienced before.

Volatility in itself does not imply risk. There does not seem to be a strong connection between crises in financial markets and the risk to the real economy

But volatility in itself does not imply risk. What do we mean by risk anyway? Financial risk should be perceived on three levels: the risks to individual consumers, the risks to a firm, along with its shareholders and investors, and the risks to the markets as a whole. Consider one of the most volatile financial experiences of the twentieth century—the global stock market crash of 1987. All three levels of risk were affected by this event. Firms and individuals suffered immediate and direct financial loss, and the knock-on effect of the crash undermined the fundamental stability of the world's economy. In more recent years there have been a number of other crises in financial markets around the globe, but it is mainly in

Japan that the financial market crisis has had a devastating effect on the economy. Elsewhere there does not seem to be a strong connection between crises in financial markets and the risk to the real economy. Thus the main sufferers are the investors. For example, in 1998 the Long Term Capital Management (LTCM) company, whose shareholders included some of the most successful Wall Street traders and most respected Nobel Prize winners, had debts of the order of $100 billion and extraordinarily highly leveraged positions amounting to approximately $1 trillion. Unfortunately, their mathematical models (which had been beating the markets consistently for a number of years) could not cope with the totally unexpected Russian debt crisis and did not prevent them from huge illiquid exposures in other markets. The US Federal Reserve bailed them out at a cost of $3.5 billion. But most of the losses were borne by LTCM's shareholders and investors.

During the last decade many banks and securities houses have also experienced very large losses. These have often been attributed to fraud, bad management or poor advice, and it is hoped that the institutions concerned will not repeat the same mistakes. But the scale of these individual losses should be put into perspective, when it is considered that the value of large multinational corporations could change by similar amounts in the course of a normal day's trading on the stock market.

The scale of these individual losses should be put into perspective, when it is considered that the value of large multinational corporations could change by similar amounts in the course of a normal day's trading on the stock market

The forces behind the measurement and control of financial risk are, therefore, extremely strong. There are internal forces to gain the optimal return on capital (where capital is risk-based) and to ensure the survival of a firm as a whole. There are external forces that are driven by competition, by the enormous growth in the risk management industry and by the increased volatility of financial markets, with new products that enable participants to increase leverage to very high levels. And there are regulatory forces to promote fair competition between firms, protect the solvency of financial institutions, and control systemic risk.

9.1.1 The 1988 Basel Accord and the 1996 Amendment

Three main tools are available to regulators for the measurement and control of financial risk: minimum risk capital requirements; inspections and reporting requirements; and public disclosure and market discipline. This section concerns only the first of these three *pillars of regulation*, the minimum risk capital requirements that are imposed by the regulatory body. The discussion focuses on the Basel Accord of 1988 and its 1996 Amendment which, though only formally adopted by the G10 countries, have had an enormous international influence.

The 1988 Basel Accord linked minimum capital standards to credit risk, and this was extended to market risks in the 1996 Amendment. The basic principle of the 1996 Amendment is to measure regulatory capital by a minimum solvency condition, the *Cooke ratio*. This is the ratio of eligible capital to risk-weighted assets, where eligible capital is the sum of tier 1 (core capital), tier 2 (complementary capital) and tier 3 (sub-supplementary capital), and risk-weighted assets are the sum of a credit risk capital requirement (CRR) and a market risk capital requirement (MRR).

Credit risk requirements apply to all positions except the equity and debt positions in a trading book, foreign exchange and commodities. At the time of writing the CRR is simply calculated as a percentage of the nominal (for on-balance-sheet positions) or a credit equivalent amount (for off-balance-sheet positions).[3] Regulators currently favour placing transactions in the banking book, where securities attract a CRR (the banking book CRR is very broadly defined to compensate for the lack of MRR). In particular, the current method used to calculate the CRR provides little incentive to diversify a portfolio or to employ other risk mitigation techniques. However, the Basel 2 Accord that is currently under discussion will define new rules for calculating the CRR, for implementation by G10 banks in 2005.

Regulators currently favour placing transactions in the banking book, where securities attract a CRR

The MRR applies to all on- and off-balance-sheet positions in a trading book. It is necessary to mark positions to market, which is easily done in liquid markets where bid and offer prices are readily available. Otherwise it is acceptable to mark the portfolio to a model price, where the value of a transaction is derived from the value of liquid instruments, or to make a liquidity adjustment that is based on an assessment of the bid–offer spread.

The standardized approach is to sum the MRRs of positions in four different categories or *building blocks*: equities, interest rates, foreign exchange and gold, and commodities. In each block the total MRR is the sum of general and specific risk requirements that are percentages of the net and gross exposures, respectively; these percentages depend on the building block.[4] The minimum solvency ratio that has been set in the 1988 Accord is 8%. That is, the eligible (tier 1, tier 2 and tier 3) capital of a firm must be at least 8% of the sum of the MRR and CRR. In this way the regulator protects the solvency of a firm by tying its total risk exposure to its capital base.

9.1.2 Internal Models for Calculating Market Risk Capital Requirements

The 1996 Amendment outlined an alternative approach to measuring the MRR, which is to use an internal model to determine the total loss to a firm when netted over all positions in its trading book (§9.1.2). Internal models for measuring the MRR must determine the maximum loss over 10 trading days at

---

[3] This percentage is determined by the type of counterparty.

[4] For example, in equities the general MRR is 8% of net exposure and the specific MRR is often 8% of gross exposure.

a 99% confidence level. They are subject to some strong qualitative and quantitative requirements. Qualitative requirements include the existence of an independent risk management function for audit and control, a rigorous and comprehensive stress testing program on the positions of the firm, and on the IT and control side the MRR model must be fully integrated with other systems. Quantitative requirements include frequent estimation of model parameters, separate assessment for the risks of linear and non-linear portfolios, rigorous model validation techniques, the use of a minimum number of risk factors and a minimum length of historic data period.

Although these models can be based entirely on scenario analysis (§9.6), many firm assess their MRR using a VaR model. VaR has been defined as *the loss (stated with a specified probability) from adverse market movements over a fixed time horizon, assuming the portfolio is not managed during this time.* So VaR is measured as a lower percentile of a distribution for theoretical profit and loss that arises from possible movements of the market risk factors over a fixed risk horizon. To see this, first note that the loss (or profit) for a portfolio that is left unmanaged over a risk horizon of h days is

$$\Delta_h P_t = P_{t+h} - P_t.$$

In other words, $\Delta_h P_t$ is the forward-looking h-day theoretical (or 'unrealized') P&L, that is, the P&L obtained by simply marking the portfolio to market today and then leaving it unchanged and marking it to market again at the risk horizon. We do not know exactly how the underlying risk factors are going to move over the next h days, but we do have some idea. For example, we might expect that historical volatilities and correlations would remain much the same. The possibilities for movements in risk factors can be summarized in a (multivariate) distribution, and this in turn will generate a distribution of $\Delta_h P_t$, as each set of possible values for the risk factors at the risk horizon are entered into the pricing models for the portfolio, weighted by their joint probabilities.

The significance level of VaR, that is, the probability that is associated with a VaR measurement, corresponds to the frequency with which a given level of loss is expected to occur. Thus a 5% 1-day VaR corresponds to a loss level that one expects to exceed, in normal market circumstances, one day in 20. And a 1% 1-day VaR is the loss level that might be seen one day in 100.[5] Now the definition of VaR above can be rephrased as follows: *the $100\alpha\%$ h-day VaR is that number x such that the probability of losing x, or more, over the next h days equals $100\alpha\%$* — in mathematical terms,

the $100\alpha\%$ h-day VaR is that number x such that $\text{Prob}(\Delta_h P_t < -x) = \alpha$.

Sometimes we use the notation $\text{VaR}_{\alpha, h}$ to emphasize the dependency of the VaR measurement on the two parameters α, the significance level, and h, the holding period. Thus,

---

[5] These are also called the 95% and 99% VaR measures, but no confusion should arise.

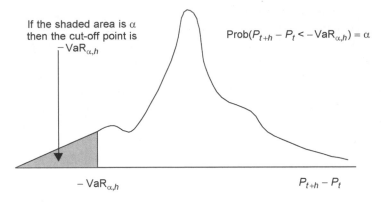

If the shaded area is α
then the cut-off point is
$-\mathrm{VaR}_{\alpha,h}$

$\mathrm{Prob}(P_{t+h} - P_t < -\mathrm{VaR}_{\alpha,h}) = \alpha$

$-\mathrm{VaR}_{\alpha,h}$

$P_{t+h} - P_t$

Figure 9.1   The P&L density and value-at-risk.

Table 9.1: VaR tables

Holding period, h	Significance level, α		
	0.01	0.05	0.1
1			
2		$\leftarrow$ VaR increases	
. . .		$\downarrow$	
10			

$$\mathrm{Prob}(\Delta_h P_t < -\mathrm{VaR}_{\alpha,h}) = \alpha \qquad (9.1)$$

is a mathematical statement that is equivalent to saying that the $100\alpha\%$ h-day VaR measurement x is the lower α quantile of the unrealized P&L distribution, as depicted in Figure 9.1.

Table 9.1 shows how VaR varies with the choice of significance level and holding period. A single VaR model will generate a whole table of VaR estimates, that will increase as the significance level increases (that is, as α decreases). From Figure 9.1 it is evident that the percentile that cuts off $100\alpha\%$ of the area under the density will move to the left as the area α decreases. The VaR will also increase as the holding period increases because the uncertainty in P&L will generally increase with holding period. In some cases the square-root-of-time rule is employed (§3.3) so that the h-day VaR is simply taken as $\sqrt{h}$ times the 1-day VaR. If the square-root-of-time rule is not invoked then the VaR measure is simply the lower percentile of the historical h-day P&L distribution or, when a covariance matrix is used, it is the VaR based on the h-day covariance matrix.[6]

$100\alpha\%$ h-day VaR measurement x is the lower α quantile of the unrealized P&L distribution

---

[6] When a covariance matrix is used in the VaR model, a 1-day covariance matrix is transformed to an h-day covariance matrix by multiplying each element in the matrix by h. In linear portfolios this is equivalent to multiplying the 1-day VaR by $\sqrt{h}$; but it is not so for option portfolios, where the square-root-of-time rule should not be used. More details are given in the help sheets for the VaR models on the CD.

The regulatory MRR is a multiple of the average of the last 60 days' 1% 10-day VaR estimates when netted across the whole firm, or the previous day's VaR estimate, whichever is greater (§9.5.1). Normally VaR models produce more realistic risk capital measurements than those obtained using the standardized approach. In fact for well-diversified or well-hedged portfolios capital requirement savings may exceed 50%. VaR models have many advantages and considerable potential for internal and external risk management and control, but there are also a number of disadvantages with their use, and these are discussed in §9.2.

9.1.3 Basel 2 Proposals

There are number of problems with the current framework for measuring risk capital. For example, the measurement of MRRs is quite complex, whereas the measurement of credit risk is still quite crude and operational risk is totally ignored. And even MRRs only focus on a few short-term risks with a single criterion of limited usefulness: market risks in the banking book are ignored. There is also no proper integration of the separate measures of market and credit risk: the two measures are simply summed, as if they were perfectly correlated (§9.3.5). But, if anything, market and credit risks will be negatively correlated. For example, with a simple instrument such as a swap, one is either owed money and therefore subject to credit risk, or one owes money and therefore subject to market risk.

There is also no proper integration of the separate measures of market and credit risk: the two measures are simply summed, as if they were perfectly correlated

In 1999 and 2001 the Basel Committee prepared three consultative papers that aimed to address some of these problems. The intention of Basel 2 is to widen the scope of its regulatory framework to cope with more sophisticated institutions and products and to cover a broader range of risks. In particular, for the first time operational risk will be included in risk capital requirements. More advanced models for measuring CRRs will be introduced, that allow better credit quality differentiation and risk mitigation techniques. Another proposal that will have a great impact is that market risk capital will be required to cover positions in the banking book. Current expectations are that the Basel 2 Amendment will be implemented in stages, starting in 2005. More details can be found on www.bis.org, www.isda.org and www.bba.org.uk.

9.2 Advantages and Limitations of Value-at-Risk

Since regulators have imposed minimum capital requirements to cover market risks that are based on internal models, VaR has become the ubiquitous measure of risk. This has many advantages. VaR can be used to compare the market risks of all types of activities in the firm, and it provides a single measure that is easily understood by senior management. The VaR concept can be extended to other types of risk, notably credit risk and operational risk. It takes into account the correlations and cross-hedging between various asset categories or risk factors, and it can be calculated according to a number of different methods. VaR may also take account of specific risks by including individual equities among risk factors or including spread risk for bonds. And it may be calculated separately by building block, although without assessed correlations between building blocks, VaR measurements are simply added.

There are, however, many disadvantages with the use of VaR. It does not distinguish between the different liquidities of market positions, in fact it only captures short-term risks in normal market circumstances. VaR models may be based on unwarranted assumptions, and some risks such as repo costs are ignored. The implementation costs of a fully integrated VaR system can be huge and there is a danger that VaR calculations may be seen as a substitute for good risk management. Furthermore, in the course of this chapter we shall see that VaR measures are very imprecise, because they depend on many assumptions about model parameters that may be very difficult to either support or contradict.

There is a danger that VaR calculations may be seen as a substitute for good risk management

9.2.1   Comparison with Traditional Risk Measures

The traditional measures of risk for a fixed income portfolio that can be represented by a cash-flow map, such as a portfolio of bonds or loans, are based on sensitivity to movements in a yield curve. For example, the standard *duration* measure is a maturity-weighted average of the present values of all cash flows.[7] Another traditional measure of yield curve risk is the *present value of a basis point move* (PVBP), the change in present value of cash flows if the yield curve is shifted up by 1 basis point.[8]

The traditional risk measures of an equity portfolio are based on the sensitivities to the risk factors, that is the portfolio 'betas'.[9] However, in §8.1 the market risk of an equity portfolio was attributed to *three* sources: the variances (and covariances) of the underlying risk factors, the sensitivities to these risk factors, and the specific variance or residual risk. Therefore the traditional 'beta' risk measure relates only to the undiversifiable part of the risk: the risk that cannot be hedged away by holding a large and diversified portfolio. The beta ignores the risk arising from movements in the underlying risk factors and the specific risks of a portfolio. One of the major advantages of VaR is that it does not ignore these other two sources of risk.

---

[7] The basic measure of duration is $\Sigma(PV_t \times M_t)/\Sigma(PV_t)$. It is a measure of interest rate risk because if interest rates rise the present value of cash flows will decrease, but the income from reinvestment will increase, and the duration marks the 'break-even' point in time where the capital lost from lower cash flows has just been recovered by the increased reinvestment income.

[8] There are 10^4 basis points in 100%, thus to convert a cash flow to PVBP terms, a simple approximation is to multiply the cash flow amount by t and then divide the result by 10^4. To see this note that the interest rate sensitivity is $-\partial \ln P/\partial r$. For a single cash flow of \$1 at time t, $P = e^{-rt}$ so $-\partial \ln P/\partial r = t$.

[9] And risk measures in option portfolios have also been based purely on sensitivities. The main risk factors in options portfolios are the price and the volatility of the underlying; the main sensitivities to these risk factors, delta, gamma and vega, are defined in §2.3.3.

Traditional risk measures cannot be compared across the different activities of the firm. For example, even though they both measure first-order changes in the portfolio as a result of movements in the underlying, the duration of a bond portfolio (which is measured in months or years) cannot be compared with the delta of an options portfolio. For comparative purposes the duration or delta can be multiplied by a notional amount and a variation in the underlying risk factor (interest rates or share price). Nevertheless it is difficult to assess which activities are taking the most risk using these sensitivity-based measures, and to allocate capital accordingly. One of the main advantages of VaR is that it takes into account the volatilities and correlations of risk factors, so it is comparable across different asset classes.

Sensitivity-based risk measures have a number of limitations. They only make sense within each trading unit, and they cannot be compared across different activities to see which area has the most risk. They cannot be aggregated to give an overall exposure across all products and currencies. They do not indicate how much could be lost, either in normal circumstances or under extreme events.

9.2.2   VaR-Based Trading Limits

Long-term capital allocation between different asset classes and different activities is normally addressed using risk-adjusted performance measures (§7.2.3). On the other hand, short-term trading limits are based only on risk and not on returns: in the short term returns can be assumed to be nearly zero. Sensitivity-based trading limits have been used for some time, but more recently there have been considerable internal and regulatory forces to implement trading limits that are based on VaR. VaR provides a risk measure that focuses on the profit and loss from different activities in the firm taken together. It is therefore natural that a firm would seek to use VaR in a unified framework for allocating capital, not just to satisfy regulatory purposes, but also to allocate capital among the different activities of the firm.

However, it is a very difficult task to replace the traditional sensitivity-based trading limits with trading limits based on VaR. Not only are traders thinking in terms of sensitivities, they have the software to calculate immediately the impact of a proposed trade on their limit. In contrast, real-time VaR systems for large complex portfolios are simply not available, unless many approximations are made (§9.4.3). Therefore, if trading limits are based on VaR, the trader will need to use both VaR- and sensitivity-based systems, at least initially, so that he knows what are the implications of a trade from all perspectives.

Real-time VaR systems for large complex portfolios are simply not available, unless many approximations are made

9.2.3   Alternatives to VaR

As a measure of risk, VaR has some limitations. First, like volatility, it is affected by 'good' risk as well as 'bad' risk. Following Dembo and Freeman

Table 9.2: Good risk, bad risk, VaR and volatility

Return:	Probability of that return in portfolio *A*	Probability of that return in portfolio *B*
−10	0.01	0.01
−7.5	0.04	0.04
−5	0.05	0.25
−2.5	0.1	0.25
0	0.5	0.3
2.5	0.15	0.1
5	0.15	0.05
Expected return	0.225	−1.775
s.d.	3.124	3.128
1% VaR	−10	−10
5% VaR	− 7.5	− 7.5

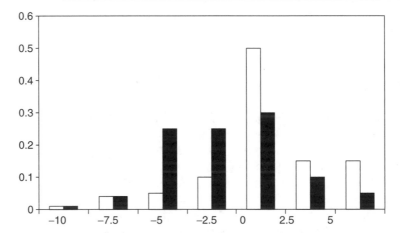

Figure 9.2   Which is more risky?

(2001), a simple example to illustrate this is given. Consider the distributions of returns for two portfolios *A* and *B* that are shown in Table 9.2 and Figure 9.2. Portfolio *A* has a greater chance of positive returns, and this is reflected in the fact that the expected return for portfolio *A* is larger than it is for portfolio *B*. However, if one only looks at the standard risk measures, these tell the same story for both portfolios. That is, the volatility (standard deviation), the 5% VaR and the 1% VaR are identical for both portfolios. Even though much of the variation in the return to portfolio *A* is concentrated on the up side, so that *A* has more 'good' risk than *B*, this is not revealed by looking at the volatility or the VaR of these portfolios.

Downside risk measures are based on the returns that fall short of a benchmark return. For example, the *semi-variance* operator introduced by Markovitz (1959) measures the variance of all returns that are less than the expected return:

$$SV = E((\min(0, \ R - E(R)))^2). \tag{9.2}$$

More generally, $E(R)$ may be replaced by any benchmark return B that can be time-varying or fixed. Dembo and Freeman (2001) advocate the use of *regret* as a measure of downside risk. The regret operator is defined as

$$\text{Regret} = -E(\min(0,\, R - B)).\tag{9.3}$$

This has the same form as the pay-off to a put option with strike equal to the benchmark return. Regret therefore has the intuitive interpretation of an insurance cost — the cost of insuring the downside risk of a portfolio. Regret will easily distinguish 'good' risk from 'bad' risk. For example, if the benchmark return $B = 0$ then the regret of portfolio A in the example above is 0.9, whereas the regret of portfolio B is 2.275.

Regret will easily distinguish 'good' risk from 'bad' risk

Artzner *et al.* (1997) have used an axiomatic approach to the problem of defining a satisfactory risk measure. They set out certain attributes that one should reasonably require of any risk measure, and call risk measures that satisfy these axioms 'coherent'. A *coherent risk measure* ρ assigns to each loss X a risk measure $\rho(X)$ such that the following conditions hold.

1. Risk is *monotonic*: if $X \geqslant Y$ then $\rho(X) \geqslant \rho(Y)$.
2. Risk is *homogeneous*: $\rho(tX) = t\rho(X)$ for $t > 0$.
3. Risk-free condition: $\rho(X + nr) = \rho(X) - n$, where r is the risk-free rate.
4. Risk is *sub-additive*: $\rho(X + Y) \leqslant \rho(X) + \rho(Y)$.

These attributes guarantee that the risk function is convex; this corresponds to risk aversion (§7.2.4).[10] The risk-free condition ensures that if an amount n of the riskless asset is added to the position then the risk measure will be reduced by n; thus capital requirements will be reduced accordingly. The last attribute is very important: it ensures that the total risk is no more than the sum of the risks of individual positions and without this there would be no incentive to diversify portfolios.

One of the great disadvantages of VaR is that it is not sub-additive

VaR is not a coherent risk measure because it does not necessarily satisfy axiom 4. The violation of axiom 4 has serious consequences for risk management, since axiom 4 allows decentralized calculation of the risks from different positions in the firm and the sum of these individual risk measures will be conservative (over-) estimate of the total risk. In a structure of limits and sub-limits for different activities or individual traders, axiom 4 implies that the respect of sub-limits will guarantee the respect of global limits. Therefore one of the great disadvantages of VaR is that it is not sub-additive.

Artzner *et al.* (1999) have introduced a new risk measure called *conditional VaR* that is a coherent risk measure, and has a simple relation to the ordinary VaR. Ordinary VaR corresponds to a lower percentile of the theoretical P&L distribution, a threshold level of loss that cuts off the lower tail of the

---

[10] That is, $\rho(tX + (1 - t)Y) \leqslant t\rho(X) + (1 - t)\rho(Y)$.

distribution. Conditional VaR is the expected loss given that the loss has exceeded the VaR threshold. That is:[11]

$$\text{Conditional VaR} = E(X|X > \text{VaR}). \qquad (9.4)$$

A simple example will illustrate the difference between VaR and conditional VaR. Suppose that 100 000 simulations of the risk factors at the risk horizon are used to generate a P&L distribution such as that in Figure 9.1, and consider the 1000 largest losses that are simulated. Then the 1% VaR is the smallest of these 1000 losses and the 1% conditional VaR is the average of these 1000 losses. So conditional VaR will always be at least as great as VaR, and usually it will be greater.

The conditional VaR risk measure will be encountered again in §10.2.1, when it will be related to the mean excess loss in the peaks over threshold model. An estimate of conditional VaR may be obtained by fitting the standard parametric distribution for excesses over a threshold, that is, the generalized Pareto distribution that is described in §10.2.1.

9.3   Covariance VaR Models

The covariance VaR methodology was introduced in October 1994 by J.P. Morgan; in fact it is the methodology that underlies the RiskMetrics daily data that are available at www.riskmetrics.com. A detailed discussion of these data, which consist of three very large covariance matrices of the major risk factors in global financial markets, has been given in §7.3.

9.3.1   Basic Assumptions

In the covariance VaR methodology the only data necessary to compute the VaR of a linear portfolio is a covariance matrix of all the assets in the portfolio. One does of course need to know the portfolio composition, but the only other data necessary are the variances and covariances of the asset returns. These can be measured using any of the standard methods — usually a moving average or GARCH methodology will be employed, as explained in Part 1 of the book — and regulators recommend that at least one year of historic data be used in their construction.

The fundamental assumption is that the portfolio P&L is normally distributed. That is, if $\Delta_h P_t = P_{t+h} - P_t$ denotes the h-day unrealized P&L, we assume[12]

---

[11] Of course conditional VaR depends on the same parameters α, the significance level, and h, the holding period, as the corresponding VaR.

[12] The validity of such an assumption is questionable, and should be investigated using some of the tests that are explained in §10.1.

$$\Delta_h P_t \sim N(\mu_t, \sigma_t^2). \tag{9.5}$$

The $100\alpha\%$ h-day Value-at-Risk is that number $\mathrm{VaR}_{\alpha,h}$ such that $\mathrm{Prob}(\Delta_h P_t < -\mathrm{VaR}_{\alpha,h}) = \alpha$. Now, applying the standard normal transformation:

$$\mathrm{Prob}([\Delta_h P_t - \mu_t]/\sigma_t < [-\mathrm{VaR}_{\alpha,h} - \mu_t]/\sigma_t) = \alpha;$$

or, since $[\Delta_h P_t - \mu_t]/\sigma_t \sim N(0, 1)$, and denoting $[\Delta_h P_t - \mu_t]/\sigma_t$ by the standard normal variate Z_t,

$$\mathrm{Prob}(Z_t < [-\mathrm{VaR}_{\alpha,h} - \mu_t]/\sigma_t) = \alpha.$$

But for a standard normal variate Z_t,

$$\mathrm{Prob}(Z_t < -Z_\alpha) = \alpha,$$

where Z_α is the 100αth percentile of the standard normal density. Therefore,

$$[-\mathrm{VaR}_{\alpha,h} - \mu_t]/\sigma_t = -Z_\alpha;$$

written another way, we have the formula for covariance VaR,

$$\mathrm{VaR}_{\alpha,h} = Z_\alpha \sigma_t - \mu_t. \tag{9.6}$$

It has already been mentioned that VaR as a risk measure is only suitable for short-term risks, so it is normal to assume that $\mu_t = 0$. Now, Z_α is simply a constant given in the standard normal tables (1.645 for $\alpha = 0.05$, 1.96 for $\alpha = 0.025$, 2.33 for $\alpha = 0.01$, and other values may be found from the tables in the back of the book). Thus it is the volatility of the P&L, that is, σ_t, that determines the portfolio VaR.

It is the volatility of the P&L that determines the portfolio VaR in the covariance method

9.3.2 Simple Cash Portfolios

The P&L volatility is easily computed for a simple cash portfolio. Recall from §7.1.1 that the variance of a linear portfolio is a quadratic form: that is, the portfolio return has a variance $\mathbf{w}'\mathbf{V}\mathbf{w}$, where $\mathbf{w}$ is the vector of portfolio weights and $\mathbf{V}$ denotes the covariance matrix of asset returns. Similarly, the portfolio P&L has a variance $\mathbf{p}'\mathbf{V}\mathbf{p}$, where $\mathbf{p}$ is the vector of nominal amounts invested in each asset. Thus if the portfolio is represented as a linear sum of its constituent assets, the covariance method gives the portfolio VaR as (9.6) with

$$\sigma_t = (\mathbf{p}'\mathbf{V}\mathbf{p})^{1/2}.$$

For example, consider a portfolio with two assets with $1 million invested in asset 1 and $2 million invested in asset 2. If asset 1 has a 10-day variance of 0.01, asset 2 has a 10-day variance of 0.005 and their 10-day covariance is 0.002, then

$$\mathbf{p}'\mathbf{V}\mathbf{p} = (1 \quad 2) \begin{pmatrix} 0.01 & 0.002 \\ 0.002 & 0.005 \end{pmatrix} \begin{pmatrix} 1 \\ 2 \end{pmatrix} = 0.038,$$

and the P&L volatility is $(\mathbf{p}'\mathbf{V}\mathbf{p})^{1/2} = 0.038^{1/2} = \$0.195$ million, so the 5% 10-day VaR is $1.645 \times 0.195 = \$0.32$ million.

Often the historic asset information is given in terms of annualized volatilities and correlations, instead of h-day variances and covariances. But the formula $\mathbf{p'Vp}$ for the P&L variance can be written equally well in terms of volatilities and correlations. Since the covariance is the correlation multiplied by the product of the square roots of the variances we have

$$\mathbf{p'Vp} = \mathbf{v'Cv},$$

where $\mathbf{C}$ is the correlation matrix and $\mathbf{v}$ is the vector of positions multiplied by the square root of the corresponding asset variance. For example, the data in the above example could have been expressed in the following form: the correlation between two assets is 0.2828, asset 1 has annualized volatility of 50% and asset 2 has an annualized volatility of 35.355%. Then one may calculate the asset 10-day standard deviations as $0.5/(250/10)^{1/2} = 0.5/5 = 0.1$ and $0.35355/(250/10)^{1/2} = 0.35355/5 = 0.0707$, respectively (assuming 250 days per year). Then

$$\mathbf{v'Cv} = \begin{pmatrix} 0.1 & 0.1414 \end{pmatrix} \begin{pmatrix} 1 & 0.2828 \\ 0.2828 & 1 \end{pmatrix} \begin{pmatrix} 0.1 \\ 0.1414 \end{pmatrix} = 0.038,$$

which is the same as $\mathbf{p'Vp}$ in the previous example.

9.3.3 Covariance VaR with Factor Models

Many linear portfolios are too large to be represented at the asset level and are instead represented by a mapping. Commonly a factor model is used for large equity portfolios or a cash-flow map is used for fixed income portfolios. In this subsection we suppose that a large equity portfolio, with n assets, has been represented by a factor model with k risk factors. Now from §7.1.1 we know that the variance of the portfolio P&L that is due to the risk factors is $\mathbf{p'BV}_X\mathbf{B'p}$, where $\mathbf{p}$ denotes the $n \times 1$ vector of nominal amounts invested in each asset, $\mathbf{B}$ is the $n \times k$ matrix of factor sensitivities (the (i, j)th element of $\mathbf{B}$ is the beta of the ith asset with respect to the jth risk factor) and $\mathbf{V}_X$ is the $k \times k$ risk factor covariance matrix appropriate to the risk horizon.

For a simple example, consider an equity portfolio with $2 million invested in US and UK stocks. Suppose the net portfolio beta with respect to the FTSE 100 is 1.5 and the net portfolio beta with respect to the S&P 500 is 2. Then the vector $\mathbf{p'B} = (3, 4)$. Suppose the 1-day risk factor covariance matrix for the FTSE 100 and the S&P 500 is

$$\begin{pmatrix} 0.0018 & 0.0002 \\ 0.0002 & 0.0012 \end{pmatrix} = 10^{-4} \times \begin{pmatrix} 18 & 2 \\ 2 & 12 \end{pmatrix}.$$

Then the variance of the P&L due to the risk factors is

$$10^{-4} \times \begin{pmatrix} 3 & 4 \end{pmatrix} \begin{pmatrix} 18 & 2 \\ 2 & 12 \end{pmatrix} \begin{pmatrix} 3 \\ 4 \end{pmatrix} = 0.0402.$$

Thus the 1% 1-day VaR due to the risk factors is $2.33 million $\times \sqrt{0.0402}$ = $0.467 million.

The specific risk of the portfolio also contributes to the P&L variance. In fact from (8.7) we have

$$\text{P\&L variance} = \mathbf{p}'\mathbf{B}\mathbf{V}_X\mathbf{B}'\mathbf{p} + \mathbf{p}'\mathbf{V}_\varepsilon\mathbf{p}, \qquad (9.7)$$

where $\mathbf{V}_\varepsilon$ is the $n \times n$ specific risk covariance matrix. There are therefore two components in the covariance VaR:

$$\text{VaR due to market risk factors} = Z_\alpha(\mathbf{p}'\mathbf{B}\mathbf{V}_X\mathbf{B}'\mathbf{p})^{1/2};$$
$$\text{Specific VaR} = Z_\alpha(\mathbf{p}'\mathbf{V}_\varepsilon\mathbf{p})^{1/2}.$$

Saving the residual covariance matrix from the factor $\mathbf{V}_\varepsilon$ model therefore allows a separate VaR measure for the specific risk of the portfolio. Risk capital charges for specific risk can be substantially reduced by this method.[13]

Note that the total VaR should not be measured as the sum of these two components.[14] The total *variance* is the sum, not the total volatility, so the total VaR is obtained from (9.7) as

$$\text{Total VaR} = Z_\alpha(\mathbf{p}'\mathbf{B}\mathbf{V}_X\mathbf{B}'\mathbf{p} + \mathbf{p}'\mathbf{V}_\varepsilon\mathbf{p})^{1/2}.$$

Similar principles are used in the **covariance VaR** spreadsheet on the CD. It calculates VaR for a dollar investor in an international equity portfolio. Total VaR is disaggregated into equity VaR and FX VaR as explained in the help sheet.

9.3.4 Covariance VaR with Cash-Flow Maps

To compute the covariance VaR of a portfolio of bonds or loans, it may be represented by a cash-flow map $\mathbf{p} = (PV_1, PV_2, \ldots, PV_k)$, where PV_t denotes the present value of the income flow at time t for fixed maturity dates $t = 1, \ldots, k$. The present value data should be translated to an absolute scale, so that VaR is measured in terms of P&L, and normally we represent the cash flow amount by its sensitivity to a 1 basis point move in interest rates. Then the covariance matrix must also refer to changes in basis points.

The present value data should be translated to an absolute scale, so that VaR is measured in terms of P&L. Normally we represent the cash flow amount by its sensitivity to a 1 basis point move in interest rates. Then the covariance matrix must also refer to changes in basis points

For example, compute the 1% 1-day VaR for a cash flow of $1 million in 3 months' time, and $2 million in 6 months' time, when both the 3-month and the 6-month interest rates are 6%, the 3-month interest rate has an annualized daily volatility of 10%, the 6-month interest rate has an annualized daily volatility of 9% and their correlation is 0.95.

---

[13] There is a limit to this reduction: the specific risk charge as measured by (9.7) cannot be less than 50% of the charge that would be made under the standardized rules.

[14] In §9.3.5 we see that it is only under very special conditions that one can aggregate covariance VaR measures.

First, the cash-flow amounts must be mapped to P&L sensitivities to changes of 1 basis point. The present value of a basis point move (PVBP) is one of the traditional risk measures that were mentioned in §9.2.1. Following footnote 8, to convert the 3-month cash flow to sensitivity terms it should be divided by 4×10^4; and to convert this to present value terms it should be discounted at the annual rate of 6% (which means dividing by approximately 1.015); similarly the 6-month cash flow should be divided by 2×10^4 and divided by 1.03 to view it in (approximate) present value sensitivity terms. Thus the 3-month cash flow has the present value of a 1 basis point move of

$$\$(10^6 \times 10^{-4})/(4 \times 1.015) = \$24.63;$$

similarly the 6-month cash flow has a present value, for a 1 basis point move, of

$$\$(2 \times 10^6 \times 10^{-4})/(2 \times 1.03) = \$97.09.$$

Secondly, the covariance matrix must refer to rate changes in basis points; if the rates are currently 6% the 10% volatility means that the 3-month rate can vary by ± 60 basis points over one year and the 9% volatility means that the 6-month rate can vary by ± 54 basis points over one year. In fact, in basis points the 1-day variances are, assuming 250 days per year, $(0.1 \times 600)^2/250 = 14.4$ and $(0.09 \times 600)^2/250 = 11.664$, respectively. Their 1-day covariance is $0.95(14.4 \times 11.664)^{1/2} = 12.312$, so the 1-day covariance matrix in basis point terms is

$$\begin{pmatrix} 14.4 & 12.312 \\ 12.312 & 11.664 \end{pmatrix}.$$

Now, recall that the h-day variance of the portfolio P&L is $\mathbf{p}'\mathbf{V}\mathbf{p}$, where $\mathbf{V}$ is the h-day $k \times k$ covariance matrix for interest rates at maturity dates $t = 1, \ldots, k$, and that the $100\alpha\%$ h-day covariance VaR of this portfolio is simply

$$\text{VaR}_{\alpha,h} = Z_\alpha (\mathbf{p}'\mathbf{V}\mathbf{p})^{1/2}.$$

Thus, in the example above, we calculate

$$\mathbf{p}'\mathbf{V}\mathbf{p} = \begin{pmatrix} 24.63 & 97.09 \end{pmatrix} \begin{pmatrix} 14.4 & 12.312 \\ 12.312 & 11.664 \end{pmatrix} \begin{pmatrix} 24.63 \\ 97.09 \end{pmatrix} = \$177\,570,$$

so the 1% 1-day VaR is $2.33 \times 177\,570^{1/2} = \$981.84$.

A standard cash-flow mapping method, where cash flows are linearly interpolated between adjacent vertices, is not appropriate for VaR models

It should be noted that a standard cash-flow mapping method, where cash flows are linearly interpolated between adjacent vertices, is not appropriate for VaR models. In fact the VaR of the original cash flow will not be the same as the VaR of the mapped cash flow if this method is used. To keep VaR constant one has to use quadratic interpolation between adjacent vertices. Consider the cash-flow X in Figure 9.3 that is between the vertices A and B. Suppose it is t_A days from vertex A and t_B days from vertex B. The linear interpolation method would be to map a proportion $p = t_B/(t_A + t_B)$ of X to A and a proportion

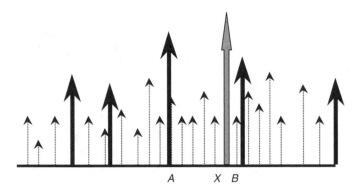

Figure 9.3 Cash-flow mapping.

$1 - p = t_A/(t_A + t_B)$ to B. But the variance of the resulting mapped cash flow will not be the same as the variance of the original cash flow. A VaR-invariant cash-flow map is to map a proportion p to vertex A and $1 - p$ to vertex B, where

$$V(X) = p^2 V(A) + (1 - p)^2 V(B) + 2p(1 - p)\text{cov}(A, B). \qquad (9.8)$$

The required proportion p is found by solving the quadratic equation (9.8), using estimates for $V(A)$, $V(B)$, $V(X)$ and $\text{cov}(A, B)$. The variances of returns at vertices A and B and their covariance can be obtained from standard covariance matrices, and the variance of the original cash flow X is obtained by linear interpolation between $V(A)$ and $V(B)$ according to the number of days:

$$V(X) = [t_B/(t_A + t_B)]V(A) + [t_A/(t_A + t_B)]V(B).$$

For example, consider a cash flow $X = \$1$ million at 1 year and 200 days. The adjacent vertices are assumed to be A at 1 year and B at 2 years, with 365 days between them. Then $t_A = 200$ and $t_B = 165$, so $t_A/(t_A + t_B) = 0.548$ and $t_B/(t_A + t_B) = 0.452$; so with linear interpolation $\$0.452$ million would be mapped to the 1-year maturity and $\$0.548$ million would be mapped to the 2-year maturity. However, this mapping would change the VaR of the cash flow. Now suppose that $V(A) = 4 \times 10^{-5}$ and $V(B) = 3.5 \times 10^{-5}$, and that $\text{cov}(A, B) = 3.3 \times 10^{-5}$. By linear interpolation $V(X) = 0.452 \times 4 \times 10^{-5} + 0.548 \times 3.5 \times 10^{-5} = 3.726 \times 10^{-5}$. So the proportion p of the cash flow that should be mapped to A to keep VaR constant is found by solving

$$3.72 = 4p^2 + 3.5(1 - p)^2 + 6.6p(1 - p)$$

or

$$0.9p^2 - 0.4p - 0.22 = 0$$

giving $p = -0.3198$ or 0.7643. Taking the positive root shows that a VaR invariant cash flow map is to map $\$0.7643$ million to A and $\$0.2357$ million to B. The fact that much more is mapped to A than under linear interpolation is due to the fact that A has a much higher volatility than B. On the other hand, if A had variance less than the variance of B, then the VaR invariant cash-flow map would map less to A than is mapped using the linear interpolation method.

9.3.5   Aggregation

Covariance VaR is determined by the volatility of the portfolio P&L, so it behaves just like a volatility. In particular, the rules for adding volatilities apply to the aggregation of covariance VaR measures and, just as one should not simply add volatilities to obtain a total volatility, it is not normally appropriate to add covariance VaR measures. To see why, we now derive a formula for adding the covariance VaR measures of two positions A and B. From the usual rule for the variance of a sum, the variance of the total position is given by

$$\sigma^2_{A+B} = \sigma^2_A + \sigma^2_B + 2\rho\sigma_A\sigma_B,$$

or

$$\sigma^2_{A+B} = (\sigma_A + \sigma_B)^2 - 2\sigma_A\sigma_B + 2\rho\sigma_A\sigma_B.$$

So

$$\text{Total VaR} = [(\text{VaR}_A + \text{VaR}_B)^2 - 2(1 - \rho)\text{VaR}_A\text{VaR}_B]^{1/2}. \qquad (9.9)$$

The total VaR is only the same as the sum of the VaRs if we assume the two positions are perfectly correlated

The total VaR is only the same as the sum of the VaRs if we assume the two positions are perfectly correlated, that is, $\rho = 1$. Note that the specific VaR in §9.3.3 should be uncorrelated with the VaR due to the market risk factors (see the comments made at the end of §8.1.1). Thus it makes little sense to add the specific VaR to the risk factor VaR. However, to err on the side of conservatism, this is exactly what regulators recommend.

This example has shown that one has to take into account the correlation, when aggregating the VaR for different portfolios. This is particularly important when there is low or negative correlation between the assets or factors, because in that case (9.9) shows that the total VaR will be much less than the sum of the individual VaRs. The interested reader should use the **covariance VaR** spreadsheet on the CD to see how equity and FX VaR are aggregated to give total VaR.

9.3.6   Advantages and Limitations

The covariance method has one clear advantage: it is very quick and simple to compute, so there is no impediment to intra-day VaR calculations and traders can perform a quick calculation to find the impact of a proposed trade on their VaR limit. However, it also has substantial disadvantages:

➢ It has very limited applicability, being suitable only for linear portfolios or portfolios that are assumed to be linear with respect to the risk factors.

➢ It assumes that the portfolio P&L distributions at any point in time are normal. This is certainly true if the returns to individual assets, or risk factors, in the portfolio are normally distributed. But often they are not.[15] If there are major differences between a covariance VaR measure and a historical simulation VaR measure for the same portfolio, it is likely that the non-normality of asset or risk factor returns distributions is a main source of error in the covariance VaR measure (Brooks and Persand, 2000).

➢ It assumes that all the historic data, including possibly very complex dependencies between risk factors, are captured by the covariance matrix. However, covariance matrices are very limited. Firstly, they are very difficult to estimate and forecast (Chapter 5). Secondly, correlation (and covariance) is only a linear measure of co-dependency (§1.1). And thirdly, unless large GARCH covariance matrices are available (§7.4) it is common to apply the square root of time rule to obtain 10-day covariance matrices. But this assumes that volatility and correlation are constant, which may be a gross simplification for the 10-day horizon.

This last point highlights the main problem with covariance VaR measures — that they are only as accurate as the risk model parameters used in the calculation. We have already noted, many times, how unreliable covariance matrices can be. Moreover, in the covariance equity VaR model, factor sensitivities are also used to compute the VaR, and these too are subject to large and unpredictable forecast errors (§8.2 and §4.5.1). Finally, in the covariance fixed income VaR model, the cash flow map itself can be a source of error — one can obtain quite different VaR measures depending on how the portfolio is mapped to the standard risk factors (§9.3.4).

This last point highlights the main problem with covariance VaR measures — that they are only as accurate as the risk model parameters used in the calculation

9.4 Simulation VaR Models

During the past few years the use of simulation methods for VaR analysis has become standard; simulation methods can overcome some of the problems mentioned in §9.3.6. Historical simulation, in particular, is an extremely popular method for many types of institutions. However, it is not easy to capture the path-dependent behaviour of certain types of complex assets unless Monte Carlo simulation is used.

Monte Carlo VaR measures require a covariance matrix and so their accuracy is limited by the accuracy of this matrix. They also take large amounts of computation time if positions are revalued using complex pricing models. Often full revaluation is simply not possible unless VaR calculations are

---

[15] In that case it is possible to adapt the covariance VaR measure to the assumption that returns are fat-tailed. In §10.3.1 it will be shown how to generalize covariance VaR so that the portfolio P&L is assumed to be generated by a mixture of normal densities. Also see the spreadsheet **normal mixture VaR** on the CD.

performed overnight, so intra-day VaR measures are often obtained using approximate pricing functions. The trade-off between speed and accuracy in the Monte Carlo VaR methods has been a focus of recent research (Glasserman *et al.*, 2001).

This section outlines the basic concepts for historical VaR and Monte Carlo VaR. It explains when and how they should be applied, and outlines the advantages and limitations of each method.

9.4.1   Historical Simulation

The absence of distributional assumptions and the direct estimation of variation without the use of a covariance matrix are the main strengths of the historical VaR model

The basic idea behind historical simulation VaR is very straightforward: one simply uses real historical data to build an empirical density for the portfolio P&L. No assumption about the analytic form of this distribution is made at all, nor about the type of co-movements between assets or risk factors. It is also possible to evaluate option prices and other complex positions for various combinations of risk factors, so it is not surprising that many institutions favour this method.

Historical data on the underlying assets and risk factors for the portfolio are collected, usually on a daily basis covering several years. Regulators insist that at least a year's data be employed for internal models that are used to compute market risk capital requirements, and recommend using between 3 and 5 years of daily data. These data are used to compute the portfolio value on each day during the historic data period, keeping the current portfolio weights constant. This will include computing the value of any options or other complex positions using the pricing models.

In a linear portfolio we represent the h-day portfolio return $\Delta_h P_t / P_t$ as a weighted sum of the returns R_i to assets or risk factors, say,

$$\Delta_h P_t / P_t = w_i R_{i,t} + \ldots + w_k R_{k,t}.$$

The w_i are the portfolio weights (so they sum to 1) or the risk factor sensitivities (§8.1.2). Historical data are obtained on each R_i, and then the portfolio price changes over h days are simulated as

$$\Delta_h P_t = \Sigma(w_i P_t) R_{i,t} = \Sigma p_i R_{i,t},$$

where the p_i are the actual amounts invested in each asset, or, in the case of a factor model, the nominal risk factor sensitivities. This representation allows h-day theoretical (or 'unrealized') P&Ls for the portfolio to be simulated from historical data on $R_1, \ldots, R_k$.

With options portfolios full valuation at each point in time is desirable, but for complex products often a price approximation such as a delta–gamma–vega approximation is used. The current portfolio deltas, gammas and vegas are

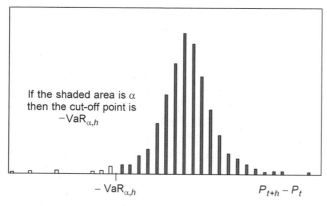

If the shaded area is α
then the cut-off point is
$-\text{VaR}_{\alpha,h}$

$-\text{VaR}_{\alpha,h}$ $P_{t+h} - P_t$

Figure 9.4   Value-at-risk from a simulated P&L density.

Table 9.3: Problems of using a long historic data period for historical VaR

Problem	Possible solution
Data on all relevant assets and risk factors may not be available.	Simulate data using a method such as principal component analysis (§6.4.2).
Full valuation using binomial trees or time-consuming numerical methods on thousands of data points may preclude the use of this method for real-time VaR calculations.	Analytic approximations may be necessary, but this introduces an additional source of error in the VaR measure.
Very long historic data periods may contain a number of extreme market events from far in the past that are not necessarily relevant to current 'normal' circumstances.	Filter out the extreme events from the historic data to obtain the VaR measure under 'normal' market circumstances that is used to calculate the MRR (but see the warning below).
The underlying assets have been trending during the historic period and this does not necessarily reflect their future performance.[16]	Mirror each upward/downward move in the data set with a downward/upward move of the same magnitude, thus doubling the size of the data set and removing any bias from trends.

The historical VaR spreadsheet on the CD illustrates how to implement the model

computed and applied to the historic series on the underlying assets and risk factors (§9.4.3).

The empirical h-day P&L density is obtained by building a histogram of the h-day differences $\Delta P_t = P_{t+h} - P_t$ for all t. Then the historical $\text{VaR}_{\alpha,h}$ is the lower 100αth percentile of this distribution, as shown in Figure 9.4. It will be sensitive to the historic period chosen. For example, if only 300 observations are used in this empirical density, the lower 1% tail will consist of only the three largest losses. The VaR will be the smallest of these three largest losses, and the

---

[16] However note that the trend over 10 days will be much smaller than the variations, so any bias introduced by trending data will be very small.

conditional VaR will be the average of these three losses. Clearly neither will be very robust to changes in the data period.

From the point of view of robustness it is obviously desirable to use a very long historic data period. But this also has a number of disadvantages, which are summarized, along with possible solutions, in Table 9.3. Also, since the portfolio composition has been determined by current circumstances, how meaningful is it to evaluate the portfolio P&L using market data from far in the past? Long ago the availability, liquidity, risk and return characteristics of the various products in the portfolio will have been quite different; the current portfolio would never have been held, so what is the point in valuing it, under these circumstances?

A word of caution on the use of exceptional events that have occurred in historic data for 'normal circumstances' VaR and for 'stress circumstances' VaR. If such events are filtered out, as suggested above, one has to be very careful not to throw out the relevant part of the data. For VaR models, the relevant part is the exceptional losses. If the exceptional event occurred far in the past and the view is taken that similar circumstances are unlikely to pertain during the next 10 days, then there should be no objection to removing them from the historic data set that is used to compute the normal circumstances VaR that forms the basis of the MRR. These events can always be substituted into the data set for the historical scenarios used to calculated stress VaR measures, for setting trading limits and so forth, possibly using the statistical bootstrap so that they occur at random times and with random frequencies in a simulation of historic data. However, if the exceptional events occurred more recently then it is not acceptable to filter them out of the data for MRR computations, setting trading limits or any other VaR application.

If such events are filtered out, one has to be very careful not to throw out the relevant part of the data. For VaR models, the relevant part is the exceptional losses

As an example of recent 'exceptional' losses that should be used in normal VaR computations, consider the daily data from 2 January 1996 to 2 October 2000 on 20 US stocks that were analysed in Table 4.1. The data showed seven extremely large negative returns among 20 stocks over about 1200 days. Over a VaR period of 10 days one should conclude that the chance of an exceptional event per stock is about $(7 \times 10)/(20 \times 1200)$ or 0.29%. Therefore if all 20 stocks are taken together, the probability of an exceptional event in the portfolio over the next 10 days will be more than 5%. One could conclude that in a portfolio of 20 US stocks an 'exceptional' return is quite 'normal'.

9.4.2 Monte Carlo Simulation

*The **Monte Carlo VaR** spreadsheet is limited to 3000 simulations*

Instead of using actual historic data to build an empirical P&L distribution, it may be more convenient to simulate the movements in underlying assets and risk factors from now until some future point in time (the 'risk horizon' of the model). Taking their current values as starting points, thousands of possible values of the underlying assets and risk factors over the next h days are

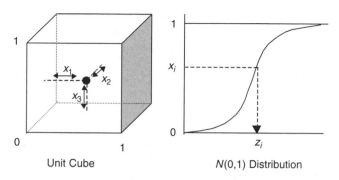

Unit Cube $N(0,1)$ Distribution

Figure 9.5 Sampling the hypercube and simulating independent $N(0, 1)$ observations.

generated using Monte Carlo methods. This very large set of scenarios is then used to obtain thousands of possible values for the portfolio in h days' time, and a histogram of the differences between these and the current portfolio value is obtained. As with the historic simulation method, the VaR measure is simply the lower percentile of this distribution.

It is necessary to generate these scenarios in a realistic manner. One should not include, for example, a scenario where the 2-year swap rate increases by 20 basis points at the same time as the 3-year swap rate decreases by 50 basis points. Not only will the volatility of an asset determine its possible future values in h days' time, one also needs to take account of the correlations between different assets in the portfolio. For this reason one usually employs an h-day covariance matrix for all the underlying assets and risk factors in the portfolio.

Monte Carlo VaR calculation can be summarized in three stages, which are now explained using the example of a portfolio that has k correlated risk factors. We denote the h-day returns to these risk factors by $R_1, \ldots, R_k$ and their covariance matrix by $\mathbf{V}$.

1. *Take a random sample on k independent standard normal variates.* First a random point in the k-dimensional unit cube is chosen, as this corresponds to a set of k independent random numbers, each between 0 and 1. The case $k = 3$ is illustrated in Figure 9.5. It shows how each random number x_i is obtained from a point in the cube and then used with the probability integral transform to obtain a random sample on the standard normal distribution. Denote this $k \times 1$ vector of independent random samples from $N(0, 1)$ by $\mathbf{z}$.[17]

2. *Use the covariance matrix to transform this sample into correlated h-day returns.* Obtain the Cholesky decomposition of $\mathbf{V}$, as explained in §7.1.2, to convert the random sample $\mathbf{z}$ to a vector of normal returns $\mathbf{r}$ that reflects the appropriate covariance structure.

---

[17] It is possible to use other forms of distribution, analytic or empirical, but the normal distribution is the usual one.

3. *Apply the pricing model to the simulated correlated h-day risk factor returns.* This will give one simulated *h*-day portfolio return, and multiplying this by the current price gives a single *h*-day profit or loss figure.

These three stages are repeated several thousand times, to obtain many P&L figures and thereby build an *h*-day P&L distribution for the portfolio. How many times will depend on the number of risk factors, that is, the dimension of the hypercube. Figure 9.6 illustrates why. If only a few hundred random points are taken from the cube it is quite possible that they will, by chance, be concentrated in one part of the cube . . . and the next time, by chance, the points could be concentrated in another area of the cube, in which case the Monte Carlo VaR measures will vary enormously each time they are recalculated.

To increase robustness of Monte Carlo VaR estimates one could, of course, take many thousands of points in the cube each time, so that sampling errors are reduced. But then the time taken for all these portfolio revaluations would be completely impractical. Jamshidian and Zhu (1997) show how principal components analysis can be used to gain enormous increases in computational efficiency in Monte Carlo VaR calculations. It is also standard to employ advanced sampling methods, such as deterministic sequences, so that the cube will be covered in a representative manner by fewer samples. But even with the aid of advanced sampling techniques or principal component analysis it will usually be necessary to employ several thousands of points in the sample.

The third stage of Monte Carlo VaR is so time-consuming that it is impossible to perform thousands of revaluations of the portfolio within a realistic time frame

Stages 1 and 2 take hardly any time, and if the third stage is also not too time-consuming there will be no impediment to using thousands of simulations to obtain accurate and robust VaR estimates. However, it is often the case that the third stage of Monte Carlo VaR is so time-consuming that it is impossible to perform thousands of revaluations of the portfolio within a realistic time frame. In that case approximate pricing functions will need to be employed, including analytic forms for complex options and Taylor approximations to portfolio value changes (§9.4.3).

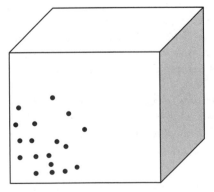

Figure 9.6 Sampling the hypercube with too few points.

The main advantages of Monte Carlo simulation are that it is widely applicable, it is able to capture path-dependent behaviour of complex products and, since simulation techniques are often already employed in the front office, it is operationally efficient to employ these models in VaR calculation also. The main disadvantages of Monte Carlo VaR are the need to use a covariance matrix, which introduces another well-known source of error, and the fact that there is considerable trade-off between speed and accuracy. Often accuracy will need to be compromised in order to complete the VaR calculations within a realistic time frame.

9.4.3 Delta–Gamma Approximations

The **Monte Carlo VaR** spreadsheet calculates the VaR for an option portfolio using full (Black–Scholes) valuation and also using a number of different Taylor approximations based on the option Greeks.

Delta approximations for options and complex instruments are, of course, very convenient. With a delta approximation the portfolio value changes are just a linear function of the underlying asset price changes. Delta approximations are simple, but the VaR obtained in this way tends to be very inaccurate, in any portfolio with gamma or convexity effects. The delta approximation is a local approximation, holding good only for small changes in the underlying price. For VaR measures we need to consider the tail of the P&L distribution, that is, the effect of large price changes. Figure 9.7 explains why the VaR approximation errors from a delta-only representation tend to be rather too large.

The *delta–gamma–theta representation* is a second-order Taylor expansion of the portfolio value change with respect to the changes in the underlying prices (denoted by the vector ΔS). That is,

$$\Delta P \approx \theta \Delta t + \boldsymbol{\delta}' \Delta \mathbf{S} + \tfrac{1}{2} \Delta \mathbf{S}' \Gamma \Delta \mathbf{S}, \qquad (9.10)$$

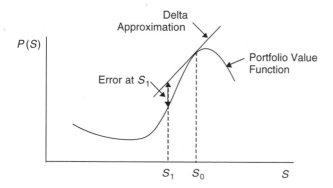

Figure 9.7 Error from delta-only approximation.

where θ is the partial derivative of the portfolio value with respect to time, $\boldsymbol{\delta}$ is a vector of first partial derivatives of the portfolio value with respect to the components of $\mathbf{S}$, and Γ is the Hessian matrix of second partial derivatives with respect to $\mathbf{S}$. Without the first term, (9.10) is the *delta–gamma representation*.

Finite differences are normally employed to compute the option sensitivities. For example, the option delta and gamma may be computed using central differences by valuing the portfolio at the current price S, giving the current value $P(S)$ and for small perturbations above and below this price, at $S + \varepsilon$ and $S - \varepsilon$ for each underlying S in the vector $\mathbf{S}$. Then the delta and gamma corresponding to S are approximated by:

$$\delta \approx [P(S + \varepsilon) - P(S - \varepsilon)]/2\varepsilon \qquad (9.11)$$

and

$$\gamma \approx [P(S + \varepsilon) - 2P(S) + P(S - \varepsilon)]/\varepsilon^2. \qquad (9.12)$$

The accuracy of the delta–gamma approximation can be tested in the usual way, by comparing the delta–gamma value changes with the full valuation value changes over a suitable historic period. If the approximation is not working sufficiently well it is normal to include volatility as another risk factor, in the *delta–gamma–vega–theta representation*

$$\Delta P \approx \theta \Delta t + \boldsymbol{\delta}' \Delta \mathbf{S} + \tfrac{1}{2} \Delta \mathbf{S}' \Gamma \Delta \mathbf{S} + \mathbf{v}' \Delta \boldsymbol{\sigma}, \qquad (9.13)$$

where $\mathbf{v}$ is a vector of first partial derivatives of the portfolio value with respect to the volatility of each component of $\mathbf{S}$, this vector of volatilities being denoted $\boldsymbol{\sigma}$.[18] Theta and the components of the vega vector are also computed using first finite differences. The procedure is the same as with the delta components, only this time using small perturbations on time and the current value of the volatility rather than the underlying price. More details can be seen on the CD.

The delta–gamma, delta–vega and delta–gamma–vega approximations are commonly employed as an approximate pricing function when full revaluation is considered too time-consuming

The delta–gamma, delta–vega and delta–gamma–vega approximations to value changes in a portfolio have an important role to play in simulation VaR models. They are commonly employed as an approximate pricing function when full revaluation is considered too time-consuming. Glasserman *et al.* (2001) show how to use them in Monte Carlo VaR, not as a pricing approximation but as a guide to sampling, with a combination of importance sampling and stratified sampling methods. Rouvinez (1997) shows how the delta–gamma approximation can be used for an analytic approximation to the VaR for an options portfolio.

---

[18] This assumes that volatility changes are independent of price changes, which is only a rough approximation (§2.3).

9.5 Model Validation

VaR models have become the primary method for calculating MRR, so regulators have set rigorous guidelines for the internal backtesting of these models. The first part of this section describes the backtesting methodology that is outlined in the 1996 Amendment and the translation of backtesting results into risk capital requirements. The second part discusses why different VaR models often give quite different results for the same portfolio, highlighting the various sources of error in each method. VaR estimates can be very sensitive to the choice of historical data period and assumptions about model parameters such as the covariance matrix. Assessment of a VaR model should therefore include an analysis of the sensitivity of results to these decisions and assumptions.

9.5.1 Backtesting Methodology and Regulatory Classification

A 1% 1-day VaR measure gives the level of loss that would be exceeded in normal market circumstances one day in every 100, if the portfolio is left unmanaged. That is, the unrealized P&L, also called the theoretical P&L, of the portfolio will show a loss greater than the 1% 1-day VaR estimate, on average, one day in every 100. So if an accurate VaR model is tested over a period of 1000 days one would expect 10 losses that exceed the level of VaR if the model is accurate. However, if the model is predicting a VaR that is too low, more than 10 exceptional losses will be observed. These 'exceptional' losses are illustrated in Figure 9.8. They form the basis of the VaR model backtests that were proposed in the 1996 Amendment to the Basel Accord.

The total number of exceptional losses may be regarded as a random variable that has a binomial distribution. The probability of 'success' (an exceptional loss) is $p = 0.01$ for a 1% VaR, and the number of trials n is the number of days for the backtest, say $n = 1000$. Then the expected number of exceptional losses

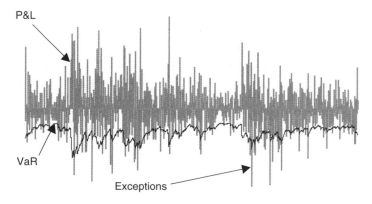

Figure 9.8 Backtests.

is $np = 10$ and the variance of the exceptional losses is $np(1 - p) = 9.9$. Therefore the standard deviation is $\sqrt{9.9} = 3.146$ and, using the fact that a binomial distribution is approximately normal when n is large and p is small, a 99% confidence interval for the number of exceptional losses, assuming that the VaR model is accurate, is approximately

$$(np - Z_{0.005}\sqrt{(np(1 - p))}, \; np + Z_{0.005}\sqrt{(np(1 - p))})$$

(see §A.2.1). In this example it becomes

$$(10 - 2.576 \times 3.146, \; 10 + 2.576 \times 3.146) = (1.896, 18.104).$$

That is, we are about 99% sure that we will observe between 2 and 18 exceptional losses if the VaR model is correct. Similarly, if the VaR model is accurate, we are 90% confident that between 5 and 15 exceptional losses will be observed in the backtest, because

$$(np - Z_{0.005}\sqrt{(np(1 - p))}, \; np + Z_{0.005}\sqrt{(np(1 - p))})$$
$$= (10 - 1.645 \times 3.146, \; 10 + 1.645 \times 3.146) = (4.825, 15.175).$$

Whether or not actual P&L gives rise to more exceptions during backtests than theoretical P&L will depend on the nature of trading

The 1996 Amendment to the Basel accord describes the form of backtests that must be undertaken by firms wishing to use a VaR model for the calculation of MRR. Regulators recommend using the last 250 days of P&L data to backtest the 1% 1-day VaR that is predicted by an internal model. The model should be backtested against both theoretical and actual P&L.[19] Whether or not actual P&L gives rise to more exceptions during backtests than theoretical P&L will depend on the nature of trading. If the main activity is hedging one should expect fewer exceptions, but if traders are undertaking more speculative trades that increase P&L volatility, then the opposite will be observed.

For each area of operations in the firm, such as equity derivatives trading, a backtest is performed by first choosing a candidate portfolio that reflects the type of positions normally taken. The portfolio is held fixed and for each of the last 250 days the VaR is compared with the P&L of the portfolio. The number of exceptional losses over the past 250 days is then recorded.

Regulators will not necessarily adhere to these rules in a hard-and-fast fashion

From the binomial model, the standard error for a 1% VaR for a backtest on 250 days is $\sqrt{(250 \times 0.01 \times 0.99)} = \sqrt{2.475} = 1.573$, so a 90% confidence interval for the number of exceptions observed if the VaR model is accurate $(2.5 \pm 1.645 \times 1.573)$. That is, one is approximately 90% confident that no more than 5 exceptions will occur when the VaR model is accurate. Thus regulators will accept that VaR models which give up to 4 exceptional losses during backtests are performing their function with an appropriate accuracy. These models are labeled 'green zone' models and have a multiplier of $k = 3$ for

---

[19] Actual includes the P&L from positions taken during the day (even when they are closed out at the end of the day), fees, commissions and so forth. Theoretical P&L is the P&L that would have been obtained if the position had been left unchanged.

Table 9.4: Multipliers for the calculation of market risk
requirements

Zone	Number of Exceptions	Multiplier k
Green	Up to 4	3
	5	3.04
	6	3.05
Yellow	7	3.65
	8	3.75
	9	3.85
Red	10 or more	4

the calculation of MRR.[20] If more than four exceptions are recorded the multiplier increases up to a maximum of 4 as shown in Table 9.4 (some 'red zone' models may in fact be disallowed). Regulators will not necessarily adhere to these rules in a hard-and-fast fashion. Some allowance may be made if markets have been particularly turbulent during the backtesting period, particularly if the model has performed well in previous backtests. It should be expected that the results of the backtests will depend on the data period chosen.

9.5.2 Sensitivity Analysis and Model Comparison

VaR estimates are highly sensitive to the assumptions of the VaR model and the other decisions that will need to be made. For example, covariance VaR models and Monte Carlo VaR models both require a covariance matrix, the generation of which requires many assumptions about the nature of asset or risk factor returns. If the same covariance matrix is employed to calculate the covariance VaR and the Monte Carlo VaR of a linear portfolio using both of these methods one should obtain the same result. The reader can verify that this is the case using the VaR spreadsheets on the CD. Differences will only arise if one drops the assumption of normality in one or other of the models (as in §10.3.1, for example), or if too few simulations are being employed in the Monte Carlo VaR.

Historical VaR models employ neither covariance matrices nor normality assumptions, so it is often the case that historical VaR estimates differ substantially from covariance or Monte Carlo VaR estimates. If this is found to be the case one should test whether the assumption of normality is warranted (§10.1). One should also investigate the accuracy of the covariance matrix forecasts, as far as this is possible (§5.1). If neither the covariance matrix nor the normality assumptions are thought to be a problem, then it is possible that it is the historical VaR estimate that is inaccurate, and this will most likely be due an inappropriate choice of historical period. It may be too short, so the

It is often the case that historical VaR measures differ substantially from covariance or Monte Carlo VaR measures

---

[20] The market risk capital charge will be either yesterday's VaR measure or k times the average of the last 60 days' VaR measures, whichever is greater.

P&L distribution is based on only a few points, in which case VaR estimates will not be robust to changes in the data. Readers should see this for themselves by choosing only a short historical period in the **historical VaR** workbook. It may be too long if there were many very extreme returns in the risk factors a long time ago which have not been repeated during the more recent past.

When attempting to validate a VaR model the risk control function will need to examine many VaR tables, along the lines of that shown in Table 9.1, where the model parameter assumptions are displayed with the table. So for each VaR table the type of covariance matrix should be clearly stated, as should the type of cash-flow maps or factor models if these are employed. In historical VaR models the historical look back period should be stated, and in Monte Carlo VaR models the number of simulations, and any advanced sampling techniques should also be mentioned.

It is the role of risk control to investigate how robust the VaR estimates are to different choices of data and parameters

It is the role of risk control to investigate how robust the VaR estimates are to different choices of data and parameters. This can be achieved using a simple visual analysis—for example, a plot of historical VaR estimates as the historical data period is increased, or a series of covariance VaR plots as certain correlations are varied (cf. Figure 5.4). Since so many assumptions will need to be made about the values of the VaR model parameters this type of sensitivity analysis is a crucial part of model development. Even if the VaR model appears to perform well in backtests, if it does not prove to be robust to small changes in parameter assumptions there is a good chance that future backtesting results will be poor, and the model will be moved into a different Basel zone.

9.6 Scenario Analysis and Stress Testing

The final part of this chapter will examine how the risk characteristics of portfolios can be assessed through scenario analysis and stress testing. Scenario analysis examines the value of a portfolio as the underlying risk factors are perturbed from their current values. Stress testing is really a part of scenario analysis, but instead of considering the sort of perturbations that are expected in normal market circumstances, one looks at the portfolio value when risk factors are moved to extreme positions.

There is much to be said for evaluating portfolios using scenario analysis. Scenario-based methods such as the mark-to-future framework (Dembo, 2000; Dembo *et al.*, 2000) do not depend on distributional assumptions and can incorporate the path-dependent behaviour of any type of security.[21] It is therefore not surprising that many banks prefer to quantify their MRR using scenario-based calculations rather than internal VaR models.

---

[21] More details are available from www.mark-to-future.com.

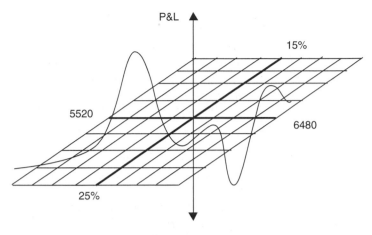

Figure 9.9 Scenario analysis.

9.6.1 Scenario Analysis

As if the building of a historic database on asset prices and risk factors that is updated in real time is not enough of a challenge, a fully functional risk management capability needs to provide a library of scenarios for use by traders and managers. The role of this library should be to allow managers to assess all risk characteristics of existing positions and to allow traders to examine the risk and return of potential trades under various scenarios. The library should consist of

A fully functional risk management capability needs to provide a library of scenarios for use by traders and managers

➤ covariance matrices (so that the portfolios can be stress-tested for extreme market conditions as described in §9.6.3);
➤ joint distributions on risk factors and volatilities (which are used to compute the expected loss of a portfolio, as described in §9.6.2);
➤ smile surfaces, including those that are particularly relevant to current market conditions (these can be generated using the method outlined in §6.3).

The 1996 Amendment to the Basel Accord laid down various guidelines if MRR is being assessed via scenario analysis.[22] Regulators require that portfolios are valued on a grid that is defined according to both country and asset class. The scenarios are for underlying risk factors and risk factor volatilities, so the grid may be envisaged in two dimensions, as shown in Figure 9.9.

Figure 9.9 shows the type of grid that could be used to revalue the net UK equity option positions. The underlying risk factors are the FTSE 100 index and the at-the-money FTSE 100 implied volatility. Their current values are

---

[22] These scenarios are much less comprehensive that those that should be considered by internal risk management.

taken as the origin of coordinates and the boundary of the grid is defined as $\pm 8\%$ for the value of the FTSE 100 and $\pm 25\%$ for ATM volatility. Thus if the FTSE index is currently at 6000, and ATM implied volatility is currently 20%, the boundaries are set at (5520, 6480) for the index and (15%, 25%) for the ATM volatility. The volatility shifts are imposed by the regulators and applied to the volatility term structure; large shifts ($\pm 30\%$) are taken for short maturities and smaller shifts are taken for longer maturities (e.g. $\pm 8\%$ for 1 year and $\pm 3\%$ for 5 years).

A fairly coarse grid is defined in this range, say at intervals of 100 points for the index and 1% for the implied volatility. In fact usually the grid will contain only 7×3 points (seven divisions for the underlying and three divisions for the implied volatility). The regulator does not impose more points but will want some justification that the maximum loss found on the grid cannot be too far from the actual maximum loss. Therefore the portfolio is revalued at each point on this grid and then potential 'hot-spots' are discovered, where the portfolio makes large losses; the grid is then refined about these points and the portfolio is revalued in these regions using the finer grid. Eventually the maximum loss of the portfolio over all possible scenarios is recorded.[23]

If all positions are cash or futures there is no need to revalue the portfolio over a grid or to account for implied volatilities, because in this case the portfolio value will be a linear function of the underlying and the maximum loss will occur at one or other extreme. Interest-rate-dependent products are treated in this way. They are banded into maturity buckets, and the net positions in each bucket are subject to yield variations from ± 100 basis points for the short buckets going down to ± 60 basis points for the long buckets. If the maximum loss occurs at $+100$ basis points for the 6–9-month bucket and -100 basis points in the 9–12-month bucket, this is a highly unlikely scenario, so there is also some netting across adjacent buckets. The rules for interest-rate-dependent products are quite complex and the interested reader should consult the current FSA Guidelines for Banking Supervision,[24] or equivalent, for further details.

This type of scenario analysis is performed for all asset types and all countries. There is netting within each asset class but not across countries, and the MRR is then the sum of all the maximum losses that are recorded from each scenario analysis.

9.6.2 Probabilistic Scenario Analysis

If a portfolio is properly hedged then the maximum loss over a scenario grid will occur at a very unlikely scenario. Suppose the maximum loss occurs when

---

[23] Useful software for performing this type of analysis is available from www.fea.com.

[24] See www.fsa.gov.uk/pubs/supervisor.

the underlying asset price is virtually unchanged at the same time as its implied volatility increases by 5%. This is very unlikely to happen: the discussion in §2.3 shows that there is often a strong negative correlation between prices and volatilities, particularly in equity markets. However, one could reduce the MRR by hedging the portfolio against this scenario. This would be costly, and of little practical importance, but it might be worth putting on the hedge if the MRR will be reduced considerably. This is one example where regulatory policy does not promote good risk management practice.

This is one example where regulatory policy does not promote good risk management practice

Although it is necessary to follow regulators' rules for market risk capital calculations, internal risk management may want to use a more sophisticated approach when assessing the risk characteristics of a portfolio. For one thing, a broader range of movements in both the underlying and the implied volatilities could be applied. Secondly, it would be more informative to compute not the maximum loss, irrespective of how likely it is to occur, but the expected loss of a portfolio, using realistic assumptions about the joint distribution of its risk factors.

It would be more informative to compute the expected loss of a portfolio, using realistic assumptions about the joint distribution of its risk factors

A simple model that employs historic data to generate a joint distribution for movements in an underlying asset and movements in its implied volatility was described in §2.3.4. A joint distribution of risk factor movements, such as those shown in Figures 2.9 and 2.10, can be used to obtain a more realistic assessment of the portfolio's risk characteristics. The expected loss of the portfolio can be obtained by multiplying the profit or loss by the relevant probability and then summing over the entire scenario range. In addition, one can compute the loss standard deviation, to indicate the accuracy of the assessment of expected loss.

9.6.3 Stress-Testing Portfolios

The 1996 Amendment also gave guidelines for the rigorous and comprehensive stress-testing of portfolios. This should include stress testing portfolios for:

➢ the repeat of an historic event, such as the global equity Black Monday crash in 1987;
➢ a breakdown in volatility and correlation that is associated with a stress event;
➢ changes in liquidity accompanying the stress event.

All three types of stress test can be performed using a covariance matrix. In the covariance and Monte Carlo VaR models all that is required is to replace the current covariance matrix by a covariance matrix that reflects the stress test. Even when the VaR model uses historic simulation, it is possible to perform the stress tests using a covariance matrix. Following Duffie and Pan (1997), let $\mathbf{r}$ denote the vector of returns that is used in the historical VaR model, and compute its equally weighted covariance matrix $\mathbf{V}$. Suppose that $\mathbf{W}$ is a stress

Even when the VaR model uses historic simulation, it is possible to perform the stress tests using a covariance matrix

covariance matrix (of one of the types defined below), and let **C** and **D** respectively denote the Cholesky decompositions of **V** and **W**. Now transform the historic returns series **r** into another vector of returns **r*** = **DC**$^{-1}$**r**. These returns will reflect the conditions of **W** rather than **V** and the stress test is performed using **r*** in the historical VaR model in place of the actual historic returns **r**.

What type of covariance matrix should be used in a stress test? If the test is against an extreme event that actually occurred, then it is simply the covariance matrix that pertained at that time. Historic data on all assets and risk factors around the time of extreme events will have to be stored so that historic covariance matrices that include data on these extreme events can be generated.

If the stress test is for a change in liquidity accompanying the stress event then the stressed matrix can be a new covariance matrix that reflects changes in holding periods associated with different asset classes. For example, consider a covariance matrix for positions in Eastern European equity markets. The risk factors that define the covariance matrix will be the relevant equity indices and the relevant exchange rates. Following an extreme event in the markets, suppose it is possible to liquidate the equity positions locally within 5 days without much effect on the bid–ask spread, but that the foreign exchange market becomes very illiquid and that it will take 25 days to hedge the currency exposure. Then an approximate stress covariance matrix can be obtained by multiplying all elements in the equity block and the equity–FX block of the matrix by 5, but the elements in the FX block by 25. Of course, it is not certain that the resulting covariance matrix will be positive semi-definite. The only way to ensure this is to use the same multiplication factor for all elements, which is in effect modelling liquidity deterioration using an h-day VaR measure for reasonably large h.

For a breakdown of volatilities and correlations it is easier to use the decomposition of a covariance matrix **V** into the product

$$\mathbf{V} = \mathbf{DCD},$$

where **C** is the correlation matrix and **D** is the diagonal matrix with standard deviations along the diagonal. Stress tests can therefore be performed by perturbing the volatilities separately from the correlations, and it is only the changes in the correlation matrix that will affect the positive definiteness of **V**.[25] Readers will observe this when using the stress VaR settings in the VaR spreadsheets on the CD. One is therefore free to change any volatilities to any (positive) level during stress tests, and the resulting VaR measures will always be non-negative. But some changes in the correlation matrix would be disallowed, and so it is important to check for positive definiteness (§7.1.3).

---

[25] **V** is positive semi-definite if and only if **x**′**Vx** ⩾ 0 for all **x** ≠ **0**. But **x**′**Vx** = **y**′**Cy** where **y** = **Dx**, and, since **D** is diagonal with positive elements, **y** ≠ **0** if and only if **x** ≠ **0**. So **V** is positive semi-definite if and only if **C** is positive semi-definite.

It is worth mentioning that principal components analysis has natural applications to both scenario analysis and stress testing portfolios (Jamshidian and Zhu, 1997). Recall from §6.1 that a principal components representation can be written $\mathbf{X} = \mathbf{PW}'$ where $\mathbf{X}$ is a set of standardized returns, $\mathbf{P}$ is a matrix of principal components and $\mathbf{W}$ is the matrix of factor weights in (6.2). Both $\mathbf{X}$ and $\mathbf{P}$ have columns that represent time series (the columns of $\mathbf{P}$ are the principal components) but $\mathbf{W}$ is a matrix of constants, which captures the correlation in the system. Stress-testing correlations can therefore be performed by changing the factor weights matrix $\mathbf{W}$. The advantages of this method include the ability to stress test for correlation breakdown without being required to use a covariance matrix.

Principal components analysis has natural applications to both scenario analysis and stress testing portfolios

Frye (1998) shows how shifts in the first few principal components are useful for the scenario analysis of interest-rate-dependent products. Yield curves lend themselves particularly well to principal component analysis, and the first principal component has the interpretation of a parallel shift in the yield curve (§6.2.1). A scenario that increases the first principal component by the equivalent of 100 basis points, for example, is therefore a computationally efficient method for evaluating the effect of parallel shift scenarios. Similarly, the second component represents a yield curve tilt and the third the curvature, so one can capture very complex scenarios on yield curve movements using just a few scenarios on the first three principal components.

Modelling Non-normal Returns

Many financial assets have high-frequency returns with non-normal distributions; in particular, they often have fatter tails than the normal distribution. That is, the probability of extreme returns that are observed empirically is higher than the probability of extreme returns under the normal distribution. This feature is referred to as *leptokurtosis*, or simply 'fat tails'.[1] There are different approaches to modelling the non-normal characteristics of financial asset returns. One possibility is to use a stochastic volatility model, where conditional returns distributions are normal but their variance changes over time. The other approach, discussed in this chapter, is to model the unconditional distribution of returns using a non-normal density function.

Section 10.1 explains the statistical tests that are commonly employed for non-normal behaviour in financial return distributions. It is shown that non-normality tends to become more pronounced as the frequency of returns increases. Excess kurtosis in particular may be quite enormous in intra-day data. As long ago as 1963, Benoit Mandelbrot observed that financial returns may have distributions that are not normal.[2] Section 10.2 describes some of the non-normal distributions that are commonly used in financial analysis A brief account of extreme value distributions (§10.2.1) and hyperbolic distributions (§10.2.2) is followed by an extensive discussion of the normal mixture distributions (§10.2.3).

As long ago as 1963, Benoit Mandelbrot observed that financial returns may have distributions that are not normal

Normal mixture distributions are a particular favourite of mine because many simple models based on normal returns may be modified quite easily to accommodate normal mixture density assumptions. Much of this chapter is focused on normal mixture density functions and their applications in finance. Covariance VaR measures that are based on normal mixture models for fat-tailed distributions are introduced in §10.3.1. The huge excess kurtosis in intra-day returns can present a serious problem for the pricing and hedging of

---

[1] In fact *leptokurtic* literally means 'thin-arched' or 'thin-centred'. Fat-tailed distributions have thin centres (see Figure 10.1). Literally translated to the Greek, 'fat-tailed' would be 'platyeschatic'.

[2] In fact Mandelbrot (1963) thought that distributions of financial asset returns would be similar to *stable Pareto* distributions. Stable distributions are so called because a sum of stable random variables is again a stable random variable. Thus the normal distribution is a special case of a stable distribution. Stable Pareto distributions are so fat-tailed that their kurtosis is infinite, and this implies that kurtosis estimates should increase with sample size; this hypothesis is not substantiated by empirical findings of kurtosis estimates that converge as the sample size increases. Kurtosis also tends to increase with sampling frequency, so the use of stable Pareto distributions has gone somewhat out of fashion for financial models, but more details may be found in Campbell *et al.* (1997).

options portfolios, and §10.3.2 shows how normal mixture densities can be applied to generate term structures of kurtosis for very high-frequency data.

At the end of Part I, in Chapter 5, we concluded that it is very difficult indeed to forecast volatility. Therefore, rather than asking 'how accurate is my volatility forecast?', we started to consider a different question: 'how much does it matter if my volatility forecast is wrong?'. In §5.3 it was shown that uncertainty in volatility can have a big effect on option prices; in fact it can explain why OTM options have higher market prices than constant volatility model option prices. That is, uncertainty in volatility can explain the volatility smile. At the end of this chapter, in §10.3.3, we shall return again to this discussion, this time to use normal mixture densities to model the uncertainty in volatility. The option price bias for simple OTM options that was explained, using Taylor expansion, in (5.7) is made concrete with an empirical model based on normal mixture densities. The effect of uncertain volatility on delta hedged portfolios that was discussed in §5.3.2 will also be revisited.

Uncertainty in volatility can explain the volatility smile. We shall use normal mixture densities to model the uncertainty in volatility

10.1 Testing for Non-normality in Returns Distributions

10.1.1   Skewness and Excess Kurtosis

The skewness τ is the standardized third moment of the distribution, and the kurtosis is the standardized fourth moment. Since the normal distribution has a kurtosis of 3 it is usual to subtract 3 from the kurtosis, so that both skewness and 'excess' kurtosis κ will be zero for a normal distribution:

$$\tau = E[(X - \mu)^3]/\sigma^3, \tag{10.1}$$

$$\kappa = E[(X - \mu)^4]/\sigma^4 - 3. \tag{10.2}$$

Positive excess kurtosis indicates more weight in both tails of the distribution than in the normal distribution. Hence the term 'fat-tailed' for distributions with positive excess kurtosis, also called leptokurtic distributions, but either way it sounds as if they have some sort of unfortunate health problem.

Precise standard errors for skewness and excess kurtosis are difficult to compute without the assumption of normality

If the underlying population is normal then standard errors for the sample estimates $\hat{\tau}$ and $\hat{\kappa}$ are approximately $\sqrt{(6/n)}$ and $\sqrt{(24/n)}$, where n is the sample size. That is, approximate standard errors for kurtosis estimates are twice the size of the standard errors of the skewness estimates. Precise standard errors for skewness and excess kurtosis are difficult to compute without the assumption of normality. Even a standard error for a variance estimate will involve computing the fourth central moment when the distribution is not normal.[3]

---

[3] The variance of the sample mean is always σ^2/n, where n is the sample size and σ^2 is the population variance; one does not need to assume normality. The variance of the sample variance s^2 is $2\sigma^4/n$, when the population is normal, but more generally it is $(\mu_4 - \sigma^4)/n$ where $\mu_4 = E((x - \mu)^4)$ is the fourth moment about the mean. The computation of standard errors for sample estimates of (10.1) and (10.2) involves a complicated matrix product of central moments when the population is not normal (see Greene, 1993).

Table 10.1: Normality statistics for the return on the DEM–USD exchange rate

	1-hour	6-hour	12-hour	1-day	1-week
Skewness	0.289	0.233	0.200	0.090	0.340
Approx. s.e.	*0.031*	*0.076*	*0.107*	*0.152*	*0.339*
Excess kurtosis	8.34	3.39	1.54	0.63	0.22
Approx. s.e.	*0.062*	*0.152*	*0.214*	*0.303*	*0.678*
JB	18245	510	54.77	4.62	1.11

The *Jarque–Bera normality test* is a form of Wald test (§A.2.5) where the null hypothesis is that the data are normal. The JB test statistic is defined in terms of sample estimates of skewness and excess kurtosis ($\hat{\tau}$ and $\hat{\kappa}$) based on a sample size n:

$$JB = n[(\hat{\tau}^2/6) + (\hat{\kappa}^2/24)] \qquad (10.3)$$

and it is asymptotically chi-squared with 2 degrees of freedom.

Table 10.1 reports the skewness and kurtosis estimates and Jarque–Bera statistics based on a year of tic data on the DEM–USD exchange rate that is bucketed into different sampling intervals. The number of observations taken to compute these statistics varies from 6264 for the hourly data down to 52 for the weekly data, so obviously their standard errors increase as the sampling frequency decreases.

Comparison of the sample estimates with their approximate standard errors (under the null hypothesis of normality) shows that there is evidence of skewness in the hourly and 6-hourly data, but not at any lower frequency. There is no evidence of leptokurtosis in the weekly data and not much in the daily data, but there is enormous excess kurtosis at the intra-day frequencies. The Jarque–Bera tests confirm this[4] — the JB statistics are significantly different from zero on the intra-day data only, and they indicate that

➤ the hypothesis of a normal distribution can be maintained for the daily and weekly returns (but there are very few observations so the power of the test is rather low);
➤ intra-day returns distributions have excess kurtosis which increases with sampling frequency.

In most liquid financial markets there is highly significant excess kurtosis in intra-day returns, which increases with sampling frequency. This is one of the stylized facts of high-frequency financial returns, which is particularly pronounced in foreign exchange markets. However, the skew in high-frequency exchange rate returns is not as pronounced as it is in high-frequency equity returns (see Hseih, 1988; Baillie and Bollerslev, 1989b; Müller *et al.*, 1990).

In most liquid financial markets there is highly significant excess kurtosis in intra-day returns, which increases with sampling frequency

---

[4] The 1% critical value of $\chi^2(2)$ is 9.21 and the 5% critical value of $\chi^2(2)$ is 5.99.

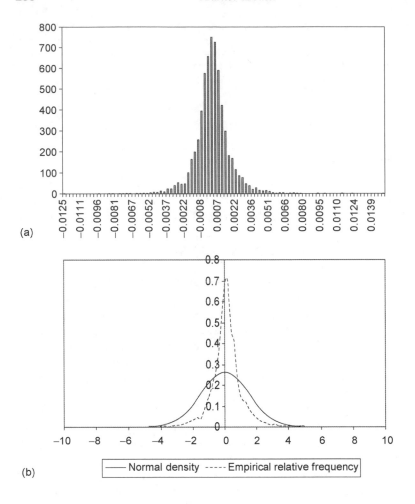

(a)

(b)

10.1.2 QQ Plots

It is also possible to observe departures from normality using some standard qualitative plots such as those shown in Figure 10.1. The first view in Figure 10.1a is of the histogram of 1-hour returns on the DEM–USD exchange rate. This is transformed to a relative frequency distribution in Figure 10.1b and compared with that of the normal density of the same mean and standard deviation. Now from Table 10.1 the skewness is 0.289 (this shows up in the extra weight in the right-hand tail of the distribution) and the excess kurtosis is 8.34. Fat-tailed densities have higher peaks — that is, more weight around the mean — as well as more weight in the tails. Note that when there is excess kurtosis the mid-range values either side of the mean have less weight than in the normal distribution. So fat-tailed densities are appropriate when market returns are likely to be very small or very large, but returns are less likely to take values in between these two extremes.

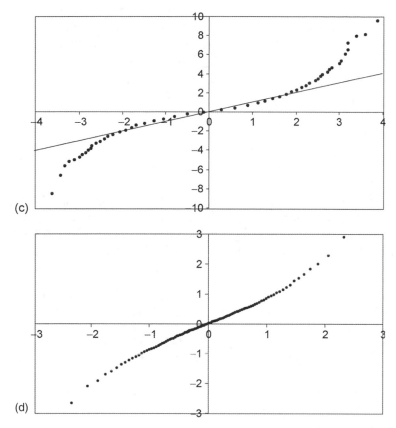

Figure 10.1 German mark–US dollar exchange rate: (a) frequency of 1-hour returns; (b) empirical versus normal density; (c) QQ plot of 1-hour returns; (d) QQ plot of daily returns.

The third view of the data in Figure 10.1c is a quantile to quantile plot or *QQ plot*.[5] This is a scatter plot of the empirical quantiles (vertical axis) against the theoretical quantiles (horizontal axis) of a given distribution. To construct a QQ plot that compares an empirical distribution with a normal distribution, apply the *standard normal transformation* to the empirical returns[6] and calculate the quantiles of the transformed empirical distribution. Then the QQ plot is simply a scatter plot of the transformed empirical and the standard normal quantiles.

Fat tails show up in QQ plots as deviations below this line at the lower quantiles, and above this line at the upper quantiles

If returns have excess kurtosis, the probability of large negative or large positive values is greater than under the corresponding normal density function. So the lower quantiles are less than the normal quantiles, and the upper quantiles are

---

[5] An α quantile of a density function is a value x such that $\text{Prob}(X < x) = \alpha$.

[6] That is, transform X_i into $Z_i = (X_i - \bar{X})/s$, where $\bar{X}$ is the sample mean and s is the sample standard deviation. Then the Z_i have a sample mean of 0 and a sample standard deviation of 1.

greater. Fat tails show up in QQ plots as deviations below this line at the lower quantiles, and above this line at the upper quantiles. The fat tails of the 1-hour returns are very evident in Figure 10.1c, although the QQ plot in Figure 10.1d shows that daily returns are much closer to being normal.

10.2 Non-normal Distributions

The normal density function is given by

$$\phi(x) = (2\pi\sigma^2)^{-1/2} \exp(-\tfrac{1}{2}(x-\mu)^2/\sigma^2), \quad -\infty < x < \infty.$$

The normal distribution $\Phi(x)$ does not have a nice functional form so we usually work with normal density functions. For non-normal distributions it depends: sometimes it is more convenient to use a density function (§10.2.2 and §10.2.3) and in other cases the distribution function makes the analysis more tractable (§10.2.1).

Normal distributions are completely determined by only two parameters: the mean μ, which measures the *location* of the distribution; and the variance σ^2, which measures the *scale* of the distribution. All normal density functions have the same shape and the function $\phi(x)$ describes the familiar bell-shaped curve. But some families of distributions will have one (or more) *shape parameter*, in addition to scale and location parameters. For example, hyperbolic densities have two shape parameters and two other parameters that determine the scale and location of the distribution (§10.2.2).

10.2.1   Extreme Value Distributions

Extreme value distributions are a class of distribution that only applies to extreme values. They are commonly used in financial risk management because they focus on extreme values of returns, or exceptional losses. These extreme returns or exceptional losses are extracted from the data, and then an extreme value distribution may be fitted to these values. There are two approaches. One either models the maximal and minimal values in a sample using the *generalized extreme value (GEV) distribution*, or one models the excesses over a predefined threshold using the *generalized Pareto distribution (GPD)*.

The difference between these approaches is illustrated in Figures 10.2 and 10.3. Figure 10.2a shows how the maximal loss data are obtained: the underlying time series, which may be thought of as a series of daily returns or of P&Ls, is filtered by extracting the maximal loss (or largest negative return) during a week, every non-overlapping week during the sample period. Figure 10.2b shows how the 'peaks over threshold' (POT) data are obtained: the same underlying time series as that of Figure 10.2a is now filtered by setting a high threshold u and taking all excesses over this threshold. Histograms of these two types of extreme value data are shown in Figure 10.3 ($u = -2$ in this example).

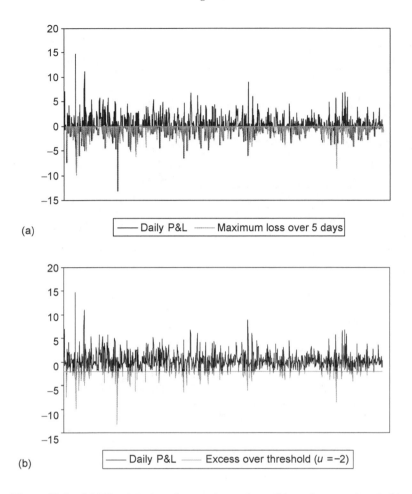

Figure 10.2 (a) Filtering data for maximum loss; (b) peaks over threshold.

Maximal loss and excess over threshold are different types of random variables, but each may be defined in terms of the underlying random variable in a straightforward way. The distributions of these two types of extreme values can be built from first principles without too much difficulty. Indeed, it is possible to understand the fundamental concepts for extreme value distributions with a basic knowledge of statistics.

First consider the case where an extreme value is defined as the maximum (or minimum) of a sample $\{x_1, \ldots, x_n\}$ of size n. The sample size depends on the non-overlapping periods specified in the model. For example, one might wish to model the maximum daily loss experienced during a week, as in Figure 10.2a. In this case the model will take a sample size $n = 5$. We start with the usual construction that each value x_i in a random sample size n can be viewed as an observation on a random variable X_i, where $X_1, \ldots, X_n$ are independent

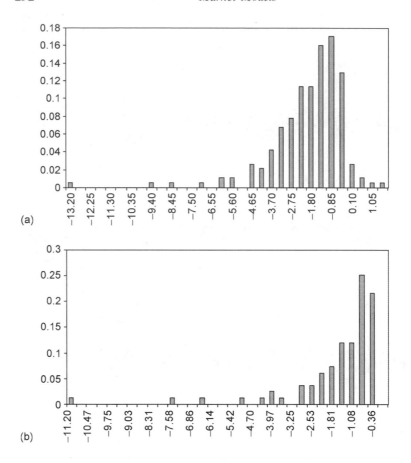

Figure 10.3   Relative frequency of: (a) maximum loss; (b) peaks over threshold.

and identically distributed random variables.[7] Since $\min(X_1, \ldots, X_n) = -\max(-X_1, \ldots, -X_n)$, we can without loss of generality derive results for the maximum in a sample (the results can easily be converted to results for the minimum). Let $M_n = \max(X_1, \ldots, X_n)$. This has the distribution function $F^n(x)$,[8] so the limiting distribution of M_n as $n \to \infty$ is degenerate. For this reason M_n is transformed into standardized extreme values by subtracting its location parameter α_n and dividing by its scale parameter β_n. With this transformation the standardized extreme values

$$Y_n = (M_n - \alpha_n)/\beta_n$$

---

[7] The X_i are independent, otherwise the sample would not be truly random, and they have the same distribution function $F(x)$=Prob(X_i<x), otherwise the sample would not be drawn from the same population.

[8] Because $\text{Prob}(M_n < x) = \text{Prob}(X_1 < x \text{ and } X_2 < x \text{ and } \ldots \text{ and } X_n < x) = \text{Prob}(X_1 < x)\text{Prob}(X_2 < x)\ldots \text{Prob}(X_i < x)$.

will have a non-degenerate distribution. In fact there are only three possible limiting distributions for the standardized extremes Y_n and all three may be expressed in the single formula,

$$F(y) = \text{Prob}(Y_n < y) = \begin{cases} \exp\{-\exp(-y)\} & \text{if } \xi = 0, \\ \exp\{-(1 + \xi y)^{-1/\xi}\} & \text{if } \xi \neq 0, \ (1 + \xi y) > 0; \end{cases} \quad (10.4)$$

hence the term 'generalized' extreme value (GEV) distributions for this type of distribution. GEVs depend on just one parameter ξ, which is called the *tail index*; ξ defines the shape in the tail of the GEV distribution. It is the reciprocal of the shape parameter of the distribution.

The tail index ξ defines the shape in the tail of the distribution

The value $\xi = 0$ corresponds to the *Gumbel distribution*. The corresponding density function has a mode at 0, positive skew and declines exponentially in the tails as n increases. It is the extreme value distribution corresponding to normal or lognormal underlying returns.

When $\xi < 0$ the formula (10.4) defines the *Weibull distribution*, whose density converges to a mass at zero as $\xi \to -\infty$. The lower tail remains finite in the Weibull density, and this is appropriate if the original returns were uniformly distributed.

When $\xi > 0$ we have the *Fréchet distribution*, whose density also converges to a mass at zero as $\xi \to \infty$, but more slowly than the Weibull. The tail in the Fréchet declines by a power as n increases. Since this is the distribution of sample maxima if returns are generated by GARCH processes, Student *t*-distributions or stable Pareto distributions, the Fréchet distribution is commonly used in financial risk management to model the maximum loss of a portfolio over a given holding period.[9]

The Fréchet is the distribution of sample maxima if returns are generated by GARCH processes, Student t-distributions or stable Pareto distributions

Figure 10.4 shows different Weibull and Fréchet density functions, depending on the tail index ξ. Of course, when ξ is small both Weibull and Fréchet densities will be approximately the same as the Gumbel density.

The theory of extreme value distributions has obvious applications to measuring portfolio risk when extreme events occur in financial markets. For example, Embrechts *et al.* (1998, 1999b) advocate the use of GEVs to estimate market VaR during market crashes. It also has applications to insurance and reinsurance (McNeil, 1997). GEV distributions may be fitted to empirical data by maximum likelihood estimation (MLE) as described in §A.6.4. However, although MLE provides consistent estimators, the size of the data set used for the optimization is generally rather small because it will only contain the extreme losses. Therefore Embrechts *et al.* (1997) suggest using the

---

[9] Note that although the Weibull has weight in the lower tail and the Fréchet has weight in the upper tail, that does not imply that the Weibull should be applied to sample minima and the Fréchet should be applied to sample maxima. Each can be applied to either sample maxima or sample minima, simply by changing the sign of the data.

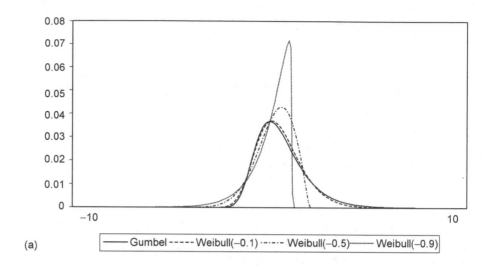

(a)

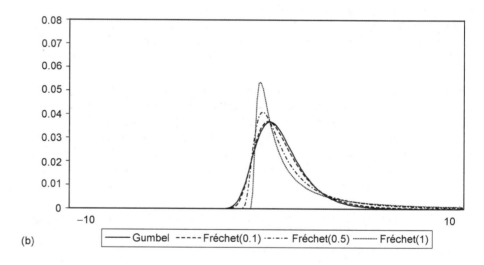

(b)

Figure 10.4 Generalized extreme value densities and the tail index ξ; (a) Weibull and Gumbel; (b) Fréchet and Gumbel.

Hill estimator; Alexander McNeil of ETHZ, Switzerland, has some free extreme value software (EVIS) for S-Plus users at www.math.ethz.ch/~mcneil.

Now let us turn to the case that extreme values are based on the POT model. Here all excess losses (or returns) over a high and predefined threshold u are recorded, as in Figure 10.2b. It is possible to state results only in terms of the excesses over a positive threshold, because results for a negative threshold follow by symmetry. The distribution function G_u of these excess losses, $X - u$, has a simple relation to the distribution $F(x)$ of X, the underlying loss (or returns) series. In fact

$$G_u(y) = \text{Prob}(X - u < y | X > u) = [F(y+u) - F(u)]/[1 - F(u)]. \qquad (10.5)$$

For many choices of underlying distribution $F(x)$ the distribution $G_u(y)$ will belong to the class of generalized Pareto distributions given by:

$$G_u(y) = \begin{cases} 1 - \exp(-y/\beta) & \text{if } \xi = 0, \\ 1 - (1 + \xi y/\beta)^{-1/\xi} & \text{if } \xi \neq 0. \end{cases} \qquad (10.6)$$

The parameters β and ξ will depend on the type of underlying distribution $F(x)$ and on the choice of threshold u. Some generalized Pareto densities for different values of β and ξ are shown in Figure 10.5. As for the GEV distributions, the effect of the tail index ξ is to increase the weight in the tails.

Generalized Pareto distributions also have useful applications to the measurement of portfolio risk. Recall that, when discussing the advantages and limitations of VaR as a risk measure in §9.2.3, it was noted that VaR is not a good risk measure because it is not 'coherent'. However, conditional VaR, which is the average of all losses that exceed VaR, is a coherent risk measure. Now consider the mean excess loss over a threshold u:

$$e(u) = E(X - u | X > u). \qquad (10.7)$$

Depending on the distribution of X, $e(u)$ can take a more or less simple functional form.[10] As mentioned above, the excess over threshold normally has a generalized Pareto distribution, and then the mean excess loss has a simple functional form. In fact under (10.6)

$$e(u) = [\beta + \xi u]/[1 - \xi]. \qquad (10.8)$$

Conditional VaR $= u + e(u)$, where $u = $ VaR, so to calculate the conditional VaR from historical data on portfolio P&L, we can take the losses in excess of the VaR level, estimate the parameters β and ξ of a generalized Pareto distribution, and compute the quantity $e(u)$ with $u = $ VaR in (10.8).

The classical (MLE) approach to fitting the parameters of the GPD model is only applicable when sample sizes are large. However peaks over a threshold are, by definition, exceptional events that occur with very low frequency. Therefore special estimation procedures for the POT model have been developed (Pickands, 1975; Bernardo and Smith, 1994). The combination of a GPD distribution for loss impact and a Poisson process for frequency is called the 'peaks over threshold' (POT) model (Leadbetter *et al.*, 1983; Smith, 1987). Recently it has found useful application in the measurement of operational risks. Alexander (2001c) gives a short review and King (2001) describes a particular model.

Peaks over a threshold are, by definition, exceptional events that occur with very low frequency. Therefore special estimation procedures for the POT model have been developed

---

[10] If X is exponentially distributed with density function $f(x) = \lambda \exp(-\lambda x)$ for $x > 0$, then $e(u)$ is a constant $1/\lambda$. If X has a distribution with fatter (thinner) tails than the exponential the mean excess increases (decreases) as u increases.

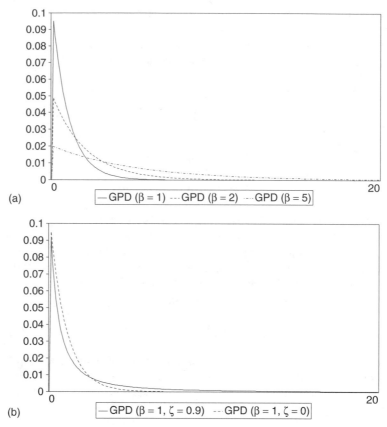

Figure 10.5 Generalized Pareto density: (a) $\xi = 0$; (b) effect of ξ.

10.2.2 Hyperbolic Distributions

Hyperbolic distributions are a class of distributions that have great potential for modelling financial asset returns and have recently attracted considerable attention (Barndorff-Nielsen, 1977; Eberlein and Keller, 1995; Eberlein, 2001). Value-at-risk estimates based on hyperbolic distributions therefore have much in common with VaR estimates based on extreme value distributions. But whereas extreme value theory concentrates only on the tails of the distribution, the hyperbolic density fits the whole range, the centre as well as the extremes.

A hyperbolic distribution is characterized by a log density function in the shape of a hyperbola

A hyperbolic distribution is characterized by a log density function in the shape of a hyperbola. The class of hyperbolic distributions contains the normal distribution, whose log density is a parabola, as a limiting case. Hyperbolic distributions can arise from quite natural assumptions about the behaviour of prices and volatility. For example, a stochastic volatility model might assume that returns are normally distributed with mean 0 and variance σ^2, where σ^2 has a generalized inverse Gaussian distribution. In this case the density function that describes returns is a two-parameter hyperbolic density

$$h(x) = (2\delta B(\alpha\delta))^{-1} \exp(-\alpha(\delta^2 + x^2)^{1/2}). \qquad (10.9)$$

The general hyperbolic density function has four parameters, two that determine its shape and two that determine scale and location.[11]

Applications of hyperbolic distributions are more wide-ranging than those of extreme value distributions. An empirical analysis of DAX stocks in Eberlein and Keller (1995) illustrates how well hyperbolic densities capture the skew and fat-tailed observed distributions of stock returns. If stock returns are assumed to be generated by hyperbolic distributions, then option pricing models should be based on hyperbolic Lévy motion rather than standard Brownian motion.[12] Eberlein *et al.* (1998) use the hyperbolic distribution to explain volatility smiles and the mispricing of options by Black–Scholes type models. They conclude that, compared with prices derived from the hyperbolic model, Black–Scholes prices are much too high for ATM options and too low for OTM and ITM options. This should be compared with the conclusions that we shall draw in §10.3.3, where Black–Scholes and normal mixture options prices are approximately the same for ATM options. In fact, we shall conclude that the Black–Scholes model only misprices OTM and ITM options.

Applications of hyperbolic distributions are more wide-ranging than those of extreme value distributions

10.2.3 Normal Mixture Distributions

Financial markets are characterized by jumps that often precede periods of high volatility. Thus a mixture of two normal densities, one with a low volatility and the other with a high volatility, has an intuitive interpretation in financial markets. A normal mixture distribution can be thought of as a model for the unconditional returns distribution when the probability of the high-volatility normal in the mixture is the probability of a jump in the market.

A normal mixture density is a probability-weighted sum of normal density functions

Another intuitive reason for modelling high-frequency financial returns with normal mixture densities is that different agents may have different expectations of very short-term volatility, although their long-term expectations are more likely to concur. This model is examined in §10.3.2 when it is used to motivate the term structure of kurtosis in very high-frequency data.

Of course an excellent empirical reason for using normal mixtures instead of normal distributions for high-frequency returns is that they are very leptokurtic. Even simple normal mixtures, for example a mixture of just two zero-mean normal densities, will fit this type of financial data much better than a normal distribution would. A normal mixture density is a probability-weighted sum of normal density functions.[13] For example, a mixture of two

---

[11] These parameters may be estimated by maximum likelihood, as described in Eberlein and Keller (1995).

[12] The hyperbolic Lévy process is purely discontinuous. That is, it changes its value only by jumps.

[13] Note the probability weighted sum is of the density functions, not of the normal variates.

normal densities $\phi_1(x) = \phi(x; \mu_1, \sigma_1^2)$ and $\phi_2(x) = \phi(x; \mu_2, \sigma_2^2)$ is the density function[14]

$$g(x) = p\phi_1(x) + (1 - p)\phi_2(x).$$

Note that there is only one random variable so it would be misleading to call the densities ϕ_1 and ϕ_2 'independent'. More generally, a mixture of n normal densities $\phi_1(x), \ldots, \phi_n(x)$ is the density

$$g(x) = p_1\phi_1(x) + \ldots + p_n\phi_n(x), \qquad (10.10)$$

where $p_1 + \ldots + p_n = 1$. The mean of a mixture distribution is just the average of the individual means,

$$E_g(x) = \sum p_i E_i(x), \qquad (10.11)$$

where $E_i(x) = \int x\phi_i(x)dx$.[15] Similarly, the variance of the mixture consists of two parts, the average of the variances and the variance of the means — that is,[16]

$$V_g(x) = \sum p_i V_i(x) + \left\{ \sum p_i E_i(x)^2 - \left[\sum p_i E_i(x) \right]^2 \right\}. \qquad (10.12)$$

With zero means the variance of the mixture is just the probability-weighted sum of the individual variances

The means and variances of the individual normal densities determine the shape and scale of the normal mixture, as illustrated in Figure 10.6. In Figure 10.6a the mixture of two normal densities with zero mean but different variances produces a density with zero skew but a fat tail. The normal distribution $\phi_1(x)$ has standard deviation 3 and the normal distribution $\phi_2(x)$ has standard deviation 2, so using (10.14) below the mixture density has excess kurtosis 3.53. Figure 10.6b shows a mixture of two normal densities with different means as well as variances. The mixture has a bimodal density with positive skew (more weight in the upper tail) and negative excess kurtosis, so it is 'thin-tailed'.

It facilitates the analysis greatly if one assumes that $E_i(x) = 0$ for every i. Non-zero means are only important for low-frequency returns, and low-frequency returns do not display significant departures from non-normality, in general. The use of normal mixture densities is most relevant for high-frequency returns, and therefore it is not very constraining to assume zero means.

In this case the second term on the right hand side of (10.12) is zero and then the variance of the mixture is just the probability-weighted sum of the individual variances. So the normal mixture density $g(x)$ has volatility σ given by:

$$\sigma = \sqrt{\left[\sum p_i \sigma_i^2 \right]}, \qquad (10.13)$$

---

[14] That is $g(x) = p[(2\pi\sigma_1^2)^{-1/2} \exp(-(x - \mu_1)^2/2\sigma_1^2)] + (1 - p) [(2\pi\sigma_2^2)^{-1/2} \exp(-(x - \mu_2)^2/2\sigma_2^2)]$.

[15] $E_g(x) = \int xg(x)dx = \Sigma p_i \int x\phi_i(x)dx$.

[16] $V_g(x) = \int x^2 g(x)dx - (\int xg(x)dx)^2$. The first term is $\Sigma p_i V_i(x) + \Sigma p_i E_i(x)^2$ and the second term is $(\Sigma p_i E_i(x))^2$.

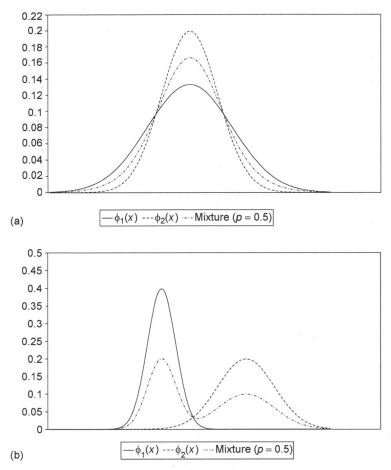

(a)

(b)

Figure 10.6 Mixture of two normal densities: (a) with zero mean; (b) with different means.

where σ_i is the volatility of $\phi_i(x)$.

Mixtures of zero-mean normal densities will have no skewness. However, it can be shown[17] that the excess kurtosis of a zero-mean normal mixture density is

$$\kappa = 3\left[\left(\sum p_i \sigma_i^4 \Big/ \left\{\sum p_i \sigma_i^2\right\}^2\right) - 1\right],\tag{10.14}$$

where p_i is the weight on the zero-mean normal $\phi_i(x)$ with volatility σ_i.

A simple example shows how a normal mixture can have positive excess kurtosis — that is, fatter tails than the normal density with the same volatility. Consider a mixture $g(x)$ of two zero-mean normal densities: $\phi_1(x)$ with

---

[17] This can be derived directly ($\kappa = \Sigma p_i E_i(x^4)/(\Sigma p_i E_i(x^2))^2 - 3$) or using the moment generating function of a mixture of n zero-mean normal densities; this is $\Sigma p_i \exp(\frac{1}{2}t^2\sigma_i^2)$. Expanding this as a power series in t, the rth moment is the coefficient of $t^r/r!$.

probability $p = 0.6$ has volatility $\sigma_1 = 5\%$ and $\phi_2(x)$ with probability $1 - p = 0.4$ has volatility $\sigma_2 = 14.58\%$. By (10.13) the mixture density $g(x)$ has volatility 10%, since $0.6 \times 5^2 + 0.4 \times 14.58^2 = 100$. But the normal mixture has positive excess kurtosis, that is, it has fatter tails than $\phi(x)$, the zero-mean normal density with volatility $\sigma = 10\%$. In fact by (10.14) the excess kurtosis is 2.535, much greater than zero.

Any mixture of normal densities with zero means will have leptokurtosis. That is, the tail probabilities will be larger than the tail probabilities of a normal with the same variance. This follows from (10.14) and the fact that $\Sigma p_i \sigma_i^4 > (\Sigma p_i \sigma_i^2)^2$.

The following illustration of the leptokurtosis of normal mixtures will form the basis of covariance VaR measures for normal mixture density functions in §10.3.1. Let $g(x) = p_1 \phi_1(x) + \ldots + p_n \phi_n(x)$, where $\phi_1(x), \ldots, \phi_n(x)$ are zero-mean normal densities, and let $\phi(x)$ be a normal density with the same volatility as $g(x)$. Suppose this volatility is σ. Then, under $\phi(x)$,

$$\mathrm{Prob}(X < -c) = \mathrm{Prob}(Z < -c/\sigma), \qquad (10.15)$$

and under $g(x)$,

$$\mathrm{Prob}(X < -c) = \int_{-\infty}^{c} g(x)dx = \sum p_i \int_{-\infty}^{c} \phi_i(x)dx$$

$$= \sum p_i \mathrm{Prob}(Z < (-c/\sigma_i)), \qquad (10.16)$$

where Z is a standard normal variate.

Figure 10.7 shows the probabilities calculated by (10.15) compared with those from (10.16) for different values of c between 1 and 26. We have used the same parameters as in the first example, that is $p = 0.6$, $\sigma_1 = 5\%$ and $\sigma_2 = 14.48\%$. Note that when c is large the probabilities under the normal mixture $g(x)$ are greater than the probabilities under the normal density $\phi(x)$. For example, when $c = 20$ the tail probabilities under $g(x)$ and $\phi(x)$ are 0.034 and 0.0228, respectively. But the probabilities nearer the centre of the distribution, for low values of c, are higher under the normal density: for example, with $c = 10$ the probabilities under $g(x)$ and $\phi(x)$ are 0.1122 and 0.1587, respectively.

The parameters of a normal mixture density can be estimated by standard distribution-fitting methods. For example, Hull and White (1998) consider a mixture of two zero-mean normal densities with standard deviation $u\sigma$ and $v\sigma$, where $u > 1$ and $v < 1$ with probability p and $1 - p$, respectively. For the weighted sum of the two variances to be equal to σ^2 the parameters p, u and v are subject to the constraint $pu^2 + (1 - p)v^2 = 1$. They are estimated by equating the theoretical and empirical densities of returns quartile by quartile.

When there are only two zero-mean normal densities in the mixture it is natural to estimate parameters by the *method of moments*. Examples may be generated using the **normal mixture estimation** spreadsheet on the CD. In the method of moments the first few sample moments are equated to the first few non-zero

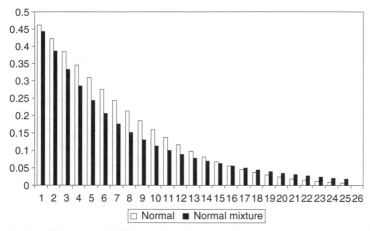

Figure 10.7 Probabilities under normal and under normal mixture distributions with the same variance.

population moments until enough equations are obtained to solve for the distribution parameters. Since there are only three parameters in a mixture of two zero-mean normal densities, only three equations are needed. For example, one might equate the second, fourth and sixth theoretical moments to their sample values based on a fixed return frequency. The second and fourth moments are easy to derive and, with a little algebra, the sixth moment can also be calculated using the moment generating function.

The method of moments may also be applied to estimate parameters of a normal mixture density function that are consistent with the observed term structures of volatility and kurtosis in very high-frequency data (§10.3.2). The three equations required for the method of moments estimation may be obtained from the second and fourth moments based on one frequency and the second or fourth moment based on another frequency (the other moment equation should be used as a check for consistency).

If more than two zero-mean normal densities are used in the mixture more sophisticated methods for estimating parameters may be suitable. Any number of normal densities, with or without zero means, could be used if a neural network is available to fit the model parameters (§14.2). Alexander and Williams (1997) find that it is optimal to use a mixture of three zero-mean normal densities to forecast excess kurtosis in foreign exchange markets. They find that the kurtosis term structure forecasts that are generated by these normal mixtures are closer to the empirical values than GARCH(1, 1) kurtosis forecasts (these are described in Bollerslev, 1986). Their findings show that the kurtosis in a normal GARCH(1, 1) model appears to be less than is empirically observed.

10.3 Applications of Normal-Mixture Distributions

Normality of returns assumptions underpin most pricing and hedging models because they are very convenient; but often these assumptions are not justified,

It is quite simple to change normal models into fat-tailed models when the fat-tailed densities are described by a normal mixture

as we have seen in §10.1. However, it is quite simple to change normal models into fat-tailed models when the fat-tailed densities are described by a normal mixture. This section shows how some basic pricing models and risk measures can be adapted when the underlying distribution is assumed to be generated by a mixture of zero-mean normal densities.

10.3.1   Covariance VaR Measures

Recall from §9.3 that the covariance VaR_α estimate is given by $Z_\alpha \sigma$ where Z_α is the critical value of a standard normal variate and σ is the P&L volatility. In this model the P&L variations are assumed to be normal, and so a simple analytic formula for VaR can be derived. If we now assume that P&L variations have normal mixture distributions there is no analytic formula for VaR. However, it is a simple matter to use a numerical algorithm to obtain a normal mixture covariance VaR estimate. Readers may use the **normal mixture VaR** spreadsheet to do this.

When P&L is distributed as a mixture of n zero-mean normal densities the covariance VaR is based on (10.16), giving the formula

$$\text{Prob}(X < -c) = \sum p_i \text{Prob}(Z < -c/\sigma_i) = \alpha. \qquad (10.17)$$

Putting in a significance level α and the probabilities and volatilities of the normal mixture, we can solve for c using numerical methods. In much the same way as we back out implied volatilities in Chapter 2, we can 'back out' the VaR number that is appropriate if P&Ls have fat-tailed distributions.

In much the same way as we back out implied volatilities in Chapter 2, we can 'back out' the VaR number that is appropriate if P&Ls have fat-tailed distributions

Table 10.2 compares the covariance VaR obtained when P&Ls are assumed to be normal and when they are assumed to be generated by a mixture of two zero-mean normal densities. The P&Ls are assumed to have the same volatility in each case, but in the second case they will be more leptokurtic. First a volatility for the normal mixture density is calculated, depending on the parameters p, σ_1 and σ_2, as the square root of the normal mixture variance (10.13). The normal covariance VaR for this volatility is shown. Beneath this is the normal mixture covariance VaR that is obtained by 'backing out' c from (10.17). In each case, $\alpha = 0.01$.

Since normal mixtures have fatter tails than normal densities of the same volatility, these normal mixture VaR estimates are greater than normal VaR estimates. But how much greater depends on the parameters of the normal mixture. The largest difference in Table 10.2 occurs in the last column, corresponding to the case where 90 per cent of the time the volatility is 10% but 10 per cent of the time the volatility is 100%. The average volatility is therefore 33% and the normal VaR with this volatility is 76.8. However, the distribution is very fat-tailed in this case, so the normal VaR is very misleading and the normal mixture VaR of 128.16 is more representative.

Table 10.2: Normal VaR and normal mixture VaR

p	0.9	0.5	0.1	0.9	0.9
Volatility 1	10	10	10	10	10
Volatility 2	30	30	30	50	100
Mixture volatility	13.42	22.36	28.64	18.44	33.02
Significance	1%	1%	1%	1%	1%
Normal VaR	31.21	52.02	66.62	42.90	76.80
Normal mixture VaR	38.54	61.61	68.60	64.08	128.16

VaR is used in daily risk management to calculate capital reserves, to set trading limits and to assess the riskiness of portfolios under different scenarios (§9.1.3, §9.2.2 and §9.6). It may seem acceptable that the assumption of normality be used for the 'normal market circumstances' VaR estimates that form the basis of market risk capital requirements, because excess kurtosis is usually small over a 10-day horizon. This is attractive, because the market risk requirement will always be lower under the assumption of normality than under the assumption of fat tails. Nevertheless normal mixture VaR estimates can be very useful for internal risk management purposes, particularly in the scenario analysis and stress testing that form the basis of limit setting, or to calculate daily VaR.

10.3.2 Term Structure Forecasts of Excess Kurtosis

As the sampling interval shortens, estimates and forecasts of both kurtosis and volatility tend to increase. We have already seen that leptokurtosis can be very pronounced in intra-day returns and intra-day volatility is well known to exceed volatility measured at daily intervals (§4.2.5, §13.1.3). However, excess kurtosis and increased volatility do not have to go hand in hand. In fact this section will show that there can be excess kurtosis in very short-term forecasts of returns even when volatility term structures are constant.

Term structure forecasts for volatility can be converted into term structure forecasts for kurtosis

The main cause of the term structure of kurtosis is nothing to do with a volatility term structure. It is a consequence of the central limit theorem.[18] If very high-frequency (log) returns over one period are denoted X_t at time t then the sum $S_T = \sum_{t=1}^{T} X_t$ is a T-period return. If 1-period returns are i.i.d., then the kurtosis of T-period returns will always be less than the kurtosis of 1-period returns; in fact the excess kurtosis of S_T is κ/T, where κ is the excess kurtosis of X_t.

If returns are fat-tailed because they are generated by a normal mixture density, term structure forecasts for volatility can be converted into term

---

[18] The central limit theorem implies that the sum of non-normal variables tends towards a normal variable: if X_i have i.i.d. distributions with mean 0, variance σ^2 and excess kurtosis κ then $Y = (X_1 + \ldots + X_n)$ has a distribution with mean 0, variance $n\sigma^2$ and kurtosis $3 + \kappa/n$, so the kurtosis approaches 3 and the excess kurtosis approaches zero as n increases.

structure forecasts for kurtosis. Formula (10.15) has been used to construct the term structure forecast of kurtosis shown in Figure 10.8. It shows a 'market volatility' term structure of a type that is not unusual in financial markets. It is relatively flat: average volatility over the next 200 hours is not much different from the average volatility over the next few hours, indicating that the current period is not particularly volatile. This type of term structure could arise if there are two types of traders in the market. Type 1 traders have expectations of volatility given by the term structure 'vol$_1$' and type 2 traders are trading on the basis of 'vol$_2$'. There is not much difference between their volatility expectations over the next one or two weeks, but over the course of the next day or so there are substantial differences. Type 1 traders expect volatility to be around 17% in the next few hours and to decline over the next week or two to average about 12%. Type 2 traders think that volatility will be around 8% in the next few hours, although the weekly average will be approaching 10%.

This type of term structure could arise if there are two types of traders in the market. Type 1 traders have expectations of volatility given by the term structure 'vol$_1$' and type 2 traders are trading on the basis of 'vol$_2$'

Suppose that traders are using zero-mean normal distributions for the underlying, and 20% of the traders are of type 1 and 80% are of type 2. Then the volatility that is observed in the market can be assumed to be generated by a mixture of two zero-mean normal densities, with a probability of 0.2 on vol$_1$ and a probability of 0.8 on vol$_2$. The 'market volatility' term structure in the figure has been constructed by taking $\sqrt{[0.2(\text{vol}_1)^2 + 0.8(\text{vol}_2)^2]}$ at every point in the term structure, as in (10.13).

The numbers in this example have been chosen in such a way that the combined expectations of volatility in the market are more or less constant. The volatility forecast is a little more than 10% for all time horizons. That is, the average volatility over the next hour, over the next week, or over more than a week is forecast to be 10%. At the same time the term structure of excess kurtosis, computed using (10.14), has been plotted on the right-hand scale. Note that excess kurtosis is around 2, much greater than 0 for the very short-term forecasts, but beyond the horizon of a few hours there is no leptokurtosis to speak of. Thus kurtosis forecasts can be very high over the next hour or so, but kurtosis term structures decrease rapidly to 0.

This subsection has shown how normal mixtures can provide a behavioural model for the rapid decline in kurtosis as the interval of time increases. Different market participants have similar expectations of volatility over longer-term horizons, although their views on volatility over the next few hours may be quite different.[19] The normal mixture model used to illustrate this point in Figure 10.7 had just two types of traders in the market. If there were many different agents, with substantially different views about volatility over the next few hours, the very short-term kurtosis forecasts might be even higher.

---

[19] Note the distinction between this assumption and that made in the next subsection. Each market participant is certain about their own view of volatility, although different participants have different views. In the next subsection we shall consider a different case, where each individual is uncertain about their own view of volatility.

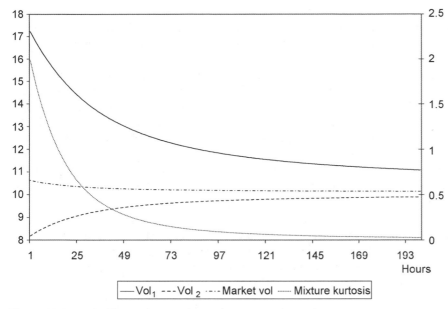

Figure 10.8 Volatility and excess kurtosis term structure forecasts.

10.3.3 Applications of Normal Mixtures to Option Pricing and Hedging

When trying to price and hedge an options book on a daily or intra-day basis, excess kurtosis will be present in the underlying market returns. However, excess kurtosis disappears when returns are measured over more than a few days (§13.1) and so has no effect on the pricing of options with maturity more than a few days. Normal mixture densities that capture the observed daily excess kurtosis may be used to price very short-term options; an example of this is given in this subsection.

Normal mixture densities may also be used to price longer-term options, and the methodology is similar to that used for very short-term options. However, the behavioural rationale is not the same. For very short-term options, where price will be affected by excess kurtosis, the behavioural model is one where different market participants have different views on volatility, but individually they are certain about their own view, as in §10.3.2. For longer-term options the excess kurtosis is negligible and will not, therefore, affect the price. What does, however, affect the price of the option is uncertainty that one individual has in his view of volatility. An option pricer may be very uncertain about volatility over a period of a few months or more; it is very difficult to predict volatility, as we have seen in Chapter 5.[20] Black–Scholes option prices will therefore need to be adjusted to account for uncertainty in volatility; in fact we have already seen that uncertainty in volatility is one of the reasons why the Black–Scholes

---

[20] In fact, experience shows that a 30% relative error in a 1-month volatility forecast is not uncommon; this is the 'shift' figure recommended by Capital Adequacy Directive regulators to take into account volatility risk in scenario-based models (§9.6.1).

formula tends to underprice OTM and ITM options (§5.3.1). The second example in this subsection shows how to modify Black–Scholes option prices using a normal mixture density that models uncertainty in volatility.

The price of an option if returns are generated by a zero-mean normal mixture, is simply the probability-weighted sum of the normal option prices

When excess kurtosis is present over the maturity of an option (so the option has maturity of no more than a few days) it will affect the price. Since the price of a European option is the expected value of a pay-off function over the probability density of the underlying asset price at maturity, if this probability density is expressed as a mixture of several density functions, then the price of the option is the weighted sum of the prices under each of the densities in the mixture. Thus the price of an option if returns are generated by a zero-mean normal mixture, is simply the probability-weighted sum of the normal option prices.[21]

In other words, the normal mixture option price is the expected value of the option over a distribution in volatilities. In mathematical terms, let $f(\sigma_i)$ be the price of an option assuming normal returns with known volatility σ_i. Then the normal mixture option price will be

$$p_1 f(\sigma_1) + \ldots + p_n f(\sigma_n).$$

If we want to calculate the price of an option under the assumption that returns are generated by a normal mixture, how should we choose the parameters of the normal mixture? Normally we would choose parameters so that the variance and the excess kurtosis under the normal mixture are the same as those observed on empirical returns.

To illustrate results throughout this subsection we shall suppose that observations on daily returns indicate an annual variance of 0.04 (corresponding to an annual volatility of 20%), but that this estimate is very uncertain. Also the excess kurtosis of daily returns is 2.53. We choose to model the uncertainty in variance by a mixture of two zero-mean normal densities: with probability $p_1 = 0.6$ the annual variance is $\sigma_1^2 = 0.01$ (annual volatility = 10%); with probability $p_2 = 0.4$ the annual variance is $\sigma_2^2 = 0.085$ (annual volatility = 29.15%). Thus the average variance is $p_1\sigma_1^2 + p_2\sigma_2^2 = 0.04$ and by (10.14) the daily excess kurtosis is 2.53. Thus our normal mixture matches the average variance and the daily kurtosis.

With this normal mixture a standard ATM 1-day European call option will have a value (as a proportion of the underlying asset price) of[22]

$$0.6 \times 0.253 + 0.4 \times 0.737 = 0.444.$$

---

[21] In their paper '*Fitting volatility smiles with analytically tractable asset price models*' Brigo and Mercurio (2001) derive a price process with a lognormal mixture density of the form $dS/S = r/\,dt + \sigma(S,t)dZ$ where the local volatility is given by $\sigma(S,\,t)^2 = \Sigma p_i^* \sigma_{i,t}^2$ and $p_i^* = p_i[\phi_{i,t}(S)/\eta_t(S)]$. The paper is available from www.fabiomercurio.it.

[22] It follows from the Black–Scholes formula that the value of a 1-day ATM option V is approximately $(1/\sqrt{2\pi})\sigma S$, where σ is the daily volatility. So if annual volatility is 10%, $V = 0.4(0.1/\sqrt{250})S = 0.0025298S$, and if annual volatility is 29.15%, $V = 0.4(0.2915/\sqrt{250}) = 0.007374S$.

For ATM options, which are approximately linear in volatility,[23] the normal mixture option price obtained above is the same as the Black–Scholes price that corresponds to the *expected volatility*:

$$0.6 \times 10\% + 0.4 \times 29.15\% = 17.66\%.$$

It is *not* the same as the Black–Scholes price based on a volatility that is equal to the square root of the expected variance.[24] In fact, the expected variance is 0.04, corresponding to the volatility 20% and this volatility gives the Black–Scholes option price as 0.506, which is very far from 0.444.

Therefore, when there is uncertainty over volatility or variance, it is the expected volatility (not the square root of the expected variance) that should be used for the Black–Scholes price, and this should be compared with the normal mixture price that is based on the whole distribution of volatility. If instead we were to use the expected variance for the Black–Scholes price, we would reach the conclusion that ATM options are very overpriced by the Black–Scholes model. Now, even though the Black–Scholes model is based on unrealistic assumptions, we should like to think that it can, at least, price a simple ATM option. Therefore, in Table 10.3, we shall compare normal mixture option prices with Black–Scholes prices that are obtained using the expected volatility and *not* the square root of the expected variance.

The above example was based on a simple ATM option, and there was no difference between the Black–Scholes price and the normal mixture price that is based on the distribution of volatilities. But in general an option price is not linear in volatility. In that case it is very important to use a model price that is based on the distribution of volatilities because this price will not be the same as the Black–Scholes price, whether it is based on the expected volatility *or* the square root of the expected variance.

Standard options are convex in volatility except when they are ATM (see Figure 2.1); some exotic options, on the other hand, may be concave in volatility (e.g. knock-out barrier options). For these options, it is very important to use a model price that is based on the distribution of volatilities (such as the price we can obtain using the normal mixture model). Exotic options will not be priced using Black–Scholes model of course, but the general option value function shown in Figure 10.9 indicates that the same conclusion can be drawn: when the variance is highly uncertain one should always calculate the option price as an expected value over the distribution of

For ATM options the normal mixture option price is the same as the Black–Scholes price that corresponds to the expected volatility. It is not the same as the Black–Scholes price based on a volatility that is equal to the square root of the expected variance

When the variance is highly uncertain one should always calculate the option price as an expected value over the distribution of volatilities, and not as a function of the expected volatility

---

[23] When $S = Ke^{-r\tau}$ then $\ln(S/Ke^{-r\tau}) = 0$ and a call option has price $C = S(\Phi(\sigma\sqrt{\tau}/2) - \Phi(-\sigma\sqrt{\tau}/2))$. Thus $\partial C/\partial \sigma = (S\sqrt{\tau})\phi(\sigma\sqrt{\tau}/2)$, where $\phi(\cdot)$ is the normal density function. For small x, $\phi(x)$ can be approximated by $\phi(0)$, so $\partial C/\partial \sigma \approx (S\sqrt{\tau})\phi(0)$ which is a constant. Figure 2.1b also shows that the price of a near to ATM option is approximately linear in volatility.

[24] The expected volatility is not equal to the square root of the expected variance, as was already noted in Chapter 3.

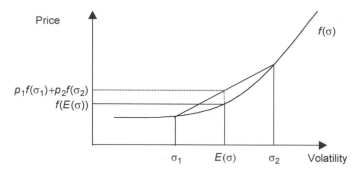

Figure 10.9 Option price under expected volatility compared with option price under distribution of volatilities.

volatilities, and not as a function of the expected volatility (or, for that matter, as a function of the square root of the expected variance).

Figure 10.9 illustrates why the option price using a distribution of volatilities will be different from the price using the expected volatility. When options are convex in volatility the option price under the distribution will be greater than the price under the expected volatility, as shown in the figure. Therefore if (Black–Scholes) option prices are calculated using the expected volatility they will be less than the (normal mixture) option prices that are calculated from the whole distribution of volatilities. Conversely, when options are concave in volatility the (normal mixture) option price under the distribution will be less than the (Black–Scholes) price under the expected volatility.

For longer-term options it is very unlikely that excess daily kurtosis will have any effect on pricing as it tends to disappear quickly. Therefore, our behavioural model of uncertainty in volatility will change. The model described in §10.3.2, with heterogeneous traders that have different short-term volatility forecasts, explains how excess kurtosis results from volatility uncertainty in the market as a whole, even though each individual has no uncertainty. However, there may still be considerable uncertainty in the volatility forecast that is held by one individual and, again, we shall model this uncertainty using a normal mixture distribution.

Suppose that we want to price a 30-day option and suppose the daily returns indicated an average annual variance of 0.04 — that is, a 20% annual volatility — as before. Suppose also that our forecast over 30 days can be approximated by the following normal mixture distribution: with probability $p_1 = 0.5$ the annual variance is $\sigma_1^2 = 0.018$ (annual volatility $= 13.41\%$); with probability $p_2 = 0.5$ the annual variance is $\sigma_2^2 = 0.062$ (annual volatility $= 24.91\%$). Thus the expected variance is again $p_1\sigma_1^2 + p_2\sigma_2^2 = 0.04$ but now the expected volatility is 19.16%. Table 10.3 compares the value of 30-day European call options with an underlying asset price of 100, priced first according to the average volatility of 19.16% and second as an average of

Table 10.3: Black–Scholes option prices with normal mixture distributions

Strike	Call price (BS)	Call price (mixture)	Difference	BS volatility (mixture)
90.00	10.055	10.107	−0.052	21.60
92.00	8.148	8.215	−0.067	20.91
94.00	6.347	6.412	−0.065	20.23
96.00	4.714	4.757	−0.043	19.66
98.00	3.314	3.328	−0.013	19.29
100.00	2.191	2.191	0.000	19.16
102.00	1.355	1.368	−0.013	19.28
104.00	0.781	0.823	−0.042	19.62
106.00	0.419	0.485	−0.066	20.12
108.00	0.209	0.283	−0.074	20.71
110.00	0.097	0.163	−0.066	21.30

options priced at the low and high volatilities of 13.41% and 24.91%. For simplicity we assume zero interest rate and no dividends.

When $K = 100$ the option price is approximately linear in volatility so the two prices are the same.[25] For other strikes the mixture prices are reflecting the uncertainty in the volatility forecast, so the mixture prices are higher than the price under the average forecast. The relationship between Black–Scholes and normal mixture prices for simple calls and puts can be investigated using the **normal mixture option pricing** spreadsheet on the CD.

For other strikes the mixture prices are reflecting the uncertainty in the volatility forecast, so the mixture prices are higher than the price under the average forecast

One of the reasons why the Black–Scholes formula tends to underprice OTM options is that large price movements have a higher probability than is assumed by a normal density and so OTM options have a greater chance of ending ITM than assumed in the Black–Scholes framework. The only way the Black–Scholes model can account for an observed market price that is greater than the model price is to 'jack up' the volatility used in the model price. This is why we observe a smile effect in Black–Scholes volatilities (§2.2.1).

Much of the observed convexity in implied volatilities can be explained by an uncertain volatility that is captured by the normal mixture model

The last column of Table 10.3 shows the Black–Scholes implied volatilities that match the normal mixture option prices. The implied volatilities display a symmetrical smile as observed in many option markets. Note that the implied skew (negative for equities, positive for commodities) has different causes, but much of the observed convexity in implied volatilities can be explained by an uncertain volatility that is captured by the normal mixture model.

We shall end this chapter with a discussion of the implications of non-normal densities for dynamic hedging. When there is excess kurtosis dynamic delta

---

[25] This is the case whatever the parameters of the normal mixture density and not just for the parameters chosen in this example. Equality of these prices is due to the fact that ATM options are linear in volatility, as shown above.

hedging may be a very uncertain activity. This is because the standard error of a delta neutral portfolio will increase with kurtosis (as well as with the volatility of the underlying). The change in MtM value of an option portfolio has a non-linear relationship with the change in the underlying, ΔS, and because of this the change in MtM value of a delta hedged portfolio as the underlying price moves will have a standard error that depends on the kurtosis as well as the volatility of the underlying returns. In fact if P is a delta hedged portfolio then

It is really the excess kurtosis in the return distribution that increases uncertainty in the value of the delta hedged portfolio

$$V(\Delta P) \approx \tfrac{1}{4}\gamma^2(\kappa + 2)\sigma^4 S^4 \Delta t^2, \tag{10.18}$$

where κ is the excess kurtosis and σ is volatility of the price process.[26] Assuming the option gamma (γ) and the volatility are constant over a small price range and time interval, formula (10.18) shows that it is really the excess kurtosis in the return distribution that increases uncertainty in the value of the delta hedged portfolio. Thus estimates of the portfolio value change can become very unreliable when returns are fat-tailed, and therefore it may be necessary to rebalance the portfolio very frequently indeed.

An optimal delta rebalancing strategy is normally designed to achieve a trade-off between the increased transaction costs that are incurred by frequent rebalancing, and the costs that may (or may not) result from uncertainty in the portfolio value. If there is much uncertainty in the value of the hedged portfolio, as there will be when returns have a large excess kurtosis, the natural tendency will be to increase the rebalancing frequency. However, this may not work, because kurtosis usually tends to increase when rebalancing intervals become shorter.

Perfect hedging may be impossible because excess kurtosis would lead to an infinite transaction volume

For example, suppose the portfolio is delta hedged twice a day and that the excess kurtosis of 12-hour returns is approximately 2. By (10.18) the standard error of the hedged portfolio will be proportional to $\gamma\sigma^2$, and if either the gamma or the volatility is large this standard error could be a problem. It may present too much uncertainty in the value of the hedge, so one would prefer more frequent rebalancing, say four times a day. But then the standard error will become even larger because the excess kurtosis will increase.[27] Therefore there will be even more uncertainty about the value of the hedge. This argument leads to the conclusion that perfect hedging may be impossible because excess kurtosis would lead to an infinite transaction volume.

The hedge uncertainty may not be reduced indefinitely by an active rebalancing strategy

It is also possible that the hedge uncertainty may not be reduced indefinitely by an active rebalancing strategy; it may have a positive minimum value. To see this, recall (footnote 18) that if returns are uncorrelated, the excess kurtosis

---

[26] To see this, use a delta-gamma approximation $\Delta P \approx \theta \Delta t + \delta \Delta S + \tfrac{1}{2}\gamma(\Delta S)^2$, where $\delta \approx 0$ for delta hedging over short time intervals. Then $V(\Delta P) = E((\Delta P)^2) - (E(\Delta P))^2 \approx \tfrac{1}{4}\gamma^2\{E(\Delta S)^4 - (E(\Delta S)^2)^2\}$. Using $\Delta S \approx S\sigma\sqrt{\Delta t}$ gives $V(\Delta P) \approx \tfrac{1}{4}\gamma^2(\kappa + 2)\sigma^4 S^4 \Delta t^2$.

[27] If the kurtosis of 6-hour returns is around 4, the standard error of the hedged portfolio will be proportional to $\sqrt{(3/2)}\gamma\sigma^2$, which is bigger than it was before (and the problem is compounded by the fact that the volatility will also increase).

observed over one time interval should revert to zero when observed over many time intervals. Conversely, if one reduces the rebalancing interval of a hedging strategy, the excess kurtosis will increase: for example, the total hedge uncertainty over a period $(0, t)$ with rebalancing every Δt would be proportional to $\gamma^2 t(2\Delta t + \kappa)$.[28] Hull and White (1997) have suggested a possible solution to this problem. Instead of trying to cope with kurtosis by increasing the frequency of the delta hedge they suggest hedging with a new Greek which captures the sensitivity of option prices to kurtosis in the underlying.

---

[28] From (10.18) and footnote 17, $V(\Delta P) \approx \gamma^2(t/\Delta t)((\kappa/\Delta t) + 2)\Delta t^2 = \gamma^2 t(\kappa + 2\Delta t)$.

Part III
Statistical Models for Financial Markets

Part III takes an econometric approach to modelling relationships between financial asset prices. Chapter 11 introduces time series models, where relationships are modelled without the confines of economic or financial theories. These models aim to find the most appropriate statistical model for the data and use this model for prediction. In this chapter autoregressive moving average (ARMA) models, unit root tests and Granger causality are introduced as essential background for the following chapter, on cointegration.

Cointegration refers not to co-movements in returns, but to co-movements in asset prices: if spreads are mean-reverting, asset prices are tied together in the long term by a common stochastic trend, and we say that the prices are 'cointegrated'. Since the seminal work of Engle and Granger (1987), cointegration has become the prevalent tool for applied economic analysis. Cointegration also arises naturally in many financial systems: within term structures, between spot and futures prices, and between international equity and bond market indices. The application of cointegration to modelling these relationships is explored in Chapter 12, and following this a new long–short equity hedge fund model based on cointegration is described in some detail.

The final chapter is about high-frequency data: time series properties and non-linear prediction models based on neural networks and nearest neighbour algorithms. This chapter has been quite selective in its coverage, to present the concepts from an advanced academic literature that are most relevant to practitioners.

11

Time Series Models

Some financial models such as the capital asset pricing model and the arbitrage pricing model described in Chapter 8 are well established for use with time series data. However, there is much to be said for analysing data without imposing constraints that are implied by a theory. The aim of time series analysis is to find the most appropriate statistical model for the data and to use this model for prediction. In this way the variables are allowed to speak for themselves, without the confines of economic or financial theories.

This chapter is about the statistical models that are used for the analysis of financial time series. In any type of data analysis it is always necessary to assume some sort of model. We have already encountered several time series models in Chapters 3 and 4. Statistical volatility and correlation models only assume that the data were generated by a process with given statistical properties; they assume nothing about the behaviour of financial markets.

The chapter begins by describing the statistical properties of univariate time series, and particular attention is drawn to the fundamentally different models that apply to stationary and non-stationary processes. In most financial markets returns are stationary and prices are non-stationary. Unit root tests that distinguish between stationary and non-stationary data are described in §11.1.4, and §11.1 concludes by explaining why it is not usually appropriate to transform prices by taking deviations from a trend line.

Variables are allowed to speak for themselves, without the confines of economic or financial theories

Section 11.2 describes autoregressive moving average (ARMA) models for stationary univariate time series and derives their autocorrelation properties. If returns are autocorrelated then it will be possible to forecast market prices at least to some extent, although the degree of forecastability may not be sufficient to make trading profits. Section 11.3 shows how to identify the right ARMA model for the data, estimate it and then use it for forecasting. The Box–Pierce test for autocorrelation is described in §11.3.2, and in §11.3.3 the 'testing down' methodology that is normally used to specify the final form of the ARMA model is described.

Section 11.4 extends the analysis to multivariate systems of time series and introduces the concept of joint stationarity that is a necessary property for statistical models of correlation. It concludes with a discussion of 'Granger causality', which is causality in the sense that one series leads or lags another (Granger, 1969). Evidence of Granger causality provides many insights into the dynamics of returns in different markets and may be used as a basis for predictive time series models.

11.1 Basic Properties of Time Series

A time series $\{y_t\}$ is a discrete time continuous state process where the variable y is identified by the value that it takes at time t, denoted y_t. For example, a *time trend*, $y_t = t$, is a very simple deterministic time series. A basic stochastic time series is *white noise*, $y_t = \varepsilon_t$, where ε_t is an independent and identically distributed (i.i.d) variable with mean 0 and variance σ^2 for all t, written $\varepsilon_t \sim$ i.i.d.$(0, \sigma^2)$. A special case is *Gaussian white noise*, where the ε_t are independent and normally distributed variables with mean 0 and variance σ^2 for all t, written $\varepsilon_t \sim \text{NID}(0, \sigma^2)$. Usually time is taken at equally spaced intervals[1] from $-\infty$ to $+\infty$ and the finite sample size T of data on y is for $t = 1, 2, 3, \ldots, T$.

The modelling procedures for return data and for price data are different. To understand why, one needs to draw the basic distinction between stationary and non-stationary time series

In financial markets the modelling procedures for return data and for price data are different. To understand why, one needs to draw the basic distinction between stationary and non-stationary time series. Daily return data on most financial markets are generated by stationary processes and consequently returns are mean-reverting in the sense defined in §11.1.2. In fact they are often rapidly mean-reverting since there is very little autocorrelation in many financial market returns. The statistical concepts and methods that apply to return data do not apply to price data. For example, volatility and correlation are concepts that only apply to stationary processes. It makes no sense to try to estimate volatility or correlation on price data. Daily (log) price data are commonly assumed to be generated by a non-stationary stochastic process. Random walks are non-stationary processes that are very often applied to log prices, or to prices themselves.

11.1.1 Time Series Operators

It will facilitate the analysis to introduce some operators that are specific to time series and to provide an understanding of the way that standard operators such as addition and multiplication are applied to time series. The first difference operator is defined by

$$\Delta y_t = y_t - y_{t-1}.$$

Note that powers of the first difference operator, such as

$$\Delta^2 y_t = \Delta y_t - \Delta y_{t-1} = y_t - 2y_{t-1} + y_{t-2},$$

---

[1]Time deformation mappings are possible, see §13.1.4.

should be distinguished from higher-order difference operators such as

$$\Delta_2 y_t = y_t - y_{t-2}.$$

Higher-order differences are useful for time series with seasonal components. For example, to eliminate seasonal effects in monthly data one can use the 12th difference operator given by

$$\Delta_{12} y_t = y_t - y_{t-12}.$$

The lag operator is defined as

$$Ly_t = y_{t-1}.$$

By defining $L^2 y_t = L(Ly_t) = Ly_{t-1} = y_{t-2}$ and more generally powers of L as $L^k y_t = y_{t-k}$, polynomials, rational functions and power series in the lag operator can be constructed. For example,

$$y_t + a_1 y_{t-1} + a_2 y_{t-2} = (1 + a_1 L + a_2 L^2) y_t.$$

The ordinary operators of algebra also apply to time series, element by element. For our purposes the values of a time series will be real numbers, so they obey the usual rules of algebra relating to the operations of scalar multiplication and addition:

$$\{y_t\} + \beta\{x_t\} = \{y_t + \beta x_t\}.$$

Volatility and correlation are concepts that only apply to stationary processes. It makes no sense to try to estimate volatility or correlation on price data

11.1.2 Stationary Processes and Mean-Reversion

Time series may have both stochastic and deterministic components; for example, a series with a deterministic trend and a stochastic white noise component is

$$y_t = \alpha + \beta t + \varepsilon_t, \tag{11.1}$$

where $\varepsilon_t \sim$ i.i.d.$(0, \sigma^2)$. Most time series models of financial markets will have a stochastic component, and so the unconditional expectation and variance of the tth observation on the time series can be calculated (§1.2). For example, in the model (11.1)

$$E(y_t) = \alpha + \beta t \quad \text{and} \quad V(y_t) = \sigma^2 \text{ for all } t.$$

Also the sth-order autocovariance of $\{y_t\}$, that is, the unconditional covariance of y_t with y_{t-s}, is

$$\operatorname{cov}(y_t, y_{t-s}) = E[(y_t - E(y_t))(y_{t-s} - E(y_{t-s}))].$$

So, for example, the time series (11.1) has $\operatorname{cov}(y_t, y_{t-s}) = E[\varepsilon_t \varepsilon_{t-s}] = 0$ for all t and $s \neq 0$.

A time series $\{y_t\}$ is *covariance-stationary* if the expectation, variance and autocovariance are the same at every date t, that is,

➤ $E(y_t)$ is a finite constant;
➤ $V(y_t)$ is a finite constant;
➤ $\mathrm{cov}(y_t, y_{t-s})$ depends only on the lag s.

This is a weak form of stationarity that is usually what is meant when a time series is said to be simply 'stationary'. A stronger form of stationarity, where not just the autocovariances but the whole joint distribution is independent of the date at which it is measured and depends only on the lag, is referred to as *strict stationarity*.

When prices appear to be trending, this is normally due to a stochastic rather than a deterministic trend

The time series (11.1) is not stationary. Even though $V(y_t)$ is a finite constant and $\mathrm{cov}(y_t, y_{t-s})$ depends only on the lag s (in fact it is zero for all t and $s \neq 0$), the unconditional mean of y_t is not independent of time. Any series with a trend in the mean will not be stationary and this is why financial asset prices, or their logarithms, tend not to be stationary. But the trends in financial markets do not normally follow the model (11.1). When prices appear to be trending, this is normally due to a stochastic rather than a deterministic trend. The basic distinction between these two models of trends is discussed in §11.1.4.

Figure 11.1 illustrates the very different behaviour of asset prices and asset returns. Whereas prices or log prices in most markets are represented by non-stationary time series models, a stationary process is used for the first difference in prices — or, more usually, the first difference in log prices since these are approximately the returns.[2] Note that although returns often exhibit autoregressive conditional heteroscedasticity, this does not normally preclude them from being stationary (§4.1).

A simple example of a stationary time series is the process generated by an *autoregressive model of order 1*, the AR(1) model. Autoregressive models for time series are discussed in detail in §11.2.1; here we use the simplest of these models to illustrate the stationarity concept. Consider a simple version of the AR(1) model that does not have a constant term,

$$y_t = \alpha y_{t-1} + \varepsilon_t, \tag{11.2}$$

where $\varepsilon_t \sim \mathrm{i.i.d.}(0, \sigma^2)$. The general AR(1) model is stable only if $|\alpha| < 1$, and in this case it defines a stationary process.[3] To verify that this is true, suppose $E(y_t) = k_1$ and $V(y_t) = k_2$ for all t, where k_1 and k_2 are finite constants. Then taking expectations and variances of (11.2) gives

$$k_1 = \alpha k_1 \quad \text{and} \quad k_2 = \alpha^2 k_2 + \sigma^2,$$

so if $|\alpha| < 1$ then, for all t,

---

[2] When x is small $\ln(1 + x) \approx x$. The return $r_t = (P_t - P_{t-1})/P_{t-1} = (P_t/P_{t-1}) - 1$, so $1 + r_t = (P_t/P_{t-1})$ and taking logs gives the return as the first difference of the log prices.

[3] This is shown in §11.2, using the moving average representation of an autoregressive model.

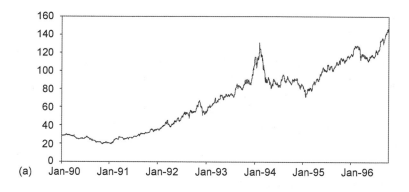

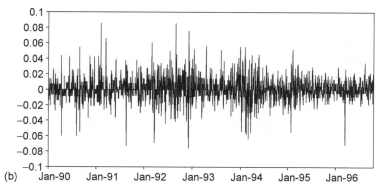

Figure 11.1 HSBC: (a) price in Hong Kong dollars; (b) daily return.

$$E(y_t) = 0 \quad \text{and} \quad V(y_t) = \sigma^2/(1 - \alpha^2). \quad (11.3)$$

Since $E(y_t) = 0$, the autocovariance at lag s is $E(y_t y_{t-s})$. Now

$$E(y_t y_{t-1}) = E((\alpha y_{t-1} + \varepsilon_t) y_{t-1}) = \alpha E(y_{t-1}^2) + E(\varepsilon_t y_{t-1})$$
$$= \alpha V(y_{t-1}) = \alpha \sigma^2/(1 - \alpha^2)$$

A stationary process can never drift too far from its mean because of the finite variance

and

$$E(y_t y_{t-2}) = E((\alpha y_{t-1} + \varepsilon_t) y_{t-2}) = \alpha E(y_{t-1} y_{t-2}) = \alpha^2 \sigma^2/(1 - \alpha^2),$$

and in general

$$E(y_t y_{t-s}) = \alpha^s \sigma^2/(1 - \alpha^2), \quad (11.4)$$

which depends only on the lag, s. So (11.2) defines a stationary time series if $|\alpha| < 1$.

The mean-reversion property of stationary series is well known. A stationary process can never drift too far from its mean because of the finite variance. The speed of mean-reversion is determined by the autocovariance: mean-reversion is quick when autocovariances are small and slow when autocovariances are large.

The speed of mean-reversion in the AR(1) model (11.2) depends on the size of α, as shown in Figure 11.2. If $\alpha = 0$ then $\{y_t\}$ is just white noise and mean-reversion is instantaneous because $\text{cov}(y_t, y_{t-s}) = 0$. As α increases in absolute value the speed of mean-reversion decreases. In the limit when $\alpha = 1$, then $\{y_t\}$ is a random walk (without drift), which is non-stationary, and there is no mean-reversion.

11.1.3 Integrated Processes and Random Walks

The efficient market hypothesis implies that the best forecast of the price on any future date is simply the price today

There is an enormous literature in financial economics concerning the validity of various forms of the 'efficient market hypothesis' (see Cuthbertson, 1996, for a review). The efficient market hypothesis implies that in liquid markets, where asset prices will be the result of unconstrained demand and supply equilibria, the current price should accurately reflect all the information that is available to the players in the market. Future changes in prices can only be the result of 'news', which by definition is unpredictable, so the best forecast of the price on any future date is simply the price today. Put another way, the price today is just yesterday's price plus a random term.

The efficient market hypothesis is related to basic option pricing models. The fundamental assumption of these models is that the underlying asset price S follows a geometric Brownian motion process,

$$dS/S = r\,dt + \sigma\,dZ, \tag{11.5}$$

where r and σ are constants representing the drift in asset prices and the volatility of returns respectively, and Z is a Wiener process. That is, increments dZ are independent and normally distributed with mean zero and variance dt.

To see how (11.5) relates to the efficient market hypothesis, apply Itô's lemma to (11.5). This gives the corresponding continuous time process that will be followed by log prices:

$$d\ln S = (r - \sigma^2/2)dt + \sigma\,dZ. \tag{11.6}$$

The discrete time version of (11.6) is $\ln P_t - \ln P_{t-1} = c + \varepsilon_t$ or

$$\ln P_t = c + \ln P_{t-1} + \varepsilon_t, \tag{11.7}$$

where $c = r - \sigma^2/2$ and the error term $\varepsilon_t \sim \text{NID}(0, \sigma^2)$, is the returns process.

The model (11.7) is the *random walk* model that is commonly applied to model log prices in efficient financial markets. In (11.7) ε_t is normally and independently distributed with mean zero and constant variance σ^2. However, market efficiency only implies that the distribution of the return conditional on

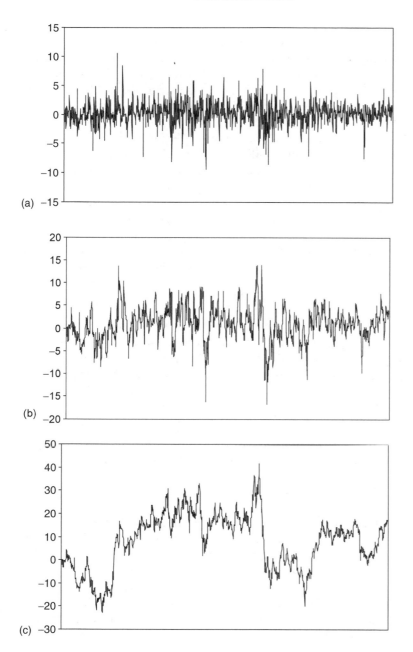

Figure 11.2 Realizations from AR(1) model: (a) $\alpha = 0.5$; (b) $\alpha = 0.9$; (c) $\alpha = 0.99$.

all information up to time t is independent and identically distributed. That is, $\varepsilon_t \mid I_t \sim$ i.i.d.$(0, \sigma^2)$, where I_t denotes the *information set* at time t. So the efficient markets hypothesis implies the model (11.7) but with a less restrictive assumption on the increments.

Market efficiency only implies that the distribution of the return conditional on all information up to time t is independent and identically distributed

The random walk model allows for trends in asset prices by including a constant term c in (11.7) that corresponds to the expected return. Thus if $c > 0$ log prices are trending upwards and if $c < 0$ they are trending downwards. Even when $c = 0$ we say that (11.7) has a *stochastic trend*. Upon visual inspection there will be no obvious drift in the data, but the term 'stochastic trend' still applies because the data are generated by an 'integrated' process.

Upon visual inspection there will be no obvious drift in the data, but the term 'stochastic trend' still applies because the data are generated by an 'integrated' process

A time series *is integrated of order n*, written $y_t \sim I(n)$, if the stochastic part is non-stationary but it becomes stationary after differencing a minimum of n times. Thus a process that is already stationary is denoted $I(0)$. Note that the deterministic trend model (11.9) is not stationary, but neither is it integrated; it is a *trend-stationary process* that is also referred to as '$I(0)$ + trend'.

A random walk is an example of an integrated process of order 1. In financial markets the general class of $I(1)$ processes is characterized by the model

$$\ln P_t = c + \ln P_{t-1} + \varepsilon_t, \tag{11.8}$$

where $\varepsilon_t \sim I(0)$. The distinction between (11.8) and (11.7) is that in the random walk model the error process is not just stationary, it is white noise. In less than fully efficient markets it is possible that log asset prices are not pure random walks because returns are autocorrelated, but they may still be $I(1)$ processes.

11.1.4   Detrending Financial Time Series Data

It is important to understand that the trend in (11.8) is *not* a deterministic trend. The $I(1)$ process (11.7) is fundamentally different from the model

$$\ln P_t = c + \beta t + \varepsilon_t, \tag{11.9}$$

which has a stationary component and a deterministic trend component. Neither (11.8) nor (11.9) is a stationary series, and the data generated by the two models may seem very similar indeed to the eye. But the transform required to make data generated by (11.8) into a stationary series is a first difference transform and for this reason the integrated process model (11.8) is also commonly referred to as a *difference-stationary process*. On the other hand, the stationarity transform for data generated by (11.9) is to take deviations from a fitted trend line, so (11.9) is called a *trend-stationary process*.

It is not unknown for technical analysis to fit a trend line to price or log price data and to take deviations from that trend as a series that can be predicted

It is not unknown for technical analysis to fit a trend line to price or log price data and to take deviations from that trend as a series that can be predicted. But fitting a trend and taking deviations will not make the series predictable if the market is efficient. All it does is to remove the drift in the random walk. The deviations from trend are still a random walk, just without the drift, but they still have a stochastic trend. They will have no mean-reversion and therefore cannot be predicted well using univariate models.

To see that taking deviations from trend of a difference-stationary process does not make it stationary, suppose the data are generated by (11.8). Repeated substitution for $\ln P_{t-1}$, $\ln P_{t-2}$, . . . gives an alternative form of (11.8):

$$\ln P_t = c_0 + ct + \sum_{i=0}^{t-1} \varepsilon_{t-i},$$

where $c_0 = \ln P_0$. The term $\sum_{i=0}^{t-1} \varepsilon_{t-i}$ is clearly non-stationary because it has a variance that increases with t.

Thus if a trend line is fitted to random walk data, or to more general data that are generated by an integrated process, the deviations from the trend will not be stationary. The appropriate way to obtain a stationary series from random walk (or integrated) data is to take first differences.

If the data were generated by a trend-stationary process (11.9) then the correct stationarity transform *is* to fit a trend and take deviations. In fact, if first differences were taken instead, the resulting series would have severe negative autocorrelation. This is easy to see, since if the true process were (11.9) then

$$\ln P_t - \ln P_{t-1} = (c + \beta t + \varepsilon_t) - (c + \beta(t-1) + \varepsilon_{t-1}) = \beta + \varepsilon_t - \varepsilon_{t-1},$$

so first differences follow an MA(1) model with first-order autocorrelation coefficient -0.5 (§11.2.1).

Figure 11.3 compares the two methods of detrending data, taking deviations from a time trend and first differencing. The year 1995 for the HSBC stock price shown in Figure 11.1a was chosen as a year with a significant trend — indeed, fitting a time trend by ordinary least squares to the price data shown in Figure 11.3a gives the model:

$$\text{HSBC} = \underset{(-58)}{-3978} + \underset{(59.6)}{0.1169t}.$$

Then Figure 11.3b compares the deviations from this fitted trend and the first differences of the price data. It is clear, just by looking at the data, that the deviations from trend are not stationary but that the first differences are, and we shall apply a simple test to confirm this in §11.1.5.

One cannot apply the usual diagnostics such as correlation or volatility analysis, information ratios and the like to deviation from trend data. They would mean nothing, because the data are not stationary. In the model above the t-statistics on the coefficients (shown in brackets) are enormous and the R^2 from the regression is 0.93. But whenever the dependent variable in a regression is non-stationary the standard diagnostics do not apply. When data have trends, deterministic or stochastic, the 'R^2' will always be close to 1 and the t-statistics are usually very biased.

When the dependent variable in a regression is non-stationary the standard diagnostics do not apply

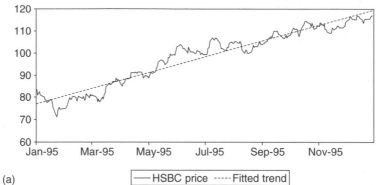

(a)

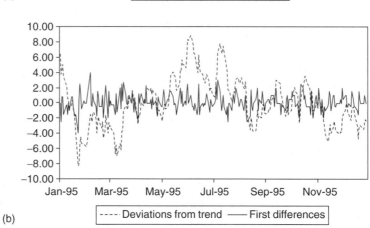

(b)

Figure 11.3   (a) HSBC price and fitted trend; (b) two types of 'detrending'.

In summary, it is very important to apply the right sort of stationarity transform to the data, if they are not already stationary. Most financial markets generate price, rate or yield data that are non-stationary because of a stochastic rather than a deterministic trend. It is hardly ever appropriate to detrend the data by fitting a trend line and taking deviations. Instead the data should be detrended by taking first differences, usually of the log prices or rates, because then the transformed stationary data will correspond to market returns.

11.1.5   Unit Root Tests

Statistical tests of the null hypothesis that a time series is non-stationary against the alternative that it is stationary are called 'unit root' tests. The name derives from the fact that an ARMA process is non-stationary if the characteristic polynomial has a root that does not lie inside the unit circle (§11.2.1).

For example, an AR(1) model (11.2) is non-stationary if $\alpha = 1$. The characteristic polynomial of the AR(1) process is $1 - \alpha x$ so it has root $1/\alpha$

which will lie on, not inside, the unit circle when $\alpha = 1$. When $\alpha = 1$ the AR(1) becomes the random walk model,

$$y_t = c + y_{t-1} + \varepsilon_t,$$

where $\varepsilon_t \sim$ i.i.d.$(0, \sigma^2)$. To test that $\alpha = 1$ it is not sufficient to estimate α and then use a simple *t*-test (§A.2.2) since these are severely biased in the case of a unit root. However, using the first difference operator, an AR(1) model can be rewritten as

$$\Delta y_t = c + (\alpha - 1)y_{t-1} + \varepsilon_t. \tag{11.10}$$

This representation of the AR(1) model gives a clue as to how the null hypothesis $\alpha = 1$ may be approached: one simply performs a regression of Δy_t on a constant and y_{t-1} and then tests whether the coefficient of y_{t-1} is significantly different from zero. Note that the test should be one-sided (§A.2.1) because the alternative hypothesis that the process is stationary is $\alpha < 1$, that is, that the lag coefficient in (11.10) is less than zero.

This type of test is called a *Dickey–Fuller* (DF) *test*. Dickey and Fuller (1979) showed that standard *t*-ratios based on (11.10) are biased and that the appropriate critical values have to be increased by an amount that depends on the sample size. For example, for a sample size of 250 the 5% critical value of the DF distribution is -2.88 and the 1% critical value is -3.46.

Let us apply this DF test for a unit root to the data shown in Figure 11.3b, to confirm that the deviations from trend are non-stationary and the first differences are stationary. First, let y_t be the first differences shown by the solid line. Take first differences of y_t and regress it on a constant and a lag, y_{t-1}. The result is the model

$$\Delta y_t = 0.122 - 0.942 y_{t-1}.$$
$${\scriptstyle(1.71)} \quad {\scriptstyle(-\mathbf{15.12})}$$

The DF statistic is the '*t*-ratio' on the lag coefficient, picked out in bold, and it far exceeds the 1% critical value of -3.46. So the null hypothesis that the data are non-stationary can be rejected in favour of the alternative hypothesis that they are stationary. However, when one applies the same test to the deviations from trend data (the dotted line) the DF regression is

$$\Delta y_t = -0.03 - 0.066 y_{t-1},$$
$${\scriptstyle(-0.47)} \quad {\scriptstyle(-\mathbf{2.11})}$$

and the DF statistic is too small to reject the null hypothesis. However this DF test is rather simple: more appropriate tests for trends are given in §11.1.6.

The standard DF test is now applied to test whether log prices are non-stationary; the DF regression is just an OLS regression of returns on the lag of log prices. For example, applying DF tests to some equity indices using daily log index prices from 16 October 1997 to 11 September 1998 gives the results in

To test whether log prices are non-stationary, the DF regression is just an OLS regression of returns on the lag of log prices

Table 11.1: Dickey–Fuller tests on equity indices

	$I(1)$ vs $I(0)$	$I(2)$ vs $I(1)$
FTSE 100	-1.61	-13.69
Nikkei 225	-2.32	-16.17
S&P 500	-1.86	-17.49
CAC	-1.27	-15.68

the first column of Table 11.1. None of the time series appear to be stationary even at 10% (the 10% critical value of DF is -2.57).

The null hypothesis that equity index prices are non-stationary cannot be rejected. This does not necessarily mean that they are generated by $I(1)$ processes: they may be non-stationary because they are generated by $I(2)$ processes, or by integrated processes of an even higher order. So the next step is to repeat the procedure but this time using Δy_t instead of y_t, that is, to test H_0: $\Delta y_t \sim I(1)$ against H_1: $\Delta y_t \sim I(0)$, or equivalently

$$H_0: y_t \sim I(2) \quad \text{against} \quad H_1: y_t \sim I(1).$$

Estimating DF regressions of the form $\Delta^2 y_t = c + \beta \Delta y_{t-1} + \varepsilon_t$ for y_t being the log equity index prices, gives the DF statistics shown in the second column of the table. The null hypothesis is obviously rejected at the highest significance level and we can conclude that these equity index log prices have followed an $I(1)$ process during the period. Readers can perform similar tests using the **ADF** workbook and the **PcGive** program provided on the CD.

In efficient markets the logarithm of prices follows a random walk, but not all markets are efficient

In efficient markets the logarithm of prices follows a random walk, but not all markets are efficient. In some energy markets prices are dominated by supply constraints (storage, transport, cartel restrictions, etc.) and by demand fluctuations (weather conditions and so on). Consider the daily data for NYMEX prompt futures prices of natural gas, from 1 January 1998 to 3 March 1999, shown in Figure 11.4.[4] Natural gas storage facilities play a crucial role in balancing supply and demand. In summer months excess production is injected into storage, and in the winter months the storage gas is withdrawn to supply the extra demand. In the winter, when demand typically exceeds production, one would expect to see spot prices rise sharply during periods of extreme cold. Futures prices may also rise because depleting storage may raise future price expectations. However, the winters of 1997/98 and 1998/99 were very mild in North America and storage was filled to capacity during the autumn months of 1997 and 1998, so futures prices responded little to daily demand fluctuations.

---

[4]The futures contract represents the price for delivery of equal volumes over the entire calendar month represented by the futures contract. Many thanks to Enron for providing these data.

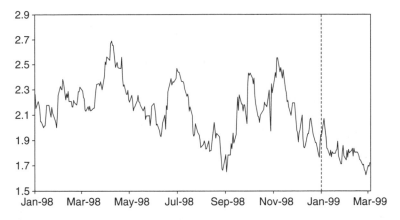

Figure 11.4 NYMEX prompt futures prices for natural gas.

ADF tests simply add lagged dependent variables to the DF regression. The number of lags included should be just sufficient to remove any autocorrelation in the errors

If the DF test is applied to the gas daily log futures prices the DF regression is

$$\Delta y_t = 0.047 - 0.063 y_{t-1},$$
$$\underset{(2.81)}{} \quad \underset{(-2.87)}{}$$

where $y_t = \ln F_t$ and F_t is the futures price as time t. The DF statistic of -2.87 allows one to accept the hypothesis that y_t is stationary at the 5% level. But this is rare. The natural gas market is an energy market that lacks efficiency, mainly because of storage and transportation constraints. Most financial markets are much more efficient, and it is unusual to find price data that are stationary.

It is fortunate that Dickey is the first named author because subsequent refinements of the test are now referred to as augmented Dickey–Fuller (ADF) tests, rather than the other way around. ADF tests simply add lagged dependent variables to the DF regression. The number of lags included should be just sufficient to remove any autocorrelation in the errors, so that OLS will give an unbiased estimate of the coefficient of y_{t-1} (§A.1.3). Slightly different critical values apply in the ADF(m) test,[5] but otherwise the general principle of testing the significance of the coefficient on y_{t-1} is similar to the DF test: Δy_t is regressed on a constant, y_{t-1} and m lags of Δy_t. The hypotheses

$$H_0: y_t \sim I(1) \quad \text{against} \quad H_1: y_t \sim I(0)$$

are equivalent to

$$H_0: \beta = 0 \quad \text{against} \quad H_0: \beta < 0$$

in the model

$$\Delta y_t = c + \beta y_t + \alpha_1 \Delta y_{t-1} + \ldots + \alpha_m \Delta y_{t-m} + \varepsilon_t. \qquad (11.11)$$

---

[5]Critical values of the ADF statistic for different values of m and different sample sizes are given in MacKinnon (1991).

The ADF test statistic is

$$\text{ADF}(m) = b/(\text{est. s.e. } b),$$

where b is the OLS estimate of β in the ADF regression (11.11).

11.1.6 Testing for the Trend in Financial Markets

If a time trend is included in the ADF regression, the test is for

$$H_0: y_t \sim I(1) \quad \text{against} \quad H_1: y_t \sim I(0) + \text{trend}.$$

This test will distinguish between a stochastic and a deterministic trend. Different critical values apply. For example, with 250 observations the ordinary DF statistic has 5% critical value of -3.43 and the 1% critical value is -3.99. But DF tests for the presence of a deterministic trend are not as powerful as other tests, such as the Durbin–Hausmann or Schmidt–Phillips tests described below.

There are a large number of unit root tests for stochastic against deterministic trends other than the basic ADF test just described, and most of them are more powerful in many circumstances

There are a large number of unit root tests for stochastic against deterministic trends other than the basic ADF test just described, and most of them are more powerful in many circumstances. The tests proposed by Durbin and Hausmann (see Choi, 1992) are uniformly more powerful than DF tests in the presence of a deterministic trend. The maintained model of the *Durbin–Hausmann test* is the same as that for DF tests of $H_0: y_t \sim I(1)$ against $H_1: y_t \sim I(0) + \text{trend}$. That is,

$$\Delta y_t = c + \alpha t + \beta y_{t-1} + \varepsilon_t.$$

The Durbin–Hausmann test statistic for $H_0: \beta = 0$ versus $H_1: \beta < 0$ is

$$\text{DH} = \frac{(b_{\text{iv}} - b)^2}{\text{est. } V(b)},$$

where b denotes the OLS estimate of β and b_{iv} denotes the instrumental variables estimate of β using y_t to instrument y_{t-1}. Another test, proposed by Schmidt and Phillips (1992), has a polynomial in the time trend in the maintained model, but since there is limited interest in presence of deterministic trends in financial data, the details are not described here.

Dickey–Fuller tests assume the errors in an ADF regression are i.i.d.$(0, \sigma^2)$, but less restrictive assumptions on the errors are possible. For example, the *Phillips–Perron test* allows errors to be dependent with heteroscedastic variance (Phillips and Perron, 1988). The theory of Phillips–Perron tests is quite complex and will not be covered here. But they are more useful than DF tests when the data have GARCH effects and they are available as an in-built procedure in standard econometrics packages. An empirical example of the application of Phillips–Perron tests is given in Corbae and Ouliaris (1986) to determine whether exchange rates follow a random walk.

The analytical results of Cochrane (1991) imply that tests for the distinction between deterministic and stochastic trends in the data can have arbitrarily low power. However, it is interesting to note that when the true data generation process contains a deterministic trend, the Durbin–Hausmann tests can detect this much more easily than DF tests. This is evident from Monte Carlo studies and in empirical tests on data from the physical sciences that have a deterministic trend (Alexander and Rendell, 1995).

There is a large literature on empirical studies of the data generation processes that govern price (and log price) data from financial markets. The overwhelming conclusion from the research on whether non-stationary behaviour is governed by trend-stationary or difference-stationary processes is that financial market data have stochastic rather than deterministic trends. That is, the model (11.7) is more appropriate than (11.9) to apply to either prices or log prices of financial assets.

The overwhelming conclusion is that financial market data have stochastic rather than deterministic trends

11.2 Univariate Time Series Models

This section describes the basic building blocks for modelling stationary univariate time series. A univariate time series model can only be explained by its own lagged values, that is with autoregressive (AR) terms as explanatory variables in its representation. If the process is stochastic and stationary the errors can be linear combinations of white noise at different lags, so the moving average (MA) part of the model refers to the structure of the error term. General stationary time series have both autoregressive and moving average parts to their representation, but before discussing these autoregressive moving average (ARMA) models, more detailed descriptions of AR models and MA models are presented separately.

11.2.1 AR Models

Autoregressive models of time series are representations of a time series by functions of its own lags. For example, the autoregressive model of order 1, the AR(1) model, is

$$y_t = c + \alpha y_{t-1} + \varepsilon_t, \tag{11.12}$$

where $\varepsilon_t \sim$ i.i.d.$(0, \sigma^2)$. The constant term c models a trend in the series either upwards $(c > 0)$ or downwards $(c < 0)$. The lag coefficient α determines the stability of the process. If $|\alpha| > 1$ the time series will explode, that is $y_t \to \pm\infty$ as $t \to \infty$. The special case $|\alpha| = 1$ gives the random walk model of §11.1.3, and it is only when $|\alpha| < 1$ that the process defined by (11.12) will be stationary. Using the lag operator (§11.1.1), an equivalent representation of (11.12) is

$$(1 - \alpha L)y_t = c + \varepsilon_t.$$

Suppose $|\alpha| < 1$. Since

$$(1 - \alpha L)^{-1} = 1 + \alpha L + \alpha^2 L^2 + \alpha^3 L^3 + \ldots,$$

another form of the AR(1) model is

$$y_t = (1 - \alpha L)^{-1}(c + \varepsilon_t) = (1 - \alpha L)^{-1}c + (1 - \alpha L)^{-1}\varepsilon_t$$

or, since $(1 - \alpha L)^{-1}\varepsilon_t = \varepsilon_t + \alpha\varepsilon_{t-1} + \alpha^2\varepsilon_{t-2} + \alpha^3\varepsilon_{t-3} + \ldots,$

$$y_t = c/(1 - \alpha) + \varepsilon_t + \alpha\varepsilon_{t-1} + \alpha^2\varepsilon_{t-2} + \alpha^3\varepsilon_{t-3} + \ldots. \tag{11.13}$$

Taking expectations and variances of (11.13) gives

$$E(y_t) = c/(1 - \alpha) \quad \text{and} \quad V(y_t) = \sigma^2/(1 - \alpha^2). \tag{11.14}$$

The autocovariances of the AR(1) model are independent of the constant term:[6]

$$E(y_t y_{t-s}) = \alpha^s \sigma^2/(1 - \alpha^2). \tag{11.15}$$

To see this, use (11.13) to write

$$\begin{aligned}
\text{cov}(y_t, y_{t-s}) = E[&(\varepsilon_t + \alpha\varepsilon_{t-1} + \alpha^2\varepsilon_{t-2} + \alpha^3\varepsilon_{t-3} + \ldots) \\
&\times (\varepsilon_{t-s} + \alpha\varepsilon_{t-s-1} + \alpha^2\varepsilon_{t-s-2} + \alpha^3\varepsilon_{t-s-3} + \ldots)]
\end{aligned}$$

and then use the fact that $E(\varepsilon_t \varepsilon_{t-s}) = 0$ unless $s = 0$ and $E(\varepsilon_t^2) = \sigma^2$.

Higher-order autoregressive models have more complex properties. For example, the AR(2) model,

$$y_t = c + \alpha_1 y_{t-1} + \alpha_2 y_{t-2} + \varepsilon_t, \tag{11.16}$$

may be written using the lag operator as

$$(1 - \alpha_1 L - \alpha_2 L^2)y_t = c + \varepsilon_t.$$

This model is only stable if the characteristic polynomial of the AR(2) model,

$$1 - \alpha_1 x - \alpha_2 x^2,$$

has roots that lie outside the unit circle in the complex plane. This is the generalization of the stationarity condition $|\alpha| < 1$ for series represented by an AR(1) model. So, for example, if a time series has the AR(2) representation

$$y_t = c + 2y_{t-1} - y_{t-2} + \varepsilon_t,$$

then it is non-stationary because the roots of $1 - 2x + x^2$ are $(1 \pm i\sqrt{3})/2$ and these have modulus 1, so they lie on the unit circle.

---

[6] So they are the same as for the AR(1) model with no constant term, already given in (11.4).

It is straightforward to calculate the mean and variance of a stationary AR(2) process, but the covariance calculations are more lengthy.[7] For the AR(p) model,

$$y_t = c + \alpha_1 y_{t-1} + \alpha_2 y_{t-2} + \ldots + \alpha_p y_{t-p} + \varepsilon_t. \qquad (11.17)$$

It follows immediately that $E(y_t) = c/(1 - \alpha_1 - \alpha_2 - \ldots - \alpha_p)$ and

$$V(y_t) = \gamma_0 = \alpha_1 \gamma_1 + \alpha_2 \gamma_2 + \ldots + \alpha_p \gamma_p + \sigma^2, \qquad (11.18)$$

where $\gamma_s = \mathrm{cov}(y_t, y_{t-s})$. For $s > 0$ the autocovariances follow the same pth-order difference equation as the process itself, that is,

$$\mathrm{cov}(y_t, y_{t-s}) = \gamma_s = \alpha_1 \gamma_{s-1} + \alpha_2 \gamma_{s-2} + \ldots + \alpha_p \gamma_{s-p}. \qquad (11.19)$$

Equations (11.18) and (11.19) can be solved to give the variance and auto-covariances of a stationary AR(p) process in terms of the model parameters α_1, $\alpha_2, \ldots, \alpha_p$ and σ^2.

The representation (11.13) shows that an AR(1) model is equivalent to an infinite moving average of white noise. The inversion of an AR(1) into an MA(∞) holds for any value of α. It is for stationarity that the condition $|\alpha| < 1$ must apply. Similar remarks apply to the general AR(p) model: it is invertible into a infinite moving average representation for any values of the coefficients, but constraints on the coefficients are necessary for stationarity.

An AR(1) model is equivalent to an infinite moving average of white noise

Note that for the AR(1) model the stationarity condition $|\alpha| < 1$ could have been expressed (less succinctly) in a similar form to the stationarity condition for an AR(2). That is, 'the root of $1 - \alpha x$ must lie outside the unit circle'. In general, the stationarity condition for the AR(p) model is that the roots of $1 - \alpha_1 x - \alpha_2 x^2 - \ldots \alpha_p x^p$ must lie outside the unit circle. Series that have AR(p) representations containing one or more roots of $1 - \alpha_1 x - \alpha_2 x^2 - \ldots \alpha_p x^p$ with modulus 1 are non-stationary.[8]

11.2.2 MA Models

Moving average models have already been encountered in Chapter 3, where they were applied to squared returns and to cross products of returns, with equal or exponentially declining weights. In this way they are used to estimate the unconditional variance or covariance of a time series of returns. In time series analysis a basic building block for models of stationary series is again a moving average, but this time of a white noise process. The first-order moving average model, MA(1), is

---

[7]The interested reader is referred to Hamilton (1994), where it is shown that autocovariances follow the same second-order difference equation as the model itself.

[8]The term 'unit root' refers to this stationarity condition.

$$y_t = c + \varepsilon_t + \beta\varepsilon_{t-1}, \qquad \qquad (11.20)$$

where $\varepsilon_t \sim$ i.i.d.$(0, \sigma^2)$. This model is a stationary representation for any values of c or β, since $E(y_t) = c$,

$$V(y_t) = (1 + \beta^2)\sigma^2 \qquad \qquad (11.21)$$

and

$$\mathrm{cov}(y_t, y_{t-s}) = \beta\sigma^2, \text{ if } s = 1 \text{ and } 0 \text{ otherwise.} \qquad (11.22)$$

Higher-order moving average models have quite simple properties and, unlike $AR(p)$, they always have a stationary representation. In the moving average model of order q, $MA(q)$, given by

$$y_t = c + \varepsilon_t + \beta_1\varepsilon_{t-1} + \ldots + \beta_q\varepsilon_{t-q},$$

a straightforward calculation gives $E(y_t) = c$,

$$V(y_t) = (1 + \beta_1^2 + \beta_2^2 + \ldots \beta_q^2)\sigma^2$$

and

$$\mathrm{cov}(y_t, y_{t-s}) = (\beta_s + \beta_1\beta_{s+1} + \beta_2\beta_{s+2} + \ldots + \beta_{q-s}\beta_q)\sigma^2,$$

$$\text{if } s \leqslant q \text{ and } 0 \text{ otherwise.}$$

We have shown that AR models are only stable under certain 'unit root' conditions but that they are always invertible to be represented by an infinite moving average. The opposite applies with MA models: they are always stable but are only invertible to an AR representation under certain conditions on the roots of a polynomial being outside the unit circle.

The invertibility conditions for an MA process are similar to the stationarity conditions for an AR process The invertibility conditions for an MA process are similar to the stationarity conditions for an AR process. For example, it is possible to write the $MA(1)$ model using the lag operator as $y_t = c + (1 + \beta L)\varepsilon_t$, or equivalently $(1 + \beta L)^{-1}(y_t - c) = \varepsilon_t$. So the $MA(1)$ is invertible into an equivalent representation as a stable $AR(\infty)$ model,

$$y_t = c/(1 + \beta) + \beta y_{t-1} - \beta^2 y_{t-2} + \beta^3 y_{t-3} - \ldots + \varepsilon_t,$$

only if $|\beta| < 1$. For the general $MA(q)$ process to be invertible to an infinite-order AR model the roots of the polynomial $1 - \beta_1 x - \beta_2 x^2 - \ldots \beta_q x^q$ must lie outside the unit circle.

11.2.3   ARMA Models

The most general model for a stationary process is an autoregressive moving average model with p autoregressive terms and q moving average terms. This is the ARMA(p, q) model given by

$$y_t = c + \alpha_1 y_{t-1} + \alpha_2 y_{t-2} + \ldots + \alpha_p y_{t-p} + \varepsilon_t + \beta_1 \varepsilon_{t-1} + \ldots + \beta_q \varepsilon_{t-q},$$

$$(11.23)$$

where $\varepsilon_t \sim$ i.i.d.$(0, \sigma^2)$. This is always invertible into an MA(∞) but is only a stationary representation if the roots of $1 - \alpha_1 x - \alpha_2 x^2 - \ldots - \alpha_p x^p$ lie outside the unit circle. It is invertible into an AR(∞) model if the roots of $1 - \beta_1 x - \beta_2 x^2 - \ldots - \beta_q x^q$ lie outside the unit circle.[9]

11.3 Model Identification

The first objective of stationary time series analysis is to identify the appropriate lags p and q for representing the data by an ARMA model. One obvious method is to compare the empirical correlogram of the data with the known autocorrelation functions for MA models and low-order AR models that are described in §11.3.1. If sample sizes are large, as they often are in financial market data modelling, the errors in the correlogram will be small. A standard test for the significance of pth-order autocorrelation in a sample size T is described in §11.3.2.

Although a simple visual inspection of the correlogram may sometimes lead to the conclusion that the series exhibits autocorrelation patterns that may be modelled by a simple AR or MA model, it is not always easy to identify the appropriate model from the correlogram. For example, the AR(2) auto-correlation function looks like a damped sine wave, but so does that of an ARMA(1,1) model, and even higher-order AR processes have autocorrelation functions that are quite difficult to identify. The last part of this section explains how to identify a time series model by testing down its specification from a high-order ARMA process.

11.3.1 Correlograms

The sth-order *autocorrelation coefficient* for a stationary time series $\{y_t\}$ is

$$\rho_s = \text{cov}(y_t, y_{t-s})/V(y_t). \qquad (11.24)$$

When attempting to identify the appropriate model for a stationary series it is convenient to represent the autocorrelations at different lags $s = 0, 1, 2, \ldots$ in a chart, which is called the correlogram. This is an estimate of the autocorrelation function based on empirical data. Obviously $\rho_0 = 1$ for any stationary series, and for a simple white noise process the autocorrelation function is 1 at lag zero and zero elsewhere.

For a simple white noise process the autocorrelation function is 1 at lag zero and zero elsewhere

---

[9]Note that if these two polynomials have a common root the ARMA model will be overparameterized and this will cause problems for model identification (Harvey, 1993).

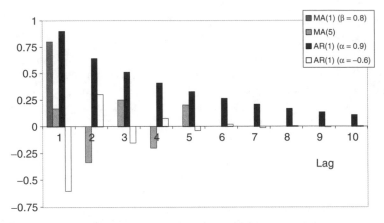

Figure 11.5 Autocorrelations in MA(q) and AR(1) models.

Figure 11.5 shows the correlograms of some simple AR and MA models. The autocorrelation functions of MA processes have a very simple shape, being non-zero only at lags less than or equal to the order of the MA representation. To see this for the MA(1) model, using (11.21) and (11.22) it is clear that the autocorrelations of an MA(1) model take the form

$$\rho_s = \beta/(1+\beta^2) \text{ for } s = 1 \text{ and } 0 \text{ otherwise,} \tag{11.25}$$

so they cut off after lag 1. An MA(2) process has autocorrelation function

$$\rho_1 = \frac{\beta_1(1+\beta_2)}{(1+\beta_1^2+\beta_2^2)},$$

$$\rho_2 = \frac{\beta_2}{1+\beta_1^2+\beta_2^2}$$

and

$$\rho_2 = 0 \text{ for } s > 2.$$

More generally, the autocorrelation functions for an MA(q) process are zero for all lags greater than q.

The autocorrelations of an AR(1) model decline geometrically as the lag increases and the signs will be oscillating if there is negative autocorrelation

It follows from (11.14) and (11.15) that the sth-order autocorrelation coefficient in the AR(1) process is α^s. So the autocorrelations of an AR(1) model decline geometrically as the lag increases and the signs will be oscillating if there is negative autocorrelation ($\alpha < 0$). The autocorrelation function of an AR(p) process with $p > 1$ is more complex. Dividing (11.19) by (11.18) gives the *Yule–Walker equations* for the AR(p) autocorrelations:

$$\rho_s = \alpha_1\rho_{s-1} + \alpha_2\rho_{s-2} + \ldots + \alpha_p\rho_{s-p} \quad \text{for } s = 1, 2, 3, \ldots .. \tag{11.26}$$

The solution of these is in terms of the sth powers of the eigenvalues of the characteristic equation $x^p - \alpha_1 x^{p-1} - \alpha_2 x^{p-2} - \ldots - \alpha_p = 0$ (Hamilton, 1994).

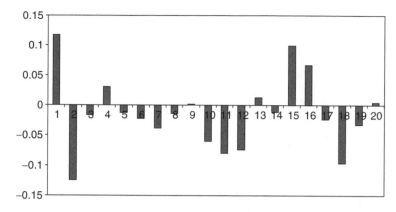

Figure 11.6 Correlogram of WTI crude oil futures returns.

Figure 11.6 shows the empirical correlogram of a typical return process, the WTI crude oil near futures returns that were analysed in §6.2.3. The largest autocorrelations occur at lag 1 and lag 2, and there are signs of negative second-order correlation. But it is not clear that they are significantly different from zero because the values here are little more than 0.1. Indeed, some of the autocorrelations at higher-order lags are almost as great as they are at lags 1 and 2. If an AR(2) model were appropriate, the estimated model would be:[10]

$$y_t = \underset{(8.47)}{0.1334} y_{t-1} - \underset{(-3.58)}{0.1373} y_{t-2} + \varepsilon_t.$$

However, it is unlikely that this model will have much predictive ability, even though the next section shows that the second-order autocorrelation is statistically significant. The forecastability of crude oil prices using ARMA models will be returned to later in this and the following chapter.

At the opposite extreme, the correlogram of the gas daily futures prices, which were found to be (weakly) stationary in §11.1.5, is shown in Figure 11.7. This has the characteristic shape of an AR(1) correlogram, and in §11.3.3 it will be shown that the AR(1) specification is more appropriate than others that are considered.

11.3.2   Autocorrelation Tests

Even in the highly efficient FX markets there is autocorrelation in returns, but not normally at the daily frequency. Like skewness and kurtosis, autocorrelation tends to increase with sampling frequency, and there is much evidence that FX markets exhibit autocorrelated returns at the intra-day frequencies (§13.1.3).

Like skewness and kurtosis, autocorrelation tends to increase with sampling frequency

---

[10]The constant term was insignificant and therefore omitted.

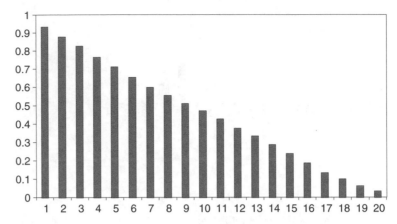

Figure 11.7 Correlogram of log futures prices for natural gas.

Table 11.2: Box–Pierce tests for autocorrelation in daily returns to WTI crude oil futures

Lag p	1	2	3	4	5	6	7	8	9	10
Q	**9.4**	**19.4**	**19.6**	**20.2**	**20.3**	**20.6**	**21.6**	**21.7**	**21.7**	**24.1**
$\chi^2_{p,0.01}$	6.63	9.21	11.3	13.3	15.1	16.8	18.5	20.1	21.7	23.2

There are a number of tests for the significance of autocorrelation, one of the most common being the *Box–Pierce test*. This test for autocorrelation up to order p is based on the statistic

$$Q = T \sum_{n=1}^{p} \varphi(n)^2, \tag{11.27}$$

where T is the sample size and $\varphi(n)$ is the nth-order sample autocorrelation

$$\varphi(n) = \frac{\sum_{t=n+1}^{T} y_t y_{t-n}}{\sum_{t=1}^{T} y_t^2}.$$

The Box–Pierce statistic is a form of Lagrange multiplier test so it is asymptotically distributed as chi-squared with p degrees of freedom (§A.2.5).

Applying Box–Pierce tests to the daily returns to the WTI crude oil near futures data shows that autocorrelations are highly significant even though they are small. The values of Q for each lag along with the 1% chi-squared

Table 11.3: Box–Pierce tests for autocorrelation in US equity returns

Stock	$Q(1)$	$Q(2)$
America Int'l Group	**8.92**	**11.8**
America Online	1.59	2.14
American Express	0.24	5.36
AT&T	0.83	0.92
Bank of America	0.09	0.49
BankOne Corp.	1.5	1.55
Boeing Corp.	0.47	4.12
Citigroup	0.61	1.86
Cisco Systems	0.59	1.14
Coca Cola Co.	2.12	7.3
Walt Disney	0.35	3.73
Exxon Mobil	4.00	**9.97**
Ford Motor Co.	**14.1**	**16.8**
General Electric Co.	0.01	5.33
Hewlitt Packard	3.91	5.25
Merrill Lynch	1.41	3.57
Microsoft Co.	1.74	2.3
Procter and Gamble	0.11	1.74
Rockwell Int.	2.06	2.06
Unicom Corp.	0.49	0.86

critical value are shown in Table 11.2. As expected from the correlogram in Figure 11.6, the autocorrelations at lags 1 and 2 are significant at 1%, but beyond that there is little increase in the value of the Q-statistic, indicating that the series is dominated by first- and second-order autocorrelation.

Since the second-order autocorrelation is very highly significant the series could have an AR(2) representation, a suggestion that is reinforced by the shape of the correlogram, although the oscillating behaviour of the correlogram could also be in line with an ARMA(1,1) representation.

Equity returns can exhibit significant autocorrelation even at a daily frequency, although this is the exception rather than the rule. Table 11.3 shows the Box–Pierce Q-statistics for lags 1 and 2 for the twenty US stocks that were discussed in Chapters 4 and 6. Only American International, Ford and perhaps Exxon show signs of autocorrelation. Readers may wish to replicate these results using the **PcGive** package on the CD.

11.3.3 Testing Down

A standard approach to ARMA model identification is to estimate the model (11.23) with a variety of lags of both autoregressive and moving average terms and then to use standard hypothesis tests on the coefficients. At the first stage several autoregressive and/or moving average terms are included as possible explanatory variables, and the model is estimated.[11] Then lags are dropped according to the significance of their coefficients. For example, estimating an AR(3) model on the log futures prices of natural gas that were shown in Figure 11.4 (and which we already know to be weakly stationary, from §11.1.5) gives:

$$y_t = \underset{(2.50)}{0.0438} + \underset{(14.34)}{0.8922 y_{t-1}} + \underset{(0.30)}{0.0250 y_{t-2}} + \underset{(0.40)}{0.0249 y_{t-3}} + \varepsilon_t.$$

The figures in parentheses are t-ratios and they indicate that while a first-order autoregressive term is significant, there is no reason to include higher-order autoregressive terms. Estimating an ARMA(1, 1) model for the same data gives:

$$y_t = \underset{(2.47)}{0.0423} + \underset{(42.43)}{0.9439 y_{t-1}} + \varepsilon_t + \underset{(0.784)}{0.0581 \varepsilon_{t-1}}.$$

As there is no good reason to include the moving average term in the model the AR(1) model is possibly the best representation of these data, and this is:

$$y_t = \underset{(2.81)}{0.0473} + \underset{(42.92)}{0.9375 y_{t-1}} + \varepsilon_t.$$

11.3.4 Forecasting with ARMA Models

Forecasting with an AR(p) model could not be easier. One simply generates the one-step-ahead forecast and then uses this for a two-step-ahead forecast and so on

Once a suitable ARMA representation of the data has been specified, the purpose of univariate time series is to use this model for predictive purposes. Forecasting with an AR(p) model could not be easier. One simply generates the one-step-ahead forecast and then uses this for a two-step-ahead forecast and so on. That is, the optimal one-step-ahead prediction at time T is the conditional expectation of y_{T+1} given $\{y_T, y_{T-1}, y_{T-2}, \dots \}$:

$$\hat{y}_{T+1} - \hat{c} = \hat{a}_1(y_T - \hat{c}) + \hat{a}_2(y_{T-1} - \hat{c}) + \dots + \hat{a}_p(y_{T-p+1} - \hat{c}),$$

and the two-step-ahead prediction is:

$$\hat{y}_{T+2} - \hat{c} = \hat{a}_1(\hat{y}_{T+1} - \hat{c}) + \hat{a}_2(y_T - \hat{c}) + \dots + \hat{a}_p(y_{T-p+2} - \hat{c}),$$

and so on.

An MA(q) model is useful for predictions only up to q steps ahead. Since ε_{T+1}, ε_{T+2}, ... are unknown they are set to zero and the s-step-ahead prediction for $s \leqslant q$ is

$$\hat{y}_{T+s} = \hat{c} + \hat{\beta}_s \varepsilon_T + \hat{\beta}_{s+1} \varepsilon_{T-1} + \dots + \hat{\beta}_q \varepsilon_{T-q+s}.$$

For an ARMA(p, q) model the s-step-ahead predictions are

---

[11]Although pure AR models may be consistently estimated by OLS, the MA part of ARMA models requires the maximum likelihood estimation method (Appendix 6). The likelihood functions for different ARMA models are given in Hamilton (1994), but most statistical packages offer ARMA model estimation by maximum likelihood as a standard routine.

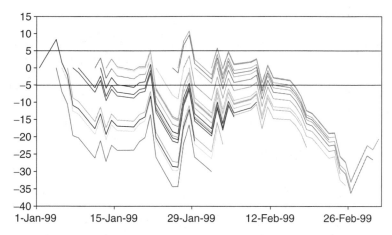

Figure 11.8 Percentage forecast error for rolling AR(1) models of log futures prices of natural gas.

$$\hat{y}_{T+s} - \hat{c} = \hat{\alpha}_1(\hat{y}_{T+s-1} - \hat{c}) + \hat{\alpha}_2(\hat{y}_{T+s-2} - \hat{c}) + \ldots + \hat{\alpha}_p(y_{T+s-p} - \hat{c})$$
$$+ \hat{\beta}_s \varepsilon_T + \hat{\beta}_{s+1} \varepsilon_{T-1} + \ldots + \hat{\beta}_q \varepsilon_{T-q-s},$$

for $s \leq q$. For $s > q$ only the AR part determines the forecasts.

Forecasting a stationary time series using ARMA models is quite straight-forward in practice.[12] To illustrate the method, the AR(1) model of natural gas futures prices has been used to provide s-step-ahead forecasts for $s = 1$, 2, . . ., 20 for the gas future price on every day from 1 January 1999 to 3 March 1999. This is the out-of-sample period indicated by the dotted line across Figure 11.4. The data from 1 January 1998 to 31 December 1999 are used to estimate the AR(1) model and then a daily forecast series is made up to 20 days ahead. The data are rolled one day at a time, and each time the AR(1) model is re-estimated and used to forecast up to 20 days ahead. In this way 24 different out-of-sample forecast series are calculated. Figure 11.8 shows the forecast errors from these 24 different forecasts over time. It shows that short-term forecasts are noticeably more accurate than long-term forecasts; in fact the forecasts generally stay within the 5% error bounds for one week ahead or even more.

The univariate approach to time series modelling can give some interesting results, but it is still only part of the story. A forecasting model for natural gas futures prices has been used to illustrate some concepts but the analysis here takes no account of any relation that these futures prices may have with the prices of other futures, or with the gas daily spot prices. Forecasting model that capture the important relationships between spot and futures prices will be explored in more detail in Chapter 12.

---

[12] ARMA model forecasting is an in-built procedure in most statistical time series packages.

11.4 Multivariate Time Series

A multivariate time series $\{\mathbf{y}_t\}$ is a vector $\{(y_{1,t}, y_{2,t}, \ldots, y_{n,t})'\}$ of n different time series processes that are measured concurrently. In addition to synchronicity of data on $y_1, \ldots, y_n$, it is normal to use time series processes that have the same basic characteristics. That is, the different processes in $\{\mathbf{y}_t\}$ should all be stationary, or have the same order of integration. The case that $\{\mathbf{y}_t\}$ contains integrated variables is discussed in Chapter 12. This section describes the basic models of stationary multivariate time series that are useful for modelling dynamic co-dependencies between the n different time series.

11.4.1 Vector Autoregressions

The general ARMA models for stationary series were introduced in §11.2. There it was shown that a moving average process of any order is invertible into an infinite AR model, so any stationary univariate time series may be modelled by an autoregressive model provided it contains sufficient lags to capture all of the dynamics.

The same is true for a multivariate time series. The generic model is a vector autoregression (VAR), which simply extends the AR model to a multivariate time series. For example, a *vector autoregression of order 1* on a bivariate system is

$$y_{1,t} = \alpha_{10} + \alpha_{11} y_{1,t-1} + \alpha_{12} y_{2,t-1} + \varepsilon_{1,t},$$
$$y_{2,t} = \alpha_{20} + \alpha_{21} y_{1,t-1} + \alpha_{22} y_{2,t-1} + \varepsilon_{2,t};$$

or, in matrix notation

$$\mathbf{y}_t = \boldsymbol{\alpha}_0 + \mathbf{A}\mathbf{y}_{t-1} + \boldsymbol{\varepsilon}_t, \tag{11.28}$$

where $\mathbf{y}_t = (y_{1,t}, y_{2,t})'$, $\boldsymbol{\alpha}_0 = (\alpha_{10}, \alpha_{20})'$, $\boldsymbol{\varepsilon}_t = (\varepsilon_{1,t}, \varepsilon_{2,t})'$ and

$$\mathbf{A} = \begin{pmatrix} \alpha_{11} & \alpha_{12} \\ \alpha_{21} & \alpha_{22} \end{pmatrix}.$$

More generally, a VAR(1) for an n-variate system is (11.28) where $\mathbf{y}_t$, $\boldsymbol{\alpha}_0$ and $\boldsymbol{\varepsilon}_t$ are $n \times 1$ vectors and $\mathbf{A}$ is an $n \times n$ matrix of coefficients. The general VAR(p) model is

$$\mathbf{y}_t = \boldsymbol{\alpha}_0 + \mathbf{A}_1 \mathbf{y}_{t-1} + \ldots + \mathbf{A}_p \mathbf{y}_{t-p} + \boldsymbol{\varepsilon}_t. \tag{11.29}$$

Estimating the parameters in a VAR model is straightforward, assuming the errors are i.i.d. processes. Each of the n equations in (11.29) may be estimated separately by OLS to give consistent and asymptotically efficient estimators (§A.1.3).

The specification procedure for a VAR model is quite simple: first determine the variables to use in the system $\{\mathbf{y}_t\}$ and then 'test down' the AR lag specification in each equation until a reasonable fit is obtained (§11.3.3). Once specified, the model may be used to gain insights into the dynamic relationships

Table 11.4: VAR(2) model for crude oil spot and futures returns

Explanatory variable	Dependent variable r_s	Dependent Variable r_f
Constant	−0.89E–03	−0.68E–03
	(−0.98)	*(−0.96)*
$r_s(-1)$	0.2727	0.9583
	(3.31)	*(15.28)*
$r_s(-2)$	0.2018	0.4796
	(2.24)	*(7.01)*
$r_f(-1)$	−0.3812	−0.9128
	(−3.62)	*(−11.42)*
$r_f(-2)$	−0.2221	−0.3823
	(−2.65)	*(−6.01)*

between the variables in the system, to look for lead–lag behaviour as described in §11.4.3 and perhaps also for predictive purposes.

As an example of a VAR model, Table 11.4 shows the estimated VAR(2) model for daily returns to WTI crude oil spot and near futures from 1 June 1998 to 26 February 1999. This model is the bivariate generalization of the AR(2) model in §11.3.1 to include spot returns in the system. Each equation is estimated separately using OLS and the *t*-statistics (in parentheses) indicate that the model fits the futures equation very well. In fact the $F_{4,666}$ statistic for goodness of fit (§A.2.4) is 66.7 for the futures equation, and this is significant at the highest level (1% $F_{4,666} = 3.35$). The *F*-statistic for the future to spot causality is only 7.2; while this is still highly significant, it is weaker than the causality from spot to future prices (§11.4.3). The results indicate that yesterdays closing crude oil spot price is a good predictor of the closing futures price today.[13] This possibility will be investigated again in the context of a much better model in §12.3.

11.4.2 Testing for Joint Covariance Stationarity

Two covariance-stationary time series $\{x_t\}$ and $\{y_t\}$ are *jointly covariance-stationary* if $cov(x_t, y_{t-s})$ depends only on the lag *s*. In particular, the contemporaneous covariance $cov(x_t, y_t)$ is a constant, irrespective of the time at which it is measured, and this means that multivariate time series that are generated by jointly covariance-stationary processes have correlation measures that will be stable over time.

The instability over time of estimates of correlation between the returns to two financial markets has been encountered throughout this book. It has been attributed to various causes, including the following:

---

[13]Spot is the first month Cushing until the future's expiry, then the second month Cushing until the 25th, then back to the first month Cushing. The 'Cushing' prices are quoted by Platts and represent market prices paid for crude to be delivered over the next (or second nearest) calendar month. Thus the underlying asset is exactly the same as that represented by the futures contract. This 'cash' market trades for only about 30 minutes each day following the close of trading in the futures contract.

➢ Co-dependencies between asset returns may be highly non-linear in nature, but correlation is a only a linear measure.
➢ Unconditional correlation is essentially a static measure, but dynamic relationships between markets may exist with a lead–lag nature.
➢ Unconditional correlation only exists when the returns are jointly covariance-stationary. It may be that correlation estimates jump around because they are being measured on non-jointly stationary series.

This subsection addresses the third of these causes of unstable correlation. It describes how a VAR representation may be used to check whether the system is jointly covariance-stationary. In fact the conditions for joint stationarity can be viewed as a simple generalization of the conditions for univariate stationarity.

Unconditional correlation only exists when the returns are jointly covariance-stationary

Recall from §11.2.1 that a univariate AR(1) model represents a stationary time series only if it is stable. That is, the coefficient α must be less than 1 in absolute value, because if $|\alpha| > 1$ the AR(1) model explodes, each successive observation increasing until $y_t \to \pm\infty$ as $t \to \infty$, and if $\alpha = 1$ the model represents a non-stationary random walk. More generally the AR(p) model represents a stationary process only if the solutions to the characteristic equation $1 - \alpha_1 x - \alpha_2 x^2 - \ldots - \alpha_p x^p = 0$ lie outside the unit circle.

Analogously, a multivariate VAR(1) model represents a jointly stationary multivariate time series only if it is stable and this will be the case if the solutions to the determinant equation

$$|\mathbf{I} - \mathbf{A}z| = 0 \tag{11.30}$$

lie outside the unit circle. Since the solutions to (11.30) are the inverse of the eigenvalues of $\mathbf{A}$,[14] an alternative characterization of the joint stationarity condition is that all eigenvalues of $\mathbf{A}$ lie inside the unit circle. A useful check for joint stationarity is therefore to fit a VAR(1) and use this condition to test for stability.[15]

In a bivariate VAR(1) the coefficient matrix $\mathbf{A}$ is a 2×2 matrix, and (11.30) reduces to the simple quadratic equation

---

[14]The eigenvalues of a square matrix $\mathbf{A}$ are those scalars λ such that $\mathbf{A}\mathbf{x} = \lambda\mathbf{x}$ for some non-zero vector $\mathbf{x}$ ($\mathbf{x}$ is called the eigenvector of λ). Thus $(\mathbf{A} - \lambda\mathbf{I})\mathbf{x} = \mathbf{0}$ for a non-zero $\mathbf{x}$, which implies that $(\mathbf{A} - \lambda\mathbf{I})$ is a singular matrix and the determinant $|\mathbf{A} - \lambda\mathbf{I}| = 0$. This equation is called the characteristic equation and the eigenvalues are the solutions.

[15]The condition for joint stationarity based on a VAR(p) representation (11.29) is that the solutions to the equation

$$|\mathbf{I} - \mathbf{A}_1 z - \mathbf{A}_2 z^2 - \ldots - \mathbf{A}_p z^p| = 0$$

If the VAR(1) representation is not stable there is little practical advantage in checking for stability in higher-order VAR models

lie outside the unit circle. This equation is not very nice to solve when $p > 2$. But if the VAR(1) representation is not stable there is little practical advantage in checking for stability in higher-order VAR models. Even if a higher-order VAR is found to be stable when a VAR(1) is not, the lack of robustness of the basic properties of the data to different VAR formulations should lead one to question this type of modelling in the first place. Also if joint stationarity is tested using a VAR(p) specification one can use the fact that a VAR(p) model has an equivalent representation as a VAR(1) model with p times as many variables, so that, in fact, joint stationarity only ever needs checking using the VAR(1) condition.

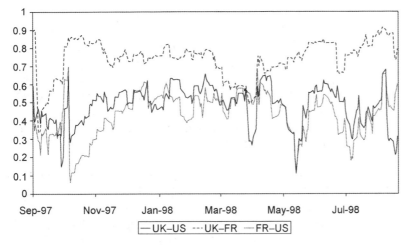

Figure 11.9 EWMA correlations of equity indices.

$$1 - \text{tr}(\mathbf{A})z + |\mathbf{A}|z^2 = 0,$$

where $\text{tr}(\mathbf{A})$ is the sum of the diagonal elements and $|\mathbf{A}|$ is the determinant of $\mathbf{A}$. So the two series are jointly covariance-stationary if the solutions of this equation lie outside the unit circle.

Some correlations between the crude oil spot and futures returns have been shown in Figure 3.4. The correlations are relatively stable over time, but could this be just an artefact of the 'historic' correlation method being applied to series with stress events? Or are these correlations stable over time because crude oil spot and near futures returns are indeed jointly covariance-stationary? To answer this question we estimate a VAR(1) representation of the crude oil spot and futures returns and obtain

The correlations are relatively stable over time, but could this be just an artefact of the 'historic' correlation method being applied to series with stress events?

$$\mathbf{A} = \begin{pmatrix} 0.196 & -0.254 \\ 0.715 & -0.536 \end{pmatrix}.$$

So $\text{tr}(\mathbf{A}) = -0.34$ and $|\mathbf{A}| = 0.07655$. The solutions of $1 + 0.34z + 0.07665z^2 = 0$ are $-2.22 \pm 2.85i$, which lie well outside the unit circle. Thus the VAR(1) model is a stable representation of spot and futures returns in WTI crude oil and it may be assumed that the series are indeed jointly covariance-stationary.

Correlations between international equity indices can also vary considerably over time (Erb *et al.*, 1994; Longin and Solnik, 1995). Exponentially weighted moving average correlations with $\lambda = 0.94$ of daily returns to the S&P 500, the CAC and the FTSE 100 index from September 1997 to September 1998 are shown in Figure 11.9. These correlations appear to vary considerably over the year. Is it possible that the S&P 500, the CAC and the FTSE 100 indices are not jointly stationary?

Estimating a VAR(1) on the S&P 500 and FT 100 daily return data gives

$$\mathbf{A} = \begin{pmatrix} 0.018534 & 0.30033 \\ 0.22758 & -0.18147 \end{pmatrix}.$$

Now the solutions to $1 - \mathrm{tr}(\mathbf{A})z + |\mathbf{A}|z^2 = 0$ are $z = -2.76719$ and $z = 5.03926$. Both lie outside the unit circle and we may conclude that the S&P 500 and the FTSE 100 returns are jointly stationary. Similar results are obtained when testing the joint stationarity of these returns with the CAC returns.

It is difficult to find examples where the assumption of joint stationarity does not hold

The correlations of individual stocks with an index can also be very unstable over time. Figure 11.10 shows EWMA correlations with $\lambda = 0.94$ of three of the main Brazilian stocks with the Ibovespa equity index. While the correlations with the main stock Telebrás are quite stable, those with two other major stocks Eletrobrás and Petrobrás are very unstable indeed. However joint stationarity tests are not rejected on these data. Indeed, it is difficult to find examples where the assumption of joint stationarity does not hold. For example, all of the US stocks in Table 11.3 (§11.3.2) pass bivariate joint stationarity tests, performed over each year and over the whole data period. The conclusion is that the observed instability of correlations between individual equities, between equities and their index, and between different equity indices is not due to lack of joint stationarity; more likely it is a result of non-linear relationships.

11.4.3   Granger Causality

After the seminal work of Granger (1988), the term 'Granger causality' means that a lead–lag relationship is evident between variables in a multivariate time series. In a bivariate system of jointly stationary time series $\{x_t\}$ and $\{y_t\}$, the variable x is said to *Granger cause* y if lagged x improves the predictions of y, even after lagged y variables have been included as explanatory variables.

'Granger causality' means that a lead–lag relationship is evident between variables in a multivariate time series

A *lead–lag* is to be expected in the co-dependent relationships that are observed between many financial markets and dynamic models of multivariate time series need to be applied if one is to gain direct insights into the nature of lead–lag relationships. This subsection shows how vector autoregressive models may be used to investigate any lead–lag behaviour between financial markets.

Consider the bivariate VAR(p) model (11.29) written out in full as:

$$x_t = c_1 + \sum_{i=1}^{p} \alpha_{1i} x_{t-i} + \sum_{i=1}^{p} \beta_{1i} y_{t-i} + \varepsilon_{1t},$$

$$y_t = c_2 + \sum_{i=1}^{p} \alpha_{2i} x_{t-i} + \sum_{i=1}^{p} \beta_{2i} y_{t-i} + \varepsilon_{2t}.$$

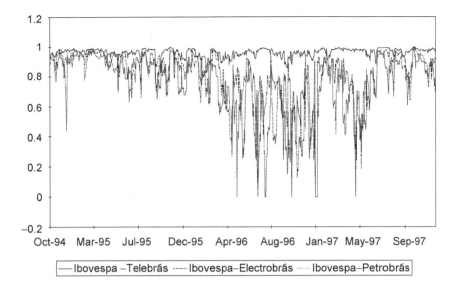

Figure 11.10 EWMA correlations in Brazilian equities.

The test for Granger causality from x to y is an F-test for the joint significance of $\alpha_{21}, \ldots, \alpha_{2p}$ in an OLS regression. Similarly, the test for Granger causality from y to x is an F-test for the joint significance of $\beta_{11}, \ldots, \beta_{1p}$.

To illustrate the method, consider testing for Granger causal flows between WTI crude oil spot and futures using the VAR(2) model of Table 11.4. Following §A.2.3, the F-statistic is calculated from residual sums of squares in the restricted and unrestricted models, and for this example $F(\text{spot} \rightarrow \text{futures}) = 118.195$ and $F(\text{futures} \rightarrow \text{spot}) = 7.197$. The 1% critical value of the $F_{2,666}$ distribution is 4.64, and so there was significant causality from futures to spot markets but a very much more significant causality from spot to futures. This model provides some very convincing empirical evidence that spot crude oil prices are good predictors of the near futures prices.

The strength of Granger causality can change over time, the direction of causality can change depending on the time that it is measured, or there can be bidirectional causality

Every empirical finding from market data modelling depends on both the length of data period used for the test and the time at which it is performed. If the finding is not robust to changes in data then it will not have much practical use, so it is important to backtest the model very thoroughly, checking the recorded Granger causal flows for stability. In fact it is always the case that the strength of Granger causality can change over time, the direction of causality can change depending on the time that it is measured, or there can be bidirectional causality.

An example of this sort of change in causal flows will be given in Chapter 12. There it is shown that although the VAR(2) model of Table 11.4 is certainly an improvement on the earlier AR(2) specification for WTI futures alone, it is still not well specified. An important variable has been omitted: these spot and futures prices are cointegrated, so they have an equilibrium relationship. Therefore a VAR model of their returns requires a variable that is defined by the equilibrium between these price series.

12

Cointegration

It is unfortunate that many market practitioners still base their analysis of the relationships between markets on the very limited concept of correlation. Trying to model the complex interdependencies between financial assets with so restrictive a tool is like trying to surf the internet with an IBM AT. It is, therefore, rather gratifying to see that more sophisticated models are now being applied to analyse relationships between financial assets. This chapter concerns an important development in this field; it introduces a multivariate time series model for the dynamic co-dependencies that are often found in financial markets.

Trying to model the complex interdependencies between financial assets with so restrictive a tool is like trying to surf the internet with an IBM AT

Cointegration refers not to co-movements in returns, but to co-movements in asset prices (or exchange rates or yields). If spreads are mean-reverting, asset prices are tied together in the long term by a common stochastic trend, and we say that the prices are 'cointegrated'. Since the seminal work of Engle and Granger (1987) cointegration has become the prevalent tool of time series econometrics. Every modern econometrics text covers the statistical theory necessary to master the practical application of cointegration, Hamilton (1994), Enders (1995) and Hendry (1996) being among the best sources. Cointegration has emerged as a powerful technique for investigating common trends in multivariate time series, and provides a sound methodology for modelling both long-run and short-run dynamics in a system.

Cointegration is a two-step process: first any long-run equilibrium relationships between prices are established, and then a dynamic correlation model of returns is estimated. This error correction model (ECM), so-called because short-term deviations from equilibrium are corrected, reveals the Granger causalities that must be present in a cointegrated system. Thus cointegration may be a sign of market inefficiency, but it can also be the result of market efficiency — as, for example, is the cointegration between spot and futures prices.

The basic building blocks for time series analysis were described in Chapter 11. Some of the empirical data that were applied there are also applied in this chapter, but this time to models of non-stationary processes to capture long-run common features such as a common stochastic trend. The first section introduces cointegration, the relationship between cointegration and correlation, and the implications of cointegration for common trends in

If spreads are mean-reverting, asset prices are tied together in the long term by a common stochastic trend, and we say that the prices are 'cointegrated'

financial data. Then §12.2 describes how to test for cointegration, with empirical examples of term structures, spot and futures prices and equity indices. Models for the dynamic relationships between returns in cointegrated systems are introduced in §12.3, with examples on equity indices and commodity spot and futures prices. A large number of cointegration models have been applied in financial markets, and this literature is surveyed in §12.4.

The relationship between the mean and the variance of portfolio returns is a corner-stone of modern portfolio theory. However, returns are short-memory processes (Granger and Hallman, 1991) and so investments that are based on the characteristics of returns alone cannot model long-run cointegrating relationships between prices. Section 12.5 examines how cointegration, applied to investment analysis, presents a modern and powerful alternative to mean-variance analysis.

A common stochastic trend is just one of many common features that multivariate time series could possess. Section 12.6 presents some empirical evidence on other common features, such as common volatility patterns and common autocorrelation properties.

12.1 Introducing Cointegration

When standard risk–return models are used, it is not possible to base any investment decision on the presence of established common trends in the data

Although empirical models of cointegrated financial time series are common-place in the academic literature, the practical implementation of these models in systems for investment analysis or portfolio risk is still in its early stages. This is because the traditional starting point for asset allocation and risk management is a correlation analysis of returns. In standard risk–return models the price data are differenced before the analysis is even begun, and differencing removes a priori any long-term trends in the data. Of course these trends are implicit in the returns data, but when standard risk–return models are used, it is not possible to base any investment decision on the presence of established common trends in the data. The fundamental aim of cointegration analysis, on the other hand, is to detect any common stochastic trends in the price data, and to use these common trends for a dynamic analysis of correlation in returns. Thus cointegration analysis is an extension of the simple correlation-based risk–return analysis that was described in Chapter 7.

Correlation is based only on return data, but a full cointegration analysis is based on the raw price, rate or yield data as well as the return data. Price, rate and yield data are not normally stationary, in fact they are usually integrated of order 1 (denoted $I(1)$, see §11.1.3). And since it is normally the case that log prices will be cointegrated when the actual prices are cointegrated it is standard, but not necessary, to perform the cointegration analysis on log prices.[1]

---

[1] Also the error correction models that are described in §12.3 have a more natural interpretation when log prices are used.

12.1.1 Cointegration and Correlation

A set of $I(1)$ series are termed 'cointegrated' if there is a linear combination of these series that is stationary. So in the case of just two integrated series:

x and y are cointegrated if $x, y \sim I(1)$ but there exists α such that $x - \alpha y \sim I(0)$.

The definition of cointegration given in Engle and Granger (1987) is far more general than this, but the basic definition presented here is sufficient for the purposes of this chapter.

Cointegration and correlation are related but different concepts. High correlation does not imply high cointegration, and neither does high cointegration imply high correlation. In fact cointegrated series can have correlations that are quite low at times. For example, a large and diversified portfolio of stocks in an equity index, where allocations are determined by their weights in the index, should be cointegrated with the index (§12.5). Although the portfolio should move in line with the index in the long term, there will be periods when stocks that are not in the portfolio have exceptional price movements. Following this, the empirical correlations between the portfolio and the index may be rather low for a time. Another example where cointegration exists without high correlation is given in the next section.

Cointegration and correlation are related but different concepts. High correlation does not imply high cointegration, and neither does high cointegration imply high correlation

The converse also holds true: returns may be highly correlated without a high cointegration in prices. An example is given in Figure 12.1, with 8 years of daily data on US dollar spot exchange rates of the German Mark (DEM) and the Dutch guilder (NLG) from 1986 to 1992. Their returns are very highly correlated, in fact the unconditional correlation coefficient over the whole period is 0.9642. The rates themselves also appear to be moving together. The spread is very stable indeed, and in fact they appear to be cointegrated, which is highly unusual for two exchange rates (Alexander and Johnston, 1992, 1994).

But suppose that extremely small, low variance, daily incremental returns are added to the spread, to create the NLG 'plus' series that is also shown in Figure 12.1. The NLG 'plus' is clearly not cointegrated with the DEM. They are not tied together by a stationary spread, instead they are diverging more and more as time goes on. But the correlation between the returns to NLG 'plus' and the DEM is still very high, at 0.9620.

Thus high correlations can easily occur when there is cointegration and when there is no cointegration. That is, correlation tells us nothing about the long-term behavioural relationship between two markets: they may or may not be moving together over long periods of time, and correlation is not an adequate tool for measuring this.

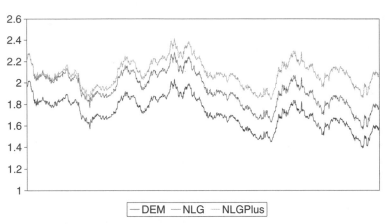

Figure 12.1 Daily German mark–US dollar and Dutch guilder–US dollar exchange rates, from January 1986 to December 1992.

Correlation is intrinsically a short-run measure

Correlation reflects co-movements in returns, which are liable to great instabilities over time. It is intrinsically a short-run measure, so correlation-based hedging strategies commonly require frequent rebalancing. Investment management strategies that are based only correlations cannot guarantee long-term performance because there is no mechanism to ensure the reversion of the hedge to the underlying. And there is nothing to prevent the tracking error from behaving in the unpredictable manner of a random walk.

Hedging methodologies based on cointegrated financial assets should be more effective in the long term. Moreover, the cointegration methodology loses none of the traditional analysis

Since high correlation is not sufficient to ensure the long-term performance of hedges, there is a need to augment standard risk–return modelling methodologies to take account of common long-term trends in prices. This is exactly what cointegration provides. Cointegration measures long-run co-movements in prices, which may occur even through periods when static correlations appear low. Therefore hedging methodologies based on cointegrated financial assets should be more effective in the long term. Moreover, the cointegration methodology loses none of the traditional analysis. It merely augments the basic correlation model to include a preliminary stage in which the multivariate price data are analysed, and then extends the correlation model to include a dynamic analysis of the lead–lag behaviour between returns.

12.1.2 Common Trends and Long-Run Equilibria

When asset price time series are random walks, over a period of time they may have wandered virtually anywhere, because a random walk has infinite unconditional variance. There is little point in modelling them individually, since the best forecast of any future value is the just value today plus the drift, but when two or more asset prices are cointegrated a multivariate model will be worthwhile because it reveals information about the long-run equilibrium in the system. For example, if a spread is found to be mean-reverting we know that, wherever one series is in several years' time, the other series will be right there along with it.

Cointegrated log asset prices have a common stochastic trend (Stock and Watson, 1988). They are 'tied together' in the long run even though they might drift apart in the short run because the spread or some other linear combination is mean-reverting. A simple example that illustrates why cointegrated series have a common stochastic trend is

$$
\begin{aligned}
x_t &= w_t + \varepsilon_{xt}, \\
y_t &= w_t + \varepsilon_{yt}, \\
w_t &= w_{t-1} + \varepsilon_t,
\end{aligned}
\tag{12.1}
$$

where all the errors are i.i.d. and independent of each other. In (12.1) the $I(1)$ variables x and y are cointegrated because $x - y \sim I(0)$. They also have a common stochastic trend given by the random walk component w. Note that the correlation between Δx and Δy is going to be less than 1, and when the variances of ε_{xt} and/or ε_{yt} are much larger than the variance of ε_t the correlation will be low.[2] So, as already mentioned above, cointegration does not imply high correlation. Of course, this example is very theoretical. It is unlikely that cointegrated series will conform to this model in practice, but it useful for illustration.

When asset prices are random walks there is little point in modelling them individually, but when two or more asset prices are cointegrated a multivariate model will provide insight

The linear combination of $I(1)$ variables that is stationary is denoted z. It is called the *disequilibrium term* because it captures deviations from the long-run equilibrium in the error correction model (ECM) (§12.3). The expectation of z gives the long-run equilibrium relationship between x and y, and short-term periods of disequilibrium occur as the observed value of z varies around its expected value. The *cointegration vector* is the vector of weights in z. So in the case of two $I(1)$ variables x and y, where $x - \alpha y \sim I(0)$, the cointegration vector is $(1, -\alpha)$. When only two integrated series are considered for cointegration, there can be at most one cointegration vector, because if there were two cointegration vectors the original series would have to be stationary.

More generally, cointegration exists between n integrated series if there exists at least one cointegration vector, that is, at least one linear combination of the $I(1)$ series that is stationary. Each stationary linear combination acts like 'glue' in the system, and so the more cointegration vectors found the greater the co-dependency between the processes. Yield curves have very high cointegration.

---

[2]This follows since $V(\Delta x) = \sigma^2 + 2\sigma_x^2$, $V(\Delta x) = \sigma^2 + 2\sigma_y^2$, and $\mathrm{cov}(\Delta x, \Delta y) = \sigma^2$, where σ^2, σ_x^2, and σ_y^2 denote the variances of ε, ε_x and ε_y respectively. So the correlation is $\sigma^2 / \sqrt{[(\sigma^2 + 2\sigma_x^2)(\sigma^2 + 2\sigma_y^2)]}$ which is small when σ^2 is much smaller than σ_y^2 and/or σ_x^2.

Table 12.1: Augmented Dickey–Fuller tests on the spreads of the US yield curve

Monthly data, 1944–1992	
Spread	ADF
1mth–3mth	-12.19
1mth–6mth	-8.16
1mth–9mth	-7.59
1mth–12mth	-7.44
1mth–18mth	-6.72
1mth–2yr	-6.40
1mth–3yr	-5.76
1mth–4yr	-5.52
1mth–5yr	-5.39
1mth–7yr	-5.28
1mth–10yr	-5.05
1mth–15yr	-4.82
1mth–20yr	-5.71
1mth–long	-4.82

Yield curves have very high cointegration. Often each of the $n-1$ independent spreads is mean-reverting, so there are $n-1$ cointegration vectors, the maximum possible number

When there are n maturities in a yield curve, often each of the $n-1$ independent spreads is mean-reverting, so there are $n-1$ cointegration vectors, the maximum possible number.

Consider the US yield curve data shown in Figure 6.1 that was used to illustrate some of the stylized facts about principal components in §6.2.1. Looking at the same data from a cointegration perspective now, note that each individual yield series is integrated and so it has infinite unconditional variance (§11.1.3). This means that, given enough time, a yield could be almost anywhere (except, of course, negative). In 1944, the beginning of the period shown in Figure 6.1, who would have guessed what the 1-month yield would be at the end of the period, almost 50 years later? However, if these yields are cointegrated it *is* known that whatever the 1-month yield is in 1992, the 3-month yield will be very close to it.

Applying a unit root test (§11.1.5) to the spread will tell us if it is stationary, that is, whether the 1-month yield and the 3-month yield are cointegrated. Table 12.1 reports ADF(1) statistics for each of the spreads with the 1-month rate. Since the 1% critical value for this test is -3.46, each spread is stationary at the 1% level.

It is important that a sufficiently long period of data is used, in order that the common long-run trends can be detected

The findings of stationarity in spreads, and consequently cointegrated yields, are quite robust to changes in data period, and to different frequency of data. But it is important that a sufficiently long period of data is used, in order that the common long-run trends can be detected. Of course, it is not necessary to use almost 50 years of data as in this example, but even when the ADF tests are performed on subsets of these data they invariably give the same type of result, provided several years of data are used.

All yield curves have a high degree of cointegration. Cointegration can also be thought of as a form of factor analysis similar to principal component analysis,[3] so it is not surprising that cointegration analysis often works very well on the term structure data that are so successfully modelled by a principal component analysis.

This example shows that cointegration is a powerful tool for the analysis of yield curves. But there are many other applications of cointegration to other financial markets. It is often the case that cointegration arises from stationary spreads, bases, or tracking errors. However, even though spreads/bases/ tracking errors may be stationary it is not always clear that they are the *most* stationary linear combination. That is, $(1, -1)$ may not be the best cointegration vector. And if the spread/basis/tracking error is not stationary that does not preclude the possibility that some other linear combination of asset prices, or log prices, is stationary.

It is only valid to regress log prices on log prices when these log prices are cointegrated

12.2 Testing for Cointegration

The first step in cointegration analysis is to use standard statistical tests for cointegration to identify stationary linear combinations of the integrated series which best define the long-run equilibrium relationships between the variables in the system, if such relationships exist. Of course, if no such relationship exists then the variables are not cointegrated and there is little point in a multivariate analysis of the price data.

The classic papers on cointegration are those of Hendry (1986), Granger (1986) and Engle and Granger (1987). Engle and Granger proposed a test for cointegration that is based on an ordinary least squares regression. In the *Engle–Granger method* one simply performs a regression of one integrated variable on the other integrated variables and then tests the residual for stationarity using a unit root test (§11.1.5). Slightly different critical values apply, as described in the help sheet for the **Engle Granger** workbook on the CD.

Now, it is not standard to do OLS regression on non-stationary data. For example, the factor models described in §8.1 were based on returns data, because the standard theory of regression is based on stationary data. If the dependent variable is non-stationary it is quite possible that residuals will be non-stationary, but the properties of OLS estimators are only established for stationary residuals (§A.1.4). However, there is only one circumstance in which a regression between integrated variables will give stationary residuals, and that is when the variables are cointegrated. Put another way, it is only valid to

There is only one circumstance in which a regression between integrated variables will give stationary residuals, and that is when the variables are cointegrated

---

[3]The connection between these two methodologies is that a principal component analysis of first differences of cointegrated variables will yield the common stochastic trend as the first principal component. But the outputs of the two analyses differ: principal components gives a few series which can be used to approximate a much larger set of series (such as the yield curve); cointegration gives all possible stationary linear combinations of a set of random walks. See Gourieroux *et al.* (1991).

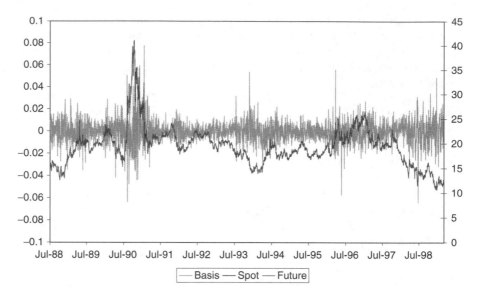

Figure 12.2 Daily average spot and future prices for WTI crude oil and the basis ($\ln F - \ln S$).

regress log prices on log prices when these log prices are cointegrated. In this case the regression will define the long-run equilibrium relationship between the log prices.

12.2.1 The Engle–Granger Methodology

The Engle–Granger test is a two-step process: first estimate an OLS regression on the $I(1)$ data, then apply a stationarity test such as the ADF test to the residuals from this regression. The critical values for this test are given in MacKinnon (1991). In the case of only two $I(1)$ variables x and y, the Engle–Granger regression is

$$x_t = c + \alpha y_t + \varepsilon_t.$$

Now x and y will be cointegrated if and only if ε is stationary. Then the cointegration vector is $(1, -\alpha)$, and the long-run equilibrium relationship between x and y is $x = c + \alpha y$. Cointegration tests will not produce sensible results if too short a data period is used: they are designed to detect common long-run trends in the variables. The data period has to be sufficiently long for a stochastic trend to be detected.

Cointegration tests will not produce sensible results if too short a data period is used: they are designed to detect common long-run trends in the variables

Daily WTI crude oil prices from 1 July 1988 to 26 February 1999 have been used to test for cointegration between spot and futures log prices using the Engle–Granger method. Looking at Figure 12.2, it is clear that these series are very closely tied together over the 11-year period (in fact, it is virtually

Table 12.2: ADF tests for a unit root in crude oil spot and future prices

	$I(1)$ vs $I(0)$	$I(2)$ vs $I(1)$
log Spot	-2.66	-24.45
log Futures	-2.66	-22.73

impossible to distinguish between the two prices on the graph) and the basis has a very high degree of stationarity because it is very rapidly mean-reverting. But before testing for cointegration it is necessary to establish that the spot and futures log prices are both $I(1)$. Following the methodology explained in §11.1.5, the ADF(1) statistics in Table 12.2 confirm this.

Moving now to an Engle–Granger cointegration test, the OLS regression of log futures prices on log spot prices gives

$$\ln F_t = 0.016404 + 0.9943 \ln S_t,$$
$$\underset{(4.05)}{} \quad \underset{(730.87)}{}$$

and the ADF test for the hypothesis $I(1)$ against $I(0)$ on the residuals from this equation indicates a high degree of stationarity (ADF(1) $= -30.97$). It may be concluded that spot and futures log prices in the crude oil market are very highly cointegrated, with cointegration vector $(1, -0.9943)$. Since this is approximately equal to $(1, -1)$, the results support the standard expectations model that the futures price is the average of all discounted expected spot prices, which implies that the basis $\ln F - \ln S$ is a stationary process.

In the more general case, an OLS regression between n different $I(1)$ cointegrated variables will estimate a linear combination of the $I(1)$ series that is stationary. The cointegration vector is $(1, -\beta_1, \ldots, -\beta_{n-1})$, where $\beta_1, \ldots, \beta_{n-1}$ are the coefficients on the $n-1$ $I(1)$ variables that are used as explanatory variables, the other $I(1)$ variable being used as the dependent variable in the Engle–Granger regression. The disequilibrium term z is given by the residuals from this regression.

When $n = 2$ it does not matter which variable is taken as the dependent variable. There is only one cointegration vector, which is the same when estimated by a regression of x on y as when estimated by a regression of y on x. But when there are more than two $I(1)$ series the Engle–Granger method can suffer from a serious bias. That is, different estimates of a cointegration vector are obtained depending on the choice of dependent variable, and only one estimate is possible even though there can be up to $n-1$ cointegration vectors. Using the stock index data provided with the **Engle–Granger** workbook, readers can investigate this bias, and compare results with those based on the more powerful Johansen method (§12.2.2).

When there are more than two $I(1)$ series the Engle–Granger method can suffer from a serious bias

Thus the Engle–Granger method cannot be used to identify all the independent cointegration vectors in a system with more than two variables. Only one

Table 12.3: ADF(1) tests for stationarity of crude oil term structure spreads

Spread	ADF for $I(1)$ vs $I(0)$
1mth–2mth	−4.79378
1mth–3mth	−3.82636
1mth–4mth	−3.47686
1mth–5mth	−3.19133
1mth–6mth	−3.14336
1mth–7mth	−3.02332
1mth–8mth	−2.92954
1mth–9mth	−2.84591
1mth–10mth	−2.77803
1mth–11mth	−2.73640
1mth–12mth	−2.67951

cointegration vector is estimated, but all of the independent cointegration vectors should be employed in the ECM (§12.3). So there are some disadvantages in using the Engle–Granger methodology for more than two variable systems.

Consider an example of the application of the Engle–Granger method to a multivariate system when it is not appropriate to do so. The term structure of crude oil futures from 1 month to 12 months, using prices quoted on NYMEX from 4 February 1993 to 24 March 1999, is illustrated in Figure 6.4. From a purely visual inspection a high degree of cointegration seems likely. Indeed, looking at the ADF(1) statistics on the 11 independent spreads with the 1-month future log price shown in Table 12.3, many of these are stationary at the 1% level. The longer spreads have less stationarity than the shorter spreads, in fact since the 5% critical value is −2.88 only the spreads up to 8 months are stationary at the 5% level.

Only one cointegration vector can be identified from an Engle–Granger regression

There will be more than one independent cointegration vector, because so many of the spreads are stationary.[4] However, only one cointegration vector can be identified from an Engle–Granger regression. So when there are more than two variables the first step in the Engle–Granger is to select a dependent variable — and in this example the choice must be arbitrary. Using the log price of the 1-month future as the dependent variable, and the other 11 log futures prices as explanatory variables, gives the OLS regression reported in Table 12.4.

The Engle–Granger test for cointegration examines whether the residuals from this model are stationary, and with an ADF(1) statistic of −18.41 it is certainly

---

[4]In fact from the results in the next section based on the Johansen methodology, it appears that there might be as many as 10 cointegration vectors.

Table 12.4: Engle–Granger regression for crude
oil futures term structure

Variable	Coefficient	*t*-ratio
Constant	0.554194E-02	0.737952
log 2mth	3.15180	46.5609
log 3mth	−2.75098	−12.2908
log 4mth	0.332182	0.987664
log 5mth	0.119571	0.291364
log 6mth	−0.058162	−0.124589
log 7mth	−0.286940	−0.590631
log 8mth	0.957277	1.89641
log 9mth	−0.570076	−1.15306
log 10mth	0.168985	0.461256
log 11mth	−0.101638	−0.608710
log 12mth	0.036000	0.286137

the case that they are. Similar regressions using other log futures prices as the
dependent variable confirm the finding of cointegration, but each of these
regressions gives a different result for the cointegration vector. So which ones
should be used to model the equilibrium relationships?

The Engle–Granger procedure is only applicable to systems with more than
two variables in very special circumstances, when there are clear answers to the
following questions:

➢ Are there several cointegration vectors, that is, several long-run equilibria?
If so, which equilibrium is being identified by the Engle–Granger regression,
and is it the most appropriate?
➢ Which variable should be chosen as the dependent variable in the Engle–
Granger regression? How different would the results be if another variable
were used as dependent variable?

*The Engle–Granger
procedure is only
applicable to systems
with more than two
variables in very special
circumstances*

12.2.2 The Johansen Methodology

Johansen's methodology for investigating cointegration in a multivariate system
has been preferred by economists. It employs a power function with better
properties than the Engle–Granger method (Kremers *et al.*, 1992), and has less
bias when the number of variables is greater than two (Johansen, 1988, 1991;
Johansen and Juselius, 1990). The Johansen tests are based on the eigenvalues of
a stochastic matrix and in fact reduce to a canonical correlation problem similar
to that of principal components. The Johansen tests seek the linear
combination which is most stationary whereas the Engle–Granger tests,
being based on OLS, seek the linear combination having minimum variance.

The Johansen tests are a multivariate generalization of the unit root tests that
were described in §11.1.5. There it was shown that an AR(1) process may be

*The Johansen tests seek
the linear combination
which is most stationary
whereas the Engle–
Granger tests seek the
linear combination
having minimum
variance*

rewritten in the form (11.10), where the first difference Δy_t is regressed on the lagged level y_{t-1}. The test for a stochastic trend is based on the fact that the coefficient on the lagged level should be zero if the process has a unit root. Generalizing this argument for a VAR(1) process motivates the Johansen tests for a *common* stochastic trend, that is, for cointegration. The VAR(1) model (11.28) may be rewritten with $\Delta \mathbf{y}_t$ as the dependent variable in a regression on $\mathbf{y}_{t-1}$:

$$\Delta \mathbf{y}_t = \boldsymbol{\alpha}_0 + (\mathbf{A} - \mathbf{I})\mathbf{y}_{t-1} + \boldsymbol{\varepsilon}_t. \tag{12.2}$$

Now if each variable in $\mathbf{y}$ is $I(1)$ then each equation in (12.2) has a stationary variable on the left-hand side. The errors are stationary and therefore each term in $(\mathbf{A} - \mathbf{I})\mathbf{y}_{t-1}$ must be stationary for the equation to be *balanced*. If $\mathbf{A} - \mathbf{I}$ has rank zero, so it is equivalent to the zero matrix, this condition implies nothing about relationships between the $\mathbf{y}$ variables. But if $\mathbf{A} - \mathbf{I}$ has rank $r > 0$, then there are r independent linear relations between the $\mathbf{y}$ variables that must be stationary. Therefore the $I(1)$ variables in $\mathbf{y}$ will have a common stochastic trend — that is, they will be cointegrated — if the rank of $\mathbf{A} - \mathbf{I}$ is non-zero; the number of cointegration vectors is the rank of $\mathbf{A} - \mathbf{I}$. The rank of a matrix is given by the number of non-zero eigenvalues, so the Johansen procedure based on (12.2) tests for the number of non-zero eigenvalues in $\mathbf{A} - \mathbf{I}$.

The model (12.2) is not the only possible maintained model for Johansen tests: a VAR(1) model with a constant may not be the most appropriate representation of the data. Returning to the univariate analogy, recall that the Dickey–Fuller regression can contain more than just a lagged levels term. It may contain a constant if there is a drift in the stochastic trend, a time trend if the process also contains a deterministic trend, and it can be augmented with sufficient lagged dependent variables to remove autocorrelation in residuals. The same applies to the Johansen test: the maintained model may or may not contain a constant or a trend term, and the number of lagged first differences is chosen so that residuals are not autocorrelated.

If a higher-order VAR(p) model is used to motivate the Johansen tests, the first difference formulation becomes

$$\begin{aligned}
\Delta \mathbf{y}_t = {} & \boldsymbol{\alpha}_0 + (\mathbf{A}_1 - \mathbf{I})\Delta \mathbf{y}_{t-1} + (\mathbf{A}_1 + \mathbf{A}_2 - \mathbf{I})\Delta \mathbf{y}_{t-2} + \cdots \\
& + (\mathbf{A}_1 + \mathbf{A}_2 + \cdots + \mathbf{A}_{p-1} - \mathbf{I})\Delta \mathbf{y}_{t-p-1} \\
& + (\mathbf{A}_1 + \mathbf{A}_2 + \cdots + \mathbf{A}_p - \mathbf{I})\mathbf{y}_{t-p} + \boldsymbol{\varepsilon}_t
\end{aligned} \tag{12.3}$$

and the Johansen method is a test for the number of non-zero eigenvalues of the matrix

$$\Pi = \mathbf{A}_1 + \mathbf{A}_2 + \cdots + \mathbf{A}_p - \mathbf{I}.$$

Johansen and Juselius (1990) recommend using the standard 'trace' test for the number r of non-zero eigenvalues in the matrix Π.[5] The test statistic for

$$H_0: r \leqslant R \text{ against } H_1: r > R$$

is

$$\text{Tr} = -T \sum_{i=R+1}^{n} \ln(1 - \hat{\lambda}_i), \qquad (12.4)$$

where T is the sample size, n is the number of variables in the system and the eigenvalues of Π are real numbers λ such that $0 \leqslant \lambda < 1$. In (12.4) the estimates of these eigenvalues are ordered so that $\hat{\lambda}_1 > \hat{\lambda}_2 > \ldots > \hat{\lambda}_n$. So the Tr statistic decreases as R increases. The Johansen method first computes the eigenvalues and then calculates the trace statistic for every $R = 0$ to $n - 1$. Critical values of the trace statistic (12.4) are given in Johansen and Juselius (1990). They depend on the specification of the underlying model, whether or not it includes a constant or trend, and the number of lags in the VAR.

The presence of the constant in (12.3) is necessary for variables that exhibit a drift in the stochastic trend and so that the cointegration test will be on the detrended data (§11.1.4). Likewise, if one or more variables is thought to contain a deterministic trend — that is they are $I(1)$ + trend — then a time trend may be included also. However, it is very unlikely that a time trend would be necessary for most financial markets. In fact the examples given in this section contain neither a constant nor a time trend, since there is no obvious trend in the data, but in many cases, when the prices do appear to be trending, a constant should be included in the Johansen test.

Table 12.5 summarizes the results of using the Johansen procedure to test for cointegration in the crude oil term structure data. The in-built Johansen cointegration procedure in the **PcGive** package on the CD gives the optimal lag length for the maintained $\text{VAR}(p)$ model, and in this example it turns out to be 3. Actually the results are so robust that their qualitative nature is more or less independent of different lag specifications, and similar conclusions may be drawn whether the actual futures prices or their logarithms are used (both are reported).

The Johansen trace statistics reject the null hypothesis that there are R cointegration vectors in favour of the alternative that there are greater than R cointegration vectors at the 1% level, for all R up to and including 10. The probability value of the trace statistic for the null hypothesis $r \leqslant 9$ against the alternative $r > 9$ is 0.004 for the price data and 0.002 for the log price data.

---

[5]Another test, the maximal eigenvalue test, is described in their paper, and some packages offer this as well as the trace test as standard output from cointegration procedure. However, the maximal eigenvalue test does not have nested hypotheses and in some cases the maximal eigenvalue and trace tests imply different conclusions. In that case the results of the trace tests should be preferred.

Table 12.5: Johansen trace tests for cointegration in the crude oil term structure

$H_0: r \leqslant R$ vs $H_1: r > R$	Trace test			Eigenvalue	
R	Price	log Price		Price	log Price
0	1387.7	1356.2	1	0.207	0.192
1	1040.3	1037.1	2	0.152	0.152
2	792.7	788.8	3	0.111	0.112
3	616.5	610.4	4	0.109	0.108
4	443.5	438.8	5	0.076	0.073
5	326.3	324.5	6	0.069	0.067
6	212.3	221.2	7	0.062	0.062
7	123.3	124.8	8	0.043	0.041
8	57.3	61.0	9	0.016	0.017
9	32.7	35.1	10	0.012	0.013
10	14.7	15.6	11	0.009	0.010
11	0.5	0.3	12	0.0003	0.0002

For $R = 10$ the hypothesis is only rejected at the 5% level, since the probability value of the trace statistic is 0.02 (price data) or 0.014 (log price data). Naturally we cannot accept the hypothesis $r > 11$ in the last row of the table since in that case the log futures prices themselves would have to be stationary. It may be concluded that there are 10 or even 11 (the maximum number) cointegration vectors in the system.

Returning to the US yield curve data of Figure 6.1 that were discussed in §12.1.2, an Engle–Granger regression using the 1-month yield as dependent variable gives an ADF(2) statistic on the residuals of -6.49, so the system is definitely cointegrated. But the Engle–Granger method gives only one long-run equilibrium, viz.

$$m1 = 0.73m2 + 0.127m3 + 0.273m6 - 0.016m12 - 0.42y2$$
$$+ 0.41y3 + 0.067y5 - 0.122y7 - 0.09y10.$$

A different estimate of a long-run equilibrium would be obtained if the 3-month yield or any other maturity were used as dependent variable. Using the Johansen procedure, Table 12.6 indicates that there are not one but seven cointegration vectors in this system (the tests reject the null for all $r \leqslant 6$, but the null hypothesis that $r \leqslant 7$ cannot be rejected in favour of $r > 7$). The conclusion is that there are seven cointegration vectors in this US yield curve with ten maturities — not the maximum number of nine, but there is still a very high level of co-dependency in the yield data.

The Johansen procedure is more informative than the Engle–Granger procedure because it finds all possible cointegrating relationships. It is commonly employed for economic problems because there are usually many variables in the system and often there is no clear indication of which should be the

Table 12.6: Johansen tests for cointegration in US yields

R	$H_0: r \leqslant R$ vs $H_1: r > R$			Eigenvalue
	Trace	Prob		
0	591.2	0	1	0.198
1	380.2	0	2	0.126
2	251.1	0	3	0.070
3	181.5	0	4	0.058
4	123.5	0	5	0.053
5	71.3	0	6	0.039
6	33.4	0.003	7	0.022
7	12.4	0.67	8	0.008
8	4.6	0.63	9	0.004
9	0.36	0.65	10	0.0003

dependent variable in an Engle–Granger regression. However, there are good reasons for choosing Engle–Granger as the preferred methodology for many financial applications of cointegration:

➤ It is very straightforward to implement and to interpret (in fact it can be done in a simple spreadsheet).
➤ From a risk management point of view the Engle–Granger criterion of minimum variance is usually more important than the Johansen criterion of maximum stationarity.
➤ There is often a natural choice of dependent variable in the cointegrating regressions, for example, in equity index tracking (§12.5).
➤ The Engle–Granger small-sample bias may not be a problem since sample sizes are generally quite large in financial analysis and the cointegration vector is super-consistent.[6]

The Johansen procedure is more informative than the Engle–Granger procedure because it finds all possible cointegrating relationships. However, there are good reasons for choosing Engle–Granger as the preferred methodology for many financial applications of cointegration

Both the Johansen and the Engle–Granger tests have been applied in extensive empirical work on cointegration in financial markets. There are many other cointegration tests: for example, Phillips and Ouliaris (1990) propose a two-step cointegration test based on the residuals from a cointegrating regression, and a test described by Engle and Yoo (1987) is based on the significance of the disequilibrium terms in the ECM.

12.3 Error Correction and Causality

The mechanism which ties cointegrated series together is a 'causality', not in the sense that if we make a structural change to one series the other will change

---

[6]In §A.1.3 a consistent estimator is defined as one whose distribution converges to the true value of the parameter as the sample size increases to infinity. A 'super-consistent' estimator is a consistent estimator with a very fast convergence.

too, but in the sense that turning points in one series precede turning points in the other. This is the concept of 'Granger causality' that was introduced in §11.4.3. It was introduced without reference to cointegration because cointegration is not necessary for causality, though it is sufficient. When time series are cointegrated there must be some Granger causal flow in the system. Cointegration is not essential for a lead–lag relationship to exist: it may be that causal flows exist between time series because they have some other common feature (§12.6).

When time series are cointegrated there must be some Granger causal flow in the system

The *Granger representation theorem* states that a vector autoregressive model on differences of $I(1)$ variables will be misspecified if the variables are cointegrated (Engle and Granger, 1987). Engle and Granger showed that an equilibrium specification is missing from a VAR representation (11.29) but when lagged disequilibrium terms are included as explanatory variables the model becomes well specified. Such a model is called an *error correction model* because it has a self-regulating mechanism whereby deviations from the long-run equilibria are automatically corrected.

The ECM is a dynamic model of correlation in returns, and the t-statistics on its estimated coefficients provide much insight into the lead–lag behaviour between returns

The ECM is a dynamic model for first differences of the $I(1)$ variables that were used in the cointegrating regression. Thus if log prices are cointegrated and the cointegration vector is based on these, the ECM is a dynamic model of correlation in returns, and the t-statistics on its estimated coefficients provide much insight into the lead–lag behaviour between returns. Note that the ECM is a short-run analysis of dynamic correlations, quite distinct from the first stage of finding cointegrating relationships in a long-run equilibrium analysis. The connection between the two stages is that the disequilibrium term z that is used in the ECM will be identified during the first stage.

The reason for the name 'error correction' is that the model is structured so that short-run deviations from the long-run equilibrium will be corrected. This is simple to illustrate in the case of two cointegrated log price series x and y. The ECM takes the form

$$
\begin{aligned}
\Delta x_t &= \alpha_1 + \sum_{i=1}^{m_1} \beta_{1i} \Delta x_{t-i} + \sum_{i=1}^{m_2} \beta_{2i} \Delta y_{t-i} + \gamma_1 z_{t-1} + \varepsilon_{1t}, \\
\Delta y_t &= \alpha_2 + \sum_{i=1}^{m_3} \beta_{3i} \Delta x_{t-i} + \sum_{i=1}^{m_4} \beta_{4i} \Delta y_{t-i} + \gamma_2 z_{t-1} + \varepsilon_{2t},
\end{aligned}
\tag{12.5}
$$

where Δ denotes the first difference operator, $z = x - \alpha y$ is the disequilibrium term and the lag lengths and coefficients are determined by testing down OLS regressions (§11.3.3).

Suppose $\alpha > 0$. The model (12.5) will only be an ECM if $\gamma_1 < 0$ and $\gamma_2 > 0$; only in that case will the last term in each equation constrain deviations from the long-run equilibrium so that errors will be corrected. To see this, suppose z is large and positive: then x will decrease because $\gamma_1 < 0$ and y will increase because $\gamma_2 > 0$;

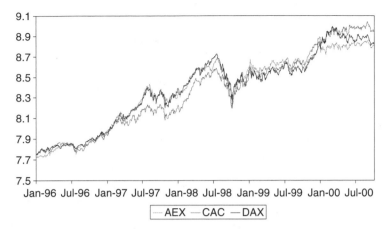

Figure 12.3 Are European equity indices cointegrated?

both have the effect of reducing z, and in this way errors are corrected. Similarly if $\alpha < 0$, for an ECM we must have $\gamma_1 < 0$ and $\gamma_2 < 0$; only then will equilibrium be maintained by the presence of the disequilibrium term.

The magnitude of the coefficients γ_1 and γ_2 determines the speed of adjustment back to the long-run equilibrium following a market shock. When these coefficients are large, adjustment is quick so z will be highly stationary and reversion to the long-run equilibrium $E(z) = E(x) - \alpha E(y)$ will be rapid. In fact a test for cointegration proposed by Engle and Yoo (1987) is based on the significance of these speed-of-adjustment coefficients.

The magnitude of the coefficients γ_1 and γ_2 determines the speed of adjustment back to the long-run equilibrium following a market shock

When x and y are cointegrated log asset prices the ECM will capture dynamic correlations and causalities between their returns. If the coefficients on the lagged y returns in the x equation are found to be significant then turning points in y will lead turning points in x. That is, y Granger causes x (§11.4.3). There must be causalities when a spread is mean-reverting and two asset prices are moving in line, but the direction of causality may change over time.

For an empirical example of cointegration and error correction modelling, consider the European equity indices shown in Figure 12.3. They are plotted as logarithms and transformed to take the same values at the beginning of 1996. The figure indicates that there is likely to be cointegration between these indices, and this is verified by the Johansen test results based on a VAR(1) model that are reported in Table 12.7.

There is clear indication of a cointegration vector (in fact it is significant at the 0.1% level) which is estimated by the Johansen procedure as

$$z = \ln(\text{AEX}) - 0.193 \ln(\text{CAC}) - 0.546 \ln(\text{DAX}).$$

Table 12.7a: Johansen tests on the AEX, CAC and DAX

R	$H_0: r \leqslant R$ vs $H_1: r > R$	
	Trace	*Prob*
0	35.88	0.0016
1	9.25	0.153
2	3.43	0.666

Table 12.7b: Error correction model for AEX, CAC and DAX

	To AEX		To CAC		To DAX	
	Coefficient	*t-statistic*	*Coefficient*	*t-statistic*	*Coefficient*	*t-statistic*
C	−4.33E-04	−0.88695	9.86E-04	2.04443	7.39E-04	1.40834
RAEX(−1)	0.055848	1.97003	−8.61E-03	−0.30703	−6.42E-03	−0.21034
RCAC(−1)	−0.0674	−1.88246	−0.09058	−2.55783	0.139623	3.62226
RDAX(−1)	**0.19267**	**5.75736**	**0.22842**	**6.90079**	−0.04725	−1.31139
Z(−1)	−0.01525	−3.80111	1.48E-03	0.373361	−7.40E-04	−0.17139

The corresponding ECM is shown in Table 12.7b. There are three columns of coefficients and *t*-statistics, corresponding to the dependent variable in the regression being the return to the AEX, CAC and DAX, respectively. The first column shows that the explanatory variables in each model are the lagged returns and the lagged cointegration vector z, given above.

The results indicate a strong positive causality from the DAX to the other two markets, and these effects have been highlighted by bold type in the table. The CAC and the AEX tend to follow the DAX, so that if today there is a large negative return on the DAX this will tend to depress the returns on the other two markets tomorrow. Similarly, if the DAX jumps up today, the other two markets are likely to see bigger returns tomorrow.

For another example of error correction modelling, return to the WTI spot and futures prices example. In §11.2.1 it was shown that they are very highly cointegrated over the period with cointegration vector approximately $(1, -1)$. That is, the basis $z = \ln F - \ln S$ defines the long-run stationary equilibrium and so, by the Granger representation theorem, the lagged basis needs to be added to VAR models on returns such as the VAR(2) model reported in Table 11.4.

Adding the basis has the effect of reducing the significance of the second-order lags in the VAR(2) model. So ECMs of the form (12.5) with only one lagged daily return to spot, and one lagged daily return to futures and one lag of the

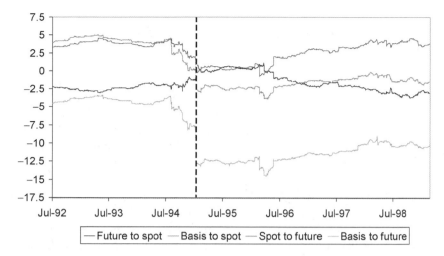

Figure 12.4 Granger causal flows between spot and future prices and the basis.

basis are used to investigate the Granger causal flows between spot and futures. During the long data period from 1 July 1988 to 26 February 1999, the bivariate ECM

$$r_{s,t} = \alpha_0 + \alpha_1 r_{s,t-1} + \alpha_2 r_{f,t-1} + \gamma_1 z_{t-1} + \varepsilon_{1,t},$$
$$r_{f,t} = \beta_0 + \beta_1 r_{s,t-1} + \beta_2 r_{f,t-1} + \gamma_2 z_{t-1} + \varepsilon_{2,t}$$

is estimated using OLS with 4 years of data. The 4-year data window is rolled over daily, and each time the model is estimated simple t-tests on the significance of the coefficients show how the lead–lag relationship between spot and futures prices evolves over time. Figure 12.4 shows these t-statistics on α_2 (future to spot), γ_1 (basis to spot), β_1 (spot to future) and γ_2 (basis to future).

Note that after the structural break on 17 January 1995, when the dramatic fall in prices on 17 January 1991 drops out of the data, part of the error correction mechanism broke down. Since $z = \ln F - \ln S$ the coefficient γ_1 should be positive for error correction, but it becomes negative after the structural break. However, the t-statistics on γ_2 are very large indeed, and negative as they should be, so the error correction mechanism is currently working through changes in futures prices.

Figure 12.4 gives a very clear message that it is futures and not spot oil prices that are being driven: there are very significant causalities from spot oil prices, and from the basis, into futures prices of crude oil on the next day. It is not surprising that futures are not good forecasts of spot prices in the crude oil market. In fact in any energy market, demand fluctuations produce an immediate response in spot prices because of the inelastic supply curve. The subsequent effect on inventory levels changes the convenience yield, but it may

There are very significant causalities from spot oil prices, and from the basis, into futures prices of crude oil on the next day

take time for futures prices to respond.[7] However, spot prices are difficult to predict, which is to be expected since demand fluctuations are governed by so many unpredictable quantities.

The generalization of an ECM to more than two variables is straightforward. The ECM has one equation for each variable in the system, where the dependent variable is the first difference, and each equation has the same explanatory variables: lagged first difference terms up to some order p, and up to r lagged 'disequilibrium terms' corresponding to the r cointegration vectors. The full specification of an ECM in vector form is therefore

$$\Delta \mathbf{y}_t = \boldsymbol{\alpha}_0 + \mathbf{B}_1 \Delta \mathbf{y}_{t-1} + \mathbf{B}_2 \Delta \mathbf{y}_{t-2} + \; \ldots \; + \mathbf{B}_p \Delta \mathbf{y}_{t-p} + \Pi \mathbf{y}_{t-1} + \boldsymbol{\varepsilon}_t. \qquad (12.6)$$

Each of the n equations in (12.6) has as regressors a constant, the lagged first differences of all variables in $\mathbf{y}$ up to order p, and all lagged disequilibrium terms because of the term $\Pi \mathbf{y}_{t-1}$. For large p this is a huge number of potential regressors, and it is unlikely that they would all be significant in every equation. OLS estimation of each equation separately will indicate which variables should be included in each equation, and when (12.6) has been specified effectively it may then be used to model the lead–lag behaviour between returns in the whole system. More details of short-run dynamics in cointegrated systems may be found in Proietti (1997) and in many of the texts already cited in this part of the book.

12.4   Cointegration in Financial Markets

It is only recently that market practitioners have found important applications of the vast body of academic research into cointegration in financial markets that goes back over a decade. In this respect financial analysts have been characteristically slow in adopting a new modelling approach. Only during the last few years have there been interesting practical developments. Asset management companies have been investing in quantitative research projects to base buy-and-hold and long–short strategies on cointegration. Commodity analysts model the lead–lag relationship between spot and futures returns using ECMs. The pricing and hedging of spread options can now be based on cointegration This section reviews some of the publications that are relevant for the implementation of cointegration modelling of financial markets.

12.4.1   Foreign Exchange

Any system of financial asset prices with a mean-reverting spread will have some degree of cointegration, even though the Granger causalities inherent in

---

[7]The closing time of the spot market is only half an hour later than the futures. It is unlikely that this time differential is the only reason for there to be such a strong causality from today's spot close to tomorrow's futures close.

such a system contradict the efficiency of financial markets (Dwyer and Wallace, 1992). Two log exchange rates are unlikely to be cointegrated since their difference is the cross rate and if markets are efficient that rate will be non-stationary. There is, however, some empirical evidence of cointegration between three or more exchange rates: see Goodhart (1988), Hakkio and Rush (1989), Baillie and Bollerslev (1989a, 1994), Coleman (1990), Alexander and Johnson (1992, 1994), Chen (1993), MacDonald and Taylor (1994) and Nieuwland *et al.* (1994).

Two log exchange rates are unlikely to be cointegrated since their difference is the cross rate and if markets are efficient that rate will be non-stationary

12.4.2   Spot and Futures

Many financial journals (the *Journal of Futures Markets* in particular) contain papers on cointegration between spot and futures prices. Since spot and futures are tied together, the basis is the mean-reverting cointegration vector. The ECM has become the focus of research into the price discovery relationship, which has been found to change considerably over time. See MacDonald and Taylor (1988), Nugent (1990), Bessler and Covey (1991), Bopp and Sitzer (1991), Chowdhury (1991), Lai and Lai (1991), Khoury and Yourougou (1991), Schroeder and Goodwin (1991), Schwartz and Laatsch (1991), Beck (1994), Lee (1994), Schwartz and Szakmary (1994), Brenner and Kroner (1995), Harris *et al.* (1995) and Alexander (1999b). This research shows that there is considerable scope for futures traders to develop ECMs that will exploit this very strong cointegration relationship.

12.4.3   Commodities

Commodity products that are based on the same underlying, such as soya bean crush and soya bean oil, should be cointegrated if carry costs are mean-reverting. However, the evidence for this seems rather weak, and the academic argument that related commodities such as different types of metals should be cointegrated is even more difficult to justify empirically. Brenner and Kroner (1995) present a useful survey of the literature in this area and conclude that the idiosyncratic behaviour of carry costs makes it very difficult to use ECMs in commodity markets. High-frequency technical traders dominate these markets, and it is unlikely that cointegration between related commodity markets is robust enough for trading.

12.4.4   Spread Options

Modelling cointegrated assets with Brownian diffusion processes is one of the many interesting problems presented at the Finance Seminars in the Newton Institute at Cambridge University during the summer of 1996. Jin-Chuan Duan and Stan Pliska took up this challenge and have recently produced an excellent study of the theory of option valuation with cointegrated asset prices (Duan and Pliska, 1998). Their discrete time model for valuing spread options has the continuous limit of a system driven by four correlated Brownian motions, one for each asset (in which the ECM is incorporated) and one for each stochastic volatility. The stochastic processes for the asset returns have an additional disequilibrium term to ensure that deviations from equilibrium are corrected, so stationary spreads are imposed. These processes are the continuous time equivalent of an ECM. Their Monte Carlo results show that cointegration can have a substantial influence on spread option prices when volatilities are stochastic. But when volatilities are constant the model simplifies to one of simple bivariate Brownian motion and the standard Black–Scholes results are recovered.

Cointegration can have a substantial influence on spread option prices when volatilities are stochastic

12.4.5 Term Structures

No financial systems have higher cointegration than term structures. In §12.2 some term structures of interest rates and futures prices were used to illustrate how cointegration should be analysed in a multivariate system. These methods lend themselves to any term structures of integrated variables, and there is a large academic literature in this area. Cointegration and correlation go together in the yield curve, and we often find strongest cointegration at the short end where correlations are highest. See Bradley and Lumpkin (1992), Hall *et al.* (1992), Alexander and Johnson (1992, 1994), Davidson *et al.* (1994), De Gennaro *et al.* (1994), Lee (1994), Boothe and Tse (1995) and Brenner *et al.* (1996).

12.4.6 Market Integration

Market indices in different countries should be cointegrated if purchasing power parity holds. There is some evidence of cointegration in international bond markets and in international equity markets, but arbitrage possibilities seem quite limited (Karfakis and Moschos, 1990; Kasa, 1992; Smith *et al.*, 1993; Corhay *et al.*, 1993; Clare *et al.*, 1995). However, in recent years the US market does appear to be somewhat of a leader in international equity and bond markets (Alexander, 1994; Masih, 1997). More cointegration has been found between international equity markets than between international bond markets, in fact in some studies international bond markets have shown no evidence of cointegration: see Andrade *et al.* (1991).

In equity markets, the analysis in §12.3 shows that the Dutch, German and French equity indices have been highly cointegrated since 1996, with most of the causality on a daily basis coming from the German market. Some time ago Taylor and Tonks (1989) used the Engle–Granger method to demonstrate a high level of cointegration between UK, Dutch, German and Japanese stock markets between 1979 and 1986, with Granger causality running from the UK to these other markets, but not vice versa. But during a similar period Andrade *et al.* (1991) found no evidence of cointegration between equities in the UK, US, Germany and Japan based on the Johansen method. However, both these papers use common currency indices, which were greatly influenced by movements in exchange rates. Cointegration between equity markets should be examined using local currency indices. Alexander and Thillainathan (1995) examine Asian-Pacific equity markets and find evidence of cointegration, but only when indices are expressed in local currency terms. GARCH volatility models of the dollar exchange rates show that FX volatility is extremely variable in the Asian-Pacific region, and would swamp any equity effects if index prices were converted to dollar amounts.

Cointegration between equity markets should be examined using local currency indices

Since an equity index is by definition a weighted sum of the constituents there should be some sufficiently large basket that is cointegrated with the index, assuming the index weights do not change too much over time (Cerchi and Havenner, 1988; Pindyck and Rothenberg, 1993). This is, in fact, the theoretical basis for cointegration index tracking models (§12.5). The sector indices within a given country should also be cointegrated when industrial sectors maintain relatively stable proportions in the economy. By the same token, a basket of equity indices in the Morgan Stanley Capital International (MSCI) world index, or the Morgan Stanley European, Asian and Far Eastern (EAFE) index, should be cointegrated with the aggregate index.

12.5 Applications of Cointegration to Investment Analysis

The cointegration methodology is a powerful tool for long-term investment analysis. If the allocations in a portfolio are designed so that the portfolio tracks an index, then the portfolio should be cointegrated with the index. The portfolio and the index can deviate in the short term, but in the long term they should be tied together. A number of asset management firms are now basing allocations on cointegration analysis.

This section describes the cointegration-based hedge fund management technology that has been developed by myself, Dr Ian Giblin and Wayne Weddington III at Pennoyer Capital Management, New York. The results presented here represent several years of model development and validation before the fund started trading in May 2000. Since then the long–short S&P 100 equity fund has returned 17.07% between May and December 2000 and between January and March 2001 (the time of writing) it returned −0.54%. This should be compared with the returns of −12.05% and −25.94% on the S&P100 during the same two periods. More details of the fund are available from www.pennoyer.net.

If the allocations in a portfolio are designed so that the portfolio tracks an index, then the portfolio should be cointegrated with the index

We have already seen that when portfolios are constructed on the basis of returns analysis, frequent rebalancing will be necessary to keep the portfolio in line with the index (§7.2.5). The power of cointegration analysis is that optimal portfolios may be constructed on the basis of common long-run trends between asset prices, and they will not require so much rebalancing. Commonly it is possible to find cointegrating baskets with relatively few stocks.

12.5.1   Selection and Allocation

*When portfolios are
based on mean–variance
analysis there is nothing
to ensure that tracking
errors are mean-
reverting*

The basic problem is still one of stock selection and asset allocation, and as such bears much relation to the mean–variance analysis described in Chapter 7. But rather than seek portfolio weights to minimize the variance of the portfolio for a given level of return, the criteria that are used in cointegration analysis are to maximize the stationarity (and minimize the variance) of the tracking error. This criterion contrasts with the efficient frontier criterion: in the Markovitz framework portfolios are based on mean–variance analysis and there is nothing to ensure that tracking errors are mean-reverting. Although the portfolios will be efficient, the tracking errors may be random walks, so the replicating portfolio could drift arbitrarily far from the benchmark unless it is frequently rebalanced.

*Any investment strategy
that guarantees
stationary tracking
errors must be based on
cointegration*

Using cointegration it is possible to devise allocations that have mean-reverting tracking errors. Indeed, any investment strategy that guarantees stationary tracking errors must be based on cointegration. When tracking errors are stationary the portfolio will be tied to the index: it cannot drift too far from the index because the tracking error is mean-reverting.

Benchmarking or index tracking models that are based on cointegration normally employ a linear regression of log prices. The dependent variable is the log index price or some other benchmark, such as LIBOR, that is used to evaluate the performance of the portfolio. In the case of tracking an index 'plus' alpha per cent per annum, the dependent variable will be the log of the index plus a small increment that amounts to $\alpha\%$ over the year. The explanatory variables are the log prices of the assets in the tracking portfolio, and the residuals are the tracking errors.

There are two parts to the problem: first select the assets, and then optimize the portfolio weights. The asset selection process is perhaps the hardest but most important part, and can be approached in a number of ways. Selection methods include a 'brute force' approach (such as when the number of assets is fixed and then linear models are fitted for all possible portfolios with this number of assets), methods that are tailored to investors' preferences over various types of stocks, and proprietary technical analysis.

The optimal allocation process uses least squares regression analysis: allocations are made according to a cointegrating regression to ensure that the fitted portfolio will be cointegrated with the benchmark and the tracking error will be stationary. Suppose a benchmark with log price index y is to be tracked with a number of assets with log prices $x_1, \ldots, x_n$. The Engle–Granger cointegration method is to regress y on a constant and $x_1, \ldots, x_n$, and then to test the residuals for stationarity. The coefficients $\alpha_1, \ldots, \alpha_n$ in the Engle–Granger regression

$$y_t = \alpha_0 + \alpha_1 x_1 + \ldots + \alpha_n x_n + \varepsilon_t \qquad (12.7)$$

are normalized to sum to 1, thereby giving the portfolio weights. So the problem of finding the optimal replicating portfolio can be solved by finding the best assets with log prices $x_1, \ldots, x_n$ to use in the cointegrating regression, and then defining allocations to give the maximum stationarity in the tracking error ε. The more stationary the tracking error, the greater the cointegration between the benchmark and the candidate portfolio.

In practice a high degree of cointegration may be found between the benchmark and the tracking portfolio; the standard ADF unit root test that was described in §11.1.5 should be sufficient to compare different portfolio specifications. When there are a large number of potential assets that could be used in a replicating portfolio it is not at all a trivial problem to test all possible portfolios to find the one that has the most stationary tracking error. If there are N assets in total one has to test $N!/n!(N-n)!$ portfolios for every $n \leqslant N$.

Note that in global asset management models where the benchmark may be a global index such as the Morgan Stanley World Index there will be two stages to the selection–allocation process. First select the country indices to track the global index and assign optimal country allocations, and then either buy/sell the country index futures (if available) or repeat the process for tracking the individual country indices with individual stocks. A single country model could also be approached in two stages: first select the industrial sectors (or style indices) and assign index weights optimally, then select the stocks within each industry sector (or style index) and optimize portfolios to track the indices.

12.5.2 Constrained Allocations

Examples of constrained allocations include the following:

➤ A fund manager may wish to go long–short in exactly 12 different countries, with the world index as benchmark. The problem then becomes one of selecting the basket of 12 countries that are currently most highly cointegrated with the world index.

➤ A small asset management company might seek a benchmark return of 5% per annum above the S&P 100 index, so in this case the benchmark index will be the S&P 100 'plus'.

➤ Assets may be selected according to quite specific preferences of investors. For example, 50% of the fund may have to be allocated to the UK, or no more than 5% of capital can be allocated to any single asset.

Equality constraints on allocations, such as 40% in technology related stocks, are simple to implement. The dependent variable just becomes $y - \omega_j x_j$, where a fraction ω_j of the fund must be assigned to the jth asset, and the other log asset prices are used as unconstrained regressors. Inequality constraints are more difficult to implement. How should one deal with the constraint of no short sales, $\omega_j > 0$ for all j? First perform an unconstrained estimation of the model by OLS, because if no constraint is violated there will be no problem.

Equality constraints on allocations, such as 40% in technology related stocks, are simple to implement

But suppose the constraints $\omega_j > 0$ for some j are violated. Then the model is restricted so that all these ω_j are set to zero, and re-estimated to ensure that no other coefficients that were originally positive have now become negative. If that is the case the resulting constrained OLS estimator is obtained, but it will of course be biased. That it is more efficient than the original estimator, because it reflects the value of further information, may be little compensation.

Problems arise when imposing the constraints causes more constraints to be violated, so that other coefficients that were positive in the unconstrained model become negative in the constrained model. The only feasible solution is to set those coefficients to zero, to re-estimate a further constrained model, and to keep shooting coefficients to zero until a purely long portfolio of assets is obtained. If many constraints have to be imposed it is not clear that any cointegrating portfolio will be found for the benchmark. However, when the benchmark is an index there are theoretical reasons for the existence of long-only cointegrating portfolios (§12.4.6) unless the index composition suddenly changes.

12.5.3   Parameter Selection

The basic cointegration index tracking model is defined in terms of certain parameters:

➢ any 'alpha' return over and above the index;
➢ the time-span of daily data that is used in the cointegrating regression (12.7) — this is called the *training period*;
➢ the number of assets in the portfolio;[8]
➢ any constraints on allocations, which will depend on the preferences of the investor.

The optimal parameter values are chosen by recording a number of in-sample and post-sample performance measures for each set of parameters. The optimal parameter set is that which gives the 'best' performance measures. The most important in-sample performance measures are the following:

➢ *ADF statistic*: This is used to test the level of cointegration between the portfolio and the benchmark during the training period: the larger and more negative the ADF statistic, the greater the level of cointegration. The 1% critical value of the ADF statistic is approximately -3.5, although much greater values than this are normally experienced in practice as, for example, in Table 12.10 and Figures 12.6d, 12.7c and 12.7d.
➢ *Standard error of the regression*: The in-sample tracking error will be stationary if the portfolio is cointegrated with the benchmark. This does not imply that the short-term deviations between the portfolio and the

---

[8] In fact the number of non-zero allocations need not be specified. Instead the number of assets chosen can depend on a bound that is set for the tracking error variance.

benchmark are necessarily small. It is also important to choose a portfolio for which the in-sample tracking error has a low volatility, and this is measured by the standard error of the regression.

➤ *Turnover*: Only those portfolios showing realistic turnover projections as the model is rolled over the backtest period should be considered.[9]

Having specified the selections and the allocations on the in-sample training period, a fixed period of data immediately following the in-sample data is used to analyse the out-of-sample performance of the portfolio (§A.5.2). This is called the *testing period*. If the strategy requires monthly rebalancing then it is normal to use a testing period of 1 or 2 months for the post-sample diagnostics. Some typical post-sample diagnostics are as follows:

➤ *Tracking error variance*: This is the variance of the daily tracking errors during the testing period. In fact the tracking error variance, if measured as an equally weighted average, is equivalent to the root mean square forecast error.
➤ *Differential return*: The difference between the portfolio return and the index return.
➤ *Information ratio*: The ratio between the mean daily tracking error and the standard deviation of the daily tracking error over the testing period. In-sample information ratios are zero by design (because the residuals from OLS regression have zero mean) but a positive post-sample information ratio is an important risk-adjusted performance measure.

Consider first a simple example of how to decide which parameters are optimal: for the problem of tracking the EAFE index with a one-year buy-and-hold strategy. The alpha over the EAFE index is fixed at 3% per annum and there are no constraints on allocations. There are only two model parameters to be chosen, the number of country indices in the portfolio (at the time of optimization the maximum number was 23) and the training period for the model. Figure 12.5 shows the 12-month out-of-sample information ratios that are obtained as the number of assets selected varies from 5 to 15 and the length of training period varies from 10 to 130 months. From the figure it seems that the highest post-sample information ratio of 3.8 occurs when the training period is between 100 and 115 months and the number of assets is between 7 and 11.

Instead of fixing the alpha over an index — or indeed under an index — it may be preferable to fix the number of assets in the portfolio. In that case this type of two-dimensional 'heat map' can be used to determine the optimal choice of the alpha over the index and the length of training period. For example, suppose a portfolio of exactly 75 stocks is to be used to track the S&P 100 index plus α% per annum. A heat map is generated by finding the 75-asset

---

[9] In contrast to mean–variance analysis, there should not be a problem with the instability of allocations because cointegration methods are based on common long-run trends.

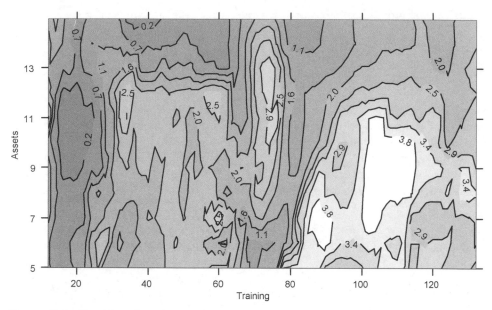

Figure 12.5 Tracking the EAFE index with a one-year buy-and-hold strategy, with fixed $\alpha = 3\%$ per annum: 12-month out-of-sample information ratio as a function of the number of assets and length of training period.

portfolio that is most highly cointegrated with the index plus $\alpha\%$ per annum for each choice of α and training period. Each time the α and the training period are changed the choice of assets and the allocations in the portfolio will change. But these allocations are not recorded at this stage. All that will be computed are some of the in-sample and out-of-sample diagnostics that have been described above.

Figure 12.6a shows the 2-month post-sample information ratios, and Figure 12.6b shows the 2-month post-sample differential returns over the index for a 75-stock portfolio in the S&P 100 index that is being optimized at the end of February 2000. Figure 12.6c is similar to Figure 12.6a, but for the 1-month information ratio, and Figure 12.6d shows the 1-month differential return. The maps are shaded so that dark areas indicate better diagnostic test results (much nicer colour plots are on the CD).

These heat maps show a clear 'hot spot' when α is negative but no more than about -7% per annum, and the training period is between 28 and 48 months. Another region that gives promising out-of-sample diagnostics is for a high, positive α and a very long training period. However, the highest differential return and information ratio are obtained within the 'hot spot' when the alpha is approximately -5% and the training period is about 3 years.

12.5.4 Long–Short Strategies

The heat maps in Figure 12.6 also have a 'cold spot', that is, a region where the parameter choices give rise to rather bad performance measures. In particular, when α is -12% and the training period is 72 months, the 1-month and 2-month out-of-sample information ratios are negative, as are the differential returns. For these parameter choices, the portfolio is (always) chosen to have the highest possible in-sample cointegration with the benchmark, but since alpha is negative it is consistently underperforming the actual index in the post-sample predictive tests. Therefore it should be possible to make money by going short this portfolio.

Note that this 'short' portfolio will itself contain long and short positions, unless the constraint of no short sales has been applied. Similarly, the 'long' portfolio, the one that has the highest information ratios and differential return, will typically also consist of long and short positions. Then a hedged portfolio is obtained by matching the amount invested in the long portfolio with the same amount being shorted with the short portfolio.

The portfolio is (always) chosen to have the highest possible in-sample cointegration and it is consistently underperforming the index in the post-sample predictive tests. Therefore it should be possible to make money by going short this portfolio

Note also that it is not, in fact, necessary for the long portfolio to outperform the index and the short portfolio to underperform the index in the post-sample predictive tests. However, it is necessary for the long portfolio to outperform the short portfolio. If this type of long–short strategy were used with a 75 asset portfolio from the S&P 100 then the heat maps in Figure 12.6 indicate that optimal parameter choices for February 2000 would be as shown in Table 12.8a. The optimal parameter choices will be different every month. For example from Figure 12.7 the optimal parameter choices for October 2000 would be as shown in Table 12.8b.

Table 12.9 shows the parameter choices that were actually used for the 75-asset long portfolio and a 75-asset short portfolio in the S&P 100 index.[10] Of course, some of the same assets will be chosen in both portfolios, and the net position in these assets will be determined by the difference between their weight (positive or negative) in the long portfolio and their weight (positive or negative) in the short portfolio.

12.5.5 Backtesting

This section describes two types of model backtests. The first type of backtest is to see how a fixed parameter set, which currently seems optimal according to 'heat maps' of the type just described, actually performs over a historic period. A simple snapshot of portfolio performance at one instance in time, as in Figures 12.6 and 12.7, may not provide sufficient evidence that parameter

---

[10]More information is available from www.pennoyer.net.

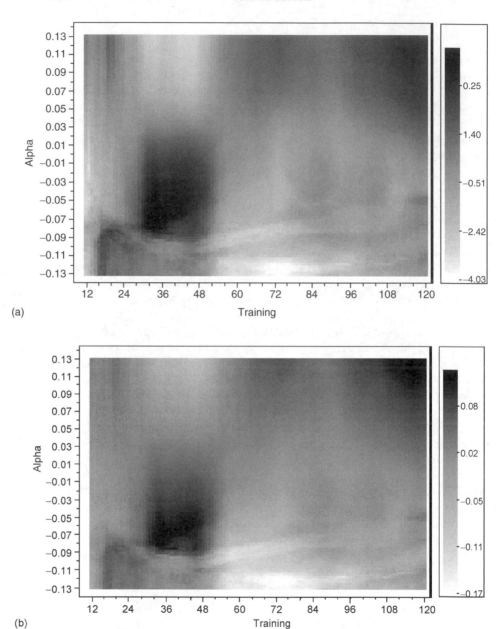

(a)

(b)

choices are optimal. Therefore, performance measures are obtained by running the model over time, for example month by month. Each month a new set of assets will be chosen and new allocations will be made, but the set of parameters remains fixed.

Table 12.10 reports the in-sample ADF, the turnover percentage, and the 1-, 2- and 3-month out-of-sample information ratios for the long and the short

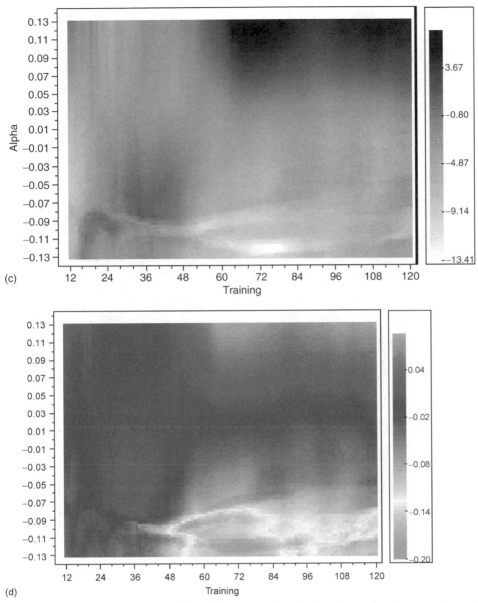

Figure 12.6 Optimizing a 75-stock portfolio in the S&P 100 index, end of February 2000: (a) heat map of the 2-month information ratio; (b) heat map of the 2-month differential return; (c) heat map of the 1-month information ratio; (d) heat map of the 1-month differential return.

Table 12.8a: Long and short portfolio parameter choices, February 2000

	Alpha	Training months
Long	−7%	36
Short	−12%	72

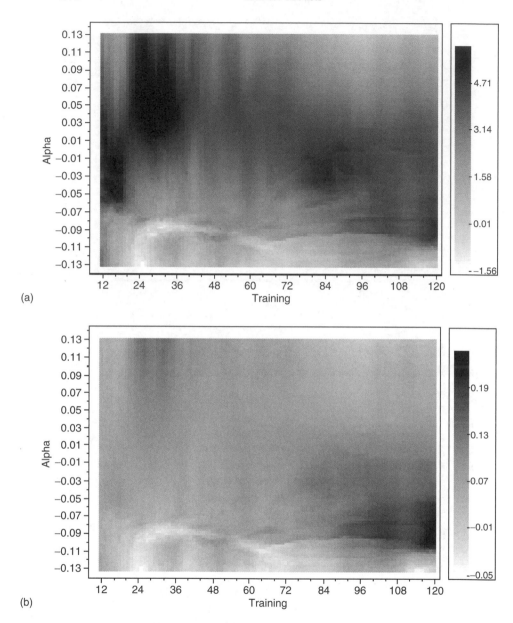

(a)

(b)

portfolios for October 2000 with the parameters given in Table 12.8b. The last line of this table corresponds to the 'snapshots' taken in October 2000 that were analysed in Figure 12.7 to obtain the parameter choices given in Table 12.8b. The rest of the table indicates how these parameter choices would have performed since January 1995. For example, the first line of the table shows that taking the portfolio parameter alpha as 5% (long) and −8% (short) and training 30 months would not have been a good choice at all in January 1995.

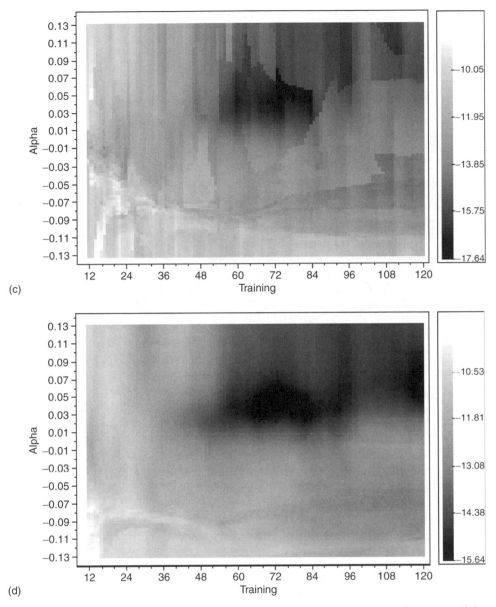

Figure 12.7 Optimizing the stock portfolio of Figure 12.6, October 2000: (a) heat map of the 2-month information ratio; (b) heat map of the 2-month differential return; (c) last ADF statistic; (d) mean ADF statistic.

Table 12.8b: Long and short portfolio parameter choices, October 2000

	Alpha	Training months
Long	5%	30
Short	−8%	30

Table 12.9: Optimal parameter choices for S&P 100

	Long		Short			Long		Short	
	Alpha	Training	Alpha	Training		Alpha	Training	Alpha	Training
Jan-95	−0.1	54	−0.06	24	Jan-98	0.04	24	−0.1	78
Feb-95	−0.12	30	0.09	30	Feb-98	0.12	90	−0.1	72
Mar-95	0.08	78	−0.05	72	Mar-98	0.12	90	−0.05	30
Apr-95	0	18	−0.05	66	Apr-98	0.12	102	−0.03	12
May-95	0.1	66	−0.05	18	May-98	0.12	84	−0.1	24
Jun-95	0.1	66	−0.1	102	Jun-98	0.12	84	−0.1	24
Jul-95	0.12	30	−0.12	102	Jul-98	0.12	12	−0.1	24
Aug-95	0.12	30	−0.12	96	Aug-98	0.12	84	−0.12	102
Sep-95	0.12	42	−0.12	36	Sep-98	0.12	30	−0.12	54
Oct-95	0.1	66	−0.07	12	Oct-98	−0.11	102	−0.1	12
Nov-95	0.12	60	−0.1	102	Nov-98	0.09	12	−0.1	12
Dec-95	0.12	54	−0.11	102	Dec-98	0.05	12	−0.04	18
Jan-96	−0.12	48	−0.12	102	Jan-99	0.12	78	−0.11	78
Feb-96	0.08	78	−0.12	102	Feb-99	0.12	102	−0.12	66
Mar-96	0.12	48	−0.05	90	Mar-99	0.03	48	−0.11	54
Apr-96	0.11	60	−0.08	96	Apr-99	0.06	102	0.04	36
May-96	0.02	72	−0.1	78	May-99	0.05	102	0.11	18
Jun-96	0.11	78	−0.09	78	Jun-99	−0.03	12	−0.08	30
Jul-96	0.12	78	−0.11	102	Jul-99	0.12	30	−0.09	30
Aug-96	0.12	78	−0.12	96	Aug-99	0.12	78	−0.12	96
Sep-96	0.01	42	0	96	Sep-99	0.12	78	−0.12	84
Oct-96	0.11	84	0	96	Oct-99	0.12	36	−0.11	102
Nov-96	0.12	78	−0.12	90	Nov-99	0.12	54	−0.1	36
Dec-96	−0.12	66	0.12	66	Dec-99	0.12	54	−0.11	96
Jan-97	0.01	24	0.11	66	Jan-00	0.12	16	−0.12	88
Feb-97	0.01	102	−0.12	54	Feb-00	0.12	6	−0.11	12
Mar-97	0.01	102	−0.12	102	Mar-00	0.12	64	−0.12	92
Apr-97	0.09	66	−0.12	30	Apr-00	0.12	64	−0.1	60
May-97	0.05	72	−0.12	12	May-00	0.12	16	−0.08	40
Jun-97	0.11	90	0	102	Jun-00	0.06	12	−0.08	28
Jul-97	0.11	96	−0.1	102	Jul-00	0.12	48	−0.1	88
Aug-97	0.11	96	−0.12	102	Aug-00	0.12	120	−0.13	20
Sep-97	−0.11	102	−0.12	36	Sep-00	0.12	120	−0.12	20
Oct-97	0.12	12	−0.11	12					
Nov-97	−0.08	12	0.12	12					
Dec-97	0	18	0.12	96					

In fact with these choices the long portfolio underperformed and the short portfolio outperformed the index!

Since the parameter choice for the current month is made on the basis of last month's performance, this autocorrelation in information ratios is a crucial performance indicator

The point of this exercise is to check the robustness of the portfolio over time, as this is fundamental to cointegration. The most important property to look for is consistency between the 1-, 2- and 3-month information ratios. Table 12.10 indicates that if the 1-month information ratio is high so also, on the whole, are the 2- and 3-month information ratios. So if a portfolio starts well for the first month, it tends to perform well over several months. Similarly, if the portfolio does not perform well during the first month, this tends to continue for subsequent months. Since the parameter choice for the current month is made on the basis of last month's performance, this autocorrelation in information ratios is a crucial performance indicator. A similar robustness check that can be done from Table 12.10 is to ensure high ADFs and relatively low turnover projections when the portfolio is rebalanced using the same fixed parameters each month.

It is evident from Table 12.9 that the same parameter selection is not generally going to be optimal for two consecutive months. In fact, the real test of the model is its actual performance, using returns that are obtained when the alpha and training periods are reoptimized every month. Table 12.11a reports the consolidated returns from applying the long–short hedge strategy to the S&P 100 during three years that have been chosen as representative of difficult market conditions: 1987, 1993 and 1998.[11]

The real test of the model is the validation of its actual performance, by analysing the returns that are obtained when the alpha and training periods are reoptimized every month

As should be expected from a successful hedge fund, the long–short strategy performs relatively well during the market crashes of October 1987 and August 1998. The returns are also much less volatile than the S&P 100 index returns, and during each of these years the fund outperformed the index.

A summary of returns, including execution costs, between 1995 and 1999 is shown in Table 12.11b. In the earlier years absolute returns were lower and less volatile than in 1998 and 1999, but the average annual return for all five years was approximately 35%. The average leverage was approximately 1.5 on both the long and the short legs of the hedge.

Barra have performed an analysis of the 1999 returns, so that the hedge strategy could be described in terms to which the market is already accustomed. It shows that the strategy derives its excess returns primarily from risk assessment items such as earnings yield, earnings variation, momentum, size, and, as one would expect, some leverage. Both 'value' and 'growth' assessment are not contributing to the return, which somewhat distinguishes the strategy from the status quo.

12.6 Common Features

When time series are cointegrated they have a common stochastic trend. The many papers cited in §12.4 demonstrate that integration is a common feature that is prevalent in many financial markets. A common trend is just one of many common features that multivariate time series may possess. This section examines the evidence for and against the existence of other common features in financial markets. In particular, the possibility of common autocorrelation and common volatility in financial markets is examined.[12]

---

[11] The returns stated include transactions costs but no other fees.

[12] Thus the time series that are analysed will be returns, rather than the prices or log prices that are analysed for cointegration.

Table 12.10: Backtesting the October 2000 parameter choices

	Long					Short				
	ADF	Turnover	1mth IR	2mth IR	3mth IR	ADF	Turnover	1mth IR	2mth IR	3mth IR
Jan-95	−10.57	0.78	−4.66	−2.47	−1.29	−10.59	0.77	9.09	2.54	2.14
Feb-95	−11.12	0.33	−4.32	−4.38	−2.80	−11.47	0.58	−0.22	4.16	1.69
Mar-95	−11.11	0.42	−0.63	−2.35	−3.31	−12.61	0.71	1.86	0.67	3.47
Apr-95	−10.93	0.47	0.13	−0.25	−1.47	−12.35	0.61	−3.22	−1.04	−0.76
May-95	−10.51	0.57	−0.32	−0.10	−0.27	−12.19	0.47	1.49	−0.85	−0.13
Jun-95	−10.74	0.36	3.79	1.39	0.93	−11.95	0.38	−4.91	−2.19	−2.50
Jul-95	−11.27	0.30	5.16	4.53	2.60	−12.16	0.64	−0.40	−2.80	−1.60
Aug-95	−10.88	0.38	3.97	4.61	4.37	−12.60	0.58	−4.74	−2.22	−3.26
Sep-95	−11.54	0.56	−2.13	0.42	1.86	−12.27	0.98	0.29	−2.29	−1.50
Oct-95	−11.57	0.39	3.50	0.75	1.57	−11.97	0.49	−6.04	−2.90	−3.54
Nov-95	−11.76	0.35	2.79	3.21	1.39	−12.33	0.99	2.26	−1.50	−0.96
Dec-95	−12.08	0.25	3.81	3.10	3.26	−12.06	0.70	1.75	2.05	−0.47
Jan-96	−11.52	0.26	3.36	3.54	3.43	−12.38	0.54	−3.32	−1.84	−0.25
Feb-96	−11.25	0.44	0.78	2.01	2.41	−12.26	0.82	−1.25	−2.46	−1.67
Mar-96	−11.94	0.42	3.77	2.06	2.52	−12.64	0.37	−0.68	−0.92	−1.81
Apr-96	−12.06	0.26	−0.35	1.56	1.27	−12.41	1.19	0.24	−0.26	−0.54
May-96	−12.65	0.38	2.68	1.15	1.96	−12.05	0.51	−2.08	−0.92	−0.84
Jun-96	−12.33	0.26	3.03	2.88	1.84	−11.57	0.87	3.85	0.83	0.64
Jul-96	−12.02	0.28	0.29	1.49	1.80	−11.62	0.60	−1.80	0.11	−0.44
Aug-96	−12.97	0.39	2.87	1.37	1.89	−12.99	1.08	−1.68	−1.74	−0.44
Sep-96	−12.28	0.53	−1.63	1.03	0.69	−12.68	0.82	−0.49	−1.18	−1.44
Oct-96	−12.19	0.26	−3.27	−2.57	−0.43	−13.18	1.03	1.38	0.60	−0.24
Nov-96	−12.26	0.23	−2.67	−3.00	−2.62	−12.40	1.19	2.79	2.04	1.32
Dec-96	−12.89	0.29	2.26	0.12	−0.89	−11.94	0.57	6.42	4.79	3.58
Jan-97	−12.00	0.31	−2.57	−0.40	−0.83	−12.07	0.76	−4.45	0.49	0.69
Feb-97	−12.48	0.17	5.54	0.10	0.80	−12.25	0.69	2.82	−0.33	1.33
Mar-97	−11.85	0.33	3.99	4.61	1.34	−12.19	0.46	−4.38	−0.54	−1.65
Apr-97	−12.79	0.26	3.06	3.50	3.93	−12.22	0.37	−2.78	−3.58	−1.30
May-97	−11.54	0.46	−0.98	1.54	2.35	−13.04	0.52	0.55	−1.23	−2.27
Jun-97	−12.32	0.26	3.40	1.38	2.09	−13.16	0.83	−0.08	0.20	−0.82
Jul-97	−11.97	0.16	1.00	2.03	1.21	−12.72	0.73	−3.94	−2.14	−1.39
Aug-97	−11.97	0.64	−3.27	−0.78	0.48	−12.26	1.01	2.46	−0.90	−0.65
Sep-97	−11.36	0.47	−2.58	−2.76	−1.52	−12.12	0.66	3.12	2.82	0.34
Oct-97	−10.67	0.64	−4.70	−3.58	−3.46	−12.62	1.50	0.96	1.87	2.06
Nov-97	−11.89	0.45	2.92	−1.13	−1.68	−12.76	1.13	−0.40	0.42	1.24
Dec-97	−11.37	0.37	2.26	2.55	0.19	−12.69	1.00	1.45	0.72	0.82
Jan-98	−12.11	0.37	1.26	2.67	3.19	−13.27	0.41	−7.46	−1.17	−1.47
Feb-98	−12.55	0.34	3.03	2.01	2.75	−13.43	0.31	−2.87	−5.25	−1.59
Mar-98	−11.95	0.39	1.47	2.13	1.82	−12.95	1.08	−2.24	−2.45	−3.81
Apr-98	−11.99	0.43	8.43	4.79	4.33	−12.64	1.26	−2.26	−2.28	−2.39
May-98	−12.44	0.32	1.63	5.14	3.85	−12.48	1.12	−4.42	−3.24	−2.88
Jun-98	−11.98	0.56	2.47	2.11	4.19	−12.08	1.08	−5.76	−5.21	−4.23
Jul-98	−11.88	0.28	3.63	3.01	2.60	−11.83	1.72	−4.47	−5.11	−4.91
Aug-98	−10.76	0.65	−4.43	−1.59	−0.47	−11.43	1.61	5.82	1.82	0.08
Sep-98	−10.45	0.42	−2.89	−3.77	−2.00	−11.39	0.93	1.31	3.82	1.67
Oct-98	−11.85	0.28	6.13	2.00	−0.42	−12.27	1.10	−3.34	−1.24	1.35
Nov-98	−11.44	0.40	−2.66	3.14	1.07	−11.96	0.71	2.33	−1.22	−0.37
Dec-98	−11.75	0.25	3.81	1.16	3.34	−11.71	0.70	−4.85	−1.31	−2.19

Continued

Table 12.10: *Continued*

	Long					Short				
	ADF	Turnover	1mth IR	2mth IR	3mth IR	ADF	Turnover	1mth IR	2mth IR	3mth IR
Jan-99	−12.48	0.47	−3.93	−1.05	−1.88	−11.06	0.66	0.81	−2.63	−1.96
Feb-99	−12.37	0.32	2.10	−1.16	−0.07	−10.90	0.97	2.54	1.60	−1.02
Mar-99	−11.78	0.43	−3.73	−0.90	−2.00	−11.53	1.46	2.80	2.68	1.96
Apr-99	−11.78	0.41	1.82	−0.70	0.14	−11.51	1.26	1.71	1.99	2.14
May-99	−11.96	0.30	2.61	2.20	0.33	−11.48	0.51	−2.80	0.30	0.92
Jun-99	−12.27	0.49	3.28	2.98	2.55	−11.51	0.88	−5.27	−4.17	−1.14
Jul-99	−11.92	0.46	−0.64	1.36	1.80	−10.98	1.27	2.71	−2.03	−2.30
Aug-99	−12.59	0.27	3.16	1.35	2.00	−11.54	0.90	−2.05	−0.23	−2.05
Sep-99	−12.30	0.17	7.87	4.97	2.97	−11.44	0.72	−7.83	−4.16	−2.24
Oct-99	−11.48	0.43	−1.66	1.52	2.07	−12.27	1.20	−3.30	−4.86	−3.83
Nov-99	−12.01	0.45	−0.35	−1.08	0.91	−12.08	0.71	−0.10	−1.93	−3.37
Dec-99	−11.49	0.54	1.15	0.63	−0.02	−12.07	0.97	−9.05	−5.21	−4.60
Jan-00	−12.03	0.35	2.65	0.95	1.07	−11.82	1.04	4.99	−0.32	−0.83
Feb-00	−12.15	0.42	−5.15	−1.31	−1.15	−11.31	0.89	−2.00	1.88	−0.82
Mar-00	−13.12	0.50	−1.55	−3.04	−1.41	−11.48	0.95	1.40	0.13	1.69
Apr-00	−13.33	0.32	2.57	0.63	−0.79	−10.94	1.39	2.67	2.01	1.02
May-00	−12.65	0.27	1.77	2.18	0.88	−11.01	1.06	3.37	3.04	2.45
Jun-00	−12.07	0.44	−0.52	0.60	1.42	−11.68	1.45	−5.59	−0.97	0.25
Jul-00	−12.48	0.45	−1.18	−0.88	−0.08	−11.68	1.06	0.65	−2.79	−0.53
Aug-00	−12.01	0.36	−3.85	−1.94	−1.46	−10.97	1.23	−0.79	−0.12	−2.13
Sep-00	−11.80	0.25	4.05	1.64	0.73	−11.40	1.13	2.28	0.68	0.67
Oct-00	**−12.45**	**0.38**	**5.62**	**4.63**	**2.85**	**−11.40**	**1.36**	**−2.54**	**−0.40**	**−0.53**

Table 12.11a: Monthly consolidated returns 1987, 1993 and 1998

1987	S&P 100	HEDGE	1993	S&P 100	HEDGE	1998	S&P 100	HEDGE
Jan-87	13.06%	1.72%	Jan-93	1.26%	−0.33%	Jan-98	2.04%	6.61%
Feb-87	3.89%	−0.37%	Feb-93	1.56%	4.54%	Feb-98	6.88%	−0.23%
Mar-87	3.31%	3.08%	Mar-93	1.69%	4.17%	Mar-98	5.30%	2.89%
Apr-87	0.68%	0.02%	Apr-93	−1.72%	−0.78%	Apr-98	1.49%	4.95%
May-87	0.68%	5.64%	May-93	2.59%	0.16%	May-98	−1.34%	3.33%
Jun-87	4.86%	0.30%	Jun-93	−0.17%	1.33%	Jun-98	4.83%	13.79%
Jul-87	4.26%	0.57%	Jul-93	−0.52%	1.84%	Jul-98	−0.54%	4.94%
Aug-87	4.50%	0.33%	Aug-93	3.31%	−0.89%	Aug-98	−15.16%	−8.83%
Sep-87	−3.09%	−1.91%	Sep-93	−1.53%	4.67%	Sep-98	5.10%	2.91%
Oct-87	−19.77%	2.27%	Oct-93	1.54%	−2.14%	Oct-98	8.78%	6.53%
Nov-87	−9.87%	−0.75%	Nov-93	−0.55%	0.42%	Nov-98	7.33%	−2.27%
Dec-87	6.00%	2.54%	Dec-93	0.88%	1.63%	Dec-98	4.73%	3.54%
Simple Return	8.51%	13.41%		8.34%	14.63%		29.46%	38.14%
Compound Return	8.88%	14.35%		8.70%	15.75%		34.26%	46.43%
Standard Deviation	8.10%	1.95%		1.52%	2.16%		6.08%	5.23%
Excess Return (Compound vs Index)		5.47%			7.05%			12.17%
Sharpe Ratio (Over Risk Free Rate 5%)		1.38			1.44			2.29

Table 12.11b: Consolidated returns 1995–1999

		Simple Return	Compound Return	Standard Deviation	Excess Return	Sharpe Ratio
1995	**SP100**	31.62%	37.18%	1.67%		
	HEDGE	16.83%	18.32%	2.26%	−18.86%	1.70
1996	**SP100**	21.58%	24.09%	2.83%		
	HEDGE	12.72%	13.57%	1.93%	−10.52%	1.28
1997	**SP100**	26.06%	29.78%	4.71%		
	HEDGE	10.94%	11.56%	3.22%	−18.22%	0.59
1998	**SP100**	29.46%	34.26%	6.08%		
	HEDGE	38.14%	46.43%	5.23%	41.43%	2.29
1999	**SP100**	29.03%	33.68%	4.04%		
	HEDGE	60.17%	82.52%	6.48%	48.84%	3.45

The general methodology introduced by Engle and Kozicki (1993) defines features and common features ('co-features') as follows: F is a *feature* if for all time series x and y:

➤ x has $F \Rightarrow a + bx$ has F;
➤ x does not have F and y does not have $F \Rightarrow x + y$ does not have F;
➤ x has F and y does not have $F \Rightarrow x + y$ has F.

Standard examples of such 'features' in time series include a trend (stochastic or deterministic), autocorrelation and conditional heteroscedasticity. A feature F is a *common feature* (or co-feature) of time series $x_1, \ldots, x_n$ if each of $x_1, \ldots, x_n$ has the feature F but there are real numbers $a_1, \ldots, a_n$ such that $y = a_1 x_1 + \ldots + a_n x_n$ does not have F. Such a linear combination is called a *co-feature combination* and $(a_1, \ldots, a_n)$ is called the *co-feature vector*.

To illustrate these definitions, consider two returns series $\{x_t\}$ and $\{y_t\}$ with the representations

$$x_t = w_t + \varepsilon_{xt},$$
$$y_t = \lambda w_t + \varepsilon_{yt},$$

where ε_{xt} and ε_{yt} are independent i.i.d. processes. If the feature is one of autocorrelation then w_t has an AR representation, and if the feature is volatility then w_t has an ARCH representation. In either case the linear combination $x - (1/\lambda)y$ will not have the feature, so the co-feature vector is $(1, -1/\lambda)$.

Testing for a common feature is quite straightforward. It consists of two stages: first the existence of the feature in each time series is established, then a linear combination of the time series is searched for that does not have the feature. The rest of this section describes some empirical applications of the tests for common autocorrelation and common volatility in securities market indices and FX markets.

12.6.1 Common Autocorrelation

Before looking for common autocorrelation it is necessary to establish that the individual series do have the feature of autocorrelation. Not all market returns are autocorrelated; it depends not only on the frequency of the return, but also on the time period of measurement and, of course, on the market itself (§11.3.2). However, daily returns to equity indices often do exhibit some autocorrelation. A possible cause of autocorrelation in equity indices is the news arrival process, where new information affects trading in some stocks before others. When daily returns are autocorrelated this may be caused by news arriving in the market during the afternoon, which affects only those stocks which are traded late in the day. The prices of other stocks in the index will not be affected until they are traded on the next or subsequent days. Important international news is likely to affect the stock indices of different countries in the same way. Thus common autocorrelation is a possible co-feature in international equity markets.

A possible cause of autocorrelation in equity indices is the news arrival process, where new information affects trading in some stocks before others

A Box–Pierce test may be used to establish that there is significant auto-correlation in the individual returns series (§11.3.2). Then a grid search is employed to find a linear combinations of the time series that do not have autocorrelation. Of course, autocorrelation is not an 'all-or-nothing' matter, so if $y - a_1 x_1 + \ldots + a_n x_n$ does not have autocorrelation, neither will $y' = a'_1 x_1 + \ldots + a'_n x_n$ for small perturbations a'_i of a_i. The linear combination y that is chosen will be the one that minimizes the Box–Pierce test statistic for autocorrelation.

The methodology of common autocorrelation testing is illustrated using daily closing prices on the Financial Times equity indices for Canada, France, Germany, Japan, the Netherlands, United Kingdom and United States from 19 June 1987 to 4 April 1993. Since the data period covers both the 1987 Black Monday crash and the 1989 mini-crash it is possible that autocorrela-tion co-features will be found that are caused by common market behaviour around these times. The effect of the October 1987 crash was evident in all the equity indices but much less so in France, which had a long bull market in equities for almost two years afterwards. From the middle of 1990 neither the Japanese nor the German market performed well. At the beginning of 1990 a sharp rise in Japanese interest rates in response to inflationary pressures preceded the bear market in equities, and the consequent slowdown in investment led to many other economic problems. On the other hand, in Germany the poor performance of equities was a result rather than a cause of economic problems: interest rates were raised in 1990 as a consequence of the effects of German unification, and German equity prices suffered. Therefore it may be expected that these two markets had less in common with the others during the period under study. Let us see.

All returns data were first converted to excess returns over the 'risk-free' 30-day Treasury bill rate. Then AR(1) models were estimated on each excess

Table 12.12: Autocorrelation and common autocorrelation tests for equity indices

	Univariate auto-correlation	Common autocorrelation tests* (parentheses indicate the λ that gives the minimum autocorrelation)				
	Q	Germany	Japan	Netherlands	UK	US
Canada	8.06	0.87 (1.6)	0.50 (0.7)	0.00003 (1.9)	0.04 (1.0)	0.13 (1.3)
Germany	3.60		1.30 (0.7)	2.05 (1.8)	1.41 (1.0)	0.63 (0.8)
Japan	5.89			0.97 (0.7)	0.70 (0.5)	0.17 (1.1)
Netherlands	12.58				0.02 (0.9)	1.05 (0.6)
UK	20.29					1.05 (0.6)
US	6.48					
France	1.10					

*Since France shows no evidence of univariate autocorrelation, it is not included in these common autocorrelation tests.

return series, and the Box–Pierce Q-statistic from each of these is reported in the first column of Table 12.12. Since the 5% and 1% critical values of χ^2 with 1 degree of freedom are 3.84 and 6.63 respectively, it is clear that Canada, Japan, the Netherlands, the UK and the US all have significant autocorrelation.

There is strong common autocorrelation in international equity indices. This is probably due to the cross-listing of major stocks and the autocorrelated news arrival process

The columns on the right of Table 12.12 report the minimum value of the autocorrelation test statistic that is obtained in an AR(1) model on the linear combination (row $- \lambda \times$ column). The λ that gives this minimum value is reported in parentheses. All the test statistics fall well below the 10% value for χ^2 with 1 degree of freedom, which is 2.71. So the results indicate that there is strong common autocorrelation in international equity indices. This is probably due to the cross-listing of major stocks and the autocorrelated news arrival process.

12.6.2 Common Volatility

The existence of common volatility has important implications for derivatives trading. Even the most straightforward of volatility trades, an at-the-money straddle, is not necessarily easy to effect. Near to ATM options may be expensive, or hard to find, but derivatives on assets which share a common volatility factor may be substituted in an ATM straddle or other volatility trade.

Unlike autocorrelation, the existence of ARCH volatility features in asset returns cannot be questioned (§4.1). Volatility 'clusters' are a well-documented feature of almost all financial markets, and the feature becomes particularly pronounced as the frequency of the returns increases. But although individual ARCH volatilities may be easy to determine, common ARCH volatility patterns seem more difficult to detect.

Tests for common volatility are just like common autocorrelation tests, but on squared returns. First the individual squared returns are tested for auto-correlation, and this may be done using a Lagrange multiplier test, such as the TR^2 from an $AR(p)$ model or the Box–Pierce Q-statistic (§11.3.2). Then, assuming ARCH features are present in two return series, some linear com-bination of these series is sought that has no ARCH effects. The linear combination is found by a grid search, and the test for no ARCH is an autocorrelation test on its squares.

Common volatility patterns have been found between international equity markets (Engle and Susmel, 1993). There is less evidence of common volatility between international bond markets (Alexander, 1994).[13] In an investigation of common volatility in FX markets, Alexander (1995) finds that good results are only obtained with weekly data. It was also found that exchange rate variability is not dominated by regional factors, in fact no common volatility patterns were found in the DEM and NLG dollar rates. The only common volatility patterns detected were in the GBP–USD and JPY–USD exchange rates; possibly these were caused by speculative dollar-dominated exchange flows.

---

[13]Daily data appeared to be too noisy for common volatility patterns to be detected.

Forecasting High-Frequency Data

There is much evidence to suggest that market prices are not completely random. Hseih (1989, 1991), Brock *et al.* (1990), LeBaron (1995), Abhyankar *et al.* (1997), de Lima (1998), Drunat *et al.* (1998) and Zhou (1998) have all tested for dependencies in financial returns, in many markets and with different frequencies. These results indicate that there are non-linear dependencies in financial returns, particularly in very high-frequency data. Lo and MacKinley (1988) and Goodhart and Figliouli (1991) also provide strong evidence that some stock prices do not follow a random walk when measured at the intra-day level.

These findings contradict the efficient markets hypothesis. The implication is that it is possible to predict market prices at high frequency, with some degree of accuracy, but because of the non-linear nature of the dependencies that have been demonstrated in high-frequency data, linear statistical models are not appropriate for high-frequency price prediction. Nevertheless there is a common perception that it is possible to develop time series models that forecast high-frequency data successfully, and a major focus of recent research has been the development of non-linear models for financial market behaviour.

It is possible to predict market prices at high frequency but because of the non-linear nature of the dependencies linear statistical models are not appropriate

Given the huge literature on forecasting high-frequency data, this chapter has been extremely selective in its coverage. The first section begins with an overview of data sources and the recent initiatives in forecasting high-frequency financial data. It describes a basic technique for high-frequency data filtering and examines the time series properties that one might expect from tic data on financial market prices. This section ends with a brief overview of some of the parametric models of high-frequency data that have been used to investigate market microstructure.

The two sections that follow cover two non-linear models that have been found useful for high-frequency financial data prediction. Section 13.2 explains the concepts that underpin the design and estimation of neural networks and surveys their applications to forecasting high-frequency financial data. My understanding of neural networks owes much to many discussions with Dr Peter Williams of Sussex University, an acknowledged expert in this field.

Recent interest in the possibility that financial markets are governed by low-dimensional but deterministic chaotic systems has precipitated a new generation of models for forecasting high-frequency data. Some of the methods that have been applied to the detection of chaos in high-frequency financial data are described in §13.3, and the chapter finishes by describing 'nearest neighbour' prediction algorithms that are based on the assumption of chaotic dynamics.

13.1 High-Frequency Data

13.1.1 Data and Information Sources

Much of the research into high-frequency financial returns has been initiated by Olsen and Associates (O&A) who have made some very useful data available to the public. One of the O&A data sets provides tic data on some major US dollar exchange rates and interest rates. They have also provided several years of tic data on the USD–DEM exchange rate from 1 January 1987 to 31 December 1993. Other information in the first O&A data set includes the identification of the institution that has given each quote, and time-stamped headline news items from *Money Market Headline News*. More recently, O&A have provided half-hourly bid–ask quote data from 1 January 1996 to 31 December 1996 on 25 exchange rates and 4 precious metals, and half-hourly transaction price data on 12 Euromarket futures, the Dow Jones Industrial Average and the S&P 500. These data sets are available for research purposes, at a nominal cost, from www.olsen.ch. O&A have also organized two highly successful international conferences on high-frequency data in finance (HFDF).[1]

Real-time tic data covering many markets are available from a number of commercial data vendors, such as Bloomberg (www.bloomberg.com), Reuters (www.reuters.com) and LIFFE (www.liffe.com). Some also provide the essential software that allows the latest information to be downloaded and formatted on a regular basis. But even with this there are enormous data management issues surrounding the storage and filtering of tic data, and of course these must be addressed before any results from a historical analysis of high-frequency time series analysis can be put into practice.

The Computer Society and the Neural Network Council of the Institute of Electrical and Electronics Engineers (www.ieee.com) produce several publications that are aimed at practitioners in financial markets and have organized a number of international conferences on computational intelligence for financial engineering. These have encompassed a number of areas in the time series analysis of high-frequency data on financial markets such as data filtering, foreign exchange forecasting and the prediction of volatility and prices.

---

[1]Proceedings of the HFDF conferences in 1995 and 1996 are available from www.olsen.ch.

13.1.2 Data Filters

A large amount of information can be filtered out of tic data on bid and ask quotes. If equally spaced time series are to be extracted, the data must be sorted within a fixed time bucket. Within each n-minute interval the open, close, high and low of the bid and ask quotes may be recorded, and the volume of quote activity. Then a closing price series is normally obtained by taking an average of the latest bid and ask quotes during the interval.[2]

Since these data are only quotes and not the actual transaction prices, some preliminary filters should be applied in order that they be analysed as if they were price series. Error filters may be applied as described in Guillaime *et al.* (1997), so that price data are not recorded from impossible or erroneous quotes. Of course it is not possible to remove all quotes that are made by players simply attempting to bid the market up or down, but rules may be applied to filter out obvious bad quotes.

It is not possible to remove all quotes that are made by players simply attempting to bid the market up or down, but rules may be applied to filter out obvious bad quotes

For example, a cleaned price series $\{p_t^*\}$ can be constructed from a price series $\{p_t\}$ by defining a suitably large price increment c. If the price changes more than this amount, but the next price does not verify this change then the price is ignored. So p_t^* is defined recursively by setting $p_1^* = p_1$ and then

$$p_t^* = p_{t-1}^* \text{ if } |p_t - p_{t-1}^*| > c \text{ but } |p_{t+1} - p_{t-1}^*| < c, \text{ and } p_t^* = p_t \text{ otherwise.}$$

Continuous tic data will also cover periods such as weekends and bank holidays where little or no activity is recorded, and it is normal to remove these periods before examining the data. Long series of zero returns will distort the statistical properties of prices and returns and make volatility and correlation modelling extremely difficult. Figure 13.1 shows the DEM–USD rate in the O&A data, where the closing price is taken as the geometric average of the latest bid and ask quotes in a 1-hour time interval and weekends have been removed.

13.1.3 Autocorrelation Properties

The autocorrelation properties of high-frequency returns have been established by a large empirical literature:

➤ There is little autocorrelation in returns, except perhaps some negative autocorrelation at very high frequency (Goodhart and Figliouli, 1991; Bollerslev and Domowitz, 1993; Zhou, 1992).
➤ There is, however, a lot of autocorrelation in squared returns, and this conditional heteroscedasticity becomes more pronounced as the sampling frequency increases (Andersen and Bollerslev, 1996; Baillie and Bollerslev,

---

[2]Prices are obtained either from the arithmetic average, price $= (\text{bid} + \text{ask})/2$, or from the geometric average, price $= (\text{bid*ask})^{1/2}$. The latter is preferable since it is the log prices that are normally applied to compute returns; however, the difference between these two averages is negligible (of the order of 10^{-5} for a bid–ask spread of 1%).

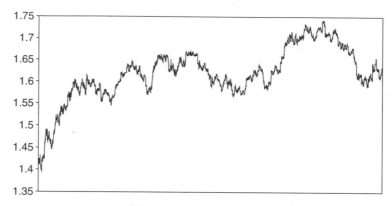

Figure 13.1 Hourly price data on the German mark–US dollar exchange rate, from 1 October 1992 to 30 September 1993.

Table 13.1: Box–Pierce autocorrelation statistics for the return on DEM–USD rates

	1-hr	6-hr	12-hr	1-day	1-week
Returns					
$Q(1)$	1.08	0.02	0.75	1.50	0.70
$Q(2)$	7.73	0.06	0.77	2.12	0.71
$Q(20)$	44.9	27.6	28.1	22.1	26.4
Squared returns					
$Q(1)$	117.0	−0.08	0.01	1.19	0.69
$Q(2)$	196.0	1.24	1.89	2.68	1.09
$Q(20)$	246.0	70.0	52.8	29.7	11.1

1990; Zhou, 1996; Drost and Nijman, 1993; Ghose and Kroner, 1995; Taylor and Xu, 1997).

These stylized facts will be supported with an example based on part of the O&A 1993 data set. Olsen and Associates have collected bid and ask quotes on the exchanges rates for the US dollar with sterling, the Deutsche Mark and the Japanese yen in real time during the period from 1 October 1992 to 30 September 1993. Each quote is time-stamped to the nearest minute and obvious error or outliers are flagged so that they can be removed.

Using the data shown in Figure 13.1, analysis of the non-overlapping returns of different frequencies from 1 hour to 1 week is shown in Table 13.1. The Box–Pierce $Q(p)$-statistics for pth-order autocorrelation that are described in §11.3.2 are computed for $p = 1$, 2 and 20 on both returns and squared returns. They are asymptotically distributed as $\chi^2(p)$, so the relevant 1% critical values are 6.63 for $Q(1)$, 9.21 for $Q(2)$ and 37.6 for $Q(20)$.

The first three rows of Table 13.1 indicate very little autocorrelation in returns, except at the highest frequency. The 1-hr data do exhibit some negative

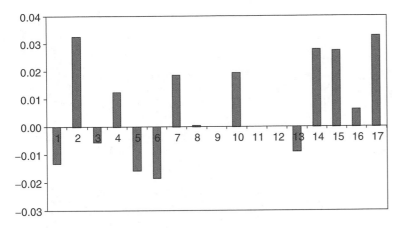

Figure 13.2 Correlogram of 1-hour returns.

autocorrelation, as shown by their correlogram in Figure 13.2. If the price series were based on transacted prices then the observed negative autocorrelation in 1-hr returns could be due to a bid–ask bounce (the transaction price is either the bid or the ask). But since the data are filtered averages of bid and ask quotes, it is probably due to heterogeneous agents responding to market events in different ways and at different times.

The autocorrelation statistics for squared returns show an entirely different pattern. There is excessively high positive autocorrelation in the 1-hr squared return data. That is, ARCH effects are quite enormous in very high-frequency data. This observation has motivated much research into GARCH volatility models for very high-frequency data (§4.2.5).

13.1.4 Parametric Models of High-Frequency Data

High-frequency data provide a rich source of information on the microstructure of financial markets, and excellent surveys of high-frequency data analysis in financial markets are found in Goodhart and O'Hara (1997) and Engle (2000a). There is a clear positive relationship between trading volume and volatility (Tauchen and Pitts, 1983; DeGennaro and Shrieves, 1995; Jones *et al.*, 1994). Figure 13.3 shows smoothed volume data on the USD–DEM spot exchange rate, and the corresponding GARCH volatility, for tic data that are bucketed into hourly intervals.

The positive relationship between volume and volatility has motivated the analysis of high-frequency data that are not sampled at regular intervals. An excellent overview of the regularly spaced and time transformation frameworks for analysing high-frequency data is given by Giot (2001). Time can be deformed by mapping calendar time to an operational time that is determined by the volume of transactions (Ghysels and Jasiek, 1995a, 1995b; Ghysels *et al.*,

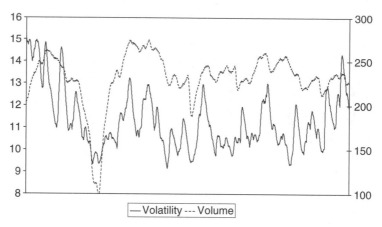

Figure 13.3 Volume and volatility.

1998) or the volatility (Zhou, 1996). The price quotes (or trades) may be sampled at irregularly spaced intervals such that the total volume of quotes (or trades) in each interval is constant. When the sampling intervals for high-frequency data are transformed using volume durations in this way, they become more amenable to standard modelling techniques (Ané and Geman, 2000).

The ACD model uses a parametric model for the time between trades that has much in common with the GARCH model; in the ACD model the expected duration between trades depends on past durations

An alternative approach to time transformation is to model the price durations, that is, the interval between trades, or between price changes that are larger than a given threshold. The *autoregressive conditional duration* (ACD) model was developed by Engle and Russell (1997) on high-frequency exchange rate data and by Engle and Russell (1998) on high-frequency stock market data. The ACD model uses a parametric model for the time between trades that has much in common with the GARCH model; in the ACD model the expected duration between trades depends on past durations. Since then a number of different ACD models have been developed, notably by Bauwens and Giot (1998) and Dufour and Engle (2000); the latter have applied the ACD model to the important area of liquidity risk by measuring the price impact of trades.

Parametric models have also been used to investigate the effect of news arrival and other public information on market activity. Almeida *et al.* (1997) show that the effect of macroeconomic news on the USD–DEM exchange rate is very short-lived, lasting little more than a few hours in most cases. Goodhart *et al.* (1991) use very high-frequency data on the GBP–USD exchange rate to investigate the effect of news announcements on GARCH volatility estimates. In line with their results, Low and Muthuswamy (1996) find strong evidence that news activity increases the volatility of returns and the volatility of the bid–ask spread. And the mechanisms by which news is carried around the world are investigated by Engle and Susmel (1994), who examine the volatility spillovers between international equity markets on an hourly basis.

When there is a common feature in financial assets there will be Granger causality; that is, there will be a lead–lag relationship between asset returns (§12.6). De Jong and Nijman (1997) find strong evidence for a lead–lag relationship between S&P 500 spot and futures returns when measured at high frequency. Low and Muthuswamy (1996) also find evidence of a lead–lag structure from the USD–DEM and USD–JPY to the DEM–JPY exchange rate.

13.2 Neural Networks

It is clear that dependencies between high-frequency returns are non-linear. There are significant linear dependencies between squared returns, but it is often more important to be able to predict the sign of a return than the magnitude of a return, so this finding is not very informative from the point of view of predictive modelling. Neural networks are comprehensive and powerful non-linear statistical models that have found applications in many disciplines, and there has been much research on the use of neural networks for modelling non-linear dependencies in financial markets (Refenes *et al.*, 1996) — notably for exchange rates (Kuan and Liu, 1995; Nabney *et al.*, 1996; Bolland *et al.*, 1998). Neural networks have also been used to develop prediction algorithms for financial asset prices, such as the technical trading rules for stocks and commodities in Fishman *et al.* (1991), Shih (1991), Katz (1992), Kean (1992), Swales and Yoon (1992), Wong (1992), Baestaens *et al.* (1996), White (1988) and Min (1999).

This section gives a brief overview of the structure of basic neural networks and the propagation algorithms that are used to estimate them. More details may be found in many text books; Azoff (1994) in particular provides an accessible introduction to the subject and some examples of financial applications. Much commercial software is available for designing and implementing neural networks, and they can now be found in many statistical packages. Useful numerical recipes for neural networks can be found in Blum (1992) and Masters (1993).

Neural networks are universal approximators in the sense that they can fit any non-linear function with any degree of accuracy. In fact neural networks have much in common with linear models (for example, the method of parameter estimation is usually some form of maximum likelihood), and neural networks have applications to every situation where linear models are used. The key idea in any neural network is a non-linear 'twist', without which the network would collapse into a standard linear statistical model. Neural networks are designed to model arbitrary non-linear effects. It is not necessary to specify any underlying model for the process. On the other hand, a greater emphasis is placed on the preprocessing of the input data than is the case in standard linear models.

Neural networks are universal approximators in the sense that they can fit any non-linear function with any degree of accuracy

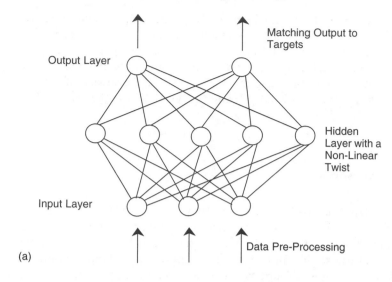

Output from this node is $x = f(w_0 + w_1x_1 + w_2x_2 + \ldots + w_n x_n)$
where f is the transfer function.

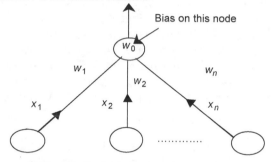

Each node j in the lower layer has output x_j.
Each connection has weight w_j.

(b)

Figure 13.4 Neural network architecture: (a) simple three-layer perceptron; (b) weights, biases and transfer functions.

13.2.1   Architecture

The architecture of a simple three-layer neural network is shown in Figure 13.4a. A neural network that has this type of layered architecture is called a *multi-layer perceptron*. It will operate by matching the outputs with targets that capture the desired response. Such neural networks have obvious applications to price forecasting, where the target for the network output would be the prices that are being forecast. Alternatively, they may be applied to estimate parameters of a distribution; in this case the output of the network would be the parameters of the distribution. The target response of the network is obtained by matching observed with predicted returns within the training data set.

In a multi-layer perceptron each set of input data is first processed into input nodes, and then passed through a series of hidden layers via the various connections of the network, to one or more output nodes. The nodes in the hidden layers contain transfer functions that give the non-linear twists that are characteristic of all neural networks. If there is more than one hidden layer, these layers are usually structured like 'sandwiches' with alternating layers of non-linear and linear transfer functions.

The nodes in the hidden layers contain transfer functions that give the non-linear twists that are characteristic of all neural networks

The structure of a neural network depends on the following:

➤ *The number of layers and nodes per layer.* Working through the network, there is the input layer, then one or more hidden layers, and finally an output layer. One hidden layer is often sufficient for most purposes, as in Figure 13.4a.
➤ *Any restrictions on the connections between the nodes.* Connections are often, but not always, made only between adjacent layers, again as in Figure 13.4a. The more connections that have non-zero weights, the more complex the neural network. Most neural networks place a penalty on over-complexity for reasons that are explained below.
➤ *The form of transfer functions.* The transfer functions, which determine the non-linear twists in the hidden layers, must be differentiable. Often they are also monotonic and *s*-shaped, like the hyperbolic tangent or the sigmoid function, so that they 'squash' the input from an infinite range to a finite interval of the real line. Each node could have a different transfer function, not necessarily because they have different functional forms, but because the parameters can differ between nodes.

Figure 13.4b illustrates how the network operates: The outputs x_j ($j = 1, \ldots, n$) from the n lower nodes are multiplied by the connection weights w_j ($j = 1, \ldots, n$) and summed, a process that is called *attenuation*. The sum is added to the 'attenuation bias' w_0 of the node in question and the result $y = w_0 + w_1x_1 + \ldots + w_nx_n$ is then passed through a transfer function f so that the output of the node is $f(y)$.

13.2.2 Data Processing

Preprocessing of the data involves normalization and data compression. Normalization of the different time series that are used as input vectors facilitates the process of tuning the parameters: they would have totally different orders of magnitude unless all inputs are normalized to lie in a similar range. This range is usually [0, 1] or [−1, 1], depending on the form of transfer function. For example, if the transfer functions are hyperbolic tangents, which have domain $(-\infty, +\infty)$, all inputs should be normalized to the range [−1, 1]. This could be achieved by putting:

$$x_t^* = 2(x_t - \min)/(\max - \min) - 1,$$

where min and max are the minimum and maximum values of the time series input $\{x_t\}$.

Note that the targets that will be matched with the network output also require normalization, independently of the input normalization. For example, if a transfer function is sigmoid with output range [0, 1], it must be matched with targets that take a similar range. Actually the sigmoid only takes the boundary values 0 and 1 when inputs are infinite, so it is usually advisable to normalize the targets to lie well within the interior of the interval.

Wavelets perform a similar function to principal components in that dimensions are reduced while all the relevant information in the input vectors is retained

Data compression is necessary for the network to cope with long historic time series. Often there is much redundant information, so the optimization procedure is facilitated when the redundancies are removed. For example, moving averages of different lengths, or discrete cosine transformations, can be applied to smooth out noisy data. Or if the data are highly collinear just the first few principal components of the vector time series can be taken as inputs (§6.1). Principal components analysis for data preprocessing is a standard option in many neural network packages. Another popular form of data compression is to use *wavelet transformations* (Press *et al.*, 1992). Unlike principal components, wavelets are not necessarily orthogonal, but they perform a similar function to principal components in that dimensions are reduced while the most important information in the input vectors is retained. Wavelet transforms are available as in-built procedures in many statistical packages.

13.2.3   Backpropagation

A training set of data is used to estimate the parameters of the network, viz. the weights on each of the connections and the attenuation biases of each node. Initial values of these parameters are set, and then the network is trained by comparing the results from the output nodes with observed targets using some type of performance measure. During training, the weights and biases are estimated by iterating on the performance measure for output results.

The process of iteration between initial and final values of network parameters is called *backpropagation* (Azoff, 1994; Ripley, 1996). The backpropagation algorithm is illustrated in Figure 13.5. It operates by first calculating a δ value for each output node, and then propagating these deltas back through the layers of the network. The delta values of the output nodes that are used in the backpropagation algorithm are calculated as $-\partial E/\partial y$, where y is the output from the output node and E is the error function (§13.2.4).

To propagate the output deltas back through the network, suppose that node j has output $f(y)$, where f is the transfer function and y is the attenuated input to that node. If the nodes above node j have deltas δ_1, δ_2, . . ., δ_k and the connection weights from node j to these nodes are w_1, w_2, . . ., w_k then the delta value for node j is

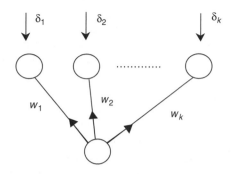

Output from this node is $x = f(y)$.
Node delta is $\delta = f'(y)(w_1\delta_1 + \ldots + w_k\delta_k)$

Figure 13.5 Backpropagation.

$$f'(y)(w_1\delta_1 + w_2\delta_2 + \ldots + w_k\delta_k).$$

Once all nodes have a delta value, these values are used to update the weights on the connections and the biases on each node. The basic form of updating weights is

$$w_{\text{new}} = w_{\text{old}} + \nu\delta x,$$

where δ is the delta on the upper node and x is the output from the lower node. The updating of biases takes a similar form,

$$w_{0,\text{new}} = w_{0,\text{old}} + \nu\delta,$$

where δ is the delta on the node.

The parameter ν is called the network *learning coefficient*. It may be modified during training if the network has an adaptive learning capability. The learning coefficient is similar to the step size of simple iterative optimization algorithms such as gradient search. In fact backpropagation is equivalent to gradient descent optimization of the error function, so any of the standard algorithms can be substituted. Some of these algorithms were described in §4.3.2, but those that are most successful for optimizing GARCH models are not necessarily as good for neural networks. The most common gradient optimization methods used for neural networks are conjugate gradients or the Broyden–Fletcher–Goldfarb–Shanno (BFGS) algorithm.

13.2.4 Performance Measurement

Any standard performance measure, such as those described in §A.5.3, may be applied when comparing the output of a neural network with its target output.

When no distributional assumptions are made — as, for example, in some neural networks that are used for price prediction — the performance of the network may be measured using a standard error function, such as the root mean square error between the observed and predicted price.

If distributional assumptions are made, it is more informative to use a likelihood than an error criterion. For example, suppose a neural network is used to estimate the parameters of a univariate normal mixture density (§10.2.3). The basic input vector, before any normalization or data compression, will be the returns time series, and the output nodes would give the parameters of the normal mixture: the probabilities, means and (log) standard deviations for each of the constituent normal densities. An appropriate performance measure is then the log-likelihood of the training data given the output parameters. We denote this by $\ln L(\mathbf{w})$ to emphasize that the value of the likelihood will depend on the weights $\mathbf{w}$ of the connections. During training the network will be optimized by minimizing the error function $E(\mathbf{w}) = -2 \ln L(\mathbf{w})$ (§A.6.3).

The old-fashioned method of preventing the network from over-fitting was just to stop the optimization before the fit became too close

Since neural networks are universal approximators, if permitted they can fit the required targets to any degree of accuracy, so that errors in the training data can be arbitrarily small. But this usually results in poor out-of-sample performance when the optimized network is run on a test data set. The old-fashioned method of preventing the network from over-fitting was just to stop the optimization before the fit became too close. This is rather crude and leaves much to the modeller's judgement of the appropriate time to switch off the network.

A more sophisticated method is to add a cost of complexity to the performance measure. For example, Williams (1995, 1996) adds a regularization term $n \ln(\Sigma |w_i|)$ to the log-likelihood function, where n is the number of connections with non-zero weights and the summation is over all the weights in the network. The regularized performance measure — that is, the error function that should be minimized — as a function of the weights $\mathbf{w}$, becomes

$$E(\mathbf{w}) = -2 \ln L(\mathbf{w}) + n \ln(\Sigma |w_i|).$$

This type of error function, which includes a penalty for over-complexity, automatically 'prunes' connections from the network with zero weights. Thus the network architecture is automatically modified during training, which avoids any need for the modeller to apply subjective tolerance levels to convergence metrics in the old-fashioned way.

13.2.5 Integration

Error functions of neural networks are usually very complex. Commonly they have many local minima and it is very hard to identify any unique global minimum. Each time the network is run, with different initial values for weights and biases, a different optimum will be achieved. So it is standard practice to run the network many times and to take some type of average over the results.

The form of average taken will depend on the type of output produced. For example, if outputs are price predictions an equally weighted arithmetic average of the results would be appropriate. But if the outputs are parameters of a distribution other types of integration over local minima may be appropriate. For example, variance parameter outputs could be averaged using the formula (10.12) for the variance of a mixture with each probability equal to $1/N$, where N is the number of different local optima in the average.

13.3 Price Prediction Models Based on Chaotic Dynamics

One of the characteristics of a chaotic dynamical system is that points on neighbouring trajectories grow apart from each other exponentially, at least in the short term. Think of the Lorenz butterfly, or some other strange attractor. If two points are distinct but infinitesimally close, they will be indistinguishable at time zero, but some time in the future they could be very far apart on opposite 'wings' of the attractor. Two points that were virtually indistinguishable nevertheless lie on different trajectories at the start; so as time passes they will diverge very rapidly.

What are the implications if deterministic chaos rather than stochastic models govern a financial market?

What are the implications if deterministic chaos rather than stochastic models govern a financial market? Very short-term predictions should be more accurate than long-term predictions, but is there anything else of practical use? Of course it would be truly wonderful if, following any positive finding for chaotic dynamics, the equations that govern the attractor could be specified. But this is extremely unlikely since the dimension of any attractor is going to be very high. In any case, financial markets are not likely to be governed by a set of purely deterministic equations. The stochastic components will be dominant, particularly in the high-frequency data that are usually necessary for the statistical tests of chaos that will be described below. Any evidence of chaos would simply tell us that a minuscule error of measurement in the data will produce large prediction errors except for very short-term forecasts. But this could be investigated directly, with or without a finding of chaotic dynamics. So although there is a large literature on the evidence for and against deterministic chaos in financial markets, it is not clear that this research is of any practical use.

Any evidence of chaos would simply tell us that a minuscule error of measurement in the data will produce large prediction errors

However, there are a number of modelling techniques that are based on chaos theory that do have useful applications for prediction purposes. The aim of this section is to present a few of the concepts from the theory of chaos that have been used as a basis for some of the more successful high-frequency data prediction models in financial markets.

13.3.1 Testing for Chaos

The concept of embedding a time series in a higher-dimensional space goes back to a theorem of Takens (1981). Takens showed that it is possible to estimate the dimension of any chaotic attractor by embedding the time series in m-dimensional space using a *time-delay embedding*. Each point x_t in the time series is mapped to a point in m-dimensional space $\Re^m$ as follows:

$$\mathbf{x}_t = (x_t, x_{t-\tau}, x_{t-2\tau}, \ldots, x_{t-(m-1)\tau}), \tag{13.1}$$

where the lag τ is some positive integer (most commonly $\tau = 1$, as in Figure 13.6b) and m is chosen to be larger than the dimension of the attractor. In this way the univariate time series is mapped to a set of points in m-dimensional space, where the time ordering is not apparent but if there *is* a strange attractor it will be revealed by the pattern generated by these points.

If the system dynamics are chaotic then they will be governed by a strange attractor that has a finite, positive *fractal dimension*. Among the many definitions of fractal dimension one of the most common is the *correlation dimension* ν (Liu *et al.*, 1992; Grassberger and Procaccia, 1993a, 1993b). The correlation dimension is related to the *correlation integral* $C(\varepsilon)$ of a time series $\{x_t\}$ of length N. The correlation integral is defined by embedding the time series in m-dimensional space $\Re^m$, where the embedding dimension m is chosen to be suitably large, so that $m > \nu$. Then $C(\varepsilon)$ is given by

$$C(\varepsilon) = \lim\{\text{number of pairs } (i, j) \text{ such that } ||\mathbf{x}_i - \mathbf{x}_j|| < \varepsilon\}/N^2 \text{ as } N \to \infty.$$

Thus the correlation integral $C(\varepsilon)$ measures the number of points in a ball of radius ε in $\Re^m$ as the length of the time series increases. The correlation dimension ν measures the rate of growth of $C(\varepsilon)$ with ε. In other words, $C(\varepsilon) \approx \varepsilon^\nu$ for small ε. The correlation dimension ν is normally estimated by finding a finite approximation to each of the correlation integrals for different ε and then estimating $d \ln C(\varepsilon)/d \ln \varepsilon$.

Another standard test for chaotic dynamics is based on the largest Lyapunov exponent λ. A *Lyapunov exponent* measures the average rate of exponential divergence of neighbouring trajectories, so it is a measure of sensitivity to initial conditions. The greater the Lyapunov exponent, the faster the divergence in trajectories. If all Lyapunov exponents are negative then all trajectories converge, so a statistical test for chaos is to estimate the largest Lyapunov exponent, and if it is negative there is no evidence for chaos. If $x_{t+1} = f(x_t)$ then the Lyapunov exponent is defined as

The greater the Lyapunov exponent, the faster the divergence in trajectories

$$\lambda = \lim(\ln |df^r/dx|/r) \text{ as } r \to \infty,$$

where the trajectory of x is $\{x, f(x), f^2(x), f^3(x), \ldots\}$. To see that λ measures the rate of divergence of neighbouring points, note that $|df^r/dx| \approx \exp(r\lambda)$, and by Taylor linearization this is approximately equal to the difference between x and $x + \varepsilon$ after r iterations.

Since the function f is unknown (all we observe are the realizations of a time series) algorithms must be designed to estimate the Lyapunov exponents

(Wolff, 1992). Estimates of the Lyapunov exponent by Abhyankar *et al.* (1997) for the S&P 500, the Nikkei 225, the DAX 30 and the FTSE 100 equity indices confirm the presence of non-linear dependence in the returns but provide no evidence of low-dimensional chaotic processes.

There are several important points to note about algorithms such as these that are designed to detect chaotic dynamics:

➤ The sample size should be upwards of 100 000 points if the algorithms are to work with any degree of accuracy. Erroneous conclusions might be drawn even with quite long data sets (Ruelle,1990; Vassilicos *et al.*, 1992).
➤ Data must not contain much noise because these methods cannot detect underlying chaos when mixed with even a small amount of noise (Smith, 1992).
➤ Correlation dimension algorithms depend on counting the number of points inside a small ball in m-dimensional space, and results can be quite sensitive to the choice of diameter for this ball (Liu *et al.*, 1992).
➤ The time series must be stationary if results are to be correctly interpreted (Casdagli, 1992).

Taken together, it should be clear that a large amount of cleaned and pre-whitened high-frequency data is necessary in order to apply these algorithms. However, not all the research that has been published for and against chaos in capital markets has been based on empirical methods that meet these stringent criteria. Therefore it is not surprising that opinions are very mixed. Those that claim to have found chaos in financial markets include Peters (1991), Medio (1992) and de Grauwe *et al.* (1993). But many more papers find no conclusive evidence of chaos, among them Scheinkman and LeBaron (1989), Hseih (1991), Tata and Vassilicos (1991), Liu *et al.* (1992), Alexander and Giblin (1994), Drunat *et al.* (1996), and Abhyankar *et al.* (1997).

Not all the research that has been published for and against chaos in capital markets has been based on empirical methods that meet these stringent criteria

13.3.2 Nearest Neighbour Algorithms

Now let us consider which concepts in the chaos detection algorithms just described could be used as a basis for high-frequency prediction models. First, since Lyapunov exponents will be positive if the series is chaotic, points on neighbouring trajectories will diverge. Chaos-based prediction algorithms can only be designed for very short-term predictions in high-frequency data. Secondly, note that the correlation dimension required embedding the time series in a higher-dimensional space and then taking points in a small ball around the current point. Such 'nearest neighbour' methods have formed the basis of some quite successful prediction algorithms for high-frequency data.

Figure 13.6 shows two different representations of the hourly returns data from a high-frequency price series. The first representation in Figure 13.6a is simply

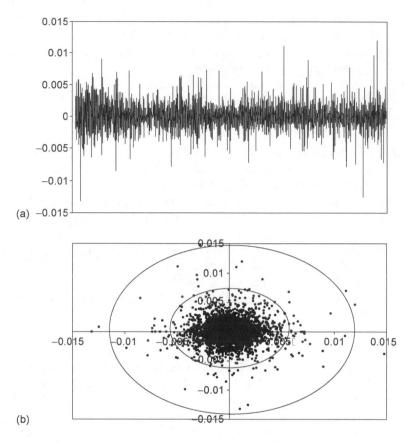

Figure 13.6 (a) Traditional time series representation; (b) two-dimensional time-delay embedding of the same series.

a time series graph, which is useful for investigating properties such as autocorrelation and conditional heteroscedasticity. The second representation in Figure 13.6b is a two-dimensional time-delay embedding, a scatter plot of current against lagged returns. This is just another view of the same data. The dimension of this embedding is only 2, far too small to reveal any strange attractor even if it were to exist; it is only used here to illustrate the concept of a time-delay embedding.

In standard nearest neighbour prediction methods, first each historic point of the time series is mapped into m-dimensional space $\Re^m$ using the time-delay embedding (13.1). This creates a 'library' of historic data in the form of a pattern of points in $\Re^m$. Then, to make a prediction for the current point in time x_t, it is mapped into the library using the same embedding. The nearest neighbours of $\mathbf{x}_t$ in $\Re^m$ are found and then the first coordinates of these points are used as data on the explanatory variable in a univariate prediction model.

Whereas conventional time series prediction uses the immediately preceding points taken at successive and equally spaced intervals in time, nearest neighbour prediction methods use a selection of points from the history of the time series. These points are chosen because they are 'similar' to the current point, in a sense that is defined by the embedding. Unless one chooses to dissect the algorithm it will not be known exactly which points are being chosen to predict any given point. They could be taken from any time during the history and they do not necessarily run consecutively through time.

Two methods of choosing nearest neighbours are possible. In the first method an *m*-dimensional ball of fixed radius is drawn around the current point as in Figure 13.6b and all points from the time series history that lie within the ball are taken. The larger the radius of the ball the more nearest neighbours; and different points will have different numbers of nearest neighbours. If the markets are behaving 'normally' there could be many points that lie within the nearest neighbour region, but during exceptional periods that may not have occurred in the past there will be very few nearest neighbours within a fixed radius ball. So the forecast will be made with many or few points, depending on the alignments associated with the current point.

Nearest neighbour prediction methods use a selection of points from the history of the time series

The second method of choosing nearest neighbours is to take a fixed number *n* of nearest neighbours. So when the markets are fairly stable the Euclidean distances between the *n* nearest neighbours and the current point will be relatively small, but when markets are jumpy these Euclidean distances will be relatively large. Both methods require computation of the Euclidean distance of each point in the library from the current point, and if the library is very large this can be quite time-consuming.

Once the points have been selected the method of forecasting could be virtually anything. For example, Casdagli (1992) uses forecasts based on fairly standard linear regression, but Nychka *et al.* (1992) use non-parametric regression, Sugihara and May (1990) use simplex projection and Alexander and Giblin (1994) use simplex projection with barycentric coordinates.

Recently nearest neighbour prediction algorithms have received some attention from the finance community. Alexandre *et al.* (1998) use time-delay embeddings to predict high-frequency returns on the DEM–FRF and USD–FRF exchange rate. Finkenstadt and Kuhbier (1995) claim some success in predicting commodity prices using this method. See also Mizrach (1992) and Jaditz and Sayes (1998).

13.3.3 Multivariate Embedding Methods

Nearest neighbour algorithms that are based on univariate series with time-delay embedding are rather limited, and the results cited above indicate that limited success has been achieved with such methods. However, it is possible

It is possible to extend the concept of univariate time-delay embedding to a multivariate setting

to extend the concept of univariate time-delay embedding to a multivariate setting, and thereby utilize much more information about the market micro-structure and the possible interdependencies with other markets. Multivariate embeddings in m-dimensional space employ lagged values of a variety of possible predictor variables. Examples of possible predictor variables include trading range, volume, and bid–ask spread and each predictor variable could be measured over a variety of possible time-frames. Furthermore, if a lead–lag relationship is thought to exist with another financial instrument then similar data on this market could also be used in the embedding.

The specification of embedding is a subjective but crucial part of the model

The specification of embedding is a subjective but crucial part of the model. Although it may seem appropriate to use microstructure data in the embedding, the perceived benefits from such an approach have to be weighed against more than a few difficulties: a very large number of different embeddings, having different dimensions, lags and predictor variables will need to be tried and tested. The model training may be analysed into three stages:

➤ specification of the embedding;
➤ stating the number of nearest neighbours, or the radius of the ball;
➤ determining the best prediction method.

For every choice of embedding, of nearest neighbours, and of prediction method, an out-of-sample data set must be produced and tested. Given the large volume of data normally employed for high-frequency analysis, the training and testing of the model is an enormous task. My interest in this area arose in 1995 after receiving details of the first international non-linear financial forecasting competition, sponsored by the *NeuroVe$t Journal* (Caldwell, 1997). I had read with much interest the accounts of the Santa Fe time series forecasting competition, which was aimed at forecasting a great variety of different time series—including even an encoding of the end of a Bach fugue (Casdagli and Eubank, 1992; Weigund and Gershenfeld, 1993). This new competition was focused exclusively on high-frequency financial data, and aimed at genetic algorithms and neural networks.[3]

At the time I was working with Peter Williams[4] on the applications of neural networks to financial market data, and so it seemed an interesting idea to enter the competition. However, when we received the data they turned out to behave in a very unusual fashion; there were a huge number of highly exceptional returns.[5] Successful forecasting of these data with a neural network seemed unlikely, and instead I worked with Ian Giblin to develop a tailor-made

---

[3]In fact the first prize included a lot of free neural network software.

[4]Dr Williams is Reader in the School of Cognitive Studies at the University of Sussex.

[5]The data provided to entrants for training the model included the time of day, the open, high, low and closing prices and the tic volume for each minute over approximately 4 years (from January 1989 to March 1993). The subsequent 2 years of data were retained for the competition organizers to test the entries. Nothing was revealed to entrants about the source of the data until after the competition, when we were informed that the data were on cotton futures prices.

forecasting model based on our research into chaotic dynamics.[6] There are many possible approaches to forecasting high-frequency data from financial markets; 'looking' at the data (as far as this is possible) is a first and very important step in deciding which approach to take.

Alexander and Giblin (1997) developed a multivariate nearest neighbour prediction algorithm for the first international non-linear financial forecasting competition. Of the 1.5 million data points provided for the competition preparation, 1 million were used for training and 0.5 million for testing. The competition rules specified that two minute-by-minute prediction series were to be generated by the program (2 hours ahead and 1 day ahead). The competition would be run on an unseen set of data on the same variable as the one provided for practice and approximately 0.5 million predictions for each time horizon had to be generated in under 4 hours' CPU time.

The practice data were very unusual. It seemed to us that although the competition was aimed primarily at neural networks it would be extremely difficult to train a neural network on these data. Instead we looked for possible embedding variables that could be extracted from the data with a view to constructing a nearest neighbour prediction algorithm. The data looked to us like a commodity future, probably a precious metal. Much of the trading in these markets is based on technical analysis so we considered some standard technical indicators as possible embedding variables (Brock *et al.*, 1992; Curcio and Goodhart, 1992; LeBaron, 1992; Murphy, 1986; Harris *et al.*, 1994).[7] For each point a fixed number of nearest neighbours were selected in the embedding space and the forecasting models for predictions 2 hours ahead and 1 day head were applied. Decisions on the embedding, the optimal number of nearest neighbours (between 100 and 1000) and the specification of the forecasting models required us to develop some sophisticated tools for choosing model parameters on the basis of forecast analysis. More details are given in Alexander and Giblin (1997).

Although the competition was aimed primarily at neural networks it would be extremely difficult to train a neural network on these data

The price dynamics in financial markets may or may not be governed by chaotic systems. It seems impossible to answer this question at present. Perhaps an answer will be found in the future and, in searching for an answer, many useful forecasting tools could be developed.

---

[6] Dr Giblin (giblin@pennoyer.net) was my ESRC-funded post-doctoral research student at the time. Our nearest neighbour algorithm won the first prize in the competition — in fact it was the only entry that beat a random walk using the metric chosen for the competition. Almost all the other 35 entries that qualified used neural networks or genetic algorithms. The results were assessed using 15 different statistical metrics (§A.5.3) and the performance measure selected for the competition was the root mean square error.

[7] The embedding variables included moving averages of different lengths and the ratio of trading volume to trading range.

Technical Appendices

These appendices have been provided with the aim of making the book self-contained for readers with no background in statistical inference and time series modelling. They are very concise and are only concerned with concepts that are fundamental to other parts of the book. Therefore they should not be viewed as a substitute for the many comprehensive texts on statistics and econometrics that provide a much more detailed and complete coverage of these topics; Greene (1998), Hamilton (1994) and Hendry (1996) are particular favourites of mine and Brooks (2002), will be specific to the econometrics of financial markets.

Appendix 1 outlines the theory of linear statistical models, from the basic principles of regression to the properties of ordinary least squares estimators under different statistical assumptions. Appendix 2 introduces basic concepts for statistical inference: hypothesis testing, confidence intervals and classical statistical tests for the parameters of regression models. Appendix 3 shows how to test the specification of a linear model using a residual analysis, and how to estimate parameters of a linear model when diagnostic tests indicate that the classical assumption of non-spherical disturbances does not hold. Appendix 4 discusses how to apply linear models to financial data that are highly collinear, measured with error, missing on some variables or subject to structural breaks. Appendix 5 shows how to test the predictive ability of statistical models with backtests, using statistical or operational performance measures. Appendix 6 describes the likelihood methods that are used to fit the parameters of many probability distributions.

Appendix 1
Linear Regression

Linear regression models are based on a relationship of the form

$$Y = \beta_1 X_1 + \beta_2 X_2 + \ldots + \beta_k X_k. \tag{A.1.1}$$

On the left-hand side is the *dependent variable*, often denoted Y, and on the right there are k *independent variables*, $X_1, X_2, \ldots, X_k$. These are also called *explanatory variables* or *regressors*. The coefficients β_1, β_2, . . ., β_k are model *parameters* and each one measures the effect that its associated independent variable has upon Y. It is conventional to assume that $X_1 = 1$, so that the model has k coefficients, including a constant β_1. The purpose of regression is to find estimates of the true parameter values and predictions of the dependent variable using data on the dependent and independent variables.

The data, which must consist of an equal number of observations on each variable, may be time series (indexed by the subscript 't'), cross-sectional (indexed by the subscript 'i'), or panel data (a mixture of cross-section and time series, indexed by the subscript 'i, t'). Most of the market models in this book have a statistical rather than an economic foundation and are estimated on daily (or even higher-frequency) time series data.

A.1.1   The Simple Linear Model

The simplest case of a linear relationship (A.1.1) is when $k = 2$ and $X_1 = 1$ for all t so that there is a constant term in the model. For convenience the constant is denoted by α (the *intercept* of the line with the vertical axis), β_2 is denoted by β (the *slope* of the line) and X_2 is replaced simply by X. This gives the equation of a line in the two-dimensional plane:

$$Y_t = \alpha + \beta X_t.$$

A *scatter plot* of the data is a plot of each pair (X_t, Y_t), for $t = 1, . . ., T$, as a point in the (X, Y) plane. It may indicate the existence of certain statistical relationships between X and Y. The points (X_t, Y_t) will not all lie along a line so one needs to add an *error process* to the right-hand side of the equation, giving the simple linear model

$$Y_t = \alpha + \beta X_t + \varepsilon_t. \tag{A.1.2}$$

Consider a linear model for the returns on a single stock Eletrobrás, Y, in the Brazilian index Ibovespa, X. Daily closing prices on the stock and index from August 1994 to December 1997 are shown in Figure A.1, along with a scatter plot of their returns. A line through the scatter plot gives a predicted or fitted value of Y for each value of X as

$$\hat{Y}_t = \hat{\alpha} + \hat{\beta} X_t,$$

where $\hat{\alpha}$ and $\hat{\beta}$ denote the estimates of the line intercept α and slope β. The difference between the actual value of Y and the fitted value of Y at time t is denoted e_t and called the *residual* at time t: $e_t = Y_t - \hat{Y}_t$. So the actual data point for Y is the fitted model value plus the residual:

$$Y_t = \hat{\alpha} + \hat{\beta} X_t + e_t. \tag{A.1.3}$$

Comparing the theoretical model (A.1.2) with the estimated model (A.1.3), note that the error process ε_t is a discrete time continuous state stochastic

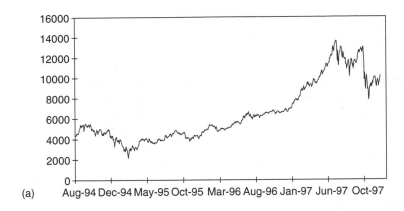

(a)

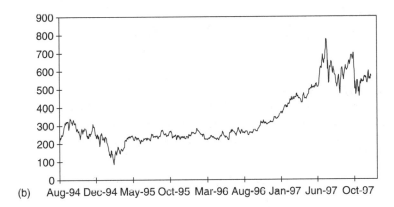

(b)

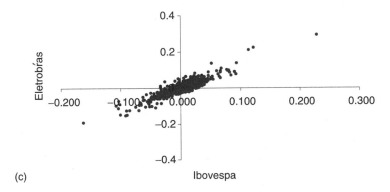

(c)

Figure A.1 Daily closing prices of (a) Ibovespa and (b) Eletrobrás, from August 1994 to December 1997; (c) scatter plot of returns to Ibovespa against returns to Eletrobrás.

process and the residuals are realizations of the error process. Each residual e_t is an observation on the random variable ε_t; the residuals will depend on the values obtained for the parameter estimates $\hat{\alpha}$ and $\hat{\beta}$.

How should these estimates be obtained? It is logical to choose a method of estimation that in some way minimizes the residuals, since then the predicted values of the dependent variable will be closer to the observed values. Choosing estimates to minimize the sum of the residuals will not work, because large positive residuals would cancel large negative residuals. The sum of the absolute residuals could be minimized, but the mathematical properties of the estimators are much nicer if we minimize the sum of the squared residuals. This is the *ordinary least squares* (OLS) criterion.

If coefficients are chosen to minimize the sum of squared residuals, the OLS estimators for coefficients in the simple linear model (A.1.2) are given by:

$$ b = \sum_t (X_t - \bar{X})(Y_t - \bar{Y}) \bigg/ \sum_t (X - \bar{X})^2, \qquad (A.1.4) $$

$$ a = \bar{Y} - b\bar{X}, \qquad (A.1.5) $$

where $\bar{X}$, $\bar{Y}$ denote the sample means (that is, the arithmetic averages) of X and Y. Thus OLS estimate of β uses an equally weighted variance estimate and an equally weighted covariance estimate, with the number of data points in the average being the number of data points used for the regression and without a zero mean assumption (§3.1):

$$ b = \text{est.cov}(X_t, Y_t)/\text{est.} V(X_t). \qquad (A.1.6) $$

In financial markets plenty of data are often available. Therefore one should choose an estimation method that gives consistent estimators (§A.1.3). OLS is widely used because it gives consistent estimators in fairly general circumstances. However, in small samples OLS will only give the 'best' estimates under certain conditions, and an alternative method of estimation should be used if residual diagnostic tests indicate that these conditions do not hold (§A.3.3).

A.1.2 Multivariate Models

The general linear statistical model is

$$ Y_t = \beta_1 X_{1t} + \beta_2 X_{2t} + \ldots + \beta_k X_{kt} + \varepsilon_t, \qquad (A.1.7) $$

and assuming the model contains a constant term then $X_{1t} = 1$ for all $t = 1, \ldots, T$. There will be T equations in the k unknown parameters β_1, $\beta_2, \ldots, \beta_k$, one equation for each date in the data. Model estimation (or 'fitting' the model) involves choosing a method for solving these equations and then using data to obtain estimates $\hat{\beta}_1, \hat{\beta}_2, \ldots, \hat{\beta}_k$ of the model parameters.

The fitted model may be used to predict the values of Y corresponding to given values of the independent variables. At a particular time t each set of values for $X_1, X_2, \ldots, X_k$ determines a predicted value of Y given by

$$\hat{Y}_t = \hat{\beta}_1 X_{1t} + \hat{\beta}_2 X_{2t} + \ldots + \hat{\beta}_k X_{kt}.$$

The difference between the actual and predicted value of Y is the residual e_t, therefore

$$Y_t = \hat{\beta}_1 X_{1t} + \hat{\beta}_2 X_{2t} + \ldots + \hat{\beta}_k X_{kt} + e_t. \tag{A.1.8}$$

Care should be taken to distinguish the model (A.1.8), where the values estimated for the coefficients and residuals depend on the data employed, from the theoretical model (A.1.7).

The general linear model may also be written using matrix notation. Let the column vector of dependent variable data be $\mathbf{y} = (Y_1, Y_2, \ldots, Y_T)'$ and arrange the data on the independent variables into a matrix $\mathbf{X}$, so that the jth column of $\mathbf{X}$ is the data on X_j. The first column of $\mathbf{X}$ will be a column of 1s if there is a constant term in the model. Denote by $\boldsymbol{\beta} = (\beta_1, \beta_2, \ldots, \beta_k)'$ the vector of true parameters and $\boldsymbol{\varepsilon} = (\varepsilon_1, \varepsilon_2, \ldots, \varepsilon_T)'$ the vector of error terms. Then the matrix form of the general linear model (A.1.7) is

$$\mathbf{y} = \mathbf{X}\boldsymbol{\beta} + \boldsymbol{\varepsilon}. \tag{A.1.9}$$

The matrix form of the equations for the OLS estimators of $\boldsymbol{\beta}$ in the general linear model (A.1.9) is[1]

$$\mathbf{b} = (\mathbf{X}'\mathbf{X})^{-1}\mathbf{X}'\mathbf{y}. \tag{A.1.10}$$

Since $\mathbf{X}$ is a $T \times k$ matrix, we need to calculate the inverse of the symmetric $k \times k$ matrix $\mathbf{X}'\mathbf{X}$, and multiply it (on the left) by the $k \times 1$ vector $\mathbf{X}'\mathbf{y}$ to get the $k \times 1$ vector of OLS estimates. Here is a simple example of the use of formula (A.1.10) that can be replicated using a hand calculator. To estimate a deterministic trend in a time series, consider the regression of Y on a constant and time:

$$Y_t = \alpha + \beta t + \varepsilon_t.$$

Suppose there are five observations on Y: $Y_1 = 10$, $Y_2 = 13$, $Y_3 = 19$, $Y_4 = 18$ and $Y_5 = 20$, and so $\mathbf{y} = (10, 13, 19, 18, 20)'$. The matrix of data on the explanatory variables $\mathbf{X}$ will be a 5×2 matrix whose first column contains 1s (for the constant) and whose second column contains 1, 2, 3, 4, 5 (for the time trend). Thus

---

[1] Note that the OLS estimators of $\boldsymbol{\beta}$ are generally denoted $\mathbf{b} = (b_1, b_2, \ldots, b_k)'$, the 'hat' notation being used to denote arbitrary estimators. Note also that in the case $k = 2$ equations (A.1.10) may be written in the summation form given for the OLS equations in (A.1.4) and (A.1.5).

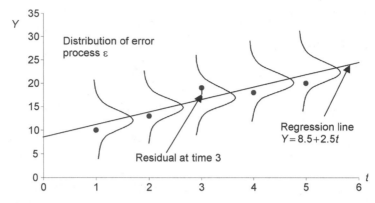

Figure A.2 Scatter plot with OLS regression line and error process.

$$\mathbf{X'y} = (80,\ 265)', \quad \mathbf{X'X} = \begin{pmatrix} 5 & 15 \\ 15 & 55 \end{pmatrix}, \quad (\mathbf{X'X})^{-1} = \begin{pmatrix} 55/50 & -15/50 \\ -15/50 & 5/50 \end{pmatrix}.$$

Applying (A.1.10), we obtain the vector $\mathbf{b} = (a,\ b)'$ of OLS estimates of $\boldsymbol{\beta} = (\alpha,\ \beta)'$ as

$$\mathbf{b} = \begin{pmatrix} 55/50 & -15/50 \\ -15/50 & 5/50 \end{pmatrix} \begin{pmatrix} 80 \\ 265 \end{pmatrix} = \begin{pmatrix} 8.5 \\ 2.5 \end{pmatrix}.$$

Therefore the OLS fitted model is $\hat{Y} = 8.5 + 2.5t$ as shown in Figure A.2.

A.1.3 Properties of OLS Estimators

When applying OLS, or any other estimation method, it should be understood that there is only one theoretical model, but there may be any number of estimated models corresponding to different data and/or different estimation methods. There is only one OLS estimator for each coefficient in the model, but there will be many different OLS estimates of any coefficient, depending on the data used.

To illustrate this point, suppose the model (A.1.2) is estimated for the Brazilian data illustrated in Figure A.1. Although there is only one model, different values for the coefficients are obtained depending on whether the data used are weekly or daily. Using the OLS formulae (A.1.4) and (A.1.5) for the same period from 1 August 1994 to 30 December 1997, one obtains

$$\hat{Y} = -9.3 \times 10^{-4} + 1.2633X$$

on weekly returns data, and

$$\hat{Y} = -2.5 \times 10^{-4} + 1.2111X$$

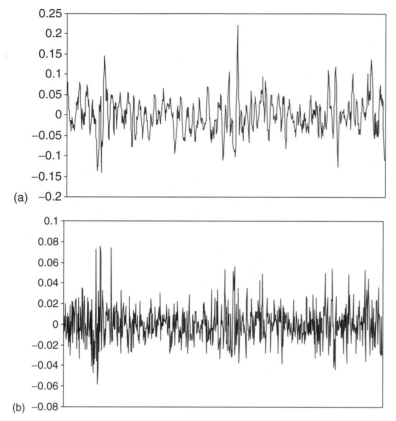

Figure A.3　Residuals from (a) weekly and (b) daily model.

on daily returns data. When the estimated coefficients change, so do the residuals. In this example they are quite different depending on whether daily or weekly data are used for the Brazilian model, as shown in Figure A.3.

The model coefficients *are not* random variables (although their values will always be unknown), but the estimators *are* random variables. Different data give different estimates, so the estimator distributions arise from differences in samples. For this reason they are called *sampling* distributions. Two types of random variables have been introduced in the context of regression: the stochastic error processes $\{\varepsilon_t\}$ are assumed to have theoretical (often normal) distributions; the coefficient estimators are random variables because different data sources, frequencies of observations, or time periods yield different values of the estimator.

The sampling distributions of the estimators may have more or less desirable properties. This will be determined by the method of estimation employed and the assumptions made about the distribution of $\{\varepsilon_t\}$. Two desirable properties for estimator distributions are *unbiasedness* and *efficiency*. Unbiasedness means that the expected value of the estimator equals the true value of the

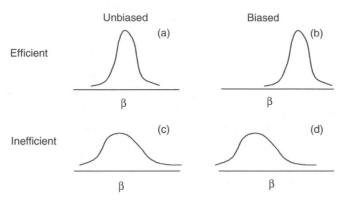

Figure A.4 Sampling distributions of estimators: (a) unbiased and efficient; (b) biased and efficient; (c) unbiased and inefficient; (d) biased and inefficient.

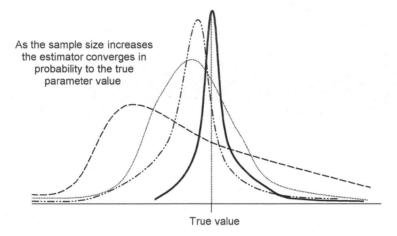

Figure A.5 Distributions of a consistent estimator.

parameter, and efficiency means that the variance of the estimator is as small as possible.

If many different estimates are obtained from an unbiased and efficient estimator, they would all be near the true parameter value, as in Figure A.4a. But if the distribution of the estimator is biased, or inefficient, or both, it would look like one of the other curves in Figure A.4. For an inefficient estimator, the estimates arising from small differences in samples are likely to vary considerably, as in Figures A.4c and A.4d. Thus estimates will not be robust even to small changes in the data. Parameter estimates may change considerably when a few more days of data are used, for no obvious reason. Perhaps the worst case is biased and efficient estimators, where most estimates lie far away from the true value, as in Figure A.4b. In this case estimates will be quite robust, changing little even when the data change a lot. But they will almost always be far above the true model parameter.

In many financial markets it is possible to obtain hundreds if not thousands of data points. The asymptotic properties of estimators are therefore particularly relevant to models of financial markets. A *consistent* estimator has a distribution such as that shown in Figure A.5, which converges to the true value of the parameter as the sample size tends to infinity. That is, the *probability limit* (plim) of the estimator distribution is the true parameter value, written plim $\hat{\beta} = \beta$. The estimator may be biased and/or inefficient for small sample sizes, but as the number of observations used to make the estimate increases the distribution converges in probability to the true parameter value.

OLS estimators are not always consistent (for example, when the model includes a time trend or the data are measured with error) but maximum likelihood estimators are almost always consistent, even though their small-sample properties may not be very good (§A.6.1)

Properties of OLS Estimators with Non-Stochastic Regressors

If possible, one should choose an estimation method that gives unbiased and efficient estimators when sample sizes are small. The *Gauss–Markov theorem* states that OLS estimators are unbiased and the most efficient of all linear unbiased estimators if:

➢ the explanatory variables are non-stochastic, and
➢ the error terms are stationary, homoscedastic, and not autocorrelated.[2]

To see this, substitute (A.1.9) into (A.1.10) to obtain

$$\mathbf{b} = \boldsymbol{\beta} + (\mathbf{X'X})^{-1}\mathbf{X'}\boldsymbol{\varepsilon}. \qquad (A.1.12)$$

Assuming that $\mathbf{X}$ is non-stochastic, taking expectations shows that the OLS estimators are unbiased:

$$E(\mathbf{b}) = E(\boldsymbol{\beta}) + (\mathbf{X'X})^{-1}\mathbf{X'}E(\boldsymbol{\varepsilon}) = \boldsymbol{\beta}.$$

The covariance matrix of $\mathbf{b}$ is

$$V(\mathbf{b}) = E((\mathbf{b} - \boldsymbol{\beta})(\mathbf{b} - \boldsymbol{\beta})').$$

Since $\mathbf{b} - \boldsymbol{\beta}$ is a $k \times 1$ vector, the covariance matrix is a symmetric $k \times k$ matrix, whose diagonal elements are the variances of each estimator, and whose off-diagonal elements are the covariances. By (A.1.12),

---

[2]A stronger assumption is that the error process be independent and identically distributed: we write $\varepsilon_t \sim$ i.i.d.$(0, \sigma^2)$, where σ^2 denotes the variance of the process. An even stronger assumption that the errors have independent normal distributions ($\varepsilon_t \sim$ NID$(0, \sigma^2)$) is usually necessary for the standard hypothesis tests that are outlined in Appendix 2.

$$V(\mathbf{b}) = E((\mathbf{X}'\mathbf{X})^{-1}\mathbf{X}'\boldsymbol{\varepsilon})((\mathbf{X}'\mathbf{X})^{-1}\mathbf{X}'\boldsymbol{\varepsilon})'$$
$$= E((\mathbf{X}'\mathbf{X})^{-1}\mathbf{X}'\boldsymbol{\varepsilon}\boldsymbol{\varepsilon}'\mathbf{X}(\mathbf{X}'\mathbf{X})^{-1})$$
$$= (\mathbf{X}'\mathbf{X})^{-1}\mathbf{X}'E(\boldsymbol{\varepsilon}\boldsymbol{\varepsilon}')\mathbf{X}(\mathbf{X}'\mathbf{X})^{-1}.$$

Under the classical assumptions $E(\boldsymbol{\varepsilon}\boldsymbol{\varepsilon}') = V(\boldsymbol{\varepsilon}) = \sigma^2\mathbf{I}$, where $\mathbf{I}$ is the $T \times T$ identity matrix, so

$$V(\mathbf{b}) = \sigma^2(\mathbf{X}'\mathbf{X})^{-1}. \tag{A.1.13}$$

From here it can be shown that if one takes an arbitrary linear unbiased estimator, its variance will always be greater than the OLS estimator variance given by (A.1.13). Therefore OLS estimators are the 'best' linear unbiased estimators, but only when the classical assumption $V(\boldsymbol{\varepsilon}) = \sigma^2\mathbf{I}$ holds. This assumption is often referred to as 'spherical disturbances'.

Large-sample properties of OLS estimators are easy to derive when the regressors are assumed to be non-stochastic. OLS estimators will be consistent unless the explanatory variables include a time trend. In the case that the model includes a trend the OLS estimators are *asymptotically unbiased* (lim $E(\mathbf{b}) = \boldsymbol{\beta}$) and *asymptotically efficient* (lim $V(\mathbf{b}) = \mathbf{0}$). Note that spherical disturbances are *not* necessary for consistency of OLS. In fact OLS will be consistent even when the error process is autocorrelated (assuming that the error covariance matrix has finite eigenvalues) or unconditionally heteroscedastic (§A.3).

Properties of OLS with Stochastic Regressors

So far it has been assumed that explanatory variables are non-stochastic, which is rather unrealistic. Introducing stochastic regressors complicates the analysis a little, but it is fairly simple to show that OLS is still unbiased if the regressors are uncorrelated with the errors. In fact we need to assume that the expectation of the errors, given all information embodied in the explanatory data, is zero. That is, there is no information about the errors in $\mathbf{X}$, or $E(\boldsymbol{\varepsilon}|\mathbf{X}) = \mathbf{0}$. This implies that each column in $\mathbf{X}$ is uncorrelated with $\boldsymbol{\varepsilon}$.

To see that OLS is unbiased when regressors are stochastic but uncorrelated with the errors, use (A.1.12) to calculate the expectation of $\mathbf{b}$, given the data on $\mathbf{X}$. Taking conditional expectations gives

$$E(\mathbf{b}|\mathbf{X}) = \boldsymbol{\beta} + (\mathbf{X}'\mathbf{X})^{-1}\mathbf{X}'E(\boldsymbol{\varepsilon}|\mathbf{X}),$$

and since $E(\boldsymbol{\varepsilon}|\mathbf{X}) = \mathbf{0}$, $E(\mathbf{b}|\mathbf{X}) = \boldsymbol{\beta}$ whatever the data in $\mathbf{X}$. From this it is intuitively clear that the unconditional expectation of $\mathbf{b}$ is $\boldsymbol{\beta}$.[3]

---

[3]The proof uses the fact that for any random variables X and Y, $E(X) = E_Y(E(X|Y))$, so $E(\mathbf{b}) = E_X(E(\mathbf{b}|\mathbf{X})) = E_X(\boldsymbol{\beta}) = \boldsymbol{\beta}$.

Although unbiased, OLS will no longer be efficient. However, it will still be consistent under certain regularity conditions on the regressors and assuming they are uncorrelated (in the limit) with the errors, that is,

$$\text{plim}\,[(\mathbf{X}'\boldsymbol{\varepsilon})/T] = \mathbf{0}.$$

Applying the plim operator to (A.1.12) gives

$$\text{plim}\,\mathbf{b} = \boldsymbol{\beta} + \text{plim}\,[(\mathbf{X}'\mathbf{X})/T]^{-1}\text{plim}\,[(\mathbf{X}'\boldsymbol{\varepsilon})/T]. \qquad (A.1.14)$$

The data regularity condition is that $\text{plim}\,[(\mathbf{X}'\mathbf{X})/T]$ is positive definite, so that its inverse in (A.1.14) exists. Then $\text{plim}\,\mathbf{b} = \boldsymbol{\beta}$ and OLS is consistent if $\text{plim}\,[(\mathbf{X}'\boldsymbol{\varepsilon})/T] = \mathbf{0}$. So when regressors are stochastic the OLS estimators will be inefficient, but they will be unbiased when the regressors are uncorrelated with the error process. They will also be consistent if the data satisfy a standard regularity condition.

When are OLS Estimators Normally Distributed?

OLS estimators are normally distributed under fairly general conditions. In the classical model where errors are normally distributed and the explanatory variables are non-stochastic, the normality of OLS estimators follows from (A.1.12). This equation implies that the distribution of $\mathbf{b}$ is determined by that of $\boldsymbol{\varepsilon}$, and so $\mathbf{b}$ has a multivariate normal distribution with mean $\boldsymbol{\beta}$ and variance $\sigma^2(\mathbf{X}'\mathbf{X})^{-1}$.

If errors are not normal, or regressors are stochastic, or both, then it is difficult to state any finite-sample results. However, OLS estimators will be asymptotically normally distributed with mean $\boldsymbol{\beta}$ and variance $\sigma^2(\mathbf{X}'\mathbf{X})^{-1}$ under certain conditions. In particular, if the errors are not necessarily normal but they all have the same distribution (with zero mean and finite variance) and if the regressors satisfy the usual regularity conditions then the asymptotic normality of OLS estimators will follow from the central limit theorem.

A.1.4   Estimating the Covariance Matrix of the OLS Estimators

The formula (A.1.13) cannot be used in practice, because the variance of the error process σ^2 is unknown. The error variance σ^2 is estimated as follows. First calculate the OLS *residual sum of squares* RSS as follows:[4]

$$\text{RSS} = \mathbf{e}'\mathbf{e} = \mathbf{y}'\mathbf{y} - \mathbf{b}'\mathbf{X}'\mathbf{y}. \qquad (A.1.15)$$

---

[4]The formula says that the residual sum of squares is the *total sum of squares*, TSS = $\mathbf{y}'\mathbf{y}$, minus the *explained sum of squares*, ESS = $\mathbf{b}'\mathbf{X}'\mathbf{y}$, so called because it is the variation in Y that is explained by the model (§A.2.4).

To obtain an unbiased estimate of σ^2, divide the RSS by the degrees of freedom in the model.[5] Thus an unbiased estimate of σ^2 is

$$s^2 = \text{RSS}/(T - k). \tag{A.1.16}$$

From (A.1.13) it follows that the estimated covariance matrix of the OLS estimators is

$$\text{est } V(\mathbf{b}) = s^2 (\mathbf{X}'\mathbf{X})^{-1}. \tag{A.1.17}$$

To illustrate formula (A.1.17), return to the simple example of the linear trend model. Here $\mathbf{y}'\mathbf{y} = 1354$, $\mathbf{b} = (8.5, 2.5)'$ and $\mathbf{X}'\mathbf{y} = (80, 265)'$, so by (A.1.19) the RSS is 11.5. There are 5 observations and 2 parameters, so we have 3 degrees of freedom and $s^2 = 11.5/3$. Finally, putting

$$(\mathbf{X}'\mathbf{X})^{-1} = \begin{pmatrix} 55/50 & -15/50 \\ -15/50 & 5/50 \end{pmatrix}$$

into (A.1.17) gives the estimated covariance matrix:

$$\text{est } V(\mathbf{b}) = \frac{11.5}{150} \begin{pmatrix} 55 & -15 \\ -15 & 5 \end{pmatrix} = \begin{pmatrix} 4.217 & -1.150 \\ -1.150 & 0.383 \end{pmatrix}$$

In the simple linear model higher estimates of the intercept are always associated with lower estimates of the slope, so the estimate of cov(a, b) is always negative in the simple linear model. In this example it is -1.150. The estimated values of $V(a)$ and $V(b)$ are 4.217 and 0.383, respectively. Note that the fact that a has greater estimated variance than does b does not imply that a is a less accurate estimate than is b: the elements of the covariance matrix, and the coefficient estimates themselves, are always in units of measurement determined by those of the corresponding variables. We could just as easily model the time trend as 10, 20, 30, 40, . . . instead of 1, 2, 3, 4, ... Then the coefficient estimate b would be ten times as large (i.e. 25) and its estimated variance would be 100 times as large (i.e. 38.3).

Changing units of measurement should not affect the properties of the model, but parameter estimates and their variances and covariances do depend on the units of measurement. Therefore a standardized form for the coefficients should be used to investigate the accuracy and specification of a regression model. It is common to standardize parameter estimates by dividing by the square root of their estimated variance. These 't-ratios' are one of the most common classical hypothesis tests; they are described in §A.2.1.

---

[5]The number of degrees of freedom would be equal to the number of observations T, but one degree of freedom is lost for every statistic that needs to be calculated in order to obtain the RSS. Since we need to calculate the k estimates in **b** to use (A.1.15), there are $T - k$ degrees of freedom left in the model.

Appendix 2
Statistical Inference

The fundamental goal of statistics is to estimate the values of model parameters and to associate a level of confidence with the results. Only when a model is properly specified and parameter estimates are robust, unbiased and efficient can the model predict well. The questions answered in this appendix concern the accuracy of parameter estimates: With what degree of confidence can we say that a model parameter takes some value, such as zero?[6] It may also be of interest to test the equality of certain parameters, or that all parameters are zero, or more general linear restrictions on several model parameters.[7]

A.2.1   Hypothesis Testing and Confidence Intervals

There are two methods of inference on the true values of model parameters: confidence intervals and hypothesis tests. The framework for hypothesis tests is conceptually very simple:

1. *Set up the null and alternative hypotheses*, H_0 *and* H_1. The null hypothesis of no change or no effect consists of one or more restrictions on the true model parameters. The alternatives may be either one-sided ($<$ or $>$) or two-sided ($\neq$).
2. *State the test statistic*, X. A variety of test statistics are often available. The most common parametric test statistics fall into one of three categories: Wald tests, Lagrange multiplier (LM) tests or likelihood ratio (LR) tests. These tests have different power properties and different distributions in small samples, although they are asymptotically equivalent (§A.2.5).
3. *Choose a significance level*, α. The level of significance with which one can state results determines the *size* of the test, which is the probability of a *type I error* (the rejection of a true null hypothesis). Increasing the significance level reduces the size, but also increases the probability of a *type II error* (the failure to reject a false null hypothesis) and so reduces its power. The *power* of a test is the probability that it will reject a false null hypothesis. When more than one test is available it is preferable to choose the most powerful test of any given size.
4. *Determine the critical region* CR_α. The critical values of the test statistic depend on the chosen significance level α. For a fixed α, and for a two-sided alternative, upper and lower critical values CV_U and CV_L give the critical region $CR_\alpha = \{(-\infty, CV_L] \text{ and } [CV_U, \infty)\}$. A one-sided ($<$) alternative has the critical region $(-\infty, CV_L]$ and a one-sided ($>$) alternative has the

---

[6]The hypothesis $\beta_i = 0$ is a particularly interesting inference in a regression model, because it implies that the associated explanatory variable X_i has no effect on the dependent variable.

[7]Non-linear hypotheses require statistical methods that are beyond the scope of this book, but they are well covered in other econometrics texts, such as Campbell *et al.* (1997).

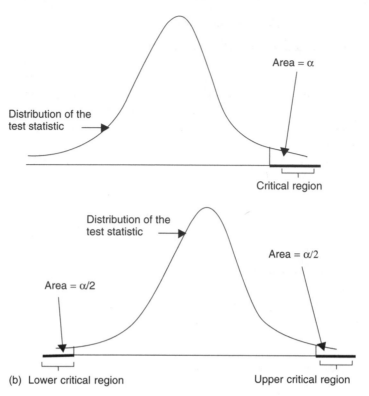

Figure A.6 Critical region of (a) a one-sided (>) statistical test; (b) a two-sided statistical test.

critical region $[CV_U, \infty)$.[8] In each case the size of the test is the area above the critical region under the density function of the test statistic as shown in Figure A.6. In the majority of cases the critical values of a test statistic are tabulated. In fact many test statistics have one of four standard sampling distributions under the null hypothesis: the normal distribution, the t-distribution, the F-distribution or the chi-squared (χ^2) distribution. Critical values for these distributions are tabulated at the end of the book.

5. *Evaluate the test statistic, X^*.* This value will be based on sample data, and it may or may not assume the values of model parameters that are given under the null and alternative hypothesis. In Wald tests the test statistic is calculated without the restrictions of the null hypothesis, but LM tests employ restricted estimators and LR tests use both unrestricted and restricted estimators.

6. *Apply the decision rule.* The decision is 'reject H_0 in favour of H_1 at $100\alpha\%$ if $X^* \in CR_\alpha$'.

---

[8]Note that, for the same value of α, the upper and lower critical values will not be the same for the one-sided test as for the two-sided test: in the latter case the critical region will be split between the tails, while in the former case it will fall entirely in one tail.

As its name suggests, a confidence interval is a range within which one is, to some degree, confident the true parameter lies. So (A, B) is a 95% confidence interval for θ if $\text{Prob}(A < \theta < B) = 0.95$. The range of the confidence interval depends on the degree of confidence and the distribution of the parameter estimator.

Confidence intervals allow error bounds to be placed on the true values of model parameters using the estimated standard errors of model parameter estimates. Consider, for example, an OLS estimator b of a parameter β in a linear regression model. The simple *t-ratio* will have a *t*-distribution if the OLS estimators are normally distributed:

$$t\text{-ratio} = (b - \beta)/(\text{est. s.e. } b) \sim t_v.$$

Here 'est. s.e.' stands for 'estimated standard error', the square root of the estimated variance given in the estimated covariance matrix (A.1.17).[9] The degrees of freedom v are $T - k$, where T is the sample size and k is the number of variables in the regression (including the constant).[10]

This *t*-statistic may be used for hypotheses with only one linear restriction on parameters, as described below. It also forms the basis of confidence intervals for β. Denote by $t_{v,0.025}$ the 2.5% critical value of the *t*-distribution on v degrees of freedom. Since

$$\text{Prob}((b - \beta)/(\text{est. s.e. } b) < -t_{v,0.025}) = 0.025$$

and

$$\text{Prob}((b - \beta)/(\text{est. s.e. } b) > -t_{v,0.025}) = 0.025,$$

we have

$$\text{Prob}(b - t_{v,0.025}(\text{est. s.e. } b) < \beta < b + t_{v,0.025}(\text{est. s.e. } b)) = 0.95.$$

Thus a two-sided 95% confidence interval for β is

$$(b - t_{v,0.025}(\text{est. s.e. } b), b + t_{v,0.025}(\text{est. s.e. } b)).$$

The size α of the critical region determines the degree of confidence, just as it does the significance level of a hypothesis test. In general, a two-sided $100(1 - \alpha)\%$ confidence interval for β is

$$(b - t_{v,\alpha/2}(\text{est. s.e. } b), b + t_{v,\alpha/2}(\text{est. s.e. } b))$$

Confidence intervals may also be one-sided, just as hypothesis tests. A one-sided upper $100(1 - \alpha)\%$ confidence interval for β is

$$(b - t_{v,\alpha}(\text{est. s.e. } b), \infty).$$

---

[9]The terminology standard error, rather than standard deviation, is used because we are referring to an estimate rather than an arbitrary random variable.

[10]One degree of freedom is lost for every constraint on the data that is necessary to calculate the estimates.

Put another way, $\text{Prob}(\beta > b - t_{v,\alpha}(\text{est. s.e. } b)) = 1 - \alpha$. Similarly, a lower $100(1 - \alpha)\%$ confidence interval is $(-\infty, b + t_{v,\alpha}(\text{est. s.e. } b))$, which is another way of saying that $\text{Prob}(\beta < b + t_{v,\alpha}(\text{est. s.e. } b)) = 1 - \alpha$.

A.2.2   *t*-Tests

To illustrate the basic idea of a *t*-test, consider the simple numerical example in Appendix 1 and perform a *t*-test of whether there is a significant deterministic trend in the data.[11] Suppose the null hypothesis H_0: $\beta = 0$ is tested against the alternative hypothesis H_1: $\beta \neq 0$. The test statistic is *t*-distributed with 3 degrees of freedom, and is given by

$$t = (b - \beta)/(\text{est. s.e. } b).$$

Evaluating *t* under the null hypothesis and given the estimated model in §A.1.2 and §A.1.4, yields a particular value for *t*, viz.

$$t^* = (2.5 - 0)/\sqrt{0.383} = 4.04.$$

Statistical tables give critical values of the t_3 distribution. For a two-sided 5% test the critical values are $\pm t_{3,0.025} = \pm 3.182$, and for a 1% test the critical values are $\pm t_{3,0.005} = \pm 5.841$. Since 4.04 lies in the 5% critical region of the t_3 distribution but not in the 1% critical region, we can reject the null hypothesis at 5% but not at 1%. We conclude that it is reasonable to include the trend in the model, but that it is not very highly significant.

When OLS regression is run in a statistical package, the estimated standard errors of the estimates and the *t*-ratios for the null hypothesis H_0: $\beta = 0$ are automatically computed. For example, estimating the daily CAPM for Eletrobrás with the Brazilian index Ibovespa gives the following Excel output for the period from 1 August 1994 to 30 December 1997:

	Coefficient	Standard error	*t-Ratio*
Intercept	-0.00025	0.000608	-0.41369
ibo	1.211073	0.021586	56.1039

With hundreds of data points, the critical values of these *t*-statistics are the same as the normal critical values ($Z_{0.05} = 1.645$, $Z_{0.025} = 1.96$, $Z_{0.01} = 2.326$). The *t*-statistic of 56.1039 shows that the index is a very highly significant determinant of Eletrobrás returns, but the intercept is not statistically significant ($t = -0.41369$), as implied by the Sharpe–Lintner model (§8.1.1).

---

[11]This is not at all a good statistical test, we use it here just to illustrate ideas. Much better tests are described in §11.1.6.

The estimated standard errors of the coefficient estimate may seem redundant in the table above: the *t*-ratio for the hypothesis that the model parameter is zero is the ratio of the coefficient estimate to its estimated standard error. The estimated standard errors are reported because this allows many other hypotheses to be tested, such as

$$H_0: \beta = 1 \text{ against } H_1: \beta < 1.$$

In the current example, this alternative hypothesis is that Eletrobrás is a 'low-risk' stock. It cannot be accepted because the critical region of the test is $(-\infty, -Z_a)$ and since $t = 0.211073/0.021586 = 9.78$ it does not lie in the critical region.

The estimated standard errors also give confidence intervals for the model parameters. For example a two-sided 95% confidence interval for β is $1.211073 \pm 1.96*0.021586$, that is, $(1.1688, 1.2534)$.

Knowledge of the estimated covariance matrix of the regression estimates makes it possible to test quite general linear hypotheses with a simple *t*-test, provided there is only one restriction. At the most general level the *t*-test statistic in a linear regression takes the form

$$t = f(\mathbf{b})/\text{est. s.e. } \mathbf{f}(\mathbf{b}) \sim \mathbf{t_{T-k}}, \tag{A.2.1}$$

where $f(\cdot) = 0$ is some linear restriction on the model parameters, and $\mathbf{b}$ are the estimated parameter values.[12] For example, if the null hypothesis is $H_0: \alpha = \beta$ then the linear restriction is $f(\alpha, \beta) = \alpha - \beta = 0$, so the test statistic is

$$t = (a - b)/\text{est. s.e.} (a - b).$$

The denominator is calculated from the square root of the estimate of $V(a - b)$. Since

$$V(a - b) = V(a) + V(b) - 2 \operatorname{cov}(a, b),$$

the estimate of $V(a - b)$ is obtained by substituting elements of the estimated covariance matrix into this formula. Similarly, for the null hypothesis $H_0: 2\alpha = \beta - 1$ the linear restriction is $2\alpha - \beta + 1 = 0$ so it has the test statistic

$$t = (2a - b + 1)/\text{est. s.e.} (2a - b + 1).$$

Again the denominator is calculated by substituting elements of the estimated covariance matrix in a variance formula, in this case using

$$V(2a - b + 1) = V(2a - b) = 4V(a) + V(b) - 4 \operatorname{cov}(a, b).$$

To see how this works in practice, again consider the deterministic trend model of Appendix 1 with the test

---

[12]The *t*-distribution of (A.2.1) is based on the normality of linear functions of OLS estimators (§A.1.3).

$$H_0: \alpha + \beta = 7 \text{ versus } H_1: \alpha + \beta > 7.$$

Since $V(a + b - 7) = V(a + b)$ the test statistic (A.2.1) is

$$t = [(a + b) - 7]/\text{est. s.e.}(a + b)$$

The estimated standard error of $a + b$ is calculated using the formula

$$V(a + b) = V(a) + V(b) + 2\,\text{cov}(a, b).$$

Putting in the estimated variances and covariances from the estimated covariance matrix in §A.1.4 and taking square roots gives

$$\text{est. s.e.}(a + b) = \sqrt{(4.217 + 0.383 - 2 \times 1.15)} = 1.517.$$

Evaluating t under H_0 and given our data gives $t^* = (11 - 7)/1.517 = 2.638$, and since $t_{3,0.05} = 2.353$ we can reject the null at 5%.

A.2.3   *F*-tests

F-tests are commonly used to test the joint significance of several explanatory variables in a linear model. For example, they can form the basis of Granger causality tests in vector autoregressions (§11.4.3).

Complex hypotheses involving more than two parameters may be formulated as a set of q linear restrictions. It is convenient to write these in matrix form as $\mathbf{R}\boldsymbol{\beta} = \mathbf{q}$, where $\mathbf{R}$ is a $q \times k$ matrix of coefficients on the model parameters and $\mathbf{q}$ is a $q \times 1$ vector of constants. For example, the null hypothesis

$$\beta_1 = \beta_2, \quad \beta_1 + \beta_3 = 0, \quad \beta_2 + 2\beta_3 = \beta_1 + 2$$

may be written

$$\begin{pmatrix} 1 & -1 & 0 \\ 1 & 0 & 1 \\ -1 & 1 & 2 \end{pmatrix} \begin{pmatrix} \beta_1 \\ \beta_2 \\ \beta_3 \end{pmatrix} = \begin{pmatrix} 0 \\ 0 \\ 2 \end{pmatrix}.$$

Complex hypotheses of the form $\mathbf{R}\boldsymbol{\beta} = \mathbf{q}$ can be tested using the *F*-statistic

$$F = [(\text{RSS}_R - \text{RSS}_U)/q]/[\text{RSS}_U/(T - k)] \sim F_{q,T-k}. \qquad \text{(A.2.2)}$$

To calculate the *F*-statistic the regression model is estimated twice, first with no restrictions to obtain the residual sum of squares RSS_U and then after imposing the q restrictions in the null hypothesis to obtain the restricted residual sum of squares RSS_R.

Here is an example that illustrates how to construct a restricted model. Suppose the test is of the null hypothesis

$$H_0: \alpha_0 = 1, \ \alpha_2 = \alpha_3 = 0, \ \alpha_5 = \alpha_6 + \alpha_7, \ \alpha_8 = 2$$

in the model $Y = \alpha_0 + \alpha_1 X_1 + \ldots + \alpha_9 X_9 + \varepsilon$. There are 10 parameters in the model so $k = 10$ in (A.2.2), and the unrestricted residual sum of squares RSS_U is obtained by first estimating the model with no restrictions on the parameters. There are 5 equalities in the null, so $q = 5$, and the restricted model is

$$Y = 1 + \alpha_1 X_1 + \alpha_4 X_4 + (\alpha_6 + \alpha_7)X_5 + \alpha_6 X_6 + \alpha_7 X_7 + 2X_8 + \alpha_9 X_9 + \varepsilon$$

or

$$[Y - 1 - 2X_8] = \alpha_1 X_1 + \alpha_4 X_4 + \alpha_6(X_5 + X_6) + \alpha_7(X_5 + X_7) + \alpha_9 X_9 + \varepsilon.$$

To estimate the restricted model a new dependent variable $[Y - 1 - 2X_8]$ is regressed on five explanatory variables: X_1, X_4, $(X_5 + X_6)$, $(X_5 + X_7)$ and X_9. The residual sum of squares from this model is the RSS_R.

For the statistic defined by (A.2.2) to be *F*-distributed it is necessary to assume that the error process is normally distributed. Otherwise even the asymptotic normality of the OLS estimators is not sufficient to invoke the *F*-distribution of (A.2.2). When errors are not normal the *Wald statistic* qF, where F is given by (A.2.2) and q is the number of restrictions, can be used in large samples (§A.2.5). In fact the *F*-distribution is a finite-sample approximation to the chi-squared distribution of Wald statistics, just as the *t*-distribution is a finite-sample approximation to the standard normal.

A.2.4 The Analysis of Variance

The 'analysis of variance' (ANOVA) describes the decomposition of the total variance of the dependent variable (as measured by the total sum of squares, TSS) into two components, the explained sum of squares, ESS, and residual sums of squares, RSS. In ANOVA the *F*-test for the null hypothesis that all parameters except the constant are zero is applied automatically. This is the 'goodness-of-fit' test of the model. The restricted model is just a constant, so RSS_R is just TSS and the numerator of (A.2.2) becomes ESS. So the *F*-statistic for 'goodness of fit' is simply measuring the same thing as the squared correlation coefficient $R^2 = \text{ESS}/\text{TSS}$.

The ANOVA table and some basic diagnostic statistics for the Eletrobrás CAPM that has been estimated in §A.2.2 are shown below (the output is from Excel):

Regression Statistics	
R Square	0.800796
Adjusted R Square	0.800542
Standard Error	0.017024
Observations	785

ANOVA

	Degrees of freedom	Sum of squares	F	Significance F
Regression	1	0.9122	3145.517	1.9E-276
Residual	783	0.226916		
Total	784	1.139116		

The explained sum of squares is 0.9122, the residual sum of squares is 0.226916 and the total sum of squares is 1.139116. So the F-statistic for goodness of fit is $0.9122/(0.226916/783) = 0.9122/0.00029 = 3145.517$ which is very highly significant (1% $F_{1,783} = 6.67$). Dividing the ESS by the TSS gives the $R^2 = 0.9122/1.139116 = 0.800796$.[13] Very few diagnostics are standard Excel output. It does report the standard error of the equation (0.017024 in the example above) and the square of this gives the estimated residual variance s^2. More advanced model diagnostic tests that are based on the residuals from the regression follow the procedures outlined in Appendix 3.

A.2.5   Wald, Lagrange Multiplier and Likelihood Ratio Tests

Linear restrictions on the model parameters can be tested in a number of ways other than the simple tests described above. Of course, F- and t-tests have many practical advantages: they are particularly simple to use in the 'testing down' procedure for model specification (§8.4), and their framework is flexible enough to admit quite general linear hypothesis. However, they do have limited applicability and they are not always as powerful as the more general Wald, Lagrange multiplier (LM) or likelihood ratio (LR) tests. The test statistics for Wald, LM and LR hypothesis tests on the parameters of a normal regression model are as follows:[14]

Test	Statistic
Wald	$(T - k)(\text{RSS}_R - \text{RSS}_U)/\text{RSS}_U$
LM	$(T - k + q)(\text{RSS}_R - \text{RSS}_U)/\text{RSS}_R$
LR	$T(\ln \text{RSS}_R - \ln \text{RSS}_U)$

---

[13]In this simple model with only one explanatory variable (plus a constant) the R^2 and the adjusted R^2, which is a modification of R^2 to take degrees of freedom into account, are roughly the same.

[14]The unrestricted sum of squares, RSS_U, and the restricted sum of squares, RSS_R, were defined in §A.2.3.

Under the null hypothesis these tests are all asymptotically distributed as chi-squared with q degrees of freedom. Wald, LM and LR tests are quite general. They can be applied to parameter testing in statistical distributions, non-linear hypotheses in linear models, or testing restrictions in general covariance matrices (see Greene, 1998; Griffiths *et al.*, 1993). They do not have to assume that errors are normally distributed. Actually the form of LR test given above does assume normal errors, but the general LR test statistic can be defined in terms of any likelihood function.

Appendix 3
Residual Analysis

The simple 'goodness-of-fit' test described in §A.2.4 goes some way towards indicating how well a linear model has been specified. But a full diagnostic analysis of residuals gives much more information about the possible omission of relevant explanatory variables, and the properties of coefficient estimators.

In an ideal world, including sufficient explanatory variables would improve a linear specification to the point that the classical assumption $V(\varepsilon) = \sigma^2 I$ can be upheld. In that case unbiased and efficient parameter estimators may be obtained by OLS. This appendix examines the residual diagnostic tests which should indicate whether this assumption is violated. Two questions will be addressed:

➤ Is $V(\varepsilon)$ diagonal? If not the errors will be autocorrelated.
➤ Is $V(\varepsilon)$ homoscedastic? In other words, does the error process have a constant variance?

These two assumptions may be tested using a wide variety of residual diagnostic tests. A brief account of the most common test procedures is given, with a description of the common causes and remedies if auto-correlation or heteroscedasticity is found in the residuals. If residuals are autocorrelated or heteroscedastic an alternative method of estimation such as generalized least squares (GLS) could be used to obtain unbiased and efficient estimators in small samples, and this is described in §A.3.3. However, since OLS is consistent under fairly general conditions, it may be applied without problems to the large samples that many of the financial applications of linear models employ. That is not to say that residual diagnostics are unnecessary for models that use large amounts of data, because the characteristics of the OLS residuals will still reveal a considerable amount about the model specification.

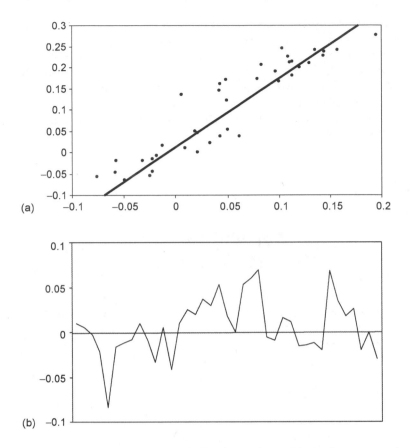

Figure A.7 (a) Structural break in data; (b) residuals from regression without dummy.

A.3.1 Autocorrelation

Common causes of autocorrelation in residuals are:

➢ *Structural breaks*. Structural breaks are very common in financial markets, since a market crash or move to a different regime may signify a structural change in the data generation process. If one attempts to fit a linear model to data with structural breaks, residuals may be autocorrelated (Figure A.7). The solution is to use a dummy variable in the regression, whose precise form depends on the type of structural break. In the example of Figure A.7, the residual autocorrelation is removed if one adds another explanatory variable to the model: a dummy variable taking the value 0 before the structural break and the value 1 at and after the structural break. The single model becomes equivalent to two models with different constant terms and/or different slope parameters, depending on how this dummy is incorporated (§A.4.4).

➤ *Omitted variables.* If the dependent variable has characteristics that are not explained by any of the included explanatory variables, those characteristics will show up in the residuals.[15]

➤ *Over- or under-differencing the data.* The usual method for transforming financial price, rate or yield data into stationary series is first differencing (§11.1.4). If this is not done, the data may have a very high degree of positive autocorrelation, and if there is no similar explanatory variable to 'balance' the model, the autocorrelation will show up in residuals. On the other hand, if first differencing is performed when it is not necessary, the data will have high negative autocorrelation. In either case, it is by no means certain that the model could explain such structural autocorrelation. It is a problem with the basic data that should already have been identified when plotting the data prior to building the model.

The *Durbin–Watson test* for autocorrelation is standard output in many statistical packages. The test statistic is

$$d = \Sigma(e_t - e_{t-1})^2 / \Sigma e_t^2.$$

Small values of d indicate positive autocorrelation in the OLS residuals, and large values indicate negative autocorrelation. In large samples $d \approx 2(1 - r)$, where r is the first-order autocorrelation coefficient estimate of the residuals (§11.3). So the approximate range for d is $[0, 4]$, and d has an expected value of approximately 2 under the null hypothesis of zero autocorrelation. No exact distribution is available, but upper and lower limits d_U and d_L for the significance levels of d are found in Durbin–Watson tables. The decision rule is: if $d < d_L$ then reject the null in favour of the alternative of positive autocorrelation; if $d > d_U$ then do not reject the null; and if $d_L < d < d_U$ the test is inconclusive.

Although positive autocorrelation is the natural hypothesis to test (being the prime indication of omitted explanatory variables), negative autocorrelation is also a concern for the application of OLS. Durbin–Watson tests of negative autocorrelation proceed in a similar way, replacing d by $4 - d$ in the decision rule above.

The basic Durbin–Watson test has limited applicability; in particular, the explanatory variables cannot be stochastic. There is an extension to the case where lagged dependent variables are included in the regression (Durbin's *h*-test). A more general framework for testing autocorrelation, in residuals from a regression model or in more general time series, is explained in §11.3.2.

If OLS residuals are found to be autocorrelated, the first step is to respecify the linear model to try to remove the autocorrelation. Assuming the data on the

---

[15]The structural break dummy just described is an example of an omitted variable causing autocorrelation. If one of the explanatory variables had the same type of structural break as the dependent variable, the residuals would not be autocorrelated. But if there is nothing else in the model to explain that sort of variation, it has to be consigned to the residuals.

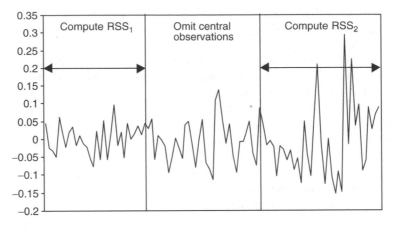

Figure A.8 Reordered data for the Goldfeld-Quandt test.

dependent variable are not over- or under-differenced, this would normally involve including more explanatory variables on the right-hand side. If none of the steps that are taken can remove the autocorrelation in OLS residuals then an alternative estimation method should be considered (§A.3.3).

A.3.2   Unconditional Heteroscedasticity

If the dependent variable has properties that are not present in any of the included explanatory variables then potential explanatory variables may have been omitted from the model. When relevant explanatory variables are omitted from the model the only term that can model those effects is the error term. Thus residuals will pick up the properties of the dependent variable that have not been captured because relevant variables have been omitted. If the omitted variables are heteroscedastic so also will be the residuals. Because of this, many tests for heteroscedasticity are based on an auxiliary regression of the squared OLS residuals on other (included or excluded) variables that are thought to be linked to the heteroscedasticity. The following are examples of such tests.

White's test of the null hypothesis of homoscedasticity is an LM test that is performed by regressing the squared residuals on all the squares and cross products of the explanatory variables (White, 1980, 1984). The LM test statistic is TR^2, where T is the number of data points used in this regression and R^2 is the squared correlation (ESS/TSS). It is asymptotically distributed as chi-squared with p degrees of freedom, where p is the number of explanatory variables in the auxiliary regression, including the constant. Although very general, White's test may have rather low power. For example, a rejection of the null hypothesis of homoscedasticity may be due to an incorrect linear functional form. The test also helps little in identifying the variables that cause heteroscedasticity.

The *Breush–Pagan test* of heteroscedasticity assumes that it is explained by some set of variables **z** that may be included in or excluded from the original regression. It is an LM test, with test statistic ESS/2, where ESS is the explained sum of squares from the auxiliary regression of normalized squared residuals[16] on the variables in **z**. It is asymptotically distributed as chi-squared with p degrees of freedom, where p is the number variables in **z**—that is, the number of variables thought to influence the heteroscedasticity.

The *Goldfeld–Quandt test* assumes that the ith residual e_i has variance $\sigma^2 x_i^2$ for some known variable x. The data are rearranged so that the first observation is the one with the smallest value for x, the second observation has the second smallest value of x, and so on. Following this, the sample is divided into three parts: under the alternative hypothesis of heteroscedasticity the residuals in the first part will have smaller variance than those in the last part. This is depicted in Figure A.8. The test statistic is the ratio, $\text{RSS}_1/\text{RSS}_2$, of the sum of squared residuals from the first part of the data, to the sum of squared residuals from the last part of the data. It is F-distributed (under the null hypothesis) with $n_1 - k, n_2 - k$ degrees of freedom, where n_1 is the number of observations in the first part and n_2 is the number of observations in the last part. Excluding observations from the test in the middle part of the reordered data decreases the probability of failing to reject a false null hypothesis (§A.2.1). But if too many observations are omitted, the power of the test to reject false null hypotheses is diminished. A rule of thumb is to exclude the middle third of the reordered data.

A.3.3   Generalized Least Squares

If there is autocorrelation and/or heteroscedasticity in the errors then $V(\varepsilon) \neq \sigma^2 \mathbf{I}$. In this case OLS will still give consistent estimators (§A.1.3), but this is only useful when sample sizes are large. What should be done if autocorrelation or heteroscedasticity is present in model residuals when the data set is relatively small? OLS estimators will still be unbiased if the explanatory variables are not correlated with the errors. But they will be inefficient, so parameter estimates will not be robust to small changes in the data.

When disturbances are not spherical, efficient estimators are provided by the GLS estimator

$$\mathbf{b}_{\text{GLS}} = (\mathbf{X}'\boldsymbol{\Omega}^{-1}\mathbf{X})^{-1}\mathbf{X}'\boldsymbol{\Omega}^{-1}\mathbf{y}, \qquad (\text{A.3.1})$$

where $\boldsymbol{\Omega}$ denotes the covariance matrix of the errors. The assumption $V(\varepsilon) = \sigma^2 \mathbf{I}$ has been replaced by $V(\varepsilon) = \sigma^2 \boldsymbol{\Omega}$ to reflect the fact that errors are either autocorrelated or heteroscedastic, or both. The GLS estimator covariance matrix is

---

[16]'Normalization' in this case is dividing by the residual variance estimate, $\Sigma e_i^2 / T$.

$$V(\mathbf{b}_{\mathrm{GLS}}) = \sigma^2 (\mathbf{X}'\mathbf{\Omega}^{-1}\mathbf{X})^{-1},$$

and estimates of this covariance matrix may be used in the hypothesis tests of linear restrictions outlined in §A.2.2.

A few lines of algebra verify that applying formula (A.3.1) directly on the data $\mathbf{X}$ and $\mathbf{y}$ is actually equivalent to applying OLS to the transformed data $\mathbf{X}^* = \mathbf{TX}$ and $\mathbf{y}^* = \mathbf{Ty}$, where $\mathbf{T}$ is the Cholesky matrix of $\mathbf{\Omega}^{-1}$ (so $\mathbf{T} = \mathbf{C}^{-1}$, where $\mathbf{CC}' = \mathbf{\Omega}$). For example, if there is heteroscedasticity and $\sigma_i^2 = \sigma^2 W_i^2$ for some known variable W, the transformation matrix is $\mathbf{T} = \mathrm{diag}(W_1^{-1}, \ldots, W_n^{-1})$. So the mth row of data in $\mathbf{X}$ and $\mathbf{y}$ is divided by W_m to get the transformed data $\mathbf{X}^*$ and $\mathbf{y}^*$, and then OLS is applied to these data. This form of GLS is called *weighted least squares*.

The precise form of $\mathbf{\Omega}$ depends on the nature of the errors process. For example, when there is heteroscedasticity but no autocorrelation, $\mathbf{\Omega}$ will be a diagonal matrix, $\mathrm{diag}(\sigma_1^2, \ldots, \sigma_n^2)$. The hypothesis of homoscedasticity, viz.

$$\sigma_1^2 = \sigma_2^2 = \ldots = \sigma_n^2,$$

will have been rejected using one or other of the tests described in §A.3.2 above. If there is autocorrelation but no heteroscedasticity, $\mathbf{\Omega}$ will take a form that is determined by the type of autocorrelation. For example, if the autocorrelation is AR(1), so

$$\varepsilon_t = \rho \varepsilon_{t-1} + v_t,$$

where ρ is the first-order autocorrelation coefficient in the residuals, then

$$\mathbf{\Omega} = \begin{pmatrix} 1 & \rho & \rho^2 & \ldots & \rho^n \\ \rho & 1 & \rho & \ldots & \rho^{n-1} \\ \rho^2 & \rho & 1 & \ldots & \rho^{n-2} \\ \ldots & \ldots & & \ldots & \ldots \\ \rho^n & \rho^{n-1} & & \ldots & 1 \end{pmatrix}.$$

Although the form of $\mathbf{\Omega}$ can be specified, depending on the type of auto-correlation or heteroscedasticity that is assumed, the actual values in $\mathbf{\Omega}$ are of course unknown. A consistent estimate of $\mathbf{\Omega}$ will normally be used in (A.3.1), to give *feasible GLS* estimators.[17] Although feasible GLS estimators may be more efficient than OLS when autocorrelation or heteroscedasticity is present, feasible GLS does not necessarily give the most efficient estimators in small samples.

Another case where GLS is often applied is to *systems of seemingly unrelated regression equations* (SURE). In general simultaneous models the explanatory variables of some equations become the dependent variable in another

---

[17]Cochrane and Orcutt (1949) describe one such consistent estimator when there is first-order autocorrelation in the residuals.

equation. In SURE models equations are related only through their disturbance terms. The arbitrage pricing model of §8.1.2 falls into this category, its general formulation being a system of equations

$$\mathbf{y}_j = \mathbf{X}_j \boldsymbol{\beta}_j + \boldsymbol{\varepsilon}_j \quad (j = 1, \ldots, n), \tag{A.3.2}$$

where $\mathbf{y}_j$ denotes the returns to asset j, $\mathbf{X}_j$ is a matrix of risk factor returns relevant for asset j, $\boldsymbol{\beta}_j$ is the vector of risk factor sensitivities and $\boldsymbol{\varepsilon}_j$ is the disturbance term specific to asset j.

For domestic portfolios it is common to assume that risk factors are the same for all assets, so $\mathbf{X}_j = \mathbf{X}$ for all j. In this case OLS is an appropriate estimation procedure. But for large international portfolios risk factors will be country-specific. In this case the more general formulation (A.3.2) should be employed.

Consider now a situation where $\mathbf{y}_j$ denotes the returns to the portfolio in country j, $\mathbf{X}_j$ is a matrix of risk factor returns relevant for country j, $\boldsymbol{\beta}_j$ is the vector of risk factor sensitivities and $\boldsymbol{\varepsilon}_j$ is the error process that is specific to country j. The whole system may be written:

$$\begin{pmatrix} \mathbf{y}_1 \\ \mathbf{y}_2 \\ .. \\ \mathbf{y}_n \end{pmatrix} = \begin{pmatrix} \mathbf{X}_1 & \mathbf{0} & .. & \mathbf{0} \\ \mathbf{0} & \mathbf{X}_2 & .. & \mathbf{0} \\ .. & .. & .. & .. \\ \mathbf{0} & \mathbf{0} & .. & \mathbf{X}_n \end{pmatrix} \begin{pmatrix} \boldsymbol{\beta}_1 \\ \boldsymbol{\beta}_2 \\ .. \\ \boldsymbol{\beta}_n \end{pmatrix} + \begin{pmatrix} \boldsymbol{\varepsilon}_1 \\ \boldsymbol{\varepsilon}_2 \\ .. \\ \boldsymbol{\varepsilon}_n \end{pmatrix}$$

or

$$\mathbf{y} = \mathbf{X}\boldsymbol{\beta} + \boldsymbol{\varepsilon},$$

where $\mathbf{y}$ is the stacked vector of data on the n different country stock returns, $\mathbf{X}$ is the block-diagonal matrix of country risk factor returns, $\boldsymbol{\beta}$ is the stacked vector of factor sensitivities according to country and to risk factor within that country, and $\boldsymbol{\varepsilon}$ is the vector of disturbances.

Applying GLS to this system will provide unbiased and efficient estimators. The assumption of country-specific risks being contemporaneously correlated becomes

$$E(\boldsymbol{\varepsilon}_i \boldsymbol{\varepsilon}_j') = \sigma_{ij}\mathbf{I},$$

where $\mathbf{I}$ is the $T \times T$ identity matrix, or in terms of a Kronecker product

$$E(\boldsymbol{\varepsilon}\boldsymbol{\varepsilon}') = \mathbf{V} = \boldsymbol{\Sigma} \otimes \mathbf{I},$$

where $\boldsymbol{\Sigma} = (\sigma_{ij})$. Then the inverse matrix $\mathbf{V}^{-1} = \boldsymbol{\Sigma}^{-1} \otimes \mathbf{I}$ should be used to calculate GLS estimators as

$$\mathbf{b}_{\mathrm{GLS}} = (\mathbf{X}'\mathbf{V}^{-1}\mathbf{X})^{-1}\mathbf{X}'\mathbf{V}^{-1}\mathbf{y}.$$

Of course in practice the cross-market covariances σ_{ij} will not be known and shall have to be estimated using some consistent method. One method is to first apply OLS to each country model separately, each time obtaining $\mathbf{e}_j$ the vector of residuals for country j, and then estimating each σ_{ij} as $\mathbf{e}'_i\mathbf{e}_j/T$.

Appendix 4
Data Problems

The rapid growth in new financial products and markets during the past decade means that good-quality data are difficult to obtain. In illiquid markets reliable daily data are not always available; inappropriate quotes might remain for several days, and in new markets data will only cover a recent period. Even in established markets one may question the reliability of data. Accountancy data from the banking or trading book can have significant measurement errors. Quoted prices may not have been traded, and when they are it is not always clear whether the quoted price is bid or offer. And often important model parameters have little or no empirical validation. So although a vast quantity of data are recorded for many financial markets, many problems may be associated with these data. This appendix deals with three of the most common data problems: highly collinear data, unreliable data, and missing data.

A.4.1   Multicollinearity

One of the problems that is common to all linear regression models is that explanatory variables can have a high degree of correlation between themselves. In this case it may not be possible to determine their individual effects. The problem is referred to as one of *multicollinearity*.

Perfect multicollinearity occurs when two (or more) explanatory variables are perfectly correlated. In this case the OLS estimators do not even exist, because $\mathbf{X}'\mathbf{X}$ has less than full rank and so is not invertible.[18] This is not really a problem. In fact it is just a fundamental mistake in the model specification: some linear transform of one of the explanatory variables has been included as another explanatory variable.

However, when there is a high degree of multicollinearity, with a large, but not perfect, correlation between some explanatory variables, there may be a real problem. The OLS estimators do exist, and they are still unbiased. They are also still the most efficient of all linear unbiased estimators. But that does not mean that their variances and covariances are small. They may be 'most

---

[18]The *rank* of a square matrix is the number of linearly independent rows (or columns). If the rank of an $n \times n$ matrix is less than n then the matrix has no inverse.

efficient', but when there is a high degree of multicollinearity, the problem is that 'most efficient' is still not very efficient.

To see why this is so, note that if some of the variables in $\mathbf{X}$ are highly (but not perfectly) collinear, the $\mathbf{X'X}$ matrix will have some very large elements in the off-diagonals corresponding to these variables. Thus the determinant of $\mathbf{X'X}$ will be small, and this has the effect of increasing all elements of $(\mathbf{X'X})^{-1}$. From (A.1.13) the covariance matrix of the estimates is governed by the matrix $(\mathbf{X'X})^{-1}$. The estimated variances and covariances of the collinear variables, in particular, will be very large. The t-ratios on their coefficient estimates will be depressed and OLS estimates of the coefficients of these collinear variables will fluctuate greatly, even when there are only small changes in the data. In short, multicollinearity implies a lack of robustness in OLS estimates.

Multicollinearity is not an 'all or nothing' thing, it is a question of degree, so there is no formal test for multicollinearity. If the intercorrelations between certain explanatory variables are too high (a rule of thumb is that they should be no greater than the R^2 from the whole regression), multicollinearity can be severe enough to distort the model estimation procedure. In that case the simple solution is to drop one of the collinear variables, and if there are more collinear variables left, continue to throw them out of the model until the multicollinearity is not a problem. However, this may not be in line with the fundamental theory of the model. Another solution is to obtain more data, or different data on the same variables. But this just may not be possible.

If none of these measures offers a feasible solution and the problem of multi-collinearity persists, the model parameters can be estimated using the *ridge estimator*

$$\mathbf{b_r} = (\mathbf{X'X} + r\mathbf{D})^{-1}\mathbf{X'y}, \qquad (A.4.1)$$

where $\mathbf{D}$ is the diagonal matrix containing the diagonal terms of $\mathbf{X'X}$ and the constant r is as small as possible. The optimal value of r can be determined by testing the model for increasing values of r until it produces stable estimates. The justification for using the ridge estimator is that since multicollinearity increases the off-diagonal elements of $\mathbf{X'X}$ in particular, one can produce more efficient results by augmenting the diagonals to be more in line with the off-diagonals. Although ridge estimators are biased they will be more precise than the OLS estimators when the regressors are highly collinear.

None of these measures for coping with multicollinearity is as powerful as that of principal component analysis (PCA). The use of PCA to cope with highly collinear explanatory variables is described in §6.4.1.

A.4.2 Data Errors

The first step towards developing any model should be to plot all the available data. This will not only reveal something of the relationships between variables, but also identify any serious errors in the data. Often prices are recorded incorrectly, and these errors can pass through even when data vendors employ proper filtering procedures.

Accounting data often have to be revised after the auditing process, which itself takes a considerable time. But however careful the audit, it will never be possible to measure certain quantities with great accuracy because too many 'guestimates' have to made. This does not only happen in book data. The accuracy of important data for credit risk and operational risk modelling leaves a lot to be desired. It is enormously difficult to obtain reliable data on credit spreads, default rates, ratings migrations, correlations and recovery rates, in fact all the processes that constitute credit loss. Similarly, for many low-frequency but high-impact operational risks, data are extremely scarce.

This subsection examines the detrimental effect that data errors will have on the parameter estimates of a linear regression model. Generally speaking, they induce an *attenuation bias*, that is, they decrease the size of parameter estimates. To see this, suppose that data on an explanatory variable X^* is not available, although data are available on $X = X^* + u$, where u is an error process. The attenuation bias may be illustrated in the framework of the very simple model

$$Y = \beta X^* + \varepsilon.$$

This model cannot be estimated, since no data are available on X^*, so let us write the model in a form that can be estimated, as

$$Y = \beta X + v,$$

where the new error process $v = \varepsilon - \beta u$. Now X is a stochastic regressor, so OLS will only give unbiased estimates if $\text{cov}(X, v) = 0$ (§A.1.3). However, $\text{cov}(X, v)$ is not 0, since both X and v contain u and so they will be correlated. In fact

$$\text{cov}(X, v) = \text{cov}(X^* + u, \varepsilon - \beta u)$$
$$= \text{cov}(X^*, \varepsilon) + \text{cov}(u, \varepsilon) - \text{cov}(X^*, \beta u) - \text{cov}(u, \beta u).$$

The first three terms are all zero, but $\text{cov}(u, \beta u) = \beta^2 V(u)$ and so $\text{cov}(X, v) = -\beta^2 V(u)$ is not zero.

This example shows that when there are errors in the data on explanatory variables the assumptions necessary for OLS to be unbiased are violated. The OLS bias will always be downwards since $\text{cov}(X, v)$ is negative. Neither is OLS consistent and the coefficient estimates will be biased downwards even in very large samples.

On the other hand, if the dependent variable is badly measured this does not cause problems with the OLS estimators: They will still be unbiased and efficient. However, it does cause problems for the validity of *any* model! If the true values of Y are never observed, a model can only be fitted to the measured values, and if the measurements are unreliable and difficult to predict, the model cannot perform well. There is little one can do about this, except try to obtain better data.

In summary, if unreliable data are used for explanatory variables the attenuation bias will tend to reduce the size of OLS parameter estimates. When data on the dependent variable are known to contain significant measurement errors there is little to be done other than to obtain better data.

A.4.3 Missing Data

Missing observations on bank holidays are usually filled by repeating the last observation, or by linear interpolation. But what should one do with new markets that have existed only for a short time, or with illiquid markets where trading occurs only sporadically? If data are available on related variables there are some measures that can be taken towards estimating the model regardless of the incomplete data, without resorting to filling in the gaps with dummy or proxy variables. One approach, based on PCA, was described in §6.4.2. This section describes an alternative approach for use in the context of regression models.

If the dependent variable in a regression model has missing data, then some auxiliary regressions of the explanatory variables can be substituted in the regression model. Divide the data on the dependent variable $\mathbf{y}$ into two parts, letting $\mathbf{y}^*$ denote the vectors of missing observations in $\mathbf{y}$ and $\mathbf{y}_c$ denote the complete observations on $\mathbf{y}$. Likewise, the explanatory data are divided into two matrices: $\mathbf{X}^*$ denotes the data on explanatory variables corresponding to the missing observations on $\mathbf{y}$, and $\mathbf{X}_c$ denotes the data on explanatory variables corresponding to the complete observations on $\mathbf{y}$.

To estimate the model on all the data, regardless of the missing observations $\mathbf{y}^*$, one proceeds as follows. First obtain parameter estimates $\mathbf{b}_c$ using the complete data vectors that are available, giving $\mathbf{b}_c = (\mathbf{X}_c'\mathbf{X}_c)^{-1}\mathbf{X}_c'\mathbf{y}_c$. Then use some estimates $\mathbf{y}^*$ of the missing observations in $\mathbf{y}$ and obtain parameter estimates $\mathbf{b}^*$ based on the incomplete data vectors, so $\mathbf{b}^* = (\mathbf{X}^{*\prime}\mathbf{X}^*)^{-1}\mathbf{X}^{*\prime}\mathbf{y}^*$. Final parameter estimates are then a weighted average of $\mathbf{b}_c$ and $\mathbf{b}^*$ given by

$$\mathbf{b}_W = \mathbf{W}\mathbf{b}_c + (\mathbf{I} - \mathbf{W})\mathbf{b}^*, \qquad (A.4.2)$$

where $\mathbf{W}$ is $(\mathbf{X}_c'\mathbf{X}_c + \mathbf{X}^{*\prime}\mathbf{X}^*)^{-1}\mathbf{X}_c'\mathbf{X}_c$.

The big question is how we should fill in the missing observations $\mathbf{y}^*$. Only if the missing data are estimated in such a way that $\mathbf{b}^*$ is unbiased will (A.4.2) give unbiased final estimates of the model parameters. Taking $\mathbf{b}^* = \mathbf{b}_c$ and

Figure A.9   The FTSE 100 index, 1986–1989.

backing out $\mathbf{y}^*$ from $\mathbf{b} = (\mathbf{X}^{*\prime}\mathbf{X}^*)^{-1}\mathbf{X}^{*\prime}\mathbf{y}^*$ is a possibility, but that does not really add any new information to the model, since then $\mathbf{b}_W = \mathbf{b}_c$ and we may just as well base the model on the complete data. Taking every element of $\mathbf{y}^*$ to be the average of the complete data on $\mathbf{y}$ is also possible, but then (A.4.2) will give biased estimates, and we may be better off just using the data set that is complete. Perhaps the most attractive alternative is to define scenarios over $\mathbf{y}^*$ that are more general than taking the average over $\mathbf{y}_c$. Then (A.4.2) can be used to estimate model parameters for a number of different $\mathbf{y}^*$, and this will give some idea of how realistic are the scenarios over $\mathbf{y}^*$. However, this method will still produce biased parameter estimates.

A.4.4   Dummy Variables

Dummy variables are proxies for explanatory variables that we know are important, but for which there are no direct data, and neither is there a suitable proxy variable. In that case all that can be done is to make up the data by creating a dummy variable. In tic data one might consider creating a dummy to model the timing of important news announcements, or a dummy corresponding to opening times in the major markets. In daily data day-of-the-week dummies are sometimes used. Structural break dummy variables are important whenever the data period covers a permanent shift arising from a change in regime, or a temporary shift due to an extreme market movement.

Dummy variables should be used prudently and only if there is a real reason, such as an important news announcement or a change in government policy. For an example of a very basic dummy, suppose an extreme event such as Black Monday occurs in the dependent variable data. Figure A.9 illustrates the FTSE 100 index during the period around Black Monday. If a model is to explain the FTSE 100 returns around Black Monday, it will have to include a variable that has similar characteristics (such as the returns on another equity index). If no similar variables are included in the model, the large returns during the Black Monday period will appear in the residuals, and this will upset the whole model because the residual variance will be increased.

A simple solution is to add a dummy variable to the model that takes the value 1 during the few days of large negative returns around Black Monday, and 0 otherwise. Denote by a the estimate of the model constant without the dummy variable. During the period that the dummy is 1, the constant will shift to $a + d$, where d is the coefficient estimate on the dummy. In this example d will be large and negative, so in effect the regression line is temporarily shifted downwards.

Dummy variables allow different regression lines to be estimated with the one set of data. For example, if there is a structural break in the data, such as in Figure A.7a, the structural break dummy D that is 0 before the break and 1 afterwards should be included in the model. There are a number of ways in which D can be included:

1. as an additional constant term as in (A.4.3a), in which case the regression line shifts parallel, as depicted in Figure A.10a;
2. as a change in slope of the regression line, which is the model (A.4.3b) and is shown in Figure A.10b;
3. or as both, which is model (A.4.3c) and is shown in Figure A.10c.

There are three ways to incorporate this type of dummy variable into the simple model:

$$Y = \alpha + \beta X + \varepsilon$$

Shift: $$Y = \alpha + \delta D + \beta X + \varepsilon \qquad (A.4.3a)$$

Slope: $$Y = \alpha + \gamma DX + \beta X + \varepsilon \qquad (A.4.3b)$$

Shift + Slope: $$Y = \alpha + \delta D + \gamma DX + \beta X + \varepsilon \qquad (A.4.3c)$$

In many cases it is sufficient to use the dummy just to shift the regression constant, as in (A.4.3a). For example, day-of-the-week effects in daily data might use day-of-the-week dummies, MON ($= 1$ on Monday and 0 otherwise), TUE ($= 1$ on Tuesday and 0 otherwise), and so on. The constant term of the model becomes $(\alpha + \alpha_1 \text{MON} + \alpha_2 \text{TUE} + \alpha_3 \text{WED} + \alpha_4 \text{THU})$ so that it takes the value $\alpha + \alpha_1$ on Mondays, $\alpha + \alpha_2$ on Tuesdays, $\alpha + \alpha_3$ on Wednesdays, $\alpha + \alpha_4$ on Thursdays, and α on Fridays. Note that only four daily dummies are used. Using five dummies would introduce perfect multicollinearity.

Dummy variables should be viewed as necessary measures for data that have structural breaks, regime shifts or seasonalities. If dummies are omitted there will be residual problems that lead to inefficient parameter estimates on the real explanatory variables. However, if too many dummies are used the power of other explanatory variables may be reduced.

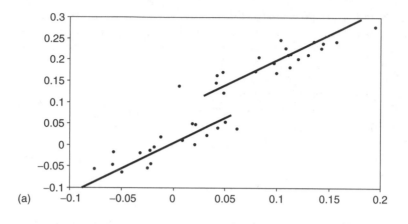

(a)

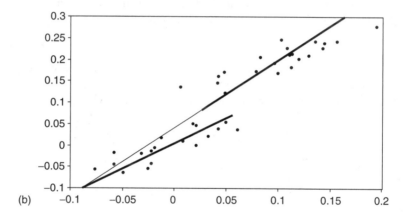

(b)

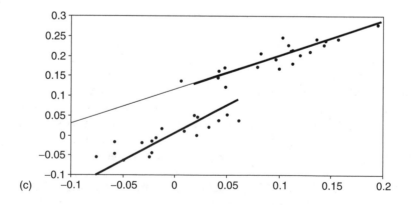

(c)

Figure A.10 Regression lines with: (a) shift dummy; (b) slope dummy; (c) shift and slope dummies.

Appendix 5
Prediction

Model specification procedures can leave much to subjective choice (§8.4). It is common that many different model specifications will be considered. Some real historic data should be retained for the purpose of evaluating the predictive performance of a model, to evaluate which is the best specification. This process is called *model validation*. One should evaluate predictions for a variety of different market conditions. A thorough *backtest* of a certain model specification would typically involve very many predictive tests. This appendix illustrates how point and confidence interval predictions are generated from a regression model. The general framework for backtesting is outlined in §A.5.2, and an overview of the statistical and operational forecast evaluation methods that are commonly employed is presented in §A.5.3.

A.5.1   Point Predictions and Confidence Intervals

A regression model generates point predictions of the expected value of the dependent variable for given values of the explanatory variables. To see how this is done, consider the general linear model (A.1.7):

$$Y_t = \beta_1 X_{1t} + \beta_2 X_{2t} + \ldots + \beta_k X_{kt} + \varepsilon_t.$$

A point forecast $\hat{Y}$ of Y is given by estimating the parameters by some method to obtain $\hat{\beta}_1, \hat{\beta}_2, \ldots, \hat{\beta}_k$ and then substituting certain values of the explanatory variables $X_1, \ldots, X_k$ into the model. A point prediction $\hat{Y}$ is the expected value of Y given that the explanatory variables take the values $X_1^*, \ldots, X_k^*$:

$$\hat{Y} = \hat{\beta}_1 X_1^* + \hat{\beta}_2 X_2^* + \ldots + \hat{\beta}_k X_k^*.$$

It is not possible to generate a point prediction of the *actual* value of Y when the explanatory variables take the values $X_1^*, \ldots, X_k^*$ because the actual value of Y is $\hat{Y} + e$, where the residual e is the value of the error term at the point of the forecast, and this value is not known. However, it is possible to generate a confidence interval for the true value of Y given that the explanatory variables take the values $\mathbf{x}^* = (X_1^*, \ldots, X_k^*)'$. This confidence interval is generated by assuming normality and using the estimated standard deviation of $Y = \mathbf{x}^{*\prime}\boldsymbol{\beta} + \varepsilon$. The forecast error is $e = Y - \hat{Y} = \mathbf{x}^{*\prime}(\boldsymbol{\beta} - \hat{\boldsymbol{\beta}}) + \varepsilon$ and so

$$V(e) = \mathbf{x}^{*\prime} V(\hat{\boldsymbol{\beta}})\mathbf{x}^* + V(\varepsilon).$$

When $\hat{\boldsymbol{\beta}} = \mathbf{b}$, the OLS estimators, then $V(\hat{\boldsymbol{\beta}}) = \sigma^2(\mathbf{X}'\mathbf{X})^{-1}$ and so

$$V(e) = \sigma^2(\mathbf{x}^{*\prime}(\mathbf{X}'\mathbf{X})^{-1}\mathbf{x}^* + 1).$$

Thus, assuming normality,

$$(Y - \hat{Y})/(\sigma\sqrt{(\mathbf{x}^{*\prime}(\mathbf{X}'\mathbf{X})^{-1}\mathbf{x}^* + 1)}) \sim N(0, 1),$$

and using the estimated value s^2 for σ^2 gives

$$(Y - \hat{Y})/(s\sqrt{(\mathbf{x}^{*\prime}(\mathbf{X}'\mathbf{X})^{-1}\mathbf{x}^* + 1)}) \sim t_{T-k}. \qquad (A.5.1)$$

This forms the basis of interval predictions for Y. A two-sided $100(1-\alpha)\%$ confidence interval for the actual value of Y when the explanatory variables take the values $\mathbf{x}^*$ is

$$(\hat{Y} - \xi, \ \hat{Y} + \xi), \text{ with } \xi = t_{T-k,\alpha/2}(s\sqrt{(\mathbf{x}^{*\prime}(\mathbf{X}'\mathbf{X})^{-1}\mathbf{x}^* + 1)}). \qquad (A.5.2)$$

Confidence intervals are used in scenario analysis, where the explanatory variable values in $\mathbf{x}^*$ may be anything, and in model validation, to ensure that real data fall into the confidence intervals predicted by the model.

A.5.2   Backtesting

It is very important that the developer should backtest the model with a large number of predictive tests. Normally the historical data are divided into two parts: the in-sample data used to specify the model, and the out-of-sample data used to evaluate model predictions. Often out-of-sample data are taken immediately after the in-sample data, in which case they are usually called 'post-sample' data.

A common form of backtest is to use a rolling window for the in-sample and post-sample data, and each time compute several in-sample and post-sample diagnostic performance measures. A reliable model will show stability in the time series of performance measures that are produced by the backtest. In-sample diagnostics can range from the basic autocorrelation and hetero-scedasticity tests that are necessary for the unbiasedness and efficiency of parameter estimates (if obtained by OLS), to more advanced in-sample diagnostics such as the unit root tests described in §11.1.5. Commonly backtests employ a number of post-sample performance measures that can be either purely statistical or operational or both. A number of out-of-sample diagnostic measures are described in §A.5.3. See also §12.5.

There may be no problem churning out the statistics, but the interpretation of backtesting results is not always straightforward. The results will depend on the diagnostics that are chosen and it is unlikely that a given model will perform well according to all possible prediction performance measures.[19] The main problem with backtesting is that results will be specific to the trading metric that is chosen for operational evaluation, or the diagnostic statistic that is chosen for statistical evaluation. The most that can be achieved is that a

---

[19]The first International Non-linear Financial Prediction Competition used 15 statistical and operational post-sample performance measures (§13.3).

model performs well according to the preferred performance measures. In a full backtest many successive diagnostic statistics should be analysed for their time series qualities. Only when backtesting results are stable and robust over time can one impart some degree of confidence in the model.

Backtests will need to include a variety of market conditions such as trending markets, stable markets and periods of extreme movements. And since the results are likely to depend on the market regime, a view has to be taken on the likelihood of each regime in the future. Some examples of backtesting a time series model can be found in §12.5.5 and §9.5.1.

A.5.3 Statistical and Operational Evaluation Methods

A predictive test is a single evaluation of the model performance based on comparison of actual data with the values predicted by the model. Some common evaluation metrics are now described. There are two types of post-sample performance measures, statistical and operational. Statistical evaluation methods compare model predictions with observable quantities, such as asset prices or returns. Common statistical performance measures include:

➢ *Information ratio* (IR): the mean prediction error divided by the standard deviation of the prediction error;
➢ *Root mean square error* (RMSE): the square root of the mean of the squared prediction errors;
➢ *Likelihood of the prediction*: the product of the likelihoods of each point predicted, assuming some form of density function for the quantities being predicted;
➢ *Mean absolute error*: the mean of the absolute values of the prediction errors;
➢ *Mean square error*: the mean of the squares of the prediction errors;
➢ *Normalized root mean square error*: the RMSE divided by the estimated standard deviation of the prediction errors;
➢ *Out-of-sample correlation coefficient*: the correlation between the predictions and the actual values, having made the appropriate stationarity transformation if necessary.[20]

There are two main concerns with the statistical approach to model evaluation:

➢ Most of these standard statistical criteria for model accuracy do not distinguish outperformance from underperformance, since they ignore the sign of the prediction error.
➢ Often the distributional assumptions that underpin statistical evaluation

---

[20]For example, in a price prediction model one would not compute the predicted–actual price correlation — it would need to be done on the respective returns.

procedures are difficult to justify. The associated hypothesis tests based on these statistics will usually only be valid under certain assumptions, such as returns being normally distributed.

A basic example of an operational evaluation method is the backtesting of a value-at-risk model by counting exceptional losses (§9.5.1). Operational evaluation methods focus on the context in which the prediction is used, by imposing a metric on prediction results. More generally, when predictions are used for trading or hedging purposes, the performance of a *trading* or *hedging metric* provides a measure of the model's success.

Most trading metrics for measuring prediction performance are variants of a profit and loss (P&L) metric. The basic framework of a *P&L metric* is to define an indicator variable for the position at time t as

$$I_t = \begin{cases} 1 & \text{if the position is long} \\ -1 & \text{if the position is short} \\ 0 & \text{if the position is neutral} \end{cases}$$

If p_t is the realized asset price at time t then $I_{t-1}(p_t - p_{t-1})$ is the gain or loss on the position at time t. Often a P&L metric includes a fixed transactions cost c, so the net profit or loss on the position at time t is

$$g_t = I_{t-1}(p_t - p_{t-1}) - c|I_t - I_{t-1}|. \tag{A.5.3}$$

The performance of price predictions may be expressed in term of total P&L up to time T (the time horizon of the post-sample test). That is, $\text{P\&L}_T = \Sigma_{t=1}^{T} g_t$. But perhaps a better statistic is the mean P&L ($\bar{g} = [\text{P\&L}_T]/T$) because it avoids the obvious scaling problem as the length of post-sample test period increases. One might also wish to adjust for risk to penalize predictions that give highly variable P&Ls during the test. A common performance measure is the normalized mean P&L over the post-sample testing period, $\bar{g}/s_g$, where s_g is the estimated standard deviation of g over the prediction period.

This is fairly standard so far, but the question of how the price predictions $\hat{p}_t$ are translated into positions has not yet been answered. The definition of the position indicator is perhaps the most flexible part of the definition of trading metric, since it should reflect as far as possible the actual trading strategy. As a simple example, one could define a single threshold τ and then put

$$I_t = \begin{cases} 1 & \text{if } \hat{p}_t > p_{t-1} + \tau \\ -1 & \text{if } \hat{p}_t < p_{t-1} - \tau \\ 0 & \text{otherwise} \end{cases}$$

Clearly many other definitions of position indicators are possible. Hedging strategies can also be defined in this framework, where rebalancing limits are placed on the option delta or the portfolio beta that is predicted by the model. An example of a P&L metric from a volatility trading perspective was given in §5.1.2.

Appendix 6
Maximum Likelihood Methods

Maximum likelihood is a standard method for fitting the parameters of a density function. It has already been mentioned in this context in §10.2. Under the classical assumptions of linear regression ordinary least squares estimation and maximum likelihood estimation are equivalent, so there is no explicit need for likelihood methods when estimating linear models or testing linear restrictions on their parameters. However, non-linear statistical models are normally estimated by maximum likelihood because maximum likelihood estimators (MLEs) are almost always consistent (§A.1.3). Models that are usually estimated by maximum likelihood include generalized autoregressive conditional heteroscedasticity (GARCH) models (Chapter 4) and neural networks (§13.2).

A.6.1 The Likelihood Function, MLE and LR Tests

The likelihood of an observation x on a random variable is the value of its density function at x, written $f(x, \theta)$, where $\theta = (\theta_1, \ldots, \theta_q)$ are the parameters of the density function. The likelihood function of an independent set of observations $(x_1, \ldots, x_n)$ on the same random variable with density function $f(\theta)$ is the product of the likelihoods of each point, that is,

$$L(\theta \mid x_1, \ldots, x_n) = \prod f(x_i, \theta). \qquad (A.6.1)$$

For given random sample data $(x_1, \ldots, x_n)$, the value of the likelihood will depend on θ. Figure A.11a illustrates the likelihood of a random sample for *two* different values of a parameter vector θ: θ_0 and θ_1. The likelihood of the sample is greater if the parameters take the values θ_1. That is, $L(\theta_0 \mid x_1, \ldots, x_n) > L(\theta_1 \mid x_1, \ldots, x_n)$ since the product of the values of the density is greater when $\theta = \theta_0$ than when $\theta = \theta_1$.

As θ ranges over all possible values for all parameters the likelihood function describes a $(q + 1)$-dimensional surface. For example, when there is a single parameter θ the likelihood function describes a curve, such as in Figure A.11b. The greater the value of the likelihood, the more probable are the parameter values, based on the given sample data. Different sample data will give different values of the likelihood, so the values of the parameters that generate the highest likelihood will depend on the choice of the sample data.

The *maximum likelihood estimator* of θ is the value of θ that maximizes the likelihood function, given the sample data:

$$\text{MLE } \theta = \arg \max L(\theta \mid x_1, \ldots, x_n).$$

The *likelihood ratio test* of a null hypothesis H_0: $\theta = \theta_0$ against H_1: $\theta = \theta_1$ is based on the statistic

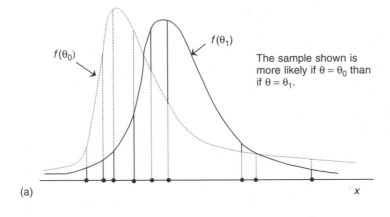

(a)

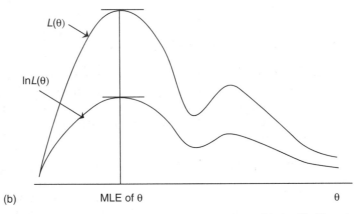

(b)

Figure A.11 (a) The likelihood of sample data; (b) the likelihood, the log-likelihood and the maximum likelihood estimator.

$$LR = L(\boldsymbol{\theta}_0)/L(\boldsymbol{\theta}_1),$$

where the conditioning statement on the sample data has been dropped for brevity of notation.[21] The general form of likelihood ratio test is given by the test statistic $-2\ln LR$, which is asymptotically chi-squared distribution with q degrees of freedom:

$$-2\ln LR = 2(\ln L(\boldsymbol{\theta}_1) - \ln L(\boldsymbol{\theta}_0)) \approx \chi_q^2. \tag{A.6.2}$$

This test has already been encountered in §A.2.5 in the context of testing a set of linear restrictions on the parameters of a linear regression model when the errors are normally distributed. If they exist the likelihood ratio tests have power properties that are better than those of the Wald and LM tests—in fact they are the uniformly most powerful tests of a given size.

---

[21]For the two-sided alternative $\boldsymbol{\theta} \neq \boldsymbol{\theta}_0$ use the MLE instead of $\boldsymbol{\theta}_1$ in the likelihood ratio.

A.6.2 Properties of Maximum Likelihood Estimators

The MLE of a parameter $\boldsymbol{\theta}$ solves

$$\partial L(\boldsymbol{\theta}|x_1, \ldots, x_n)/\partial\theta_i = 0 \quad (i = 1, \ldots, q),$$

provided the matrix of second derivatives is negative definite. But, being a product of density functions which are typically fairly complex, it is not straightforward to calculate the derivatives of $L(\boldsymbol{\theta}|x_1, \ldots, x_n)$. It is much easier to differentiate the log-likelihood function $\ln L(\boldsymbol{\theta}|x_1, \ldots, x_n)$, that is, the sum of the log densities:

$$\ln L(\boldsymbol{\theta}|x_1, \ldots, x_n) = \sum \ln f(x_i, \boldsymbol{\theta}). \qquad (A.6.3)$$

Since the optima of L are the same as those of $\ln L$, it is standard to find the MLE as the value of $\boldsymbol{\theta}$ that maximizes the log-likelihood (see Figure A.11b).

MLEs do not necessarily have good small-sample properties — for example, the variance estimator in (A.6.5) below is biased. However, under standard data regularity conditions, MLEs are consistent, asymptotically normally distributed and asymptotically efficient. That is, they have the lowest variance of all consistent asymptotically normal estimators. In fact the asymptotic covariance matrix of MLEs achieves the *Cramér Rao lower bound* for the variance of unbiased estimators. This bound is the inverse of the *information matrix* $\mathbf{I}(\boldsymbol{\theta})$, where

$$\mathbf{I}(\boldsymbol{\theta}) = -E[\partial^2 \ln L(\boldsymbol{\theta})/\partial\boldsymbol{\theta}\partial\boldsymbol{\theta}'],$$

that is, minus the expected values of the second derivatives of the log-likelihood function. In large samples MLEs have the minimum variance property, with covariance matrix $\mathbf{I}(\boldsymbol{\theta})^{-1}$. Statistical inference on MLEs follows from the convergence of their distribution to the multivariate normal $N(\boldsymbol{\theta}, \mathbf{I}(\boldsymbol{\theta})^{-1})$.

Another feature that makes MLEs among the best of the classical estimators is that the MLE of any continuous function $g(\theta)$ of a parameter θ is $g(\hat{\theta})$, where $\hat{\theta}$ is the MLE of θ. Thus it is a simple matter to find MLEs of standard transformations or products of parameters if the individual parameter MLEs are known.

A.6.3 MLEs for a Normal Density Function

Financial returns are often assumed to be generated by normal distributions. The probability density function for a normal random variable with mean μ and variance σ^2 is

$$f(x) = (1/\sqrt{(2\pi\sigma^2)}) \exp(-(x - \mu)^2/2\sigma^2),$$

so

$$\ln f(x) = -\tfrac{1}{2}\ln(2\pi) - \tfrac{1}{2}\ln\sigma^2 - \tfrac{1}{2}(x-\mu)^2/\sigma^2$$

or

$$-2\ln f(x) = \ln(2\pi) + \ln\sigma^2 + (x-\mu)^2/\sigma^2.$$

and the simplest form for the normal likelihood is

$$-2\ln L(\mu,\sigma^2\mid x_1,\ldots,x_n) = n\ln(2\pi) + n\ln\sigma^2 + \sum (x_i-\mu)^2/\sigma^2. \qquad \text{(A.6.4)}$$

For this reason the maximum likelihood estimates of normal density parameters are usually found by minimizing $-2\ln L$. Differentiating (A.6.4) gives

$$\partial(-2\ln L)/\partial\mu = -(2/\sigma^2)\sum (x_i-\mu),$$

$$\partial(-2\ln L)/\partial\sigma^2 = n/\sigma^2 - (1/\sigma^4)\sum (x_i-\mu)^2.$$

Therefore the two first-order conditions for maximization are

$$\sum (x_i-\mu) = 0$$

and

$$n\sigma^2 = \sum (x_i-\mu)^2.$$

Solving for μ and σ^2 gives the familiar estimators that are the MLEs of the mean and variance parameters of a normal density:

$$\begin{aligned}\hat{\mu} &= \sum (x_i)/n = \bar{x} \\ \hat{\sigma}^2 &= \sum (x_i-\bar{x})/n\end{aligned} \qquad \text{(A.6.5)}$$

To find the standard errors of these estimators and make inference on models estimated by MLE we need to compute their covariance matrix. This is estimated by putting the MLE values for θ into the inverse information matrix $I(\theta)^{-1}$ — see §A.6.2. For a normal density the matrix of second derivatives of the log-likelihood is

$$[\partial^2 \ln L(\theta)/\partial\theta\partial\theta'] = -\begin{pmatrix} n/\sigma^2 & \sum (x_i-\mu)/\sigma^4 \\ \sum (x_i-\mu)/\sigma^4 & \sum (x_i-\mu)^2/\sigma^6 - n/2\sigma^4 \end{pmatrix},$$

so multiplying by -1 and taking expectations, we obtain

$$I(\theta) = \begin{pmatrix} n/\sigma^2 & 0 \\ 0 & n/2\sigma^4 \end{pmatrix}.$$

Finally, the asymptotic covariance matrix of the MLEs is the inverse of this,

$$\mathbf{I}(\boldsymbol{\theta})^{-1} = \begin{pmatrix} \sigma^2/n & 0 \\ 0 & 2\sigma^4/n \end{pmatrix}. \qquad (A.6.6)$$

A.6.4   MLEs for Non-normal Density Functions

Maximum likelihood estimation is a very flexible method for estimating the parameters of any distribution. Distributions of returns in financial markets are often fat-tailed, that is, they have positive excess kurtosis (§10.1). This is particularly apparent in high-frequency data in foreign exchange markets, but in other markets, particularly equity markets, market crashes or other 'extreme' events produce outliers that give far more weight in the tails that can be modelled by a single normal distribution. In §10.2 a number of different distributions were introduced to model the fat-tailed nature of financial returns, and the parameters of these distributions are normally estimated by maximum likelihood.

Many financial distributions are skewed as well as fat-tailed, particularly those that relate to credit risk. With a typical portfolio of many credits, each having a very small probability of loss, the credit loss distribution will be heavily skewed. When a credit loss is modelled by exposure, recovery rate and default probability distributions, each of these distributions can be regarded as skewed and fat-tailed. Because normal probability measures are inappropriate, some models characterize these distributions by beta or gamma distributions, and maximum likelihood estimation of their parameters is standard.

When non-normal distributions are assumed, the computation of second derivatives for the covariance matrix of MLEs can be a very tricky problem. For normal variates substituting in (A.6.6) the MLE of σ^2 gives the estimated covariance matrix, and the information matrix was particularly easy to compute in this case. But for non-normal densities the information matrix may be non-diagonal and the expected values of the second derivatives of the log-likelihood very complex. Often they have to be approximated by taking their actual values, rather than expected values, at the maximum likelihood estimates. Analytic second derivatives may be impossible to compute, in which case an alternative form for the information matrix

$$\mathbf{I}(\boldsymbol{\theta}) = E[\partial \ln L(\boldsymbol{\theta})/\partial\boldsymbol{\theta}][\partial \ln L(\boldsymbol{\theta})/\partial\boldsymbol{\theta}']$$

can prove most useful computationally. An estimated covariance matrix is obtained taking the inverse of the estimated information matrix above, evaluated at the MLEs. Only the first derivatives of the log-likelihood are required, and these have to be computed anyway for the first-order conditions that define the MLEs.

Maximum likelihood estimation is a standard procedure in statistical packages. It is not as straightforward as least squares, since the likelihood optimization is an iterative procedure (often a gradient method) and it may not converge. For example, if there are many parameters in the model then the likelihood is a multi-dimensional surface that can be very flat indeed. In such circumstances an iterative search algorithm can yield a local rather than a global optimum, or it may hit a boundary if there are constraints on parameters. Because differences in starting values and optimization methods, as well as sometimes small differences in sample data can all lead to different results, a maximum likelihood procedure should always be monitored more closely than its simple least squares relative.

References

Abhyankar, A., Copeland, L.S. and Wong, W. (1997) 'Uncovering nonlinear structure in real-time stock-market indexes: The S&P 500, the DAX, the Nikkei 225, and the FTSE-100'. *Journal of Business and Economic Statistics* **15**, 1–14.

Alexander, C.O. (1994) 'Cofeatures in international bond and equity markets'. University of Sussex Discussion Papers in Economics no. 94/1, available from *www.ismacentre.rdg.ac.uk*

Alexander, C.O. (1995) 'Common volatility in the foreign exchange market'. *Applied Financial Economics* **5**(1), 1–10.

Alexander, C.O. (1996) 'Evaluating the use of RiskMetrics™ as a risk measurement tool for your operation: What are its advantages and limitations'. *Derivatives Use, Trading and Regulation* **2**(3), 277–285.

Alexander, C.O. (1997) 'Splicing methods for generating large covariance matrices' in *Learning Curve of Derivatives Week, Volume 3*. Institutional Investor. Also in *Derivatives Week*, June 1997.

Alexander, C.O. (1999a) 'Optimal hedging using cointegration'. *Philosophical Transactions of the Royal Society A* **357**, 2039–2058.

Alexander, C.O. (1999b) 'Cointegration and correlation in energy markets' in *Managing Energy Price Risk* (2nd edition), Chapter 15, pp. 291–304. RISK Publications.

Alexander, C.O. (2000a) 'Orthogonal methods for generating large positive semi-definite covariance matrices'. ISMA Centre Discussion Papers in Finance 2000-06, University of Reading, UK, available from *www.ismacentre.rdg.ac.uk*

Alexander, C.O. (2000b) 'Principal component analysis of implied volatility smiles and skews'. ISMA Centre Discussion Papers in Finance 2000-10, University of Reading, UK, available from *www.ismacentre.rdg.ac.uk*

Alexander, C.O. (2001a) 'Principles of the skew'. *RISK* **14**(1), S29–S32. Also available from *http://www.risk.net/supplements/supplements.html*

Alexander, C.O. (2001b) 'Orthogonal GARCH' in C.O. Alexander (ed.), *Mastering Risk Volume 2*. Financial Times–Prentice Hall.

Alexander, C. (2001c) 'The Bayesian approach to measuring operational risks' in C.O. Alexander (ed.), *Mastering Risk Volume 2*. Financial Times–Prentice Hall.

Alexander, C.O. and Chibumba, A. (1996) 'Multivariate orthogonal factor GARCH'. University of Sussex Discussion Papers in Mathematics.

Alexander, C.O. and Giblin, I. (1994) 'Chaos in the system?' *RISK* **7**(6), 71–76

Alexander, C.O. and Giblin, I. (1997) 'Multivariate embedding methods: Forecasting high-frequency data in the first INFFC'. *Journal of Computational Intelligence in Finance* **5**(6), 17–24

Alexander, C.O. and Johnson, A. (1992) 'Are foreign exchange markets really efficient?' *Economics Letters* **40**, 449–453.

Alexander, C.O. and Johnson, A. (1994) 'Dynamic links'. *RISK* **7**(2), 56–61.

Alexander, C.O. and Leigh, C. (1997) 'On the covariance matrices used in VaR models'. *Journal of Derivatives* **4**(3), 50–62.

Alexander, C.O. and Rendell, H. (1995) 'Data generation processes of spatial series: Analysis of ephemeral channel form'. *Geographical Analysis* **27**(1), 78–93.

Alexander, C.O. and Thillainathan, R. (1995) 'The Asian connection'. *Emerging Markets Investor* **2**(6), 42–46.

Alexander, C.O. and Williams, P.M. (1997) 'Term structure forecasts of foreign exchange volatility and kurtosis: A comparison of neural network and GARCH methods'. Unpublished manuscript, available from *www.ismacentre.rdg.ac.uk*

Alexandre, H., Girerd-Potin, I. and Taramasco, O. (1998) 'High frequency exchange rate forecasting by the nearest neighbours method' in C. Dunis and B. Zhou (eds), *Non-linear Modelling of High Frequency Financial Time Series*. Wiley.

Almeida, A., Goodhart, C.A.E. and Payne, R. (1998) 'The effect of macroeconomic "news" on high frequency exchange rate behaviour'. *Journal of Financial and Quantitative Analysis* **33**(3).

Amin, K. and Ng, V. (1993) 'Option valuation with systematic stochastic volatility'. *Journal of Finance* **48**, 881–910.

Andersen, T.G. and Bollerslev, T. (1996) 'DM–dollar volatility: Intraday activity patterns, macroeconomic announcements and longer run dependencies'. Working paper no. 217, Kellog Graduate School of Management, Northwestern University, available from the Financial Economics Network (FEN) at *www.ssrn.com*

Andersen, T.G. and Bollerslev, T. (1998) 'Answering the skeptics: Yes, standard volatility models do provide accurate forecasts'. *International Economic Review* **39**(4), 885–905.

Andersen, T., Bollerslev, T., Diebold, F.X. and Labys, P. (1999a) 'The distribution of exchange rate volatility'. Working paper no. W6961, Kellog Graduate School of Management, Northwestern University, available from the Financial Economics Network (FEN) at *www.ssrn.com*

Andersen, T., Bollerslev, T., Diebold, F.X. and Ebens, H. (1999b) 'The distribution of stock returns volatility'. Working paper No. W7933, Kellog Graduate School of Management, Northwestern University, available from the Financial Economics Network (FEN) at *www.ssrn.com*

Andrade, I., Clare, A.D. and Thomas, S.H. (1991) 'Cointegration and the gains from international portfolio diversification in bonds and equities'. Dept of Economics Discussion Paper Series, No. 9119, University of Southampton.

Ané, T. and Geman, H. (2000) 'Stochastic volatility and transaction time: An activity-based estimator of stochastic volatility'. *Journal of Risk* **2**, 57–69.

Artzner, P., Delbaen, F., Eber, J.-M. and Heath, D. (1997) 'Thinking coherently'. *RISK* **10**(11), 68–72.

Artzner, P., Delbaen, F., Eber, J.-M. and Heath, D. (1999) 'Coherent measures of risk'. *Mathematical Finance* **9**, 203–228.

Azoff, E.M. (1994) *Neural Network Time Series Forecasting of Financial Markets*. Wiley.

Baestaens, D.E., van den Berg,W.M. and Vaudrey, H. (1996) 'Money market headline news flashes, effective news and the DEM/USD swap rate: An intraday analysis in operational time'. Paper presented at the 3rd Forecasting Financial Markets Conference, London.

Baillie, R.T. and Bollerslev, T. (1989a) 'Common stochastic trends in a system of exchange rates'. *Journal of Finance* **44**(1), 167–181.

Baillie, R.T. and Bollerslev, T. (1989b) 'The message in daily exchange rates: A conditional-variance tale'. *Journal of Business and Economic Statistics* **7**(3), 297–305.

Baillie, R.T. and Bollerslev, T. (1990) 'Intra-day and inter-market volatility in foreign exchange rates'. *Review of Economic Studies* **58**, 565–585.

Baillie, R.T. and Bollerslev, T. (1994) 'Cointegration, fractional cointegration, and exchange rate dynamics'. *Journal of Finance* **49**(2), 737–745.

Baillie, R.T. and Myers, R.J. (1991) 'Bivariate GARCH estimation of the optimal commodity futures hedge'. *Journal of Applied Econometrics* **6**, 109–124.

Barndorff-Nielsen, O.E. (1977) 'Exponentially decreasing distributions for the logarithmic of particle size'. *Proceedings of the Royal Society of London A* **353**, 401–419.

Bauwens, L. and Giot, P. (1998) 'The logarithmic ACD model: An application to the bid/ask quotes process of two NYSE stocks'. CORE Working Paper no. 9789, Centre for Operations Research and Economics, Catholic University of Louvain.

Beck, S.E. (1994) 'Cointegration and market efficiency in commodities futures markets'. *Applied Economics* **26**(3), 249–257.

Bernardo, J.M. and Smith, A.F.M. (1994) *Bayesian Theory*. Wiley.

Bessler, D.A. and Covey, T. (1991) 'Cointegration — some results on cattle prices'. *Journal of Futures Markets* **11**(4), 461–474.

Black, F. (1972) 'Capital market equilibrium with restricted borrowing'. *Journal of Business* **45**, 444–454.

Black, F. and Scholes, M. (1973) 'The pricing of options and corporate liabilities'. *Journal of Political Economy* **81**, 637–654.

Blum, A. (1992) *Neural Networks in C^{++}*. Wiley.

Bolland, P.J., Connor, J.T. and Refenes, A.-P. (1998) 'Application of neural networks to forecast high frequency data: Foreign exchange' in C. Dunis and B. Zhou (eds), *Non-linear Modelling of High Frequency Financial Time Series*. Wiley.

Bollerslev, T. (1986) 'Generalised autoregressive conditional heteroskedasticy'. *Journal of Econometrics* **31**, 307–327.

Bollerslev, T. (1987) 'A conditional heteroskedasticity time series model for security prices and rates of return data'. *Review of Economics and Statistics* **69**, 542–547.

Bollerslev, T. (1990) 'Modelling the coherence in short-run nominal exchange rates: A multivariate generalized ARCH model'. *Review of Economics and Statistics* **72**, 498–505.

Bollerslev, T. and Domowitz, I. (1993) 'Trading patterns and prices in the interbank foreign exchange market'. *Journal of Finance* **48**, 1421–1443.

Bollerslev, T., Chou, R. and Kroner K. (1992) 'ARCH modelling in finance'. *Journal of Econometrics* **52**, 5–59.

Bollerslev, T., Englc, R.F. and Nelson, D.B. (1994) 'ARCH models' in R.F. Engle and D.L. McFadden (eds), *Handbook of Econometrics*, Vol. 4. North-Holland.

Booth, G. and Tse, Y. (1995) 'Long memory in interest rate futures markets: A fractional cointegration analysis'. *Journal of Futures Markets* **15**(5).

Bopp, A.E. and Sitzer, S. (1987) 'Are petroleum prices good predictors of cash value?' *Journal of Futures Markets* **7**, 705–719.

Bradley, M. and Lumpkin, S. (1992) 'The Treasury yield curve as a cointegrated system'. *Journal of Financial and Quantitative Analysis* **27**, 449–463.

Brailsford, T.J. and Faff, R.W. (1996) 'An evaluation of volatility forecasting techniques'. *Journal of Banking and Finance* **20**(3), 419–438.

Brenner, R.J. and Kroner, K.F. (1995) 'Arbitrage, cointegration, and testing the unbiasedness hypothesis in financial markets'. *Journal of Financial and Quantitative Analysis* **30**(1), 23–42.

Brenner, R.J., Harjes, R.H. and Kroner, K.F. (1996) 'Another look at alternative models of the short term interest rate'. *Journal of Financial and Quantitative Analysis* **31**(1), 85–108.

Broadie M. and Glasserman, P. (1996) 'Estimating security price derivatives using simulation'. *Management Science* **42**(2), 269–285.

Broadie, M. and Glasserman, P. (1998) 'Simulation for option pricing and risk management' in C. Alexander (ed.), *Risk Management and Analysis* (2nd edition), *Volume 2: Measuring and Modelling Financial Risk*, pp. 173–208. Wiley.

Brock, W.A., Hseih, D.A. and LeBaron B. (1990) *A Test for Non-linear Dynamics*. MIT Press.

Brooks, C. (2002) *Introduction to Financial Econometrics*. Cambridge University Press.

Brooks, C., Burke, S.P. and Persand, G. (2001) 'Benchmarks and the accuracy of GARCH model estimation'. *International Journal of Forecasting* **17**(1), 45–56.

Brooks, C. and Persand G. (2000) 'The pitfalls of VaR estimates'. *RISK* **13**(5), 63–66.

Campbell, J.Y., Lo, A.W. and MacKinlay, A.C. (1997) *The Econometrics of Financial Markets*. Princeton University Press.

Casdagli, M. (1992) 'Chaos and deterministic vs stochastic non-linear modelling'. *Journal of the Royal Statistical Society B* **54**, 303–328.

Casdagli, M. and Eubank, S. (eds) (1992) *Non-linear Modelling and Forecasting*, Santa Fe Institute Proceedings Vol. XII. Addison-Wesley.

Cecchetti, S.G., Cumby, R.E. and Figlewski, S. (1988) 'Estimation of the optimal futures hedge'. *Review of Economics and Statistics* **70**, 623–630.

Cerchi, M. and Havenner, A. (1988) 'Cointegration and stock prices'. *Journal of Economic Dynamics and Control* **12**, 333–346.

Chen, Z. (1993) 'Cointegration and exchange rate forecasting: A state space model'. LSE Financial Markets Group Discussion Paper no. 156.

Choi, I. (1992) 'Durbin–Hausman tests for a unit root'. *Oxford Bulletin of Economics and Statistics* **54**(3), 289–304.

Chowdhury, A.R. (1991) 'Futures market efficiency: Evidence from cointegration test'. *Journal of Futures Markets* **11**(5), 577–589.

Chriss, N.A. (1997) *Black–Scholes and Beyond: Option Pricing Models*. Irwin.

Clare, A.D., Maras M. and Thomas, S.H. (1995) 'The integration and efficiency of international bond markets'. *Journal of Business Finance and Accounting* **22**(2), 313–322.

Cochrane, J.H. (1991) 'A critique of the application of unit root tests'. *Journal of Economic Dynamics and Control* **15**, 275–284.

Coleman, M. (1990) 'Cointegration-based tests of daily foreign exchange market efficiency'. *Economics Letters* **32**, 53–59.

Coleman, T.S., Fisher, L. and Ibbotson, R.G. (1993) 'US Treasury Yield Curves 1926–1992'. Moody's Investors Service Inc.

Corbae, D. and Ouliaris, S. (1986) 'Cointegration and tests of purchasing power parity'. *Review of Economics and Statistics* **68**, 508–511.

Corhay, A., Tourani Rad, A. and Urbin, J.-P. (1993) 'Common stochastic trends in European stock markets'. *Economics Letters* **42**, 385–390.

Covey, T. and Bessler, D.A. (1992) 'Testing for Granger's full causality'. *Review of Economics and Statistics* **74**, 146–153.

Cumby, R., Figlewski, S. and Hasbrouk, J. (1993) 'Forecasting volatility and correlations with EGARCH models'. *Journal of Derivatives* **1**(3), 51–63.

Cuthbertson, K. (1996) *Quantitative Financial Economics: Stocks, Bonds and Foreign Exchange*. Wiley.

Dacoragna, M., Müller, U., Olsen, R. and Pictet, O. (1998) 'Modelling short term volatility with GARCH and HARCH models' in C. Dunis and B. Zhou (eds), *Non-linear Modelling of High Frequency Financial Time Series*. Wiley.

Dacorogna, M., Müller, U.A., Jost, C., Pictet, O.V., Olsen, R. and Ward, J.R. (1996) 'Heterogeneous real-time trading strategies in the foreign exchange market' in C. Dunis (ed.), *Forecasting Financial Markets*. Wiley.

Davidson, J., Madonia, G. and Westaway, P. (1994) 'Modelling the UK gilt-edged market'. *Journal of Applied Econometrics* **9**(3), 231–253.

de Grauwe, P, Dewachter, H. and Embrechts, M. (1993) *Exchange Rate Theory: Chaotic Models of Foreign Exchange Markets*. Blackwell.

De Jong, F. and Nijman, T. (1995) 'High frequency analysis of lead–lag relationships between financial markets'. *Journal of Empirical Finance* **4**(2), 259–278.

De Lima, P.J.F. (1998) 'Nonlinearities and nonstationarities in stock returns'. *Journal of Business and Economic Statistics* **16**, 227–236.

DeGennaro, R.P and Shrieves, R.E. (1995) 'Public information releases, private information arrival and volatility in the FX market' in *HFDF-1: First International Conference on High-Frequency Data in Finance*, Volume 1. Olsen and Associates, Zurich.

DeGennaro, R.P., Kunkel, R.A. and Lee, J. (1994) 'Modeling international long-term interest rates'. *Financial Review* **29**(4), 577–597.

Dembo, R. (2000) 'Mark-to-future: A framework for measuring risk and reward' in C. Alexander (ed.), *Visions of Risk*, pp. 74–85. Financial Times–Prentice Hall.

Dembo, R.C. and Freeman, A. (2001) *The Rules of Risk*. Wiley.

Dembo, R., Aziz, A., Rosen, D. and Zerbs, M. (2000) *Mark-to-Future: A Framework for Measuring Risk and Reward*. Algorithmics Publications (available from *www.mark-to-future.com*).

Derman, E. (1999) 'Volatility regimes'. *RISK* **12**(4), 55–59.

Derman, E. and Kamal, M. (1997) 'The patterns of change in implied index volatilities'. Quantitative Strategies Research Notes, Goldman Sachs.

Derman, E. and Kani, I. (1994) 'Riding on a smile' *RISK* **7**(2), 32–39.

Dickey, D.A. and Fuller, W.A. (1979) 'Distribution of the estimates for autoregressive time series with a unit root'. *Journal of the American Statistical Association* **74**, 427–429.

Diebold, F.X. and Lopez, J.A. (1996) 'Forecast evaluation and combination', in G.S. Maddala and C.R. Rao (eds), *Handbook of Statistics, Vol. 14: Statistical Methods in Finance*, pp. 241–268. North-Holland.

Diebold, F.X. and Mariano, R.S. (1995) 'Comparing predictive accuracy'. *Journal of Business & Economic Statistics* **13**, 253–263.

Dimson, E. and Marsh, P. (1990) 'Volatility forecasting without data snooping'. *Journal of Banking and Finance* **14**, 399–421.

Ding, Z. (1994) 'Time series analysis of speculative returns'. PhD thesis, University of California, San Diego.

Ding, Z., Granger, C.W.J and Engle, R.F. (1993) 'A long memory property of stock market returns and a new model'. *Journal of Empirical Finance* **1**, 83–106.

Drost, F.C. and Nijman, T.E. (1993) 'Temporal aggregation of GARCH processes'. *Econometrica* **61**(4), 900–927.

Drunat, J., Dufrenot, G., Dunis, C. and Mathieu, L. (1996) 'Stochastic or chaotic dynamics in high frequency exchange rates?' in C. Dunis (ed.), *Forecasting Financial Markets*. Wiley.

Drunat, J. Dufrenot, G. and Mathieu, L. (1998) 'Testing for linearity: A frequency domain approach' in C. Dunis and B. Zhou (eds), *Non-linear Modelling of High Frequency Financial Time Series*. Wiley.

Duan, J-C. (1995) 'The GARCH option pricing model'. *Mathematical Finance* **5**(1), 13–32.

Duan, J.C. (1996) 'Cracking the smile'. *RISK* **9**(12).

Duan, J.-C. (1999) 'Analytic approximation for GARCH option pricing'. Unpublished manuscript, available from *www.bm.ust.hk/~jcduan/index.html*

Duan, J.-C. and Pliska, S. (1998) 'Option valuation with cointegrated asset prices'. Unpublished manuscript, available from *www.bm.ust.hk/~jcduan/index.html*

Duan, J.C. and Wei, J.Z. (1999) 'Pricing foreign currency and cross-currency options under GARCH'. Unpublished manuscript, available from *www.bm.ust.hk/~jcduan/index.html*

Duan, J.-C., Gauthier, G. and Simonato, J.G. (1998) 'An analytical approximation for the GARCH option pricing model'. Unpublished manuscript, available from *www.bm.ust.hk/~jcduan/index.html*

Duffie, D. and Pan, J. (1997) 'An overview of value at risk'. *Journal of Derivatives* **4**(3), 7–49.

Dufour, A. and Engle, R.F. (2000) 'Time and the price impact of a trade'. *Journal of Finance* **55**, 2467–2498.

Dwyer, G.P. and Wallace, M.S. (1992) 'Cointegration and market efficiency'. *Journal of International Money and Finance* **11**, 318–327.

Eberlein, E. (2001) 'Recent advances in more realistic market and credit risk management: The hyperbolic model' in C. Alexander (ed.), *Mastering Risk Vol. 2*. Financial Times–Prentice Hall.

Eberlein, E. and Keller, U. (1995) 'Hyperbolic distributions in finance'. *Bernoulli* **1**, 281–299.

Eberlein, E., Keller, U. and Prause, K. (1998) 'New insights in smile, mis-pricing and value-at-risk: The hyperbolic model'. *Journal of Business* **71**, 371–406.

Embrechts, P., Klüppelberg, C. and Mikosch, T. (1997) *Modelling Extremal Events for Insurance and Finance*. Springer-Verlag.

Embrechts, P., Resnick, S.I. and Samorodnitsky, G. (1998) 'Living on the edge', *RISK* **11**(1), 96–100.

Embrechts, P., McNeil, A.J. and Straumann, D. (1999a) 'Correlation and dependency in risk management: Properties and pitfalls'. Working Paper, Dept. Mathematik, ETHZ, Zurich.

Embrechts, P., Resnick, S.I. and Samorodnitsky, G. (1999b) 'Extreme value theory as a risk management tool'. *North American Actuarial Journal* **3**(2), 30–41.

Enders, W. (1995) *Applied Dynamic Econometrics*. Wiley

Engle, R.F. (1982) 'Autoregressive conditional heteroscedasticity with estimates of the variance of UK inflation'. *Econometrica* **50**, 987–1007.

Engle, R.F. (2000a) 'The econometrics of ultra-high frequency data'. *Econometrica* **68**, 1–22.

Engle, R.F. (2000b) 'Dynamic conditional correlation — a simple class of multivariate GARCH models'. PDF version available from *http://weber.ucsd.edu/∼mbacci/engle/cv.html*

Engle, R.F. and González-Riviera, G. (1991) 'Semi-parametric GARCH models'. *Journal of Business and Economic Statistics* **9**, 345–359.

Engle, R.F. and Granger, C.W.J. (1987) 'Co-integration and error correction: Representation, estimation, and testing'. *Econometrica* **55**, 251–276.

Engle, R.F. and Kozicki, S. (1993) 'Testing for common features'. *Journal of Business and Economic Statistics* **11**, 369–395 (with discussions).

Engle, R.F. and Kroner, K.F. (1993) 'Multivariate simultaneous generalized ARCH'. *Econometric Theory* **11**, 122–150.

Engle, R.F. and Lee, G.G.J. (1993a) 'Long run volatility forecasting for individual stocks in a one factor model'. Working Paper 93-30, Department of Economics, University of California, San Diego, July, p. 20.

Engle, R.F. and Lee, G.G.J. (1993b) 'A permanent and transitory component model of stock return volatility' UCSD discussion paper, October.

Engle, R.F. and Mezrich, J. (1995) 'Grappling with GARCH'. *RISK* **8**(9), 112–117.

Engle, R.F. and Mustafa, C. (1992) 'Implied ARCH models from option prices'. *Journal of Econometrics* **52**, 289–311.

Engle, R.F. and Ng, V.K. (1993) 'Measuring and testing the impact of news on volatility'. *Journal of Finance* **48**, 1749–1778.

Engle, R.F. and Rosenberg, J. (1994) 'Hedging options in a GARCH environment: Testing the term structure of stochastic volatility models'. UCSD discussion paper, October.

Engle, R.F. and Rosenberg, J. (1995) 'GARCH gamma'. *Journal of Derivatives* **2**, 47–59.

Engle, R.F. and Russell, J.R. (1997) 'Forecasting the frequency of changes in the quoted foreign exchange prices with the autoregressive conditional duration model'. *Journal of Empirical Finance* **4**, 187–212.

Engle, R.F. and Russell, J.R. (1998) 'Autoregressive conditional duration: A new model for irregularly spaced transaction data'. *Econometrica* **66**, 1127–1162.

Engle, R.F. and Susmel, R. (1993) 'Common volatility in international equity markets'. *Journal of Business and Economic Statistics* **11**, 167–176.

Engle, R.F. and Yoo, B.S. (1987) 'Forecasting and testing in co-integrated systems'. *Journal of Econometrics* **35**, 143–159.

Engle, R.F., Ng, V. and Rothschild, M. (1990) 'Asset pricing with a factor ARCH covariance structure: Empirical estimates for treasury bills'. *Journal of Econometrics* **45**, 213–238.

Erb, C.B., Harvey, C.R. and Viskanta, T.E. (1994) 'Forecasting international equity correlations'. *Financial Analysis Journal,* November–December, 32–45.

Fengler, M., Härdle, W. and Villa, C. (2000) 'The dynamics of implied volatilities: A common principal component approach'. Preliminary version (September) available from *fengler@wiwi.hu-berlin.de*

Figlewski, S. (1997) 'Forecasting volatility'. *Financial Markets, Institutions and Instruments* **6**, 1–88.

Finkenstadt, B. and Kuhbier, P. (1995) 'Forecasting nonlinear economic time series: A simple test to accompany the nearest neighbor approach'. *Empirical Economics* **20**, 243–263.

Fishman, M.B., Barr, D.S. and Loick, W.J. (1991) 'Using neural nets in market analysis'. *Technical Analysis of Stocks and Commodities* **9**(4).

Fitzgerald, M.D. (1996) 'Trading volatility' in C.O. Alexander (ed.), *Handbook of Risk Management and Analysis*. Wiley.

Frennberg, P. and Hansson, B. (1996) 'An evaluation of alternative models for predicting stock volatility: Evidence from a small stock market'. *Journal of International Financial Markets, Institutions and Money* **5**, 117–134.

Frye, J. (1998) 'Monte Carlo by day'. *RISK* **11**(11), 66–71.

Galbraith, J.W. and Zinde-Walsh, V. (2000) 'Properties of estimates of daily GARCH parameters based on intra-day observations'. Economics Dept. Working Papers, McGill University, available from *www.arts.mcgill.ca/programs/econ/Working_Papers.html*

Gallant, A.R., Hseih, D. and Tauchen, G. (1991) 'On fitting a recalcitrant series: The pound/dollar exchange rate 1974–83' in W. Barnett, J. Powell and G.Tauchen (eds), *Nonparametric and Semiparametric Methods in Econometrics and Statistics*. Cambridge University Press.

Ghose, D. and Kroner, K.F. (1995) 'Temporal aggregation of high frequency financial data' in *HFDF-1: First International Conference on High-Frequency Data in Finance*, Volume 2. Olsen and Associates, Zurich.

Ghysels, E. and Jasiak, J. (1995a) 'Stochastic volatility and time deformation: An application to trading volume and leverage effects'. Working paper, Université de Montréal.

Ghysels, E., and Jasiak, J. (1995b) 'Trading patterns, time deformation and stochastic volatility in foreign exchange markets'. Working paper, Université de Montréal.

Ghysels, E., Gourieroux, C. and Jasiak, J. (1998) 'High frequency financial time series data: Some stylised facts and models of stochastic volatility' in C. Dunis and B. Zhou (eds), *Non-linear Modelling of High Frequency Financial Time Series*. Wiley.

Giot, P. (2001) 'Time transformations, intraday data, and volatility models'. *Journal of Computational Finance* **4**(2), 31–62.

Glasserman, P., Heidelberger, P. and Shahabuddin, P. (2001) 'Efficient Monte Carlo methods for Value-at-Risk' in C. Alexander (ed.), *Mastering Risk Vol. 2*. Financial Times–Prentice Hall.

Glosten, L.R., Jagannathan, R. and Runkle, D.E. (1993) 'On the relation between expected value and the volatility of excess returns on stocks'. *Journal of Finance* **48**, 1779–1801.

Goodhart, C. (1988) 'The foreign exchange market: A random walk with a dragging anchor'. *Economica* **55**, 437–460.

Goodhart, C.A.E. and Figliouli, L. (1991) 'Every minute counts in financial markets'. *Journal of International Money and Finance* **10**, 23–52.

Goodhart, C.A.E. and O'Hara, M. (1997) 'High frequency data in financial markets: Issues and applications'. *Journal of Empirical Finance* **4**, 73–114.

Goodhart, C.A.E., Hall, S.G., Henry, S.G.B. and Pesaran, B. (1991) 'News effects in a high frequency model of the sterling–dollar exchange rate'. LSE Financial Markets Group Discussion Paper No. 119.

Gourieroux, C., Monfort, A. and Renault, E. (1991) 'A general framework for factor models'. Working Paper No. 9107, Institut National de la Statistique et des Etudes Economiques.

Granger, C.W.J. (1969) 'Investigating causal relations by econometric models and cross spectral methods'. *Econometrica* **37**, 424–438.

Granger, C.W.J. (1986) 'Developments in the study of cointegrated economic variables'. *Oxford Bulletin of Economics and Statistics* **42**(3), 213–227.

Granger, C.W.J. (1988) 'Some recent developments on a concept of causality'. *Journal of Econometrics* **39**, 199–211.

Granger, C.W.J. and Hallman, J. (1991) 'Long memory processes with attractors'. *Oxford Bulletin of Economics and Statistics* **53**, 11–26.

Granger, C.W.J. and Ramanathan, R. (1984) 'Improved methods of combining forecasts'. *Journal of Forecasting* **3**, 197–204.

Granger, C.W.J. and Teräsvirta, T. (1993) *Modelling Nonlinear Economic Relationships*. Oxford University Press.

Grassberger, P. and Procaccia, I. (1983a) 'Characterisation of strange attractors'. *Physical Review Letters* **50**, 346–349.

Grassberger, P and Procaccia, I. (1983b) 'Measuring the strangeness of strange attractors'. *Physica D* **9**, 189–208.

Greene, W.H. (1998) *Econometric Analysis* (4th edition). Macmillan.

Griffiths, W.E., Carter Hill, R. and Judge, G.C. (1993) *Learning and Practicing Econometrics*. Wiley.

Guillaume, D.M., Dacorogna, M. and Pictet, O.V. (1994) 'From the bird's eye to the microscope: A survey of new stylised facts of the intra-daily foreign exchange markets'. Discussion paper DMG 1994-04-06, Olsen and Associates, Zurich.

Guillaume, D.M., Dacorogna, M. and Pictet, O.V. (1995) 'On the intra-day performance of GARCH processes' in *HFDF-1: First International Conference on High-Frequency Data in Finance*, Volume 3. Olsen and Associates, Zurich.

Hafner, C.M. and Härdle, W. (2000) 'Discrete time option pricing with flexible volatility estimation'. *Finance and Stochastics* **4**, 189–207.

Hagerud, G.E. (1997) 'Modeling Nordic stock returns with asymmetric GARCH models'. Stockholm School of Economics Working Paper Series in Economics and Finance No.164.

Hakkio, C.S. and Rush, M. (1989) 'Market efficiency and cointegration: An application to the sterling and Deutschmark exchange markets'. *Journal of International Money and Finance* **8**, 75–88.

Hall, A.D., Anderson, H.M. and Granger, C.W.J. (1992) 'A cointegration analysis of Treasury bill yields'. *Review of Economics and Statistics* **74**, 116–126.

Hamilton, J.D. (1994) *Time Series Analysis*. Princeton University Press.

Hamilton, J.D. and Susmel, R. (1994) 'Autoregressive conditional heteroskedasticity and changes in regime'. *Journal of Econometrics* **64**, 307–333.

Harris, F.deB., McInish, T.H., Shoesmith, G.L. and Wood, R.A. (1995) 'Cointegration, error correction, and price discovery on informationally linked security markets'. *Journal of Financial and Quantitative Analysis* **30**(4).

Harris, L, Sofianos, G. and Shapiro, J.E. (1994) 'Program trading and intraday volatility'. *Review of Financial Studies* **7**, 653–685.

Harvey, A. (1993) *Time Series Models*. Harvester-Wheatsheaf.

Hendry, D.F. (1986) 'Econometric modelling with cointegrated variables: An overview'. *Oxford Bulletin of Economics and Statistics* **48**(3), 201–212.

Hendry, D.F. (1996) *Dynamic Econometrics*. Oxford University Press.

Heynen, R., Kemna, A. and Vorst, T. (1994) 'Analysis of the term structure of implied volatilities'. *Journal of Financial Quantitative Analysis* **29**(1), 31–56.

Hseih, D.A. (1988) 'The statistical properties of daily foreign exchange rates: 1974–1983'. *Journal of International Economics* **24**, 129–145.

Hseih, D.A. (1989) 'Testing for non-linear dependence in daily foreign exchange rates'. *Journal of Business* **62**, 339–369.

Hseih, D.A. (1991) 'Chaos and non-linear dynamics: Application to financial markets'. *Journal of Finance* **46**, 1839–1877.

Hull, J. and White, A. (1987) 'The pricing of options on assets with stochastic volatilities'. *Journal of Finance* **42**, 281–300.

Hull, J. and White, A. (1997) 'Evaluating the impact of skewness and kurtosis on derivatives prices'. *NetExposure* **3** (December).

Hull, J. and White, A. (1998) 'Taking account of the kurtosis in market variables when calculating VAR'. *Journal of Derivatives*, **5**(3), 9–19.

Jaditz, T. and Sayers, C.L. (1998) ' Out-of-sample forecast performance as a test for nonlinearity in time series'. *Journal of Business and Economic Statistics* **16**, 110–117.

Jamshidian, F. and Zhu, Y. (1997) 'Scenario simulation: Theory and methodology'. *Finance and Stochastics* **1**(1), 43–68.

Johansen, S. (1988) 'Statistical analysis of cointegration vectors'. *Journal of Economic Dynamics and Control* **12**, 231–254.

Johansen, S. (1991) 'Estimation and hypothesis testing of cointegration vectors in Gaussian vector autoregressive models'. *Econometrica* **59**, 1551–1580.

Johansen, S. and Juselius, K. (1990) 'Maximum likelihood estimation and inference on cointegration — with applications to the demand for money'. *Oxford Bulletin of Economics and Statistics* **52**(2), 169–210.

Jolliffe, I.T. (1986) *Principal Component Analysis*. Springer-Verlag.

Jones, C.M., Kaul, G. and Lipton, M.L. (1994) 'Transactions, volume and volatility'. *Review of Financial Studies* **7**(4), 631–651.

Karfakis, C.J. and Moschos, D.M. (1990) 'Interest rate linkages within the European monetary system: A time series analysis'. *Journal of Money, Credit, and Banking* **22**(3), 388–394.

Kasa, K. (1992) 'Common stochastic trends in international stock markets'. *Journal of Monetary Economics* **29**, 95–124.

Katz, J.O. (1992) 'Developing neural network forecasters for trading'. *Technical Analysis of Stocks and Commodities* **10**(4).

Kean, J. (1992) 'Using neural nets for intermarket analysis'. *Technical Analysis of Stocks and Commodities* **10**(11).

Khoury, N.T. and Yourougou, P. (1991) 'The informational content of the basis: Evidence from Canadian barley, oats and canola futures markets'. *Journal of Futures Markets* **11**(1), 69–80.

King, J. (2001) *Operational Risk: Measurement and Modelling*. Wiley.

Klaassen, F. (2000) 'Have exchange rates become more closely tied? Evidence from a new multivariate GARCH model'. Centre for Economic Research discussion paper, University of Tilburg.

Kremers, J.J.M., Ericsson, N.R. and Dolado, J.J. (1992) 'The power of cointegration tests'. *Oxford Bulletin of Economics and Statistics* **54**(3), 325–348.

Kroner, K.F. and Claessens, S. (1991) 'Optimal dynamic hedging portfolios and the currency composition of external debt'. *Journal of International Money and Finance* **10**, 131–148.

Kroner, K.F. and Ng, V.K. (1998) 'Modeling asymmetric comovements of asset returns'. *Review of Financial Studies* **11**, 817–844.

Kuan, C-M. and Liu, T. (1995) Forecasting exchange rates using feedforward and recurrent neural networks. *Journal of Applied Econometrics* **10**, 347–364.

Lai, K.S. and Lai, M. (1991) 'A cointegration test for market efficiency'. *Journal of Futures Markets* **11**, 567–576.

Leadbetter, R., Lindgren G. and Rootzen, H. (1983) *Extremes and Related Properties of Random Sequences and Processes*. Springer-Verlag.

LeBaron, B. (1992) 'Forecast improvements using a volatility index'. *Journal of Applied Econometrics* **7**, 137–149.

LeBaron, B. (1995) 'Chaos and nonlinear forecastability in economics and finance' in H. Tong (ed.), *Chaos and Forecasting*, Vol. 2. World Scientific.

Lee, T.-H. (1994) 'Spread and volatility in spot and forward exchange rates'. *Journal of International Money and Finance* **13**(3), 375–383.

Lien, D. and Luo, X. (1994) 'Multiperiod hedging in the presence of conditional heteroskedasticity'. *Journal of Futures Markets* **14**(8), 927–955.

Lintner, J. (1965) 'The valuation of risk assets and the selection of risky investments in stock portfolios and capital budgets'. *Review of Economics and Statistics* **47**, 13–37.

Liu, T., Granger, C.W.J. and Heller, W.P. (1992) 'Using the correlation exponent to decide whether an economic series is chaotic'. *Journal of Applied Econometrics* **7**, 25–39.

Lo, A.W. and MacKinlay, A.C. (1988) 'Stock market prices do not follow random walks: Evidence from a simple specification test'. *Review of Financial Studies* **1**(1), 41–66.

Longin, F. and Solnik, B. (1995) 'Is the correlation in international equity returns constant: 1960–1990?' *Journal of International Money and Finance* **14**(1), 3–26.

Low, A. and J. Muthuswamy (1996) 'Information flows in high-frequency exchange rates' in C. Dunis (ed.), *Forecasting Financial Markets*. Wiley.

Lumsdaine, R.L. (1995) 'Finite sample properties of the maximum likelihood estimation in GARCH(1, 1) and IGARCH (1, 1) models: A Monte Carlo investigation'. *Journal of Business Economics and Statistics* **13**(1), 1–10.

MacDonald, R. and Taylor, M. (1988) 'Metals prices, efficiency and cointegration: Some evidence from the London Metal Exchange'. *Bulletin of Economic Research* **40**, 235–239.

MacDonald, R. and Taylor, M.P. (1994) 'The monetary model of the exchange rate: Long-run relationships, short-run dynamics and how to beat a random walk'. *Journal of International Money and Finance* **13**(3), 276–290.

MacKinnon, J.G. (1991) 'Critical values for cointegration tests' in R.F. Engle and C.G. Granger (eds), *Long-Run Economic Relationships: Readings in Cointegration*. Oxford University Press.

Makridakis, S. (1993) 'Accuracy measures: Theoretical and practical concerns'. *International Journal of Forecasting* **9**, 527–529.

Mandelbrot, B. (1963) 'The variation of certain speculative prices'. *Journal of Business* **36**, 394–419.

Markovitz, H. (1959) *Portfolio Selection: Efficient Diversification of Investments*. Wiley.

Masih, R. (1997) 'Cointegration of markets since the '87 crash'. *Quarterly Review of Economics and Finance* **37**(4).

Masters, T. (1993) *Practical Neural Network Recipes in C^{++}*. Academic Press.

McNeil, A.J. (1997) 'Estimating the tails of loss severity distributions using extreme value theory'. *ASTIN Bulletin* **27**, 117–137.

Medio, A. (1992) *Chaotic Dynamics, Theory and Applications to Economics*. Cambridge University Press.

Mizrach, B. (1992) 'Multivariate nearest-neighbor forecasts of EMS exchange rates'. *Journal of Applied Econometrics* **7** (Suppl. Dec.), 151–163.

Morgan, J.P. and Reuters (1996) *RiskMetrics Technical Document*, 4th edition. Morgan Guaranty and Reuters. Available from *www.riskmetrics.com* or from *www.jpmorgan.com/RiskManagement/RiskMetrics/RiskMetrics.html*

Müller, U.A., Dacoragna, M., Olsen, R., Pictet, O.V., Schwarz, M. and Morgenegg, C. (1990) 'Statistical study of foreign exchange rates, empirical evidence of a price change scaling law, and intraday analysis'. *Journal of Banking and Finance* **14**, 1189–1208.

Müller, U.A., Dacoragna, M., Davé, R.D., Olsen, R., Pictet, O.V. and von Weizsäcker, J.E. (1997) 'Volatilities of different time resolutions — analysing the dynamics of market components'. *Journal of Empirical Finance* **4**, 213–239.

Murphy, J. (1986) *Technical Analysis of the Futures Markets*. Prentice Hall.

Nabney, I., Dunis, C., Rallaway, R., Leong, S. and Redshaw, W. (1996) 'Leading edge forecasting techniques for exchange rate prediction' in C. Dunis (ed.), *Forecasting Financial Markets*. Wiley.

Nelsen, R.B. (1999) *An Introduction to Copulas*, Lecture Notes in Statistics 139. Springer-Verlag.

Nelson, D.B. (1988) 'The time series behaviour of stock market volatility and returns'. Doctoral dissertation, Massachusetts Institute of Technology, Cambridge, MA.

Nelson, D.B. (1990) 'ARCH models as diffusion approximations'. *Journal of Econometrics* **45**, 7–38.

Nelson, D.B. (1991) 'Conditional heteroskedasticity in asset returns: A new approach'. *Econometrica* **59**, 347–370.

Nieuwland, F.G.M., Verschoor, W., Willen, F.C. and Wolff, C.C.P. (1994) 'Stochastic trends and jumps in EMS exchange rates'. *Journal of International Money and Finance* **13**(6), 669–727.

Noh, J., Engle, R.F. and Kane, A. (1994) 'Forecasting volatility and option prices of the S&P500 index'. *Journal of Derivatives* **2**, 17–30.

Nugent, J. (1990) 'Further evidence of forward exchange market efficiency: An application of cointegration using German and U.K. data'. *Economic and Social Reviews* **22**, 35–42.

Nychka, D., Ellner, S., McCaffrey, D. and Gallant, A.R. (1992) 'Finding chaos in noisy systems'. *Journal of the Royal Statistical Society B* **54**, 399–426.

Palm, F.C. (1996), 'GARCH models of volatility', in G.S. Maddala and C.R. Rao (eds), *Handbook of Statistics* (Vol. 14), *Statistical Methods in Finance*, pp. 209–240. North-Holland.

Park, T.H. and Switzer, L.N. (1995) 'Bivariate GARCH estimation of the optimal hedge ratios for stock index futures: A note'. *Journal of Futures Markets* **15**(1), 61–67.

Peters, E.E. (1991) *Chaos and Order in the Capital Markets*. Wiley.

Phillips, P.C.B. and Ouliaris, S. (1990) 'Asymptotic properties of residual based tests for cointegration'. *Econometrica* **58**, 165–193.

Phillips, P.C.B. and Perron, P. (1988) 'Testing for a unit root in time series regressions'. *Biometrika* **75**, 335–346.

Pickands, J. (1975) 'Statistical inference using extreme order statistics'. *Annals of Statistics* **3**, 119–131.

Pindyck, R.S. and Rothemberg, J.J. (1993) 'The comovement of stock prices'. *Quarterly Journal of Economics* **108**, 1073–1103.

Press, W.H., Teukolsky, S.A., Vetterling, W.T. and Flannery, B.P. (1992) *Numerical Recipes in C: The Art of Scientific Computing* (2nd edition). Cambridge University Press.

Proietti, T. (1997) 'Short-run dynamics in cointegrated systems'. *Oxford Bulletin of Economics and Statistics* **59**(3).

Qi, Min (1999) 'Nonlinear predictability of stock returns using financial and economic variables'. *Journal of Business and Economic Statistics* **17**, 419–429.

Refenes, A.-P., Abu-Mostafa, Y., Moody, J. and Weigend, A. (eds) (1996) *Neural Networks in Financial Engineering,* Proceedings of the Third International Conference on Neural Networks in the Capital Markets. World Scientific.

Ripley, B.D. (1996) *Pattern Recognition and Neural Networks*. Cambridge University Press.

Ross, S. (1976) 'The arbitrage theory of capital asset pricing'. *Journal of Economic Theory* **13**, 341–360.

Rouvinez, C. (1997) 'Going Greek with VAR'. *RISK* **10**(2), 57–65.

Ruelle, D. (1990) 'Deterministic chaos: The science and the fiction'. *Proceedings of the Royal Society of London, A* **427**, 241.

Scheinkman, J.A. and LeBaron, B. (1989) 'Non-linear dynamics and stock returns'. *Journal of Business* **62**, 311–328.

Schmidt, P. and Phillips, P.C.B. (1992) 'LM tests for a unit root in the presence of deterministic trends'. *Oxford Bulletin of Economics and Statistics* **54**(3), 257–288.

Schroeder, T.C. and Goodwin, B.K. (1991) 'Price discovery and cointegration for live hogs'. *Journal of Futures Markets* **11**(6), 685–696.

Schwarz, T.V. and Laatsch, F.E. (1991) 'Dynamic efficiency and price discovery leadership in stock index cash and futures markets'. *Journal of Futures Markets* **11**(6), 669–684.

Schwarz, T.V. and Szakmary, A.C. (1994) 'Price discovery in petroleum markets: Arbitrage, cointegration, and the time interval of analysis'. *Journal of Futures Markets* **14**(2), 147–167.

Schweizer, B. and Sklar, A. (1958) 'Espaces métriques aléatoires'. *Comptes Rendues de l'Académie des Sciences de Paris* **247**, 2092–2094.

Sentana, E. (1995) 'Quadratic ARCH models'. *Review of Economic Studies* **62**, 639–661.

Sharpe, W. (1964) 'Capital asset prices: A theory of market equilibrium under conditions of risk'. *Journal of Finance* **19**, 425–442.

Sharpe, W. (1970) *Portfolio Theory and Capital Markets*. McGraw-Hill.

Shih, Y.L. (1991) 'Neural nets in technical analysis'. *Technical Analysis of Stocks and Commodities* **9**(2).

Skiadopoulos, G., Hodges, S. and Clewlow, L. (1998) 'The dynamics of implied volatility surfaces'. Financial Options Research Centre Preprint 1998/86, Warwick Business School, University of Warwick.

Smith, K.L., Brocato, J. and Rogers, J.E. (1993) 'Regularities in the data between major equity markets: Evidence from Granger causality tests'. *Applied Financial Economics* **3**, 55–60.

Smith, R. (1987) 'Estimating tails of probability distributions'. *Annals of Statistics* **15**, 1174–1207.

Smith, R.L. (1992) 'Estimating dimension in noisy chaotic time series'. *Journal of the Royal Statistical Society B* **54**, 329–352.

Stock, J.H. and Watson, M.W. (1988) 'Testing for common trends'. *Journal of the American Statistical Association* **83**(404), 1097–1107.

Sugihara, G. and May, R.M. (1990) 'Non-linear forecasting as a way of distinguishing chaos from measurement error in a data series'. *Nature* **344**, 734–741.

Swales, G.S. and Yoon, Y. (1992) 'Applying artificial neural networks to investment analysis'. *Financial Analysts Journal* **48**(5).

Swidler, S. and Diltz, J.D. (1992) 'Implied volatilities and transaction costs'. *Journal of Financial and Quantitative Analysis* **27**(3), 437–447.

Takens, F. (1981) 'Detecting strange attractors in fluid turbulence' in D. Rand and L.-S. Young (eds), *Dynamical Systems and Turbulence*, Lecture Notes in Mathematics 898. Springer-Verlag.

Tata, F. and Vassilicos, C. (1991) 'Is there chaos in economic time series? A study of the stock and the foreign exchange markets'. LSE Financial Markets Group Discussion Paper No. 120.

Tauchen, G.E. and Pitts, M. (1983) 'The price variability–volume relationship on speculative markets'. *Econometrica* **51**, 485–505.

Taylor, S.J. and Xu X. (1997) 'The incremental volatility information in one million foreign exchange quotations'. *Journal of Empirical Finance* **4**, 317–340.

Taylor, M.P. and Tonks I. (1989) 'The internationalisation of stock markets and the abolition of UK exchange control'. *Review of Economics and Statistics*, **71**, 332–336.

Taylor, S.J. (1994) 'Modeling stochastic volatility: A review and comparative study'. *Mathematical Finance* **4**(2), 183–204.

Teräsvirta, T. (1996) 'Two stylized facts and the GARCH(1,1) model'. Stockholm School of Economics Working Paper Series in Economics and Finance No. 96.

Vassilicos, J.C., Demos, A. and Tata, F. (1992) 'No evidence of chaos but some evidence of multifractals in the foreign exchange and the stock market'. LSE Financial Markets Group Discussion Paper No. 143.

Weigund, A.S. and Gershenfeld, N.A. (eds) (1993) *Time Series Prediction: Forecasting the Future and Understanding the Past*. Addison-Wesley.

West, K.D. and Cho, D. (1995) 'The predictive ability of several models of exchange rate volatility'. *Journal of Econometrics* **69**, 367–391.

White, H. (1980) 'A heteroscedasticity-consistent covariance matrix estimator and a direct test for heteroscedasticity'. *Econometrica* **48**, 817–838.

White, H. (1984) *Asymptotic Theory for Econometricians*. Academic Press.

White, H. (1988) 'Economic predictions using neural networks: The case of IBM daily stock returns'. *Proceedings of IEEE International Conference on Neural Networks*, Vol. 2, pp. 451–458.

Williams, P.M. (1995) 'Bayesian regularization and pruning using a Laplace prior'. *Neural Computation* **7**, 117–143.

Williams, P.M. (1996) 'Using neural networks to model conditional multivariate densities'. *Neural Computation* **8**, 843–854.

Wolff, R.C.L. (1992) 'Local Lyapunov exponents: Looking closely at chaos'. *Journal of the Royal Statistical Society B* **54**, 353–372.

Wong, F.S. (1992) 'Fuzzy neural systems for stock selection'. *Financial Analysts Journal* **48**, 47–52.

Wooldridge, J.M. (1991) 'On the application of robust regression-based diagnostics to models of conditional means and conditional variances'. *Journal of Econometrics* **47**, 5–46.

Zakoian, J.-M. (1994) 'Threshold heteroscedastic models'. *Journal of Economic Dynamics and Control* **18**, 931–955.

Zhou, B. (1996) 'High frequency data and volatility in foreign exchange markets'. *Journal of Business and Economic Statistics* **14**, 45–52.

Zhou, B. (1998) '*F*-consistency, devolatilization and normalization of high frequency financial data' in C. Dunis and B. Zhou (eds), *Non-linear Modelling of High Frequency Financial Time Series*. Wiley.

Tables

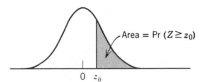

Area = Pr $(Z \geq z_0)$

0 z_0

1 Standard Normal, Cumulative Probability in Right-Hand Tail (For Negative Values of z, Areas are Found by Symmetry)

	NEXT DECIMAL PLACE OF z_0									
z_0	0	1	2	3	4	5	6	7	8	9
0.0	.500	.496	.492	.488	.484	.480	.476	.472	.468	.464
0.1	.460	.456	.452	.448	.444	.440	.436	.433	.429	.425
0.2	.421	.417	.413	.409	.405	.401	.397	.394	.390	.386
0.3	.382	.378	.374	.371	.367	.363	.359	.356	.352	.348
0.4	.345	.341	.337	.334	.330	.326	.323	.319	.316	.312
0.5	.309	.305	.302	.298	.295	.291	.288	.284	.281	.278
0.6	.274	.271	.268	.264	.261	.258	.255	.251	.248	.245
0.7	.242	.239	.236	.233	.230	.227	.224	.221	.218	.215
0.8	.212	.209	.206	.203	.200	.198	.195	.192	.189	.187
0.9	.184	.181	.179	.176	.174	.171	.169	.166	.164	.161
1.0	.159	.156	.154	.152	.149	.147	.145	.142	.140	.138
1.1	.136	.133	.131	.129	.127	.125	.123	.121	.119	.117
1.2	.115	.113	.111	.109	.107	.106	.104	.102	.100	.099
1.3	.097	.095	.093	.092	.090	.089	.087	.085	.084	.082
1.4	.081	.079	.078	.076	.075	.074	.072	.071	.069	.068
1.5	.067	.066	.064	.063	.062	.061	.059	.058	.057	.056
1.6	.055	.054	.053	.052	.051	.049	.048	.047	.046	.046
1.7	.045	.044	.043	.042	.041	.040	.039	.038	.038	.037
1.8	.036	.035	.034	.034	.033	.032	.031	.031	.030	.029
1.9	.029	.028	.027	.027	.026	.026	.025	.024	.024	.023
2.0	.023	.022	.022	.021	.021	.020	.020	.019	.019	.018
2.1	.018	.017	.017	.017	.016	.016	.015	.015	.015	.014
2.2	.014	.014	.013	.013	.013	.012	.012	.012	.011	.011
2.3	.011	.010	.010	.010	.010	.009	.009	.009	.009	.008
2.4	.008	.008	.008	.008	.007	.007	.007	.007	.007	.006
2.5	.006	.006	.006	.006	.006	.005	.005	.005	.005	.005
2.6	.005	.005	.004	.004	.004	.004	.004	.004	.004	.004
2.7	.003	.003	.003	.003	.003	.003	.003	.003	.003	.003
2.8	.003	.002	.002	.002	.002	.002	.002	.002	.002	.002
2.9	.002	.002	.002	.002	.002	.002	.002	.001	.001	.001

z_0	DETAIL OF TAIL (.$_2$135, FOR EXAMPLE, MEANS .00135)									
2.	.$_1$228	.$_1$179	.$_1$139	.$_1$107	.$_2$820	.$_2$621	.$_2$466	.$_2$347	.$_2$256	.$_2$187
3.	.$_2$135	.$_3$968	.$_3$687	.$_3$483	.$_3$337	.$_3$233	.$_3$159	.$_3$108	.$_4$723	.$_4$481
4.	.$_4$317	.$_4$207	.$_4$133	.$_5$854	.$_5$541	.$_5$340	.$_5$211	.$_5$130	.$_6$793	.$_6$479
5.	.$_6$287	.$_6$170	.$_7$996	.$_7$579	.$_7$333	.$_7$190	.$_7$107	.$_8$599	.$_8$332	.$_8$182
	0	1	2	3	4	5	6	7	8	9

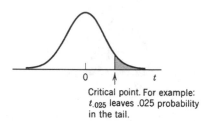

Critical point. For example:
$t_{.025}$ leaves .025 probability
in the tail.

2 *t* Critical Points

d.f.	$t_{.25}$	$t_{.10}$	$t_{.05}$	$t_{.025}$	$t_{.010}$	$t_{.005}$	$t_{.0025}$	$t_{.0010}$	$t_{.0005}$
1	1.00	3.08	6.31	12.7	31.8	63.7	127	318	637
2	.82	1.89	2.92	4.30	6.96	9.92	14.1	22.3	31.6
3	.76	1.64	2.35	3.18	4.54	5.84	7.45	10.2	12.9
4	.74	1.53	2.13	2.78	3.75	4.60	5.60	7.17	8.61
5	.73	1.48	2.02	2.57	3.36	4.03	4.77	5.89	6.87
6	.72	1.44	1.94	2.45	3.14	3.71	4.32	5.21	5.96
7	.71	1.41	1.89	2.36	3.00	3.50	4.03	4.79	5.41
8	.71	1.40	1.86	2.31	2.90	3.36	3.83	4.50	5.04
9	.70	1.38	1.83	2.26	2.82	3.25	3.69	4.30	4.78
10	.70	1.37	1.81	2.23	2.76	3.17	3.58	4.14	4.59
11	.70	1.36	1.80	2.20	2.72	3.11	3.50	4.02	4.44
12	.70	1.36	1.78	2.18	2.68	3.05	3.43	3.93	4.32
13	.69	1.35	1.77	2.16	2.65	3.01	3.37	3.85	4.22
14	.69	1.35	1.76	2.14	2.62	2.98	3.33	3.79	4.14
15	.69	1.34	1.75	2.13	2.60	2.95	3.29	3.73	4.07
16	.69	1.34	1.75	2.12	2.58	2.92	3.25	3.69	4.01
17	.69	1.33	1.74	2.11	2.57	2.90	3.22	3.65	3.97
18	.69	1.33	1.73	2.10	2.55	2.88	3.20	3.61	3.92
19	.69	1.33	1.73	2.09	2.54	2.86	3.17	3.58	3.88
20	.69	1.33	1.72	2.09	2.53	2.85	3.15	3.55	3.85
21	.69	1.32	1.72	2.08	2.52	2.83	3.14	3.53	3.82
22	.69	1.32	1.72	2.07	2.51	2.82	3.12	3.50	3.79
23	.69	1.32	1.71	2.07	2.50	2.81	3.10	3.48	3.77
24	.68	1.32	1.71	2.06	2.49	2.80	3.09	3.47	3.75
25	.68	1.32	1.71	2.06	2.49	2.79	3.08	3.45	3.73
26	.68	1.31	1.71	2.06	2.48	2.78	3.07	3.43	3.71
27	.68	1.31	1.70	2.05	2.47	2.77	3.06	3.42	3.69
28	.68	1.31	1.70	2.05	2.47	2.76	3.05	3.41	3.67
29	.68	1.31	1.70	2.05	2.46	2.76	3.04	3.40	3.66
30	.68	1.31	1.70	2.04	2.46	2.75	3.03	3.39	3.65
40	.68	1.30	1.68	2.02	2.42	2.70	2.97	3.31	3.55
60	.68	1.30	1.67	2.00	2.39	2.66	2.92	3.23	3.46
120	.68	1.29	1.66	1.98	2.36	2.62	2.86	3.16	3.37
∞	.67	1.28	1.64	1.96	2.33	2.58	2.81	3.09	3.29
	$= z_{.25}$	$= z_{.10}$	$= z_{.05}$	$= z_{.025}$	$= z_{.010}$	$= z_{.005}$	$= z_{.0025}$	$= z_{.0010}$	$= z_{.0005}$

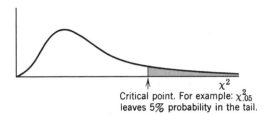

Critical point. For example: $\chi^2_{.05}$
leaves 5% probability in the tail.

3 χ^2 Critical Points

d.f.	$\chi^2_{.25}$	$\chi^2_{.10}$	$\chi^2_{.05}$	$\chi^2_{.025}$	$\chi^2_{.010}$	$\chi^2_{.005}$	$\chi^2_{.001}$
1	1.32	2.71	3.84	5.02	6.63	7.88	10.8
2	2.77	4.61	5.99	7.38	9.21	10.6	13.8
3	4.11	6.25	7.81	9.35	11.3	12.8	16.3
4	5.39	7.78	9.49	11.1	13.3	14.9	18.5
5	6.63	9.24	11.1	12.8	15.1	16.7	20.5
6	7.84	10.6	12.6	14.4	16.8	18.5	22.5
7	9.04	12.0	14.1	16.0	18.5	20.3	24.3
8	10.2	13.4	15.5	17.5	20.1	22.0	26.1
9	11.4	14.7	16.9	19.0	21.7	23.6	27.9
10	12.5	16.0	18.3	20.5	23.2	25.2	29.6
11	13.7	17.3	19.7	21.9	24.7	26.8	31.3
12	14.8	18.5	21.0	23.3	26.2	28.3	32.9
13	16.0	19.8	22.4	24.7	27.7	29.8	34.5
14	17.1	21.1	23.7	26.1	29.1	31.3	36.1
15	18.2	22.3	25.0	27.5	30.6	32.8	37.7
16	19.4	23.5	26.3	28.8	32.0	34.3	39.3
17	20.5	24.8	27.6	30.2	33.4	35.7	40.8
18	21.6	26.0	28.9	31.5	34.8	37.2	42.3
19	22.7	27.2	30.1	32.9	36.2	38.6	32.8
20	23.8	28.4	31.4	34.2	37.6	40.0	45.3
21	24.9	29.6	32.7	35.5	38.9	41.4	46.8
22	26.0	30.8	33.9	36.8	40.3	42.8	48.3
23	27.1	32.0	35.2	38.1	41.6	44.2	49.7
24	28.2	33.2	36.4	39.4	32.0	45.6	51.2
25	29.3	34.4	37.7	40.6	44.3	46.9	52.6
26	30.4	35.6	38.9	41.9	45.6	48.3	54.1
27	31.5	36.7	40.1	43.2	47.0	49.6	55.5
28	32.6	37.9	41.3	44.5	48.3	51.0	56.9
29	33.7	39.1	42.6	45.7	49.6	52.3	58.3
30	34.8	40.3	43.8	47.0	50.9	53.7	59.7
40	45.6	51.8	55.8	59.3	63.7	66.8	73.4
50	56.3	63.2	67.5	71.4	76.2	79.5	86.7
60	67.0	74.4	79.1	83.3	88.4	92.0	99.6
70	77.6	85.5	90.5	95.0	100	104	112
80	88.1	96.6	102	107	112	116	125
90	98.6	108	113	118	124	128	137
100	109	118	124	130	136	140	149

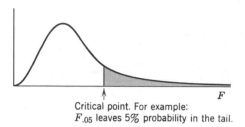

Critical point. For example:
$F_{.05}$ leaves 5% probability in the tail.

4 *F* Critical Points

		DEGREES OF FREEDOM FOR NUMERATOR										
		1	2	3	4	5	6	8	10	20	40	∞
1	$F_{.25}$	5.83	7.50	8.20	8.58	8.82	8.98	9.19	9.32	9.58	9.71	9.85
	$F_{.10}$	39.9	49.5	53.6	55.8	57.2	58.2	59.4	60.2	61.7	62.5	63.3
	$F_{.05}$	161	200	216	225	230	234	239	242	248	251	254
2	$F_{.25}$	2.57	3.00	3.15	3.23	3.28	3.31	3.35	3.38	3.43	3.45	3.48
	$F_{.10}$	8.53	9.00	9.16	9.24	9.29	9.33	9.37	9.39	9.44	9.47	9.49
	$F_{.05}$	18.5	19.0	19.2	19.2	19.3	19.3	19.4	19.4	19.4	19.5	19.5
	$F_{.01}$	98.5	99.0	99.2	99.2	99.3	99.3	99.4	99.4	99.4	99.5	99.5
	$F_{.001}$	998	999	999	999	999	999	999	999	999	999	999
3	$F_{.25}$	2.02	2.28	2.36	2.39	2.41	2.42	2.44	2.44	2.46	2.47	2.47
	$F_{.10}$	5.54	5.46	5.39	5.34	5.31	5.28	5.25	5.23	5.18	5.16	5.13
	$F_{.05}$	10.1	9.55	9.28	9.12	9.10	8.94	8.85	8.79	8.66	8.59	8.53
	$F_{.01}$	34.1	30.8	29.5	28.7	28.2	27.9	27.5	27.2	26.7	26.4	26.1
	$F_{.001}$	167	149	141	137	135	133	131	129	126	125	124
4	$F_{.25}$	1.81	2.00	2.05	2.06	2.07	2.08	2.08	2.08	2.08	2.08	2.08
	$F_{.10}$	4.54	4.32	4.19	4.11	4.05	4.01	3.95	3.92	3.84	3.80	3.76
	$F_{.05}$	7.71	6.94	6.59	6.39	6.26	6.16	6.04	5.96	5.80	5.72	5.63
	$F_{.01}$	21.2	18.0	16.7	16.0	15.5	15.2	14.8	14.5	14.0	13.7	13.5
	$F_{.001}$	74.1	61.3	56.2	53.4	51.7	50.5	49.0	48.1	46.1	45.1	44.1
5	$F_{.25}$	1.69	1.85	1.88	1.89	1.89	1.89	1.89	1.89	1.88	1.88	1.87
	$F_{.10}$	4.06	3.78	3.62	3.52	3.45	3.40	3.34	3.30	3.21	3.16	3.10
	$F_{.05}$	6.61	5.79	5.41	5.19	5.05	4.95	4.82	4.74	4.56	4.46	4.36
	$F_{.01}$	16.3	13.3	12.1	11.4	11.0	10.7	10.3	10.1	9.55	9.29	9.02
	$F_{.001}$	47.2	37.1	33.2	31.1	29.8	28.8	27.6	26.9	25.4	24.6	23.8
6	$F_{.25}$	1.62	1.76	1.78	1.79	1.79	1.78	1.77	1.77	1.76	1.75	1.74
	$F_{.10}$	3.78	3.46	3.29	3.18	3.11	3.05	2.98	2.94	2.84	2.78	2.72
	$F_{.05}$	5.99	5.14	4.76	4.53	4.39	4.28	4.15	4.06	3.87	3.77	3.67
	$F_{.01}$	13.7	10.9	9.78	9.15	8.75	8.47	8.10	7.87	7.40	7.14	6.88
	$F_{.001}$	35.5	27.0	23.7	21.9	20.8	20.0	19.0	18.4	17.1	16.4	15.8
7	$F_{.25}$	1.57	1.70	1.72	1.72	1.71	1.71	1.70	1.69	1.67	1.66	1.65
	$F_{.10}$	3.59	3.26	3.07	2.96	2.88	2.83	2.75	2.70	2.59	2.54	2.47
	$F_{.05}$	5.59	4.74	4.35	4.12	3.97	3.87	3.73	3.64	3.44	3.34	3.23
	$F_{.01}$	12.2	9.55	8.45	7.85	7.46	7.19	6.84	6.62	6.16	5.91	5.65
	$F_{.001}$	29.3	21.7	18.8	17.2	16.2	15.5	14.6	14.1	12.9	12.3	11.7
8	$F_{.25}$	1.54	1.66	1.69	1.66	1.66	1.65	1.64	1.63	1.61	1.59	1.58
	$F_{.10}$	3.46	3.11	2.92	2.81	2.73	2.67	2.59	2.54	2.42	2.36	2.29
	$F_{.05}$	5.32	4.46	4.07	3.84	3.69	3.58	3.44	3.35	3.15	3.04	2.93
	$F_{.01}$	11.3	8.65	7.59	7.01	6.63	6.37	6.03	5.81	5.36	5.12	4.86
	$F_{.001}$	25.4	18.5	15.8	14.4	13.5	12.9	12.0	11.5	10.5	9.92	9.33
9	$F_{.25}$	1.51	1.62	1.63	1.63	1.62	1.61	1.60	1.59	1.56	1.55	1.53
	$F_{.10}$	3.36	3.01	2.81	2.69	2.61	2.55	2.47	2.42	2.30	2.23	2.16

DEGREES OF FREEDOM FOR DENOMINATOR

		DEGREES OF FREEDOM FOR NUMERATOR										
		1	2	3	4	5	6	8	10	20	40	∞
	$F_{.05}$	5.12	4.26	3.86	3.63	3.48	3.37	3.23	3.14	2.94	2.83	2.71
	$F_{.01}$	10.6	8.02	6.99	6.42	6.06	5.80	5.47	5.26	4.81	4.57	4.31
	$F_{.001}$	22.9	16.4	13.9	12.6	11.7	11.1	10.4	9.89	8.90	8.37	7.81
10	$F_{.25}$	1.49	1.60	1.60	1.59	1.59	1.58	1.56	1.55	1.52	1.51	1.48
	$F_{.10}$	3.28	2.92	2.73	2.61	2.52	2.46	2.38	2.32	2.20	2.13	2.06
	$F_{.05}$	4.96	4.10	3.71	3.48	3.33	3.22	3.07	2.98	2.77	2.66	2.54
	$F_{.01}$	10.0	7.56	6.55	5.99	5.64	5.39	5.06	4.85	4.41	4.17	3.91
	$F_{.001}$	21.0	14.9	12.6	11.3	10.5	9.92	9.20	8.75	7.80	7.30	6.76
12	$F_{.25}$	1.56	1.56	1.56	1.55	1.54	1.53	1.51	1.50	1.47	1.45	1.42
	$F_{.10}$	3.18	2.81	2.61	2.48	2.39	2.33	2.24	2.19	2.06	1.99	1.90
	$F_{.05}$	4.75	3.89	3.49	3.26	3.11	3.00	2.85	2.75	2.54	2.43	2.30
	$F_{.01}$	9.33	6.93	5.95	5.41	5.06	4.82	4.50	4.30	3.86	3.62	3.36
	$F_{.001}$	18.6	13.0	10.8	9.63	8.89	8.38	7.71	7.29	6.40	5.93	5.42
14	$F_{.25}$	1.44	1.53	1.53	1.52	1.51	1.50	1.48	1.46	1.43	1.41	1.38
	$F_{.10}$	3.10	2.73	2.52	2.39	2.31	2.24	2.15	2.10	1.96	1.89	1.80
	$F_{.05}$	4.60	3.74	3.34	3.11	2.96	2.85	2.70	2.60	2.39	2.27	2.13
	$F_{.01}$	8.86	5.51	5.56	5.04	4.69	4.46	4.14	3.94	3.51	3.27	3.00
	$F_{.001}$	17.1	11.8	9.73	8.62	7.92	7.43	6.80	6.40	5.56	5.10	4.60
16	$F_{.25}$	1.42	1.51	1.51	1.50	1.48	1.48	1.46	1.45	1.40	1.37	1.34
	$F_{.10}$	3.05	2.67	2.46	2.33	2.24	2.18	2.09	2.03	1.89	1.81	1.72
	$F_{.05}$	4.49	3.63	3.24	3.01	2.85	2.74	2.59	2.49	2.28	2.15	2.01
	$F_{.01}$	8.53	6.23	5.29	4.77	4.44	4.20	3.89	3.69	3.26	3.02	2.75
	$F_{.001}$	16.1	11.0	9.00	7.94	7.27	6.81	6.19	5.81	4.99	4.54	4.06
20	$F_{.25}$	1.40	1.49	1.48	1.46	1.45	1.44	1.42	1.40	1.36	1.33	1.29
	$F_{.10}$	2.97	2.59	2.38	2.25	2.16	2.09	2.00	1.94	1.79	1.71	1.61
	$F_{.05}$	4.35	3.49	3.10	2.87	2.71	2.60	2.45	2.35	2.12	1.99	1.84
	$F_{.01}$	8.10	5.85	4.94	4.43	4.10	3.87	3.56	3.37	2.94	2.69	2.42
	$F_{.001}$	14.8	9.95	8.10	7.10	6.46	6.02	5.44	5.08	4.29	3.86	3.38
30	$F_{.25}$	1.38	1.45	1.44	1.42	1.41	1.39	1.37	1.35	1.30	1.27	1.23
	$F_{.10}$	2.88	2.49	2.28	2.14	2.05	1.98	1.88	1.82	1.67	1.57	1.46
	$F_{.05}$	4.17	3.32	2.92	2.69	2.53	2.42	2.27	2.16	1.93	1.79	1.62
	$F_{.01}$	7.56	5.39	4.51	4.02	3.70	3.47	3.17	2.98	2.55	2.30	2.01
	$F_{.001}$	13.3	8.77	7.05	6.12	5.53	5.12	4.58	4.24	3.49	3.07	2.59
40	$F_{.25}$	1.36	1.44	1.42	1.40	1.39	1.37	1.35	1.33	1.28	1.24	1.19
	$F_{.10}$	2.84	2.44	2.23	2.09	2.00	1.93	1.83	1.76	1.61	1.51	1.38
	$F_{.05}$	4.08	3.23	2.84	2.61	2.45	2.34	2.18	2.08	1.84	1.69	1.51
	$F_{.01}$	7.31	5.18	4.31	3.83	3.51	3.29	2.99	2.80	2.37	2.11	1.80
	$F_{.001}$	12.6	8.25	6.60	5.70	5.13	4.73	4.21	3.87	3.15	2.73	2.23
60	$F_{.25}$	1.35	1.42	1.41	1.38	1.37	1.35	1.32	1.30	1.25	1.21	1.15
	$F_{.10}$	2.79	2.39	2.18	2.04	1.95	1.87	1.77	1.71	1.54	1.44	1.29
	$F_{.05}$	4.00	3.15	2.76	2.53	2.37	2.25	2.10	1.99	1.75	1.59	1.39
	$F_{.01}$	7.08	4.98	4.13	3.65	3.34	3.12	2.82	2.63	2.20	1.94	1.60
	$F_{.001}$	12.0	7.76	6.17	5.31	4.76	4.37	3.87	3.54	2.83	2.41	1.89
120	$F_{.25}$	1.34	1.40	1.39	1.37	1.35	1.33	1.30	1.28	1.22	1.18	1.10
	$F_{.10}$	2.75	2.35	2.13	1.99	1.90	1.82	1.72	1.65	1.48	1.37	1.19
	$F_{.05}$	3.92	3.07	2.68	2.45	2.29	2.17	2.02	1.91	1.66	1.50	1.25
	$F_{.01}$	6.85	4.79	3.95	3.48	3.17	2.96	2.66	2.47	2.03	1.76	1.38
	$F_{.001}$	11.4	7.32	5.79	4.95	4.42	4.04	3.55	3.24	2.53	2.11	1.54
∞	$F_{.25}$	1.32	1.39	1.37	1.35	1.33	1.31	1.28	1.25	1.19	1.14	1.00
	$F_{.10}$	2.71	2.30	2.08	1.94	1.85	1.77	1.67	1.60	1.42	1.30	1.00
	$F_{.05}$	3.84	3.00	2.60	2.37	2.21	2.10	1.94	1.83	1.57	1.39	1.00
	$F_{.01}$	6.63	4.61	3.78	3.32	3.02	2.80	2.51	2.32	1.88	1.59	1.00
	$F_{.001}$	10.8	6.91	5.42	4.62	4.10	3.74	3.27	2.96	2.27	1.84	1.00

DEGREES OF FREEDOM FOR DENOMINATOR

Index